Protection of Geographic Names in International Law and Domain Name System

Information Law Series (INFO)

VOLUME 30

Editor

Objective & Readership

Publications in the Information Law Series focus on current legal issues of information law and are aimed at scholars, practitioners, and policy makers who are active in the rapidly expanding area of information law and policy.

Introduction & Contents

The advent of the information society has put the field of information law squarely on the map. Information law is the law relating to the production, marketing, distribution, and use of information goods and services. The field of information law therefore cuts across traditional legal boundaries, and encompasses a wide set of legal issues at the crossroads of intellectual property, media law, telecommunications law, freedom of expression, and right to privacy. Recent volumes in the Information Law Series deal with copyright enforcement on the Internet, interoperability among computer programs, harmonization of copyright at the European level, intellectual property and human rights, public broadcasting in Europe, the future of the public domain, conditional access in digital broadcasting, and the 'three-step test' in copyright.

The titles published in this series are listed at the end of this volume.

Protection of Geographic Names in International Law and Domain Name System

Second Edition

Heather Ann Forrest

Wolters Kluwer

Published by:
Kluwer Law International B.V.
PO Box 316
2400 AH Alphen aan den Rijn
The Netherlands
Website: www.wolterskluwerlr.com

Sold and distributed in North, Central and South America by:
Wolters Kluwer Legal & Regulatory U.S.
7201 McKinney Circle
Frederick, MD 21704
United States of America
Email: customer.service@wolterskluwer.com

Sold and distributed in all other countries by:
Quadrant
Rockwood House
Haywards Heath
West Sussex
RH16 3DH
United Kingdom
Email: international-customerservice@wolterskluwer.com

ISBN 978-90-411-8839-7

e-book: ISBN 978-90-411-8920-2
web-PDF: ISBN 978-90-411-8960-8

About the Author

Heather Ann Forrest is an attorney, academic, researcher and active participant in ICANN policy development. She is a member of ICANN's Intellectual Property Constituency (IPC) and has twice been elected to represent the IPC on ICANN's GNSO Council, the body responsible for managing policy development in respect of generic top-level domains. She served as a co-chair of the CWG on the Use of Country and Territory Names as Top-Level Domains and member of its predecessor ccNSO Study Group. She is an Associate Professor of Law at the University of Tasmania and an Associate Professor of Law (Adjunct) at Murdoch University. *Protection of Geographic Names in International Law and Domain Name System Policy* documents her doctoral thesis undertaken at the University of Berne, Switzerland. It was awarded the Swiss National Professor Walther Hug Preis in 2014 and is recognized as the global authority on legal rights in geographic names and their use in the internet Domain Name System.

Table of Contents

Foreword

The World Wide Web, conceived in the 1980s as a specialized tool facilitating computer-based information flows among a few professionals, exponentially grew in recent years and became a principal tool of general communication, indispensable to business, government, science and society at large with some 205 million second-level domain names by 2010. The network grew without a proper legal framework – perhaps thanks to that, it rapidly conquered the world beyond all initial expectations. It was not designed to fit the law, nor was the law ready for it. This is true both in domestic and international law.

When ICANN's Board of Directors announced preparations for new top-level domain names in 2008, largely with a view to meet new demands and to diversify an overstretched .com top-level, it was by no means clear whether the possibility of recourse to geographical names was compatible with international law and law in general. This book undertakes to assess the legal regime accompanying geographical top-level domain names. Is it lawful and possible to allocate names such as .asia, or .europe, or a particular locality, such as .newyork, as a prime organizational structure for the internet Domain Name System? Who is entitled to use these denominations?

Given the global dimension of the internet, this study seeks to answer these questions from a perspective of international law. The author examines the implications of positive international law with a view to assess to what extent geographical names are currently protected by different titles, and to what extent they can be exclusively claimed by governments in defence of territorial prerogatives under the principle of sovereignty. In doing so, this book walks a number of avenues, ranging from intellectual property to unfair competition and to human rights. It offers a comprehensive analysis of a field which raises more questions than clear answers can be provided, given the flux and novelty of the field.

The author concludes her survey in finding that States cannot claim exclusive rights, and a great number of different factors will need to be taken into account in shaping future rules on the subject. Her work offers a most valuable contribution to this effort, as it sets out all the different legal facets which internet law should take into account in the field of internet domain name allocation.

This book is of great interest both to practitioners and to academics focusing on internet governance and its challenges in the process of legal globalization. It is based upon a thesis submitted to the Faculty of Law at the University of Bern, Switzerland in 2011. Working with Heather Forrest during regular visits to the World Trade Institute was a pleasure, as well as an experience of gradually understanding an entirely new and emerging field of international economic law, thanks to the effort of the author of this highly commendable work.

Prof. Thomas Cottier

> *"In the absence of justice, what is sovereignty but organized robbery?" Saint Augustine*

Since the first edition of Heather's book which was published three years ago, the world of ICANN has become surprisingly unpredictable. Whether you are an IP attorney or a policy advisor, a representative of civil society or a government official, if you are seeking truth and certainty in regard to the protection of geographic names in the domain name system, the road ahead is long and winding.

When the stewardship of IANA transferred away from the US Government to the private sector in October 2016, there was much talk in ICANN, the IGF and even the ITU about accountability and transparency. This unexpectedly positive manifestation of multi-stakeholderism was accompanied by mutual back-slapping and bonhomie. We were all friends with the common goal of cyberspace stability, and we wanted the best result for the most.

Unfortunately, the willingness of parties to engage in respectful debate and reasoned argument dissipates all too rapidly when the focus turns to the more esoteric subject of geographical name protection.

Perhaps it is something to do with the recent rise of populism and its less savoury companion, nationalism. Were we naïve to expect anything else when sovereignty slouched out of the shadows to commandeer the ballot box in elections across 2016?

Whatever the reason, there is a need now more than ever for clarity in the creation of cyber-policy and the allocation of terms of geographic significance. Heather's book looks at the hard questions relating to international law and geographic names on the internet. Her crisp analysis lays a trail you can follow even whilst the democratic and the demagogic tussle for control over such terms and identifiers.

Her conclusion is clear. Nation States cannot claim exclusive rights in geographical terms – at least not yet. She examines the issue from the perspective of custom and general principle, intellectual property protection, human rights, unfair competition and related commercial rights, international and soft law and more. The time may come when States seek to change international law because technology cannot be outside the law, but that is in the future.

Along the way, Heather considers the likelihood of a globally applicable solution emerging within ICANN that Nation States and intellectual property owners alike will accept. She also outlines factors which must be taken into account as the internet community lays the foundation for Round Two / Subsequent Procedures of the new gTLD program.

Echoing Saint Augustine 1500 years after his death, Kemal Ataturk said, 'Sovereignty is not given, it is taken'. This position holds true in the age of the internet. The Working Groups developing policy and practice wherever internet governance is debated – and indeed all of us interested in fairness and the rule of law – need to recognize this. Thanks to Heather and her meticulous research, we can at least start on the right track.

Nick Wood
Managing director of Com Laude & Valideus

Preface and Acknowledgements

The catalyst for the study documented in this book was the June 2008 decision of the Board of Directors of the Internet Corporation for Assigned Names and Numbers (ICANN) to commence a new round of expansion at the top-level of the internet Domain Name System. This book is the product of a doctoral thesis commenced at the University of Bern, Switzerland under the supervision of Professor Thomas Cottier, now Emeritus Professor of Law and Senior Research Fellow of the World Trade Institute at the University of Bern, and then Director of the World Trade Institute and Institute for European and International Economic Law. Professor Cottier's inestimable experience in intellectual property and trade law pushed me to new levels of understanding and enquiry, inspired me to draw connections where previously I had not even considered that these existed, and encouraged me to look beyond the microcosm of ICANN policy-making to the larger world in which it operates.

This study was additionally guided by Professor Dr Jürgen Bröhmer, then-Head of the School of Law at the University of New England, now Dean of the School of Law at Murdoch University and Visiting Professor at the Europa Institute, Saarbrücken University. Professor Bröhmer's early support encouraged me to turn mere wonderings about the legality of domain name policy into a doctoral study. His input and insight at so many stages along the journey have inspired me to question fundamental assumptions; he has thus contributed much to the rigour of this work, particularly as respects the role of human rights law in the protection of geographic names.

Thanks to Professor Cottier and Professor Bröhmer, I had the great pleasure of undertaking several months of research in residence at the Institute of European and International Economic Law at the University of Bern, Switzerland. I am particularly grateful to Dr Mira Burri, Dr Christian

Häberli, Dr Dannie Jost, Professor Marion Panizzon and Dr Susan Brown-Shafii for their support and interest in my work. I am also grateful to them for having introduced me to Dr Ueli Buri of the Swiss Federal Intellectual Property Institute and Professor Rolf Weber of the University of Zürich, who generously offered input in their respective areas of specialization and provided me with an opportunity to test my ideas. Further, the successful completion of this study also owes much to Wulfhard Stahl, Institute librarian, and the Institute staff, in particular Rosemarie Cöppicus and Gaby Hofer. It has been a pleasure to keep in touch with several of my fellow doctoral candidates and to be introduced to newly commencing candidates, all of whom I wish tremendous happiness and success in their future endeavours.

The first edition of this work was blessed with moral support from colleagues at the School of Law at the University of New England and the Thomas More Academy of Law at Australian Catholic University. The second edition has benefitted from the support of the Faculty of Law at the University of Tasmania, and particularly Dean Margaret Otlowski and Deputy Dean Rick Snell. LL.B. candidate Sophie Hey's research skills and attention to detail have contributed to the precision of citations and the expanded bibliography in this second edition.

For offering me the opportunity to revisit this work and produce a second edition, I am grateful to Wolters Kluwer and Professor P. Bernt Hugenholtz, General Editor of the Information Law Series. Miriam Weemhoff has cheerfully and patiently kept both the first and second editions on track. Certainly, without the support the first edition received from lawyers, academics, governments and new gTLD applicants around the world, this second edition would not have been contemplated.

Looking back over the ten years since I first became involved in the ICANN multi-stakeholder community, I am fascinated by the slow but steady transition of that organization into a more mature, more globally and legally aware policy-making body. So many within ICANN have contributed to the likewise slow but steady increase in my understanding of the DNS. We spend countless hours together on conference calls, in windowless conference rooms, on airplanes and in airports travelling to and from public meetings, to the point that each public meeting feels, in some way, like a family reunion. When I started my ICANN journey, there were no formal welcoming or induction structures as there are now, and finding my place was not easy. Most particularly, I have the Intellectual Property Constituency to thank. Representing the IPC on the GNSO Council alongside two incredibly talented lawyers, Brian Winterfeldt and Paul McGrady, has truly been an honour and a privilege. To my fellow Councilors and our outstanding ICANN support staff, here is my opportunity to resoundingly thank you for everything (and in particular your kind consideration of Australian Eastern Daylight Time when scheduling meetings).

Despite the tremendous distances between us, friends scattered across the globe have provided motivation and moral support throughout the life of this project, and often at exactly the moments I needed it most. With good humour, food and wine they have more than once pulled me back from the brink of ICANN overload.

What was said in the first edition is truer today; this journey could not have been sustained without the support of my family, immediate and extended. My husband, Jani Myöhänen, carries the heaviest burden, and does so with unfailing love, understanding, tolerance and companionship. He still makes all things seem possible.

Finally, I remain unable to articulate here the commitment that my parents, Teryle A and Mary Catharine Forrest, have made to their only child's education. This second edition is another milestone that is as much theirs as it is mine, and it is to them that I continue to dedicate this book.

Heather Ann Forrest, Dr. (Ius)
Associate Professor of Law, University of Tasmania, Australia
Associate Professor of Law (Adjunct), Murdoch University, Australia

Preface and Acknowledgements to First Edition

The catalyst for the study documented in this book was the June 2008 decision of the Board of Directors of the Internet Corporation for Assigned Names and Numbers (ICANN) to commence a new round of expansion at the top-level of the internet Domain Name System. This book is the product of a doctoral thesis commenced at the University of Berne, Switzerland under the supervision of Professor Thomas Cottier, Director of the World Trade Institute and Institute for European and International Economic Law. Professor Cottier's inestimable experience in intellectual property and trade law pushed me to new levels of understanding and enquiry, inspired me to draw connections where previously I had not even considered that these existed, and encouraged me to look beyond the microcosm of ICANN policy-making to the larger world in which it operates.

This study was additionally guided by Professor Jürgen Bröhmer, then-Head of the School of Law at the University of New England, now Dean of the School of Law at Murdoch University and Visiting Professor at the Europa Institute, Saarbrücken University. Professor Bröhmer's early support encouraged me to turn mere ideas about the legality of domain names into a doctoral study. His input and insight at so many stages along the journey have inspired me to question fundamental assumptions; he has thus contributed much to the rigour of this work, particularly as respects the role of human rights law in the protection of geographic names.

Thanks to Professor Cottier and Professor Bröhmer, I had the great pleasure of undertaking several months of research in residence at the Institute of European and International Economic Law at the University of Berne, Switzerland. I am particularly grateful to Dr Mira Burri, Dr Christian

Häberli, Dr Dannie Jost, Professor Marion Panizzon and Dr Susan Brown-Shafii for their support and interest in my work. I am also grateful to them for having introduced me to Dr Ueli Buri of the Swiss Federal Intellectual Property Institute and Professor Rolf Weber of the University of Zürich, who generously offered input in their respective areas of specialization and provided me with an opportunity to test my ideas. Further, the successful completion of this study also owes much to Wulfhard Stahl, Institute librarian, and the Institute staff, in particular Rosemarie Cöppicus and Gaby Hofer. I also wish to thank my fellow doctoral candidates for their perceptive and insightful comments and suggestions at our annual conferences and I wish them happiness and success in their future endeavours.

There are many whom I wish to thank for their day-to-day encouragement, beginning with my former colleagues in the School of Law at the University of New England and my current colleagues in the Faculty of Law at Australian Catholic University. Despite the tremendous distances between us, friends scattered across the globe provided motivation and moral support, often at exactly the moments I needed it most. Anna Jondelius and Tim Eavis in particular have, without hesitation, rearranged their lives, holidays and home to support the European phases of this project.

This journey could not have been sustained without the support of my family, immediate and extended. My husband, Jani Myöhänen, has carried the heaviest burden but done so with unfailing understanding, tolerance and companionship; he makes all things seem possible.

Finally, I could not possibly hope to articulate here the commitment that my parents, Teryle A and Mary Catharine Forrest, have made to their only child's education. The achievement of this milestone is as much theirs as it is mine, and it is to them that I dedicate this book.

Introduction

To get to basics, the Internet, and its associated domain name system, derives from engineering, not from the magisterium of the law. So, when an engineer looks at an arch, for instance, or a span, or a girder, he looks at the thing for its suitability to a task. He uses a design idea, he assembles the design into the plan for the bridge, and builds the bridge. Likewise with software, he uses what comes to hand or mind to achieve his goals. He is not looking for authority to use them. His right to use the words of the english [sic] language, or the mathematical or design ideas of his predecessors in the field, is unquestioned, as long as it has not become the intellectual property of someone else. ... The issue, as I see it, is that lawyers need to be cautious about extending the reach of their concepts into areas such as engineering, or anything else, for that matter, where their application may serve no useful purpose. The use of concepts such as of 'rights', 'title', 'record' evince a tendency to subject what were originally sensible design decisions to the claims of law and the pretensions of legal theory.[1]

Three decades have passed and a new century has dawned since the implementation of the internet Domain Name System, commonly referred to by its acronym 'DNS', with the launch of eight generic top-level domains, amongst which are .net, .edu and the now ubiquitous .com. Since then the internet has expanded at an unforeseen rate, absorbing millions of new sources of information and users across the globe. In its first twenty-five years, the system evolved to accommodate an increasingly high volume of use and users, in particular through the carefully planned and monitored creation of fifteen additional generic top-level domains (or 'gTLDs'). This was largely done in order to ease perceived congestion in the .com domain,

1. Timothy Denton, *RE: [gnso-rn-wg] Comments on ICANN/IANA Reserved Names Reports, 28 Feb. 2007*, http://forum.icann.org/lists/gnso-rn-wg/msg00169.html.

consistently the most populous[2] since its launch even, ironically, after the near twofold increase in top-level domain options specifically intended to reduce .com's popularity.

While actual demand for new gTLDs has long been disputed, many in the global internet community have argued that the DNS could and should offer more users and interests space (or, to use the appropriate terminology, 'domains') in which to identify and express themselves online.[3] After considerable consultation and following two 'proof of concept' expansion rounds commenced in 2000 and 2003, the Internet Corporation for Assigned Names and Numbers ('ICANN'), the body charged with operational and policy authority over the DNS, announced in June 2008 that it would commence another round of expansion at the system's top-level.[4] This expansion round would go significantly further than the 'proof of concept' rounds had: it would be an open and uncapped round in which not just a handful of carefully selected new top-level domains would be created, but rather all applications fulfilling a set of prescribed criteria would be successful. Useful estimates of just how many new gTLD applications would be lodged proved elusive. In a pamphlet published and distributed in 2009 in the New gTLD Program policy implementation process, ICANN projected 'anything from hundreds to thousands';[5] ultimately, 1,930 applications were received.[6]

ICANN's Board of Directors' justifications for proceeding with expansion at the top-level of the DNS in this manner were twofold. First, the 'proof of concept' rounds were broadly deemed successful, and there were no indications that the DNS could not absorb a higher volume of growth in a shorter period of time without losing stability. Second, an open round in which the internet community named and designed its own domains furthered ICANN's mandate to support 'the functional, geographic and cultural diversity of the Internet'.[7] For the first time in the as-yet relatively brief history of the internet, otherwise unrepresented groups would have a real probability of success in staking their own claim in cyberspace by

2. Verisign, *The Domain Name Industry Brief 9(2), Jul. 2012*, 2, http://www.verisigninc.com/assets/domain-name-brief-july2012.pdf.
3. ICANN, *New gTLDs Proposed Final Applicant Guidebook Public Comment Summary,* http://www.icann.org/en/topics/new-gtlds/summary-analysis-proposed-final-guidebook-21feb11-en.pdf (21 Feb. 2011).
4. ICANN, *Board of Directors Resolution 2008.06.26.02, Adopted Board Resolutions, Paris,* https://www.icann.org/resources/board-material/resolutions-2008-06-26-en (26 Jun. 2008).
5. ICANN, *New gTLD Program: New gTLD Program in Brief,* https://archive.icann.org/en/topics/new-gtlds/factsheet-new-gtld-program-oct09-en.pdf (2009).
6. ICANN, *Reveal Day 13 June 2012: New gTLD Applied-For Strings*, https://www.icann.org/news/announcement-2012-06-13-en (13 Jun. 2012).
7. ICANN, *Bylaws*, Art. 1, s. 2, Provision 4, https://www.icann.org/resources/pages/governance/bylaws-en (as amended 1 Oct. 2016).

clearly identifying a space as their own with a name representative of their interest or community.

Yet with the benefits of increasing the number of internet top-level domains also came certain challenges. In particular, more top-level domains means more opportunities for conflict to arise between holders of legal rights in names (what might be termed 'offline' rights in names) and registrants of internet domain names comprised of those same names (what might be termed 'online' rights in names). The New gTLD Program has particularly concerned trademark holders, whose resources were already overextended in policing their offline rights within .com and the twenty-one other legacy generic top-level domains,[8] plus the then-nearly 300 country code top-level domains ('ccTLDs') such as Canada's .ca and Germany's .de. The addition of new gTLDs to the DNS creates an additional – and potentially overwhelming – burden for trademark holders by giving rise to the need to police not only the applications for new gTLDs themselves (a new .bmw or .nike, for example) but also all of the lower level domain names that will be registered within each new top-level domain (a registration for the name 'sony' in a new .music gTLD, for example: www.sony.music).

Trademarks are not, however, the only vulnerable type of name in an enlarged DNS. The World Intellectual Property Organization ('WIPO'), the United Nations ('UN') body that administers the major international treaties respecting intellectual property rights ('IPRs'), identified as early as 1999 as a 'problem of bad faith, abusive domain registrations that violate IPRs other than trademarks or service marks',[9] amongst which are geographical indications and other geographic identifiers. WIPO confirmed two years later the significant incidence of such registrations 'by persons who might be considered not to be properly entitled to use the identifiers in question',[10] but concluded that the principal international treaty on the protection of intellectual property, the Agreement on Trade-Related Aspects of Intellectual

8. *See for example*, Intellectual Property Constituency, *The Intellectual Property Constituency Impact Statement Regarding the Introduction of New gTLDs*, Principle A, http://www.ipconstituency.org/assets/ipc-position-papers/2007/IPC%20Impact%20Statement%20re%20new%20gTLDs.pdf ('Based on past experience, the addition of new gTLDs will likely result in numerous defensive registrations of otherwise unnecessary domain names by IP owners (which we note include all trademark owners such as Registrars, Registries, ISPs, etc.). Such an introduction not only places a significant burden and cost to IP owners, it results in absolutely no value whatsoever to IP owners, not to mention Internet users in general.').

9. WIPO, *Final Report of the WIPO Internet Domain Name Process: The Management of Internet Names and Addresses: Intellectual Property Issues*, viii, http://www.wipo.int/amc/en/processes/process1/report/index.html (30 Apr. 1999) (hereinafter, 'WIPO I Report').

10. WIPO, *The Recognition of Rights and the Use of Names in the Internet Domain Name System: Report of the Second WIPO Internet Domain Name Process*, vi, http://www.wipo.int/amc/en/processes/process2/report/html/report.html (3 Sep. 2001) (hereinafter, 'WIPO II Report').

Property Rights (the 'TRIPS Agreement'),[11] did not expressly recognize what governments viewed as legitimate, superior interests in their countries' names or offer sufficient protection to geographical indications to prevent their unauthorized registration as domain names. In the years since, disputes between governments asserting rights in geographic names and unauthorized registrants of geographic domain names have not been consistently resolved. Efforts to limit the registration of geographic domain names through DNS policy were, prior to the New gTLD Program, implemented on an ad hoc basis.

ICANN's decision to undertake large scale expansion at the top-level of the DNS presented as an opportunity to finally develop and apply clear, predictable, consistent policy on various issues,[12] including the treatment of geographic names. There has never been any doubt that applications for geographic new gTLDs would be made during this open, uncapped expansion in light of the success of two particular applications in the second 'proof of concept' round: the Catalan linguistic community's application for .cat and the Dot Asia Organisation's application for .asia were both approved and added to the system in 2004. Applications for other geographic and linguistic new gTLDs were being prepared for .berlin,[13] .gal (representing the Galician linguistic community)[14] and .cym (representing the Welsh community),[15] amongst others, in some cases years before the ICANN Board of Directors' June 2008 decision to approve and launch a new expansion round.

With this in mind, during the New gTLD Program policy development process, the Governmental Advisory Committee ('GAC') within ICANN recommended that the creation of new gTLDs of national significance be avoided 'unless in agreement with the relevant governments or public authorities'.[16] This recommendation led to ICANN's implementing in the *gTLD Applicant Guidebook*, the policy instrument that sets out the rules of the expansion program, measures to prevent any new gTLDs comprising country and territory names, or other forms of geographic name without the

---

11. Agreement on Trade-Related Aspects of Intellectual Property Rights, Marrakesh Agreement Establishing the World Trade Organization, Annex 1C (15 Apr. 1994), 1869 U.N.T.S. 299, 33 I.L.M. 1197 (hereinafter, the 'TRIPS Agreement').
12. Jacqueline D. Lipton, *Bad Faith in Cyberspace: Grounding Domain Name Theory in Trademark, Property, and Restitution*, 23(2) Harvard J.L. & Tech. 447, 450 (2010).
13. dotBERLIN GmbH & Co. KG was founded in 2005 for the purpose of lodging a .berlin application; dotBERLIN GmbH & Co. KG, *.berlin: Die Top-Level-Domain Für Berliner*, http://dotberlin.de.
14. The Asociación PuntoGal was founded in 2006 for the purpose of obtaining the .gal top-level domain representing the Galician language and culture. *See* Asociación PuntoGal, *Official Web[site] of Asociación PuntoGal*, http://www.puntogal.org.
15. Public seminars on a proposed bid for a .cym top-level domain representing Welsh-language and culture were organized by the Institute of Welsh Affairs in early 2007; *see* dotCYM, *April 2007 Newsletter*, http://www.dotcym.org/home/?p=56.
16. GAC, *Principles Regarding New gTLDs*, 2.2, https://archive.icann.org/en/topics/new-gtlds/gac-principles-regarding-new-gtlds-28mar07-en.pdf (28 Mar. 2007).

documented authorization of relevant governments.[17] Implicit in this policy is an assumption that governments possess exclusive rights in geographic names. There is cause, however, to question the legal basis for this assumption, particularly in light of WIPO's earlier conclusions as to the legality of governments' claims to rights.

That such rights *should* be recognized was considered indubitable to some countries' representatives participating in the First[18] and Second[19] Special Sessions of WIPO's Standing Committee on the Law of Trademarks, Industrial Designs and Geographical Indications. These sessions were held following the release of the WIPO II Report with its conclusions on the lack of protection for geographic names. What became clear in these sessions was that 'the question of the appropriateness of the registration of country names as domain names is inextricably linked by some governments to what they perceive to be their national sovereign interest.'[20] Simply put, governments expected to be able to register their country names as domain names and, as a corollary, to prevent third parties from doing so. These expectations remain, and have since grown to encompass a much wider scope of names of geographic, linguistic and cultural interest.

This book has its origins in a doctoral thesis in Law written during the development and implementation of New gTLD Program policy. The first edition was published six months after ICANN's reveal of the 1,930 applied-for strings. As the internet's DNS embarked on a critical (perhaps the *most* critical) stage in its development, this work began by acknowledging the following fundamental points, which – curiously – remain unresolved:

(1) The use of geographic names in the DNS has been considered problematic since the system's early days. Nevertheless, policy and scholarship around legal rights recognition in the DNS has focused

17. ICANN, *gTLD Applicant Guidebook: Version 2012-01-11*, 2.2.1.4, http://newgtlds.icann.org/en/applicants/agb/guidebook-full-11jan12-en.pdf (11 Jan. 2012). Unless otherwise noted, all references to the *gTLD Applicant Guidebook* in this book are to *Version 2012-01-11*, which was the operative version during the new gTLD application period (which ran from 12 Jan. to 30 May 2012).
18. WIPO Standing Committee on the Law of Trademarks, Industrial Designs and Geographical Indications, *First Special Session on the Report of the Second WIPO Internet Domain Name Process, Geneva, November 29 to December 4,* 2001, SCT/S1/6, http://www.wipo.int/amc/en/processes/sct/documents/index.html (7 Dec. 2001) (hereinafter, 'First Special Session').
19. WIPO Standing Committee on the Law of Trademarks, Industrial Designs and Geographical Indications, *Second Special Session on the Report of the Second WIPO Internet Domain Name Process, Geneva, May 21-24, 2002,* SCT/S2/8, http://www.wipo.int/amc/en/processes/sct/documents/index.html (24 May 2002) (hereinafter, 'Second Special Session').
20. WIPO, *General Assembly Twenty-Eighth (13th Extraordinary) Session, Geneva, 23 Sep. – 1 Oct. 2002*: *Internet Domain Names*, WIPO Doc. WO/GA/28/3, para. 27, http://www.wipo.int/meetings/en/details.jsp?meeting_id=4650 (24 Jun. 2002,).

mainly on recognizing rights in trademarks at the system's second level.

(2) ICANN adopted the recommendation of its internal advisory group, the Generic Names Supporting Organization ('GNSO'), to ensure that new gTLDs added to the DNS do not 'infringe the existing legal rights of others that are recognized or enforceable under generally accepted and internationally recognized principles of law'.[21] ICANN also acted upon the recommendation of another of its internal advisory groups, the Governmental Advisory Committee, to prevent geographic new gTLDs from being created without the authorization of relevant governments.

(3) The immediately preceding point gives rise to a potential inconsistency in new gTLD policy respecting geographic names that had not been evaluated prior to the study documented in this book. On the one hand, the *gTLD Applicant Guidebook* assumes governments' rights in geographic names. It does this by preventing the creation of new gTLDs with country and territory names and by requiring that applicants for strings comprised of other types of 'geographic names', as that term is expansively defined, demonstrate the consent or acquiescence of the governments relevant to such name. On the other hand, the same rules provide for the challenge of applications on grounds of existing legal rights, yet the only rights holders granted standing to object are trademark holders and international intergovernmental organizations. Legal rights in geographic names, to the extent that these are indeed recognized under international law (a point which was ignored by ICANN's Board of Directors in approving the conflicting recommendations of its internal policy developing Generic Names Supporting Organization and the advice-issuing Governmental Advisory Committee), are not actionable against applied-for new gTLDs.

(4) Even now, after the evaluation of nearly 2,000 new gTLD applications and the entry of more than half of those into the DNS, there is no clear, predictable policy framework consistent with international law to govern the use of geographic terms in the DNS. The *gTLD Applicant Guidebook* expressly left open the future treatment of country and territory names, but as the disputes discussed in Chapter 1 evidence, existing policy on other types of geographic name simply cannot be said to be sufficient or appropriate. This final point should weigh heavily on the ICANN community now that policy

---

21. GNSO, *Final Report on the Introduction of New Generic Top-Level Domains*, Recommendation 3, http://gnso.icann.org/issues/new-gtlds/pdp-dec05-fr-parta-08aug07.htm (8 Aug. 2007).

development efforts are underway to develop the 'Subsequent Procedures' applicable to future applications.[22]

The study documented in this book addressed these points in its first edition by evaluating, at the point of launch of ICANN's New gTLD Program, the extent to which rights in geographic names were 'recognized or enforceable under generally accepted and internationally recognized principles of law',[23] and the consistency of the treatment of geographic names in the *gTLD Applicant Guidebook* with that recognition or lack thereof. This second edition revisits and extends this analysis to take account of developments since ICANN's evaluation of applications, the resolution of various competing applications, the generation – and, in some cases, resolution – of disputes between new gTLD applicants and ICANN, and the introduction of more than 1,000 new gTLDs into the DNS.[24] So much having happened in the four short years separating these first and second editions, the fact that the four foundational points raised above continue to raise more questions than answers is rather inexplicable.

Related to this study are issues of internet governance, which in turn affect the applicability of international law to the DNS. As to internet governance, Chapter 2 of this book serves as an introduction to the DNS by tracing the system's development from US government research project to a standard universally relied upon for global communications. Issues about the legitimacy, transparency and representativeness of ICANN, a California, USA-based non-profit public benefit corporation, are raised in that discussion. Significant developments in ICANN's status as an independent entity arising since the first edition of this study are examined, but it remains the case that governance issues are not pursued in great depth because they lie beyond the aim of this work, which is to identify and analyse legal rights in geographic names. Where the first edition questioned whether ICANN's handling of the New gTLD Program would be a catalyst for changes to its authority over the DNS, this has squarely (at least for now) since been resolved in favour of ICANN's continued existence and mandate.[25] It is still the case, as in the first edition of this work, that no attempt is made here to predict future changes; rather, focus lies squarely upon the status quo both as to the substance of ICANN DNS policy and its interaction with international *lex lata*.

---

22. ICANN GNSO, *Council Resolution 20151217: Initiation of a Policy Development Process (PDP) on New gTLD Subsequent Procedures*, https://gnso.icann.org/en/council/resolutions#201512 (17 Dec. 2015).
23. *Ibid.*
24. ICANN, *A 'Grand' Milestone: New gTLD Program Reaches 1,000th Delegation*, https://www.icann.org/news/blog/a-grand-milestone-new-gtld-program-reaches-1-000th-delegation (25 May 2016).
25. The current legal status and role of ICANN are discussed in Part I Chapter 2 at s. 2.2.3 and in Part II Chapter 4 at s. 4.2.4.3.

The applicability of international law to the DNS is an issue that also demands addressing from the outset. ICANN is, as just noted in the previous paragraph, a private corporation based in the state of California in the United States of America ('USA'). As such, it is subject to California state and United States ('US') federal law. As to the appropriateness of this situation given the importance of the internet and its DNS to the entire world, the (now formerly) responsible agency of the US government once notoriously offered that a private corporation tasked with overseeing the internet 'must be headquartered somewhere, and similar objections would inevitably arise if it were incorporated in another location'.[26] This remark highlights the fact that the idea of privatizing the internet was formed within a decidedly domestic paradigm. By contrast, States (as in the US, rather than the state of California) are the principal subjects of international law,[27] and ICANN is clearly not a State. Now that it is no longer even a private entity sub-contracted by the US government, any argument that may have once been made for its being a governmental organization of the US is now untenable, as is explained in detail in Chapter 2.

International law is thus the benchmark in this study not because ICANN is obliged to adhere to it, but rather because ICANN's Board of Directors committed the organization to do so by adopting[28] the GNSO's recommendation to avoid the creation of new gTLDs that infringe rights 'recognized or enforceable under generally accepted and internationally recognized principles of law'.[29] Had this recommendation not been adopted, it would be necessary to identify some other legal basis for challenging the consistency of new gTLD policy (which has the form of a private contract between ICANN and a new gTLD applicant) with international law. The recognition of geographic names under domestic law enters this particular study only by means of general principles of international law; this is introduced in Chapter 4 and then considered where relevant in each of the succeeding chapters. Domestic law otherwise lies beyond the scope of this work, but is nevertheless something that will require consideration in the future given the role that domestic trademark registration standards and norms of morality and public order play in new gTLD policy.

This book is divided into three parts. The first part, comprising Chapters 1 and 2, provides an identification of the issues raised by geographic names' use in the DNS and an understanding of the context surrounding those issues. New to this second edition are examples of conflicts involving geographic

---

26. NTIA, *Management of Internet Names and Addresses*, 63 Fed. Reg. 31,741, 31,745 (10 Jun. 1998) (hereinafter, the 'White Paper').
27. The subjects and sources of international law are discussed in Part II Chapter 4.
28. ICANN, *Board of Directors Resolution 2008.06.26.02: GNSO Recommendations on New gTLDs*, https://www.icann.org/resources/board-material/resolutions-2008-06-26-en (26 Jun. 2008).
29. GNSO, *Final Report on the Introduction of New Generic Top-Level Domains*, Recommendation 3.

gTLDs applied for in the 2012 New gTLD Program applications period. Chapter 2 seeks particularly to contextualize the New gTLD Program within the trajectory of the DNS's development. It does this by tracing the steps that have led to this point, beginning with the design of the system and the role of names within it attributed by its architects. Chapter 2 ends by identifying issues arising in New gTLD Program policy; in some cases these issues are not new to the DNS, but were nevertheless new to its top-level at the time of launch of the New gTLD Program.

Part II, which is comprised of Chapters 3 and 4, explores the existing policy and legal frameworks respecting the recognition of rights in names, in particular geographic names. Chapter 3 addresses the past and present policy of recognizing rights in names in the DNS. It begins with the lawlessness that prevailed immediately after the system's implementation and tracks the mechanisms that have since been put into place in an attempt to limit the unauthorized registration of names the subject of 'offline' legal rights as domain names. Many of these mechanisms are the result of concerted efforts of the intellectual property community, particularly trademark owners; the scope of rights currently protected in the DNS is therefore, unsurprisingly, largely limited to trademark rights. Where these mechanisms presently or could in the future offer scope for protecting rights in geographic names, this is highlighted.

Chapter 4 proceeds by setting out the legal framework underpinning the recognition of rights in names under international law. It begins by identifying the sources of international law, of which only treaties have been given close consideration in previous efforts to elucidate rights in geographic names and control their use in the DNS. Beyond the formal sources of law, the dynamism of the internet and the forums in which norms respecting it are taking shape necessitate an exploration of the notion of 'soft law'. It is posited that an answer to the question of whether rights are recognized under international law in geographic names in large part depends upon the role that one attributes to 'soft law' and the contributions of non-State actors such as ICANN, the WIPO and the World Trade Organization ('WTO'). This study thus implicates broader doctrinal questions about the formation and formalization of international norms respecting the internet.

Part III of this book proceeds by applying the legal analytical framework presented in Chapter 4 to identify and analyse rights recognized in geographic names under international law. This final part is comprised of five chapters, each of which explores a different basis for legal rights in geographic names. Chapter 5 leads this by considering first, whether geographic names fit within the notion of intellectual property and second, the extent to which rights in geographic names are recognized in trademark law. Standard, collective and certification marks are discussed, and the benefits of trademark registration in the DNS context are identified. Chapter 6 then examines rights in geographic names as such; principal areas of focus are Article 6*ter* of the Paris Convention for the Protection of Industrial

Property (the 'Paris Convention') and the principle of sovereignty. Chapter 7 considers the special legal category of geographical indications, which are names that represent products originating from a specific geographic location. The multiple existing treaty frameworks recognizing geographical indications are examined along with developing treaty and customary international law in this area. Chapter 8 then considers rights that can be derived from geographic names' commercial use, arising in particular from the prevention of unfair competition. The focus in this analysis is mainly on Articles 10 and 10*bis* of the Paris Convention; relevant provisions of the General Agreement on Tariffs and Trade ('GATT') are also discussed. Chapter 9 explores the potential of international human rights as encompassing rights in geographic names; specifically, rights to national identity, self-determination, freedom of expression, culture, language and property are explored, along with the doctrine of common heritage of mankind. A summary of findings and conclusions is lastly presented after Chapter 9.

This edition is current to the conclusion of the 57th ICANN Public Meeting and Annual General Meeting held in Hyderabad, India in early November 2016. One notable downside to the remarkable dynamism of the internet and its DNS is that addresses change frequently; the many internet sources referenced and relied upon in this work were updated and their addresses confirmed live as of 11 November 2016, but inevitably, in time, some of these will change. Any unintentional errors or mistakes in the chapters that follow are, with regret, the fault of the author's.

Part I

Geographic Names in the Developing Domain Name System

Chapter 1

Assumptions of Rights in Geographic Names

The language of rights is so central to modern political and judicial discourse that to be recognized as a true 'right' is an important victory in itself. ... All manner of interests and claims can loosely be classified as 'rights'. Such casual application of language, however, only serves to obfuscate the true legal status of these interests.[1]

1.1 'OFFLINE' VERSUS 'ONLINE' RIGHTS IN NAMES

Names lie at the heart of the internet's Domain Name System ('DNS'), a system built upon the premise that its human users find it easier to remember addresses constituted of names than those of numbers.[2] Certain types of names, most notably trademarks and trade names, have long been subjects of proprietary rights under domestic and international legal frameworks. Yet when the DNS's early architects declined to constrain the system with geopolitical or topographical borders,[3] they likewise rejected fitting the system into the existing legal frameworks that are based on and derive their authority from the acknowledged legitimacy of those borders. Without these

1. John Cahir, *The Public Domain: Right or Liberty?*, in *Intellectual Property: The Many Faces of the Public Domain* 35 (Hector Macqueen & Charlotte Waelde eds, Edward Elgar 2007).
2. CSTB, *Signposts in Cyberspace: The Domain Name System and Internet Navigation* 40 (National Academies Press 2005).
3. Jon Postel & J. Reynolds, *Domain Requirements: RFC 920*, http://www.rfc-editor.org/rfc/rfc920.txt (October 1984).

constraints, the DNS would be free to develop globally along creative rather than political lines; innovations would be implemented after consultation not with bureaucrats and lawyers but with peers in a burgeoning 'Internet community'.[4]

The use of names in the DNS was seen as something apart from the legal frameworks the system's architects avoided. Such a view is a logical extension of the distinctly different contexts involved, IPRs being domestic legal constructs constrained by national borders and domain names being information source identifiers in a borderless, global communications medium. Collision of the two was not apparently anticipated by the technical community, who envisioned the choice of names to be guided by mnemonic rather than semantic value.[5] In hindsight, however, the attempt to construct the DNS outside of existing legal (in particular trademark) frameworks came to be viewed as a 'sure recipe for conflict'.[6]

Prior to the large-scale expansion of the DNS that culminated in an open global applications round in the first half of 2012, the focus in the scholarship and policy debate in this area was largely directed at the use of trademarks in second-level domain names. This can be explained by two things: first, the cohesiveness of the legal rights framework protecting trademarks and the global community of trademark holders, and second, by the actual path of DNS development to that point. These ideas are concisely introduced in this chapter, because while the volume of disputes generated by competing applications for new top-level domains and the objection processes built into the applications process has – of necessity – broadened the focus, a retrospective remains key to understanding the context underpinning New gTLD Program policy. Chapter 2 then explains DNS expansion and its past, present and potential future relevance by exploring in detail the system's development and the role of names in that progression.

1.1.1 Trademarks and the Domain Name System

Trademarks have been recognized in international law as rights in the nature of private property since the late nineteenth century, and in many nations' domestic law for considerably longer. They have long benefited from a general attitude of consensus, rather unique when considered against other IPRs, about the subject matter, duration and criteria of protection. The 1883 Paris Convention for the Protection of Industrial Property (the 'Paris

4. Milton L. Mueller, *Ruling the Root: Internet Governance and the Taming of Cyberspace* 73 (MIT Press 2002).
5. 'The motivation is to provide an organization name that is free of undesirable semantics.' Postel & Reynolds, 2.
6. IAHC, *Memorandum of Understanding on the Generic Top-Level Domain Space of the Internet Domain Name System (gTLD-MoU)*, archived at http://www.archive.org/web/web.php (28 Feb. 1997).

Convention')[7] required signatories to prevent third parties from making use of a mark without the authorization of its right holder, while also recognizing and preserving the domestic nature of this protection by allowing Member States to maintain their own registration criteria. Critically, the Paris Convention imposed in Article 2 the principle of national treatment, with the result that rights conferred by a national system in relation to registration of and limited monopoly rights over trademarks must be made available at no disadvantage to nationals of other Member States. More than a century later, the TRIPS Agreement,[8] which incorporates and binds signatories to uphold the Paris Convention and to which all WTO Member States are bound, harmonized in Article 15(1) the by-then relatively consistent registration criteria of distinctiveness and use on or in connection with specified goods or services.

This longstanding, cohesive recognition of rights at the international level has facilitated the formation of a similarly cohesive global community of domestic legal rights holders. That community has systematically refused to accept the notion that the DNS is some sort of separate, parallel universe in which trademark rights can be ignored. This sentiment was, however, surprisingly slow burning at first: ten years after the launch of the DNS, as few as one-third of Fortune 500 companies had registered 'the most desirable forms of their trademarks' as domain names.[9] This delay would exacerbate the collision between their existing 'offline' rights in names and the use by others of those same names in the new 'online' environment:

> Once it became clear that the Internet was important, even essential to business, a bunch of companies had decided to get themselves an Internet domain and found that the ones they wanted had already been registered by someone else under Network Solutions' first-come-first-served registration policy. They were outraged. They sued. Some won; some lost.[10]

That the global trademark community would come to play a vital role in shaping DNS policy is, in hindsight, no surprise as brand owners united to achieve the recognition of their commercially valuable rights in the new communications medium. Intellectual property interests have been formally

7. Paris Convention for the Protection of Industrial Property (20 Mar. 1883, last revised 14 Jul. 1967 and as amended 28 Sep. 1979), 828 U.N.T.S. 305.
8. Agreement on Trade-Related Aspects of Intellectual Property Rights, Marrakesh Agreement Establishing the World Trade Organization, Annex 1C (15 Apr. 1994), 1869 U.N.T.S. 299, 33 I.L.M. 1197 (hereinafter, the 'TRIPS Agreement').
9. J. Theodore Smith, Student Author, *'1-800-RIPOFFS.COM': Internet Domain Names Are the Telephone Numbers of Cyberspace*, 1997 U. Ill. L. Rev. 1169, 1185 n. 135 (1997).
10. Jessica Litman, *Essay: The DNS Wars: Trademarks and the Internet Domain Name System*, 4 J. Small & Emerging Bus. L. 149, 152–153 (2000) (internal citations omitted).

recognized in ICANN's structure from that organization's earliest days;[11] today, the Intellectual Property Constituency ('IPC') contributes to policy-making as a component of the Generic Names Supporting Organization ('GNSO'), one of the three policy-development bodies within ICANN. Members of the wider internet community, ranging from corporate multinationals to single local brand owners, are also active in their individual capacities or through representatives as direct individual participants in ICANN policy development.

This level of cohesion and cooperation explains why trademark interests have come to be acknowledged in the DNS, but it also helps (at least partly) to explain why other legal rights holders have not achieved the same result. Trademarks' commercial value is undoubtedly the key motivation for the resources expended in policy development, law-making and scholarship to secure their recognition in the DNS, while the non-commercial nature of geographic, cultural, and other names of national significance is likely the key reason for their lack of recognition, both online and offline. The communities represented by geographic and cultural names are more diverse than the community of trademark owners, and their interests are not collectively represented[12] or lobbied on a scale anywhere near the capabilities of such international organizations as the International Trademark Association ('INTA') and the Association of European Trade Mark Owners ('MARQUES'). Yet the gravest point of distinction between trademarks and names of geographical and cultural significance, as later chapters of this book reveal, is the lack of express, cohesive or harmonized support for their protection under international law.

1.1.2 The Impact of DNS Development on Naming Issues

The development and use of the DNS up to the point of the New gTLD Program also helps to explain the focus in DNS naming policy on the use of trademarks in second-level domain names. Before progressing further, a high-level understanding of terminology is necessary: domain names are addresses that identify an information source's location on the internet. They are the public's point of everyday interaction with the DNS, which otherwise operates largely hidden from the average internet user's view. Similar to the way in which a postal address identifies the path that a parcel needs to travel to reach its destination via a particular country, then state, province or county,

11. ICANN, *Preliminary Report: ICANN Meeting in Berlin 27-29 May 1999*, http://archive.icann.org/en/meetings/berlin/berlin-resolutions.html#1 (ICANN's Board unanimously adopting a resolution to recognize six constituencies, including a constituency representing intellectual property interests, of the Domain Names Supporting Organization, predecessor to today's Generic Names Supporting Organization).
12. *See generally,* Mancur Olson, *The Logic of Collective Action: Public Goods and the Theory of Groups* (Harv. U. Press 1971).

then city and street, the component parts of a domain name, separated by dots, identify the path that electronic data must travel to reach its destination. Like the standardized system of postal addressing, the purpose of the DNS is to structure and organize all of the sending and receiving destinations in the system to ensure that information can reliably and accurately travel between destinations. In the case of the DNS, these destinations are not geographic locations, but computers that store information. They are organized into areas called 'domains', and each is assigned a name by which to identify it. Thus what we have come to call a 'domain name' is not one name, but actually several names strung together, being the names of the multiple domains through which requests must travel to reach the desired source of information. These names are separated by the '.' character, which is colloquially referred to as a 'dot'.

At the highest point in this organizing structure is a database that identifies the name and location of what are referred to as 'top-level domains' or 'TLDs'. Each TLD in turn maintains a database that records all of the domains registered directly within it. These 'registrants' within a TLD form the next (second) level in the hierarchy, and so the structure continues down the hierarchy.

Domain name registrations have grown exponentially since their initial commercial availability:[13] as the applications period opened in January 2012 for the creation of new top-level domains, the DNS reportedly comprised more than 225 million second-level domain names.[14] Once brand owners awoke to the possibilities of the internet as a new environment for placing brand messages before consumers, conflicts arose with those who had already registered second-level domain names constituting their trademarks. While progress has been made, these conflicts still arise as the number of second-level registrations continually grows; four years on from the 2012 applications period and with more than 1,000 new generic top-level domains added to it, the DNS reached the 300 million milestone in the first quarter of 2016.[15]

The top-level domain space is so significantly smaller because, prior to the New gTLD Program, it was not open to large-scale public registration ('registration' is not the term normally used in this context for technical and practical reasons that are fully explained in Chapter 2, but nevertheless its use in this foundational introduction to the technology offers a helpful analogy to the second level) and its development was tightly controlled by ICANN. As of January 2012, there were a total of approximately 330 top-level domains, of which only twenty-two were categorized as generic, in

---

13. On the growth of the .com domain, *see* Table 2.4 in Part I, Chapter 2, below.
14. Verisign, *The Domain Name Industry Brief 9(1)*, 2, https://www.verisign.com/assets/domain-name-brief-march2012.pdf (Mar. 2012).
15. Verisign, *The Domain Name Industry Brief 13(2)*, 2, https://www.verisign.com/assets/domain-name-report-july2016.pdf (Jul. 2016).

addition to nearly fifty test or operative Internationalized Domain Names ('IDNs') in non-Latin scripts, and the remainder called 'country code TLDs'. The country code TLDs (or 'ccTLDs', for example, the United Kingdom's (hereinafter 'UK') .uk, Switzerland's .ch and Japan's .jp) derive their names from an existing naming convention maintained by the International Standardization Organization ('ISO'), while the initial set of eight generic TLDs (or 'gTLDs') was selected and named by the DNS's architects.[16] The initial gTLDs' three-letter names were fittingly generic rather than proprietary in character, broadly reflecting the activity of their potential registrants: arpa (named after the US Department of Defense ARPA project out of which the DNS originated), com (commercial), edu (education), gov (government), int (international), mil (military), net (networks), and org (organizations). Conflicts with legal rights holders over the names of these aptly called 'generic' top-level domains did not arise.

Two subsequent 'proof of concept' expansion rounds added fifteen more gTLDs to the system. In the first, which commenced in the year 2000, forty-four applications were lodged requesting more than 200 new gTLDs.[17] Conflicts with legal rights were not an issue for the vast majority of these applied-for gTLD names (which are frequently referred to not as 'names' but as 'strings') because, like the initial eight gTLDs, they were of a generic, non-proprietary character and suggestive of an activity or industry, for example: .books, .hotel, .insurance and .xxx. A select few of the applied-for strings in this first 'proof of concept' round could be interpreted more narrowly and problematically as representing not a field of activity but rather the identity of a particular applicant, for example: .nyc, .africa and .times. These few names had a proprietary, rather than plainly generic, connotation. Ultimately, none of the seven strings approved and selected for delegation during this round[18] were of this potentially problematic type. Issues of conflicting third-party rights were addressed only in the context of preventing clashes at the second level in the newly delegated gTLDs.[19]

---

16. Jon Postel, *Domain Name System Structure and Delegation: RFC 1591*, 2, http://www.rfc-editor.org/rfc/rfc1591.txt (March 1994).
17. ICANN, *TLD Applications Lodged: 2 Oct. 2000*, http://www.icann.org/en/tlds/tld-applications-lodged-02oct00.htm (corrected to 10 Oct. 2000).
18. These seven were: .museum, .aero, .coop, .biz, .info, .name and .pro. ICANN, *Status Report on the sTLD Evaluation Process*, https://archive.icann.org/en/tlds/stld-apps-19mar04/stld-status-report.pdf (19 Mar. 2004).
19. Applications for new gTLDs were evaluated against nine criteria, of which the eighth related to conflict with existing legal rights, but the emphasis being on 'appropriate protections of rights of others in connection with the operation of the TLD. In introducing new TLDs, care should be taken to ensure that the rights of third parties are appropriately protected. Examples of matters to be examined in this regard include:
    (a) Does the proposal have a well-thought-out plan for allocation of names during the start-up phase of the TLD in a way that protects the legitimate interests of significant stakeholders, including existing domain name holders, businesses with legally protected names, and others with which conflict is likely?

The perceived success of this initial attempt at top-level expansion, particularly with respect to new gTLDs targeting a defined community of users, led to the launch of a second 'proof of concept' expansion round in 2003 in which only 'sponsored' gTLD applications were called for. Proposed strings were required to '[c]ategorize[] a broad and lasting field of human, institutional, or social endeavour or activity' and '[r]epresent[] an endeavour or activity that has importance across multiple geographic regions'.[20] Neither of these criteria was inherently conducive to applications for distinctive names of a proprietary nature, but they did not expressly bar them, either, as is reflected in the ten applied-for strings: .asia, .cat, .jobs, .mail, .mobi, .post, .tel (two applications), .travel and .xxx.[21] All were ultimately accepted and delegated with the exception of .mail and one of the two competing .tel applications.[22]

As in the first 'proof of concept' expansion round, evaluation criteria in this second round were explicitly directed at measures to avoid conflict with existing (primarily trademark) rights in the operation of the proposed new namespace, including restrictions on eligibility for registration of second-level domain names, compliance with applicable trademark laws, implementation of the Uniform Domain Name Dispute Resolution Policy ('UDRP')[23] to combat bad faith trademark infringing registrations and, where appropriate, additional safeguards.[24] Applicants were required to demonstrate the appropriateness of their chosen string relative to the scope of the community

---

(b) Does the proposal provide for a reasonably accessible and efficient mechanism for resolving domain name disputes?
(c) Has the proponent considered intellectual property interests or otherwise designed protections for third party interests?
(d) Does the proposal make adequate provision for Whois service that strikes an appropriate balance between providing information to the public regarding domain name registrations in a convenient manner and offering mechanisms to preserve personal privacy?
(e) Does the proposal incorporate policies that are likely to discourage abusive registration practices?

ICANN, *Criteria for Evaluating New TLD proposals*, http://www.icann.org/en/tlds/tld-criteria-15aug00.htm (15 Aug. 2000).

20. ICANN, *sTLD Application Process Appendix A: sTLD Selection Criteria*, http://www.icann.org/en/tlds/stld-apps-19mar04/PostAppA.pdf (19 Mar. 2004).
21. ICANN, *Status Report on the sTLD Evaluation Process*.
22. ICANN, *Information Page for Sponsored Top-Level Domains: A Summary of Documents and Reports Associated with the Second 'Proof of Concept' Top-level Domain Expansion Round*, http://www.icann.org/en/tlds/stld-apps-19mar04/. The much-disputed application for a new .xxx gTLD was ultimately approved by ICANN's Board of Directors on 18 Mar. 2011. ICANN, *Board of Directors Resolutions 2011.03.18.23-2011.03.18.25 Approval of ICM Registry Application for .XXX: Adopted Board Resolutions, Silicon Valley/San Francisco*, https://www.icann.org/resources/board-material/resolutions-2011-03-18-en#5 (18 Mar. 2011).
23. The UDRP is discussed in Part II, Chapter 3, s. 3.3.1 below.
24. ICANN, *sTLD Application Process Appendix A: sTLD Selection Criteria*.

represented by it, as well as the 'broad-based support' of that community for the application.[25] An applicant's right to apply for a string could presumably be inferred from the demonstration of community support, but as in the first 'proof of concept' expansion round, none of the selection criteria addressed the potential for the name of the applied-for TLD string itself to be the subject of or conflict with existing legal rights.

Such an inquiry would have been moot for the applicants of .jobs, .mail, .mobi, .post, .tel, .travel and .xxx given their strings' plainly generic nature. The same cannot be said, however, of the .asia and .cat strings. Both applications presented support from their relevant communities: the .asia application was made by the Dot Asia Organisation, which sought Asian-region ccTLD registries as members,[26] while the .cat application was formally endorsed by the Institute of Catalan Studies, which is 'the Catalan equivalent of the French or Spanish royal academies', as well as by the governments of Spain and Andorra, countries in which Catalan is declared an official language at the national or regional level.[27] The public portions of these applications contain no indication of enquiries having been made into the legal rights of the applicants, or indeed the national governments and ccTLD administrators that supported them, in these names.

It is clear why the conflict between offline and online rights at the top-level of the DNS did not arise prior to the second 'proof of concept' expansion round, but it is not clear why conflict did not arise during or after that point. The .asia and .cat new gTLD applications set a dangerous precedent not (as ICANN's Board of Directors feared) because they opened the door to a flood of applications for geographical, cultural and linguistic strings,[28] but because they demonstrated ICANN's willingness to delegate new gTLDs comprised of names of geographical or cultural significance without questioning the applicants', their official supporters', or third parties' legal rights in such names. Going one step further, the .asia and .cat applications also demonstrated ICANN's willingness to delegate new gTLDs comprised of names of geographical or cultural significance without a reliably clear or comprehensive policy for the allocation of such names, setting an unfortunate precedent that continues today.

---

25. *Ibid.*
26. ICANN, *New sTLD RFP Application: .asia Part B Application Form*, http://archive.icann.org/en/tlds/stld-apps-19mar04/asia.htm.
27. ICANN, *New sTLD RFP Application: .cat Part B Application Form*, http://archive.icann.org/en/tlds/stld-apps-19mar04/cat.htm. Peter Gerrand, *Cultural Diversity in Cyberspace: The Catalan Campaign to Win the New .cat Top Level Domain*, 11(1–2) First Monday (2006).
28. Members of the ICANN Board of Directors are reported as having asked of the .cat application: 'But doesn't .cat create a precedent for thousands of minority languages, all wanting a TLD?' Concern was also reportedly expressed 'that UNESCO might fund 5,000 new cultural sTLDs.' To this, Amadeu Abril i Abril, the 'mastermind behind the campaign for ".cat"', replied: 'What is the problem if someone pays?' *Ibid.*

Fundamentally underpinning this study is the view that the *gTLD Applicant Guidebook*, the document that sets out ICANN's policy on new gTLDs, is a missed opportunity that took ICANN further down the path of implicit assumptions about the existence and exclusivity or supremacy of governments' rights in geographic names, and wilful blindness of the potential existence of third parties' rights in such names. These implicit assumptions sparked the questions that gave rise to the study documented in the first edition of this book, the manuscript of which was completed in 2012 soon after the New gTLD Program applications were revealed, but before any application had undergone evaluation or been added to the DNS. It was appropriate and overdue then to question the validity of ICANN's assumptions about rights in geographic names, particularly in light of ICANN's Board having voluntarily undertaken to avoid creating new gTLDs that infringe the rights of others as recognized under international law. One thousand new gTLDs in the root later, it remains appropriate to raise these questions: indeed, the starting point of this second edition is the view that acknowledging and addressing the problems generated by the faulty assumptions made in the *gTLD Applicant Guidebook* is the only way to resolve the disputes that have embroiled applications made in 2012 for names of a perceived geographic nature, and the only way to prevent similar disputes in future top-level expansion initiatives. Exemplary disputes are discussed after the next section, which sets out the applicable ICANN policy that gave rise to them.

1.2 THE *G*TLD APPLICANT GUIDEBOOK AND GEOGRAPHIC NAMES

1.2.1 GEOGRAPHIC NAMES DEFINED AND STATES' RIGHTS IMPLIED

It could easily be taken for granted, but the term 'geographic name' is not so easy to define because geographic names take many forms. There are the long-form names that formally represent a country's identity in the international diplomatic sphere, such as 'United Kingdom of Great Britain and Northern Ireland' and 'United States of America'. There are also short-form names that are in many cases more commonly used than long-form names, such as 'United Kingdom' or 'Great Britain', and 'United States'. There are also further shortened, colloquial names such as 'Britain' and 'America', acronyms such as 'GB', 'UK' and 'USA', translations such as 'Grande Bretagne', 'Royaume-Uni' and 'Estados Unidos', and transliterations such as 'Great Brittain' and 'Untied States'. With this in mind, it is not surprising that geographic names have yet to be subjected to the line-drawing exercise needed to develop a precise legal definition.

The development of a policy on geographic names and their use in the context of new gTLDs unavoidably required just such an exercise. A definition of 'geographic names' first appeared in the third draft of ICANN's *gTLD Applicant Guidebook*; it encompassed many of the forms identified in the previous paragraph, plus others.[29] With subsequent drafts of the *gTLD Applicant Guidebook* came revised versions of this definition, the most significant being the removal of country and territory names in order to completely bar applicants from applying for them.[30] The other categories of geographic name remained in the 11 January 2012 version of the *gTLD Applicant Guidebook* operative during the New gTLD Program 2012 applications period, with some changes to the scope of excluded country names and included city and supranational names:

> 1. An application for any string that is a representation, in any language, of the *capital city name* of any country or territory listed in the ISO 3166-1 standard.
> 2. An application for a *city name*, where the applicant declares that it intends to use the gTLD for purposes associated with the city name.
>
> ... ;

29. Country or territory names, meaning:
    - an alpha-3 code listed in the ISO 3166-1 standard;
    - a long- or short-form name listed in the ISO 3166-1 standard, or a translation of the long- or short-form name in any language;
    - a long- or short-form name associated with a code that has been designated as 'exceptionally reserved' by the ISO 3166 Maintenance Agency;
    - a 'separable component of a country name' designated on a list based on the ISO 3166-1 standard;
    - a 'permutation or transposition' of any of the above, where 'permutations include removal of spaces, insertion of punctuation, and addition or removal of grammatical articles like "the"'. A transposition is considered a change in the sequence of the long- or short-form name, for example, 'RepublicCzech' or 'IslandsCayman'.

    'Exact matches of a sub-national place name, such as a county, province, or state, listed in the ISO 3166-2 standard.
    A representation, in any language, of the capital city name of any country or territory listed in the ISO 3166-1 standard.
    A city name, where the applicant declares that it intends to use the gTLD for purposes associated with the city name.
    The name of a continent or UN region appearing on the "Composition of macro geographical (continental) regions, geographical sub-regions, and selected economic and other groupings' list."'
    ICANN, *Draft Applicant Guidebook, version 3*, 2.1.1.4.1, https://archive.icann.org/en/topics/new-gtlds/draft-rfp-clean-04oct09-en.pdf (2 Oct. 2009).
30. ICANN, *gTLD Applicant Guidebook*, 2.2.1.4.1. Notably, the definition of excluded 'country names' was amended at a late stage to include the names by which countries are commonly known.

3. An application for any string that is an exact match of a *sub-national place name*, such as a county, province, or state, listed in the ISO 3166-2 standard.
4. An application for a string listed as a UNESCO region or appearing on the 'Composition of macro geographical (continental) regions, geographical sub-regions, and selected economic and other groupings' list.[31]

Amendments made after the applications process which resulted in a final version of 4 June 2012 of the *gTLD Applicant Guidebook*[32] made no changes to this definition, which will continue to apply to future expansion initiatives unless it is amended in the interim.[33]

The breadth of this definition of 'geographic names' is notable because it includes much more than just country names, which had previously been the main target of ICANN's Governmental Advisory Committee. The above definition includes supra- and subnational geographic names and also captures geographical indications, which are a distinct legal category of geographic name that serve to identify a product as originating from a particular geographic location.[34]

The *gTLD Applicant Guidebook* protects geographic names in two distinct ways. First, it prevents applicants from applying for strings comprised of country or territory names.[35] Second, it imposes upon applicants of other so-defined 'geographic names' a requirement to demonstrate the support or non-objection of the governments or public authorities relevant to the applied-for string. Applications failing to meet the support or non-objection requirement are to be rejected during the initial application evaluation phase in a process called 'string review'.[36] Also relevant to

31. *Id.*, 2.2.1.4.2.
32. ICANN, *Applicant Guidebook: New gTLD Applicant Guidebook 4 June 2012*, https://newgtlds.icann.org/en/applicants/agb.
33. ICANN, *Public Meetings: GNSO New gTLD Subsequent Procedures PDP WG – Transcript [EN]*, https://meetings.icann.org/en/marrakech55/schedule/thu-new-gtld-subsequent-procedures/transcript-new-gtld-subsequent-procedures-10mar16-en.pdf (10 Mar. 2016) (*see* remarks of Jeff Neuman, co-Chair of the GNSO Subsequent Procedures PDP, noting that the Applicant Guidebook is 'currently the GNSO policy on new gTLDs. So if there were subsequent TLDs introduced, whether in rounds or going forward in another way, these policies would still apply unless we as a group, as the PDP, decide by consensus to change any of those, modify those, take some out, add some. So the reason why we're spending a lot of time on this is because this is still the policy unless we all decide to change it.').
34. Geographical indications are discussed in Part III, Chapter 7.
35. ICANN, *gTLD Applicant Guidebook*, 2.2.1.4.1. A study group was formed within ICANN to identify issues relating to the registrability of country and territory names as a starting point for developing policy to apply in future application rounds. ccNSO, *Non-PDP Study Group on Use of Names for Countries and Territories*, http://ccnso.icann.org/workinggroups/unctwg.htm.
36. ICANN, *gTLD Applicant Guidebook*, 2.2.1.3.1.

geographic names' eventual delegation as new gTLDs is the availability of review and an 'early warning' by the GAC, whereby concerns about an application can be formally raised to ICANN's Board of Directors.[37] Examples involving the use of these procedures are provided in the case studies set out in section 1.3 of this chapter, below.

ICANN's definition of and limitations upon geographic domain names as contained in the *gTLD Applicant Guidebook* is thus consistent with the recommendation made to the Board of Directors by the GAC, membership of which is made up of 'national governments, distinct economies as recognized in international fora, and (as Observers) multinational governmental organisations and treaty organisations',[38] to prevent the creation of geographic new gTLDs without the authorization of relevant governments. The legal basis for government control over applications for geographic new gTLDs is not addressed by, or specifically challengeable under, the *gTLD Applicant Guidebook*. As the next section of this chapter explains, objection grounds are available, but these offer only limited scope for challenging geographic new gTLD applications.

1.2.2 Grounds of Objection to New gTLD Applications

A limited selection of grounds for challenging new gTLD applications that survive the initial 'string review' phase[39] is provided by the *gTLD Applicant Guidebook*; these grounds are each discussed in the subsections that follow. It must simultaneously be borne in mind that applications for geographic strings not demonstrating the requisite support or non-objection of relevant governments will be rejected irrespective of objections being filed against them.

---

37. *Id.*, 1.1.2.4. ICANN, *New gTLD Program Explanatory Memorandum: GAC and Government Objections; Handling of Sensitive Strings; Early Warning*, https://archive.icann.org/en/topics/new-gtlds/gac-objections-sensitive-strings-15apr11-en.pdf (15 Apr. 2011).
38. GAC, *About the GAC*, https://gacweb.icann.org/display/gacweb/About+the+GAC (2011).
39. Note that the *gTLD Applicant Guidebook* mandates rejection of applications for geographic strings not demonstrating the requisite support or non-objection of relevant governments irrespective of objections being filed against them. ICANN, *gTLD Applicant Guidebook*. ICANN, *gTLD Applicant Guidebook*, 2.2.1.4.2 Geographic Names Requiring Government Support ('The following types of applied-for strings are considered geographic names and must be accompanied by documentation of support or non-objection from the relevant governments or public authorities') and 2.2.1.4.4 Review Procedure for Geographic Names ('if the applicant has not produced the required documentation by the required date … the application will be considered incomplete and will be ineligible for further review.')

1.2.2.1 Objection on Community Grounds

Standing to object to any new gTLD application on community grounds is available to '[e]stablished institutions associated with clearly delineated communities' with a strong association to the applied-for string.[40] Objections can also be raised by a designated Independent Objector, who 'does not act on behalf of any particular persons or entities, but acts solely in the best interests of the public who use the global Internet'.[41] The *gTLD Applicant Guidebook* makes no inquiry into the legal rights of either objectors or community based applicants to their applied-for names; on the contrary, these are effectively assumed on satisfaction of the standing requirements.

This objection is directed at situations in which a 'significant portion of the community to which the gTLD string may be explicitly or implicitly targeted' raises 'substantial opposition'.[42] To clarify, all applicants for new gTLD strings are required to designate their application for a new gTLD as either 'standard' or 'community based'. The term 'standard', alternatively termed 'open' in drafts prior to version 3 of the *gTLD Applicant Guidebook*,[43] by contrast simply signifies applications that are not community based. The second draft version of the *gTLD Applicant Guidebook* offered an explanation of the community based designation as a gTLD intended to be 'operated for the benefit of a defined community consisting of a restricted population.'[44] Accordingly, an applicant for a community based new gTLD is required to 'substantiate its status as a representative of the community it names in the application.'[45] Forty-two of the 1,930 applications received by ICANN in 2012 were designated as community based, although not all of these have been successful in relying upon that designation.[46] Table 1.1 below identifies applications designated as community based for strings comprising names of geographic places. This table additionally notes whether the applicant identified the applied-for string as 'geographic' pursuant to the *gTLD Applicant Guidebook* definition cited earlier in this chapter in section 1.2.1. The Asian Spa and Wellness Promotion Council Limited's community based application for .spa[47] is notable here for its

40. ICANN, *gTLD Applicant Guidebook*, 3.2.2.4.
41. ICANN, *gTLD Applicant Guidebook*, 3.2.5.
42. *Id.*, 3.2.1 ('Community Objection').
43. The appropriateness of the characterization 'open' was questioned as it suggested that community based gTLDs were somehow 'antithetical to … openness'. *Id.*, 1.2.2.1.
44. ICANN, *Draft Applicant Guidebook, version 2*, Glossary, https://archive.icann.org/en/topics/new-gtlds/draft-rfp-clean-18feb09-en.pdf (18 Feb. 2009).
45. *Ibid.*
46. *See for example*, New gTLD Program Community Priority Evaluation Report (.GAY), https://www.icann.org/sites/default/files/tlds/gay/gay-cpe-rr-1-1713-23699-en.pdf (8 Oct. 2015).
47. ICANN, New gTLD Application Submitted to ICANN by: Asian Spa and Wellness Promotion Council Limited, https://gtldresult.icann.org/application-result/application status/applicationdetails:downloadapplication/123?t:ac=123 (13 Jun. 2012).

having been targeted by the GAC as requiring coordination with and agreement from the city of Spa, Belgium,[48] despite the application's having successfully passed Initial Evaluation and being considered not to 'fall within the criteria for a geographic name contained in the Applicant Guidebook Section 2.2.1.4.'[49]

Table 1.1 Community Based Applications (2012) for Names Corresponding to Geographic Places

Applied-for String	*Applicant*	*Designated by Applicant as Geographic Yes/No*
.paris[50]	City of Paris	Yes
.berlin[51]	dotBERLIN GmbH & Co. KG	Yes
.wien[52]	punkt.wien GmbH	Yes
.madrid[53]	Communidad de Madrid	Yes
.quebec[54]	PointQuébec Inc	Yes
.osaka[55]	Interlink Co., Ltd.	Yes
.hamburg[56]	Hamburg Top-Level-Domain GmbH	Yes

48. ICANN Governmental Advisory Committee, GAC Communiqué – Singapore, https://gacweb.icann.org/display/GACADV/2014-03-27-spa (27 Mar. 2014).
49. ICANN, New gTLD Program – Initial Evaluation Report (SPA), https://newgtlds.icann.org/sites/default/files/ier/0riusp5e5hoes40ji6vlayi6/ie-1-1309-81322-en.pdf (7 Jun. 2013).
50. ICANN, New gTLD Application Submitted to ICANN by: City of Paris, https://gtldresult.icann.org/application-result/applicationstatus/applicationdetails:downloadapplication/1450?t:ac=1450 (13 Jun. 2012).
51. ICANN, New gTLD Application Submitted to ICANN by: dotBERLIN GmbH & Co. KG, https://gtldresult.icann.org/application-result/applicationstatus/applicationdetails:downloadapplication/1777?t:ac=1777 (13 Jun. 2012).
52. ICANN, New gTLD Application Submitted to ICANN by: punkt.wien GmbH, https://gtldresult.icann.org/application-result/applicationstatus/applicationdetails:downloadapplication/1564?t:ac=1564 (13 Jun. 2012).
53. ICANN, New gTLD Application Submitted to ICANN by: Communidad de Madrid, https://gtldresult.icann.org/application-result/applicationstatus/applicationdetails:downloadapplication/416?t:ac=416 (13 Jun. 2012).
54. ICANN, New gTLD Application Submitted to ICANN by: PointQuébec Inc, https://gtldresult.icann.org/application-result/applicationstatus/applicationdetails:downloadapplication/556?t:ac=556 (13 Jun. 2012).
55. ICANN, New gTLD Application Submitted to ICANN by: Interlink Co., Ltd., https://gtldresult.icann.org/application-result/applicationstatus/applicationdetails:downloadapplication/1781?t:ac=1781 (13 Jun. 2012).
56. ICANN, New gTLD Application Submitted to ICANN by: Hamburg Top-Level Domain GmbH, https://gtldresult.icann.org/application-result/applicationstatus/applicationdetails:downloadapplication/1351?t:ac=1351 (13 Jun. 2012).

Applied-for String	*Applicant*	*Designated by Applicant as Geographic Yes/No*
.corsica[57]	Collectivité Territoriale de Corse	No
.tirol[58]	punkt Tirol GmbH	Yes
.barcelona[59]	Municipi de Barcelona	Yes
广东 (Guangdong)[60]	Xinhua News Agency Guangdong Branch 新华通讯社广东分社	Yes

From the limited number of entries in Table 1.1 it can also be deduced that not all of the sixty-six applications characterized by ICANN as 'geographic' were designated by their applicants to be community based.[61]

Designating an application as standard (i.e., not community based) under the *gTLD Applicant Guidebook* notably does not prevent an applicant from imposing eligibility restrictions or other limitations on domain name registrants within the proposed new gTLD. This means that an application for a domain name of geographic significance, for example representing a linguistic or cultural community or a producer of products identified by a geographical indication,[62] could be designated as either standard or community based. A community based example from applications lodged in 2012 is

57. ICANN, New gTLD Application Submitted to ICANN by: Collectivité Territoriale de Corse, https://gtldresult.icann.org/application-result/applicationstatus/applicationdetails:downloadapplication/1697?t:ac=1697 (13 Jun. 2012).
58. ICANN, New gTLD Application Submitted to ICANN by: punkt Tirol GmbH, https://gtldresult.icann.org/application-result/applicationstatus/applicationdetails:downloadapplication/461?t:ac=461 (13 Jun. 2012).
59. ICANN, New gTLD Application Submitted to ICANN by: Municipi de Barcelona, https://gtldresult.icann.org/application-result/applicationstatus/applicationdetails/320 (13 Jun. 2012).
60. ICANN, New gTLD Application Submitted to ICANN by: Xinhua News Agency Guangdong Branch 新华通讯社广东分社, https://gtldresult.icann.org/application-result/applicationstatus/applicationdetails:downloadapplication/140?t:ac=140 (13 Jun. 2012).
61. Examples of standard geographic applications include GMO Registry, Inc.'s application for .TOKYO (https://gtldresult.icann.org/application-result/applicationstatus/applicationdetails:downloadapplication/1790?t:ac=1790 (13 Jun. 2012); The State of New South Wales, Department of Premier and Cabinet's application for .sydney, https://gtldresult.icann.org/application-result/applicationstatus/applicationdetails:downloadapplication/200?t:ac=200 (13 Jun. 2012); and Generalitat de Catalunya's application for .catalonia, https://gtldresult.icann.org/application-result/applicationstatus/applicationdetails:downloadapplication/318?t:ac=318 (13 Jun. 2012).
62. Interestingly, no gTLD applications intended to comprise a geographical indication were lodged in 2012, but ongoing negotiations over the use of geographical indications at the second-level in the proposed .wine and .vin new gTLDs amply illustrate the challenges. *See for example* ICANN, *.WINE and .VIN: Where Does ICANN Stand?*, https://www.icann.org/news/blog/wine-and-vin-where-does-icann-stand (14 May 2014).

the .scot gTLD, applied-for by Dot Scot Registry Limited 'in name and on behalf of the Scottish community, composed of individuals and organizations linked to the community on a cultural or business basis, or by any other activity conducive to the welfare of the Scottish community'.[63] A standard application example is the .cymru gTLD, applied for by Nominet UK 'to provide an innovative, relevant and trusted internet top level domain (TLD) for the use and benefit of the citizens and businesses of Wales.'[64]

Nor does the designation of an applied-for string as standard (i.e., not community based) insulate it from objection on community grounds, as is demonstrated by the Independent Objector's objection to an application for .indians,[65] and objections by the Ministry of Foreign Affairs of Argentina and the Independent Objector against an application for .patagonia.[66] An objection on community grounds against a government-endorsed geographic new gTLD application seems to be the only means available to an affected community to express opposition; this approach was taken in 2012 in only one instance, against an application designated as geographic but lacking the requisite evidence of government support or non-objection.[67]

The choice of an application's community or standard designation is affected by the availability only to community based applicants of an optional community priority evaluation in the resolution of conflicting applications. The community priority evaluation is a process in which the

63. ICANN, New gTLD Application Submitted to ICANN by: Dot Scot Registry Limited, https://gtldresult.icann.org/application-result/applicationstatus/applicationdetails:downloadapplication/417?t:ac=417 (13 Jun. 2012). Other examples include Better Living Management Company's application for .thai, https://gtldresult.icann.org/application-result/applicationstatus/applicationdetails:downloadapplication/27?t:ac=27 (13 Jun. 2012) and the Swiss Confederation's application for .swiss, https://gtldresult.icann.org/application-result/applicationstatus/applicationdetails:downloadapplication/906?t:ac=906 (13 Jun. 2012).
64. ICANN, New gTLD Application Submitted to ICANN by: Nominet UK, https://gtldresult.icann.org/application-result/applicationstatus/applicationdetails:downloadapplication/1420?t:ac=1420 (13 Jun. 2012).
65. ICANN, *New Generic Top Level Domains: Application Details (INDIANS)*, https://gtldresult.icann.org/application-result/applicationstatus/applicationdetails/1005 (application status shows a community objection filed ('Prof. Alain Pellet, Independent Objector vs Reliance Industries Limited – Community') but the objection documentation is not made available).
66. ICANN, *New Generic Top Level Domains: Application Details (PATAGONIA)*, https://gtldresult.icann.org/application-result/applicationstatus/applicationdetails/1466 (application status shows two community objections filed but the objection documentation is not made available).
67. ICANN, New gTLD Application Submitted to ICANN by: Guangzhou YU Wei Information Technology Co., Ltd., https://gtldresult.icann.org/application-result/applicationstatus/applicationdetails:downloadapplication/1379?t:ac=1379 (13 Jun. 2012); ICANN, New gTLD Program – Initial Evaluation Report (广州 – Guangzhou), https://newgtlds.icann.org/sites/default/files/ier/driuswlu8rlevoagl5ml1si9/ie-1-1121-22691-en.pdf (6 Sep. 2013).

relative strength of the articulation of community support within the new gTLD application is scored and compared.[68] Standard applications are eliminated from contention sets by qualified conflicting community based applications, 'regardless of how well qualified' the standard application is.[69] The *gTLD Applicant Guidebook* provides that contention amongst remaining community applications is to be resolved, if not otherwise achieved between the parties, by an auction process.[70]

As the examples provided in this section show, designation as community based is logical for applications for new gTLDs comprised of names of geographical or cultural significance because the very nature of such names is that they are representative of a particular community, such as producers of a product associated with a particular region or the residents of a particular geographic location. In all cases, the applicant (whether a government, an applicant acting on government authority, or an applicant acting without government authority or affiliation) must demonstrate support from the community associated with the string. Also implicit in the examples provided is the fact that the question of whether requisite support can be secured is answerable only on a case-by-case basis; larger, less cohesive or clearly delineated communities present greater challenges than smaller, cohesive, clearly delineated communities in this regard. The *gTLD Applicant Guidebook* gives a qualifying community based application priority over standard applications for the same string, but the prioritized application could still end up in a contention set with one or more other qualifying community based applications. Community designation is not, therefore, a cure-all.

For completeness, it should lastly be noted that the New gTLD Program introduced a new dispute mechanism available to community members who are harmed by the registry's failure to operate the new gTLD on behalf of the community designated in its application.[71] The complaint at the heart of this mechanism is not, however, a challenge to the registry operator's right to the TLD string itself. Rather, it is a challenge to the registry operator's failure to operate the new gTLD for the community's benefit as proposed in the original application and incorporated into the Registry Agreement with ICANN.

---

68. *See for example*, ICANN, New gTLD Program – Community Priority Evaluation Report (.OSAKA), https://www.icann.org/sites/default/files/tlds/osaka/osaka-cpe-1-901-9391-en.pdf (29 Jul. 2014). *See generally*, ICANN, *New Generic Top-Level Domains: Community Priority Evaluation*, https://newgtlds.icann.org/en/applicants/cpe.
69. ICANN, *gTLD Applicant Guidebook*, 4.2.3.
70. *Id.*, 4.2.2.
71. ICANN, *New Generic Top-Level Domains – Applicant Guidebook*, https://newgtlds.icann.org/en/applicants/agb (scroll to Module 5 and click 'Registry Restriction Dispute Resolution (RRDRP) to download). As of 1 Nov. 2016, the mechanism had not yet been utilized against any new gTLD registry operator.

1.2.2.2 Legal Rights Objection

In addition to objection on community grounds, applications for new gTLDs can be challenged on grounds of 'existing legal rights'.[72] Yet even as the *gTLD Applicant Guidebook* assumes rights in geographic and community names, it fails to recognize those rights as bases of objection on the ground of existing legal rights. That opportunity is reserved only to 'rightsholders': trademark owners and international intergovernmental organizations.[73] While standing to object depends on possession of legal rights 'which may include either registered or unregistered trademarks',[74] only one of the eight 'non-exclusive factors' to be evaluated by WIPO, as the selected dispute resolution service provider to administer this objection, makes any reference to legal rights other than trademark rights:[75]

> 6. Whether the applicant has marks or **other intellectual property rights** (emphasis added) in the sign corresponding to the gTLD, and, if so, whether any acquisition of such a right in the sign, and use of the sign, has been bona fide, and whether the purported or likely use of the gTLD by the applicant is consistent with such acquisition or use.

This focus on trademark rights in new gTLD policy implementation is a further reflection of the trademark community's involvement in the policy development process, but the apparent lack of recognition of legal rights in non-trademark names sits uneasily against the assumptions of rights made elsewhere in the *gTLD Applicant Guidebook.* It is also incongruent with the recommendation of ICANN's GNSO, as adopted by the Board of Directors, that new strings be rejected if they:

> infringe the existing legal rights of others that are recognized or enforceable under generally accepted and internationally recognized principles of law. Examples of these legal rights that are internationally recognized include, but are not limited to, rights defined in the Paris Convention for the Protection of Industrial Property (in particular trademark rights), the Universal Declaration of Human Rights (UDHR) and the International Covenant on Civil and Political Rights (ICCPR) (in particular freedom of expression rights).[76]

Public comments to that effect submitted during the *gTLD Applicant Guidebook* drafting process went unheeded.[77]

---

72. ICANN, *gTLD Applicant Guidebook*, 3.2.2.2.
73. *Ibid.*
74. *Ibid.*
75. *Id.*, 3.5.2.
76. GNSO, *Final Report on the Introduction of New Generic Top-Level Domains*, Recommendation 3.
77. *See for example,* Heather A. Forrest, *Comments on the Scope of the Legal Rights*

The limited scope of the legal rights objection sits in stark and inexplicable contrast to the assumptions elsewhere in the *gTLD Applicant Guidebook* about rights in geographic and community names. Legal rights in geographic names and geographical indications, if these are recognized under international law, plainly fall within the spirit of the GNSO's recommendation. If rights in geographic names are recognized under international law, the *gTLD Applicant Guidebook* improperly denies the holders of such rights standing to object on the basis of those rights, while elsewhere implicitly assuming and recognizing the existence of such rights.

The technical conflict between assumed rights and existing rights can be illustrated by reference to any geographic name that is also a brand name. From the applications submitted in 2012 come the following examples arising from a list of names, which includes the separable country names 'Cartier Island' and 'Virgin Islands', forming an Annex of Module 2 of the *gTLD Applicant Guidebook*. Applications by trademark holders (e.g., Cartier jewellers and the Virgin Group) were not prevented by the operation of the exclusion from registrability under section 2.2.1.4.1, which incorporates names identified in the Annex list in the definition of prohibited country and territory names. This can only be attributed to the fact that both strings (for obvious reasons) omit the term 'island/s'; that the brand names themselves are a 'separable *component* (emphasis added) of a country name designated on the "Separable Country Names List"' provided as an Annex to Module 2 of the Guidebook must have been ignored. Applications for both .cartier and .virgin were not only made, but have been approved by ICANN.[78] Under the Governmental Advisory Committee's Geographic Names Working Group's ('GAC Geographic Names Working Group') proposal which expands the definition of 'geographic name' even further, in future expansion initiatives, such applications would likely be subjected to consent requirements, if not prevented outright.[79]

Another area of potential conflict arises in applications for geographical indications, which by their very nature are based on and in most cases identical to geographic names. Should the *gTLD Applicant Guidebook* apply

---

Objection [3gtld-dispute] Chronological Index, http://forum.icann.org/lists/3gtld-dispute/ (23 Nov. 2009).

78. ICANN, *New Generic Top-Level Domains: Application Details VIRGIN*, https://gtldresult.icann.org/application-result/applicationstatus/applicationdetails/378; ICANN, *New Generic Top-Level Domains: Application Details CARTIER*, https://gtldresult.icann.org/application-result/applicationstatus/applicationdetails/1152.

79. GAC, GAC Working Group to Examine the Protection of Geographic Names in Any Future Expansion of gTLDs: Working Papers (https://gacweb.icann.org/display/gacweb/GAC+Working+Group+to+Examine+the+Protection+of+Geographic+Names+in+any+Future+Expansion+of+gTLDs?preview=/39944662/41944013/GAC%20Geo-names%20WG%20-%20Working%20Papers%20.pdf (27 Jun. 2016). Trevor Little, 'Think Geographic Name Protection in New gTLDs Won't Impact Your Brand? Think Again', World Trademark Law Review, http://www.worldtrademarkreview.com/Blog/detail.aspx?g=63cc4191-082f-431e-87bb-980bbf02b7b6 (16 Oct. 2014).

to future applications in its present form, geographical indication new gTLDs constituting a country or territory name will be rejected by the operation of section 2.2.1.4.1. An applied-for string comprising a geographical indication falling within the definition of 'Geographic Names Requiring Government Support' in section 2.2.1.4.2 would be subjected to the government support or non-objection requirement. Even if it did not fall within the section 2.2.1.4.2 definition, a string comprising a geographical indication would very likely be flagged by a member or members of the GAC in an 'early warning' review.[80] An applied-for string comprising a geographical indication would also almost certainly be restricted by an amended *gTLD Applicant Guidebook* that adopted the Governmental Advisory Committee Geographic Names Working Group's restrictive proposal, which advises: 'Governments should keep the right to oppose the delegation of a top level domain (even if it is not included on that list) on the basis of its sensitivity to national interests. Furthermore, that right should be enhanced for future rounds.'[81]

Critically, the legal rights objection is available only to those with trademark rights in geographic names, of which there are relatively few due to the inherent difficulties in registering such trademarks.[82] Governments have no need of the legal rights objection to challenge geographic new gTLD applications because of the availability to them of other challenge mechanisms (including 'early warning' through their GAC representatives) as well as to the priority afforded applications made or consented to by relevant governments. Yet there is no reason why other, non-governmental holders of legal rights in geographic names, if these exist, should be denied standing to object, provided there is a verifiable legal basis for such objection.

It may be possible to resolve conflict between new gTLD applicants and governments on an application-by-application basis, but the overarching conflict between the recognition and non-recognition of rights in geographic names in the *gTLD Applicant Guidebook* remains, as the case studies provided in section 1.3 of this chapter unequivocally illustrate. It is not logical on the one hand to confer priority on the basis of rights without first establishing that such rights are indeed recognized, nor is it logical at other opportunities within the same policy instrument to disallow the recognition of such rights. This is a conundrum that can only be resolved by first determining whether rights in geographic names are actually 'recognized or

80. ICANN, *gTLD Applicant Guidebook*, 1.1.2.4. ICANN, *New gTLD Program Explanatory Memorandum: GAC and Government Objections*.

81. ICANN GAC, 'The protection of geographic names in the new gTLDs [sic] process: V3 – August 29 2014', https://gacweb.icann.org/display/gacweb/Community+Input+-+The+protection+of+Geographic+Names+in+the+New+gTLDs+process?preview=/35455403/35622234/Geo%20names%20in%20new%20gTLDs%20Updated%20%20V3%20%2029%20august%202014%5B4%5D.pdf (29 Aug. 2014).

82. On the availability of trademark protection to geographic names, *see* Part III, Chapter 5, s. 5.2 below.

enforceable under generally accepted and internationally recognized principles of law'; such a determination facilitates clarification and requires amendment of existing ICANN policy to resolve current and prevent future conflicts.

1.2.2.3 Conflict with Country Code TLDs

Also of continuing concern for applicants of geographic new gTLD strings – entirely apart from the requirement that applications demonstrate government support or non-objection – are the country code TLDs ('ccTLDs') and Internationalized Domain Name ('IDN') ccTLDs. As introduced earlier in this chapter and discussed in detail in the next chapter, ccTLDs have been incorporated in the DNS from its inception, being added slowly at first but then with increasing frequency to reach the nearly 300 that are currently in existence. Their creation and naming is directly tied to the ISO's 3166-1 list of 'English country names and code elements' (the 'ISO 3166-1 list'),[83] which assigns two-letter 'country codes' to the official name of each of the countries[84] listed in the UN Terminology Bulletin Country Names and the Country and Region Codes for Statistical Use of the UN Statistics Division.

As a starting point, the *gTLD Applicant Guidebook* prohibits, at Module 2, section 3.1, 'two-character ASCII strings … to avoid conflicting with current and future country codes based on the ISO 3166-1 standard.'[85] The future availability of two-character strings depends in large part upon how the ICANN community ultimately chooses to define 'geographic name'; the inclusion of two-character TLDs in the scope of both a ccNSO Study Group[86] and a Cross-Community Working Group on the Use of Country and Territory Names as TLDs[87] evidences a perceived association between them and country codes. Notably, the Cross-Community Working Group's preliminary recommendation, still under discussion at the time of publication of this second edition, proposes that the restriction against two-character ASCII strings be maintained in future applications processes, but justifies this on the basis of reliance upon an externally developed and maintained standard with widespread application outside of the DNS context, while expressly rejecting restriction on the basis of government claims to proprietary rights.[88]

83. ISO, *Online Browsing Platform (OBP)*, https://www.iso.org/obp/ui/#search.
84. For simplicity, the term 'country' is used here and throughout this work when referring to country code TLDs and their nexus to the ISO 3166-1 list. It must be acknowledged that although the list is entitled 'English country names and code elements', some if its entries correspond to sub- or supranational territories. The 'eu' (European Union) and 'hm' (Heard and Marshall Islands) country codes illustrate this.
85. ICANN, *gTLD Applicant Guidebook*, 3.1.
86. ICANN ccNSO, *Non-PDP Study Group on Use of Names for Countries and Territories*.
87. ICANN ccNSO, *Cross-Community Working Group on Use of Country/Territory Names as TLDs*, http://ccnso.icann.org/workinggroups/ccwg-unct.htm.
88. ICANN, *Cross-Community Working Group – Framework for Use of Country and Territory Names as TLDs (CWG-UCTN) {Strawman} Options Paper*, 21, https://com

Beyond this prohibition of two-letter new gTLDs, new gTLD applications for strings that are visually similar to any country code on the ISO 3166-1 list are at risk of objection on grounds of confusion with another string. This ground of objection targets the situation 'where a string so nearly resembles another that it is likely to deceive or cause confusion.'[89] All existing TLD operators have standing to object on this ground, as do other new gTLD applicants provided that the alleged similarity has not already been raised during initial evaluation. This suggests that the basis for challenge is actually a priority of rights in the proposed name rather than technical stability or an intention to minimize user confusion.

New Internationalized Domain Name ('IDN') ccTLDs could likewise be the basis of objection to applications for geographic new gTLDs on confusing similarity grounds. IDN ccTLDs have been created through a process by which a select number of ccTLDs in non-Latin scripts were delegated to requesting governments. The timing of the launch of the 'fast track' IDN ccTLD applications process vis-á-vis the New gTLD Program was hotly debated during 2009. The first process to launch naturally created priority rights for its applicants, whose strings would stand in the way of future TLD applications for identical and confusingly similar strings: the decision of ICANN's Board of Directors at the end of its 36th public meeting in October 2009 to launch the IDN ccTLD 'fast track'[90] ended the priority debate in IDNs' favour, while the launch of the New gTLD Program would be delayed until 2011. As a result, new gTLD applicants have both existing ISO 3166-1 country code and IDN ccTLD strings as potential bases of objection on confusing similarity grounds. As the top-level continues to expand, each new entrant will inherently pose some degree of threat to future applicants.

1.2.2.4 Other Objection Grounds

Another potentially applicable objection to new gTLD strings comprised of geographic names is the so-called limited public interest objection,[91] which in early draft versions of the *gTLD Applicant Guidebook* was called the 'morality and public order objection'.[92] This objection is directed at strings that are 'contrary to general principles of international law for morality and

munity.icann.org/display/CWGOUCNT/Output+and+Draft+Documents?preview=/49354211/56143211/Options%20Paper%2015%20October%202015%20.doc (21 Sep. 2015).

89. ICANN, *gTLD Applicant Guidebook*, 2.2.1.1.2.

90. ICANN, *ICANN Bringing the Languages of the World to the Global Internet*, http://www.icann.org/en/announcements/announcement-30oct09-en.htm (30 Oct. 2009).

91. ICANN, *gTLD Applicant Guidebook*, 3.2.1.

92. *See for example,* ICANN, *Draft Applicant Guidebook*, version 2, 3.1.2.3.

public order.'[93] Specific grounds proved a challenge to articulate and only first appeared in the third draft of the *gTLD Applicant Guidebook*. These were developed 'following extensive legal research that examined restrictions in a representative sample of countries, which included Brazil, Egypt, France, Hong Kong, Malaysia, South Africa, Switzerland and the United States of America'.[94] The concept ultimately came to be expressed as:

- incitement to or promotion of violent lawless action;
- incitement to or promotion of discrimination based upon race, color, gender, ethnicity, religion or national origin, or other similar types of discrimination that violate generally accepted legal norms recognized under principles of international law;
- incitement to or promotion of child pornography or other sexual abuse of children; or
- a determination that an applied-for gTLD string would be contrary to equally generally accepted identified legal norms relating to morality and public order that are recognized under general principles of international law.[95]

The experience of the .cat new gTLD application in the second 'proof of concept' round suggests the potential applicability of this objection to applications for geographic strings. Although initially proposed as .ct, representing the name of the Spanish geographic region of Catalonia, this sponsored gTLD application's proponents realized early on that such an identifier could be interpreted as an incitement of separatist sentiment and political uprising in a historically fractious region of the country and, on that basis, formally opposed by the Spanish government.[96] The string .cat, representing the name of the less politically or geographically charged Catalan linguistic community, proved less contentious. One can envision other situations in which an alternative name for a community is not practicable or does not exist. The potential relevance of this objection to geographic new gTLD applications is only determinable on a case-by-case

93. ICANN, *gTLD Applicant Guidebook*, 3.5.3. Curiously, the wording of this objection in the *gTLD Applicant Guidebook* mirrors the wording of the GNSO's Recommendations, whilst the wording of the wording of the legal rights objection does not, omitting the phrase 'under general principles of international law'. This point was raised in the public comment period relating to the third draft of the *gTLD Applicant Guidebook*, but did not provoke change in later drafts. Forrest, *Comments on the Scope of the Legal Rights Objection*.
94. Letter from Peter Dengate Thrush, Chairman of ICANN Board, to Janis Karklins, Chairman of the Governmental Advisory Committee and Ambassador of Latvia to France, 20, https://www.icann.org/en/system/files/files/dengate-thrush-to-karklins-22sep09-en.pdf (22 Dec. 2009).
95. ICANN, *gTLD Applicant Guidebook*, 3.5.3.
96. Gerrand, *Cultural Diversity in Cyberspace*.

basis, taking into consideration the historical, political and cultural context underpinning the string in question.

1.3 THE *gTLD APPLICANT GUIDEBOOK* AND DISPUTED 'GEOGRAPHIC' APPLICATIONS

The study documented in this book was motivated by a prediction that ICANN's implicit validation, without legal substantiation, of governments' assertions to rights in geographic names through the *gTLD Applicant Guidebook* would result in disputes between governments and private parties. Sadly, this prediction was borne out in the applications lodged in 2012. The applications highlighted and analysed in this final section of this chapter serve to illustrate this and highlight the necessity of reforming the *gTLD Applicant Guidebook*'s provisions on geographic names before new gTLD applications are called for again.

The examples provided here have been selected because they are each illustrative of particular failings in the *gTLD Applicant Guidebook*. These are not the only geographic name disputes to have arisen out of the 1,930 applications lodged in 2012, but the significant publicity each of them has generated serves to highlight the complexity of the problems they represent. The risk of eroding public trust and further wasting of resources should put additional pressure on the entire ICANN community to resolve the existing gaps between the *gTLD Applicant Guidebook* and the international legal norms examined in Part III of this book.

1.3.1 .wine/.vin

A surprising non-issue from the 2012 New gTLD Program applications was geographical indications. As noted earlier in this chapter, geographical indications principally relate to comestible products. Many inherently implicate geographic names because the link between a product and its cultural and territorial origin is signalled by the use of the geographical name as an identifier. They benefit in some countries from distinct legal classification and absolute protection. The international legal framework is discussed in detail in Part III at Chapter 7.

Interestingly, no applications were lodged in 2012 for names constituting a geographical indication. Such an application could have implicated the requirement in section 2.2.4.1.2 of the *gTLD Applicant Guidebook* for evidence of government support or non-objection by reason of an applied-for name's inclusion in a country's ISO 3166-2 list. For example, Italy's ISO 3166-2 list includes the province 'Asti',[97] while 'Asti' is registered in the

97. UNECE, *UN/LOCODE Code List by Country: Italy*, http://www.unece.org/fileadmin/DAM/cefact/locode/Subdivision/itSub.htm.

Lisbon System of Appellations of Origin[98] by the Ministero delle Politiche Agricole, Alimentari e Forestali and the Consorzio per la tutela dell'Asti.[99]

The complexities surrounding applications for new .wine and .vin gTLDs show, however, that geographical indication issues have not been entirely avoided. Rather, critical questions have simply been pushed down to the next level in the DNS hierarchy, the level at which domain names are registered. A legal opinion commissioned by the ICANN Board's New gTLD Program Committee appropriately noted that 'apart from the fact that a wine does not necessarily have a geographical indication, the common nouns "vin" and "wine" and the gTLDs ".vin" and ".wine" clearly do not refer to a specific geographical indication. The situation would be similar if one applicant were to apply for the ".cheese" or ".fromage" gTLDs.'[100] Yet at the second level, the problem arises that 'the domain names reserved by the third parties in the registry of the new gTLD ".wine" or ".vin" may contain an element identical or similar to the name of a geographical indication for wine', and furthermore that 'a party reserving such a domain name does not necessarily have the right to use the geographical indication in question for wines or products or another type which it sells on the website identified under the domain name in question.'[101] That the top-level strings were not geographical indications but generic terms, however, was not necessarily a dependency; the opinion concludes, consistent with the conclusions reached in Chapter 7 below, that 'there is no rule of the law of geographical indications, nor any general principle which obliges ICANN to reject the applications or accept the applications under certain specific conditions.'[102]

Apart from the required 'initial' reservation through the draft New gTLD Registry Agreement[103] of country and territory names at the second and lower levels in which registrations are made available, the *gTLD Applicant Guidebook* rules on geographic names are directed only at the top-level. This results in both unpredictability for applicants during the Initial Evaluation process and the risk of inconsistent rules on the use of the same name at different levels of the DNS. Although ultimately advising the

98. Detailed information is provided in Part III, Chapter 7, section 7.1, below.

99. WIPO, *Search Appellations of Origin (Lisbon Express)*, http://www.wipo.int/ipdl/en/search/lisbon/search-struct.jsp (enter 1017 in 'number' search field).

100. Opinion Report of Jérôme Passa, https://www.icann.org/en/system/files/files/analysis-wine-vin-22mar14-en.pdf (22 Mar. 2014) 3.

101. Opinion Report of Jérôme Passa, https://www.icann.org/en/system/files/files/analysis-wine-vin-22mar14-en.pdf (22 Mar. 2014) 3.

102. *Ibid.*

103. Specification 5 of the Base Registry Agreement provided by the *gTLD Applicant Guidebook* 'initially' reserves country and territory names at the second and all other levels open for registration. ICANN, *gTLD Applicant Guidebook*, New gTLD Agreement.

implementation of additional safeguards against possible abuse in the .vin application[104] and the three competing applications for .wine,[105] the Governmental Advisory Committee ('GAC') advised ICANN's Board of Directors to permit the applications to 'proceed through the normal evaluation process' while respecting 'the legally complex and politically sensitive' issues surrounding the use of geographical indications.[106] An Early Warning initiated by GAC representatives of France[107] did not lead, as France proposed, to withdrawal of Holly Shadow, LLC's ultimately successful application for .vin.[108] Publicly, the ultimately successful[109] albeit delayed applications, both backed by large portfolio applicant company Donuts, committed to Public Interest Commitments (commonly referred to as 'PICs') strengthening the above-noted reservation of country and territory names required by Specification 5 of the Registry Agreement:

> Pursuant to Specification 5 of this Registry Agreement, Registry Operator will transmit to the registrars the list of geographic names prohibited from second-level registration. Registry Operator will periodically review this list to ensure it is identical to that maintained by ICANN. Should Registry Operator seek to release these reserved names,

---

104. ICANN, New gTLD Application Submitted to ICANN by: Holly Shadow, LLC, https://gtldresult.icann.org/application-result/applicationstatus/applicationdetails/679 (13 Jun. 2012).
105. ICANN, New gTLD Application Submitted to ICANN by: June Station, LLC, https://gtldresult.icann.org/application-result/applicationstatus/viewstatus:viewapplicationdetails/706 (13 Jun. 2012); ICANN, New gTLD Application Submitted to ICANN by: dot Wine Limited, https://gtldresult.icann.org/application-result/applicationstatus/viewstatus:viewapplicationdetails/1204 (13 Jun. 2012); ICANN, New gTLD Application Submitted to ICANN by: Afilias plc, https://gtldresult.icann.org/application-result/applicationstatus/viewstatus:viewapplicationdetails/1831 (13 Jun. 2012).
106. ICANN GAC, *GAC Communiqué – Buenos Aires, Argentina* (20 Nov. 2013), https://gacweb.icann.org/download/attachments/28278854/FINAL_Buenos_Aires_GAC_Communique_20131120.pdf?version=1&modificationDate=1390424520000&api=v2.
107. ICANN, GAC Early Warning – Submittal Vin-FR-23177, https://gacweb.icann.org/display/gacweb/GAC+Early+Warnings?preview=/27131927/27197919/Vin-FR-23177.pdf (20 Nov. 2012).
108. No Early Warnings were filed against any of the .wine applications within the filing deadline (ICANN GAC, GAC Early Warnings, https://gacweb.icann.org/display/gacweb/GAC+Early+Warnings) but GAC representatives of Iran filed an Early Warning against dot Wine Limited's (ultimately unsuccessful) application on ethical grounds after the deadline (GAC Early Warning – Submittal ---, https://gacweb.icann.org/display/gacweb/Early+Warnings+received+from+GAC+Member%28s%29+after+the+EW+Deadline?preview=/27132095/27197596/GAC%20EW%20Submission-Iran-1-1223-37711%20(WINE).docx (undated)).
109. ICANN, *Resolutions – Applications for .vin and .wine/GAC Communiqué-Singapore*, https://features.icann.org/applications-vin-and-wine-gac-communiqu%C3%A9-%E2%80%93-singapore (4 Apr. 2014).

> it will consult with ICANN's Governmental Advisory Committee and obtain any permissions necessary from ICANN for such release.[110]

Donuts reportedly privately reached an undisclosed[111] agreement with wine industry stakeholders,[112] leading some to attribute the resolution of the dispute to the vigilance of the French Deputy Minister for Digital Affairs and his insistence upon a list of protected names, a protection that apparently applies uniquely amongst new gTLDs to .wine and .vin.[113] Yet celebrating the triumph of 'the political pressure applied on ICANN' over the *gTLD Applicant Guidebook* in so-called solutions[114] such as this continues ICANN on the course of ad hoc, inconsistent, unpredictable decision-making on geographic domain names.

1.3.2 .bar

The application for a new .bar gTLD made by Mexican company Punto 2012 Sociedad Anonima Promotora de Inversion de Capital Variable[115] ('Punto 2012') highlights the illogical and inconsistent results arising from the *gTLD Applicant Guidebook*'s definition of 'geographic names'. On its face, Punto 2012's application reads much as one would expect:

> The .bar gTLD is expected to appeal to all entities who identify themselves with the word or the concept of a 'bar,' including but not limited to: sushi, espresso or tapas bars (places where food is served and consumed); juice, smoothie, cocktail, martini, and espresso bars (places where drinks are served and consumed); nail, wax or beauty bars (places where beauty treatments are performed); sports, jazz or beach bars

110. Specification 11: Public Interest Commitments (Donuts), https://gtldresult.icann.org/application-result/applicationstatus/applicationdetails:downloadpicposting/706?t:ac=706.
111. Kevin Murphy, 'Donuts makes private deal with wine-makers', Domain Incite, 21 Jun. 2015, http://domainincite.com/18739-donuts-makes-private-deal-with-wine-makers.
112. Scott Gerien and Christopher Passarelli, 'Challenges for Geographical Indications (GIs) in the Context of the ICANN New Generic Top-Level Domains (gTLDs): A Manual for GIs Groups to Navigate the New Environment', oriGIn, http://www.origin-gi.com/images/stories/PDFs/English/oriGIn_Publications_2010/GI_gTLDs_JAN2016_WEB_VERSION.pdf (2016).
113. Jean Guillon, '.WINE New gTLD is Here, Thanks to Politicians', CircleID, http://www.circleid.com/posts/201451005_wine_new_gtld_is_here_thanks_to_politicians/ (5 Oct. 2015).
114. Jean Guillon, '.WINE New gTLD is Here, Thanks to Politicians', CircleID, http://www.circleid.com/posts/201451005_wine_new_gtld_is_here_thanks_to_politicians/ (5 Oct. 2015).
115. ICANN, New gTLD Application Submitted to ICANN by: Punto 2012 Sociedad Anonima Promotora de Inversion de Capital Variable, https://gtldresult.icann.org/application-result/applicationstatus/applicationdetails:downloadapplication/246?t:ac=246 (13 Jun. 2012).

> (places where people gather to drink and be entertained); candy, chocolate and energy bars (products); and related products and entities. Thanks to its broad spectrum of uses, it will provide a designated namespace where these entities and those that provide corollary products and services can register short and intuitive domain names related to their activities while allowing consumers to search for and easily locate them.[116]

ICANN's own case study on the .bar gTLD application adds the following:

> While .BAR is specifically geared for bars, pubs and nightclubs in the traditional sense, the domain is also applicable to guides, critics, delivery services and wine and liquor establishments, as well as other industries and businesses that feel their interest will be best represented by the .BAR domain. From sushi and tapas bars, to sports and beach bars, and even ice bars, the opportunities for .BAR can be limitless.[117]

Punto 2012's assertion that '[t[he word "bar" represents many different types of establishments, products, services and activities'[118] is unassailable, but what proportion of internet users understand 'bar' *not* as a place to consume food or beverages, receive beauty treatments or enjoy social entertainments, but rather as a geographic place? The question must be asked given that: first, Punto 2012 designated its application as geographic; second, according to the application's Initial Evaluation Report, Punto 2012 provided the requisite evidence of government support or non-objection;[119] and third, a competing application for .bar[120] was withdrawn[121] by its applicant United TLD Holdco

---

116. ICANN, New gTLD Application Submitted to ICANN by: Punto 2012 Sociedad Anonima Promotora de Inversion de Capital Variable, https://gtldresult.icann.org/application-result/applicationstatus/applicationdetails:downloadapplication/246?t:ac=246 (13 Jun. 2012).
117. ICANN, Case Study: .BAR, https://newgtlds.icann.org/en/announcements-and-media/case-studies/bar-us-letter-11nov15-en.pdf (11 Nov. 2015).
118. ICANN, New gTLD Application Submitted to ICANN by: Punto 2012 Sociedad Anonima Promotora de Inversion de Capital Variable, https://gtldresult.icann.org/application-result/applicationstatus/applicationdetails:downloadapplication/246?t:ac=246 (13 Jun. 2012).
119. ICANN, New gTLD Program – Initial Evaluation Report (BAR), https://newgtlds.icann.org/sites/default/files/ier/98l2hf75ri5droaslu2iacie/ie-1-1870-98363-en.pdf (4 Oct. 2013). Kevin Murphy, 'Told You So? Four New gTLDs Given Geographic Surprise, Others Given a Pass', Domain Incite, http://domainincite.com/12166-told-you-so-four-new-gtlds-given-geographic-surprise-others-given-a-pass (7 Mar. 2013).
120. ICANN, New gTLD Application Submitted to ICANN by: United TLD Holdco Ltd., https://gtldresult.icann.org/application-result/applicationstatus/applicationdetails:downloadapplication/1121?t:ac=1121 (13 Jun. 2012).
121. ICANN, *New Generic Top-Level Domains: Application Details* (Application ID: 1-1255-43729 BAR), https://gtldresult.icann.org/application-result/applicationstatus/applicationdetails/1121.

Ltd after it was found to have failed to provide evidence of relevant government support.

The new gTLD application required, at Question 21, that applicants declare Yes/No to identifying the application as for a geographic name.[122] The Attachment to Module 2 of the *gTLD Applicant Guidebook* setting out the evaluation questions and criteria provides the following guidance in answering this question:

> An applied-for gTLD string is considered a geographic name requiring government support if it is (a) the capital city name of a country or territory listed in the ISO 3166-1 standard; (b) a city name, where it is clear from statements in the application that the applicant intends to use the gTLD for purposes associated with the city name; (c) a sub-national place name listed in the ISO 3166-2 standard; or (d) a name listed as a UNESCO region or appearing on the 'Composition of macro geographic (continental) or [sic] regions, geographic sub-regions, and selected economic and other groupings' list. See Module 2 for complete definitions and criteria.
>
> An application for a country or territory name, as defined in the Applicant Guidebook, will not be approved.

ICANN Initial Evaluation Reports disclose only the outcome of the Geographic Names Panel's determination, not the underlying reasoning. In the case of .bar, this Report states: 'The Geographic Names Panel has determined that your application falls within the criteria for a geographic name contained in the Applicant Guidebook Section 2.2.1.4, and the documentation of support or non-objection provided has met all relevant criteria in Section 2.2.1.4.3 of the Applicant Guidebook.'[123] Rationalizing an application's designation as geographic therefore requires applying the Module 2 Attachment guidance and working through each element of the definition of 'geographic names requiring government support' set out in section 2.2.1.4.2 in turn. In this case:

- The string 'bar' is not a 'string that is a representation, in any language, of the <u>*capital city name*</u> of any country or territory listed in the ISO 3166-1 standard.'[124]
- Punto 2012's application was, as excerpted in relevant part above, directed at the common English-language meaning of the word 'bar', not a city name, and did not declare an intention to use the gTLD for

122. ICANN, *gTLD Applicant Guidebook*, Attachment to Module 2 – Evaluation Questions and Criteria.
123. ICANN, New gTLD Program – Initial Evaluation Report (BAR), https://newgtlds.icann.org/sites/default/files/ier/9812hf75ri5droaslu2iacie/ie-1-1870-98363-en.pdf (4 Oct. 2013).
124. ICANN, *gTLD Applicant Guidebook*, 2.2.1.4.2 cl 1 (emphasis in original).

purposes associated with a city name.[125] Nowhere in the publicly disclosed portion of the application, other than the one-word response 'Yes' to Question 21, does Punto 2012's application address anything having to do with the name of a geographic place. United TLD Holdco Ltd's application was similarly directed at the common English-language meaning of the word 'bar', not a city name, and it likewise did not declare an intention to use the gTLD for purposes associated with a city name.[126]

- The string 'bar' is, nevertheless, 'an exact match of a *sub-national place name*, such as a county, province, or state, listed in the ISO 3166-2 standard',[127] in this case the municipality of Bar, Montenegro.[128]
- Finally, 'bar' is not 'listed as a UNESCO region or appearing on the "Composition of macro geographical (continental) regions, geographical sub-regions, and selected economic and other groupings" list.'[129]

Bar, in the official language Montenegrin, is written: Бар. English is not an official language of Montenegro. Bar Province reportedly comprises less than 14,000 households for a total population of roughly 42,000 citizens.[130]

Attachments in support of an applicant's answer to Question 21 are not made publicly available by ICANN. It must be presumed that Punto 2012 sought and received a declaration of support or non-objection from the government/s of the Republic of Montenegro, the Principality of Бар, and/or the principality's capital city, also named Бар.[131]

---

125. ICANN, *gTLD Applicant Guidebook*, 2.2.1.4.2 cl 2.
126. ICANN, New gTLD Application Submitted to ICANN by: United TLD Holdco Ltd., https://gtldresult.icann.org/application-result/applicationstatus/applicationdetails:downloadapplication/1121?t:ac=1121 (13 Jun. 2012) ('The desired reputation of.bar is that of an open namespace where everyone is welcomed as engaged participants. As such, we expect that participants will create innovative and specialized products and services that connect with their audience. For example, local owners of drinking establishments may promote their businesses to consumers. Merchants might market specialized products and services, such as preparatory classes for law school students to pass the state bar exam').
127. ICANN, *gTLD Applicant Guidebook*, 2.2.1.4.2 cl 3 (emphasis in original).
128. United Nations Economic Commission for Europe, UN/LOCODE Country Subdivisions ISO 3166-2 – Montenegro, http://www.unece.org/fileadmin/DAM/cefact/locode/Subdivision/meSub.htm.
129. ICANN, *gTLD Applicant Guidebook*, 2.2.1.4.2 cl 4 (internal footnotes omitted).
130. Statistical Office of Montenegro, *Statistical Yearbook 2015: Review by Municipalities*, http://www.monstat.org/eng/publikacije_page.php?id=1312 (Chapter 28.4 (Review by Municipalities, Population and Households by Municipalities), based on 2011 census data).
131. Kevin Murphy, 'Ten More New gTLDs Get ICANN Contracts', Domain Incite, http://domainincite.com/15299-ten-more-new-gtlds-get-icann-contracts (13 Dec. 2013) ('The gTLD was originally contested, but Demand Media's [sic] United TLD withdrew following an RFP held by the government of Montenegro, which had an effective veto

The .bar example, which ICANN lauds as an example of best practice,[132] is problematic for several reasons even apart from the question of whether international law recognizes any rights that might be asserted by the Republic of Montenegro, the Principality of Бар, and/or the City of Бар in the name 'bar'. First, 'bar' is an English-language term the plain meaning of which is recognized and relied upon by Punto 2012 in its application and by ICANN in its case study.[133] The risk of overlap with generic meanings is expressly addressed in the *gTLD Applicant Guidebook* in relation to city names: 'City names present challenges because city names may also be generic terms or brand names, and in many cases city names are not unique.'[134] This point is validly made where the city and the generic meaning are both well-known, since confusion simply cannot result unless both meanings are known. In the context of a subnational place name that is not well-known, it must be said that confusion is far less likely to result. Furthermore, when English is not the language used by the population of the subnational place and the place name in the local language differs from its representation in the English language, the risk of confusion is further minimized or even eliminated.

The .bar example heralds the possible end of new gTLD expansion if applicants must fear that an application for an unquestionably generic term, to be used in an unquestionably generic sense, must nevertheless be designated geographic and can, on that basis, be impeded by government. A lack of consistency only adds to this fear: as journalist Kevin Murphy pointed out on announcing the surprise findings of the Geographic Names Panel for .bar, .tata and .tui, applications for .delta, .est and .capital, which correspond to subnational place names in Nigeria, Burkina Faso and Denmark, respectively, were not deemed geographic by the Geographic Names Panel.[135]

1.3.3 .patagonia

The experience of the Patagonia outdoor clothing company in filing a new gTLD application under the *gTLD Applicant Guidebook* rules highlights the risks to applicants who interpret those rules with a plain meaning approach.

---

over the string "Bar" due to a match with the protected name of one of its administrative regions. I gather Montenegro will be paid in some way from the .bar registry pot.').

132. Kevin Murphy, 'The Price of .bar Was $100,000 to a school', Domain Incite, http://domainincite.com/17002-the-price-of-bar-was-100000-to-a-school (30 Jun. 2014).
133. ICANN, Case Study: .BAR, above n. 117.
134. ICANN, *gTLD Applicant Guidebook*, 2.2.1.4.2 cl 2.
135. Kevin Murphy, 'Told You So? Four New gTLDs Given Geographic Surprise, Others Given a Pass', Domain Incite, 7 Mar. 2013, http://domainincite.com/12166-told-you-so-four-new-gtlds-given-geographic-surprise-others-given-a-pass.

Patagonia, Inc. lodged an application for .patagonia,[136] its principal brand which is registered as a trademark in numerous countries worldwide.[137] The company had planned to use the .patagonia domain 'to provide the general public, the outdoor industry, and potential (sic) as well as existing consumers of our products and services with an authenticated and more secure experience, to protect our Patagonia brand, and to promote our company.'[138] These plans were set aside when the application was abandoned in mid-July 2013,[139] following the issuance in late 2012 of an 'Early Warning' initiated by GAC representatives of Argentina.[140]

Patagonia, Inc. must have determined that its proposed string fell outside the *gTLD Applicant Guidebook* definitions of 'geographic name' in section 2.2.1.4, and therefore applied without designating the application as 'geographic' or seeking government support or non-objection. 'Patagonia' is not a 'country or territory name' falling within section 2.2.1.4.1 of the *gTLD Applicant Guidebook*. Nor is 'Patagonia' a city name, a 'sub-national place name listed in the ISO 3166-2 standard', or other name falling within the definition of 'geographic name requiring government support' set out in section 2.2.1.4.2. 'Patagonia' is, as Argentina's Early Warning objection itself states, a 'region of Argentina';[141] 'Patagonia' is not specified in Argentina's ISO 3166-2 standard. As such, the application should not have been subjected to the *gTLD Applicant Guidebook*'s government support or non-objection requirement. Argentina's complaint that the various provincial governments 'never authorized the use of the name "Patagonia" to be used [sic] as a new generic top level domain, of any kind, to any company or to any other organization or government' and 'were never contacted by any

136. ICANN, New gTLD Application Submitted to ICANN by: Patagonia, Inc., https://gtldresult.icann.org/application-result/applicationstatus/applicationdetails/1466 (13 Jun. 2012).

137. *Ibid* ('We have invested significant resources in protecting our Patagonia(r) mark. We own hundreds of trademark registrations for the Patagonia mark in nearly half the countries in the world. In addition, we have registered more than 200 second-level domain names that contain or consist of our Patagonia mark, although the vast majority are defensive registrations against cybersquatting.').

138. *Ibid.*

139. The Economist, 'New internet addresses: .patience', http://www.economist.com/blogs/schumpeter/2013/07/new-internet-addresses-0 (25 Jul. 2013).

140. ICANN, GAC Early Warning – Submittal Patagonia-AFR-78254, https://gacweb.icann.org/display/gacweb/GAC+Early+Warnings?preview=/27131927/27197990/Patagonia-AR-78254.pdf (20 Nov. 2012); *subsequently amended by* ICANN, GAC Early Warning – Submittal Patagonia-AFR-78254, https://gacweb.icann.org/download/attachments/27131927/GAC%20EW%20Submission%20PATAGONIA%202.pdf?version=1&modificationDate=1356054993000&api=v2.

141. ICANN, GAC Early Warning – Submittal Patagonia-AFR-78254, https://gacweb.icann.org/download/attachments/27131927/GAC%20EW%20Submission%20PATAGONIA%202.pdf?version=1&modificationDate=1356054993000&api=v2, 1.

company or organization that has the intention to use the name "Patagonia" as a new generic top level domain, of any kind'[142] are procedurally irrelevant.

On the face of the *gTLD Applicant Guidebook* rules, therefore, Patagonia, Inc. was not compelled to withdraw its application, yet it did so reportedly 'because it expected ICANN's board (sic) would not resist pressure to deny the application.'[143] The legal basis upon which ICANN's Board could have made such a decision is not addressed in the Argentinian GAC Early Warning, nor is this supported by the comprehensive legal analysis provided by Part III of this book.

1.3.4 .amazon

This final case study involves another global enterprise, but one that opted not to stand down in the face of GAC pressure on ICANN's Board of Directors. The trajectory of its application provides the worst-case scenario for new gTLD applicants who rely upon the plain meaning of the definitions of 'geographic name' in the *gTLD Applicant Guidebook* and the treatment of such names under international law. This is arguably the most publicized new gTLD dispute,[144] pitting globally recognized technology company Amazon and its application for .amazon in the English, and Chinese and Japanese languages against ICANN's GAC and Board of Directors, starting with an 'Early Warning' from GAC members Peru and Brazil in late 2012[145] and still ongoing as of late 2016.

Application of the *gTLD Applicant Guidebook* Module 2 Attachment guidance and each element of the definition of 'geographic names requiring government support' set out in section 2.2.1.4.2 to the name 'Amazon' and its Chinese and Japanese equivalents yields the following analysis:

142. *Ibid.*

143. The Economist, 'New internet addresses: .patience', http://www.economist.com/blogs/schumpeter/2013/07/new-internet-addresses-0 (25 Jul. 2013).

144. *See for example,* Jonathan Watts, 'Amazon v the Amazon: internet retailer in domain name battle', The Guardian, 25 Apr. 2013, http://www.theguardian.com/environment/2013/apr/25/amazon-domain-name-battle-brazil; John Ribeiro, US lawmakers back Amazon.com's bid for .amazon domain, PCWorld, 24 Jun. 2015, http://www.pcworld.com/article/2940032/us-lawmakers-back-amazoncoms-bid-for-amazon-gtld.html; Brian Fung, 'Amazon Wants to Control '.amazon.' But so Does Half of South America.', The Washington Post, 23 Jun. 2015, https://www.washingtonpost.com/news/the-switch/wp/2015/06/23/amazon-wants-to-control-amazon-but-so-does-practically-half-of-south-america/.

145. ICANN, GAC Early Warning – Submittal Amazon-BR-PE-58086, https://gacweb.icann.org/download/attachments/27131927/Amazon-BR-PE-58086.pdf?version=1&modificationDate=1353452622000&api=v2.

- The string 'amazon' is not a 'string that is a representation, in any language, of the <u>*capital city name*</u> of any country or territory listed in the ISO 3166-1 standard.'[146]
- Amazon EU S.à.r.l.'s application was intended '[t]o provide a unique and dedicated platform for Amazon while simultaneously protecting the integrity of its brand and reputation'.[147] The application at no point expressly or impliedly declares an intention to use the .amazon gTLD for purposes associated with a city name.[148]
- The string 'amazon' is not 'an exact match of a <u>*subnational place name*</u>, such as a county, province, or state, listed in the ISO 3166-2 standard'.[149] That standard contains entries for 'Amazonas' as subnational place names of Brazil, Peru, Colombia and Venezuela, but 'Amazonas' is not an 'exact match' of 'Amazon'. The *gTLD Applicant Guidebook* notably does not define the term 'exact match', but the use of this phrase in section 2.2.1.4.2 must be interpreted in light of, and therefore contrasted with, other provisions of the section 2.2.1.4 in which it falls. The express mention in other categories of the definitions in 2.2.1.4 of 'a translation'[150] and 'a representation, in any language'[151] demand that 'exact match' be interpreted as requiring something identical, and not being satisfied by translations or approximates.
- Finally, 'amazon' is not 'listed as a UNESCO region or appearing on the "Composition of macro geographical (continental) regions, geographical sub-regions, and selected economic and other groupings" list.'[152]

Like 'Patagonia', the name 'Amazon' clearly falls outside of the definition of 'geographic names requiring government support' under section 2.2.1.4.2 of the *gTLD Applicant Guidebook*. The name 'Amazon' is likewise not a name that falls within the definition of 'country or territory names' under section 2.2.1.4.1 of the *gTLD Applicant Guidebook*. These conclusions

146. ICANN, *gTLD Applicant Guidebook*, 2.2.1.4.2 cl 1 (emphasis in original); *Amazon EU S.à.r.l. v. ICANN (.AMAZON)*, International Centre for Dispute Resolution, Expert Report of Professor Heather Ann Forrest, 23, https://www.icann.org/en/system/files/files/irp-amazon-export-report-forrest-02mar16-en.pdf (26 Feb. 2016).
147. ICANN, New gTLD Application Submitted to ICANN by: Amazon EU S.à.r.l., https://gtldresult.icann.org/application-result/applicationstatus/applicationdetails:downloadapplication/984?t:ac=984 (13 Jun. 2012); *Amazon EU S.à.r.l. v. ICANN (.AMAZON)*, Expert Report of Professor Heather Ann Forrest.
148. *Cf.* ICANN, *gTLD Applicant Guidebook*, 2.2.1.4.2 cl 2.
149. ICANN, *gTLD Applicant Guidebook*, 2.2.1.4.2 cl 3 (emphasis in original).
150. ICANN, *gTLD Applicant Guidebook*, 2.2.1.4.1 cl ii, iii, and v.
151. ICANN, *gTLD Applicant Guidebook*, 2.2.1.4.2 cl 1.
152. *Id.*, 2.2.1.4.2 cl 4 (internal footnotes omitted).

are notably consistent with the finding of the Geographic Names Panel, which advised applicant Amazon in the Initial Evaluation of its application: 'The Geographic Names Panel has determined that your application does not fall within the criteria for a geographic name contained in the Applicant Guidebook Section 2.2.1.4.'[153]

The ICANN Board nevertheless rejected the .amazon application, not on the basis of its being a 'geographic name', as that term is defined by the *gTLD Applicant Guidebook*, but rather on the basis of GAC Advice and the report of an expert commissioned by ICANN to answer the question of whether 'ICANN would be bound … to assign the new gTLD in question to its applicant, or, to the contrary, … to refuse to assign it in order to protect prior rights'.[154] The precise articulation of this question is, however, unhelpful and misleading, given that at no point does the *gTLD Applicant Guidebook* require applicants to prove that they are the only valid possible applicant, or that ICANN is legally obligated to assign a new gTLD to the particular applicant.

While the *gTLD Applicant Guidebook* does not oblige the Board to seek independent legal advice, it does state the following in relation to GAC Advice:

> The GAC may provide public policy advice directly to the ICANN Board on any application. … If the Board receives GAC Advice on New gTLDs stating that it is the consensus of the GAC that a particular application should not proceed, this will create a strong presumption for the ICANN Board that the application should not be approved. If the Board does not act in accordance with this type of advice, it must provide rationale for doing so.[155]

In seeking an independent review before the International Centre for Dispute Resolution, Amazon argued, *inter alia*, that:

> ICANN accepted the GAC advice simply because it created a 'strong presumption' that the Applications should not proceed. The GAC advice was nothing more than an attempt to veto the .AMAZON Applications contrary to the [Applicant Guidebook]. Thus, the [Board's] decision to accept that advice was an arbitrary expression of prejudice.[156]

153. ICANN, New gTLD Program – Initial Evaluation Report (AMAZON), http://newgtlds.icann.org/en/program-status/application-results/ie-1-1315-58086-en.pdf (12 Jul. 2013).
154. ICANN, Letter from Stephen D. Crocker, Chair, ICANN Board of Directors, to Heather Dryden, Chair, Governmental Advisory Committee, https://www.icann.org/en/system/files/correspondence/crocker-to-dryden-07apr14-en.pdf (31 Mar. 2014).
155. ICANN, *gTLD Applicant Guidebook*, 1.1.2.7.
156. *Amazon EU S.à.r.l. v. ICANN (.AMAZON)*, International Centre for Dispute Resolution, Request by Amazon EU S.à.r.l. for Independent Review, 19–20, https://www.icann.org/en/system/files/files/irp-amazon-request-redacted-02mar16-en.pdf (1 Mar. 2016).

These complaints are reinforced and exacerbated by the Board's failure to invalidate other new .brand gTLDs with geographically meaningful names, including .ipiranga, .lasalle and .rocher.[157]

An International Centre for Dispute Resolution panel will ultimately decide the fate of the .amazon applications. What is clear even before that occurs is that the present treatment of geographic names in the *gTLD Applicant Guidebook* is not sufficient to prevent resource- and time-consuming disputes that threaten the perceived legitimacy of DNS expansion and ICANN's role in that process. Future applicants must weigh the risk of unpredictable, inconsistent decision-making against the benefits of a unique online presence.

In summary, the *gTLD Applicant Guidebook* assumes governments' exclusive or superior rights in geographic names without questioning whether those rights are recognized under international law. The *gTLD Applicant Guidebook* offers scant opportunity to challenge these assumed rights, while at the same time failing to extend standing to object on the ground of legal rights to the private party holders of any such rights if these are recognized. This is an incongruous situation that has, predictably and inevitably, generated conflict. This conflict and the disputes arising as a result validate the existence of the perceived problem that sparked the doctoral study documented in this book, as well as its most fundamental conclusion: conflict is the result of divergence between international law and the *gTLD Applicant Guidebook*, a policy framework that is based on assumptions, rather than legal conclusions, about rights in geographic names.

The starting point to unravelling this problem is to explain in detail the context in which the issues introduced in this chapter have arisen. The next chapter, Chapter 2, thus contextualizes the treatment of geographic names in past and present DNS policy by tracing the development of the DNS and the use of names within it.

---

157. ICANN, New gTLD Application Submitted to ICANN by: Ipiranga Produtos de Petroleo S.A., https://gtldresult.icann.org/application-result/applicationstatus/applicationdetails:downloadapplication/1509?t:ac=1509 (13 Jun. 2012); ICANN, New gTLD Application Submitted to ICANN by: Jones Lang LaSalle Incorporated, https://gtldresult.icann.org/application-result/applicationstatus/applicationdetails:downloadapplication/1160?t:ac=1160 (13 Jun. 2012); ICANN, New gTLD Application Submitted to ICANN by: Ferrero Trading Lux S.A., https://gtldresult.icann.org/application-result/applicationstatus/applicationdetails:downloadapplication/1371?t:ac=1371 (13 Jun. 2012). *Amazon EU S.à.r.l. v. ICANN (.AMAZON)*, Expert Report of Professor Heather Ann Forrest.

Chapter 2
The Expanding Domain Name System

[A]ny implementation undertaken now should be based on an assumption of a much larger Internet. - David D. Clark, MIT Laboratory for Computer Science, July, 1982[1]

2.1 ORIGINS OF THE DOMAIN NAME SYSTEM

2.1.1 WHY REVISIT THE ORIGINS OF THE DOMAIN NAME SYSTEM?

The Domain Name System, commonly referred to by its acronym 'DNS', has been in a constant state of evolution since its implementation in 1984, but the change initiated by ICANN's New gTLD Program is arguably the most significant to date. Simply put, the 1,930 applications received in 2012 will expand the top-level of the DNS by at least threefold, more growth in only a few years than was experienced over the entire first two and a half decades of the DNS's existence. It is this dramatic change and its extent and impact that give rise to the questions at the heart of this study.

Fundamental to answering these questions is an understanding of the DNS's origins and development leading up to this catalytic point. These matters are explored in this chapter in order to contextualize the questions

1. David D. Clark, *RFC814: Name, Addresses, Ports and Routes*, http://www.rfc-editor.org/rfc/rfc814.txt (Jul. 1982).

posed in the previous chapter and pursued in subsequent chapters. Terminology relevant to the DNS is identified and explained in order to substantiate its use in this study and to further clarify the scope and relevance of the questions being posed. Acronyms and abbreviations, of which there are unfortunately very many in use in the ICANN environment, are introduced in this chapter; these are also listed at the start of this book for quick reference. Consistent with ICANN best practice, efforts have been taken throughout this book not to rely excessively upon acronyms with the intention of reducing confusion in an already complex area and making ICANN's work more accessible to newcomers. This chapter begins with an account of the origins of the DNS and the reasons for its implementation. It becomes evident in this discussion that the current state of the DNS has been, and its future development will likely continue to be, influenced by those who exercise authority over it. While an in-depth exploration of the many and varied issues relating to internet governance lies beyond the scope of this work, a concise discussion of the evolution of authority over the DNS helps to identify the reasons for expanding it and specifically explain ICANN's role in that process.

As its name suggests, the 'Domain Name System' is a system that involves the use of names in an environment partitioned into regions called 'domains'; why and how domains are named and their relationship to what we call a 'domain name' is the next subject explored in this chapter. The second part of this chapter focuses particularly on the area referred to as the 'top level' of the DNS, because it is this level of the system's hierarchical structure at which the growth that gives rise to the questions posed in this book is taking place. Issues arising from this growth are identified at the end of this chapter for deeper exploration in later chapters.

2.1.2 COMPUTERS TALKING TO COMPUTERS

In its nascence, the network of machines and users that would develop into what we now call the 'internet' was populated by a handful of research scientists working with enormous, costly mainframe computers. During the mid-twentieth century, the size, cost, capabilities and scarcity of mainframe computers in existence made shared access to them highly attractive. There were efficiencies to be gained from having one machine serve multiple organizations, but remote access required that computers be able to effectively communicate with each other across distances.

Transmitting information from one computer to another as one long, continuous sequence of data over a dedicated communications line proved slow, inefficient and impractical. The US Department of Defense's Advanced Research Projects Agency Network ('ARPANET) project was the first to embrace on a workable scale a theory first proposed in 1961 by Massachusetts Institute of Technology's Leonard Kleinrock, called 'packet switching'.[2] Rather than send long sequences of binary data, packet switching proposed that long data sequences be broken into shorter sets, dubbed 'packets'. The reduced size of a data packet offers the advantage of a relatively short transmission time and the added efficiency of enabling a single transmission line to carry data from more than one data sequence rather than be wholly devoted for a lengthy period to transmitting a single continuous sequence.

After being broken up and transmitted in this manner, data packets need to regroup and reassemble at the receiving computer. Ensuring a stable, reliable way for data packets to be transmitted and re-assembled was an obvious priority, because this new means of data transmission was useless if packets reached their destination in an altered state or not at all. With this in mind, Robert Kahn and Vinton Cerf, two key contributors to the ARPANET project, developed what would come to be called the Transmission Control Protocol/Internet Protocol ('TCP/IP'). TCP/IP directed a consistent means of identifying computers connected to the network, termed 'hosts', by assigning to each host a unique numerical address, termed an 'Internet Protocol' (or 'IP') address. The numerical digits of the IP address identify the network to which a host is connected and the host's location within that network.[3]

With each host thus uniquely identified, reliable transmission of data packets is achieved by adding to each data packet – not conceptually dissimilar to the way in which the intended recipient's address is added to a postal parcel – the IP address of the destination host. The IP address is read by routers, which are devices placed at intersections of the communications network through which data packets pass, and which direct packets towards the location of their destination host.[4] With the implementation of packet switching and TCP/IP, the manner in which information moved through communications networks took on the semblance of a highway system offering multiple, converging and intersecting routes to a final destination. At each intersection of multiple highways stands a router to direct packets towards their respective destinations. While the precise analogy may not be

---

2. L. Kleinrock, *Information Flow in Large Communication Nets*, RLE Quarterly Progress Report, http://www.lk.cs.ucla.edu/data/files/Kleinrock/Information%20Flow%20in%20Large%20Communication%20Nets0.pdf (July 1961). On the fundamental concepts of packet switching theory, *see* (film) Robert X. Cringely, *Nerds 2.0.1*, available at http://www.sci.sdsu.edu/~stewart/cs440/nerds_2_0_1.html.
3. Barry M. Leiner et al., *A Brief History of the Internet*, Internet Society, http://www.internetsociety.org/internet/what-internet/history-internet/brief-history-internet.
4. Mueller, *Ruling the Root*, 33–34.

as appropriate to the contemporary internet,[5] it remains a useful metaphor for the fundamental, progressive ideas from which it evolved.

2.1.3 Humans Talking to Computers

The numerical IP address gives computers a way to consistently locate and communicate with each other, but the network's human users would find them difficult to remember. To solve this problem, it was recommended that hosts be given short, unique, mnemonic names.[6] Each host thus had two separate but related identifiers: one used by computers and the other used by humans. Together these enabled hosts to communicate in the budding ARPANET network.

It was not sufficient to assign a host a name and an IP address, however, for it to become part of the network. In order for existing hosts to be able to communicate with a new host, they had to be informed of the new host's existence. Simply put, it was impossible to be found if others did not know that there was something to look for. Existing hosts therefore required notification of new hosts' connection to the network. This was achieved by maintaining and circulating a master list of names and addresses, what was called the hosts.txt file. If a host's name and address were not included on this list, that host would be unknown, and therefore inaccessible, to hosts on the list.

The US Department of Defense contracted with a private company linked to Stanford University, the Stanford Research Institute ('SRI'), with which Vinton Cerf and other ARPANET project participants were associated, to maintain and host the hosts.txt file.[7] This task was referred to as running the Network Information Center of the Defense Data Network ('DDN-NIC'), eventually simply called the 'NIC'. The task of assigning IP addresses was separately contracted by the Department of Defense to the Information Sciences Institute ('ISI') of the University of Southern California. In practice, it was Jon Postel who personally assumed this responsibility at ISI from the creation of the role in 1977 until his death twenty-one years later.[8]

The small community of government, academic and private research organizations aware and capable of connecting to the network meant that the task of maintaining, updating and circulating the hosts.txt file was not over-burdensome at first. As the concepts and technologies of network

5. Peter Sevcik & Rebecca Wetzel, *Stop Comparing the Internet to the Highway System*, NetworkWorld (6 Aug. 2008) (available at http://www.networkworld.com/article/2345535/data-center/stop-comparing-the-internet-to-the-highway-system.html).
6. Richard W. Watson, *RFC 273: More on Standard Host Names*, http://www.rfc-editor.org/rfc/rfc273.txt (18 Oct. 1971).
7. Mueller, *Ruling the Root*, 77, 81. *See also* CSTB, 74.
8. Information Sciences Institute USC Viterbi School of Engineering, *About Jon Postel*, http://www.postel.org/postel.html (16 Sep. 2008).

connectivity developed and were shared, however, this began to change. The volume of new additions to the hosts.txt file and the growing administrative burden associated with maintaining it provoked discussions about how the network could grow in a more efficient manner. It was from these discussions that the concept of the Domain Name System evolved.

2.1.4 The Domain Name System ('DNS')

The practicality of having and maintaining a single list that identified every host in the network was questioned in 1981, at which point the hosts.txt file had only a few hundred entries.[9] The concern was that if the network continued to attract hosts as the ARPANET project participants hoped it would, the relatively mundane task of updating the file would consume valuable time and energy at the expense of innovation, testing and development. The preferred solution, attributed to Paul Mockapetris at the University of Southern California's ISI, was to divide and apportion the responsibility of keeping track of the hosts connected to network.[10]

The genius lay not just in the relatively simple idea of apportioning responsibility, but in the logic underpinning its apportionment. The network would be structured into defined areas, or 'domains', with responsibility parsed and delegated accordingly. An entity with authority over a particular domain would be responsible for keeping track of all of the hosts connected to that domain of the network; it would assume the role of maintaining and hosting an equivalent of the hosts.txt file, but for that domain only.[11] There would no longer be one single, authoritative list of all of the hosts in the network but numerous such lists, each limited in scope to disclosing the connections within a particular, defined area of the network.

This means of allocating responsibility lent itself naturally to a hierarchical, 'tree structured'[12] system comparable to the depiction in Figure 2.1, below. At the top of the hierarchy, what can be envisioned as the trunk of the tree, sits the authority responsible for maintaining the list of all of the large branches connected to the trunk. These large branches comprise the top-level domains; they are commonly referred to by their acronym 'TLD'. Each TLD authority is responsible for keeping track of all of the branches that connect directly to it. These connecting branches are two levels removed from the trunk, and so are referred to as 'second-level domains'. The authority for each second-level domain is responsible for keeping track of the branches that connect to it, and so on down the hierarchy.

9. David L. Mills, *RFC 799: Internet Domain Names*, http://www.rfc-editor.org/rfc/rfc799.txt (September 1981).
10. Leiner et al.
11. Clark, 3.
12. Zaw-Sing Su & Jon Postel, *RFC 819: The Domain Naming Convention for Internet User Applications*, 1, http://www.rfc-editor.org/rfc/rfc819.txt (1 Aug. 1982).

Figure 2.1 The Tree-Structured DNS

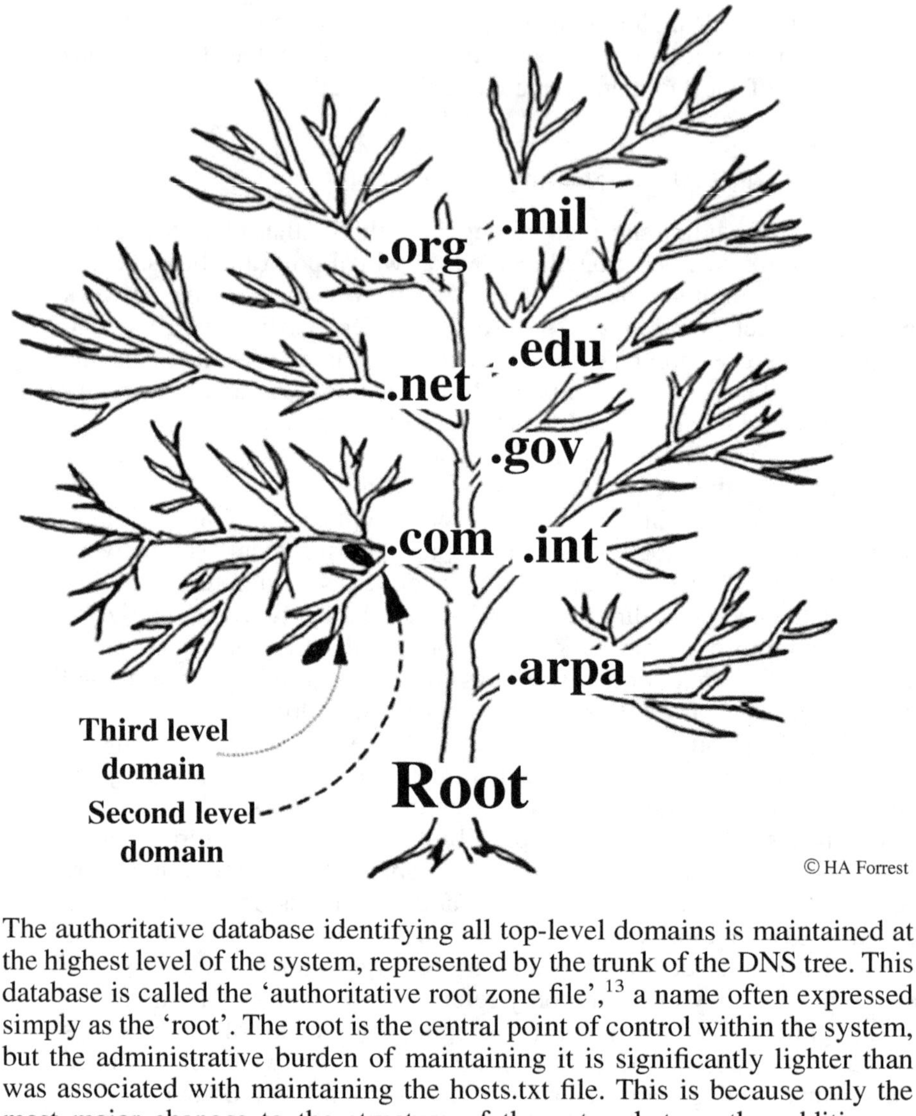

The authoritative database identifying all top-level domains is maintained at the highest level of the system, represented by the trunk of the DNS tree. This database is called the 'authoritative root zone file',[13] a name often expressed simply as the 'root'. The root is the central point of control within the system, but the administrative burden of maintaining it is significantly lighter than was associated with maintaining the hosts.txt file. This is because only the most major changes to the structure of the network tree, the addition or removal of top-level domains, require action at the level of the root. The root is the main point of authority in the DNS; access to the servers on which it is stored equates to an ability to add entries to or remove them from this most

13. Mueller, *Ruling the Root*, 50–51.

authoritative of files. Exclusion from the root has the same consequence as exclusion from the hosts.txt file, but on a significantly grander scale: TLDs not in the root are invisible to TLDs in the root, and the potentially hundreds, thousands or millions of hosts connected to an invisible TLD are likewise all invisible to the hundreds of millions of hosts connected to the TLDs in the root.

The DNS presupposes only one root, and the conflicts arising out of this solitary point of authority and control are numerous and ongoing. It is not within the scope of this study to explore these in detail, and in any event to do so would be duplicative of existing works, of which several are cited in this chapter. A focused, concise discussion of the prior and current authority for the DNS is needed, however, in order to put its current and potential future expansion into context.

2.2 ADMINISTRATION AND OPERATION OF THE DNS

2.2.1 BEFORE ICANN

The US Department of Defense, through its research projects arm ARPA, funded and directed the ARPANET project. As noted in the previous section, the Department of Defense bifurcated and delegated the operational and policy roles necessary to the network's functioning by contracting with the Stanford Research Institute ('SRI') to host and maintain the hosts.txt file and with the University of Southern California's Information Sciences Institute ('ISI') to set network policy. This remained the state of affairs following the DNS's implementation in the early 1980s and then onwards through the end of that decade.

In the early 1990s, the source of funding for the ARPANET project shifted within the US government from the Department of Defense to the National Science Foundation ('NSF'). With this transition, the fundamental character of the project shifted from military to civilian,[14] assisted by the NSF's early decision to connect all American universities to the network.[15] Yet while its character and source of funding changed, the entities contracted to facilitate the project did not. The 'policy-setting authority'[16] undertaken by Jon Postel at ISI remained with him until his death in 1998. He called this role the Internet Assigned Numbers Authority ('IANA'), a name with which

14. 'By 1990, ARPANET was completely phased out.' NTIA, *White Paper*, 31,741.
15. *Ibid.* Mueller, *Ruling the Root*, 85; CSTB, 75.
16. Mueller, *Ruling the Root*, 93.

he would become synonymous,[17] and announced in RFC 1083[18] IANA's authority to manage the protocols standardized by the internet community. Exactly when IANA was formed[19] and the basis of its authority are unclear,[20] but it continues to this day in this role, albeit without Postel.

The Stanford Research Institute, later called SRI International, also retained its role as the NIC up to the start of the 1990s under Department of Defense contract.[21] In 1992, SRI International sub-contracted the NIC to another private company, Network Solutions, Inc. (sometimes referred to as 'Network Solutions' or by its acronym, 'NSI'). When the National Science Foundation took up the reins from the Department of Defense, it retained Network Solutions in this role. The status quo was preserved even through the next transition in authority within the US government from the National Science Foundation to the National Telecommunications and Information Administration ('NTIA'), a division of the US Department of Commerce, in 1997.[22]

This highlights the fact that the DNS was not the product of a particular government department so much as of particular, collaborating individuals such as Jon Postel, Steve Crocker, Robert Kahn, Vinton Cerf and Paul Mockapetris, who stayed on even as authority over the project transitioned from one department to another. At first they were a small cadre of mainly university-based researchers with access to the large, expensive mainframe computers that made connectivity so desirable in the first place. As technology progressed and computers became smaller and cheaper, with each new host that connected to the growing network, an 'internet community' came into existence.

Much of the development of the network arose out of collaboration between the members of this growing community, who initially communicated by post but later by files published on the network they together helped to create.[23] These communications, distributed as the 'Internet Request for Comments' (or 'RFC') series, serve as a chronicle of the collaborative process that eventually resulted in the implementation of TCP/IP, the DNS and subsequent protocols and standards. The RFCs also offer insight into some of the tension that developed between new members of the 'internet

17. *See for example*, Vint Cerf's tribute to Postel following his death in 1998, in which he wrote 'Jon, our beloved IANA, is gone.' Vint Cerf, *RFC 2468: I Remember IANA*, http://www.rfc-editor.org/rfc/rfc2468.txt (17 Oct. 1998).
18. Jon Postel, *RFC 1083: IAB Official Protocol Standards*, http://www.rfc-editor.org/rfc/rfc1083.txt (December 1988).
19. One account sets IANA's creation at 1983, five years before the publication of RFC 1083. Andrew D. Murray, *The Regulation of Cyberspace: Control in the Online Environment* 97 (Routledge-Cavendish 2007).
20. Mueller, *Ruling the Root*, 93.
21. CSTB, 76.
22. *Id.*, 76–77.
23. The history of RFCs is chronicled in Leiner et al.

community' and its founders, many of whom maintained positions of authority as members of the Department of Defense's Internet Advisory (later, Activities, and ultimately, Architecture) Board ('IAB') throughout the 1980s.

When the National Science Foundation took control, it preserved the project structure then in place, with the effect of cementing the IAB's and its influential members' position of influence well into the 1990s.[24] The IAB has since been described as 'a self-selecting group of the original internet people with no legal identity. ... Jon Postel was the "defacto Internet standards process" and the "IAB served as his reviewing team".'[25] The IAB's influential members attempted to rectify their lack of legal identity through the formation in 1992 of a non-profit organization called the Internet Society (it would come to be referred to by its acronym 'ISOC'), but this addition to the administrative structure only reinforced the latent tensions in internet governance.[26]

2.2.2 ICANN the US Government Contractor

By the end of the twentieth century, with the mounting unrest in the growing and increasingly internationalized internet community, discontent was directed at the US government as a result of its de facto control over the root through its contracts with Network Solutions and IANA. It fell on the Clinton administration to address these growing concerns, which it attempted to do with the release of the 'Framework for Global Electronic Commerce'.[27] President Clinton tasked the Department of Commerce's National Telecommunications and Information Administration ('NTIA'), which had assumed responsibility for the government's interests in the internet in 1997, with increasing competition in the internet environment while also promoting international involvement.[28] The Framework further specifically directed: 'The private sector should lead'.[29]

The NTIA's greatest challenge in implementing President Clinton's 'Framework' lay in addressing challenges from an increasingly vocal international community to perpetuation of US government control over the

24. IAB, *A Brief History of the Internet Advisory/Activities/Architecture Board*, http://www.iab.org/about/history.html (describing the history of the IAB and listing all former and current members). NSF Network Technical Advisory Group, *RFC 985: Requirements for Internet Gateways [Draft]*, http://www.rfc-editor.org/rfc/rfc985.txt (May 1986).
25. Craig Partridge, quoted in Mueller, *Ruling the Root*, 90.
26. *Id.*, 94–98.
27. William J. Clinton & Albert Gore Jr, *A Framework For Global Electronic Commerce*, Office of the Executive, http://clinton4.nara.gov/WH/New/Commerce/.
28. *Ibid.* CSTB, 76–77.
29. Clinton & Gore Jr, *A Framework For Global Electronic Commerce*, Principle 1.

core functions of the DNS. Its 'Proposal to Improve the Technical Management of Internet Names and Addresses',[30] today referred to as the 'Green Paper', asserted that the future of the internet lay in principally private hands supported by the stability, reliability and security of the American legal system. More specifically, it proposed the creation of a non-profit corporation headquartered in the United States that would assume from the US Federal Government the following authority:

(1) to set policy for and direct the allocation of number blocks to regional number registries for the assignment of Internet addresses;
(2) to oversee the operation of an authoritative root server system;
(3) to oversee policy for determining, based on objective criteria clearly established in the new organization's charter, the circumstances under which new top-level domains are added to the root system; and
(4) to coordinate the development of other technical protocol parameters as needed to maintain universal connectivity on the Internet.[31]

The Green Paper proposed that the transition of authority to this new corporation would be completed 'as soon as possible and in no event later than September 30, 2000'.[32]

The White Paper produced later in 1998 reported strong support for the idea of the new corporation while noting that 'the proposal to headquarter the new corporation in the United States' had been interpreted by some as 'an inappropriate attempt to impose American law on the Internet as a whole.'[33] The NTIA proffered in reply three justifications for basing the corporation in the United States:[34]

> Because of the significant US-based DNS expertise and in order to preserve stability, it makes sense to headquarter the new corporation in the United States. Further, the mere fact that the new corporation would be incorporated in the United States would not remove it from the jurisdiction of other nations. Finally, we note that the new corporation must be headquartered somewhere, and similar objections would inevitably arise if it were incorporated in another location.

Jon Postel took the immediate lead in the initiative to set up the new corporation, but in doing so, clashed with Network Solutions, the company

30. NTIA, Improvement of Technical Management of Internet Names and Addresses, 63 Fed. Reg. 8826–8833 (20 Feb. 1998) (hereinafter, the 'Green Paper').
31. *Id.*, 8828.
32. *Ibid.*
33. NTIA, White Paper, 31,744.
34. *Id.*, 31,745.

still operating the NIC.[35] The final outcome of this complex process[36] was the formation at the end of 1998 of the Internet Corporation for Assigned Names and Numbers ('ICANN'), a California non-profit public benefit corporation. The Department of Commerce and ICANN entered into a Memorandum of Understanding in which they jointly undertook to further the development and privatization of the DNS.[37]

Despite seemingly earnest statements to the contrary in both the Green and White Papers, the US government retained a key (if no longer as prominent) stake in the DNS for nearly two decades after ICANN's formation. The Memorandum of Understanding was replaced in 2006 by an agreement that, according to then-ICANN CEO and President Dr Paul Twomey, 'recognizes [ICANN] as being responsible for the management of the Internet's system of unique identifiers on an ongoing basis. It means ICANN is more autonomous.'[38] Twomey trumpeted key changes in the relationship brought about by the new agreement, including ICANN no longer having to report regularly to the Department of Commerce and the Department no longer prescribing ICANN's activities.

To the extent that ICANN interpreted this as the beginning of the end of its formal relationship with the US government, this hope would have been dampened by recommendations made in early 2009 by the Chairman of the House Committee on Energy and Commerce and the Chairman of the Internet Subcommittee to strengthen that relationship through 'a permanent instrument'.[39] The seventh amendment to the original Memorandum of Understanding was then followed by an 'Affirmation of Commitments' between ICANN and the Department of Commerce.[40] In this agreement, the Department of Commerce affirmed 'its commitment to a multi-stakeholder, private sector led, bottom-up policy development model for DNS technical

35. Mueller, *Ruling the Root*, 175–184.

36. For a detailed account of the ICANN formation process, *see* Mueller, *Ruling the Root*, 163–184.

37. US Department of Commerce and ICANN, *Memorandum of Understanding Between the US Department of Commerce and Internet Corporation for Assigned Names and Numbers*, https://www.ntia.doc.gov/page/1998/memorandum-understanding-between-us-department-commerce-and-internet-corporation-assigned-.

38. ICANN, *New Agreement Means Greater Independence in Managing the Internet's System of Unique Identifiers*, https://www.icann.org/news/announcement-2006-09-29-en (29 Sep. 2006).

39. CircleID, *Key Members of Congress Call for Permanent ICANN-US Tie, CircleID Internet Infrastructure*, http://www.circleid.com/posts/key_members_of_congress_call_for_permanent_icann_us_tie/ (5 Aug. 2009).

40. US Department of Commerce and ICANN, *Affirmation of Commitments by the United States Department of Commerce and the Internet Corporation for Assigned Names and Numbers*, https://www.icann.org/resources/pages/affirmation-of-commitments-2009-09-30-en (30 Sept. 2009).

coordination that acts for the benefit of global Internet users' and pledged continued support for and participation in ICANN's Governmental Advisory Committee (the 'GAC').[41] In actuality, the Affirmation of Commitments codified the then-status quo insofar as the United States' role in DNS authority was concerned. Comments made at subsequent ICANN public meetings to suggest that this new agreement cast further doubts as to ICANN's legitimacy within the international internet community received cool response from ICANN leadership.[42]

2.2.3 An Independent ICANN

Faced with renewed global pressures in relation to its perceived control over the DNS specifically and the internet more generally, the National Telecommunications and Information Administration of the US Department of Commerce announced in March 2014 its intention to end its contractual relationship with ICANN.[43] The NTIA's announcement signalled the long-awaited transition to a fully independent ICANN: 'Transitioning NTIA out of its role marks the final phase of the privatization of the DNS as outlined by the U.S. Government in 1997.'[44] The ICANN community was asked to work together to deliver a transition plan demonstrating the organization's sufficient maturity to undertake, without US government oversight, the previously contracted functions of operating the DNS. Almost exactly two years later, in March 2016, ICANN's Board of Directors delivered a plan,[45] pursuant to which ICANN remains a California public benefit non-profit corporation, accountable in the carrying out of the IANA functions not to the US government, but to a committee of community-selected representatives.

A last-minute attempt by four US State Attorneys General to delay the transition was denied,[46] and the Affirmation of Commitments simply expired on 30 September 2016.

41. *Ibid.*
42. ICANN, *Transcript: Affirmation of Commitments Consultation*, http://sel.icann.org/node/7481 (27 Oct. 2009).
43. National Telecommunications and Information Administration – US Department of Commerce, *Press Release: NTIA Announces Intent to Transition Key Internet Domain Name Functions*, https://www.ntia.doc.gov/press-release/2014/ntia-announces-intent-transition-key-internet-domain-name-functions (14 Mar. 2014).
44. *Ibid.*
45. ICANN, *ICANN Board Transmits IANA Stewardship Transition Proposal and Enhancing ICANN Accountability Recommendations to NTIA*, https://www.icann.org/resources/pages/board-ntia-transmissions-2016-06-13-en (10 Mar. 2016).
46. *State of Arizona et. al. v. NTIA et. al.*, Case 3:16-cv-00274 (28 Sep. 2016); Elizabeth Weise, 'Judge denies block on Internet address transfer', USA Today (1 Oct. 2016), http://www.usatoday.com/story/tech/news/2016/09/30/judge-denies-block-internet-address-transfer-icann-iana-ip-address-texas/91349184/.

In developing the transition plan and corresponding amended corporate bylaws,[47] numerous, complex existential issues were raised in relation to ICANN's continuing role and responsibility vis-à-vis the DNS. These issues – many of which remain under discussion in a second 'work stream'[48] – lie beyond the scope of this study. While none expressly targets ICANN policy or decision-making in relation to geographic names, the new accountability mechanisms[49] are mentioned here because they will apply in future disputes raised by new gTLD applicants against ICANN's Board of Directors.

2.3 DOMAIN NAME COMPONENTS AND RELATED TERMINOLOGY

Throughout this turbulent evolution of authority over and responsibility for the system of unique identifiers that underpins the internet, the actual use and development of that system, the Domain Name System, carried on. What began as ideas for more efficiently keeping track of the hosts in the network developed into a logical, hierarchically structured system based on identifiers that can be understood by both humans and machines. Yet it was recognized early on that humans and machines have different needs and preferences when it comes to identifiers; computers understand numbers, long series of which are less intuitive or meaningful to human users. The DNS solves this problem by assigning each host two identifiers: a numerical IP address to be used by computers and a mnemonic, alphanumeric name, called a 'domain name', to be used by humans. The translation of one to another is achieved through the use of a program called a 'resolver'.[50]

It is helpful to return to the image of the DNS tree (as previously depicted in Figure 2.1, above) to explain how the naming convention works. The root occupies the highest place in the hierarchy, and is represented by the trunk of the DNS tree. The main branches that connect to it are the top-level domains ('TLDs'). Since the inception of the DNS, top-level domains have been broadly classified into two categories and named accordingly: generic TLDs ('gTLDs', such as .com, .net and .int) and country code TLDs

47. ICANN, *Bylaws for Internet Corporation for Assigned Names and Numbers (As amended 1 October 2016)*, https://www.icann.org/resources/pages/governance/bylaws-en.
48. CCWG Accountability, *Supplemental Final Proposal on Work Stream 1 Recommendations*, https://www.icann.org/en/system/files/files/ccwg-accountability-supp-proposal-work-stream-1-recs-23feb16-en.pdf (23 Feb. 2016) (Recommendation #12: Committing to Further Accountability Work in Work Stream 2).
49. *Ibid.*
50. Paul Mockapetris, *RFC 882: Domain Names Concepts and Facilities*, 3 and 8, http://www.rfc-editor.org/rfc/rfc882.txt (November 1983). CSTB, 44–45.

('ccTLDs', such as .nz (New Zealand), .ch (Switzerland) and .jp (Japan)).[51] The distinction between the two is discussed in more detail in the next section of this chapter. Prior to the official launch of the New gTLD Program with the ICANN Board of Directors' adoption in June 2011 of the *gTLD Applicant Guidebook*,[52] the internet 'tree' had 325 such large branches, of which twenty-two were categorized as gTLDs, forty-eight as test or operative IDNs in non-Latin scripts, and the remainder as ccTLDs.[53]

Top-level domains are not sources of information, but rather portals to the information that internet users create and store on host computers situated at the second and lower levels of the system. As explained above, a host becomes part of the DNS only when it is identified with an IP address and a domain name. Second-level domain names are offered to the public by companies called 'registrars'.[54] Applicants self-select a unique domain name and that name is assigned an IP address. The requirement of absolute uniqueness in domain names means as a practical matter that applicants are prevented from registering a domain name that already exists. This was not a significant problem in the early days of the DNS, but increasingly became one as the internet attracted more users from around the globe. When the applications period for new gTLDs opened in early 2012, the DNS reportedly comprised more than 233 million domain name registrations across all TLDs.[55] Four years on and 1,000 new gTLDs having been added to the root,[56] the total number of domain name registrations in the DNS has further grown by roughly 100 million.[57] Each of these registrations must, due to the requirements of the system, be totally unique.

Returning to the image of the DNS tree, the leaves of the tree represent the computers that store (or 'host') the information that internet users create; these are the ultimate sources to which the root and branches of the tree point. As Figure 2.1 illustrates, in some cases a source of information resides at the second level, while at others it resides at a lower level in the hierarchy. Some TLD authorities have implemented a taxonomic structure at the second

---

51. Postel & Reynolds. RFC 920 identified the 'initial set of top level domain names'; the labels 'generic' and 'country code' came to be applied later. Postel, *Domain Name System Structure and Delegation*, 1.
52. ICANN, *Approval of the New gTLD Program: Resolution 2011.06.20.01*, https://www.icann.org/resources/board-material/resolutions-2011-06-20-en (20 Jun. 2011).
53. IANA, *Root Zone Database: List of TLDs and administrators*, http://www.iana.org/domains/root/db#.
54. ICANN, *New gTLD Program*, 4 (Glossary and useful terms).
55. Verisign, *The Domain Name Industry Brief 9(2)*, 2.
56. ICANN, *A 'Grand' Milestone: New gTLD Program Reaches 1,000th Delegation*, https://www.icann.org/news/blog/a-grand-milestone-new-gtld-program-reaches-1-000th-delegation (25 May 2016).
57. Verisign, *The Domain Name Industry Brief 13(2)*, 2, https://www.verisign.com/assets/domain-name-report-july2016.pdf (Jul. 2016).

level,[58] so that the registration of domain names by the public occurs at the third-level; Australia's .au is an example of this. Some TLDs that were initially established in this manner (i.e., registration at the third-level) have in recent years opened registration at the second level; the United Kingdom's .uk is an example of this.[59]

The structure of a tree is thus clearly replicated in the naming convention for which the DNS is well-known: 'The domain name of a … leaf is the path from the root of the tree to the … leaf.'[60] In other words, a domain name is comprised of the names of all of the branches in the hierarchical tree through which a request for information must route in order to find the desired source of information, from the name of the most specific location at the far left of the address to the least specific, the root (represented by an invisible dot), at the far right.[61] The additional 'www' component of the address signifies the World Wide Web software application, the use of which facilitates the linkage and visual appearance of information stored 'online'.[62] The component names that make up a domain name are separated by dots, where each component name is a sub-domain of the name to its right. This is depicted in Table 2.1.

Table 2.1 Parts of a Domain Name

www	.		.	myname	.	com	(.)
www	.		.	myname	.	ch	(.)
www	.	myname	.	com	.	au	(.)
		Third-Level Domain		**Second-Level Domain**		**Top-Level Domain**	**Root (invisible)**

The database of second-level domain names registered within a TLD and their corresponding IP addresses is called a 'registry', and the entity responsible for maintaining it is also called the 'registry' or, alternatively, 'registry operator'.[63] Domain names, although unique, are not owned, but rather are licensed by registrants. There is no one standard form domain name registration agreement, but registrars for .com, .net and .org along with

58. Owen Vaughan, *RFC 2240: A Legal Basis for Domain Name Allocation*, http://www.rfc-editor.org/rfc/rfc2240.txt (November 1997) ('The allocation of sub-domains under these TLDs is entirely up to the registry for that TLD. The registry may decide to allocate further levels of structure or merely allocate domains in a "flat" manner.').
59. Nominet, *Second Level Registration in .uk: Nominet Consultation Document*, https://ico.org.uk/media/about-the-ico/consultation-responses/2013/2135/consultation-second-level-domain-registration-in-uk-july-2013.pdf (1 Jul. 2013).
60. Mockapetris, 6.
61. *Id.*, 7.
62. Mueller, *Ruling the Root*, 107.
63. ICANN, *New gTLD Program*, 4 (Glossary and Useful Terms).

all of the gTLDs added to the root since ICANN's formation are required to be accredited by ICANN. The terms of their domain name registration agreements are guided by ICANN's overarching Registrar Accreditation Agreement.[64] Across other TLDs there is much wider variance due, as the remainder of this chapter explains, to the manner in which the TLD space has developed over the three decades since the DNS's implementation.

2.4 DEVELOPMENT OF THE TOP-LEVEL DOMAIN SPACE

2.4.1 DISTINGUISHING GENERIC AND COUNTRY CODE TOP-LEVEL DOMAINS

Published in 1984, RFC 920: Domain Requirements[65] announced the creation of two types of top-level domain: generic ('gTLD') and country-code ('ccTLD'). The architects of the DNS saw no functional or technological difference between them; any distinction was said to be purely of an administrative nature in the delegation of their oversight.[66] Administration of the eight initial gTLDs was delegated to individuals and entities with links to the ARPANET project, while ccTLDs were delegated to individuals and entities associated with the territory represented by a country code.[67]

It is said that in actual practice, TLDs were offered by Jon Postel (in the role of IANA) to his own contacts, and that this created some degree of bad sentiment and distrust amongst those outside that circle.[68] The publication in March 1994 of TLD delegation guidelines authored by Postel in the form of RFC 1591 was not entirely positively received, with some interpreting this as effectively codifying Postel's authority to make arbitrary delegations.[69] Much has been written about RFC 1591 and the manner in which the delegation guidelines it established were implemented and, at times, ignored by IANA.[70] These discussions feed into the broader issues described above

64. ICANN, *2013 Registrar Accreditation Agreement,* https://www.icann.org/resources/pages/approved-with-specs-2013-09-17-en (17 Sep. 2013). These contractual relationships are depicted in Figure 3.1 at Part II, Chapter 3, s. 3.3, below.
65. Postel & Reynolds.
66. Mockapetris.
67. Postel & Reynolds, 2.
68. Erica Schlesinger Wass, *Introduction: Lots of Dots*, in *Addressing the World: National Identity and Internet Country Code Domains* xii (Erica Schlesinger Wass ed., Rowman & Littlefield 2003).
69. Mueller, *Ruling the Root*, 126.
70. *Id.*, 125–127. *See also* John C. Klensin, *Reflections on the DNS, RFC 1591, and Categories of Domains*, http://tools.ietf.org/html/draft-klensin-1591-reflections-03 (29 Jan. 2011).

relating to DNS administration and authority, so will not be discussed further here.[71]

Specifically relevant to the development of the top-level of the DNS, however, is the direct impact that RFC 1591 has had on the management and, as a result, use of top-level domains. It imposed few requirements on top-level domain administrators, and these were of a primarily technical nature to ensure that adequate infrastructure was in place to reliably and responsibly operate a TLD. Governments had no role in the technologically focused delegation process, even in respect of country code TLDs. Suggestions that the top-level domain categories were designated in recognition of geopolitical borders or deference to legal jurisdiction were flatly rejected; TLDs were simply a way to logically partition responsibility at that level of the network.[72] The semantics of domain names would nevertheless have a significant impact upon the creation, naming and administration of both country code and generic TLDs.

2.4.2 Creation, Delegation, and Administration of ccTLDs

The creation of new ccTLDs is specifically constrained by IANA's adoption in RFC 1591 of the International Standardization Organization's ISO 3166-1 list of 'English country names and code elements'[73] (the 'ISO 3166-1 standard') as the exclusive naming convention of ccTLDs. The ISO 3166-1 standard provides a set of two-letter codes corresponding to the official name of each of the countries listed in the UN Terminology Bulletin Country Names and the Country and Region Codes for Statistical Use of the UN Statistics Division.[74] 'Once a country name or territory name appears in either of these two sources, it will be added to ISO 3166-1 by default',[75] and then is automatically available for designation as a ccTLD and delegation to an appropriate registry operator. New ccTLDs for countries not already on

71. For information about ccTLD conflicts in particular, *see* Kim G. Von Arx & Gregory R. Hagen, *Sovereign Domains: A Declaration of Independence of ccTLDs from Foreign Control*, 9 Richmond J.L. & Tech 4 (2002).
72. 'Domains are administrative entities. … There are no geographical, topological, or technological constraints on a domain. … The motivation is to provide an organization name that is free of undesirable semantics.' Postel & Reynolds, 1.
73. ISO, *Country Codes: ISO 3166*, http://www.iso.org/iso/home/standards/country_codes.htm#2012_iso3166_MA.
74. Listing in the Country Names Bulletin requires that a territory is either: a member country of the UN, a member of one of its specialized agencies, or a party to the *Statute of the International Court of Justice*. ISO, *Country Codes: ISO 3166*.
75. IANA, *Qualifying top-level domain strings: Eligible countries for country-code TLDs*, http://www.iana.org/help/eligible-tlds.

the ISO 3166-1 standard cannot simply be requested or petitioned from IANA or the ISO. Indeed, IANA highlights that the ISO has described such requests as 'absolutely futile'.[76]

The decision to embrace an existing international standard[77] expediently removed Postel as IANA from messy political and diplomatic conflicts, thus enabling him to focus his energies on IANA's broader policy-setting role.[78] ICANN has preserved this approach and so absolutely avoids any responsibility for determinations of what is considered a 'country' for the purposes of the ISO 3166-1 standard, an attitude commended by the ISO as 'prudent'.[79] Although there have been a few deviations from the ISO 3166-1 standard, including .uk (United Kingdom) and .eu (European Union ('EU')), these are exceptions to otherwise consistent compliance.

Once deemed able to manage their TLD in 'an equitable, just, honest and competent' manner in accordance with RFC 1591, the registry operators to whom the early ccTLDs were delegated were free to operate the ccTLD and establish, implement and enforce policies relating to it as they saw fit. The result of this uncoordinated, unregulated approach is the lack of a uniform framework of ccTLD operation and policy in an environment constrained only by best practice guidelines.[80] Relationships between ccTLD registry operators and national governments also vary. Further, not all ccTLDs operate with a formal relationship with ICANN,[81] a situation that ICANN has been attempting to address since its formation.[82] Where once concerns were expressed about the potential impact that this might have upon ICANN's perceived legitimacy and its future ability to assume full control of the root,[83] in the context of an ICANN independent of the US government the question crystallizes, and as it does so, it shifts from 'whether' to 'why not'. In other words: on what grounds can ccTLDs legitimately refuse to formalize their relationship with ICANN now that ICANN has severed its contractual ties with the US Department of Commerce and become a fully independent entity?

---

76. *Ibid.*
77. The ISO 3166-1 two-letter codes have been adopted by various international organizations including the International Atomic Energy Agency, the International Telecommunication Union and the Universal Postal Union. ISO, *Country Codes: ISO 3166.*
78. Mueller, *Ruling the Root*, 79.
79. ICANN, *ICP-1: Internet Domain Name System Structure and Delegation (ccTLD Administration and Delegation)*, http://www.icann.org/en/icp/icp-1.htm.
80. CENTR, *CENTR Best Practice Guidelines for ccTLD Managers: Version 2 Adopted 10 May 2001*, http://www.icann.org/en/cctlds/centr-2nd-best-practices-20may01.htm.
81. ICANN, ccTLD Agreements, http://www.icann.org/en/cctlds/agreements.html.
82. The challenges of getting agreements into place are described in Peter K. Yu, *The Origins of ccTLD Policymaking*, 12 Cardozo J. Intl & Compar. L. 387 (2004).
83. CSTB, 10–11.

2.4.3 Creation, Delegation, and Administration of gTLDs

RFC 1591 announced the creation of seven generic TLDs plus the 'arpa' domain, a transitional TLD for ARPANET hosts. These are identified in Table 2.2, below. Five were deemed 'international in nature',[84] while registration in the remaining two, .mil and .gov, was restricted to the US Armed Forces and Federal Government, respectively. All were named to represent 'general categories'[85] of expected use, and all are still in existence and use today, including the .arpa TLD, which is now used to support internet infrastructure.[86]

Table 2.2 Generic TLDs Established by RFC 1591

ARPA	ARPANET hosts
GOV	US Federal Government
MIL	US Armed Forces
EDU	Education institutions
COM	Commercial enterprises
ORG	Organizations not fitting within other categories
NET	Network providers
INT	Organizations established by international treaty and international databases

An immediate and unexpected development arising out of this initial offering of gTLDs was the overwhelming popularity of one, .com, over all the others, even including the entire range of ccTLDs. The .us ccTLD, by notable contrast, was almost categorically ignored by American registrants; it is not without irony that many simply assumed that .com was the United States' country code.[87] The .com gTLD attracted commercial and non-commercial domain name registrants alike, and was for a time the default when names were typed into internet browsers without TLDs.[88] This single gTLD came to represent the phenomenon of the internet, lending its name to the most significant global financial events of the late twentieth century, the 'dot com boom' and 'bust', successively.

84. Postel, *RFC 1591*, 1.
85. Postel & Reynolds, 2.
86. Network Working Group, *RFC 3172: Management Guidelines & Operational Requirements for the Address and Routing Parameter Area Domain ('arpa')*, http://www.rfc-editor.org/rfc/rfc3172.txt (September 2001).
87. Erica Schlesinger Wass, *The United States' .US: Striving for the American Dream*, in *Addressing the World: National Identity and Internet Country Code Domains* 126 (Erica Schlesinger Wass ed., Rowman & Littlefield 2003).
88. Mueller, *Ruling the Root*, 108–109.

The overwhelming popularity of .com was unanticipated, as is evident from the DNS's design. Nor was the DNS used in the manner in which its architects had planned. Postel and Reynolds, the authors of RFC 920: Domain Requirements, envisioned vertical growth of the DNS tree in which '[t]here are very few top-level domains, each of these may have many second-level domains' and 'each second level domain may have many third-level domains, etc..'[89] The planned result was that content would be stored in the smaller branches of the tree, several levels distant from the root. What actually occurred was lateral growth through a high volume of second-level domain name registrations. The popularity of .com further distorted the shape of the system, with many leaves stemming from .com and significantly fewer from the other TLD branches. This is depicted in Figure 2.2 below.

Figure 2.2 Domain Name Registrations in .com, .net and .org Before Top-Level Expansion

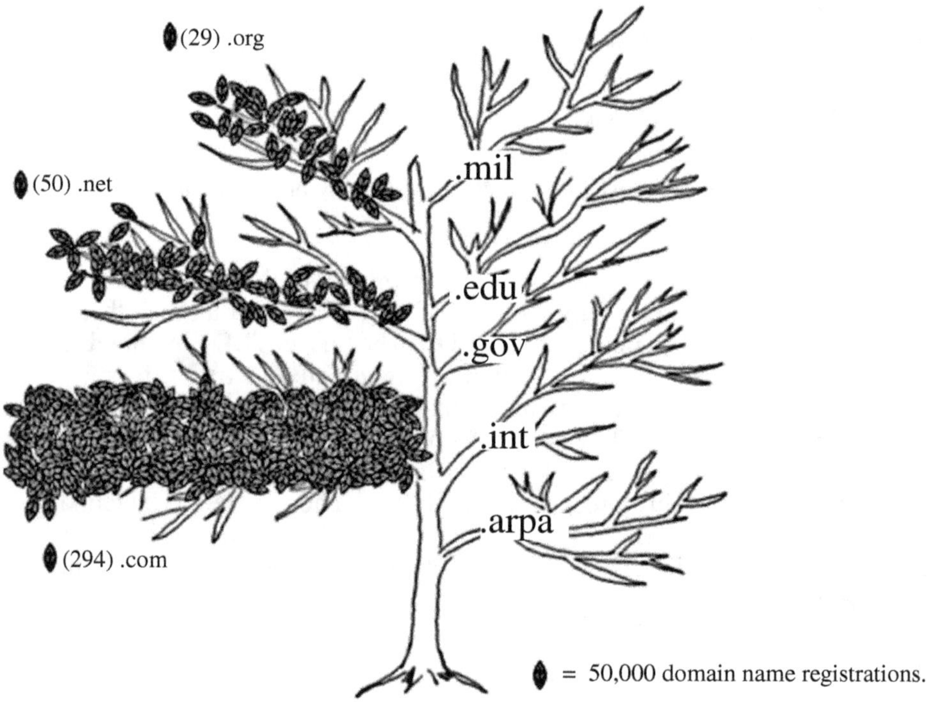

This gave rise to two chief concerns about the sustainability of the system as a whole. First, it was argued that .com had become overcrowded. An ICANN

89. Postel & Reynolds, 7.

working group reported in March, 2000 on a survey conducted in 1999 that found 'of 25,000 standard English-language dictionary words, only 1760 were free in the .com domain.'[90] Second, there were relatively few alternatives to .com, of which by that point only .net and .org were open to public registration.[91] An obvious solution to this problem, posited with increasing frequency as the twentieth century drew to a close, was the addition of new gTLDs to the system.

These discussions were also fuelled by the fact that the lopsided shape of the DNS tree benefited one member of the internet community in particular: Network Solutions. Network Solutions had resisted ICANN's creation and then its authority once created. It still operated the NIC under US government contract and 'controlled almost all of the retail registration business under *.com* but was not itself an [ICANN] accredited registrar.'[92] A deal was struck in which Network Solutions agreed to split its registry and registrar businesses, maintaining the registry role for .com, .net and .org pursuant to a registry agreement with ICANN, while surrendering the registrar role.[93] The deal effectively paved the way for increased competition in the market for .com domain name registrations, but this did not quell interest, which was by no means universal but nevertheless held by a substantial and vocal portion of the internet community, in alternatives to .com.

Talk of creating new gTLDs was already under way when ICANN was in formation, which explains the reference in the National Telecommunications and Information Administration's Green Paper to the new corporation having the authority to 'oversee policy for determining, based on objective criteria clearly established in the new organization's charter, the circumstances under which new top-level domains are added to the root system'.[94] In line with that authority, on 16 June 2000, ICANN's nascent Board of

---

90. ICANN, *Report (Part One) of Working Group C (New TLDs) Presented to Names Council, ICANN* (21 Mar. 2000), https://archive.icann.org/en/dnso/wgc-report-21mar00.htm. The survey referred to was conducted by online news group Wired.com: Declan McCullagh, *Domain Name List is Dwindling*, Wired.com, http://archive.wired.com/science/discoveries/news/1999/04/19117 (14 Apr. 1999).
91. Registration of domain names in the.edu gTLD, while initially intended for all educational institutions, was in practice limited to American universities. In 2001, the contract between the US Department of Commerce and Verisign, the purchaser of Network Solutions as the registrar of the .edu TLD, expired. A new contract was awarded to Educause, a US-based non-profit association that promotes the use of information technology in the higher education sector. The Cooperative Agreement between Educause and the US Department of Commerce formalized the prior practice by expressly limiting registration in the .edu TLD to American post-secondary educational institutions. The .edu Cooperative Agreement and its subsequent amendments (last amended 16 Oct. 2007) are no longer accessible at http://www.ntia.doc.gov/ntiahome/domainname/educa, but they are archived at http://www.archive.org/web/web.php.
92. Mueller, *Ruling the Root*, 194.
93. *Ibid.*
94. NTIA, *Green Paper*.

Directors adopted the recommendation of the Names Council of its internal policy development authority, the Domain Names Supporting Organization ('DNSO', predecessor to today's Generic Names Supporting Organization, or 'GNSO'), 'that a policy be established for the introduction of new TLDs in a measured and responsible manner.'[95] An applications round commenced soon thereafter, but potential applicants were forewarned:

> The effort and cost of preparing a sufficient proposal should not be underestimated. The proposal must be based on a thoroughly formulated plan for the establishment and viable long-term operation of the TLD. The application should clearly and effectively describe the plan, show that the necessary resources have been arranged (or that firm commitments have been obtained) to implement the plan, and demonstrate that the proposal would be superior to others in promoting the goals of the new-TLD policy.[96]

In the face of these admonitions, forty-four applications requesting more than 200 domain strings[97] were received and evaluated by ICANN, which made it clear that it intended to select 'only a few of these … for negotiations toward registry sponsor and operator agreements'.[98] The selection process was guided by nine broadly formulated criteria:[99]

(1) The need to maintain the Internet's stability.
(2) The extent to which selection of the proposal would lead to an effective 'proof of concept' concerning the introduction of top-level domains in the future.
(3) The enhancement of competition for registration services.
(4) The enhancement of the utility of the DNS.
(5) The extent to which the proposal would meet previously unmet types of needs.
(6) The extent to which the proposal would enhance the diversity of the DNS and of registration services generally.
(7) The evaluation of delegation of policy-formulation functions for special-purpose TLDs to appropriate organizations.
(8) Appropriate protections of rights of others in connection with the operation of the TLD.

95. Letter from Fiona M. Alexander, Associate Administrator International Affairs, NTIA, to Rod Beckstrom, President and CEO, ICANN (2 Dec. 2000) (available at http://forum.icann.org/lists/5gtld-guide/msg00013.html).
96. ICANN, *New TLD Application Process Overview*, http://www.icann.org/en/tlds/application-process-03aug00.htm (3 Aug. 2000).
97. ICANN, *TLD Application Review Update*, http://www.icann.org/en/tlds/tld-review-update-13oct00.htm (13 Oct. 2000); ICANN, *TLD Applications Lodged 2 Oct. 2000.*
98. ICANN, *Criteria for evaluating new TLD proposals.*
99. *Ibid.*

(9) The completeness of the proposals submitted and the extent to which they demonstrate realistic business, financial, technical, and operational plans and sound analysis of market needs.

Only seven new TLDs were created and delegated in that first, cautious attempt at top-level DNS expansion: three (.museum, .aero, and .coop) had been applied for and were delegated as 'sponsored gTLDs' and four (.biz, .info, .name, and .pro) as 'unsponsored gTLDs'. Sponsored TLDs were intended to serve a defined and delineated community; applicants were required to appoint a 'sponsoring organization' to represent the needs and interests of the community represented by the string. The sponsoring organization would have authority to set policy in the new gTLD, including the formulation of second-level domain name registration eligibility restrictions.[100] Unsponsored gTLDs, by contrast, were geared towards new TLDs open to the public without restrictions.

All seven new gTLDs launched during the year 2000, and in the span of about a year, the top level of the DNS had doubled in size. The next step was simply to wait and watch how the system and the internet community would respond to this growth.

2.4.4 A Second Test of Expansion at the Top-Level

The first expansion round was a real-time experiment in DNS development, and the seven new gTLDs that resulted from it were selected, as the second application criterion specified, as a 'proof of concept' to flush out the technical, practical and policy issues associated with top-level growth. It was made clear that these efforts were being taken with further expansion in mind provided the DNS proved capable. To this end, a New TLD Evaluation Process Planning Task Force was formed, and it promptly recommended a comprehensive evaluation of the newly created gTLDs, to be conducted over a twelve-month period, with preliminary consideration of steps towards initiating future expansion rounds.[101] In August 2002, ICANN's Board of Directors directed the then-CEO and President of ICANN, Dr. M. Stuart Lynn, to prepare a 'plan for action' for implementing that report.[102]

---

100. ICANN, *New TLD Application Process Overview* ('Because restricted TLDs require definition and implementation of policies concerning naming restrictions, which are most appropriately addressed by subsets of the global Internet community, proposals for restricted TLDs should ordinarily provide for a sponsoring organization.').
101. ICANN, *New TLD Evaluation Process Planning Task Force Final Report*, https://archive.icann.org/en/committees/ntepptf/final-report-31jul02.htm (31 Jul. 2002).
102. ICANN, *Minutes of Special Meeting of the Board of Directors: Resolution 02.97A*, https://www.icann.org/resources/board-material/minutes-2002-08-23-en (23 Aug. 2002).

Lynn's personal recommendation was that proposals should be sought and considered for adding up to three more sponsored gTLDs.[103] He reasoned that this would be a relatively safe way to proceed with testing growth because sponsored gTLDs were likely to generate lower domain name registration volumes due to their focus on a delineated segment of the internet community. This would minimize trademark infringement issues, competing applications for the same domain name, and other 'business concerns'.[104] To the extent that problems did arise, Lynn further noted, these could be addressed by the TLD's sponsoring organization.

Another decision to be made was whether the second test round should be open to all or limited to applicants who had been unsuccessful in the first 'proof of concept' round.[105] ICANN's Board of Directors opted for the former and resolved[106] to commence an application round seeking a limited number of new sponsored TLDs that '[c]ategorize a broad and lasting field of human, institutional, or social endeavor or activity' and '[r]epresent an endeavor or activity that has importance across multiple geographic regions'.[107]

After public comment on a draft version, ICANN released a 'Request for Proposals for Sponsored Top Level Domain Names'.[108] Broader concerns about developing a long-term policy for new gTLDs were set aside for the future. The second expansion round was treated instead as an extension of the first, following the 'same groundrules' [sic].[109] In addition to technical standards and a detailed list of information to be provided in applicants' business plans, applications were adjudged against their ability to demonstrate added value to the internet community, including, *inter alia*, the significance and longevity of the proposed TLD, '[e]nhanced diversity of the Internet name space' and '[e]nrichment of broad global communities'.[110] As in the first 'proof of concept' expansion round, applicants were required to give assurances of adequate means to protect third party rights, but expectations were heightened by a specific requirement to implement the Uniform Domain Name Dispute Resolution Policy ('UDRP').[111]

---

103. Stuart Lynn, *A Plan for Action Regarding New gTLDs*, http://www.icann.org/en/committees/ntepptf/new-gtld-action-plan-18oct02.htm (18 Oct. 2002).
104. *Ibid.* Analysis.
105. ICANN, *Status Report on the sTLD Evaluation Process.*
106. ICANN, *ICANN Resolutions » 2003-10-31 - Adoption of GNSO Council Domain Deletion Policy Recommendations*, https://features.icann.org/2003-10-31-adoption-gnso-council-domain-deletion-policy-recommendations (31 Oct. 2003).
107. ICANN, *sTLD Application Process Appendix A: sTLD Selection Criteria.*
108. ICANN, *New sTLD Application*, http://www.icann.org/en/tlds/new-stld-rfp/new-stld-application-parta-15dec03.htm (15 Dec. 2003).
109. Lynn, *A Plan for Action Regarding New gTLDs.*
110. ICANN, *New sTLD Application*, Part A: Explanatory Notes and Selection Criteria.
111. *Ibid.* The UDRP is discussed in detail in Part II, Chapter 3, s. 3.3.1.

Of the ten applications received, eight (.asia, .cat, .jobs, .mobi, .post, .tel, .travel and .xxx) were delegated,[112] raising the total number of top-level domains to twenty-three. Table 2.3 identifies all gTLDs delegated, as recorded by IANA, when the applications process for the New gTLD Program opened in 2012.[113]

Table 2.3 gTLDs in the Root Before the New gTLD Program

TLD	*Eligible Second-Level Domain Name Registrants*	*IANA Root Zone Delegation*
.arpa	Internet infrastructure	1985
.gov	US Federal Government	1985
.mil	US Armed Forces	1985
.edu	Post-secondary educational institutions accredited by an agency on the US Department of Education's list of Nationally Recognized Accrediting Agencies	1985
.com	Public	1985
.org	Public	1985
.net	Public	1985
.int	Organizations established by international treaty and international databases	1988
.museum	Museums	2001
.aero	Air transport industry members	2001
.coop	Cooperative associations	2001
.biz	Business and commercial use	2001
.info	Public	2001
.name	Individuals	2001
.pro	Credentialed professionals	2002
.jobs	Human resource managers	2005
.cat	Catalan linguistic and cultural community	2005
.mobi	Mobile products and services industry	2005
.travel	Travel industry	2005
.asia	Pan-Asian community	2007

112. Applications for .mail and .xxx were rejected along with a competing application for.tel. Of these, .xxx has received the most publicity. A thorough description of the applications process, individual applications and applicants in the 2004 round is set out in ICANN, *Information Page for Sponsored Top-Level Domains*.

113. IANA Internet Assigned Numbers Authority, *Root Zone Database*, http://www.iana.org/domains/root/db.

TLD	Eligible Second-Level Domain Name Registrants	IANA Root Zone Delegation
.tel	Businesses and individuals (for online publishing of contact details)	2007
.xxx	Adult entertainment industry	2011
.post	Entities providing postal services	2012

Thus, during the first decade of the twenty-first century, the number of main branches on the DNS tree increased threefold, offering the internet community, and in some cases narrowly defined segments of the community, a limited selection of alternatives to .com. ICANN's second test expansion of the TLD space had notably been referred to as an 'interim round',[114] a clear hint at yet further expansion.

2.4.5 THE 'NEW GTLD PROGRAM'

Any further expansion of the top-level space was quite logically predicated upon the success of the two test expansion rounds. ICANN's Board of Directors' authorization of the so-called interim round in 2003 was prima facie an indication that the challenges that had arisen in the first 'proof of concept' round were not considered so serious as to warrant a halt in progress towards ICANN's mission of expanding the DNS.

One of the challenges to expansion that remained unsettled was demand for new gTLDs.[115] For all that demand for registrations in the original gTLDs, of which .com in particular, may have been underestimated in the early days of the DNS, demand for domain name registrations in the new gTLDs added to the root between 2001 and 2012 was significantly overestimated. Reports filed with ICANN by the first 'proof of concept' round new gTLD registry operators reveal that demand forecasts made in new gTLD applications grossly exceeded the actual volume of second-level domain name registrations within those gTLDs; of the seven gTLDs created in that round, only .info managed to meet even the most conservative four-year post-launch targets set out in its application, but in twice as many

114. ICANN, *Status Report on the sTLD evaluation process.*

115. *See* GNSO, *GNSO Issues Report: Introduction of New Top-Level Domains Draft version 1.3*, paras 16 and 18, http://gnso.icann.org/issues/new-gtlds/gnso-issues-rpt-gtlds-05dec05.pdf (5 Dec. 2005). ('Usage patterns are developing and studies from both the OECD and the NRC show that proven demand for new top-level domains is inconclusive, with contentions about advantages claimed by some in stark contrast to the drawbacks purported by others. … Additional TLDs are requested by many that see a business opportunity in running a new TLD. Whether there is true market demand for new TLDs from end-users is another matter and is likely to be conditional on multiple factors.').

years.[116] ICANN demonstrated a certain willingness to accept gTLD applicants' inability to more accurately forecast demand, perhaps in recognition of its own inability to precisely estimate demand; the existence of actual (as contrasted with perceived or presumed) demand was a much-debated 'overarching issue' throughout the new gTLD policy development and implementation processes.[117]

Fuel to this fire was provided by data that challenged the assumption that new gTLDs achieved any lightening of the burden in ever-popular .com. A 2004 report by the Organisation for Economic Co-operation and Development ('OECD') concluded that the seven gTLDs added during the first 'proof of concept' expansion round broadly contributed to a competitive TLD market, but also that the 'significant reduction in the number of registrations under the original gTLDs (.com, .org, .net) at the time of the introduction of the new gTLDs' was only temporary.[118] Similar concerns were articulated in an evaluation conducted by Summit Strategies International.[119] Further, the fears of overcrowding in .com to the point of exhausting that domain, the chief motivator for top-level expansion, simply did come to pass; in the decade after studies warned of an exhausted .com space, that TLD alone grew more than tenfold.[120] By way of comparison, by the end of 2008, the *total* number of second-level domain name registrations in *all* new gTLDs combined equalled approximately 9 million, while Table 2.4 below shows that the number of registrations in .com on several occasions between 2000 and 2010 grew by that amount in one year or less.[121]

---

116. Forecasted demand is set out in each new gTLD application, the non-confidential parts of which are accessible on ICANN's website at ICANN, *New gTLD Program Application Process Archive*, http://archive.icann.org/en/tlds/app-index.htm; ICANN, *Information Page for Sponsored Top-Level Domains*, http://archive.icann.org/en/tlds/stld-apps-19mar04/. Actual registration volume has been derived from the various TLD operators' reports, which are also available on ICANN's website at ICANN, *Registry Report Monthly Reports*, https://www.icann.org/resources/pages/registry-reports.
117. ICANN, *Welcome to the New gTLD Applicant Guidebook Version 2 (V2) Public Comment Forum*, http://archive.icann.org/en/topics/new-gtlds/comments-2-en.htm (2009).
118. OECD Working Party on Telecommunication and Information Services Policies, *Generic Top Level Domain Names: Market Development and Allocation Issues*, DSTI/ICCP/TISP(2004)2/FINAL, 21, http://www.oecd.org/dataoecd/56/34/32996948.pdf (13 Jul. 2004).
119. Summit Strategies International, *Evaluation of New gTLDs: Policy and Legal Issues*, http://archive.icann.org/en/tlds/new-gtld-eval-31aug04.pdf (10 Jul. 2004).
120. Total registration volumes in .com from 2000 to 2009 are published by ZookNIC Internet Intelligence, *History of gTLD Domain Name Growth*, http://www.zooknic.com/Domains/counts.html. Data from 2010 to 2012 has been provided by Professor Matthew Zook. Email from Professor Matthew Zook to Heather Forrest, *Domain Counts* (15 Sep. 2012) (on file with author).
121. Pre-2009 calculations are based on .com registration data recorded on approximately 15 December of each year at ZookNIC Internet Intelligence, *History of gTLD Domain Name*

Table 2.4 Year-on-year .com Domain Name Registration Growth Between ICANN's Formation and the Launch of the New gTLD Program

2011	*7,881,722*
2010	7,844,281
2009	5,239,569
2008	7,263,354
2007	11,180,186
2006	14,136,444
2005	13,327,170
2004	6,855,116
2003	3,858,170
2002	-1,206,882
2001	2,546,477

This is not to suggest that the .com space was not crowded prior to the New gTLD Program, but the fact that registrations volumes have remained consistently high belies a greater availability of names and a higher degree of creativity on the part of domain name registrants than previously thought possible. Registration volumes in the 'proof of concept' new gTLDs have improved over time with increased public awareness and longevity, but they simply cannot be characterized as serious competitors to .com. These empirical issues notwithstanding, ICANN maintained the view that top-level expansion through the two 'proof of concept' rounds had been a success,[122] as supported by the fact that the DNS and the infrastructure on which it relies withstood without cataclysmic incident threefold growth during the ten-year period 2001 to 2011. In addition to creating new space for the world's internet users, the call for sponsored generic TLDs opened the door to distinct linguistic, cultural and industry-specific communities having their own branch on the DNS tree, enabling them to take advantage of the many communications, cultural and commercial opportunities the internet has to offer.

When tasked with advising ICANN's Board of Directors on the feasibility and appropriateness of forging ahead, the GNSO, successor to the DNSO as ICANN's internal body on matters of policy regarding gTLDs,

Growth. Post-2009 calculations are based on Verisign's.com monthly reports of total domains under management in December of 2010 and 2011, available at ICANN, *Monthly Registry Reports*, https://www.icann.org/resources/pages/registry-reports.

122. ICANN, *New gTLD Program*, ('ICANN has successfully carried out two previous rounds for new gTLDs … .').

recommended in late 2007 that gTLD expansion 'must' continue.[123] This recommendation was based on a wide-ranging consultation process and deemed 'consistent with the reasons articulated in 1999 when the first proof of concept round was initiated'.[124] It was pointed out that '[n]o compelling reason has been articulated not to proceed with accepting applications for new top-level domains.'[125] The Board's adoption[126] of the GNSO's recommendations in June 2008 thus signalled the official start of implementation of the GNSO's policy framework underpinning a third top-level expansion initiative.

Concerns about procedural clarity and consistency would finally be addressed in this third initiative. The GNSO's policy development process was used to develop a 'systemized and ongoing mechanism'[127] for future, continued expansion of the top-level domain space. Key policy changes aimed at 'fairness, transparency and non-discrimination'[128] were intended to distinguish the New gTLD Program from the previous two experimental initiatives. First, acting on advice from the technical community about the DNS's ability to withstand larger scale growth, ICANN's Board of Directors decided that the New gTLD Program would be open and uncapped, meaning that all applications satisfying the application criteria would be successful.[129] ICANN then found itself in the position of previous new gTLD applicants, finding it difficult to forecast demand; initially 'anything from hundreds to thousands of applications' was predicted.[130] Second, the Board embraced the recommendation of the GNSO[131] not to impose a defined taxonomy on the expanding DNS. This idea of forcing the DNS into a particular structure through pre-designated TLD categories (such as .retail and .cars) is a suggestion that had been made before[132] but set aside then and again in 2007 in favour of allowing market forces to determine which TLDs get added to the root.

---

123. GNSO, *Final Report on the Introduction of New Generic Top-Level Domains*, Recommendation 1.
124. *Id.*, Recommendation 1 Discussion, para. 7(i).
125. *Id.*, Recommendation 1 Discussion, para. 7(v).
126. ICANN, *Board of Directors Resolution 2008.06.26.02*.
127. GNSO, *Final Report on the Introduction of New Generic Top-Level Domains*.
128. *Ibid.*
129. ICANN, *Board of Directors Resolution 2008.06.26.02*, citing ICANN, *DNS Stability: The Effect of New Generic Top Level Domains on the Internet Domain Name System*, available at http://archive.icann.org/en/topics/dns-stability-draft-paper-06feb08.pdf (6 Feb. 2008).
130. ICANN, *New gTLD Program: New gTLD Program in Brief*, 2, https://archive.icann.org/en/topics/new-gtlds/factsheet-new-gtld-program-oct09-en.pdf (2009).
131. GNSO, *Final Report on the Introduction of New Generic Top-Level Domains*, Background para 13.
132. *See for example*, Lynn. TLD categorization is discussed further in Part II, Chapter 3, s. 3.4.2.

Thus applicants in 2012 had considerable freedom to self-select the name of their applied-for TLD. This was not necessarily new policy, since applicants in the two 'proof of concept' rounds were able to do this, but the fact that ICANN opted not to artificially limit the number of new gTLDs added to the root meant, practically speaking, that ICANN had less control over naming choices. As a result, the New gTLD Program gave rise to new issues that had not yet been faced at the top-level, including: multiple competing applications for identical TLD strings, confusion with existing TLDs, confusion with new IDN ccTLDs in non-Latin scripts, and conflicts with existing 'offline' legal rights in names. The GNSO foreshadowed each of these in its Principles and Recommendations to ICANN's Board of Directors,[133] but the issues raised in the final section of this chapter and the disputes highlighted at the end of the previous chapter[134] clearly illustrate the gaps between these Principles and Recommendations and Board-approved *gTLD Applicant Guidebook* and decision-making pursuant to it. These gaps must be resolved before further expansion occurs if future applicants are to have sufficient confidence in ICANN's implementation of the outcomes of Bylaws-mandated bottom-up policy development.

2.5 THE NEW GTLD PROGRAM AND NEW ISSUES AT THE TOP-LEVEL

The trajectory of development leading up to the New gTLD Program as described in this chapter portrays a measured and deliberate response to a perceived problem of overcrowding at the top-level of the DNS and an opportunity to adapt from the system's architects' unrealized expectations about how it would be used. It is undeniably the case that the two 'proof of concept' top-level expansion rounds were not entered into lightheartedly, but it would be inaccurate to suggest that they were unanimously approved or welcomed. On the contrary, creating new gTLDs was initially declared to be, and indeed remained only a 'consensus position'[135] in a debate with ardently opposed participants.

Certain points of opposition, amongst which actual demand for new gTLDs and the perceived overcrowding of the .com TLD, remain unsettled

133. The initial stage of this process, during which applications would be accepted, was scheduled to run from 12 Jan. to 12 Apr. 2012. ICANN, *Approved Board Resolutions - Singapore*, https://www.icann.org/resources/board-material/resolutions-2011-06-20-en (20 Jun. 2011). Repair of a 'glitch' in the online application system software forced an extension of the application window to 30 May. ICANN, *Statement on TLD Application System*, https://newgtlds.icann.org/en/announcements-and-media/announcement-2-12apr12-en (12 Apr. 2012); ICANN, *TAS Interruption: Update (21 May 2012)*, https://newgtlds.icann.org/en/announcements-and-media/announcement-21may12-en.

134. *See* above Part I, Chapter 1, s. 1.3.

135. ICANN, *Report (Part One) of Working Group C (New TLDs).*

even today, nearly five years after applications were submitted under the *gTLD Applicant Guidebook* framework, and after 1,000 new gTLDs borne of that process have been added to the root.[136]

Certain concerns, on the other hand, have proven moot: most critically, the DNS and its infrastructure have withstood the addition of domains at the top-level and a sustained high rate and volume of growth at the second level. The internet community has developed from a close cadre from mainly American universities contracted by the US Department of Defense to a global citizenry whose interests are now represented by the non-profit public benefit California corporation ICANN, now wholly independent from the US government that formed it at the turn of the twenty-first century.[137]

Having missed the opportunity to develop clear, conclusive, legally consistent policy on geographic names in the first 'round' of the New gTLD Program, this task now falls to the next iteration of policy development; the GNSO's New gTLD Subsequent Procedures Policy Development Process, initiated in December 2015,[138] notably includes within its scope the following: 'Review whether geographic names requirements are appropriate.'[139] This policy development process is notably also dependent upon other activities within ICANN, including another GNSO Policy Development Process, the Review of All Rights Protection Mechanisms in All gTLDs,[140] and the Competition, Consumer Trust and Consumer Choice Review[141] (a legacy of the now-expired Affirmation of Commitments between ICANN and the US Department of Commerce), which may also develop recommendations directly or indirectly affecting the use of geographic names in the DNS.

The decision made by ICANN's Board in June 2008 to proceed with expansion of the top-level DNS space pursuant to the GNSO's policy framework and then implementation of that framework were informed by the multitude of interests within the global internet community. Yet what is said to be technically possible – large scale expansion over a short time frame – nevertheless generates serious procedural (in terms of ICANN's ability to handle a large volume of applications and crafting a firm and achievable

136. ICANN, *A "Grand" Milestone: New gTLD Program Reaches 1,000th Delegation*, https://www.icann.org/news/blog/a-grand-milestone-new-gtld-program-reaches-1-000th-delegation (25 May 2016).

137. *See* above in this Chapter at s. 2.2.3.

138. ICANN GNSO, *Council Resolution 20151217-1: Initiation of a Policy Development Process (PDP) on New gTLD Subsequent Procedures*, https://gnso.icann.org/en/council/resolutions#201512 (17 Dec. 2015).

139. ICANN, *Working Group (WG) Charter: New gTLD Subsequent Procedures*, https://gnso.icann.org/en/issues/new-gtlds/subsequent-procedures-charter-21jan16-en.pdf, 4 (21 Jan. 2016).

140. ICANN GNSO, *PDP Review of All Rights Protection Mechanisms in All gTLDs*, https://gnso.icann.org/en/group-activities/active/rpm.

141. ICANN, *New Generic Top Level Domains: Competition, Consumer Trust and Consumer Choice Review*, https://newgtlds.icann.org/en/reviews/cct.

timeline for doing so) as well as substantive (in terms of conflicts generated by applicants' choice of TLD strings) pressures. Multiple conflicting applications, confusion and conflicts with existing legal rights were largely avoidable when ICANN hand-picked a limited number of applications in the two 'proof of concept' expansion rounds. The New gTLD Program, on the other hand, squarely introduced to the top-level of the system issues of conflicting strings and legal rights. Existing legal rights have been a matter of concern in DNS policy from the system's early days, and the sorts of naming conflicts that came to light with open expansion at the top-level had since long before been experienced at the second level. These experiences are evaluated in the next chapter as a platform from which to explore in Part III the current and future resolution of conflicting claims to legal rights in geographic names.

Part II

Recognition of Rights in Names in DNS Policy and International Law

Chapter 3

Recognition of Rights in Names in DNS Policy

The resultant conflicts over who has rights to use particular domain names has enmeshed and continues to enmesh apparently technical naming processes in economic, public policy and legal issues.[1]

3.1 THE EMERGENCE OF BAD ACTORS

Names are a principal component of the DNS, but they have come to play a different role within the system than its architects had planned: 'Names at all levels were conceived as names for network resources – primarily host computers – not for people, organizations, documents, or products.'[2] In other words, domain names were intended to direct computers, not their users. It was their mnemonic rather than semantic quality that made names such a logical and integral component to the system, but indeed their semantic possibilities that endeared them to the human user and as a result, spurred the system's uptake and growth.[3]

The first domain name, www.symbolics.com, was registered on 15 March 1985 by Symbolics, Inc., a Massachusetts, US-based computer

1. CSTB, *Signposts in Cyberspace*, 63.
2. Mueller, *Ruling the Root*, 78. CSTB, x–xi ('The original purpose of the DNS was to provide identifiers for network objects that are more easily remembered and enduring than the numerical addresses and port numbers used by the network infrastructure. However, domain names are now often used for purposes for which they were not originally intended, such as searching, corporate identification and marketing.').
3. Mueller, *Ruling the Root*, 108.

manufacturer.[4] Other registrants similarly selected second-level domain names that did not so much assign a simple moniker to the host computer on which their information was stored as identify the content or source, in a proprietary more than technical sense, of that information. Information seekers responded to this by using domain names as a navigational aid to find content for which an address was unknown. In this way, domain names quickly acquired not only meaning but commercial value, the best names being the most easily guessable.[5]

Navigability in the online environment has thus come to depend upon one's choice of domain name; names that are clearly representative of the registrant's identity (whether personal or commercial), products or other identifying characteristics are more likely to be found by those looking for them. This is neither a new or surprising phenomenon in human communications, particularly in the commercial context: consumers' searches for goods and services have long been facilitated by brand names. A logical extension of internet users' use of domain names as a navigational aid, therefore, is brand owners' use of domain names as a means of communicating branding messages to consumers. Non-commercial names expressing personal, cultural, political and other forms of identity have also made the transition to the online environment.

A registrant's choice of second-level domain name is constrained in three principal ways: practically by the available TLDs in which to register (although with the introduction of new gTLDs, this constraint is diminishing); procedurally by eligibility requirements (if any) within TLDs; and technically by the number and type of characters a domain name may contain and the requirement of absolute name uniqueness. Legal constraints on name choice, on the other hand, have had a relatively limited effect on domain name registration, with infringement of trademarks being the primary concern. It was decided early on in the development of the DNS that the desired ease and efficiency of the second-level domain name registration process, not to mention the complications of legal jurisdiction in the adjudication of disputes, rendered pre-registration scrutiny of applications for infringements of legal rights impracticable.[6] This decision, when coupled with a first-come, first-served approach to registration, rather quickly gave rise to disputes between legal rights holders keen to preserve and extend their rights in the DNS and domain name registrants who were quicker to register trademark names. Self-policing was soon proven ineffective by registrations

4. Symbolics.com, About Symbolics, http://symbolics.com/about-symbolics/.
5. Mueller, *Ruling the Root*, 109 (describing a process of 'Webification' of domain names and the impact this had upon their acquiring a value); CSTB, 26.
6. Postel, *RFC 1591*, 6 ('In case of a dispute between domain names registrants as to the rights to a particular name, the registration authority shall have no role or responsibility other than to provide the contact information to both parties. The registration of a domain name does not have any trademark status. It is up to the requester to be sure he is not violating anyone else's trademark.').

such as journalist Joshua Quittner's for the domain name www.mcdonalds.com. Quittner reportedly registered the name simply 'to see if he could do it', and then offered to ransom it to the McDonald's Corporation in exchange for a USD 3,500 donation to a New York City school.[7]

Many brand owners had simply assumed that their trademark rights would extend automatically to the online environment. They further assumed that consumers would share in this thinking: 'For most of us, it is a reasonable assumption that the owner of a trademark in the real world that you rely on to provide authentic goods or services is also the owner of a website that you find under the corresponding domain name.'[8] This notion of an automatic extension of rights was not universally considered axiomatic, however. What brand owners and courts ultimately termed 'cybersquatting' others viewed as a business opportunity.[9]

Cybersquatting developed into an industry unto itself in the registration and use of trademarks as internet domain names. Other practices such as 'phishing', 'kiting', and 'tasting'[10] (to name but a few) have developed alongside advances in technology and users' savvy. It is not clear whether, or the extent to which, the system's architects foresaw these behaviours or contemplated in detail how they might be addressed, but as they began to surface it became clear that mechanisms were needed to bridge the gap between offline and online rights in names. Any attempts to do so would also, it was acknowledged early on, need to 'balance the value of avoiding confusion or preventing illegal or otherwise undesired appropriation of

---

7. Smith, 1189, quoting James W. Morando & Christian H. Nadan, *Can Trademark Law Regulate the Race to Claim Internet Domain Names*, 13 Computer Lawyer 10, 10 (1996).
8. IRT, *Final Report on Trademark Protection in new gTLDs*, 1, http://www.icann.org/en/topics/new-gtlds/irt-final-report-trademark-protection-29may09-en.pdf (29 May 2009) (hereinafter 'Final Report').
9. *See for example*, *Avery Dennison Corp. v. Sumpton*, 999 F.Supp. 1337, 1338 (C.D. Cal. 1999) *rev'd*, 189 F.3d 868 (9th Cir. 1999) ('Like all "cybersquatters," defendants merely "squat" on their registered domain names until someone else comes along who wishes to use them. Like all "cybersquatters," defendants usurp all of the accepted meanings of their domain names, so as to prevent others from using the same domain names in any of their accepted meanings. And like all "cybersquatters," defendants seek to make a financial return by exacting a price before consenting to allow others to use the domain names on which they have chosen to "squat".'). The title of an article featured on Wired.com succinctly sums up the business opportunist's perspective: Joshua Quittner, *Billions Registered: Right Now, There Are No Rules to Keep You from Owning a Bitchin' Corporate Name as Your Own Internet Address*, Issue 2.10 Wired.com (October 1994) (available at https://www.wired.com/1994/10/mcdonalds/).
10. 'Phishing' involves a 'Web site fraudulently presenting itself as a trusted brand in order to deceive Internet users into divulging sensitive information (e.g., online banking credentials, email passwords).' 'Kiting' occurs where registrants 'abuse the Add Grace Period through continual registration, deletion, and reregistration of the same names in order to avoid paying the registration fees.' 'Tasting' occurs where a registrant uses the five-day grace period to test the 'the monetization potential of a domain.' ICANN, *Registration Abuse Policies Working Group Initial Report*, http://gnso.icann.org/issues/rap-wg-initial-report-12feb10-en.pdf (12 Feb. 2010).

identity against the value of free expression, open communication, and fair use.'[11] Such weighty considerations make for tremendous challenges in striking a balance, something both sides could claim has not yet been achieved.

While the global trademark community has achieved much in terms of protecting its interests in the online environment, a universal approach to rights protection across the TLD space has up to now been quite simply impossible owing to the way in which that has developed, the variety of approaches to managing TLDs and the variety of communities they serve. Some are open to registration by all, while others are limited to use by a specifically identified community. Some are intended to be commercial in nature, while others are not. Even prior to the New gTLD Program the WIPO acknowledged the impact of this diversity,[12] as has ICANN's Intellectual Property Constituency, highlighting the lack of 'consensus on what constitutes "Best Practice" when it comes to measures to protect intellectual property and the rights of others' in the DNS.[13]

As a result of this diversity among top-level domains, the development and application of rights protection mechanisms has occurred on an ad hoc basis, with the merits and failings of mechanisms being noted along the way for their potential future utilization and improvement. This chapter captures that distinct part of the development of DNS policy relating to rights protection mechanisms in order to understand the extent of the recognition of legal rights in the DNS up to and including the New gTLD Program's *gTLD Applicant Guidebook*. To date, two opportunities to protect rights have emerged: before and after registration of a second-level domain name. The mechanisms employed in the former stage are considered first, followed by mechanisms employed in the latter stage. All mechanisms, which are primarily trademark-based, are scrutinized in order to determine their current or future scope for protecting rights in geographic names to the extent that these are determined in Part III below to be recognized by international law.

3.2 *EX ANTE* RIGHTS RECOGNITION

Procedural mechanisms geared toward the recognition of 'offline' legal rights in names prior to the allocation of those names in the online environment can be characterized as *ex ante* rights protection mechanisms. Their role is to prevent or at least reduce the number of registrations of domain names that

11. CSTB, 63.
12. WIPO, *ccTLD Best Practices for the Prevention and Resolution of Intellectual Property Disputes: version 1*, 2, http://www.wipo.int/export/sites/www/amc/en/docs/bestpractices.pdf (20 Jun. 2001).
13. IPC & Marques, *The Perfect Sunrise? How Pre-launch Rights Protection Mechanisms and Successful Registry Operations Go Hand in Hand*, 4, https://archive.icann.org/en/topics/new-gtlds/perfect-sunrise-jun08-en.pdf (June 2008).

infringe existing legal rights and thereby reduce the need for and number of post-registration disputes. Inherent in all *ex ante* mechanisms is the priority status afforded to the holder of existing legal rights. It must from the outset be acknowledged that trademarks have been treated with priority status for most of the DNS's existence; to change that position would necessitate a fundamental shift in DNS policy with untold consequences. Accepting this status quo allows the focus to be turned away from *whether* – as a general principle – rights should be recognized and protected in the DNS to the question of *what* rights are recognized and *how* their protection is achieved.

To date, the use of *ex ante* rights protection mechanisms has principally occurred at the second level of the DNS. This is attributable to the sheer volume of second-level domain name registrations and their availability to the general public, while the controlled manner in which top-level expansion has taken place up to the point of the New gTLD Program rendered such mechanisms largely unnecessary at that level. As the top-level transitions to a higher volume space through open and uncapped expansion initiatives, however, it is appropriate to evaluate the experience of rights protection mechanisms at the second level in order to identify some of the challenges that lie ahead.

3.2.1 Reserved Names

One way to avoid conflicts between offline and online rights in names is simply to exclude potentially conflict-generating names from registration, whether by preventing their registration entirely or by reserving them for designated registrants. Because the focus of this book is on the recognition of legal rights in names, the notion of restriction (i.e., restricting a name from registration by *anyone*) should be distinguished from the notion of reservation (i.e., reserving a name for *a particular applicant*): restriction may but need not infer legal rights, and need not be based upon a claim to ownership, while reservation is inherently a proprietary-based conferment of priority on one party over all others.[14] In the DNS context, both of these concepts, restriction and reservation, tend unhelpfully to be captured by the term 'reserved names'.

Reservations have been in place since the early days of the DNS, most frequently applied below the top-level. This is because domain names are ordinarily open to public registration at lower levels, while ICANN's strict control of the development of the top-level space prior to the New gTLD Program rendered the need for explicit policy on reservations there largely unnecessary. ICANN's Board of Directors' decision to conduct an open and

14. The authority of ICANN or any other body to remove names from open registration is a live issue, but nevertheless one that lies beyond the scope of this work. Mueller raises interesting arguments on this point in *Ruling the Root,* 232.

uncapped new gTLD expansion round brought the concept of reserved names squarely into view at the top-level, and it is with this in anticipation that the GNSO formed a Reserved Names Working Group in 2007 to review the use of reservations in the DNS. In its report,[15] the Working Group identified eight broad categories of names subject to reservation in gTLDs, of which one of the longest in existence is names such as 'IANA' and related essential DNS bodies and functions. In the absence of documentation from those early days, the Working Group assumed that these names had been set aside by the internet architects in order to prevent the creation of top and lower level domain names with the potential to disrupt DNS stability.[16] Table 3.1 identifies this and other reservation categories that have likewise been justified on the basis of system security, stability and integrity.

Table 3.1 Names Historically Reserved for Reasons of DNS Stability and Security

Category	*Names*
ICANN & IANA-related	aso, gnso, icann, internic, ccNSO, afrinic, apnic, arin, example, gtld-servers, iab, iana, iana-servers, iesg, ietf, irtf, istf, lacnic, latnic, rfc-editor, ripe, root-servers
NIC, WHOIS, www	nic, whois, www
Tagged	All names with hyphens (-) in both the third and fourth character positions
Single Character	For example, www.**a**.com and www.zenith.**z**
Two Character	For example, www.**be**.com; www.name.**go**

Notably, ICANN has not in any gTLD created prior to the New gTLD Program required reservation for the express purpose of protecting proprietary rights. This protection mechanism has more than once been discussed for trademarks, most recently in the form of a globally protected trademarks list, as is discussed later in this chapter. It nevertheless seems likely that proprietary concerns have at least to some degree motivated certain reservations otherwise expressly or impliedly justified on technical grounds. The name 'icann' is, for example, the name of a corporation, and 'iana' is the name of the entity responsible for a critical function of internet operations. That ICANN should be able to reserve its own corporate name from the public registration process, as one member of the Reserved Names Working

15. GNSO, *Reserved Names Working Group Final Report*, http://gnso.icann.org/issues/new-gtlds/final-report-rn-wg-23may07.htm (23 May 2007).
16. *Id.*, 42.

Group pointed out, is at odds with the way in which other proprietary names are treated in the DNS.[17]

One might, on the other hand, simply accept the reservation of 'icann', 'iana' and similar names as a practical matter that owes much to the way and spirit in which the DNS was created:

> When reserved names were devised for IANA, ICANN or registries, the engineers simply looked about for useful tools and found words like iana, ietf, whois, www and said: there is plenty of reason for us to reserve them and no particular reason why, out of the infinitude (or vast number) of available word strings, these several should not be reserved. Is it sensible on its face to reserve 'ietf' for the unincorporated IETF? Of course it is, but I wager that those who reserved it gave not a thought to the IETF's unincorporated status when they did so. They had no concern for a dispute resolution process that probably did not exist at the time. It was handy, it fitted the task of identifying the IETF, so the letter-string ietf was reserved.[18]

Even if reservation is accepted as an appropriate approach for the names of entities involved in the internet's functions, such an argument cannot so easily be made for geographic names, which have been (and are currently) reserved in various gTLDs, and 'controversial names', which have not traditionally been reserved in gTLDs. Reservation of these two categories of name is closely examined in the subsections that follow.

3.2.1.1 'Geographic and Geopolitical' Names

In its review, the GNSO's Reserved Names Working Group characterized reservations for geographic and geopolitical names 'a relatively new class of reservations', tracing their origin to 10 September 2001 resolutions[19] of the ICANN Board of Directors regarding the then-newly delegated .info gTLD.[20] The new .info gTLD's 'very special nature' had provoked concern amongst members of the GAC within ICANN, which advised 'that interim ad hoc measures should be taken by ICANN and the Registries' whereby 'the use of names of countries and distinct economies as recognized in international fora as second level domains in the *.info* TLD should be at the

17. GNSO, *Reserved Name Working Group Report: Working Document 16 Mar. 2007*, 54–55 (quoting Mike Rodenbaugh) http://gnso.icann.org/drafts/rn-wg-fr19mar07.pdf.
18. Denton, *RE: [gnso-rn-wg] Comments on ICANN/IANA Reserved Names Reports.*
19. ICANN, *Regular Meeting of the Board Minutes*, Resolutions 01.92 and 01.93 https://www.icann.org/resources/board-material/minutes-2001-09-10-en (10 Sep. 2001).
20. GNSO, *Reserved Names Working Group Final Report*, at *Annex Five: Geographical and Geopolitical Names Sub-group Report.*

discretion of the respective governments and public authorities.'[21] ICANN's Board of Directors acted on this advice and obliged Afilias, the .info registry operator, to incorporate a reservation at all levels of registration in the following terms:[22]

> **E. Geographic and Geopolitical Names.** All geographic and geopolitical names contained in the ISO 3166-1 list from time to time shall initially be reserved at both the second level and at all other levels within the TLD at which the Registry Operator provides for registrations. All names shall be reserved both in English and in all related official languages as may be directed by ICANN or with the GAC.
>
> In addition, Registry Operator shall reserve names of territories, distinct geographic locations, and other geographic and geopolitical names as ICANN may direct from time to time. Such names shall be reserved from registration during any sunrise period, and shall be registered in ICANN's name prior to start-up and open registration in the TLD. Registry Operator shall post and maintain an updated listing of all such names on its website, which list shall be subject to change at ICANN's direction. Upon determination by ICANN of appropriate standards and qualifications for registration following input from interested parties in the Internet community, such names may be approved for registration to the appropriate authoritative body.

The life of this supposedly 'temporary measure'[23] was extended in 2002 by a subsequent resolution of ICANN's Board of Directors directing 'the 329 country names reserved under resolution 01.92 should be made available for registration by the governments and public authorities of the areas associated with the names … according to procedures established by the GAC.'[24] Governments were given until the end of 2003 to act on this, a deadline which the then-GAC Chair, Mohamed Sharil Tarmizi, urged his colleagues to

---

21. GAC, *Meeting 10 Communique: Montevideo 7-8 September 2001*, https://gacweb.icann.org/display/gacweb/GAC+10+Meeting+Montevideo%2C+Uruguay+-+7-8+September+2001.
22. ICANN, *.info Registry Agreement (signed 11 May 2001)*, https://www.icann.org/resources/unthemed-pages/index-d0-2001-05-11-en.
23. ICANN, *Regular Meeting of the Board Minutes*, Geographic and Geopolitical Names in.info, https://www.icann.org/resources/board-material/minutes-2001-09-10-en (10 Sep. 2001).
24. ICANN, *Board of Directors Resolution 02.43: Geographic and Geopolitical Names in.info*, https://www.icann.org/resources/board-material/minutes-2002-03-14-en (14 Mar. 2002). The proposed procedure, described in a circular letter from the GAC Chair, called upon the relevant government or public authority to notify the GAC of its request to register the name. The GAC Secretariat would 'authenticate' the request and transfer it to the ICANN staff and the .info registry operator. Mohamed Sharil Tarmizi, *Reservation of Country Names in Dot Info: ICANN Board Resolutions of 10 September 2001 and 14 March 2002* (9 Sep. 2003) (web address no longer available, hard copy on file with author).

bear in mind as the year drew to a close and 'most reserved names ha[d] still not been registered by the governments and public authorities concerned.'[25] The reservation of 'geographic and geopolitical' names took on a life of its own when ICANN mirrored the language of Clause E of the .info Registry Agreement in the .asia Registry Agreement, and then incorporated it with few changes in the other second round 'proof of concept' new gTLD registry agreements including, several years later, those of .post and .xxx.[26]

Developments in other forums following the conclusion of WIPO's Second Internet Domain Name Process ('WIPO II') informed consideration within ICANN of geographic names' reservation, in particular the conclusions reached in two special sessions of WIPO's Standing Committee on the Law of Trademarks, Industrial Designs and Geographical Indications.[27] Formed to consider in detail the recommendations of the WIPO II Report, this ad hoc working group explored such key questions as whether country names and geographical indications should be protected in the DNS and if so, by what protection mechanisms, in which TLDs, with what effect on existing registrations, etc. The group found it difficult to reach consensus on the issue of geographical indications, but it was concluded by the Chair that most delegations, with the US, Canada and Australia as notable exceptions, 'favored some form of protection for country names against registration or use by persons unconnected with the constitutional authorities of the country in question.'[28] In October, 2002, the General Assembly of WIPO decided that the Standing Committee should continue discussions 'with a view to reaching a final position'.[29]

---

25. 'It is possible that some of the governments, distinct economies and public authorities may not be familiar with the message contained in this letter, but for the uninitiated, I urge you to read on. It is about protecting your country name in the generic top level domain name in Dot Info e.g., www.[country name].info.' Tarmizi, *Reservation of Country Names in Dot Info*.
26. ICANN, *.asia Registry Agreement (6 Dec. 2006)*, https://www.icann.org/resources/unthemed-pages/asia-2012-02-25-en; ICANN, *.jobs Registry Agreement (5 May 2005)*, https://www.icann.org/resources/unthemed-pages/jobs-agreement-2012-02-25-en; ICANN, *.cat TLD Sponsorship Agreement (signed 23 Sept. 2005)*, https://www.icann.org/resources/unthemed-pages/cat-agreement-2005-09-23-en; ICANN, *.mobi TLD Sponsorship Agreement (signed 10 July 2005)*, https://www.icann.org/resources/unthemed-pages/mobi-2012-02-25-en; ICANN, *.travel Sponsored TLD Registry Agreement (signed 5 May 2005)*, https://www.icann.org/resources/unthemed-pages/travel-agreement-2006-04-12-en; ICANN, *.tel Registry Agreement (30 May 2006)*, https://www.icann.org/resources/unthemed-pages/tel-2012-02-25-en; ICANN, *.post Sponsored TLD Agreement (11 Dec. 2009)*, https://www.icann.org/resources/unthemed-pages/post-2015-10-30-en; ICANN, *.xxx Registry Agreement (31 Mar. 2011)*, https://www.icann.org/resources/agreement/xxx-2011-03-31-en.
27. WIPO, *First Special Session*; WIPO, *Second Special Session*.
28. WIPO, *Second Special Session*, para. 210.
29. WIPO General Assembly, *Report of the Twenty-Eighth (13th Extraordinary) Session, WIPO Doc. WO/GA/28/7 CORR*, para. 81, http://www.wipo.int/edocs/mdocs/govbody/en/wo_ga_28/wo_ga_28_7.pdf (1 Oct. 2002).

The form of protection ultimately recommended was not reservation of country names from domain name registration, however, but incorporation of country names into the scope of the Uniform Domain Name Dispute Resolution Policy ('UDRP').[30] The UDRP is an administrative dispute resolution procedure for challenging bad faith domain name registrations comprised of trademarks; it is discussed in detail in the next section of this chapter along with other *ex post* rights protection mechanisms. These recommendations were again highlighted by WIPO in mid-2016 in response to ICANN staff-developed proposals that legitimized and acted upon, without legal basis, governments' claims to superior interests in two-letter country codes.[31] The legal effect of these recommendations is also discussed in Chapter 4 as a basis for deeper examination in the chapters that comprise Part III of this book.

Many WIPO Member States had openly expressed reluctance to use reservation to protect geographic names from unauthorized registration as domain names.[32] Nevertheless, in 2007, ICANN's GAC called for the adoption of reservation as a standard practice in all new gTLDs through procedures to block 'at no cost and upon demand of governments, public authorities or IGOs, names with national or geographical significance at the second level of any new gTLD', with associated challenge procedures.[33] Shortly thereafter, the Reserved Names Working Group was formed by the GNSO, the body charged with policy development in relation to gTLDs, and all of this history surrounding the reservation of 'geographical and geopolitical' names fell under that group's lens.

A sub-group of the Reserved Names Working Group focusing specifically on the category of geographic and geopolitical name reservations found it impossible to support the GAC's recommendation of reservation for these names. Echoing the concerns expressed by WIPO in its WIPO II Report, the group stressed the need to 'ensure that "there is a solid and clear basis in existing international law which can be applied so as to prevent erosion of the integrity of geographical indicators and enhance the creditability of the

---

30. WIPO Standing Committee on the Law of Trademarks, Industrial Designs and Geographical Indications, *Report of the Ninth Session, Geneva, November 11 to 15, 2002, SCT/9/9*, para. 149, http://www.wipo.int/edocs/mdocs/sct/en/sct_9/sct_9_9.pdf (2 May 2003).
31. Brian Beckham, *WIPO Arbitration and Mediation Center observations on ICANN's Proposed Measures for Letter/Letter Two-Character ASCII Labels to Avoid Confusion with Corresponding Country Codes, ICANN Email List Archives*, https://forum.icann.org/lists/comments-proposed-measures-two-char-08jul16/msg00006.html (4 Aug. 2016).
32. WIPO Standing Committee on the Law of Trademarks, Industrial Designs and Geographical Indications, *Report of the Ninth Session, Geneva, November 11 to 15, 2002, SCT/9/9*, para. 149.
33. GAC, *Principles Regarding New gTLDs*, Principle 2.7, https://archive.icann.org/en/topics/new-gtlds/gac-principles-regarding-new-gtlds-28mar07-en.pdf (28 Mar. 2007).

DNS".'[34] On this basis, it was agreed[35] that the practice of reserving geographic domain names should be discontinued unless national law required otherwise or a country expressly supported the guidelines of WIPO's Standing Committee on Law of Trademarks, Industrial Designs and Geographical Indications. This notably brought GNSO policy recommendations into direct conflict with GAC advice; the GNSO's recommendations have since been implemented only, ironically, in the .info TLD Schedule of Reserved Names,[36] the gTLD in which geographic name reservations first were made. Prior to the New gTLD Program, all Registry or Sponsorship Agreements for new gTLDs created during the second 'proof of concept' expansion round reserved geographic and geopolitical names, including the much delayed .xxx gTLD.[37]

Looking ahead to new gTLDs created through the New gTLD Program, the Reserved Names Working Group sub-group deemed it sufficient that challenge mechanisms be implemented to prevent user confusion, reinforced by a representation made by a domain name applicant 'that the use of the proposed string is not in violation of the national laws in which the applicant is incorporated.'[38] This is not, however, the approach adopted by ICANN in its implementation of GNSO policy recommendations. Specification 5 of the base Registry Agreement provided by the *gTLD Applicant Guidebook* comprises the 'Schedule of Reserved Names'.[39] It requires all new gTLD registry operators to reserve (with the potential for release upon agreement with relevant government/s):

- short form of country and territory names on the ISO 3166-1 list (including the European Union, which is exceptionally reserved in the ISO 3166-1 list);
- the names of countries in the United Nations Group of Experts on Geographical Names, Technical Reference Manual for the Standardization of Geographic Names; and
- the names of UN Member States in the six official UN languages.

This reservation affects second and lower level domain name registrations in all new gTLDs delegated from 2012.

Specification 5 envisages that 'the reservation of specific country and territory names (including their IDN variants according to the registry

34. GNSO, *Reserved Names Working Group Final Report*, at *Annex Five: Geographical and Geopolitical Names Sub-group Report* (quoting WIPO, *WIPO II Report*, para. 238).
35. GNSO, *Reserved Names Working Group Final Report*, Recommendation 22.
36. ICANN, *.INFO Agreement Appendix 6: List of Reserved TLD Strings*, https://www.icann.org/en/system/files/files/info-appx-06-pdf-22aug13-en.pdf (8 Dec. 2006). Other gTLD agreements are as identified in n. 26 above.
37. ICANN, *.xxx Registry Agreement*, Schedule 6.
38. GNSO, *Reserved Names Working Group Final Report*, Recommendation 20.
39. ICANN, Registry Agreement, https://newgtlds.icann.org/sites/default/files/agreements/agreement-approved-09jan14-en.htm (9 Jan. 2014).

operator IDN registration policy, where applicable) may be released to the extent that Registry Operator reaches agreement with the applicable government(s).'[40] It was not until December 2014 that ICANN launched a release process.[41] Two-character combinations other than letter-letter were released without further restriction, as these were 'determined not to raise significant security, stability or competition concerns', and there were no objections 'from governments, country code top-level domain managers, and members of the technical community or rights holders'.[42] Letter-letter combinations, on the other hand, became subject to a sixty-day review and comment process, during which time a request might be objected to by a member or members of the GAC. Registry operators were given an opportunity to respond to objections with 'mitigation measures'.[43]

Within a mere six months, more than 16,000 objecting comments were filed by GAC members against new gTLD registry release requests, some governments having filed hundreds of such comments against both brand and non-brand new gTLDs.[44] Large volume objectors include Portugal, the UK, Singapore and Russia. Non-commenters include the US, Australia and Canada, an outcome notably consistent with the position of these countries in the earlier WIPO debates.[45] To introduce efficiencies and reduce administration in light of the enormous number of comments received, in July 2016, ICANN staff published for public comment a proposed threshold list of measures which, if adopted, would bind all new gTLD registries and enable the release of all two-letter second-level domain names.[46] These measures included a thirty-day period in which two-letter registrations would 'be made exclusively available to the applicable country-code manager or government'.[47] Various comments filed in response to these proposals rejected or recommended strict limitation of the exclusive availability pre-registration period, voicing concerns about the lack of legal basis for governments' priority claims to country codes.[48] Taking these concerns into

40. *Ibid.*
41. ICANN, *ICANN Finalizes Process for Requests for Release of Two-Character ASCII Labels*, https://www.icann.org/news/announcement-2014-12-01-en (1 Dec. 2014).
42. *Ibid.*
43. ICANN GAC, Two-Letter Second-Level Domains, https://gacweb.icann.org/display/gacweb/Two-Letter+Second-Level+Domains.
44. ICANN, Two-Character Letter/Letter Label Comments and Mitigation Measures, https://www.icann.org/resources/two-character-comments.
45. *See* above n. 28 and related text.
46. ICANN, *Proposed Measures for Letter/Letter Two-Character ASCII Labels to Avoid Confusion with Corresponding Country Codes*, https://www.icann.org/en/system/files/files/proposed-measures-two-char-08jul16-en.pdf (Jul. 2016).
47. *Ibid.*
48. *See for example*, IPC, *IPC Comments on Proposed Measures for Letter/Letter Two-Character ASCII Codes*, https://ipc.memberclicks.net/assets/ipc-position-papers/2016/2016_08august_17%20ipc%20comments%20on%20letter%20letter%20ascii%20codes.pdf (17 Aug. 2016); Donuts, *Comment on Proposed Measures for Letter/Letter*

consideration, in November, 2016, the ICANN Board resolved to adopt a revised version of the proposals which make the exclusive availability period voluntary rather than mandatory.[49]

At the top level of the DNS, section 2.2.1.4 of the *gTLD Applicant Guidebook* operates for governments and relevant public authorities as a presumptive reservation that the Reserved Names Working Group and WIPO's Standing Committee on the Law of Trademarks, Industrial Designs and Geographical Indications advised against. The only recommendation of the GNSO's Reserved Names Working Group actually implemented in the New gTLD Program policy implementation framework is the disuse of the term 'geopolitical names',[50] which is presumably now encompassed in the broad definition of 'geographic names' contained in section 2.2.1.4.1 of the *gTLD Applicant Guidebook.*

The reservation of geographic names from registration at the top and second level in the *gTLD Applicant Guidebook* gives rise to questions involving sovereignty or other legal principles as a basis for governments' claims, as well as the recognition of third parties' legal rights in such names. These questions remain unanswered, even after years of policy development and implementation for the New gTLD Program. These questions lie at the heart of this study and are explored in detail in the chapters comprising Part III of this book in order to inform future policy-making and facilitate resolution of the problems that have arisen as a result. What should be noted at this point is that the procedural history in DNS policy-making discussions regarding the reservation of geographic names is as complex as the substantive legal questions themselves. That the *gTLD Applicant Guidebook* adopts a reservation-type approach as the means of protecting geographic names at the top-level simply adds to this complexity.

3.2.1.2 'Controversial Names'

The reservation from domain name registration of so-called controversial names has its conceptual roots in the domestic regulation of broadcast media in the US respecting a group of words commonly referred to as the 'Network Seven'. The 'Network Seven' gained notoriety through a comedic

Two-Character ASCII Codes, https://forum.icann.org/lists/comments-proposed-measures-two-char-08jul16/pdfNH7eezpMIp.pdf (17 Aug. 2016); ICANN, *Registry Stakeholder Group Statement on Proposed Measures for Letter/Letter Two-Character ASCII Codes*, https://forum.icann.org/lists/comments-proposed-measures-two-char-08jul16/msg00014.html (16 Aug. 2016).

49. ICANN, *Adopted Board Resolutions: Regular Meeting of the ICANN Board 8 November 2016 - Resolution 2016.11.08.15*, https://www.icann.org/resources/board-material/resolutions-2016-11-08-en#2.a.rationale.

50. GNSO, *Reserved Names Working Group Final Report*, Recommendation 21.

monologue called 'Seven Dirty Words' by comedian George Carlin.[51] The airing of Carlin's monologue by a radio station owned by the Pacifica Foundation during an afternoon broadcast prompted the filing of a complaint with America's communications regulatory body, the Federal Communications Commission ('FCC'). The FCC deemed seven of the words in Carlin's broadcasted monologue 'indecent' and thus prohibited from broadcast pursuant to §1464 of the Communications Act 1934, which forbids the broadcast of 'any obscene, indecent, or profane language by means of radio communications.'

The FCC's finding gave it grounds to issue an order rendering the radio station owner potentially subject to administrative sanctions. The station challenged the FCC's order in a case that was ultimately granted certiorari[52] by the US Supreme Court. Interpreting 'indecent' to mean 'nonconformance with accepted standards of morality', five Justices deemed the monologue as broadcasted to fall within that meaning.[53] The Supreme Court's decision had the effect of removing the seven words at issue from broadcasting at times when children could be expected to be in the audience, a position maintained to this day[54] despite the suggestion that society's sense of propriety has moved on.[55]

Against this backdrop, Network Solutions (the first gTLD registry/registrar, as discussed above in Part I Chapter 2, section 2.2) voluntarily adopted a policy in 1996 of reserving the 'Network Seven' from registration as domain names in .com, .net and .org. Network Solutions attributed to itself 'a right founded in the First Amendment to the US Constitution to refuse to register, and thereby publish, on the Internet registry of domain names words that it deems to be inappropriate'.[56] Two separate challenges were raised in

51. *Federal Communications Commission v. Pacifica Foundation et. al.*, 438 U.S. 726, 740 (U.S. Sup. Ct. 1978).

52. *Federal Communications Commission v. Pacifica Foundation*, 434 U.S. 1008 (U.S. Sup. Ct. 1978).

53. *Federal Communications Commission v. Pacifica Foundation et. al.*, 438 U.S. 726, 740 (U.S. Sup. Ct. 1978). Chief Justice Burger and Justices Rehnquist, Blackmun, and Powell joined parts I, II, III, and IV-C of Justice Stevens' opinion.

54. But *see Federal Communications Commission v. Fox Television Stations, Inc.*, 132 S. Ct. 2037, 2321 (2012) (per Justice Ginsburg, *concurring*: 'In my view, the Court's decision in *FCC v Pacifica Foundation* ... was wrong when it issued. Time, technological advances, and the Commission's untenable rulings in the cases now before the Court show why *Pacifica* bears reconsideration.').

55. Sheila Marikar, *Do Carlin's 'Seven Dirty Words' Still Shock? Comedians Argue for More Curses on TV, Critics Say It Won't Happen Soon*, ABC News (24 Jun. 2008) (available at http://abcnews.go.com/Entertainment/story?id=5229910&page=1). Timothy Bella, *The '7 Dirty Words' Turn 40, but They're Still Dirty*, The Atlantic (24 May 2012) (available at http://www.theatlantic.com/entertainment/archive/2012/05/the-7-dirty-words-turn-40-but-theyre-still-dirty/257374/).

56. InternetNews.com, *NSI Faces Seven Filthy Words Suits*, http://www.internetnews.com/bus-news/article.php/109461/NSI+Faces+Seven+Filthy+Words+Suits.htm (3 May 1999). The National Association for the Advancement of Colored People (NAACP) and

US Federal Courts against Network Solutions, one in California by Seven Words LLC,[57] and the other in New Hampshire by National A-1 Advertising, Inc.[58] The California case was ultimately transferred to the District Court of New Hampshire to be dealt with in connection with the *National A-1* case, to which Seven Words LLC reacted by bringing a second action[59] in California raising only state law claims.

The procedural history of these cases, described in detail in the decision of the US Court of Appeals for the Ninth Circuit in its dismissal[60] of Seven Words LLC's second California case, is convoluted. Matters were further complicated by the incorporation of ICANN in 1998 and the divesting from Network Solutions of its role as the exclusive registrar of .com, .net and .org domain names. In its decision, the court noted that by the time argument had commenced before the Ninth Circuit Court of Appeals, all sixteen of the names disputed by Seven Words LLC and National A-1 had been made available for registration by newly appointed registrars.

No gTLD has been required by ICANN to reserve socially or morally controversial names. Some ccTLD registries have reserved names at the second and lower levels on public policy grounds, reflecting the fundamentally domestic nature of such concerns. Standards of morality have long been formally acknowledged in trademark law as grounds for denying registration of a trademark, dating back at the international level to the 1883 Paris Convention.[61] It is this foundation that some have proposed to build upon in the context of domain names. Once again, the fundamental differences between the trademark system (a territorial system of proprietary legal rights the conferment of which is predicated upon use in the territory on or in connection with goods or services offered for sale) and the DNS (a global communications system that does not distinguish between commercial and non-commercial use or expressly confer any legal right in names) stand in the way of a wholesale application of a trademark approach in the DNS context. This is noted in comments to the Reserved Names Working Group's Final Report.[62]

---

other American civil rights groups registered racially sensitive terms to prevent their registration by others. Paul Festa, *Controversial Domains Go to Civil Rights Groups*, CNET News (1 May 1998) (available at https://www.cnet.com/news/controversial-domains-go-to-civil-rights-groups/).

57. *Seven Words LLC v. Network Solutions, Inc. (Seven Words I)*, D.C. No. CV-99-02816-SVW (C.D. Cal. 1999).
58. *National A-1 Advertising, Inc. v. Network Solutions, Inc.*, 121 F.Supp. 2d 156 (Dist. Ct. N.H. 2000).
59. *Seven Words LLC v. Network Solutions, Inc. (Seven Words II)*, D.C. No. CV-99-06722-SVW (C.D. Cal. 1999).
60. *Seven Words LLC v. Network Solutions*, 260 F.3d 1089 (9th Cir. Ct. App. 2001).
61. Paris Convention, Art. 6 para 4 provided: 'Le depot pourra être refuse, si l'objet pour lequel il est demandé est considéré comme contraire à la morale ou à l'ordre public.'
62. Comments of Avri Doria (in consultation with Victoria McEvedy) in GNSO, *Reserved Name Working Group Report*, 132–133.

The trouble with imposing at a global level a policy that has its roots in one country's domestic law and policy decisions about social morality is hinted at in the 'dirty words' cases brought against Network Solutions. The FCC's prohibition against the broadcast of those words and indeed Network Solutions' own justifications for extending that policy to internet domain name registration has as its heart the very specific language of the free speech guarantee of the First Amendment of the US Constitution, which places limitations on the protection of obscene communications.[63] Domestic contexts are logically and appropriately taken into account in ccTLD policy given the purpose of those domains as supporting a local internet community,[64] yet this is achievable only on a country-by-country basis. Such a reservation can be proscriptive and expressly reserve names of specific and particular concern within the country or it can, like the United States' .us ccTLD domain name registration terms and conditions, provide for reservations as and when deemed necessary by the .us registry, *inter alia*, 'to comply with any applicable laws, government rules or requirements, requests of law enforcement, in compliance with any dispute resolution process;' and 'to avoid any liability, civil or criminal'.[65]

Agreement on a national standard of morality is difficult enough to achieve, but the internet is a global resource and most gTLDs are directed at a global pool of registrants. Universal standards of morality are, some argue, impossible to articulate – if they exist at all.[66] The media attention surrounding ICM's application in the 'proof of concept' top-level expansion

---

63. 'Obscene materials have been denied the protection of the First Amendment because their content is so offensive to contemporary moral standards. But the fact that society may find speech offensive is not a sufficient reason for suppressing it. Indeed, if it is the speaker's opinion that gives offense, that consequence is a reason for according it constitutional protection. For it is a central tenet of the First Amendment that the government must remain neutral in the marketplace of ideas. If there were any reason to believe that the Commission's characterization of the Carlin monologue as offensive could be traced to its political content – or even to the fact that it satirized contemporary attitudes about four-letter words – First Amendment protection might be required. But that is simply not this case. These words offend for the same reasons that obscenity offends. Their place in the hierarchy of First Amendment values was aptly sketched by Mr Justice Murphy when he said: '[Such] utterances are no essential part of any exposition of ideas, and are of such slight social value as a step to truth that any benefit that may be derived from them is clearly outweighed by the social interest in order and morality.' *FCC v. Pacifica Foundation*, 438 U.S. at 745–746.
64. Postel, *RFC 1591*, 4 ('The designated manager is the trustee of the top-level domain for both the nation, in the case of a country code, and the global Internet community.').
65. NeuStar Inc., *.US Domain Name Registration Terms and Conditions Version 2.1*, http://web.neustar.biz/policies/docs/neustar_registrar_terms.pdf.
66. The concept of a morality and public order exception is notably embedded in both the General Agreement on Tariffs and Trade (GATT) at Art. XX(a) and the General Agreement on Trade in Services (GATS) at Art. XIV(a). On the scope of these exceptions, *see United States – Measures Affecting the Cross-Border Supply of Gambling and Betting Services*, WT/DS285/AB/R AB-2005-1 (W.T.O. D.S.B. App. Body 2005);

rounds for the .xxx gTLD lend support to this view.[67] In spite of these acknowledged challenges, in developing new gTLD policy, the Controversial Reserved Names sub-group of the GNSO's Reserved Names Working Group pointed to Articles 6*quinques* (B)(3) of the Paris Convention and Article 19 of the UN Convention on Human Rights as support at the level of international law for agreement on certain fundamental aspects of 'public policy and morality'.[68] The group ultimately recommended that '[t]here should not be a new reserved names category for Controversial Names',[69] but that '[t]here should be a list of disputed names created as a result of the dispute process to be created by the new gTLD process.'[70] This is the approach taken by various ccTLD registries, amongst which South Africa's .za domain.[71]

It is imperative to acknowledge the impact that the definition of the term 'controversial name' has on the scope and effect of any future reservation or ground of objection. The Reserved Names Working Group's report defined 'controversial names' as those otherwise qualifying 'as a TLD under the then prevailing String Criteria' but not falling 'under any other Reserved Name category and is disputed for reasons other than that it either falls under any other Reserved Name category or that it infringes on the prior legal rights of others.'[72] This definition effectively precludes challenging a proposed string on grounds of both infringing existing legal rights and being contrary to morality and public order. The *gTLD Application Guidebook* does not, however, impose such a limitation. As noted above in Chapter 1, the potential relevance of the 'limited public interest' objection to new gTLD strings of geographic and cultural significance is determinable only on a case-by-case basis, but as a general matter, the possibility of couching claims to legal rights as objections to politically or culturally controversial names on morality and public order grounds clearly exists.

China – Measures Affecting Trading Rights and Distribution Services for Certain Publications and Audiovisual Entertainment, WT/DS363/AB/R AB-2009-1 (W.T.O. D.S.B. App. Body 2009).

67. On the.xxx application, *see* above Part I, Chapter 1, n. 22.
68. GNSO, *Reserved Name Working Group Report*, 124–126.
69. GNSO, *Reserved Names Working Group Final Report*, Recommendation 24.
70. *Id.*, Recommendation 25.
71. Clause 1.13.2 of the .ZA Second Level Domain General Policy defines a 'blocked name' as 'a name that is considered to be offensive on the basis of race, colour, religion, sex, gender or any other grounds that are in the public interest', while clause 1.13.4 gives .zadna the authority to 'implement a policy that outlines, inter alia, the criteria and procedures for classifying names as reserved or offensive, and compile a list of reserved and blocked names, or require the Registry for that SLD to compile such a list and ensure that names in the list are not available for registration.' .zadna, *Second Level Domain General Policy* – 1 Apr. 2015, http://www.zadna.org.za/uploads/files/ZA_SLD_General_Policy_final_1_April_2015.pdf.
72. GNSO, *Reserved Names Working Group Final Report*, Definitions.

3.2.1.3 Famous and Well-Known Trademarks

The reservation of trademarks from registration as second-level domain names has long been suggested but not implemented in any new gTLD to date. Nevertheless, the detailed consideration given to this option in New gTLD Program policy development and implementation justifies its inclusion here as a high potential future reservation. Weighing against treating trademarks as reserved names in the DNS is the fundamental nature of marks as a domestic legal right to use a name in connection with particular goods or services offered for sale in a particular jurisdiction. Discussions about reserving trademarks' registrability as domain names have gained some foothold, however, in the context of famous and well-known marks the use and recognition of which transcends national borders. Such marks can be characterized as global in nature and therefore deserving of protection at the supranational level.

The special legal status of well-known trademarks has for a relatively long time been agreed. The earliest attempt to proscribe the use of well-known marks at an international level was the 1925 amendment of the Paris Convention to include Article 6*bis*,[73] but the scope of that provision was limited in that it applied only to trade (not service) marks. This limitation, as well as a broadening to include dissimilar goods and services, was addressed by Article 16(3) of the TRIPS Agreement as follows:[74]

> Article 6bis of the Paris Convention (1967) shall apply, mutatis mutandis, to goods or services which are not similar to those in respect of which a trademark is registered, provided that use of that trademark in relation to those goods or services would indicate a connection between those goods or services and the owner of the registered trademark and provided that the interests of the owner of the registered trademark are likely to be damaged by such use.

73. **Paris Convention Art. 6*bis*:**

> (1) The countries of the Union undertake, ex officio if their legislation so permits, or at the request of an interested party, to refuse or to cancel the registration, and to prohibit the use, of a trademark which constitutes a reproduction, an imitation, or a translation, liable to create confusion, of a mark considered by the competent authority of the country of registration or use to be well known in that country as being already the mark of a person entitled to the benefits of this Convention and used for identical or similar goods. These provisions shall also apply when the essential part of the mark constitutes a reproduction of any such well known mark or an imitation liable to create confusion therewith.
> (2) A period of at least five years from the date of registration shall be allowed for requesting the cancellation of such a mark. The countries of the Union may provide for a period within which the prohibition of use must be requested.
> (3) No time limit shall be fixed for requesting the cancellation or the prohibition of the use of marks registered or used in bad faith.

74. Georg Hendrik Christiaan Bodenhausen, *Guide to the Application of the Paris Convention for the Protection of Industrial Property as revised at Stockholm in 1967* 89–93 (United Bureaux for the Protection of Intellectual Property 1968).

Key terminology in these articles (and, as a result, many domestic trademark laws) is unclear and inconsistently used. In particular, the terms 'well-known' and 'famous' are generally understood as synonymous.[75] Article 16(2) of the TRIPS Agreement and Article 6*bis* (2) of the Paris Convention both use the term 'well-known', but neither defines it. To address this deficiency, in 1999 the Assembly of the Paris Union for the Protection of Industrial Property and the General Assembly of WIPO issued a Joint Recommendation Concerning Provisions on the Protection of Well-Known Marks (the 'Joint Recommendation').[76] The Joint Recommendation provides guidelines on how Member States may determine and protect well-known marks, setting out the following non-exclusive factors for determining whether a mark is well-known:

- degree of knowledge or recognition of the mark in the relevant sector of the public;
- duration, extent and geographical area of any use of the mark;
- duration, extent and geographical area of any promotion of the mark, including advertising or publicity and the presentation, at fairs or exhibitions, of the goods and/or services to which the mark applies;
- duration and geographical area of any registrations, and/or any applications for registration, of the mark, to the extent that they reflect use or recognition of the mark;
- record of successful enforcement of rights in the mark, in particular, the extent to which the mark was recognized as well-known by competent authorities; and
- value associated with the mark.

Even to the extent that it is agreed that well-known trademarks should have a special status in domestic law, such a decision would not have any automatic impact on the registrability of such marks as domain names. This is a logical corollary of the broader policy decision to separate trademark registration from domain name registration such that one does not automatically give rise to the other. Article 3(1) of the Joint Resolution addresses this point by expressly requiring Member States to 'protect a well-known mark against conflicting marks, business identifiers and domain names, at least with effect from the time when the mark has become well known in the Member State', while Article 6 offers specific instruction on how marks are to be protected in the DNS:

75. David Tatham, *Well Known Trade Marks: A CLIP Seminar Report* (Intellectual Property Institute 1997).
76. WIPO, *Joint Recommendation Concerning Provisions on the Protection of Well-Known Marks, WIPO Doc. A/34/13*, http://www.wipo.int/edocs/pubdocs/en/marks/833/pub833.pdf.

(1) [Conflicting Domain Names] A domain name shall be deemed to be in conflict with a well-known mark at least where that domain name, or an essential part thereof, constitutes a reproduction, an imitation, a translation, or a transliteration of the well-known mark, and the domain name has been registered or used in bad faith.
(2) [Cancellation; Transfer] The owner of a well-known mark shall be entitled to request, by a decision of the competent authority, that the registrant of the conflicting domain name cancel the registration, or transfer it to the owner of the well-known mark.

The problem of bad faith registration of famous and well-known trademarks as domain names was an agenda item of WIPO's First Internet Domain Name Process ('WIPO I'); a full section of the WIPO I Report was devoted to the topic.[77] In the Interim Report of that process, reservation was recommended as the preferred way to recognize the special status of famous and well-known marks. This idea was said to be 'widely supported in the commercial and intellectual property sectors as an appropriate means of reflecting established international principles in the DNS.'[78] Opponents of reservation offered two principal arguments: first, that such a move would effectively extend the scope of protection offered to well-known marks under existing trademark law; and second, that this extension would result in 'the erosion of the DNS through the removal of large numbers of names from its ambit.'[79] The mechanics of reservation also proved contentious: proposed quantitative thresholds of domestic trademark registrations were rejected as 'wrong in principle' for not giving proper consideration to whether a mark was, in fact, 'well-known'.[80] A proposed quota on the total number of reserved trademark names was also rejected on concerns of arbitrariness.[81]

Despite these procedural and substantive challenges, the final report of the WIPO I process maintained the recommendation for reservation of well-known trademarks, relying on the clear legal basis for 'special protection'[82] offered by Article 6*bis* of the Paris Convention. Both concerns raised by objectors could, it was proposed, be addressed through rigorous qualification criteria, namely a requirement that a mark be deemed 'famous or well-known across a widespread geographical area and across different classes of goods and services',[83] and a limitation of protection to cases where

77. WIPO, *WIPO I Report*, paras 245–303.
78. *Id.*, para. 249.
79. *Id.*, para. 250.
80. *Id.*, para. 266. The WIPO I Report affirmed the factors set out in the Joint Recommendation while also recommending at para. 285 the addition of another factor: 'evidence of the mark being the subject of attempts by non-authorized third parties to register the same or misleadingly similar names as domain names.'
81. *Id.*, para. 269.
82. *Id.*, para. 263.
83. *Id.*, para. 274.

a domain name string is identical to the famous mark.[84] The argument that this treatment would extend the protection normally afforded famous marks 'across an undifferentiated space' was rejected, with WIPO expressing the view 'not that exclusions extend such protection, but that they give expression to it in the DNS.'[85]

The final WIPO I Report further recommended that the reservation of well-known marks should form the basis of an evidentiary presumption against third-party registrations of misleadingly similar names. This recommendation is best understood in light of the primary significance of the WIPO I Report, which was the establishment of the framework for an administrative post-registration dispute resolution procedure that would ultimately develop into the now firmly established Universal Domain Name Dispute Resolution Policy ('UDRP'), which procedure is discussed in detail in the next section of this chapter. What is notable at this point is that the final version of the UDRP did not include the proposed evidentiary presumption in favour of well-known marks,[86] nor does it provide for their reservation.[87] Neither did ICANN require that trademarks be reserved from registration in any of the pre-2012 'proof of concept' new gTLDs.

With talk of a third gTLD expansion round came the start of a new policy development process in which to debate a reservation for trademarks. Trademark owners' opposition to further DNS expansion and the sheer volume of potential applications for new top-level domains that could result from an open, uncapped round added a sense of urgency to this discussion. Comments made by ICANN's Intellectual Property Interests Constituency (which later came to be known as the Intellectual Property Constituency, or 'IPC') on the first draft of the *gTLD Applicant Guidebook* [88] highlighted ICANN's failure to impose specific requirements upon new gTLD applicants to adopt particular pre-launch rights protection mechanisms 'such as an expanded reserved names list' for trademarks, well-known or otherwise.[89] The IPC urged ICANN to '[p]rovide incentives for new TLDs to employ

84. *Id.*, para. 276.
85. *Id.*, para. 270.
86. David Lindsay, *International Domain Name Law: ICANN and the UDRP* 106–109 (Hart Publishing 2007).
87. This decision was informed by the consensus conclusion of an internal review of the WIPO I Report recommendations that exclusion of famous and well-known marks was not needed. *See* DNSO Working Group B, *Working Group B (WG-B) Report*, http://www.dnso.org/wgroups/wg-b/Arc00/msg00963.html (presented to DNSO Names Council on 15 May 2000). On the UDRP, *see* Part II, Chapter 3, s. 3.3.1 below.
88. ICANN, *Draft New gTLD Agreement Specification 5: Schedule of Reserved Names at the Second Level in gTLD Registries*, https://archive.icann.org/en/topics/new-gtlds/reserved-names-24oct08-en.pdf (24 Oct. 2008).
89. ICANN Intellectual Property Interests Constituency, *Comments of Intellectual Property Interests Constituency Re: 'Draft Applicant Guidebook' for New gTLDs*, 5, http://ipconstituency.org/PDFs/IPC%20comments%20re%20new%20TLD%20DAG%20submitted%20121508%20%282060018%29.pdf (15 Dec. 2008).

reserved names lists that include globally famous marks'.[90] Continued debate about the adequacy of rights protection measures in the second draft of the *gTLD Applicant Guidebook* led ICANN's Board of Directors to direct the IPC to form an ad hoc team it called the Implementation Recommendation Team (commonly referred to as the 'IRT') to investigate these matters more closely.[91] On conclusion of its review, the IRT reported that it 'had considered and rejected the idea of a single, all-encompassing Trademark Reserved Names List as a universal protective mechanism.'[92] The team instead recommended an 'IP Clearinghouse', essentially a repository of IPR claims with a verification service to ensure the integrity of claims and a means of disseminating this information to affected parties. The proposed IP Clearinghouse is not itself a rights protection mechanism, but rather a repository of information about legal rights to support and facilitate a range of rights protection mechanisms, including the proposed Globally-Protected Marks List (or 'GPML', as it is commonly referred to).

The Globally-Protected Marks List was 'not intended to be a reserved list by which trademark owners will be able to simply block pending domain applications or reserve domain names in advance.'[93] Nor did the IRT intend that the list 'possess any precedential value in any dispute or resolution proceeding in relation thereof' or be interpreted as 'a consolidated list of what may constitute "well known" or "famous" marks under national trademark laws'.[94] Yet the actual mechanics of the proposed marks list picked up the thread of earlier debates about reservation of famous and well-known marks: reminiscent of WIPO's earlier debates, the IRT's proposed criteria for inclusion on the list are quantitative and geographical in nature (e.g., a specified number of registrations currently in use in each of the five ICANN regions). Not unlike a reserved names list, the effect of a mark's inclusion on the Globally-Protected Marks List would be to limit the creation of identical or confusingly similar top-level and identical second-level domain names to particular applicants.[95]

The IRT's final report generated considerable debate at ICANN's 35th public meeting in June 2009, at which it was tabled for community discussion. Subsequent discussion shifted away from the Globally-Protected

---

90. *Ibid.*
91. ICANN, *Board of Directors Resolution 2009.03.06.06*, item 7, http://www.icann.org/en/minutes/resolutions-06mar09.htm#07 (6 Mar. 2009).
92. IRT, *Final Report*, 12. 'The primary reasons were that (1) such a list could not accommodate the various types (and corresponding scope of legal protection) of protected marks or the possibility of calibrating the recommended RPM to these differing types and scope of protection; (2) designing workable, specific, flexible and inclusive criteria for a single, all-encompassing Trademark Reserved Names List would be extremely difficult – if possible at all; and (3) such a one-size-fits-all solution would not be acceptable to the ICANN community.'
93. *Id.*, 16.
94. *Ibid.*
95. *Id.*, 17.

Marks List and focused on the implementation of the concept of a rights clearinghouse (discussed in the next section). The GPML concept was raised in the May, 2011 US Congressional oversight hearing on new gTLDs, in response to which ICANN's Senior Vice President for Stakeholder Relations cited concerns expressed by WIPO as to the mechanics of such a list and opposition from ICANN's Governmental Advisory Committee as chief obstacles to its implementation in new gTLD policy.[96] He concluded: 'The time, commitment and resources (from ICANN and the community) needed to create and maintain such a list would provide only marginal benefits as such a list would apply to only a small number of names and only for identical matches of those names.'[97]

The concept was not ultimately included in the Board of Directors'-approved version of the *gTLD Applicant Guidebook*, but proposals to require new gTLD registries' reservation of trademarks from registration as domain names were re-enlivened in late 2012 during Trademark Clearinghouse implementation.[98] The most significant development ultimately came not through consensus policy requirements but through voluntarily adopted additional protections at the second-level implemented across the more than 300 new gTLDs applied for by large portfolio new gTLD applicant Donuts, Inc. The attractiveness of its Domains Protected Marks List, or 'DPML', is enhanced by its availability across the entire Donuts portfolio, enabling trademark holders to block domain name registrations of their trademarks in all Donuts-owned new gTLDs.[99]

3.2.2 IP/Trademark Clearinghouse

The 'IP Clearinghouse' concept proposed by the IRT is not in itself a rights protection measure. Rather, it underpins and is designed to facilitate various other rights protection measures[100] by storing information on claims to IPRs

96. Letter from Kurt Pritz, ICANN Senior Vice President for Stakeholder Relations, to The Honorable Robert Goodlatte, US House of Representatives, *Response to Questions* (7 Jun. 2011) (available at http://www.icann.org/en/correspondence/pritz-to-goodlatte-07jun11-en.pdf).
97. *Ibid.*
98. ICANN, *Transcription ICANN Toronto Meeting: Commercial Stakeholder Group (CSG) Meeting Tuesday 16 October 2012 at 9:45 local time*, http://archive.icann.org/en/meetings/toronto2012/bitcache/Transcript_%20Commercial%20Stakeholder%20Group%20(CSG)-vid=42195&disposition=attachment&op=download.pdf.
99. Donuts, *Domains Protected Marks List Overview*, http://www.donuts.domains/services/dpml/dpml-overview.
100. STI, *Recommendations*, 4, https://gnso.icann.org/en/issues/sti/sti-wt-recommendations-11dec09-en.pdf (11 Dec. 2009) (reporting consensus 'among the members of the STI that though this was not a rights protection mechanism, the creation of a Trademark Clearinghouse (TC) to be operated by an arms-length contractor, would be a beneficial implementation tool for rights protection mechanisms, such as sunrise or TM Claims, and therefore should be included in the New gTLD program').

in names and making this available to parties affected by the registration of a corresponding domain name. The IRT emphasized that the clearinghouse would merely capture information about existing trademark rights in a single location, and not create legal rights.[101] Although this information already exists, it is scattered across a large number of national and regional trademark registry databases. The key aim of the clearinghouse was therefore data centralization facilitated by electronic submissions made by trademark owners, top-level domain registries or registrars.

While the concept of a clearinghouse proved broadly acceptable during New gTLD Program policy development, the actual mechanics of its implementation and operation appeared less so. In the months that followed the release of the IRT's report, ICANN staff developed a modified version of the IP Clearinghouse proposal, which was re-named 'Trademark Clearinghouse', better reflecting the scope of eligible rights.[102] ICANN's then-Chairman and CEO directed[103] the GNSO Council to review and make recommendations on both proposals; the Special Trademarks Issues Review Team ('STI') was formed with representatives from all GNSO constituencies to undertake these tasks.[104]

By the time of formation of the STI, the question of *whether* to have a clearinghouse appeared to have been settled. The STI's recommendations therefore went directly to how and by whom the clearinghouse should be implemented and operated. Relevant to this discussion is the STI's unanimous recommendation that new gTLD registries be required to recognize rights in a clearinghouse the scope of includable rights in which should be limited to trademarks only.[105] The *gTLD Applicant Guidebook*[106] deems the following forms of mark eligible for inclusion:

- Nationally or multi-nationally registered word marks from all jurisdictions.
- Any word mark that has been validated through a court of law or other judicial proceeding.

101. IRT, *Final Report*, 17.
102. ICANN, *For GNSO Consideration: Trademark Clearinghouse*, http://www.icann.org/en/topics/new-gtlds/draft-proposed-procedure-tm-clearinghouse-04oct09-en.pdf (Oct. 2009).
103. Letter from Peter Dengate Thrush, ICANN Chairman, and Rod Beckstrom, ICANN President and CEO, to GNSO Council Members (12 Oct. 2009) (available at http://gnso.icann.org/correspondence/beckstrom-to-gnso-council-12oct09-en.pdf).
104. GNSO, *Motion on Selected Trademark Issues from the ICANN Board of Directors: GNSO Council Resolution 20091028-3*, http://gnso.icann.org/resolutions/#200910 (28 Oct. 2009).
105. STI, *Recommendations*, 4. A complete record of the group's conclusions is set out in table format in the STI Recommendations report, pp. 4–25. Due to their length, they are not reproduced here.
106. ICANN, *gTLD Applicant Guidebook*, Trademark Clearinghouse, s. 3.2.

- Any word mark protected by a statute or treaty in effect at the time the mark is submitted to the Clearinghouse for inclusion.
- Other marks that constitute intellectual property.[107]

Authentication is easiest for registered trademarks, the act of registration being considered prima facie proof of the claim of ownership; unsurprisingly, a review of all rights protection mechanisms in new gTLDs conducted by ICANN staff in 2012 found that of the nearly 38,000 verified marks in the Clearinghouse as of 4 August 2015, 'most ... are nationally or regionally or registered trademarks, with the U.S. having the greatest number of registered trademarks recorded.'[108]

Clearly there is no express provision of eligibility for geographic names, and within the four specified categories of eligibility noted above, the options are limited. The conceptual difficulties inherent in recognition of geographic trademarks are described in detail in Part III, Chapter 6, below. The data required to authenticate 'other marks' are not specified, but rather are left to be 'determined by the registry operator and the Clearinghouse based on the services any given registry operator chooses to provide.'[109] Evidentiary challenges come into play in respect of unregistered and 'other' marks (which could potentially include geographical indications and other geographic names, character and personal names, book titles, etc.). The extent to which the Trademark Clearinghouse operator is required to address these challenges depends as a starting point on whether any new gTLD registry operators' policies recognize rights in names other than trademarks.

Insofar as rights in geographic names are determined to be derived from legal bases outside of the four categories of includable 'mark' eligible for inclusion in the Trademark Clearinghouse, this raises significant questions for future policy development initiatives. Further, to the extent that utilization of rights protection mechanisms in new gTLDs is conditioned – whether mandatorily in ICANN consensus policy or voluntarily in TLD-specific policy – upon inclusion in the Trademark Clearinghouse, decisions about the eligibility for inclusion of 'other marks that constitute intellectual property' will have a significant impact on the ability of the holders of rights in those marks to exercise rights in new gTLDs. It is therefore notable that ICANN's GNSO embarked in early 2016 upon a new policy development process to review all existing rights protection mechanisms.[110] One of the notable potential issues identified to be addressed by that review is not whether the

107. *Id.*, Trademark Clearinghouse, s. 3.2.5.
108. ICANN, *Rights Protection Mechanisms Review: Revised Report 11 September 2015*, 4, https://newgtlds.icann.org/en/reviews/rpm/rpm-review-11sep15-en.pdf.
109. ICANN, *gTLD Applicant* Guidebook, Trademark Clearinghouse, s. 3.6.
110. ICANN, *Charter for Proposed PDP to Review all Rights Protection Mechanisms in All gTLDs*, http://gnso.icann.org/en/drafts/rpm-charter-15mar16-en.pdf (15 Mar. 2016).

protection of the Trademark Clearinghouse is too narrow, but rather whether it is too broad.[111]

3.2.3 Sunrise Registration Period

The cause of many rights holders' headaches in the early years of the DNS was the decision to allocate domain names on a 'first-come, first-served' basis.[112] This policy, coupled with the technical limitation of absolute name uniqueness, has the practical effect of limiting the registration of any particular combination of alphanumeric characters to one registrant alone, that being the one who registers first. When brand owners embraced the internet as an environment in which to expand brand exposure, they lamented this procedure because it often left them challenging large numbers of domain names the use of which by their registrants would not otherwise be permitted under trademark law. Even after the implementation of the Uniform Domain Name Dispute Resolution Policy ('UDRP') in 1999, rights holders held the view that a post-registration rights protection mechanism (even an effective one, as the UDRP is broadly seen to be) was not the only or most efficient way of tackling unauthorized registrations of trademarks as domain names.[113]

Aside from reserving trademark domain names for trademark owners, an obvious solution to the problem of unauthorized domain name registrations was to move trademark owners ahead in the first-come, first-served registration queue. This notion would come to be known as a 'sunrise' period, meaning a set period of time for a defined category or categories of prospective applicants to register domain names before the opening up of registration to the general public.[114] So hopeful was the Intellectual Property Constituency within ICANN of the utility of this measure that it reportedly 'wanted sunrise in all the new gTLDs.'[115]

---

111. ICANN, *Review of all Rights Protection Mechanisms (RPMs) in all gTLDs PDP Working Group – Questions Raised in the Charter*, https://community.icann.org/display/RARPMRIAGPWG/Questions+raised+in+the+Charter (last modified on 15 Mar. 2016). The policy development working group's timeline foresees focusing on the Trademark Clearinghouse in the latter half of 2016, with work concluded on this mechanism in early January, 2017. ICANN, *Draft Work Plan for Phase One of the PDP on Review of all RPMs in all gTLDs – 12 July 2016*, https://community.icann.org/display/RARPMRIAGPWG/Work+Plan?preview=/59643840/60491167/Work%20Plan%20-%2012%20July.pdf.
112. NSI's first-come, first-served domain name registration policy is discussed in *Avery Dennison Corp. v. Sumpton*, 999 F.Supp. 1337, 1338 (C.D. Cal. 1999) *rev'd*, 189 F.3d 868 (9th Cir. 1999).
113. Christopher P. Rains, *A Domain By Any Other Name: Forging International Solutions for the Governance of Internet Domain Names*, 13 Emory Int'l L. Rev. 355, 384 (2000).
114. Lindsay, *International domain name law: ICANN and the UDRP*, 120.
115. James Nurton, *Top Level Domains: Mapping a TLD strategy*, July/August 2001 Managing Intellectual Property 17–18 (quoting Jane Mutimear, IPC Deputy Chair).

Four of the seven new gTLDs created in the first 'proof of concept' expansion round (.coop, .info, .name and .pro) implemented a rights-based sunrise registration period. Of those .info,[116] .name and .pro[117] based eligibility in the sunrise period on ownership of trademark rights.[118] In the second 'proof of concept' expansion round, three new gTLDs (.asia,[119] .mobi[120] and .tel[121]) utilized a sunrise period with eligibility based on trademark rights leading to 'live' domain name registrations. 'Defensive' registrations were available in .cat.[122] When it launched some years after the others in that round, the .xxx domain also based its sunrise on trademark rights that could be called upon to pre-register names or defensively block others' registrations.[123]

The chaos of the .info launch, the first in which a sunrise period was utilized, demonstrated that at a minimum, validation of eligibility claims was necessary in order for the sunrise process to be effective.[124] This was a lesson learned the hard way: .info launched with a self-policing sunrise in which

116. INFO, History of .INFO, http://info.info/why-info/history-info. James Nurton, *Sunrise meets sunset for.info*, September 2001 Managing Intellectual Property 36–37; PROWG, *Protecting the Rights of Others Working Group (PROWG) Final Report: Annex One Registry Summaries*, 57, http://gnso.icann.org/files/gnso/drafts/GNSO-PRO-WG-final-01Jun07.pdf (1 Jun. 2007) (hereinafter 'Final Report: Annex One').
117. A priority period was conferred on trademark owners in .pro and .name, but registrations made during this period were 'defensive', meaning that mark owners could block other applicants from registering a particular name. Global Name Registry, *What Is .name: Defensive Registrations*, http://www.gnr.com/whatis.htm (2001, archived at http://www.archive.org/web/web.php); PRNewswire, *New .Pro Internet Registry Now Accepting Defensive Registrations for Trademarks and Brand Names: 'Sunrise' Period Allows Major Brands, Others to Protect Names*, http://www.prnewswire.com/news-releases/new-pro-internet-registry-now-accepting-defensive-registrations-for-trademarks-and-brand-names-72334052.html (5 Apr. 2004). PROWG, *Final Report: Annex One*, 72–78.
118. Sunrise eligibility in .coop was restricted to organizations that were involved in the creation of the .coop domain. A separate 'Brandsafe' reservation program blocked registered trademark holders' names from registration. PROWG, *Final Report: Annex One*, 36–37. *New dotCoop Internet Domain Offers Trademark/Brand Protection for Companies Who Can't Get .coop Sites*, Biofuels Journal (15 May 2002) (available at http://www.biofuelsjournal.com/articles/new_dotcoop_internet_domain_offers_trademark_brand_protection_for_companies_who_can_t_get__coop_sites-15011.html).
119. DotAsia Organisation, *.ASIA Sunrise Policies,* http://www.dot.asia/policies/DotAsia-Sunrise-Policies--COMPLETE-2007-08-10.pdf (10 Aug. 2007).
120. Public Domain Registry, *Dotmobi: When Can I Start Registering?*, http://www.publicdomainregistry.com/dotmobi/. PROWG, *Final Report: Annex One*, 63–64.
121. Archived at Domein Registreren, *.tel Sunrise terms & conditions,* (Jun. 2008) https://www.domein-registreren.nl/tel-voorwaarden_533.html.
122. Fundació PuntCat, *Registration Agreement (English version)*, http://fundacio.cat/sites/default/files/cat-registrationagrmt.pdf.
123. IPRota, *Taking Control: Safeguarding Brand Owners' Rights in .XXX*, http://eo2.commpartners.com/users/inta/downloads/110803_XXX-Whitepaper.pdf (May 2011).
124. Nurton, *Top Level Domains: Mapping a TLD Strategy*, 17 (quoting Nicholas Wood of registrar NetSearchers: 'Setting up.info has not been quite as smooth as it might be, which is understandable as there are difficult concepts.').

'trade mark proprietors had to root out false applications and such false applications could be subject to a Sunrise Challenge process, administered by WIPO.'[125] In 2008, in anticipation of further expansion at the top-level of the DNS, ICANN's Intellectual Property Constituency in cooperation with the Association of European Trade Mark Owners ('MARQUES') prepared a best practice guide for new gTLD applicants entitled 'The Perfect Sunrise? How pre-launch Rights Protection Mechanisms and successful registry operations go hand in hand'.[126] In addition to .info and other 'proof of concept' gTLDs, this guide was informed by the launch of the .eu and re-launch of the .us ccTLDs and interviews with brand owners. This work was then reinforced and augmented the following year by the IPC's Implementation Recommendation Team, whose recommendations set out specific components of an effective sunrise process. Those recommendations are (logically, given their drafters) directed towards the protection of trademarks.[127]

In practice, where sunrise eligibility has been granted on the basis of legal rights, the legal rights in question are nearly always limited to trademark rights. A notable exception, although not one involving a gTLD, is the European Union's .eu ccTLD, the application procedures for which conferred sunrise priority on '[h]olders of prior rights recognized or established by national and/or Community law', defined to include (but not limited to) trade names, business identifiers, company names, family names and distinctive titles of protected literary and artistic works.[128] Among pre-2012 new gTLDs, .jobs launched with a sunrise-like priority period in which holders of trade names were eligible.[129]

The *gTLD Applicant Guidebook* makes a sunrise period mandatory in the launch of all new gTLDs[130] for 'all word marks':

> nationally or regionally registered and for which proof of use – which can be a declaration and a single specimen of current use – was submitted to, and validated by, the Trademark Clearinghouse; or (ii) that

125. Olsen et al., *Domain Names: Global Practice and Procedure*, Introduction/56–57 (Sweet & Maxwell 2007) (citing Afilias press release of 15 Aug. 2001). Nurton, *Sunrise Meets Sunset for .info.*
126. IPC & Marques.
127. IRT, *Final Report*, 23. The recommended components are: Eligibility cut-off dates, pre-validation of rights, premium name schemes, reconsiderations or challenge mechanisms, usage requirements and eligibility requirements for goods or services in a particular class ('e.g., the .shoe registry could restrict participation in its Sunrise process to owners of trademark registrations that cover shoes or other goods in International Class 25').
128. Commission Regulation (EC) No 874/2004 of 28 Apr. 2004 laying down public policy rules concerning the implementation and functions of the .eu Top Level Domain and the principles governing registration, OJ/L 162, 30.4.2004 p. 40 (2004), Art. 10(1).
129. Employ Media, *Trade Name Period version 1.0*, http://www.employmedia.com/tradenameperiod.html (2005, archived at http://www.archive.org/web/web.php).
130. ICANN, *gTLD Applicant Guidebook*, Registry agreement, s. 2.8 and Trademark Clearinghouse, s. 6.

have been court-validated; or (iii) that are specifically protected by a statute or treaty currently in effect and that was in effect on or before 26 June 2008.[131]

This is notably a more limited scope than the full range of rights eligible for inclusion in the Trademark Clearinghouse, but one that picks up on the concern expressed in the IRT's final report that 'other legal rights must be capable of being authenticated and must be recognized under the laws of the country in which the registry is organized.'[132] With this in mind, recognition of non-trademark rights in a sunrise process is possible, although patently less practicable, than recognition of registered trademarks the registration of which is proof of ownership.

3.2.4 IP/Trademark Claims Service

As an alternative to a sunrise registration period, when the new .biz gTLD launched a procedure was implemented to recognize the priority rights of trademark holders through a claim notification system. In a 'Start-up Period' prior to general public registration, trademark owners were given the opportunity to file claims asserting their trademark rights in a particular name.[133] 'This step was intended to protect the rights of trademark holders, although such claims did not themselves grant preferential rights to particular domain names.'[134] Rather, the filing of a claim offered the advantage of triggering a notice to those who applied for a domain name comprising an identical match to the claimed name. The applicant so notified was then given the option of either withdrawing or proceeding with its application.[135] If the applicant opted to proceed, the applied-for name was placed on hold for thirty days, and the trademark owner was notified and given twenty days in which to file a complaint against the application.

The filing of an 'IP claim', another misleading name given its application only to trademarks, was the first of three steps in the .biz Start-up Period procedure.[136] As a second step, would be applicants filed a 'pre-registration' application. As a third step, applications were processed and delegated in random order as opposed to order of filing. These latter two steps were the subject of litigation against ICANN, the .biz registry operator

131. *Id.*, Trademark Clearinghouse, s. 7.2.

132. IRT, *Final Report*, 23.

133. WIPO, *General Information on STOP*, http://www.wipo.int/amc/en/domains/gtld/biz/stop/index.html .

134. Minqin Wang, *Regulating the Domain Name System: Is the '.BIZ' Domain Name Distribution Scheme an Illegal Lottery?*, U. Ill. L. Rev. 245, 260 (2003).

135. NeuLevel Inc., *Start-up Trademark Opposition Policy and Rules for .biz*, http://www.wipo.int/amc/en/docs/stoprules.pdf (adopted 11 May 2001). Lindsay, *International Domain Name Law: ICANN and the UDRP*, 120–121.

136. Lindsay, 120–121.

NeuLevel and .biz registrars in a case alleging that the procedure constituted an illegal lottery under California State and US Federal law.[137] NeuLevel settled the dispute in March 2003,[138] but not without first generating a considerable amount of publicity and being issued a preliminary injunction.[139] Critically, the first step of the procedure, the so-called IP claims service, was not implicated in the litigation.

IP claims in the .biz new gTLD were limited to 'registered and common law trademarks or service marks'.[140] Unlike a sunrise process, the .biz IP claims service offered 'no early advantage'[141] to trademark holders. It merely 'provided what might be called an automated "watch service" for trademark owners who, in order to qualify for obtaining the corresponding domain name, still had to submit a domain name application against a separate fee.'[142] Nor did the generation of a notice that an applied-for domain name matched a trademark claim prevent the would-be applicant from registering a domain name. The applicant could choose to go ahead by representing and warranting, *inter alia*, its possession of 'a right or legitimate interest in that domain name' and 'that it will not use the domain name in bad faith as described in the UDRP'.[143]

The approach of the .xxx gTLD to rights protection at launch is also noteworthy, as it was the most recently launched gTLD preceding the New gTLD Program. The .xxx gTLD utilized both a pre-registration reservation service and a claims notification procedure whereby '[a]t the close of the Sunrise period, if more than one Sunrise application is made for a domain name, all Sunrise Applicants for that domain name will be notified of the claims made by the other Sunrise Applicants for that name.'[144]

The final reports of both the IRT and STI supported new gTLDs' implementation of an IP claims service facilitated by a rights clearinghouse, though the STI's support went to requiring use of the clearinghouse to

137. *Smiley v. ICANN*, No. BC254659 (Cal. Super. Ct. filed 23 Jul. 2001). A second case was brought only against NeuLevel and the .biz registrars: *ePrize v. NeuLevel*, No. BC257632 (Cal. Super. Ct. filed 10 Sep. 2001).
138. Mark Berniker, *NeuLevel Settles Internet Domain Class-Action Suit*, InternetNews.com (2 Jan. 2003) (available at http://www.internetnews.com/xSP/article.php/1563201/NeuLevel+Settles+Internet+Domain+ClassAction+Suit.htm).
139. Molly McDonough, *Tightening Domain Reins: California Court Puts a Damper on '.biz' Addition, Calls Application Process a Lottery*, ABA Journal 23 (December 2001).
140. NeuLevel Inc., *IP Claims Service: Terms of Use*, clause 1, http://www.webfusion.co.uk/terms-and-conditions/biz-terms/.
141. Nurton, *Top Level Domains: Mapping a TLD Strategy*, 17 (quoting Nick Wood).
142. IPC & Marques, 16. NeuLevel Inc., *IP Claims Service: Terms of Use*, 2 ('USE OF THE SERVICE DOES NOT GUARANTEE THAT AN OWNER WILL BE AWARDED THE.BIZ EXTENSION FOR ITS TRADEMARK.').
143. IRT, *Final Report*, 22.
144. ICM Registry, *Launch Plan and Related Policies*, https://www.icmregistry.com/about/policies/launch/Launch-Plan-and-Related-Policies.pdf.

facilitate either (but not both) a sunrise process or a claims service.[145] The template Registry Agreement incorporated in the *gTLD Applicant Guidebook* requires the use of the clearinghouse to facilitate *both* a sunrise process and claims service.[146] Also notable is the fact that the Trademark Claims process as set out in the *gTLD Applicant Guidebook* was enhanced during its implementation to facilitate the triggering of a claims notice on attempts to register not just exact matches of Trademark Clearinghouse entries, but other related names the subject of prior abuse. The so-called Strawman Solution permitted rights holders to link to an existing Trademark Clearinghouse entry up to fifty additional names found through a UDRP challenge or court proceeding to be abusive, thus widening the scope of a claims notice.[147]

3.2.5 *Ex Ante* Challenge Mechanisms

Recognition of legal rights before the point of domain name registration has the distinct and obvious objective and potential advantage of preventing post-registration disputes. This is not to suggest, however, that the implementation of any of the *ex ante* rights protection mechanisms described above has been completely effective at preventing disputes, or that the costs to rights holders of *ex ante* mechanisms have been offset by a corresponding decrease in post-registration dispute costs.[148] On the contrary, the use of *ex ante* rights protection mechanisms has the potential even to generate disputes, as in the case of an applicant who challenges a rejection of its eligibility to participate in a sunrise period. If such a dispute is to be addressed before the domain name in question is actually created and allocated to its registrant, *ex ante* rights protection mechanisms must logically incorporate *ex ante* challenge procedures, because *ex post* rights protection mechanisms such as the UDRP are not available until after a domain name has been registered.

It is interesting to note that to date, where sunrise and general eligibility challenge policies have been implemented, this has primarily been achieved

145. *Id.*, 13; STI, *Recommendations*, Recommendation 5.1.
146. ICANN, *gTLD Applicant Guidebook,* Registry agreement clause 2.8 and Trademark Clearinghouse, s. 6.
147. ICANN, *Memorandum on the Trademark Clearinghouse 'Strawman Solution'*, 2–3, https://newgtlds.icann.org/en/about/trademark-clearinghouse/strawman-solution-memo-20mar13-en.pdf (20 Mar. 2013).
148. It is not surprising, therefore, that one of the general issues raised by the charter of the GNSO's Review of all Rights Protection Mechanisms (RPMs) in all gTLDs Policy Development Process Working Group is: 'How can costs be lowered so end users can easily access RPMs?' ICANN, *Review of all Rights Protection Mechanisms (RPMs) in all gTLDs PDP Working Group – Questions Raised in the Charter*, https://community.icann.org/display/RARPMRIAGPWG/Questions+raised+in+the+Charter (last modified on 15 Mar. 2016).

as an *ex post* mechanism. This is likely a reflection of the prevailing view that it is not practical or efficient to scrutinize domain name applications prior to registration.[149] The availability of an *ex ante* sunrise reconsideration proceeding in .tel,[150] the Pioneer Challenge Process in .asia,[151] and the formal and informal registration dispute resolution procedures in .travel[152] are notable but not heavily publicized exceptions.

3.3 *EX POST* RIGHTS RECOGNITION

Mechanisms geared towards the recognition of 'offline' legal rights in names after their allocation as domain names can be characterized as '*ex post*' rights recognition mechanisms. Domain name allocation at all levels of the DNS is achieved through contractual relationships; the agreement in respect of the management and operation of a top-level domain is referred to as a Registry (or, for a few 'proof of concept' new gTLDs, Sponsorship) Agreement, while agreements for the registration of second and lower level domain names are typically called Domain Name Registration Agreements. Once a domain is 'assigned' (the frequently used term for a top-level domain) or 'registered' (the frequently used term for second- and lower-level domain names), the sorts of malicious and unauthorized practices described at the start of this chapter are then addressed through the contractual relationship.

As with the *ex ante* mechanisms discussed in the preceding section of this chapter, *ex post* rights protection mechanisms can be used at any level of the DNS, but in practice they have largely been targeted below the top-level, at domain name registrants directly.[153] The Uniform Domain Name Dispute Resolution Policy ('UDRP'), sunrise and registrant eligibility dispute resolution policies, and Uniform Rapid Suspension ('URS'), a new procedure for rapid domain name suspension, all fall within this characterization. This is

149. Graham J.H. Smith, *Internet Law and Regulation* 90 (3d ed., Sweet & Maxwell 2002).

150. Domein Registreren, *.tel Sunrise Terms & Conditions*, s. 12.

151. The Pioneer Challenge Procedure offered the opportunity to challenge expressions of interest in 'Pioneer Domains', of which there were three categories: Community Pioneers, Global Brand Pioneers and Partner Pioneers. The DotAsia Organisation, *.ASIA Pioneer Domains Program Policies version 2.0*, http://pioneer.domains.asia/ascii/policies/DotAsia-PDP-Policies--2007-07-11.pdf (2007).

152. Tralliance, *.travel Registry Policies*, s. 5.2.1 Denial of Eligibility and Informal Resolution and 5.2.2 Denial of Name Registration and TTPC-Review, http://www.travel.travel/wp-content/uploads/2008/12/122008trmcpoliciesfinal.pdf.

153. WIPO, *ccTLD Best Practices for the Prevention and Resolution of Intellectual Property Disputes*, 3–4 (positing that 'the registration agreement offers a prime opportunity to establish certain terms and conditions aimed at alleviating potential conflicts that may arise between the domain name registration and any third party intellectual property rights').

not to suggest that registries and registrars are entirely exempt from the onus of *ex post* rights protection mechanisms, because both are required through their respective contractual relationship with ICANN to ensure that the *ex post* mechanisms agreed in consensus policy are in place and applicable to domain name registrants.

Figure 3.1 Recognizing Rights in the DNS Through Contractual Relationships – Pre-New gTLD Program

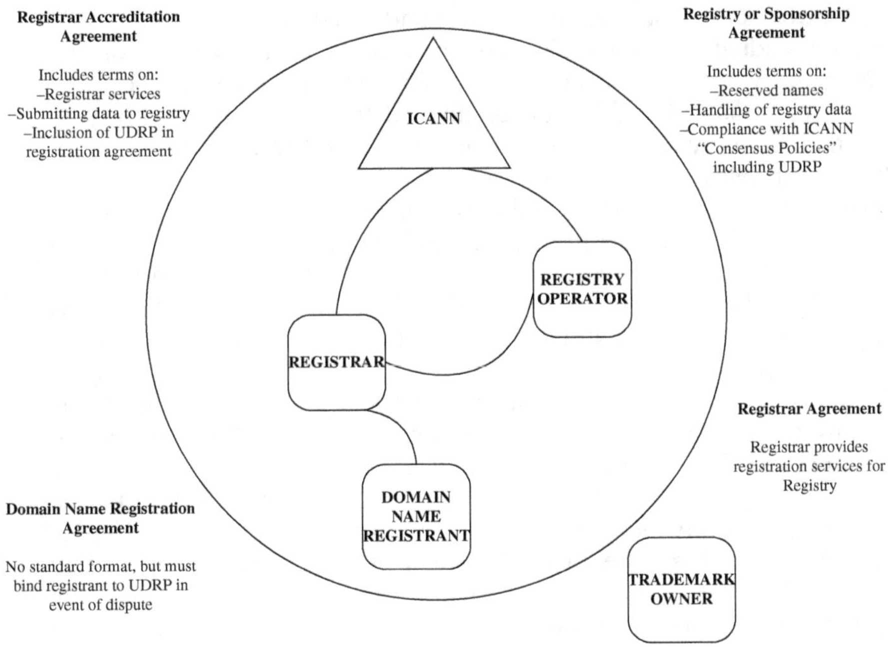

Figure 3.1 above depicts the pre-New gTLD Program status quo in terms of *ex post* liability. By contrast, the New gTLD Program marks a turning point in terms of an increased responsibility on registries to curb registrants' malicious or unauthorized registration and use of domain names. The reality is that the generally agreed success of the UDRP is continually tested by the increasing technological savvy of bad actors in the DNS, making it necessary (in the view of some, but by no means all) to broaden efforts to combat such behaviours. The remaining sections of this chapter explore the UDRP and other more recently implemented *ex post* mechanisms in order to complete the picture of the recognition of legal rights in ICANN's DNS policy up to and including the New gTLD Program.

3.3.1 UNIFORM DOMAIN NAME DISPUTE RESOLUTION POLICY ('UDRP')

3.3.1.1 Development of the UDRP

Prior to the formation of ICANN, Network Solutions had in place a dispute resolution policy which it adopted in July, 1995 and applied to registrations within the .com, .net and .org top-level domains.[154] The policy in its earliest form was actionable only by holders of US federal trademarks that had been registered prior to the activation of the challenged domain name. Only domain names identical to a registered mark could be challenged, during which Network Solutions placed the domain name at issue 'on hold'.[155] Subsequent revisions of the policy broadened the scope of eligibility to include other countries' registered trademarks and later, additional remedies.[156] Nevertheless, the policy was ineffective at resolving disputes between domain name registrants and trademark holders. The opinion of US District Court Judge Pregerson in the landmark 1996 case *Panavision International, LP v. Toeppen* pointed this out, also going on to remark that it was 'clear beyond question that the policy's sole purpose' was not to protect trademark owners or the registrant public, but rather, 'to protect [Network Solutions].'[157]

The question of how to deal with abusive and bad faith domain name registrations was pressing when the discussions that would ultimately lead to the formation of ICANN were taking place. In its Green Paper, the US Department of Commerce's National Telecommunications and Information Administration recommended that the new corporation adopt a dispute resolution policy and require that all domain name registrants submit to and be bound by it.[158] WIPO was then called upon to assist in the development of such a policy through an international process that would

154. This policy is no longer operative or directly accessible but it is electronically archived by 'Lectric Law Library, *NSI Domain Dispute Resolution Policy*, http://www.lectlaw.com/files/inp08.htm.

155. Marie-Emmanuelle Haas, *The Origin of the UDRP: NSI's 1995 Domain Name Dispute Policy*, DomainesInfo (23 Jul. 2009) (available at http://www.domainesinfo.fr/english/302/the-origin-of-the-udrp-nsi-s-1995-domain-name-dispute-policy.php).

156. NSI's revised policies, as archived by 'Lectric Law Library, are illustrative. 'Lectric Law Library, *NSI Domain Dispute Policy, Rev. 01*, http://www.lectlaw.com/files/inp13.htm (effective 23 Nov. 1995); NSI *Domain Name Dispute Policy Revision 02* (effective 9 Sep. 1996) (reproduced in Michael Tanner, *Trademarks, Internet Domain Names, and the NSI: How Do We Fix a System that is Already Broken?*, 3(2) J. Tech. L. & Pol'y, Appendix).

157. *Panavision Int'l v. Toeppen*, 141 F.3d 1316, 1318 (9th Cir. 1998).

158. The Green Paper is discussed in detail in Part I, Chapter 2, s. 2.2 above.

come to be known as the First Internet Domain Name Process, or colloquially, 'WIPO I'.[159] The most significant recommendations made in the final report of that process went to the establishment of a mandatory administrative procedure for the cancellation or transfer of domain names deemed abusively registered in violation of a third party's trademark rights by a registrant with no rights or legitimate interests in the domain name. This recommendation was adopted by the Board of Directors of the newly formed ICANN at its first public meeting in August, 1999.[160] The resulting administrative procedure, named the Uniform Domain Name Dispute Resolution Policy, now commonly referred to by its acronym 'UDRP', was implemented by the registrars of .com, .org and .net during the period of December, 1999 through January, 2000.[161] Today the UDRP is applicable to all of the pre-2012 'proof of concept' new gTLDs by force of a contractual obligation upon registry operators to use only ICANN-accredited registrars,[162] who in turn are contractually obligated to incorporate the UDRP in their domain name registration agreements.[163] The *gTLD Applicant Guidebook* and its incorporated Registry Agreement extended this obligation to all post-2012 New gTLD Program registry operators.

A distinguishing feature of the UDRP is that it expressly leaves open the right to resort to litigation in national courts,[164] upon which UDRP

---

159. The results of this process are documented in WIPO, *Final Report of the WIPO Internet Domain Name Process*. Jeffrey M. Samuels & Linda B. Samuels, *Internet Domain Names: The Uniform Dispute Resolution Policy*, 40 Am. Bus. L. J. 885, 889 (2003).

160. ICANN, *Minutes of the Meeting of the Initial Board*, https://www.icann.org/resources/board-material/minutes-1999-08-26-en (26 Aug. 1999). ICANN, *Second Staff Report on Implementation Documents for the Uniform Dispute Resolution Policy*, http://archive.icann.org/en/udrp/udrp-second-staff-report-24oct99.htm (24 Oct. 1999) (described by Lindsay at 105 as an 'important source of background information on the policy deliberations that eventually resulted in the final form taken by the UDRP'); DNSO Working Group-A, *DNSO WG-A Final Report to the Names Council*, http://www.dnso.org/dnso/notes/19990729.WGA-report.html (29 Jul. 1999).

161. Smith, *Internet Law and Regulation*, 100.

162. ICANN, Registry Agreement, clause 2.9, https://newgtlds.icann.org/sites/default/files/agreements/agreement-approved-09jan14-en.htm.

163. ICANN, *2013 Registrar Accreditation Agreement, Clause* 3.8, https://www.icann.org/resources/pages/approved-with-specs-2013-09-17-en (2013). On the peculiarities of the UDRP contractual relationship and the lack of privity between complainant and domain name registrant, *see* Warren B. Chik, *Lord of Your Domain, But Master of None: The Need to Harmonize and Recalibrate the Domain Name Regime of Ownership and Control*, 16 Int'l J. L. Info. Tech. 8, 64–65 (2008).

164. 'While the establishment of the UDRP was in large part driven by the perceived and anticipated difficulties of litigating domain name cases in courts, the UDRP is not intended in any way to eliminate or diminish such court options. Indeed, the fact that courts have tended to respect the UDRP mechanism and process as such probably owes much to the deference which the UDRP itself expresses in relation to the full role of the courts. This is not only a question of principle, but has practical reasons as well. In some circumstances, courts can offer benefits which this ADR mechanism cannot. These include the conduct of an evidentiary process that takes account of the full range of facts

panellists' decisions are not binding.[165] A further distinguishing feature of the UDRP is that although WIPO played a critical role, the policy was drafted and implemented through ICANN's unique multi-stakeholder governance framework, and is therefore not an instrument that is based in international agreement.

3.3.1.2 Scope and Application of the UDRP

The UDRP is actionable on proof of all of the following three elements, which equate to a finding that a registration is abusive:

(i) the registrant's domain name is identical or confusingly similar[166] to a trademark or service mark in which the complainant has rights; and
(ii) the registrant has no rights or legitimate interests in respect of the domain name; and
(iii) the registrant's domain name has been registered and is being used in bad faith.[167]

This makes clear the strictly limited scope of the UDRP: proof of the existence of a valid and enforceable trade or service mark, which has been interpreted to include unregistered marks, is a prerequisite.[168] Early suggestions that the policy cast a wider net went unheeded. In 1997, the International Ad Hoc Committee ('IAHC'), a pre-ICANN group, had

---

and arguments which parties may present by various means over time. A court is not a priori limited either in its procedural options or in the sanctions which it may issue. Also, while the public posting of UDRP decisions creates its own deterrent effect, this effect may be even stronger with court proceedings' (internal citations omitted). Nicholas Smith & Erik Wilbers, *The UDRP: Design Elements of an Effective ADR Mechanism*, 15(2) Am. Rev. Int'l Arb. 215, 218 (2004). A less favourable view is offered by Chad D. Emerson, *Wasting Time in Cyberspace: The UDRP's Inefficient Approach Toward Arbitrating Internet Domain Name Disputes*, 34 U. Baltimore L. Rev. 161, 173 (2004) (positing that the 'domain name registrant's ability to circumvent, or even completely avoid, mandatory participation in the UDRP undermines the efficiency of the UDRP').

165. *See for example*, *Weber-Stephen Products Co. v. Armitage Hardware & Building Supply, Inc.*, No. 00 C 1738, 2000 U.S. Dist. LEXIS 6335 (N.D. Ill. 2000).
166. Lindsay explains, citing Froomkin, that this wording was chosen over the WIPO I Report's recommended phrase 'identical or misleadingly similar' in order to accord with the wording in the United States federal trademark statute, the Lanham Act. Lindsay, 106. A. Michael Froomkin, *ICANN's Uniform Dispute Resolution Policy: Causes and (Partial) Cures*, 67 Brooklyn L. Rev. 605, 654 (2002).
167. Lindsay highlights 'relatively minor drafting changes' to the WIPO I Report recommendations to clarify factors indicating evidence of bad faith. Lindsay, 107.
168. Samuels and Samuels note that 'many panels have made an independent evaluation of whether the complainant has rights in the mark', citing by way of example *402 Shoes, Inc. v. Weinstock*, Case No. D2000-1223 (WIPO December 2000). Samuels & Samuels, 899–900.

recommended the establishment of 'Administrative Domain Name Challenge Panels' to hear claims respecting second-level domain names deemed 'identical or closely similar to names which are, for the purposes of the Internet, internationally known, and for which demonstrable intellectual property rights exist'.[169] The WIPO I Interim Report similarly recommended that the policy apply to 'any dispute concerning the domain name arising out of the alleged violation of an intellectual property right.'[170]

Such broad language was also used in the predecessor agreement to the 2001 and 2009 Registrar Accreditation Agreements. The earlier agreement required at section III.J.7.g that registrars impose the following obligation upon domain name registrants: 'The SLD [second-level domain] holder shall represent that, to the best of the SLD holder's knowledge and belief, neither the registration of the SLD name nor the manner in which it is directly or indirectly used infringes the *legal rights* of a third party.'[171] (emphasis added) Later versions replaced this clause with the obligation to have in place and adhere to the UDRP.[172]

The UDRP requires domain name registrants to represent and warrant that: '(b) to your knowledge, the registration of the domain name will not infringe upon, or otherwise violate the rights of any third party;' and '(d) you will not knowingly use the domain name in violation of any applicable laws or regulations. It is your responsibility to determine whether your domain name registration infringes or violates someone else's rights.'[173] Disputes that can be resolved using the UDRP, however, are much narrower in scope than these undertakings suggest, given that a claim can only be based on a trade or service mark.

The case for extending the scope of the UDRP to include geographic names was made during the WIPO II process. WIPO declined in its report to

169. IAHC, *Final Report of the International Ad Hoc Committee: Recommendations for Administration and Management of gTLDs*, 7.1.2: Administrative Domain Name Challenge Panels, http://www.iahc.org/draft-iahc-recommend-00.html (4 Feb. 1997) (archived at http://www.archive.org/web/web.php) (hereinafter '*Final Report*').

170. WIPO, *Interim Report of the WIPO Internet Domain Name Process, The Management of Internet Names and Addresses: Intellectual Property Issues*, 151, http://www.wipo.int/amc/en/processes/process1/rfc/3/index.html (23 Dec. 1998).

171. ICANN, *Statement of Registrar Accreditation Policy*, http://www.icann.org/en/registrars/policy_statement.html#lllj.

172. The 2001 and 2009-versions of the Policy also provided the following at s. 3.8: 'Domain-Name Dispute Resolution. During the Term of this Agreement, Registrar shall have in place a policy and procedures for resolution of disputes concerning Registered Names. Until different policies and procedures are established by ICANN under s. 4, Registrar shall comply with the Uniform Domain Name Dispute Resolution Policy identified on ICANN's website (www.icann.org/general/consensus-policies.htm).' ICANN, *Registrar Accreditation Agreement*, https://www.icann.org/resources/unthemed-pages/raa-2001-05-17-en (17 May 2001); ICANN, *Registrar Accreditation Agreement*, https://www.icann.org/resources/pages/ra-agreement-2009-05-21-en (21 May 2009).

173. ICANN, *Uniform Domain Name Dispute Resolution Policy (adopted 26 Aug. 1999)*, clause 2, http://www.icann.org/en/udrp/udrp-policy-24oct99.htm.

recommend that path on account of having reached the conclusion that the TRIPS Agreement offers insufficient support for the recognition of rights in non-trademark names, including geographic names.[174] Complainants have, as a result, had little success over the years in applying the UDRP to geographic names: it has been said that UDRP challenges involving geographic names have been 'overwhelmingly unsuccessful',[175] with complainants succeeding 'in only a few exceptional cases.'[176] Their largely non-commercial nature ordinarily prevents geographic names from being registrable as trademarks, although their use in a commercial context can (but does not always) tip the balance, for example in the case of certification marks or geographical indications such as Champagne,[177] trade names incorporating geographic names,[178] sporting club names,[179] and geographic names used in connection with tourism and the provision of public services.[180] In these cases, the registered trademark holder has no exclusive

174. WIPO, *WIPO II Report*, 8 at Executive summary para. (iv).

175. Olsen et al., Introduction/65.

176. *Domain Name Law and Practice: An International Handbook* 1015 (Torsten Bettinger ed., Oxford University Press 2005).

177. *See for example, Veuve Clicquot Ponsardin v. Net-Promotion, Inc.*, Case No. D2000-0347 (WIPO Arbitration and Mediation Center 14 Jun. 2000) (available at http://www.wipo.int/amc/en/domains/decisions/html/2000/d2000-0347.html) (involving the trademark VEUVE CLICQUOT and the domain names champagneclicquot.com, champagne-clicquot.com, champagnecliquot.com and champagne-cliquot.com, with the outcome that the domain names were transferred to the complainant).

178. *See for example, Skipton Building Society v. Peter Colman*, Case No. D2000-1217 (WIPO Arbitration and Mediation Center 1 Dec. 2000) (available at http://www.wipo.int/amc/en/domains/decisions/html/2000/d2000-1217.html) (involving UK trademark SKIPTON and domain name skipton.com, with the outcome that the domain names were transferred to the complainant); *BAA plc, Aberdeen Airport Limited v. Mr H Hashimi*, Case No. D2004-0717 (WIPO Arbitration and Mediation Center 21 Oct. 2004) (available at http://www.wipo.int/amc/en/domains/decisions/html/2004/d2004-0717.html) (involving the domain name aberdeenairport.com and recognizing common law rights in the name ABERDEEN AIRPORT, with the domain name deemed not confusingly similar).

179. *See for example, FC Bayern München AG v. Peoples Net Services Ltd*, Case No. D2003-0464 (WIPO Arbitration and Mediation Center 15 Jul. 2003) (available at http://www.wipo.int/amc/en/domains/decisions/html/2003/d2003-0464.html) (involving the registered trademark FC BAYERN MÜNCHEN E.V. and domain names bayernmuenchen.net and bayernmunchen.net, with the outcome that the domain names were transferred to the complainant).

180. *See for example, Brisbane City Council v. Warren Bolton Consulting Pty Ltd*, Case No. D2001-0047 (WIPO Arbitration and Mediation Center 7 May 2001) (available at http://www.wipo.int/amc/en/domains/decisions/html/2001/d2001-0047.html) (involving an Australian composite mark including the words 'BRISBANE CITY WORKS' and the domain name brisbanecity.com, but complaint denied for lack of confusing similarity); *Excelentisimo Ayuntamiento de Barcelona v. Barcelona.com Inc.*, Case No. D2000-0505 (WIPO Arbitration and Mediation Center 4 Aug. 2000) (available at http://www.wipo.int/amc/en/domains/decisions/html/2000/d2000-0505.html) (involving the domain name barcelona.com and multiple Spanish registered trademarks comprising or including the name 'Barcelona', with the outcome that the domain name was transferred to the

right in the geographic name per se, so cannot prevent others from using it.[181] This makes it difficult for complainants to prove that a challenged registrant has 'no legitimate right' to use the geographic name in question.[182]

It is also difficult for complainants to prove unregistered rights in a trademark as a basis for making a challenge.[183] Whether complainants even have the option of basing a claim on unregistered marks depends on domestic law. In a notable challenge brought by the Government of the Spanish region of Catalonia, the name 'Generalitat de Catalunya' was deemed protectable based on its well-known status as a result of Spanish law's providing that 'the same rights deriving from a trademark registration shall be granted to an unregistered well-known trademark in Spain, in accordance with Article 6*bis*

---

complainant). *But see Brisbane City Council v. Joyce Russ Advertising Pty Ltd*, Case No. D2001-0069 (WIPO Arbitration and Mediation Center 14 May 2001) (available at http://www.wipo.int/amc/en/domains/decisions/html/2001/d2001-0069.html) (involving the domain name brisbane.com, with the outcome that the Complainant was found not to have trademark rights in the name Brisbane or Brisbane City). *See generally*, Heather Ann Forrest, *Domain Name Allocation and Government Super-Prioritization: Lessons Learned from the UDRP Keep ICANN Out of the Business of Deciding What Is or Is Not a Country*, 18(1) Vanderbilt J. Ent. & Tech. L. 1 (2015).

181. *See for example*, *Puerto Rico Tourism Company v. Virtual Countries, Inc.*, Case No. D2002-1129 (WIPO Arbitration and Mediation Center 14 Apr. 2003) (available at http://www.wipo.int/amc/en/domains/decisions/html/2002/d2002-1129.html) (involving the domain name puertorico.com and finding that rights in the name 'Puerto Rico' had been disclaimed in the Claimant's trademark registrations). *But see*, *Barcelona v. Barcelona.com, WIPO Case No. D2000-0505*. *See generally*, Forrest, *Domain Name Allocation and Government Super-Prioritization*.

182. *See for example*, *Kur-und Verkehrsverein St Moritz v. StMoritz.com*, Case No. D2000-0617 (WIPO Arbitration and Mediation Center 17 Aug. 2000) (available at http://www.wipo.int/amc/en/domains/decisions/html/2000/d2000-0617.html) (involving the domain name stmoritz.com and registered trademarks in twenty-seven countries for the name ST MORITZ, finding no bad faith use and registration); *Deer Valley Resort Company v. Intermountain Lodging and Registration Center*, Case No. FA474344 (National Arbitration Forum 27 Jun. 2005) (available at http://www.adrforum.com/domaindecisions/474344.htm) (involving the US trademark DEER VALLEY and the domain name deervalleylodging.info, finding for respondent and noting 'there is a conflict between the rights Complainant has by way of trademark registration and the rights of the community at large to use the geographic indicator outside the scope of the trademark registrations'); *City of Hamina v. Paragon International Projects Ltd*, Case No. D2001-0001 (WIPO Arbitration and Mediation Center 12 Mar. 2001) (available at http://www.wipo.int/amc/en/domains/decisions/html/2001/d2001-0001.html) (involving the domain name portofhamina.com and the city's asserted unregistered trademark rights under Finnish law in the name 'Port of Hamina', with a finding for the Respondent, who was deemed to have a legitimate interest in the name by offering websites providing information about the port). *See generally*, Forrest, *Domain Name Allocation and Government Super-Prioritization*.

183. Forrest, *Domain Name Allocation and Government Super-Prioritization*.

of the Paris Convention'.[184] This outcome appears to be the exception rather than the rule, however.

Where rights have been found, this is more commonly attributable to the geographic name at issue having taken on the significance of identifying a business rather than a particular geographic location, as for example in the case of the names 'Wembley Stadium',[185] 'Sydney Markets',[186] and 'Sydney Airport'.[187] On the other hand, the vast majority of cases in respect of geographic names face a difficulty that has long been acknowledged in trademark law, a difficulty that is succinctly explained in the decision to a challenge to the domain name www.paris.org:[188]

> It is absolutely inconceivable that anyone, at first instance, hearing this term would think of anything other than that particular city. Accordingly, not only does this term not have any common law significance as a trademark, it strains reason to even contemplate that this term could ever obtain such significance.

This fundamental principle of trademark law is built into the second element that must be satisfied in all UDRP challenges, thus carving out respondents who have been commonly known by a name and therefore have a right or legitimate interest in that name even if they hold no trade or service mark rights. While there is scope for the application of this defence of legitimate interest in the context of generic names, abbreviations and slang terms,[189] as

184. *Generalitat de Catalunya v. Thomas Wolf*, Case No. D2002-1124 (WIPO Arbitration and Mediation Center 14 Apr. 2003) (available at http://www.wipo.int/amc/en/domains/decisions/html/2002/d2002-1124.html). The applicability of Art. 6*bis* to geographic names is discussed in detail in Part III, Chapter 8, s. 8.3 below.
185. *Wembley National Stadium Limited v. Bob Thomson*, Case No. D2000-1233 (WIPO Arbitration and Mediation Center 16 Nov. 2000) (available at http://www.wipo.int/amc/en/domains/decisions/html/2000/d2000-1233.html).
186. *Sydney Markets Limited v. Nick Rakis*, Case No. D2001-0932 (WIPO Arbitration and Mediation Center 8 Oct. 2001) (available at http://www.wipo.int/amc/en/domains/decisions/html/2001/d2001-0932.html).
187. *Sydney Airport Corporation v. John Crilly*, Case No. D2005-0989 (WIPO Arbitration and Mediation Center 22 Nov. 2005) (available at http://www.wipo.int/amc/en/domains/decisions/html/2005/d2005-0989.html).
188. *The Paris Pages v. Woohoo T&C Ltd*, Case No. FA110763 (National Arbitration Forum 10 Jul. 2002) (available at http://www.adrforum.com/domaindecisions/110763.htm) (challenging the registration of paris.org by an American applicant to promote tourism in Paris, France and held, that the name had not acquired secondary meaning). WIPO has come to a similar conclusion in its overview of UDRP decisions: 'It is very difficult for the legal authority of a geographical area to show unregistered trademark rights in that geographical term based on secondary meaning.' WIPO, *WIPO Overview of WIPO Panel Views on Selected UDRP Questions: 1.5 Can a complainant show rights in a geographical term or identifier?*, http://www.wipo.int/amc/en/domains/search/overview/index.html#15.
189. Ryan Shewchuk, *The UDRP and the ACPA: What Are They, and Which Should Be Used?*, 2 Asper Rev. Int'l Bus. & Trade L. 85, 91–92 (2002).

well as names and acronyms of IGOs, geographic,[190] cultural and linguistic names, it is not particularly likely that a UDRP claim would be raised in these situations, given that the policy is not actually intended to address situations in which the respondent patently has a legitimate right to the name in question.

3.3.1.3 The Future of the UDRP

Despite concerns about bias towards complainants[191] and inappropriate application of trademark principles,[192] the UDRP is widely hailed as a success story in the fight against bad actors in the DNS.[193] In its first decade, the UDRP broadly achieved the aims set out for it in the WIPO I process by offering a 'quick and inexpensive procedure ... that is simpler and more cost-effective than legislation' without foreclosing the option of resorting to national courts. The subsequent WIPO II Report and discussion since make clear, however, that the UDRP is not the much sought after silver bullet: where once it was said that 'with the advent of UDRP, the days of the .com infringer are numbered',[194] such a result has unfortunately failed to materialize. Even before the introduction of New gTLD Program domains, the policy showed signs of strain under the weight of a substantial case load that reduces its efficiency and expediency. New gTLDs have added further to that load, although perhaps not as significantly as was feared.[195]

As to its limited applicability, there are those who continue to support the idea of expanding the scope of the UDRP to cover other bases of legal rights.[196] The decision to limit actionable rights to trademarks was reportedly

190. Forrest, *Domain Name Allocation and Government Super-Prioritization*, 33–35.
191. *See for example*, Michael Geist, *Fair .com? An Examination of the Allegations of Systemic Unfairness in the ICANN UDRP*, http://aix1.uottawa.ca/~geist/geistudrp.pdf; Milton L. Mueller, *Rough Justice: A Statistical Assessment of ICANN's Uniform Dispute Resolution Policy*, 17(3) Information Society (2001).
192. Victoria Holstein-Childress, *Lex Cyberus: The UDRP as a Gatekeeper to Judicial Resolution of Competing Rights to Domain Names*, 109 Penn St. L. Rev. 565 (2004).
193. ICANN Meeting Transcript, *Current State of the UDRP*, http://archive.icann.org/en/meetings/singapore2011/bitcache/The%20Current%20State%20of%20the%20UDRP-vid=26007&disposition=attachment&op=download.txt (22 Jun. 2011); ICANN, *Workshop on the Current State of the UDRP: Overview & Analysis of the Preliminary Issue Report*, http://archive.icann.org/en/meetings/singapore2011/bitcache/Workshop%20on%20the%20Current%20State%20of%20the%20UDRP_%20Overview%20&%20Analysis%20of%20the%20Preliminary%20Issue%20Report-vid=25871&disposition=attachment&op=download.pdf (22 Jun. 2011).
194. Olsen et al., Introduction/47.
195. Doug Isenberg, *WIPO Domain Name Dispute Filings Rise 4.5% in 2015*, http://www.gigalaw.com/2016/01/13/wipo-udrp-2015/ (13 Jan. 2016) (positing that the introduction of the new Uniform Rapid Suspension mechanism 'may have kept the number of UDRP filings from increasing even more than 4.5 percent.').
196. Samuels & Samuels, 903–904.

an initial position, to be subsequently revisited.[197] ICANN's Registrar Accreditation Agreement is broader in scope than only trademarks in that it obliges registrars to require that domain name registrants affirm non-violation of third parties' 'legal rights'.[198] Naturally, the New gTLD Program generated an opportunity to re-enliven discussion of the UDRP's scope, but it was not until after delegation of New gTLD Program gTLDs into the root had begun that any firm steps were taken: a GNSO Policy Development Process was chartered to address concerns about third-party registration of names and acronyms belonging to intergovernmental organizations ('IGOs') and international non-governmental organizations ('INGOs'). This group recommended broadening the scope of the UDRP for use by IGOs.[199] Cautionary comments on this recommendation advised that, as this 'would amount to extending the scope of [the UDRP] beyond pure trademark disputes', '[c]are should be taken to not expand their workings beyond what is necessary to ensure IGO and INGO protections tailored specifically to the W[orking] G[roup]'s recommendations.'[200]

While the legal basis for extending the UDRP is not immediately clear, other domain name dispute resolution policies offer models of how this could potentially be achieved. The European Union's .eu Dispute Resolution Policy, for example, protects names 'in respect of which a right is recognized or established by national and/or Community law', amongst which 'registered national and community trademarks, geographical indications or designations of origin, and, in as far as they are protected under national law in the Member State where they are held: unregistered trademarks, trade names, business identifiers, company names, family names, and distinctive titles of protected literary and artistic works.'[201] Domestic legislation can also serve as a model. The US Anticybersquatting Prevention Act, for example, requires courts' consideration of certain non-exhaustive enumerated factors when determining whether a registration was made in bad faith, the first of which is 'the trademark *or other intellectual property rights* of the person, if any, in the domain name'[202] (emphasis added). This is proof that

197. It is reported that Chateau Neuf du Pape supported a broader scope, but the 'preponderance of views' was in support of a limited scope 'at least initially'. WIPO, *Final Report of the WIPO Internet Domain Name Process*, 52–53.
198. ICANN, *Registrar Accreditation Agreement (2001)*, s. 3.7.7.9; ICANN, *Registrar Accreditation Agreement (2009)*, s. 3.7.7.9; ICANN, *Registrar Accreditation Agreement (2013)*, s. 3.7.7.9.
199. ICANN, *Final Report on the Protection of IGO and INGO Identifiers in All gTLDs*, 17, http://gnso.icann.org/en/issues/igo-ingo-final-10nov13-en.pdf (10 Nov. 2013).
200. *Id.*, 68.
201. Regulation (EC) No 874/2004 Arts 10(1), 21. Other examples include Nominet's .uk Dispute Resolution Policy and Ireland's .ie Dispute Resolution Policy. Some ccTLD policies use a broader term than just trademarks, but in practice, their applicability has been limited by dispute resolution providers to trade and service marks. Examples of this are Singapore and Hong Kong. Chik, 28–31.
202. Anticybersquatting Consumer Protection Act, 15 U.S.C. § 1125(d) (1)(b)(i)(I).

rights in non-trademark geographic names, to the extent recognized by law, could be and in some cases are being protected through *ex post* mechanisms.

Another option still, and perhaps far easier, is to expressly provide in domestic trademark law for geographic names' registrability as trademarks or for their recognition as unregistered marks. Such a move would transform geographic names from a position of no protection to priority in the DNS, making their bad faith registration and use as second-level domain names actionable under the UDRP as well as the new rights protection mechanisms implemented under the *gTLD Applicant Guidebook*, plus their use as a basis for a Legal Rights Objection against a new gTLD application. The profound effect of such a change in domestic law would be to effectively render the names in question protected at the international level. Notable here are, for example, changes made in 2011 to Swiss trademark law to recognize geographic trademarks.[203] A broad range of names, including commercial names (trade names and registered trademarks), municipality names, and geographical indications are protected under the dispute resolution policy that applies to Switzerland's .ch country code TLD.[204] This protection is of no effect in other top-level domains, however. The recognition of a new geographic form of trademark has the broader impact just described in terms of making the unauthorized registration and use of such marks in the DNS actionable, and far beyond Switzerland's borders.

With the New gTLD Program on its agenda, the ICANN community had little time or energy to devote to an overhaul of the UDRP, but the merits of launching a policy development process on this issue were raised.[205] A major milestone in the life of the UDRP was reached when the GNSO Council, the body responsible (as per ICANN's Bylaws[206]) for developing policy relating to gTLDs, voted in early 2016 in favour of including the UDRP in the scope of a policy development process to review rights protection mechanisms:[207]

> to determine whether modifications to the existing RPMs (including but not limited to the UDRP) are needed and, if so, what they should be. The outcome of the PDP may lead to (i) amendments or replacement of

203. L'Assemblée Fédérale, Loi sur la protection des marques et loi sur la protection des armoiries: Vers une réglementation différenciée, 11 Nov. 2011, http://www.parlament.ch /f/mm/2011/pages/mm-rk-n-2011-11-11.aspx.
204. SWITCH, *Legal Information: Legal basis and Dispute Resolution Service for.ch domain names*, https://www.nic.ch/terms/.
205. ICANN, *Workshop on the Current State of the UDRP: Overview & Analysis of the Preliminary Issue report*; ICANN, *Current State of the UDRP*.
206. ICANN, *Bylaws*, https://www.icann.org/resources/pages/governance/bylaws-en/#article11 (as amended 1 Oct. 2016), Art. 11, s. 11.1.
207. ICANN GNSO, *Council Resolution 20160218-3: Initiation of a Policy Development Process (PDP) on a Review of All Rights Protection Mechanisms in All Generic Top-Level Domains (gTLDs)*, http://gnso.icann.org/en/council/resolutions#20160218-3 (18 Feb. 2016).

existing policies, principles or procedures; (ii) the development of new or additional policy recommendations; and/or (iii) the creation of new implementation guidance to supplement existing policies or procedures.

The Council opted to bifurcate the policy development process into two 'phases',[208] with newly introduced New gTLD Program mechanisms to be evaluated in phase 1, followed by the UDRP in phase 2. While some have criticized the delay that will result from this bifurcation,[209] to some degree these criticisms detract from the significance of the UDRP's inclusion in the review at all, given that this is the first review of the policy since its implementation at the time of ICANN's formation.

In the interim, a review of the new injunctive relief-type *ex post* rights protection mechanism called 'Uniform Rapid Suspension', or 'URS' as it is commonly referred to in ICANN documentation, in the first phase of the review will shed some light on the UDRP, since it is both substantively and procedurally based upon the UDRP. This is not the first instance of a new *ex post* mechanism being based upon the UDRP, however, so before turning to the URS, it is relevant to consider the lessons that have been learned from the experience of .biz with its Start-up Trademark Opposition Policy.

3.3.2 Start-up Trademark Opposition Policy ('STOP')

As noted earlier in this chapter, the new .biz gTLD launch involved innovative but controversial new rights protection mechanisms. To support its 'IP Claims' service, .biz applied a 'Start-up Trademark Opposition Policy' ('STOP') which offered trademark holders who had filed an 'IP Claim'[210] (called 'IP Claimants') a thirty-day period in which to challenge applicants who chose to proceed with a .biz domain name application despite having received notice of third-party rights in the applied-for name.[211]

The STOP process was highly automated and conducted entirely online.[212] A total of 801 complaints were filed.[213] The grounds for challenge under the STOP were significantly less novel than the overall concept, as they were based on the tried and tested grounds of the UDRP.[214] To be

208. *Ibid.*

209. ICANN, *Transcript GNSO Council Public Meeting Marrakech – 9 March 2016 at 13:30 UTC*, https://webcache.googleusercontent.com/search?q=cache:fKxMYHvf-60J:https://meetings.icann.org/en/marrakech55/schedule/wed-gnso-council/transcript-gnso-council-09mar16-en.pdf+&cd=1&hl=en&ct=clnk&gl=au (see comments of Heather Forrest, Edward Morris and Philip Corwin).

210. The .biz IP claims service is discussed in Part II, Chapter 3, s. 3.2.4 above.

211. Lindsay, 121.

212. WIPO, *General Information on STOP*.

213. Lindsay, 121.

214. WIPO, *General Information on STOP*.

successful, IP Claimants were required to satisfy all three of the following conditions:[215]

(1) The domain name was identical to a trademark or service mark in which the Complainant had rights.
(2) The domain name registrant had no rights or legitimate interests in respect of the domain name.
(3) The domain name was either registered or used in bad faith.

The key differences between these grounds and those of the UDRP were the lowering of the burden of proof to bad faith registration *or* use and the limitation of actionable marks to those which are identical. The UDRP requires, by contrast, proof of bad faith registration *and* use, and is actionable in respect of confusingly similar marks.[216] Despite the fact that the STOP was only utilized in a single TLD, it remains relevant because decisions under the STOP are occasionally (and unsurprisingly, given the relative similarity of the two procedures) referred to by UDRP panellists.[217]

3.3.3 Uniform Rapid Suspension ('URS') Procedure

The Implementation Recommendation Team formed within ICANN's Intellectual Property Constituency recommended in its June 2009 Final Report the creation of a new mechanism to quickly resolve 'those cases in which there is no genuine contestable issue as to the infringement and abuse that is taking place.'[218] The Uniform Rapid Suspension or 'URS' procedure, as this new mechanism is called, is 'intended to supplement and not replace the UDRP.'[219] The same substantive standards as those of the UDRP apply save that a higher evidentiary burden of proof is imposed upon the complainant, who is required to demonstrate to a standard of clear and convincing evidence that there is 'no genuine issue of material fact.'[220] As is obvious from the similarity between it and the UDRP, the Uniform Rapid Suspension procedure is not intended to address cases in which the challenged domain name registrant has a legitimate right to use the domain name in question. Neither is it intended for 'questionable cases of alleged infringement (e.g., use of terms in their generic sense) or for anti-competitive purposes or denial of free speech'.[221] Rather, its application is strictly limited to 'clear-cut'[222] cases of 'abusive use of trademarks where there is no genuine contestable

215. NeuLevel Inc., *Start-up Trademark Opposition Policy and Rules for.biz.*
216. The UDRP is discussed in detail in Part II, Chapter 3, s. 3.3.1 above.
217. Lindsay, 121.
218. IRT, *Final Report,* 25.
219. *Ibid.*
220. ICANN, *gTLD Applicant Guidebook,* Uniform Rapid Suspension, s. 8.3.
221. IRT, *Final Report,* 25.
222. *Id.*, 26.

issue as to the infringing or abusive use of a mark in a domain name and in connection with a site that represents abusive use (i.e., not a fair use or commentary situation nor a situation involving questions of whether the registrant is or is not authorized or selling, for example, legitimate, non-counterfeit goods).'[223]

Both the Implementation Recommendation Team and the Special Trademark Issues review team recommended that implementation of the Uniform Rapid Suspension procedure be made mandatory for all new gTLDs going forward.[224] This position was ultimately adopted by ICANN's Board in the *gTLD Applicant Guidebook* [225] despite lingering opposition generally to the concept of the URS, and specifically to the adequacy of notice provided to challenged registrants and the potential for of abuse of the system by trademark owners.[226] As to the latter concern, initial feedback from rights holders indicates some 'have opted not to use this service due to the "clear and convincing" standard being seen as too strict and the URS remedy being limited to suspension only, thus not justifying the costs.'[227]

Procedurally, upon filing of a complaint, the registry operator is required to lock the disputed domain against changes and notify the domain name's registrant. The registrant then has fourteen days to submit a response. Initial data notably shows that more than half of URS determinations are reached by default arising from a registrant's failure to respond.[228]

This mechanism can be supported by the new Trademark Clearinghouse, another of both teams' recommendations: a right validated in the clearinghouse can be presented as the basis for a URS claim just as it can for a UDRP claim.[229] Indeed, the desirability of leveraging Trademark Clearinghouse data is a clear point of feedback received by ICANN staff in an early review of the URS. [230]

Consistent with the aim of the procedure to address obvious cases of trademark cybersquatting, the URS protects only trade and service marks.[231] The holders of rights in geographic names are not able to access the instant relief provided by Uniform Rapid Suspension unless those rights are

223. *Id.*, 25.
224. *Id.*; STI, *Recommendations*, 16 (Recommendation 2.4).
225. ICANN, *gTLD Applicant Guidebook,* Specification 7 s. 2b.
226. ICANN, *New gTLD Program: Uniform Rapid Suspension (URS) Summary and Analysis of Public Comments*, 14, http://www.icann.org/en/topics/new-gtlds/summary-analysis-urs-comments-04oct09-en.pdf (4 Oct. 2009).
227. ICANN, *Rights Protection Mechanisms Review: Revised Report*, 103, https://newgtlds.icann.org/en/reviews/rpm/rpm-review-11sep15-en.pdf (11 Sep. 2015).
228. *Id.*, 105.
229. ICANN, *gTLD Applicant Guidebook,* Uniform Rapid Suspension, s. 1.2.6.1.a. The Trademark Clearinghouse is discussed in detail in Part II, Chapter 3, 3.2.2 above.
230. ICANN, Rights Protection Mechanisms Review: Revised Report, 101.
231. ICANN, *gTLD Applicant* Guidebook, Uniform Rapid Suspension, s. 1.2.5.

recognized in the form of a trademark. On the other hand, given the expedited nature of the process and the harsh consequences of a successful proceeding (the abusive domain name is suspended for the remaining term of the domain name registration),[232] the potential existence of other legitimate rights in geographic names renders this challenge mechanism otherwise inapplicable.

3.3.4 OTHER *EX POST* MECHANISMS

Where registration of a second-level domain name in a TLD or participation in a sunrise registration period is conditional on satisfying certain criteria, a decision must be taken as to whether an applicant satisfies those criteria. Sunrise and registrant eligibility challenge policies have not been implemented by all of the gTLDs in which those mechanisms are used. Where they have been used, however, this has in the past primarily been directed at challenging eligibility after a disputed domain name is allocated. Notable exceptions highlighted earlier in this chapter are the *ex ante* sunrise reconsideration proceeding in .tel, the Pioneer Challenge Process in .asia, and the formal and informal registration dispute resolution procedures in .travel. Yet even where they are implemented as an *ex post* mechanism, challenge policies can have a profound impact on registration volumes. This is demonstrated by the .info Sunrise Challenge Policy, under which almost half of the total number of 51,764 registrations 'were either successfully challenged or cancelled without challenge.'[233]

Different eligibility criteria mean the possibility, although not necessity, of different approaches to resolving eligibility disputes. Certainly the procedural aspects of eligibility challenges can be shared across TLDs despite potentially diverse eligibility criteria. The pre-2012 'proof of concept' new gTLDs .aero, .coop, .museum and .travel demonstrated this through their shared Charter Eligibility Dispute Resolution Policy and related Rules.[234] This policy allows any person or entity (not only registrants) to challenge a registered domain name on grounds that the registrant does not meet the registrability requirements applicable to the particular gTLD.

232. *Id.*, Uniform Rapid Suspension, s. 10.

233. Lindsay, *International Domain Name Law: ICANN and the UDRP*, 121. The unverified, self-policing nature of the sunrise process (as described in nn 124 and 125 above and accompanying text) undoubtedly contributed to this outcome.

234. ICANN, *Charter Eligibility Dispute Resolution Policy*, https://www.icann.org/resources/pages/cedrp-2012-02-25-en; ICANN, *Charter Eligibility Dispute Resolution Policy Rules*, https://www.icann.org/resources/pages/rules-fd-2012-02-25-en. The DotAsia General Policies also incorporate the Charter Eligibility Dispute Resolution Policy. The DotAsia Organisation, *.ASIA General Registry Policies Final Draft*, 4.2, http://www.dot.asia/draft/DotAsia-General-Policies--FINALDRAFT-v-1-0.pdf (2007). Lindsay, 121.

Similar but TLD-specific policies were applied in the .asia,[235] .biz,[236] .cat,[237] and .pro[238] 'proof of concept' gTLDs.

No gTLD created prior to the New gTLD Program has conditioned eligibility to register domain names on holding an IPR. A link between domain name registrant eligibility and ownership of an intellectual property or other legal right is nevertheless easily envisioned in the example of a new trademark or brand-specific gTLD (an idea which is discussed in detail in the final section of this chapter) or for new gTLDs comprising geographical indications at the top (e.g., .champagne) or second (e.g., .wine and .vin) level.

Where applied-for names are supported by a trademark, these can potentially be challenged under the UDRP and, in some cases, gTLD-specific challenge policies. For example, a challenge can be raised against the registration of a domain name constituting the name of a fictional character that is protected as a trade or service mark under the 'proof of concept' .name Eligibility Requirements Dispute Resolution Policy.[239] As another pre-New gTLD Program example, defensive registrations made in the .pro gTLD on the basis of the existence of a trade or service mark can be challenged pursuant to an Intellectual Property Defensive Registration Challenge Policy.[240] These policies complement, without limiting the application of, the UDRP.

As noted in the discussion of sunrise registration procedures earlier in this chapter, proof of the existence of a trademark was a cornerstone of sunrise eligibility in several of the new gTLDs created by the two 'proof of concept' expansion rounds. Of those, all four in which the trademark sunrise application resulted in a live (rather than defensive) registration, .asia, .info, .mobi and .tel, provided procedures for challenging sunrise eligibility decisions.[241]

---

235. The DotASIA Organisation, *.ASIA Charter Eligibility Requirement Policies*, http://www.dot.asia/policies/DotAsia-Charter-Eligibility--COMPLETE-2007-08-15.pdf (15 Aug. 2007).

236. ICANN, *Restrictions Dispute Resolution Policy*, at https://www.icann.org/resources/pages/rdrp-2012-02-25-en. This policy provides for challenges to a domain name on the ground that it is not being and will not be used primarily for bona fide business or commercial purposes. Lindsay, 121.

237. Fundació.cat, *Normativa del domini.cat*, http://fundacio.cat/ca/domini/sobre-el-cat/normativa. Lindsay, 121.

238. ICANN, *Qualification Challenge Policy*, https://www.icann.org/resources/pages/proqcp-2012-02-25-en. Lindsay, 121.

239. ICANN, *Eligibility Requirements Dispute Resolution Policy*, https://www.icann.org/resources/pages/erdrp-2012-02-25-en. Lindsay, 121.

240. ICANN, *Intellectual Property Defensive Registration Challenge Policy*, https://www.icann.org/resources/pages/ipdrcp-2012-02-25-en. Lindsay, 122.

241. These rules are no longer posted by.INFO, but information is available at WIPO, *WIPO Arbitration and Mediation Center - Domain Name Disputes (New gTLDs: WIPO Guide to the Afilias Sunrise Registration Challenge Policy for .info,* http://www.wipo.int/amc

The Implementation Recommendation Team recommended that all new gTLDs utilizing a sunrise procedure be required to adopt a standardized procedure that incorporates a related dispute resolution policy with a minimum four grounds of challenge.[242] The ICANN Board-approved *gTLD Applicant Guidebook* incorporates and slightly expands the IRT's recommended grounds to include challenge on the basis of registrations of regional effect, and marks that are 'court-validated or protected by statute or treaty'.[243] While the door is open to New gTLD Program registries to adopt detailed eligibility policies with built-in pre-registration scrutiny processes, the existing trend of delaying the availability of challenge mechanisms until after a contested domain name has been registered facilitates unencumbered registration, and thus more rapid growth of a new domain.

3.3.5 *Ex Post* Challenges Against Registry Operators

All of the *ex post* rights recognition mechanisms described to this point in this chapter are targeted at the actions of second-level domain name registrants, but one should not discount the effect that the actions or inactions of registrars and, higher up the DNS chain, registries have upon their registrants' ability to misuse the system. WIPO has for some time 'strongly advocated'[244] the adoption of an *ex post* administrative procedure to challenge the actions of registries that facilitate, countenance or advocate

/en/domains/gtld/info/sunrise/guide.html; The DotASIA Organisation, *DotAsia Sunrise Challenge Policy,* http://www.dot.asia/draft/DotAsia-Sunrise-Challenge--DRAFT.pdf (effective 31 Oct. 2007); WIPO, *WIPO End Report on Case Administration under the Sunrise Challenge Policy for .mobi and the Premium Name Trademark Application Rules for .mobi*, http://www.wipo.int/amc/en/domains/reports/mobi/report/index.html; Domein Registreren, *.tel Sunrise Terms & Conditions*.

242. The four grounds, as set out in the IRT Final Report (at 23–24) are as follows:
    - at the time the challenged domain was registered, the domain name registrant did not own a trademark registration of national effect;
    - the domain name is not identical to the trademark on which the domain name registrant based its Sunrise registration;
    - the trademark registration on which the domain name registrant based its Sunrise registration is not of national effect; and
    - the trademark registration on which the domain name registrant based its Sunrise registration did not issue on or before [the date of the Registry Agreement] and was not applied for on or before [the date that ICANN publishes the list of applications received in the round].

243. ICANN, *gTLD Applicant Guidebook*, at Trademark Clearinghouse, clause 6.2.4. *See also* n. 130 above in this chapter.

244. Letter from WIPO to ICANN regarding Proposed New gTLDs Procedure (13 Mar. 2009) (available at http://www.wipo.int/export/sites/www/amc/en/docs/icann130309.pdf).

their registrants' cybersquatting activities. Both WIPO and ICANN's Implementation Recommendation Team have deemed such a measure a necessary component of a broader rights protection strategy in the DNS.[245]

With the introduction of open and uncapped expansion at the top-level, the dynamics of the DNS and the nature of roles within it are changing. The pre-New gTLD Program state of remoteness between registries and registrants depicted in Figure 3.1 at the start of section 3.3 of this chapter can be replaced by a much closer relationship; an obvious example is a .brand TLD, where a company is both contracted to ICANN as a gTLD registry operator and is only domain name registrant in the TLD. This is made possible by the ICANN Board of Directors' decision[246] to end the policy of forced separation of registries and registrars, and implemented specifically in relation to .brand new gTLDs through Specification 13 to the Registry Agreement. This optional late-stage addition to the agreement exempts .brand registry operators from restrictions against, *inter alia*, registering domain names in their own right.[247]

The changing roles and relationships brought about by these new policies hold registries more accountable than has previously been the case. The ICANN Board-approved version of the *gTLD Applicant Guidebook* includes, for example, a Trademark Post-Delegation Dispute Resolution Procedure (or 'Trademark PDDRP')[248] that targets the harm caused to a trademark by a registry's affirmative conduct in its operation or use of a gTLD string or its affirmative bad faith conduct as regards domain name registrants within the registry. These grounds are closely aligned with classic intellectual property infringement doctrines. Following the general pattern of other rights protection mechanisms in the *gTLD Applicant Guidebook*, the Trademark PDDRP protects only trademarks that are registered, court-validated or 'specifically protected by a statute or treaty at the time the PDDRP complaint is filed'.[249] As of November 2016, the Trademark PDDRP had not yet been utilized.

Another *ex post* dispute resolution mechanism developed after the New gTLD Program applications process closed and implemented through the base New gTLD Registry Agreement is the Public Interest Commitment Dispute Resolution Procedure at Specification 11 of the Registry

245. *Id.*, 3 ('Without such a procedure, we believe it will be difficult to ensure adequate and ongoing protection of intellectual property rights … .'); IRT, *Final Report,* 38.
246. ICANN, *Board of Directors Resolution 2010.11.05.02: New gTLDs Cross-Ownership Issues for Registries and Registrars*, http://www.icann.org/en/minutes/resolutions-05nov10-en.htm (5 Nov. 2010).
247. *See for example, .aarp Registry Agreement: Specification 13 .BRAND TLD Provisions*, https://www.icann.org/sites/default/files/tlds/aarp/aarp-spec13-21may15-en.pdf (21 May 2015).
248. ICANN, *gTLD Applicant Guidebook,* at Trademark PDDRP.
249. *Id.*, at Trademark PDDRP, s. 9.2.1.

Agreement.[250] This procedure is actionable by those harmed by a registry's failure to comply with its Public Interest Commitments (commonly referred to as 'PICs') to ICANN.[251] PICs facilitate enforcement of general commitments relating to security and prevention of harm and specific commitments made in new gTLD applications by incorporating these into the Registry Agreement. An example is the new .airforce gTLD Registry Agreement, which incorporates a PIC binding the registry to, *inter alia*, 'operating an "open" registry where no restrictions shall be placed on registrant's eligibility to register a .airforce web address for legitimate and lawful purposes', implementing a Domain Protected Marks List, and placing restrictions on the use of privacy/proxy services.[252] Specification 11 thus provides a potential vehicle for capturing and enforcing throughout the life of the TLD commitments to recognize legal rights in non-trademark (including geographic) names.

3.4 CONCLUSIONS AND CATEGORIZATION

3.4.1 Conclusions on Existing Rights Protection Mechanisms in DNS Policy

Having considered the various rights protection mechanisms that have been utilized up to and including the New gTLD Program, it is clear that much of the effort in and attention to the recognition of legal rights in names in the DNS to date has focused on trademark rights. Only ICANN-mandated reservation from domain name registration currently offers any protection to non-trademark geographic names against unauthorized registration as a domain name, but the ad hoc approach taken there to date risks an unpredictable, imprecise approach that may deter future new gTLD applicants.[253] This is clearly seen in the New gTLD Program application conflicts highlighted at the end of Chapter 1. Discontinuation of the reliance on reservations has appropriately been recommended out of concern for a lack of support under international law.

Yet in most cases there is no reason why existing mechanisms could not be used to protect non-trademark rights in the DNS to the extent that these rights are legally recognized. Issues of authentication and validation may arise, but these should not be considered insurmountable obstacles. On the

250. ICANN, *Public Interest Commitment Dispute Resolution Procedure*, https://newgtlds.icann.org/en/applicants/agb/picdrp-19dec13-en.pdf (19 Dec. 2013).
251. *Id.*, clause 1.1.
252. ICANN, *New gTLD Agreement Specifications AIRFORCE: Specification 11 Public Interest Commitments*, https://gtldresult.icann.org/application-result/applicationstatus/applicationdetails:downloadpicposting/1109?t:ac=1109.
253. *See generally*, Forrest, *Domain Name Allocation and Government Super-Prioritization.*

other hand, to the extent that it is determined through this study that rights do not exist in geographic names, then changes to reflect such rights in DNS rights protection policy are not required.

3.4.2 Categorization of the DNS: A Solution to Rights Protection Problems?

DNS rights protection mechanisms (which would in fact be more accurately referred to as 'DNS *trademark* protection mechanisms', given their focus to date on trademark rights) have been implemented to address two chief concerns. These are – not coincidentally – reflective of the twin aims of trademark law: on the one hand, limiting unfair commercial behaviour, and on the other, preventing consumer confusion. The way that the public has come to blend in its mind 'offline' brands and 'online' domain names, and to depend on domain names as a navigational aid (an outcome unintended by the DNS's architects) has served to increase the likelihood of their confusion.

One possible solution to the twin problems of users not being able to find what they are looking for and legal rights being infringed is categorization at the top-level of the DNS. The imposition of set categories of use or user as top-level domains would have clearly structured the system, making it easier to access known addresses or locate unknown addresses while at the same time preventing duplication.[254] Users would know to look for Ford, Volvo and Ferrari in a .cars gTLD, for example, but could reasonably expect that a 'ford' in another non-automobile-related gTLD was not related to the Ford Motor Company.

The counter argument is that the forced expansion of the DNS through a structured, top-down approach may not reflect the market's needs or adequately serve all of the members of the global internet community in the way that an unregulated, applicant-driven name selection process can.[255] Nor is categorization the only way to prevent duplication within the system; restrictions on the delegation of confusingly similar names illustrate how this can otherwise be achieved. For these reasons and more, calls to impose such a rigid topography upon the DNS have been rejected since the system's early days.

Although categorization may not be a practicable overarching solution to the problem of user confusion, it could have, in a specific context made some inroads while also limiting abuse of rights in names. That specific context is a trademark-only TLD space, which could have taken shape in at least three different ways, as illustrated by Figure 3.2. As proposed more than a decade ago by the pre-ICANN International Ad Hoc Committee ('IAHC'),

254. On categorization, *see* Litman, *The DNS Wars*, 9.
255. CSTB, 240–241.

a branded space could also be designated at the second level within an existing gTLD or ccTLDs.[256]

Figure 3.2 Trademark Domain Options

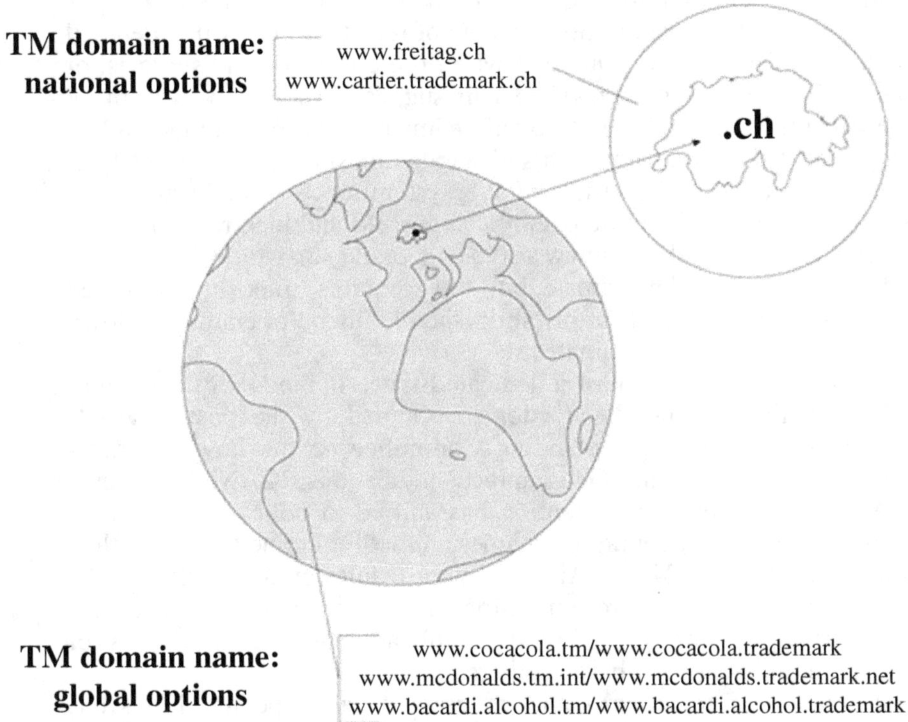

Registration in a national trademark domain could easily reflect the rights recorded in a national trademark register, while registration in a global trademark domain could, although more controversially and conceptually difficult to implement, have the appearance of a global trademark registration register. Either could save the internet user from having to guess the TLD string in a domain name, but for those consumers who use a domain name to search for unknown information sources, their potential confusion is likely only shifted down a level in the DNS hierarchy. Nor is it clear how any of these model names, of which the global in particular, would have handled the potentially high volume of confusingly similar names. It bears noting that the

256. In 1997, the IAHC proposed the creation of seven new broadly categorical gTLDs: .arts, .firm, .info, .nom, .rec, .store and .web. The IAHC's proposal was made at a time of great flux in the DNS, coterminous with the US Government's release of the Green and White Papers. The ultimate decision to create ICANN and bestow upon it policy making authority in respect of DNS development resulted in no further action being taken on the IAHC report. IAHC, *Final Report*.

.tm domain already exists as the country code of Turkmenistan, but attempts to attract global trademark holders as domain name registrants have not been overwhelmingly successful.

More than a decade ago, the IAHC suggested that 'each trademark owner should be entitled to a unique domain name which contains its trademark, even if there are multiple owners of registrations for the identical trademark (e.g., for use in conjunction with different goods and services, or registrations in different countries).'[257] This suggestion was, however, made at a time when the total volume of domain name registrations numbered less than 1 million;[258] the feasibility of this idea today must be questioned in light of the exponential growth and use of the system since then. Further, this suggestion implies that the more deeply categorized and hierarchical names (e.g., www.burberry.tm.uk or www.volvo.cars.brand.se) would have functioned better than broader names, but this requires imposing a forced taxonomy in lower levels and simply shifts the likelihood of confusion down to those levels rather than eliminates it.

Proposals for the creation of a dedicated space in the DNS for country names[259] have likewise not been adopted. Guided by the post-WIPO II special sessions of the WIPO Standing Committee on the Law of Trademarks, Industrial Designs and Geographical Indications, ICANN's Governmental Advisory Committee's attention has shifted to policy to reserve or block registrations of geographic names, broadly defined, rather than quarantine them in the DNS.[260] An equivalent result could nevertheless be procedurally achieved in future expansion initiatives without the need for express reservations simply by inviting applications for certain types of strings (i.e., .brands or .geos before others).

The creation of trademark- and geographic name-specific TLDs has never progressed beyond speculative discussion. With the open and uncapped nature of the New gTLD Program, the idea of a TLD space limited to brands ceded to brand-specific new gTLDs (e.g., a new .volvo gTLD instead of a volvo.brand, volvo.tm or volvo.trademark). The principal difference between the New gTLD Program approach and that of the two previous 'proof of concept' rounds is that the global internet community is truly now able to decide which gTLDs it wants added to the root; rejection

257. *Id.*, 8.2.

258. Robert Hobbes Zakon, *Hobbes' Internet Timeline Version 10.1*, http://zakon.org/robert/internet/timeline/#Growth (last updated 15 Dec. 2010) (reporting the total number of domains at January 1997 as 828,000).

259. ICANN, *Board of Directors Resolution 02.44*, https://www.icann.org/resources/board-material/minutes-2002-03-14-en (14 Mar. 2002).

260. GAC, GAC Working Group to Examine the Protection of Geographic Names in Any Future Expansion of gTLDs: Working Papers (https://gacweb.icann.org/display/gacweb/GAC+Working+Group+to+Examine+the+Protection+of+Geographic+Names+in+any+Future+Expansion+of+gTLDs?preview=/39944662/41944013/GAC%20Geo-names%20WG%20-%20Working%20Papers%20.pdf (27 Jun. 2016).

of imposed categorization has finally been put to the test. Time will tell which new gTLDs succeed and which fail, and with more than 1,000 diverse New gTLD Program new gTLDs in the root, failure of a TLD for the first time in the DNS's history is not simply an abstract and unlikely possibility, but an eventual certainty.

To the extent that we accept as a fundamental principle that offline rights warrant recognition in the online environment, this will continue to impose certain limitations on a fully free market approach to expanding the DNS. This basic premise lies at the heart of the recommendation of the GNSO, the ICANN body charged with developing gTLD policy, against the creation of new top-level domains that 'infringe the existing legal rights of others that are recognized or enforceable under generally accepted and internationally recognized principles of law.'[261] As a first step, therefore, it must be determined *whether rights in geographic names are even recognized in international law*. This is the task taken up in Part III of this book. Before delving into that analysis, there is one more foundational step: identification of the international legal framework that underpins the exposition of rights in names under international law. This is undertaken in the next chapter.

261. GNSO, *Final Report on the Introduction of New Generic Top-Level Domains*, Recommendation 3.

Chapter 4

Legal Framework for Challenging Assumptions of Rights in Geographic Names

[R]ights cannot be presumed to exist merely because it might seem desirable that they should ... .[1]

4.1 FITTING RIGHTS IN GEOGRAPHIC NAMES INTO THE INTERNATIONAL LAW FRAMEWORK

4.1.1 LEGAL RIGHTS IN GEOGRAPHIC NAMES: AN UNANSWERED QUESTION

The previous chapters establish the context of this book by identifying how legal rights have been recognized and protected in DNS policy in the past and are now being assumed. This chapter explores the framework of international law and seeks to establish how that framework should be employed to determine whether legal rights in geographic names are recognized such that they should be accounted for in DNS policy. This question of rights in geographic names and their recognition in international law has gone unanswered for some time. It was notably on the agenda of the

1. *South West Africa Cases (Ethiopia v. South Africa; Liberia v. South Africa) (Second Phase)*, 4 I.C.J. 48, para. 91 (I.C.J. 1966).

1980 Diplomatic Conference for the Review of the Paris Convention,[2] but no changes to the Paris Convention ultimately resulted from those discussions. It took the introduction of the DNS a few years later to transform what may have been said previously to be a largely theoretical question into a live dispute. WIPO considered the registration and use of geographic domain names an area of concern in its 1999 Report of the First Internet Domain Name Process ('WIPO I').[3] As a result, geographic names and other forms of non-trademark names were deemed to warrant further investigation in a Second Internet Domain Name Process ('WIPO II'). In 2001, the WIPO II Report confirmed the existence of (and characterized as problematic) the practice of registering geographic names and geographical indications as second- and third-level domain names 'by persons who might be considered not to be properly entitled to use the identifiers in question'.[4]

A significant conclusion of the WIPO II Report was that international law fell short of offering support for governments' assertions of exclusive or priority rights in geographic names to prevent their use by others as domain names. In particular, the TRIPS Agreement, which is the principal international treaty recognizing IPRs, and the suite of intellectual property treaties it incorporates,[5] were found lacking.[6] This conclusion has subsequently been supported by commentators[7] and relied upon by an ICANN policy development process.[8] The WIPO II Report is not, however, conclusive as to the question of rights in geographic names under international law. Its focus on rights in the nature of intellectual property leaves unexplored other legal bases of rights. Further, its apparent focus on rights derived from international treaties leaves unexplored other likewise authoritative sources of international law.

The study documented in this book fills those gaps while also expanding the scope of the question to the top-level of the DNS. The New

2. WIPO Diplomatic Conference on the Revision of the Paris Convention, Doc PR/DC/4, 30 Aug. 1979 (available at http://www.wipo.int/mdocsarchives/PR_DC_1%20to%2020_1980/PR_DC_4_E.pdf).
3. WIPO, *WIPO I Report*, Executive Summary (b) page (viii).
4. WIPO, *WIPO II Report*, vi.
5. Berne Convention for the Protection of Literary and Artistic Works (9 Sep. 1886), 828 U.N.T.S. 221; Paris Convention for the Protection of Industrial Property (20 Mar. 1883, last revised 14 Jul. 1967 and as amended 28 Sep. 1979), 828 U.N.T.S. 305; International Convention for the Protection of Performers, Producers of Phonograms and Broadcasting Organisations (26 Oct. 1961, entered into force 18 May 1964), 496 U.N.T.S. 43; Treaty on Intellectual Property in Respect of Integrated Circuits (26 May 1989), 28 I.L.M. 1477.
6. WIPO, *WIPO II Report*, paras 239–243.
7. *See for example*, Milton L. Mueller, Speech, *Governments and Country Names: ICANN's Transformation into an Intergovernmental Regime* (Pacific Telecommunication Council, January 2002); A. Michael Froomkin, *When We Say US™, We Mean It!*, 41 Houston L. Rev. 839 (2004–2005).
8. *See* above Part II, Chapter 3, nn. 34 and 35, and accompanying discussion on the GNSO Reserved Names Working Group.

gTLD Program invites and necessitates these expansions in the ICANN community's thinking. Thus each of the chapters in Part III explores a different basis of rights under international law in respect of which the full range of 'sources' of international law is considered. Before embarking on that analysis, however, fundamental questions such as why and how international law is relevant to this enquiry must be answered.

4.1.2 Why International Law?

ICANN is itself responsible for the relevance of international law to this study, not because it is itself a subject of international law (this issue is explored in-depth later in this chapter in the context of the role of non-State actors) but rather because its Board of Directors resolved[9] upon launching the New gTLD Program in June 2008 to adopt the recommendations of the Generic Names Supporting Organization, amongst which Recommendation 3:

> Strings must not infringe the existing legal rights of others that are recognized or enforceable under generally accepted and internationally recognized principles of law.
>
> Examples of these legal rights that are internationally recognized include, but are not limited to, rights defined in the Paris Convention for the Protection of Industrial Property (in particular trademark rights), the Universal Declaration of Human Rights (UDHR) and the International Covenant on Civil and Political Rights (ICCPR) (in particular freedom of expression rights).[10]

By adopting Recommendation 3, the Board of Directors effectively undertook to ensure that ICANN policy and procedures respecting the creation and delegation of new gTLD strings, which are set out in the *gTLD Applicant Guidebook*, are consistent with international law's recognition of rights in the names applied for as gTLD strings. This, it is worth emphasizing, is not something ICANN would otherwise be obliged to do: the *gTLD Applicant Guidebook* creates a private contractual relationship between ICANN and gTLD applicants. That ICANN should undertake to ensure that new gTLD strings not infringe the existing rights of others under international law is nevertheless not entirely surprising, given the unique circumstances (as described in Chapter 2) in which ICANN was created, its organizational structure, and its mandate to 'operate for the benefit of the Internet

9. ICANN, *Board of Directors Resolution 2008.06.26.02*.
10. GNSO, *Final Report on the Introduction of New Generic Top-Level Domains*.

community as a whole, carrying out its activities in conformity with relevant principles of international law and applicable international conventions … .'[11]

Having undertaken to ensure that new gTLD strings do not infringe rights recognized under international law, it is appropriate to consider whether ICANN has achieved this in the *gTLD Applicant Guidebook*, the instrument that encapsulates new gTLD policy. An immediate concern arises when one turns to the treatment of geographic names. Priority rights are extended to governments such that new gTLD applicants are prevented from applying for:

- new top-level domains comprising country and territory names; and
- other geographic names without the consent of relevant governments.

Is this protection of geographic names in new gTLD policy consistent with the recognition of rights in geographic names under international law, and thus GNSO Recommendation 3? This question lies at the heart of this study and is the focus of Part III of this book, which is comprised of Chapters 5, 6, 7, 8 and 9. Each chapter addresses a potential basis of legal rights in geographic names: intellectual property, rights of statehood, rights in geographical indications, unfair competition and related commercially derived rights, and finally, human rights.

To the extent that it is revealed that ICANN's treatment of geographic names is inconsistent with rights afforded (or not) under any of these bases, it will be relevant to question as a next step the extent to which ICANN could be compelled, if it is not otherwise willing, to modify its private agreements accordingly. Pressure from the global internet community may prove sufficient to motivate it to do so voluntarily. Counter to this is the inevitable pressure from the Governmental Advisory Committee ('GAC'), which throughout New gTLD Program policy development and implementation seemingly conditioned continued willingness to respect ICANN's authority in DNS policy development on Board deference to GAC positions. As policy development gets underway for a continuation of the New gTLD Program, certain GAC members have expressed desires for even greater levels of protection for geographic names than the *gTLD Applicant Guidebook* currently offers.[12] Part III of this book reveals that achieving this will either require change in international law to conform even to the *gTLD Applicant*

11. ICANN, *Bylaws for Internet Corporation for Assigned Names and Numbers (As amended 1 October 2016)*, s. 1.2(a), https://www.icann.org/resources/pages/governance/bylaws-en.

12. *See for example*, GAC, *GAC Indicative Scorecard on New gTLD Outstanding Issues Listed in the GAC Cartagena Communiqué*, http://www.icann.org/en/topics/new-gtlds/gac-scorecard-23feb11-en.pdf (23 Feb. 2011) (hereinafter '*GAC indicative scorecard*'). Letter from Janis Karklins, Governmental Advisory Committee Chairman to Paul Twomey, ICANN CEO and President (26 May 2009) (available at http://www.icann.org/en/correspondence/karklins-to-twomey-26may09-en.pdf).

Guidebook status quo, or change in the *gTLD Applicant Guidebook* to conform to the legal status quo.

4.1.3 Accountability of an Independent ICANN

Before the New gTLD Program, the answer to the question of whether ICANN could be compelled to change its policy on new gTLDs depended on ICANN's accountability under the laws of the state of its incorporation and its contractual relationship with the US government. Post-New gTLD Program, the situation has changed, although only tangentially (if at all) because of the New gTLD Program itself. In 2014, in response to another wave of foreign government discontent with the US government's controlling role in the internet, the National Telecommunications and Information Agency of the US Department of Commerce announced the US government's intention to end its agreement with ICANN, leaving ICANN an independent entity with sole responsibility for the various technical and policy functions underpinning the DNS's operation.[13] Under the agreement in place at that point, the Affirmation of Commitments (often represented in writing as the 'AoC'), ICANN was accountable for 'ensur[ing] as it contemplates expanding the top-level space, the various issues that are involved (including competition, consumer protection, security, stability and resiliency, malicious abuse issues, sovereignty concerns, and rights protection) will be adequately addressed prior to implementation.'[14] A failure by ICANN to adequately address these in the *gTLD Applicant Guidebook* and its implementation could – at least in principle – have been deemed a breach of that contractual obligation.

The previous Memorandum of Understanding between the US Department of Commerce and ICANN provided for assignment to the Department of ICANN's rights under existing contracts with registries and registrars in the event that the Department 'withdraws its recognition of ICANN or any successor entity'.[15] Though the Affirmation of Commitments did not contain such a provision on breach, its contractual history is at least suggestive of an

---

13. National Telecommunications and Information Administration, *NTIA Announces Intent to Transition Key Internet Domain Name Functions*, https://www.ntia.doc.gov/press-release/2014/ntia-announces-intent-transition-key-internet-domain-name-functions (14 Mar. 2014).
14. US Department of Commerce and ICANN, *Affirmation of Commitments by the United States Department of Commerce and the Internet Corporation for Assigned Names and Numbers*, Art. 9.3, http://www.icann.org/en/documents/affirmation-of-commitments-30sep09-en.htm (30 Sep. 2009).
15. ICANN, *Amendment 1 to ICANN/DOC Memorandum of Understanding*, https://archive.icann.org/en/nsi/amend1-jpamou-04nov99.htm (approved 4 Nov. 1999, signed 10 Nov. 1999); ICANN, *Amendment 3 to ICANN/DOC Memorandum of Understanding*, https://www.icann.org/resources/unthemed-pages/amend3-jpamou-2001-05-25-en (entered 25 May 2001).

authority on the part of the US government to remove ICANN from its role. In line with this, just prior to the Board of Directors' decision to launch the New gTLD Program, ICANN's Senior Vice President for Stakeholder Relations made a point to defend ICANN's compliance with the Affirmation of Commitments before the House Subcommittee on Intellectual Property, Competition and the Internet.[16]

Even free of its contractual obligations to the US government, an independent ICANN may notably not be entirely beyond the reach of the US government: antitrust law could potentially be relied upon to justify intervention in ICANN contracts. This would be justifiable only to the extent that the *gTLD Applicant Guidebook* (i) intentionally impairs competition or (ii) denies access to an essential facility.[17] Beyond this, freedom of contract largely preserves ICANN's rights to dictate the terms of new gTLD creation and allocation. These issues lie beyond the scope of this work, but are identified here for deeper consideration elsewhere.

4.2 THE 'SOURCES' OF INTERNATIONAL LAW

4.2.1 The Process of Identifying International Law

The process of identifying the law on any given question is fraught with doctrinal disputes as to where and how one looks, how one addresses perceived biases, and indeed what one perceives the law to be. When dealing with laws respecting the internet, to these already challenging questions one must also add concerns about the multiplicity of levels of governance, jurisdictions and parties involved and the frequency and rapidity with which the technology itself changes. With all of this in mind, the approach taken in this study is guided by the questions to be answered, which seek first to

---

16. Testimony of Kurt Pritz, ICANN Senior Vice President, Stakeholder Relations, before the US House Committee on the Judiciary, Subcommittee on Intellectual Property, Competition and the Internet, Hearing on New Generic Top-Level Domains (gTLD) (4 May 2011) (available at https://www.gpo.gov/fdsys/pkg/CHRG-112shrg74251/html/CHRG-112shrg74251.htm.
); Letter from Kurt Pritz, ICANN Senior Vice President for Stakeholder Relations, to The Honorable Robert Goodlatte, US House of Representatives, *Response to Questions*.

17. *Morris Communications Corp. v. PGA Tour, Inc.*, 364 F.3d 1288 (11th Cir. 2004), *cert. denied*, *Morris Communications Corp. v. PGA Tour, Inc.*, 543 U.S. 919, 125 S.Ct. 87, 160 L.Ed.2d 203 (US Sup. Ct. 2004). On the essential facilities doctrine and its history in US antitrust law, *see* Robert Pitofsky et al., *The Essential Facilities Doctrine Under U.S. Antitrust Law*, 70 Antitrust L.J. 443 (2002). Reliance on the essential facilities doctrine is likely constrained, however, by the Supreme Court's decision in *Verizon Communications Inc. v. Law Offices of Curtis v. Trinko, LLP*, 540 U.S. 398, 410-411 (2004). *But see* Brett Frischmann & Spencer Weber Waller, *Revitalizing Essential Facilities*, 75 Antitrust L.J. 1, 8 (2008) (positing that the doctrine may yet have some application to the internet).

identify and then to apply the existing international legal framework to a particular situation, namely the DNS, and then to evaluate the effects of the application of that legal framework to this situation. These questions are expository in nature: they seek to identify and apply the law as an objective reality (*lex lata*), as opposed to how it could or should be (*lex ferenda*).

Expository studies in international law have traditionally tended towards a positivist approach, though the appropriateness of that approach in the context of the internet is justifiably questioned for reasons that will shortly be explained. In the early days of twentieth century international legal scholarship it was assumed that a positivist approach was the only one possible.[18] Positivism's reliance on the concepts of State and sovereignty align squarely with the questions posed in this study; these concepts lie at the heart of States' claims to rights in what they view as 'their' geographic names and their support of subnational governments' claims to rights in subnational geographic names. These claims are increasingly made in order to assert control over the use of geographic names in the online environment; in many cases they are clear and observable, and presumably in all cases voluntary. Positivism derives international law from such observable acts – and only from such observable acts. It presumes the development of norms arising out of independent States acting collectively and freely as evidenced by their having consented to rules or practices.[19] An exercise in the exposition of the rules of law, as is the aim of this study, is therefore one of the interpretation of States' expressions of consent.[20] This approach is exemplified by the judgment of the Permanent Court of International Justice ('PCIJ', predecessor of the International Court of Justice (hereinafter 'ICJ')) in the *Lotus* case:[21]

> International law governs relations between independent States. The rules of law binding upon States therefore emanate from their own free will as expressed in conventions or by usages generally accepted as expressing principles of law and established in order to regulate the relations between these co-existing independent communities or with a view to the achievement of common aims.

---

18. *See for example*, Lassa Oppenheim, *Science of International Law: Its Tasks and Method*, 2(2) Am. J. Int'l L. 313, 327 (1908) ('How is it possible to offer a body of firm, distinct, and clear-cut rules of law, if rules of morality and of religion, if political aspirations and chimerical schemes for a better future, are constantly mixed up with what is really law?'). For a recent expression of this view, *see* Karen Petroski, *Special Issue: The Many Fates of Legal Positivism – Is Post-Positivism Possible?*, 12 *German L. Rev.* 663 (2011).
19. Ian Brownlie, *Principles of Public International Law* 3–5 (7th ed., Oxford University Press 2008).
20. Bruno Simma & Andreas L. Paulus, *Symposium on Method in International Law, The Responsibility of Individuals for Human Rights Abuses in Internal Conflicts: A Positivist View*, 93(2) Am. J. Int'l L. 302, 304 (1999).
21. *The Case of the S.S. 'Lotus'*, Ser. A., no. 10, p. 18 P.C.I.J. 18 (P.C.I.J. 1927).

Yet the ways and places in which States are asserting themselves in respect of rights in geographic names and their exercise in the DNS often do not conform to the traditional positivist 'sources' of international law as enumerated in Article 38(1) of the Statute of the International Court of Justice[22] (hereinafter, the 'Statute of the ICJ'). Article 38(1) may be 'generally regarded as a complete statement'[23] of the sources of international law, but as is discussed in the next section of this chapter, resort to it exclusively demands discounting the vast majority of norm-generating acts and activities relating to the DNS and its development that do not fall within the formal sources of law described by Article 38(1). An answer to the question of whether international law recognizes rights in geographic names thus hinges less on the traditional inventory of international conventions, custom, general principles or judicial decisions and teachings than on the role that one attributes to so-called soft law and the actions of the intergovernmental and non-governmental organizations ('IGOs' and 'NGOs', respectively) most active in the internet domain name environment. In this way, this study highlights broader doctrinal questions about the formation and formalization of norms at the international level respecting the internet. The subsequent sections of this chapter set out the means by which international law respecting rights in geographic names can be identified, while exposing the challenges inherent in the exposition of international law when the underlying factual premise is the internet.

4.2.2 The 'Sources' of International Law

Article 38(1) of the Statute of the ICJ[24] provides a well-travelled starting point for any exposition of international law because it identifies the agreed upon ways in which States express consent to be bound to rules of the international community.[25] In this way, it codifies positivism's link between law and the observable, voluntary acts of States. Yet just as positivism has come under fire for not keeping up with the modern legal order by

22. Statute of the ICJ (26 Jun. 1945, entered into force 24 Oct. 1945), 3 Bevans 1179; 59 Stat. 1031; T.S. No. 993; 39 A.J.I.L. Supp. 215.
23. Brownlie, 5.
24. Article 38(1) The Court, whose function is to decide in accordance with international law such disputes as are submitted to it, shall apply:
    (a) international conventions, whether general or particular, establishing rules expressly recognized by the contesting states;
    (b) international custom, as evidence of a general practice accepted as law;
    (c) the general principles of law recognized by civilized nations;
    (d) subject to the provisions of Art. 59, judicial decisions and the teachings of the most highly qualified publicists of the various nations, as subsidiary means for the determination of rules of law.
25. Simma & Paulus, 304.

sociological schools of jurisprudence,[26] so has Article 38(1), with critics calling it 'dated and increasingly misleading'.[27] Nevertheless, there is reported to be broad consensus among contemporary legal scholars that Article 38(1) does at least 'contain a list of sources of international law, although perhaps not an exhaustive statement of such sources.'[28] It therefore serves this work as a starting – but not an ending – point in the exposition of international law recognizing rights in geographic names.

4.2.2.1 International Conventions

Of the 'sources' of international law set out Article 38(1) only the first, international conventions, has been comprehensively reported on in connection with rights in non-trademark names in the DNS. The WIPO II Report and the work of ICANN's policy development body, the GNSO, have focused in particular on the TRIPS Agreement and the Paris Convention for the Protection of Industrial Property, both of which expressly concern rights in names. A comprehensive evaluation of rights under these and other potentially relevant treaties in accordance with Articles 31 and 32 of the Vienna Convention on the Law of Treaties[29] is a logical starting point in an exposition of rights in names under international law, but should not be its boundary, because 'one cannot have a very coherent idea of the essence of international law by reading treaties alone.'[30]

Further, treaties' placement at the top of Article 38(1)'s list has been interpreted as not suggesting their supremacy over other sources.[31] While the other sources of law identified in Article 38(1) of the Statute of the ICJ are more dynamic and perhaps less immediately discernible evidence of States'

26. *See for example*, Siegfried Wiessner & Andrew R. Willard, *Symposium on Method in International Law, Policy-Oriented Jurisprudence and Human Rights Abuses in Internal Conflict: Toward a World Public Order of Human Dignity*, 93 Am. J. Int'l L. 316, 320 (1999). Wiessner and Willard remark that positivism's 'focus on "existing" rules, emanating solely from entities deemed equally "sovereign," does not properly reflect the reality of how law is made, applied and changed. Positivism remains fixated on the past, trying to reap from words laid down, irrespective of the context in which they were written, the solution to a problem that arises today or tomorrow in very different circumstances.'
27. Alan Boyle & Christine Chinkin, *The Making of International Law* 211 (Oxford University Press 2007). José E. Alvarez, *Positivism Regained, Nihilism Postponed*, 15 Michigan J. Int'l L. 747 (1994).
28. Andrew D. Mitchell, *Legal Principles in WTO Disputes* 19 (Cambridge University Press 2008). Gennadiĭ Mikhaĭlovich Danilenko, *Law-making in the international community* 31 (Martinus Nijhoff 1993).
29. Vienna Convention on the Law of Treaties (23 May 1969, entered into force 27 Jan. 1980), 1155 U.N.T.S. 331.
30. Martti Koskenniemi, *From Apology to Utopia: The Structure of International Legal Argument* 389 (Cambridge University Press 2005) quoting Clive Parry, *The Sources and Evidences of International Law* 34–35 (Manchester University Press 1965).
31. Brownlie, 5.

consent to be bound, they are nevertheless considered sources of international law. Given the conclusions of the WIPO II Report as to the inadequacy of existing treaty obligations respecting rights in geographic names, these other sources of law are highly relevant to this inquiry.

4.2.2.2 Customary International Law

Even without treaty recognition, to the extent that States in their practice honour each other's assertions of rights in 'their' respective geographic names out of a sense of legal obligation,[32] this can constitute customary international law. Yet challenges arise in identifying customary law respecting the internet and the DNS; this may explain why previous analyses of legal rights in geographic names and their use in the DNS have not specifically addressed custom. Certain of the four key elements in proving custom, namely the duration, uniformity and consistency, generality of the practice and *opinio juris et necessitatis*,[33] are difficult to prove in this context, leading some to doubt the likelihood of formation of customary international law of the internet.[34]

It is important to bear in mind, however, that while the internet gives rise to the questions posed in this study, the answer to those questions lies beyond the internet, seeking more generally to determine whether international law recognizes rights in geographic names. This is not a study of international internet law, but a study of international law. Rights in names are seemingly static, while the factual constellations in which those rights are asserted are seemingly dynamic. Some clarification is needed, however: rights in names derived from international conventions are static, but customary international law is based on practice, and practice necessarily changes as the environment in which actions are taken changes. This study reveals that the context in which actions are being taken as regards geographic names is primarily the highly dynamic environment of the internet. Even so, not all of the bases of legal rights analysed in this study suffer the difficulties of proving the existence of customary international law that will now be discussed.

4.2.2.2.1 Duration

Duration of State practice is difficult to prove in the DNS context because of the relatively short duration of the internet's existence and the dynamism of

---

32. James Leslie Brierly, *The Law of Nations: An Introduction to the International Law of Peace* 61 (6th ed. revised, Oxford University Press 1963); Brownlie, 6.
33. Brownlie, 8 (meaning States' compliance with practice out of a sense of legal obligation 'as opposed to motives of courtesy, fairness, or morality').
34. *See for example*, Rolf H. Weber, *Shaping Internet Governance: Regulatory Challenges* 15 (Schulthess Juristische Medien 2009).

its development – difficult but not impossible, as the ICJ has already determined as regards the law of the sea. In that context, the Court opined:[35]

> Although the passage of only a short period of time is not necessarily, or of itself, a bar to the formation of a new rule of customary international law on the basis of what was originally a purely conventional rule, an indispensable requirement would be that within the period in question, short though it might be, State practice, including that of States whose interests are specially affected, should have been both extensive and virtually uniform in the sense of the provision invoked … .

Yet a distinction can reasonably be made between the seas and the internet: the former changes on a planetary, evolutionary timescale, but the latter changes almost daily. So while it is theoretically possible for custom to develop in a short time, whether this is in practice possible in respect of the internet is questionable given the fact that the technology, the thing that the law attempts to define and manage, changes so rapidly and frequently that there may not be sufficient time to generate the requisite 'extensive' practice. On the other hand, the potential for custom to develop almost instantaneously (so-called instant custom), an idea originating in the context of outer space law,[36] is increasingly accepted by international law scholars.[37] This new thinking offers greater scope for the formation of an international customary law of the internet than would previously have been thought possible, though the dynamism of the environment means that instantly formed law might be practically relevant only for a short period of time.

4.2.2.2.2 Opinio Juris et Necessitatis

Even where instantaneous development of custom occurs, it is still required that this 'occurred in such a way as to show a general recognition that a rule of law or legal obligation is involved.'[38] It is not always clear that State practice in the internet environment is borne out of the observation of a legal obligation rather than technological or practical necessity. There is only one DNS root and only one entity in control of it; that entity, ICANN, is primarily responsible for setting the terms of the global internet public's use of that resource.[39] There may be only one way in which to achieve a particular

---

35. *North Sea Continental Shelf Cases (Federal Republic of Germany/Denmark; Federal Republic of Germany/Netherlands)*, I.C.J. 43 para. 74 (I.C.J. 1969).
36. Bin Cheng, *United Nations Resolutions on Outer Space: 'Instant' International Customary Law?*, 5 Indian J. Int'l L. 23 (1965).
37. *See for example*, Hiram E. Chodosh, *Neither Treaty nor Custom: The Emergence of Declarative International Law*, 26 Texas Int'l L.J. 87, 101 (1991) (declaring the requirement of long duration to be 'now practically a dead letter').
38. *North Sea Continental Shelf Cases*, 43.
39. On control of the root and ICANN's role, *see* Part I, Chapter 2, s. 2.2 above.

outcome, or where multiple ways are possible, perhaps only one is selected and implemented by ICANN. Alternate practice in such an environment is impossible. It is therefore difficult to say with certainty that actions arising out of such limited practical or technological options are taken on the basis of a sense of legal obligation.

4.2.2.2.3 *Uniformity and Consistency, and Generality*

The absence of practical or technical alternatives could, on the other hand, be said to contribute to the formation of customary international law in that this facilitates the requisite uniformity and consistency, and generality of practice. Some time is needed for this to occur, however, making it less likely to happen 'in such a lively and short-lived environment as cyberspace.'[40] Even where uniformity, consistency and generality are achieved, the practical consequence may be quite limited, again because of the highly dynamic environment of the internet. A particular practice, though uniform, consistent and general, may very quickly become obsolete as the technology itself or use of it changes. For example, a custom of States communicating by telegram in particular situations would certainly now be obsolete, perhaps replaced by a custom of communicating by fax or telex, which would likely have been replaced by email, which could quickly be replaced by a newer technology. Here again is a distinction between natural environments and cyberspace; in the former, practices are simply likely to transition to obsolescence at a slower pace.

The internet is not the first or only arena in which the law has struggled to keep pace with human development.[41] The operative question is whether internet technology is simply moving too much and too quickly to be captured by customary international law; in response it is posited that there may at least be scope for the application of more general customary rules to the internet.[42] In such a dynamic environment, uncrystallized, gestational norms assume a greater significance and force than they otherwise would. Some characterize this as the difference between 'hard' law and 'soft' law, although the latter term suffers (as do many core terms in the international law lexicon) from a lack of clear definition.[43] The topic of 'soft' law and the role that it plays in the recognition of rights in names is taken up in detail later in this chapter.

---

40. Weber, 15.
41. Thomas Cottier, *The Impact of New Technologies on Multilateral Trade Regulation and Governance*, 72 Chicago-Kent L. Rev. 415, 415–416 (1996).
42. Weber, 17.
43. Daniel Thürer, *Soft Law*, in *Max Planck Encyclopedia of Public International Law* para. 8 (Rüdiger Wolfrum ed., Oxford University Press 2010).

4.2.2.3 General Principles of Law

General principles of law are principles 'which can be derived from a comparison of the various systems of municipal law, and the extraction of such principles as appear to be shared by all, or a majority of them.'[44] As the use of the term 'general' implies, the quantitative aspect of what constitutes a general principle is somewhat flexible: 'universality is not a prerequisite', though it is 'equally clear that a single system of municipal law' is insufficient.[45] General principles become particularly relevant when there are no applicable international conventions or customs. In the context of rights in geographic names it has already been posited by WIPO that conventions are only of limited assistance; this immediately makes it more likely that general principles might be called upon in this study.

The way to elucidate general principles of international law is to conduct comparative studies across all or at least a majority of domestic legal orders in order to identify commonalities between them.[46] This has been done before the ICJ[47] but practically speaking, such studies are cumbersome. Alternatively, what tends to happen is that the task of validating the existence of a general principle falls to the Judges of the ICJ themselves, with the understanding that they were 'elected so as to ensure "the representation of the main forms of civilization and the principal legal systems of the world"',[48] and thus can be called upon to attest to the existence of a particular general principle in their home jurisdiction.

International law scholars point out that the ICJ has relied upon general principles in only a limited way,[49] and that general principles apply more often to procedural and interpretative matters than substantive issues. Yet the questions in this study are substantive in nature, seeking a general principle of international law recognizing an exclusive right of States to geographic names or, in the alternative, a right of others to geographic names that disproves an exclusive right of States to geographic names. Weighing against this is the argument that it is questionable whether general principles of international law can be the basis of exclusive substantive rights, bearing in mind that there is:

> a striking lack of evidence in international practice and jurisprudence of claims of a specific right of a concrete nature being asserted or upheld

---

44. Hugh Thirlway, *The Sources of International Law*, in *International Law* 109 (Malcom D. Evans ed., Oxford University Press 2010). F.A. Mann, *Reflections on a Commercial Law of Nations*, 33 British Y.B. Int'l L. 20, 36 (1957).
45. Mann, 38.
46. *Id.*, 37–40; Michel Virally, *The Sources of International Law*, in *Manual of Public International Law* 143–148 (Max Sorensen ed., Macmillan 1968).
47. *See for example*, *Right of Passage over Indian Territory (Portugal v. India)*, Merits Judgment I.C.J. Reports (I.C.J. 1960), discussed in Thirlway, 107–109.
48. Virally, 146, quoting Statute of the ICJ, Art. 9.
49. Brownlie, 17–18.

> on the basis simply of the general principles of law. It may be that such a phenomenon is inconsistent with the nature of such principles; in any event, this particular source of law is of less practical importance in determining the rights and obligations of States in their regular relations.[50]

These remarks suggest that general principles of this nature may have an ancillary status in this study, but where evidence is collected and readily available as to consistencies in the ways in which States recognize proprietary rights in geographic names, this is identified in each of the analytical chapters in Part III. Surveys conducted by WIPO regarding members' domestic protection of geographic names are instructive in this regard, as is the longstanding general attitude towards the registrability of geographic names as trademarks. These things are discussed in particular in Chapter 5, which explores the relationship between geographic names and IPRs, and Chapter 7, which examines the law relating to geographical indications.

Where it can be concluded in Part III that international law recognizes (by general principles of law or otherwise) rights of both States and non-State third parties in geographic names, as a next step it must logically be asked whether the exercise of States' rights conflicts with the recognized rights of others, and vice versa. The general principles of good faith and abuse of rights are relevant in this context. By acting on the provisions of ICANN's *gTLD Applicant Guidebook*, are, for example, States 'exercising a right either in a way which impedes the enjoyment by other States of their own rights or for an end different from that for which the right was created, to the injury of another State'?[51] By answering these questions, a complete picture of rights in geographic names can be drawn, addressing not only *whether such rights are recognized*, but also *whether they inhere exclusively or preferentially in States*, as has simply been assumed in ICANN's *gTLD Applicant Guidebook.*

4.2.3 The Role of 'Soft' Law

The difference between so-called soft law and the formal 'sources' of international law lies in soft law rules not being accepted as law by a generality of States. 'Soft' laws 'represent a form of international law, albeit a tentative and nascent one.'[52] The lack of a clear definition of 'soft' law is reflective of the problem of line-drawing:[53] it is certainly not so easy as

50. Thirlway, 109.
51. Alexandre Kiss, *Abuse of Rights*, in *Encyclopedia of Public International Law* vol. 1, 4 (R. Bernhardt ed., North-Holland 1992).
52. Chodosh, 90.
53. Thürer, para. 8.

declaring legal acts and instruments not falling within Article 38(1) of the Statute of the ICJ to be 'soft'. Rather:

> [T]he legal form is decisive: treaties that have entered into force are by definition hard law, at least for the parties. So are mandatory UN Security Council Resolutions adopted under Chapter VII of the UN Charter, because all UN member states have agreed to accept and carry out these decisions. ... The question is one of substance and intent; the label attached to the instrument is not decisive. Moreover, an agreement involving a state and another entity may be binding, even if it is not a treaty, so the distinction between hard and soft agreements is not simply synonymous with the distinction between treaties and other instruments. Furthermore, once soft law begins to interact with binding instruments its non-binding character may be lost or altered.[54]

With this in mind, certain essential characteristics can be attributed to 'soft' law: it is largely the product of international relations, so in addition to treaties, the activities of IGOs are relevant.[55] Though it is not a formal 'source' of international law, like those sources, 'soft' law is created by States, 'in contrast to commercial customs and rules such as codes of conduct set up by private organizations or companies.'[56] Because they cannot be traced to the formal 'sources' of international law, 'soft' law rules are not legally binding. They nevertheless may benefit from 'an element of good faith commitment, evidencing in some cases a desire to influence state practice or expressing some measure of law-making intention and progressive development.'[57]

As between treaty and 'soft' law (though treaties should not be assumed always to be 'hard' law[58]) where the subject matter of the law is highly dynamic as it is in internet context, 'soft' law may pose significant advantages over a treaty: the formation of 'soft' law rules need not follow particular procedural steps and they require no formal ratification.[59] This is particularly useful in highly dynamic areas in which there is uncertainty as to the future effects of technological development and other factors.[60] While 'soft' law rules may ultimately lead to the drafting and ratification of a treaty, they may be equally effective as non-binding normative standards of behaviour.

In the context of intellectual property norms at the international level, it is clear that the TRIPS Agreement and the suite of international

54. Boyle & Chinkin, 213 (internal citations omitted).
55. Thürer, para. 9.
56. *Ibid.* In light of this, the relevance of actions taken by ICANN is explored later in this chapter.
57. Boyle & Chinkin, 214.
58. *Id.*, 220.
59. *Id.*, 225.
60. Thürer, para. 6.

conventions it incorporates impose certain binding, 'hard' obligations upon signatories. That said, the reluctance and relative infrequency with which the intellectual property community has agreed upon and implemented amendments to the Paris Convention and the length of time devoted to negotiating treaty provisions respecting rights in, for example, geographical indications, cultural expressions and traditional knowledge underscore the difficulties in achieving consensus at a global level.[61] 'Soft' law instruments provide a potential means of overcoming these impasses, and they may do so in respect of rights in geographic names as well. 'Soft' law instruments do not obviate the need for consensus,[62] but they do remove the formal (if not the informal) pressure of adherence, and thus perhaps improve chances of achieving consensus.[63] It is likely for this reason that WIPO's efforts at regulating rights in the internet context have largely taken the form of non-binding guidelines, such as its ccTLD Best Practices for the Prevention and Resolution of Intellectual Property Disputes,[64] rather than amendments to the Paris Convention.

It is a core proposition of this study that an answer to the question of whether international law recognizes rights in geographic names ultimately depends upon the weight that one attributes to 'soft' law. Although a positivist approach aligns with States' claims to rights in geographic names based on State theory and the principle of sovereignty, a strict adherence to positivism would necessitate rejecting the normative effects of the non-binding acts and instruments which predominate in this area. In short, a strict positivist approach would remove much, if not most, of the expressions of consensus regarding the internet from the radar of consideration. Such a formal, rigid view of positivism cannot helpfully underpin scholarship of international law pertaining to rights and their protection in the DNS because it effectively reduces to a bare minimum the potential of there ever coming into being an international law of the internet. Technology is said to be moving too quickly for law to crystallize in custom, while States are reluctant to act in an area they still do not understand, in which they have law and policy-makers scattered across various government departments and portfolios, and about which they cannot adequately predict the longevity, utility or consequences of their formally binding actions. Furthermore, strict positivism would fail to acknowledge the significant role that informal mechanisms of protection such as the UDRP have already played in this context.

A less rigid view of positivism, one that accepts the formal sources of law as authoritative while acknowledging the role that freely and voluntarily made non-binding obligations have on normative behaviour, addresses this

61. Protection of geographical indications is discussed in Part III Chapter 7 and of cultural expressions and traditional knowledge in Chapter 9.
62. Boyle & Chinkin, 225.
63. Thürer, para. 6.
64. WIPO, *ccTLD Best Practices*.

problem. Such a view could draw the line (as undesirable as the activity of line-drawing may be) between *the law* and those things which are not yet *the law* but nevertheless impact upon the ways in which States and others behave. It would accept that changes in behaviour, while not themselves binding in a formal way, could ultimately influence the formal, observable, voluntary assertions of consensus by States needed to bring about a change in the law, or at the very least could identify gaps and insufficiencies in the law prompting the parties to devise means – binding or otherwise – to work around those insufficiencies. It is this less rigid notion of positivism that drives the legal analysis conducted in Part III of this book.

Support for this approach can be found emanating from the WTO Appellate Body, which in the *Shrimp-Turtle* [65] case looked beyond international conventions to non-binding resolutions when interpreting the term 'exhaustible natural resources' in Article XX(g) of the GATT.[66] In that case it was concluded that that term in question was dynamic and developing, 'to be read by a treaty interpreter in the light of contemporary concerns of the community of nations about the protection and conservation of the environment.'[67] A similar 'evolutionary' approach could be adopted in the interpretation of the TRIPS Agreement.[68] Had the Panel in the *Canada – Patent Protection of Pharmaceutical Products (Generic Medicines)* [69] utilized such an approach, it has been suggested,[70] a new balance could have been struck between rights holders and technology users.

Upsetting established balances is not inherently a bad thing, and the potential for doing so should not be a reason to ignore the many informal acts and instruments establishing norms in respect of the developing DNS. Put another way, to ignore the non-binding resolutions, reports, statements and guidelines emanating from States' participation in the multi-stakeholder environment that is the DNS, as it is presently governed, would be to ignore the context in which the law in fact operates, in which 'new concepts of private property rights'[71] and other non-property bases of legal rights are emerging alongside vast and rapid technological advances.

---

65. *United States – Import Prohibition of Certain Shrimp and Shrimp Products*, WT/DS58/AB/R, AB-1998-4 (W.T.O. D.S.B. App. Body 12 Oct. 1998) (available at http://www.wto.org/english/tratop_e/dispu_e/58abr.pdf).
66. General Agreement on Tariffs and Trade 1994 (15 Apr. 1994, entered into force 1 Jan. 1995), 1867 U.N.T.S. 187; 33 I.L.M. 1153.
67. *United States – Import Prohibition of Certain Shrimp and Shrimp Products*, para. 130.
68. Lawrence R. Helfer, *Regime Shifting: The TRIPS Agreement and New Dynamics of International Intellectual Property Lawmaking*, 29 Yale J. Int'l L. 1, 77 (2004).
69. *Canada – Patent Protection of Pharmaceutical Products (Generic Medicines)*,WT/DS114/R (W.T.O. D.S.B. Panel 17 Mar. 2000) (available at http://www.wto.org/english/tratop_e/dispu_e/cases_e/ds114_e.htm).
70. Robert Howse, *The Canadian Generic Medicines Panel: A Dangerous Precedent in Dangerous Times*, 3 J. World Int. Prop. 493 (2000).
71. Cottier, *The Impact of New Technologies on Multilateral Trade Regulation and Governance*, 425.

4.2.4 The Role of Non-State Actors in Generating Norms in the DNS

The internet has a tremendous levelling effect; it has broken down traditional barriers between content providers and users.[72] It could also be said that the internet, or more precisely its DNS, has served to break down a barrier between States and private actors, in that all are treated as equal competitors for scarce resources (domain names) in this global communications platform. The internet architects' devotion to cross-fertilization of ideas without regard to borders, reinforced by the privatization of the internet and the participation of non-State actors in its management and development, have created an environment in which reliance on the formal sources of international law is only so productive.

While international law has traditionally been a sphere reserved only for States, the internet serves as a clear example of an area of concern to States in which norm-setting activities have occurred largely at the fringes or outside of the sphere of direct State action. Where such activities would in the past not have been considered to have legal significance, contemporary scholars advise that a 'focus solely on state actions gives a misleading picture of international law-making. Account must also be taken of the role and influence in multilateral law-making of the state-based intergovernmental organizations (IGOs)'.[73] Given the role of the private sector in internet policy development, it is necessary also to be mindful of the role of the California public benefit non-profit corporation ICANN in DNS norm generation. ICANN's contribution is not legally equivalent to that of States or IGOs, nor is ICANN's function in creating new spaces in the DNS an unequivocally governmental one.[74] Nevertheless, ICANN itself is hugely significant in this unique multi-stakeholder model of governance.

Several key players in the setting of standards regarding rights in internet domain names have been identified in Chapter 2 in the discussion of the development of the DNS and its governance. ICANN and the WIPO feature most prominently, and within each, certain constituent or advisory bodies such as ICANN's Governmental Advisory Committee and Generic Names Supporting Organization, and WIPO's Standing Committee on the Law of Trademarks, Industrial Designs and Geographical Indications have particular influence and relevance to the recognition of rights in geographic

72. Nicholas Garnham, *Constraints on Multimedia Convergence*, in *Information and Communication Technologies: Visions and Realities* 104–106 (William H. Dutton ed., Oxford University Press 2001).
73. Boyle & Chinkin, 41. Malgosia Fitzmaurice, *Actors and Factors in the Evolution of Treaty Norms (An Empirical Study)*, 4 Austrian Rev. Int'l & Eur. L. 1, 12–13 (1999) (on the role in treaty-making of intergovernmental organizations as distinguished from the independent actions of States). *See generally*, José E. Alvarez, *International Organizations as Law-makers* (Oxford University Press 2005).
74. *See* below in this chapter at n. 98 and accompanying text.

names. The WTO is another relevant body by virtue of its role in intellectual property law-making through the TRIPS Agreement. There are certainly other organizations involved in the broader agendas of internet governance and technical standards-setting whose actions have an impact on internet technology and its use,[75] but detailed consideration of the impact of *all* non-State actors in the internet environment on the formation of international law respecting every facet of the technology would constitute a study unto itself. The intention here is rather to identify the principal non-State actors with direct involvement in norm generation respecting internet domain names, and to highlight the issues arising out of their involvement for bearing in mind in the identification and analysis of the law that follows in the remainder of this book.

4.2.4.1 World Intellectual Property Organization ('WIPO')

WIPO is a specialized agency of the UN. It administers the major international conventions respecting intellectual property (amongst which the Paris Convention for the Protection of Industrial Property). Its membership was comprised in 2016 of 189 States.[76] Its importance in the context of internet domain name standard-setting lies not in its status as an IGO or in its high membership numbers, but in its members' specific expertise.[77] In particular, members of the Standing Committee on the Law of Trademarks, Industrial Designs and Geographical Indications (hereinafter the 'WIPO Standing Committee') are key contributors to debates about internet domain names precisely because of their understanding of both the relevant law and technology.

From a law-making perspective, WIPO cannot itself amend the conventions it administers; rather, amendments must come through and from the convention parties themselves. Several of the conventions under its custody have been incorporated by reference into the TRIPS Agreement, which is a WTO agreement not administered by WIPO.[78] As will become evident in Chapter 6 in the context of Article 6*ter* of the Paris Convention, WIPO's Standing Committee and its General Assembly have been active in recent years in the area of geographic names and their use in the DNS. It must be noted from the outset, however, that their actions do not alone create new law: resolutions of the UN General Assembly 'do not ipso facto create new rules of customary law',[79] so this must surely also be the case for resolutions

75. Examples include the Internet Architecture Board (IAB), the Internet Engineering Task Force (IETF), and the Internet Governance Forum (IGF).
76. WIPO, *Member States*, http://www.wipo.int/members/en/.
77. Boyle & Chinkin, 125.
78. These conventions are identified above in this chapter at n. 5.
79. International Law Association Committee on Formation of Customary (General) International Law, *Statement of Principles Applicable to the Formation of General*

of specialized UN bodies such as WIPO.[80] This does not mean, however, that WIPO General Assembly resolutions have no bearing on the formation of customary international law. On the contrary:

> Resolutions of more restricted conferences may (in appropriate circumstances) provide rebuttable evidence of the opinions of their participants as to the content of existing customary law, or even help to create new particular customary law for those voting in favour; but the lack of generality of participation will prevent such resolutions from becoming general law (unless the participation is nevertheless sufficiently widespread and representative and/or subsequent practice widens the scope of the rule's recognition and application).[81]

The role of WIPO is in recent times said to be 'best understood as international standard-setting.'[82] Examples include its 'ccTLD Best Practices for the Prevention and Resolution of Intellectual Property Disputes'[83] and its assistance to ICANN in the drafting of the Uniform Domain Name Dispute Resolution Policy ('UDRP') and administration of UDRP disputes.[84] In fact, it can be observed that WIPO's role in international intellectual property law generally and internet domain names specifically has increased with its greater involvement in generating 'soft' law-type standards. These standards lack the binding force of international law, but they 'have found their way into TRIPS-plus bilateral agreements, opinions of national jurists, and proposals for formal WIPO treaties … .'[85]

It is not possible in many cases for the decisions of WIPO's General Assembly to crystallize into 'hard' law obligations respecting the DNS simply because DNS governance, currently in the hands of the private body ICANN, is outside of States' control. This is exemplified by the outcome of the two special sessions of the WIPO Standing Committee convened following the WIPO II Report,[86] the result of which was a recommendation

---

Customary International Law: Final Report of the Committee on Formation of Customary (General) International Law, s. 28 (2000).

80. *Id.* Part V Introductory Remarks, n. 144: '[G]iven that the UN is the only universal organization with a general remit, the contribution of such organizations will necessarily be more limited in any event. And in practice, instances seem hard to find.'
81. *Id.* s. 33 Comment (b).
82. Boyle & Chinkin, 125. *But see* Don MacLean, Speech, *Herding Schrödinger's Cats: Some Conceptual Tools for Thinking about Internet Governance* (ITU Workshop on Internet Governance, 26–27 Feb. 2004) (available at www.itu.int/osg/spu/forum/intgov 04/contributions/itu-workshop-feb-04-internet-governance-background.pdf) (characterizing WIPO as a purely 'hard' law contributor to this field).
83. WIPO, *ccTLD Best Practices for the Prevention and Resolution of Intellectual Property Disputes*.
84. The UDRP is discussed in detail in Part II, Chapter 3, 3.3.1, above.
85. Graeme B. Dinwoodie, *The International Intellectual Property Law System: New Actors, New Institutions, New Sources*, 98 Am. Soc. Int'l L. Proc. 213, 215 (2004).
86. WIPO, *First Special Session*; WIPO, *Second Special Session*.

made by WIPO's General Assembly to add country names to the scope of the UDRP.[87] This recommendation is problematic from a law-making perspective because it does not place an obligation on States; the UDRP is an ICANN policy that is incorporated into its private contracts with registries and registrars.[88] This logic applies not just to the UDRP, but to all of the IPRs protection mechanisms applicable to new gTLDs as provided for in the *gTLD Applicant Guidebook*.[89] It is likely with this in mind that WIPO's Standing Committee highlights[90] the need for support from ICANN.

4.2.4.2 World Trade Organization ('WTO')

The WTO plays an increasing role in international intellectual property norm-setting. The TRIPS Agreement, which forms an Annex to the Agreement Establishing the World Trade Organization, brought IPRs within the agenda of global trade and in so doing, into the realm of GATT/GATS ('General Agreement on Trade in Services') trade agreements. Less publicized but no less important in this regard is the cooperation agreement between WIPO and the WTO, which is said to be 'facilitating the incorporation of WIPO-created norms into the WTO process.'[91]

Like the World Intellectual Property Organization, the WTO is an intergovernmental organization responsible for a suite of international conventions. It has a large membership, with 164 members and 20 observer governments as of mid-2016.[92] The WTO must answer to the States that are its members and, like WIPO, it cannot undertake law-making activities other than through its members.[93] That said, the WTO arguably itself engages in law-making in two ways: '[f]irst, … it is in effect a regulatory agency. … Second, and very unusually for an international organisation, the WTO itself has exclusive compulsory jurisdiction over disputes arising under the relevant agreements (covered agreements).'[94] This is limited, however, by the fact that the Appellate Body's decisions can be overturned by the General Council or effectively overruled by the Ministerial Council.[95] The WTO's

87. WIPO Standing Committee on the Law of Trademarks, Industrial Designs and Geographical Indications, *Report of the Ninth Session, Geneva, November 11 to 15, 2002*, WIPO Doc. SCT/9/9, para. 149.
88. ICANN's contractual relationships are illustrated in Figure 3.1.
89. The scope of the UDRP is discussed in Part II, Chapter 3, s. 3.3.1.2, above.
90. WIPO, *First Special Session*, para. 36.
91. Dinwoodie, 215.
92. WTO, *Understanding the WTO: The Organization, Members and Observers, 164 members since 29 July 2016 (with dates of membership)*, https://www.wto.org/english/thewto_e/whatis_e/tif_e/org6_e.htm.
93. Boyle & Chinkin, 135 (noting that '[l]ike other such [intergovernmental] organisations, it has an influential secretariat, but it is in no sense an autonomous regulatory or law-making body').
94. *Id.*, at 135–136.
95. *Id.*, 125.

law-making capacity in the context of rights in internet domain names is further limited from a practical perspective by the unlikelihood that a dispute, even if falling within the covered agreements, would be raised before the Dispute Settlement Body. Past practice in this regard is instructive; to date, disputes over internet domain names have been addressed through ICANN's contract-based UDRP, the Bylaws-based Independent Review Process,[96] and domestic courts, not through the WTO agreements and the Dispute Settlement Body.

The Doha Ministerial Conference of November, 2001 is relevant to the discussion of rights in geographic names insofar as it returned provisions of the TRIPS Agreement respecting the international protection of geographical indications to the forefront of the global trade negotiations agenda. Two particular issues were raised: first, an international notification system for wines and spirits, which has lingered on the global trade agenda since 1998, and second, extension of the higher level protection currently afforded wines under the TRIPS Agreement to non-wine products, on the agenda since 2000. The status of these discussions and their impact upon the recognition of rights at the international level in geographical indications are discussed in detail in Chapter 7.

4.2.4.3 Internet Corporation for Assigned Names and Numbers ('ICANN')

In terms of international law-making capacity, ICANN cannot be understood as an equal of the World Intellectual Property Organization and the World Trade Organization. Unlike those organizations, ICANN is a domestic corporation, not a treaty-based intergovernmental organization. Its exclusive authority in respect of the DNS could ultimately come to be seen to justify its being treated as a subject of international law in a manner similar to the 'functional international personality' of the International Committee of the Red Cross, but at this time ICANN's involvement in diplomatic relations is only nascent, and it lacks recognition in and authority to conclude any treaty.[97] These factors significantly distinguish ICANN from the International Committee of the Red Cross and its status in international law, and will likely continue to do so for the near future.

Arguments for ICANN's being a subject of international law by virtue of its having contractually assumed governmental authority from the US are blunted by the lapsing in September 2016 of the contractual relationship that underpinned ICANN's formation in 1999. Yet even prior to this catalytic point, it may have been difficult to argue that ICANN acted as or on behalf

---

96. An example is the Independent Review Process dispute raised by Amazon EU S.à.r.l., as discussed above in Part I, Chapter 1, s. 1.3.4.
97. Andrew Clapham, *Human Rights Obligations of Non-State Actors* 76 (Oxford University Press 2006).

of the US government in its oversight of top-level expansion of the DNS. First, there is the difficult question of whether expanding the DNS is a governmental function.[98] Second, the Affirmation of Commitments expressly attributed to ICANN policy-making authority in respect of new gTLDs, noting: 'Nothing in this document is an expression of support by DOC [the US Department of Commerce, the relevant agency of the US government responsible for ICANN's oversight] of any specific plan or proposal for the implementation of new generic top level domain names (gTLDs)'.[99] The US government's input into the process would thus be limited to its participation, as an equal alongside other governments, in ICANN's Governmental Advisory Committee; no superior authority would be wielded by virtue of the Memorandum of Understanding or Affirmation of Commitments. Further, the New gTLD Program was funded entirely by new gTLD applicants, not the US Department of Commerce or any other branch of US government.

Freed of its contractual relationship with the US government, ICANN's current legal accountability as a California non-profit public benefit corporation is derived solely from the laws of the state of its incorporation and applicable federal law. It is (at least for now) a private body, albeit one with an expressly global accountability;[100] revising ICANN's Bylaws in 2016 in anticipation of its privatization provided an opportunity to clarify and emphasize this unique responsibility.[101]

Since long before its transition to independence, and indeed before the launch of the New gTLD Program, ICANN has sought to avoid being characterized as an international law-making body:

> In fact, ICANN has generally denied its engagement in the governance of the Internet. For a long time, the organization positioned itself as a standards setting and technical coordination entity. This perception has been subject to harsh criticism, since it seems clear that important public policy choices are made within the entity. For example, ICANN's adding of new TLD's to the root does not only have technical implications, but also requires value choices.[102]

98. Clapham, 11 (arguing that 'it is now no longer clear what are the traditional functions of the state').
99. ICANN, *Affirmation of Commitments by the United States Department of Commerce and the Internet Corporation for Assigned Names and Numbers*, clause 5, https://www.icann.org/resources/pages/affirmation-of-commitments-2009-09-30-en (30 Sep. 2009).
100. Thomas M. Lenard & Lawrence J. White, *Improving ICANN's governance and accountability: A policy proposal*, 23(2) Info. Econ. & Pol'y 189 (2011).
101. ICANN, *Bylaws for Internet Corporation for Assigned Names and Numbers (As amended 1 October 2016)*, Art. 4 (Accountability and Review) and Art. 6 (Empowered Community), https://www.icann.org/resources/pages/governance/bylaws-en.
102. Weber, 61 (internal citations omitted). *See also* Mueller, *Governments and Country Names*, 10 (characterizing ICANN as 'a policy making structure that can create and destroy rights and interests as they intersect with the domain name system').

Certainly, the New gTLD Program offered fuel for the fire of these criticisms: the open, uncapped new gTLD expansion program influenced at all stages by public comments effectively allowed ICANN to mask far-reaching policy choices behind purely technical, administrative and fiscal standards, giving the appearance of leaving the difficult policy choices to the global internet community. By grounding the entire New gTLD Program in contract, ICANN avoided 'making someone do something he does not choose to do or preventing him from doing what he wishes to do',[103] while also presumably attempting to avoid the spectre of regulatory action.[104]

ICANN's independence is likely to shift attention away from its role in international law through its relationship with one government, the US, and instead generate interest in ICANN's role in international law through the participation of all governments in its policy development. The independent ICANN's revised Bylaws leave unchanged the prohibition against government officials as members of the Board of Directors,[105] and also leave in place the internal advisory body, the Governmental Advisory Committee, whose members voluntarily represent their home countries. The official status and authority of members as representatives of their respective governments varies,[106] so while there is future potential for GAC activities to provide evidence of State attitudes on the matters before the group, it has to date been considered 'very hard to argue seriously that the GAC's view alone can state anything more than a snapshot of evolving practice, and this is certainly not now a hardened norm.'[107] Nothing in the new accountability structure of ICANN suggests that this will change in the near term.

As to its role in ICANN, the GAC is one of several internal groups advising the Board of Directors, which is not obliged to follow GAC advice. ICANN's revised post-independence Bylaws provide at Article 12.2(a):

> (x.) The advice of the Governmental Advisory Committee on public policy matters shall be duly taken into account, both in the formulation and adoption of policies. In the event that the Board determines to take an action that is not consistent with Governmental Advisory Committee advice, it shall so inform the Governmental Advisory Committee and state the reasons why it decided not to follow that advice. Any

---

103. David M. Lawrence, *Private Exercise of Governmental Power*, 61 Indiana L.J. 647, 648 (1985–1986).
104. *But see* A. Michael Froomkin, *Wrong Turn in Cyberspace: Using ICANN to route around the APA and the Constitution*, 50 Duke L.J. 17 (2000) (arguing that '[a]lthough the ICANN-DoC contracts speak of cooperation and research, some of the most significant outputs from ICANN are government regulation in all but name.'). On the IANA contract, *see* Milton Mueller, *NTIA Plays Chicken with the IANA Contract*, http://www.internetgovernance.org/2012/03/10/ntia-plays-chicken-with-the-iana-contract/ (10 Mar. 2012).
105. ICANN, *Bylaws (As amended 1 October 2016)*, Art. 7.4(a).
106. Froomkin, *When We Say US™, We Mean It!*, 862–863.
107. *Id.*, 866.

Governmental Advisory Committee advice approved by a full Governmental Advisory Committee consensus, understood to mean the practice of adopting decisions by general agreement in the absence of any formal objection ('GAC Consensus Advice'), may only be rejected by a vote of 60% of the Board, and the Governmental Advisory Committee and the ICANN Board will then try, in good faith and in a timely and efficient manner, to find a mutually acceptable solution.

(xi) If no such solution can be found, the Board will state in its final decision the reasons why the Governmental Advisory Committee advice was not followed, and such statement will be without prejudice to the rights or obligations of Governmental Advisory Committee members with regard to public policy issues falling within their responsibilities.

The 60% threshold is an attempt to formalize the relationship between the Board and the GAC and address latent tensions that erupted during New gTLD Program policy development and implementation. These tensions came to a head at extraordinary face-to-face meetings in Brussels a few weeks prior to the 40th public meeting in San Francisco held in March 2011, when the GAC presented to ICANN's Board of Directors a 'scorecard' of issues regarding new gTLDs that its members believed were unresolved, amongst which the treatment of geographic names.[108] Many of these issues were still live at the subsequent public meeting held in Singapore in June 2011, by which point it was evident that a change had occurred in terms of the GAC's role within ICANN. At that meeting, ICANN's Senior Vice President for Public Affairs described the New gTLD Program as having been the catalyst of an 'unintended ... paradigm shift'[109] within the corporation in terms of the way it works and its various internal bodies cooperate. This would, he predicted, come to be seen as important a result of the New gTLD Program as the addition of new gTLDs to the root.[110]

The *gTLD Applicant Guidebook's* complete removal of country and territory names from eligibility, the expansive definition of other 'geographic names' and their reservation from registration without government sanction are the clearest and widest-reaching manifestations of GAC advice on geographic names' use in the DNS to date. It would be wrong, however, to consider the protection offered to geographic names the product of 'the

108. GAC, *GAC Indicative Scorecard*; ICANN, *Updated: New gTLDs: Briefing Papers for ICANN Board-GAC Consultations,* https://www.icann.org/news/announcement-6-2011-02-21-en (21 Feb. 2011, updated 23 Feb. 2011); ICANN, *ICANN Board Notes on the GAC New gTLD Scorecard*, http://www.icann.org/en/topics/new-gtlds/board-notes-gac-scorecard-04mar11-en.pdf (4 Mar. 2011).

109. Kurt Pritz, Comments, *New gTOLD [sic] Session*, 12 (ICANN 40, 13 Mar. 2011) (available at http://archive.icann.org/en/meetings/siliconvalley2011/bitcache/Transcript_%20New%20gTLD%20Session-vid=23275&disposition=attachment&op=download.pdf).

110. *Ibid.*

GAC's view alone';[111] the *gTLD Applicant Guidebook* was produced through numerous drafts, each of which involved a period of public comment. That it ultimately withstood such an extensive and intrusive drafting process suggests the existence, at least in theory, of some degree of consensus support in the global internet community for the protection of geographic names in the DNS in this manner. That said, the *gTLD Applicant Guidebook* policies on geographic names, implemented under a previous version of the Bylaws that did not define 'GAC Consensus Advice' or impose a threshold on Board votes on that advice, clearly favour the GAC's position over the directly contrary conclusions of the GNSO.

As to the broader role of ICANN in international law-making, perhaps whilst not de jure binding as rules of international law, the standards, procedures and guidelines developed by ICANN are, for all practical purposes, nevertheless de facto binding for two key reasons. First, as a practical matter, ICANN alone controls the DNS's root and, by virtue of that control, has the exclusive authority to set rules as to how one goes about being included and staying in it. An argument, for example, that the *gTLD Applicant Guidebook* is not binding on applicants would be unthinkable due to the technical control that ICANN has over the DNS. Put simply, if one wants to add a new gTLD to the root as we know it, one must follow ICANN's policies and procedures for doing so, ICANN being the only entity so empowered and there being only one DNS root. Second, this state of affairs is underpinned and reinforced by ICANN's network of private contractual relationships. In this way, practical, standard-setting, contract-based solutions such as the UDRP are effectively 'hardened' into norms because of their 'functional advantages' to those who use them.[112] This structure effectively ensures that ICANN-generated standards are binding on DNS participants and thus highly influential on certain aspects of State practice involving the DNS, but nevertheless beyond States' reach.[113]

4.2.5 Conclusions on International Law and Law-Making in the DNS Context

The role of non-State actors in international law-making is an increasingly debated topic for which ICANN offers a test-bed given its indispensability to the development of norms respecting the DNS. ICANN's GAC has increasingly significant influence over new gTLD policy respecting geographic names and thus the way that States and others use the DNS in actual practice. To suggest that GAC advice in the development of norms respecting geographic names and their use in the DNS should be disregarded in this study would be short-sighted.

---

111. On the nature of GAC advice, *see* n. 107 above in this chapter and accompanying text.
112. Dinwoodie, 215.
113. Weber, 106.

Furthermore, expressions of GAC members on the issue of rights in names may offer useful insight onto the views of the States they represent, despite the fact that members may not themselves be in possession of delegated authority to engage in international law-making activity and the fact that their activities, like recent developments in the field of human rights, 'do not fit neatly into the categories of state practice under the traditional conception of customary international law.'[114] There is growing acceptance of the notion that expressions of State practice in an informal setting such as ICANN are worth considering, provided that one recognizes their limitations: 'Of course, private opinio iuris alone cannot bind states. But – to a certain extent – commonly held private opinion, channelled, e.g., through non-governmental organizations or laid down in standards, might influence state practice and thus the development of customary international law.'[115] To this end, ICANN's revised Bylaws provide a needed opportunity to increase the transparency and accountability of GAC decision-making, not simply for the benefit of the ICANN community, but the broader international legal community.

It must be acknowledged that the involvement of so many different participants in DNS norm-setting creates the risk of dissonance that could actually prevent the development of custom, as well as a risk of cafeteria-style norm development whereby States selectively hear and advance only the views that support their own interests. Beyond this, there is a risk that a handful of influential States, 'whose beliefs as to the legality of their actions largely remain in the eye of the beholder',[116] declare their supported position to be the law on a given issue.

These problems, when considered alongside ICANN's lack of international treaty oversight and formal law-making capacity, make it difficult to predict when[117] and if the standards ICANN develops will harden into norms having the force of binding customary international law or be implemented in domestic legal orders and thus evolve into general principles of international law. Where conclusions can be drawn about the hardening of legal norms into customary international law or their evolution through domestic legal orders into general principles of international law, this is specified in the next part of this book, though it is helpful to bear in mind at those points the issues raised in this chapter about the difficulties inherent in the formation of international law in the DNS context.

Applying the legal framework laid down in this chapter, this study now turns to identifying and analysing bases of legal rights in geographic names

114. S. James Anaya, *Customary International Law*, 92 Am. Soc. Int'l L. Proc. 41, 42 (1998).
115. Juliane Kokott, *Soft Law Standards under Public International Law*, in *International Standards and the Law* 26 (Peter Nobel ed., Staempfli 2005).
116. Chodosh, 104–105.
117. Weber, 5 (arguing that 'it has to be kept in mind that Internet technology itself has an accelerating effect on the process of globalization of legal rules').

under international law. Chapter 5 considers the fundamental challenges to geographic names falling within the clearly articulated definitions of intellectual property law and the specific subject matter of trademarks. Chapter 6 considers whether rights subsist in geographic names as such due to their exclusion from trademark registrability or inclusion in the principle of sovereignty. Chapter 7 then explores the recognition afforded in international law to rights in geographical indications. Chapter 8 addresses rights in geographic names arising out of their commercial use. Lastly, Chapter 9 completes this study by identifying connections between geographic names and human rights, exploring specific human rights and related doctrines that may encompass a right of individuals or peoples in geographic names.

Part III

Rights in Geographic Names under International Law

Chapter 5

Intellectual Property Rights in Geographic Names

Domain names are not intellectual property rights.[1]

5.1 GEOGRAPHIC NAMES AS 'INTELLECTUAL PROPERTY'

Governments at national and subnational levels have used the phrase 'legitimate interests'[2] when asserting exclusive rights in geographic names, but prior to this study it had yet to be determined what rights international law actually recognizes in respect of geographic names, let alone their exclusivity. IPRs are an obvious potential basis for recognizing rights in geographic names due to the strong similarities between geographic names and other intellectual property subject matter, as well as the fact that names have long been protected through intellectual property law as trademarks. The fundamental aim of this study is, however, to dispel reliance on assumptions. A thorough analysis is therefore undertaken to determine conclusively whether geographic names fall within the general subject matter

1. Smith, *Internet Law and Regulation* 89, 3-042.
2. *See for example, St Moritz v. StMoritz.com,* WIPO Case No. D2000-0617; *Sydney Airport v. Crilly,* WIPO Case No. D2005-0989; *Her Majesty the Queen, in right of her Government in New Zealand v. Virtual Countries*, WIPO Case No. D2002-0754. The use of this particular phrase is owed at least in part to the possession of 'rights or legitimate interests' in the name in question being a ground of contention under the UDRP (clause 4(a)(ii)). The exclusivity of State interests in geographic names is explored in-depth in Part III, Chapter 6.

of intellectual property law as recognized in international law, or within the specific subject matter protected by trademark law.

It is a mistake to assume from the outset that all intangibles that derive value from their contribution to human culture, information or entertainment fall within the scope of what is broadly termed 'intellectual property'. Intellectual property is not a refuge for all creative or potentially profit-generating expression or innovation. While rights in certain types of names have long been recognized as 'intellectual property', this does not mean that all names are or should be characterized as such. Rather than be assumed, the obviousness or common sense nature of an IPR in geographic names should be questioned. In the context of similar assumptions about a right of publicity it has been said: 'What appears to be "common sense" may be nothing but the particular view of a matter that most strongly supports and expresses the interests of powerful social groups, or that fits most snugly with other deeply rooted and unexamined beliefs.'[3] So may it be for geographic names as intellectual property.

The first part of this chapter examines the scope and definitions of intellectual property. It is shown that geographic names are not expressly provided for as intellectual property subject matter save in a strictly limited context. Their inclusion as a general category of names falling within the general notion of intellectual property subject matter hinges upon States taking the initiative to do so. The second part of this chapter explores geographic names' imperfect fit within trademark law. Even if '[m]arks indicating the geographic origin of goods were the earliest type of trademark',[4] trademark law (as distinguished from rights in geographical indications, which are separately recognized in international law and therefore addressed as a separate chapter of this book) has to date largely prevented geographic names from receiving protection.[5] It is curious, therefore, that contemporary concerns about the use of geographic names in the DNS should be primarily characterized in terms of trademark law. Conclusions as to the recognition within international law of IPRs generally and trademark rights particularly in geographic names are summarized at the end of this chapter.

---

3. Michael Madow, *Private Ownership of Public Image: Popular Culture and Publicity Rights*, 81 Cal. L. Rev. 127, 136 (1993).
4. Bernard O'Connor, *The Law of Geographical Indications* 21 (Cameron May 2004), citing F. I. Schechter, *The Historical Foundation of the Law Relating to Trade-Marks* (1925). S.A. Diamond, The Historical Development of Trademarks, 73 Trademark Rep. 22 (1983); M.G. Coerper, *The Protection of Geographical Indications in the United States of America, with Particular Reference to Certification Marks*, 29(7/8) Industrial Property 232, 232 (1990).
5. Albrecht Conrad, *The Protection of Geographical Indications in the TRIPS Agreement*, 86 Trademark Rep. 11, 40 (1996).

5.1.1 CHARACTERISTICS OF INTELLECTUAL PROPERTY AND GEOGRAPHIC NAMES

It is true that geographic names possess certain common characteristics attributed to intellectual property subject matter generally. Names, like other intellectual property subject matter, are intangible in the sense that they are merely human expression and not something that has physical embodiment, such as a house, a car, or a chair. Names are ideas that have as their raw material the human mind rather than such physical, tangible raw materials as wood, steel or clay. This is the case for all names, geographic or otherwise. Like intellectual property generally, all names are non-perishable; they will not rot or spoil if left unused, and they can be used over and over again without physical depletion, damage or depreciation.

Names are also non-rivalrous resources: the use of a name by one person, like the use of language[6] or ideas but unlike the use of a car, plot of land or machine, does not prevent others from using it simultaneously.[7] While the physical materials in or onto which names are expressed are constrained by exclusivity of use (in other words, the can onto which the brand name of a soft drink is printed or a book on whose pages ideas are expressed can be exploited by only one individual at a time), the ideas themselves are not.

That said, perhaps the DNS, with its technical requirement of absolute name uniqueness, forces re-thinking this long-held belief about the nature of names as non-rivalrous resources. When they are components of a domain name, names are in fact constrained by a certain degree of exclusivity because there can only be one registrant of the name www.myname.com. There is no technological impediment to another party's registering the name 'myname' in another top-level domain (e.g., www.myname.org), but absolute name uniqueness demands simply that there cannot be more than one www.myname.com. In this example, the name 'myname' is not subject to exclusivity, but the complete domain name www.myname.com can be registered by only one registrant. Thus, in the context of the DNS, names do not entirely lose their characteristic of non-exclusivity, but they do sacrifice some of it.

Another divergence of names from the broad conceptual characteristics of intellectual property is that in order to receive protection, they need not be the product of creative genius or original thought. This is an interesting characteristic that the law has traditionally been willing to overlook in the

6. Lawrence Lessig, *The Future of Ideas: The Fate of the Commons in a Connected World* 21 n. 6 (Random House 2001).
7. On the rivalrous nature of intellectual property, *see* Christine Greenhalgh & Padraig Dixon, *The Economics of Intellectual Property: A Review to Identify Themes for Future Research*, University of Oxford Department of Economics Discussion Paper Series No. 135, December 2002, 4–5 (available at http://www.economics.ox.ac.uk/Research/wp/pdf/paper135.pdf).

case of trademarks but require in respect of other intellectual property subject matter.[8] Geographic names have nevertheless not historically been considered inherently registrable as trademarks, as will be explained in detail in the next section of this chapter.

5.1.2 INTELLECTUAL PROPERTY SUBJECT MATTER

With the exception of geographical indications, which are a specifically defined category of origin-connoting geographic names (these are discussed in detail in Chapter 7), geographic names are not expressly stated to fall within the scope of the TRIPS Agreement's definition of 'intellectual property' in Article 1(2) as: 'all categories of intellectual property that are the subject of sections 1 through 7 of Part II.' This definition has been characterized as 'pragmatic', but it 'excludes from general TRIPS obligations forms of intellectual property (or of protection that some would consider as being a part of intellectual property). Such as sui generis or new forms of protection.'[9] Geographic names generally, not simply the narrow subset in geographical indications, may be one such exclusion. It is also relevant to note as a tangential matter that in terms of the ownership of rights recognized under the TRIPS Agreement, governments' claims as rights holders under that agreement are not contemplated in the wording of Articles 1(3) or 42.[10]

The interpretation of the definition of 'intellectual property' in Article 1(2) was directly at issue in the WTO dispute *United States – Section 211 Omnibus Appropriations Act of 1998*.[11] The Panel in that case concluded that trade names did not fall within the list of categories articulated in Article 1(2), but the Appellate Body disagreed, interpreting 'intellectual property' to

---

8. Rosemary J. Coombe, *The Cultural Life of Intellectual Properties: Authorship, Appropriation, and the Law* 61 (Duke University Press 1998). Coombe explains: 'Although trademarks are not conventionally understood to have "authors" because they require no necessary genius, originality, or creativity, the legal recognition that trademark "owners" have a proprietary interest in marketing signs increasingly relies upon a reenactment of the author-function as described by Foucault. This is evident in judicial acceptance of the belief that through investment, labor, and strategic dissemination, the holder of a trademark creates a set of unique meanings in the minds of consumers and that this value is produced solely by the owner's efforts' (internal citations omitted).
9. Daniel Gervais, *The TRIPS Agreement: Drafting History and Analysis* 177 (4th ed., Sweet & Maxwell 2012).
10. Art. 1(3) of the TRIPS Agreement identifies beneficiary rights holders as 'the nationals of other Members.' Note 1 to Art. 1 indicates that 'nationals' means 'persons, natural or legal, who are domiciled or who have a real and effective industrial or commercial establishment in that customs territory.' Note 11 to Art. 42 of the TRIPS Agreement clarifies that 'federations and associations having legal standing to assert' rights are considered rights holders for the purposes of enforcement.
11. *United States – Section 211 Omnibus Appropriations Act of 1998*, 41 I.L.M. 654 (W.T.O. D.S.B. App. Body 2 Jan. 2002).

include not only the categories indicated in each title of each section of Part II of the TRIPS Agreement, but also categories of intellectual property subject to each section of Part II. Applying this reasoning, trade names can be distinguished because geographic names (other than geographical indications) are not even mentioned in the TRIPS Agreement. Furthermore, as the Appellate Body pointed out, trade names are expressly recognized in Article 8 of the Paris Convention for the Protection of Industrial Property, which is incorporated into the TRIPS Agreement by reference.

Geographic names, by contrast, are not expressly provided for in the Paris Convention, the definition of 'industrial property'[12] in which is considered:

> a traditional but not entirely exact denomination for certain exclusive rights, resembling property rights, regarding creative ideas or distinguishing signs or designations in the industrial or commercial field, supplemented by certain rules against unfair behavior in the same field. The term is inexact because 'industrial property' presents no more than an analogy with normal property; further, because it covers more than industrial subjects only; and, finally, because the rules against unfair behavior are not necessarily related to property at all.[13]

This interpretation allows for the recognition of rights in non-commercial names by the Paris Convention, but beyond their possible recognition as trademarks, geographic names fall within that agreement's covered subject matter only insofar as they constitute indications of source or appellations of origin, or give rise to an unfair competition claim. Their ability to do the latter is explored in detail in Chapter 8 of this book, but at this stage it can be concluded that geographic names are not provided for as such within the protected subject matter of the Paris Convention.

Nor do geographic names as such fall expressly within the scope of the broader definition of 'intellectual property' set out at Article 2 of the Convention Establishing the World Intellectual Property Organization:[14]

---

12. **Paris Convention Art. 1:**

> ...
> (2) The protection of industrial property has as its object patents, utility models, industrial designs, trademarks, service marks, trade names, indications of source or appellations of origin, and the repression of unfair competition.
> (3) Industrial property shall be understood in the broadest sense and shall apply not only to industry and commerce proper, but likewise to agricultural and extractive industries and to all manufactured or natural products, for example, wines, grain, tobacco leaf, fruit, cattle, minerals, mineral waters, beer, flowers and flour.
> ...

13. Bodenhausen, 20. WIPO Standing Committee on the Law of Trademarks, Industrial Designs and Geographical Indications, *Report Adopted by the Standing Committee*, WIPO Doc. SCT/21/8 (26 Nov. 2009) para. 317 (comments of South Africa) (available at http://www.wipo.int/edocs/mdocs/sct/en/sct_21/sct_21_8.pdf).
14. Convention Establishing the World Intellectual Property Organization (14 Jul. 1967, entered into force 26 Apr. 1970), 828 U.N.T.S. 3.

(viii) 'intellectual property' shall include the rights relating to:

- literary, artistic and scientific works,
- performances of performing artists, phonograms, and broadcasts,
- inventions in all fields of human endeavor,
- scientific discoveries,
- industrial designs,
- trademarks, service marks, and commercial names and designations,
- protection against unfair competition,

and all other rights resulting from intellectual activity in the industrial, scientific, literary or artistic fields.

Their primarily non-commercial use separates geographic names from classification as 'industrial' alongside trade and service marks, while the fact that their creation requires no particularly creative or inventive thought isolates them from the other catch-all 'intellectual' fields.

There is therefore scant express support for a claim to rights in the nature of intellectual property in geographic names at the international level. This does not stop WTO Member States from treating geographic names as protectable intellectual property, yet for this to be considered a general principle of international law it must be relatively consistent and widespread. The most obvious means by which States might do so is through registrability as a trademark.

5.2 GEOGRAPHIC NAMES AS TRADEMARKS

The recognition of rights in names under international law has historically focused primarily on the intellectual property subject matter of trademarks and trade names; these have been expressly protected since 1883 by the Paris Convention on the Protection of Industrial Property (the 'Paris Convention'). In addition to the minimum standards framework laid down in the Paris Convention, trademarks' protection at the international level was helpfully clarified[15] and harmonized by the TRIPS Agreement, while administrative measures pertaining to the international recognition of rights in trademarks are provided for by the Nice Agreement Concerning the International Classification of Goods and Services for the Purposes of the Registration of

15. Thomas Cottier, *The Prospects for Intellectual Property in GATT*, 28 Common Mkt. L. Rev. 383, 403–404 (1991).

Marks,[16] the Madrid Agreement concerning the International Registration of Marks,[17] the Protocol relating to the Madrid Agreement concerning the International Registration of Marks,[18] and the Trademark Law Treaty.[19]

Geographic names have long struggled to satisfy trademark registration criteria, which today are harmonized by Article 15(1) of the TRIPS Agreement:

> Any sign, or any combination of signs, capable of distinguishing the goods or services of one undertaking from those of other undertakings, shall be capable of constituting a trademark. Such signs, in particular words including personal names, letters, numerals, figurative elements and combinations of colours as well as any combination of such signs, shall be eligible for registration as trademarks. Where signs are not inherently capable of distinguishing the relevant goods or services, Members may make registrability depend on distinctiveness acquired through use. Members may require, as a condition of registration, that signs be visually perceptible.

From this provision can be distilled the three fundamental requirements of trademark registrability: first, the subject matter of protection must be a sign; second, that sign must be distinctive; third, it must be used on or in connection with commercial goods or services. It is clear from the second sentence of Article 15(1) that word names fall within the meaning of the term 'sign'; this criterion has never proved an obstacle to geographic names being protected as trademarks. The remaining two criteria of trademark registrability have, however, historically been and continue to be obstacles. The reasons for this are explored in the subsections that follow.

5.2.1 The Requirement of Distinctiveness

The heart of a trademark's registrability lies in its capacity to distinguish the goods or services of one trader from those of another, termed 'distinctiveness'.[20] Article 15(1) of the TRIPS Agreement provides that protectable signs may either be 'inherently capable of distinguishing the relevant goods or services' or acquire distinctiveness through use. Inherent distinctiveness refers to whether a mark on its face indicates that the goods or services to

16. Nice Agreement Concerning the International Classification of Goods and Services for the Purposes of the Registration of Marks of 15 Jun. 1957, as revised at Stockholm on 14 Jul. 1967 (entered into force 12 Nov. 1969), 828 U.N.T.S. 191.
17. Madrid Agreement Concerning the International Registration of Marks (14 Apr. 1891, entered into force 23 Oct. 1983) 828 U.N.T.S. 389.
18. Protocol Relating to the Madrid Agreement Concerning the International Registration of Marks (28 Jun. 1989, entered into force 1 Dec. 1995), 82 Trademark Rep. 58.
19. Trademark Law Treaty (27 Oct. 1994, entered into force 1 Aug. 1996) 2037 U.N.T.S. 35.
20. *See generally*, Charles Martin, *The Meaning of Distinctiveness in Trade-mark Law*, 45(5) Ill. L. Rev. 535 (1950–1951).

which it is applied refer to those of the applicant and no one else. Acquired distinctiveness offers signs with multiple meanings an opportunity to crystallize in the mind of the consuming public the identity of the applicant in connection with the goods or services to which the sign is applied. It has not always been the case that applicants have had this opportunity to demonstrate acquired distinctiveness, and this proved fatal for many applications for geographic trademarks.

Geographic names lack inherent distinctiveness because – irrespective of any other connotations a commercial enterprise might wish for them – they bring to mind a particular geographic location. Names of actual or even likely places of production, manufacture or origin of goods are unavoidably inherently descriptive of the goods they represent rather than indicative of the trader responsible for putting them on the market. This historically rendered geographic marks per se unregistrable.[21] Distinctiveness can only come about, if at all, because the consuming public learns over time to associate the geographic name in question with something other than a geographic location: specifically, a link must be made in the consumer's mind between a geographic name and a particular trader and its particular offering of goods and/or services.

Following revisions to the Paris Convention in 1967 at Stockholm, Article 6*quinquies* (B)(2) provided for the invalidation or refusal of registrations of marks 'when they are devoid of any distinctive character'. This was qualified by subsection (C)(1), which provided: 'In determining whether a mark is eligible for protection, all the factual circumstances must be taken into consideration, particularly the length of time the mark has been in use.' This required the consideration of circumstances in which 'a trademark which originally was not distinctive has, in the long run, through use, acquired a "*secondary meaning*" which makes it distinctive.'[22]

Today, the opportunity provided by Article 15(1) of the TRIPS Agreement to demonstrate acquired distinctiveness makes it possible (although by no means simple) for geographic names to be registered as trademarks. A geographic name always calls to mind a geographic location and therefore leads the consumer to question whether a connotation of origin or some other connection to the geographic location is the primary message being conveyed. Still, it is open to the trader through extensive commercial use of the name in connection with particular goods or services to try to override that inherent connotation of geography and put in its place a branding-type message that brings to mind the trader and its offering. There is no guarantee that these efforts will be successful, and this helps to explain why trademarks constituted only of geographic names are not particularly

21. Heather A. Forrest, *The New Frontier: Country Brands and Their Legal Status under Australian Trade Mark Law*, 20(3) Austl. Intell. Prop. J. 127, 138–140 (2009).
22. Bodenhausen, 118.

common.[23] If the changes enacted in 2011 to Swiss trademark law[24] to create a new geographic type of trademark are indicative of a future general domestic law trend, then in time this will change. The practical benefits arising out of such changes to the owners of geographic marks, which include their being actionable under the UDRP and other priority rights accorded trademark holders in DNS policy, should not be underestimated.

5.2.2 The Requirement of Use in Connection with Goods or Services

Another obstacle to geographic names' registrability as trademarks is the requirement that a sign be used on or in connection with particular goods or services. The protection of names at the level of international law has always been based upon use in a commercial context. This can be deduced from the negotiating history of the Paris Convention for the Protection of Industrial Property, which records the Chair of the convention as opening the drafting conference with reference to the scope of their work: 'Messieurs, vos etudes et vos recherché auront un vaste champ: brevets d'invention, dessins et modèles industriels, marques de fabrique, noms et raisons de commerce, tells seront les sujets principaux de vos entretiens.'[25] Indeed, the name of the resulting convention is suggestive of, even if not definitive on,[26] the sorts of subject matter that the convention's drafters set out to protect.

The requirement that signs be used on or in connection with particular goods or services is a logical extension of the requirement of distinctiveness, which demands recognition by the consumer of a triangular relationship between a mark, a particular trader and its particular goods or services. Registered marks receive protection only in respect of the goods or services specified in their registration, and it is principally only in connection with those goods or services that the mark's use is protected.[27] While geographic and cultural names can be used to identify commercial goods or services, more often they are used to identify a place or cultural concept. The

---

23. For specific data on the presence of geographic marks on the Australian trademarks register, for example, *see* Forrest, *The New Frontier*.
24. Loi fédérale sur la protection des marques et des indications de provenance, nouveau Art. 27a. *See* detailed discussion below at Part III, Chapter 5, s. 5.4.
25. Ministère des Affaires Étrangères de la France, *Conférence Internationale pour la Protection de la Propriété Industrielle* 13 (Imprimerie Nationale 1880).
26. *See* above n. 13 and accompanying discussion.
27. Defensive registrations and the protection of well-known marks are notable exceptions to this general rule that marks are only protected against competing use in relation to the same or similar goods and services. Arguments for treating well-known marks specially in the DNS are explored in Part II Chapter 3, s. 3.2.1.3 above. The protection offered to well-known marks under international law against dilution is discussed in detail in Part III Chapter 8, s. 8.3.1 below.

commercial uses of geographic names must logically outweigh their non-commercial uses, and this is rare; most commonly, they serve an informational purpose on maps and globes, on road signs and in official documents. The infrequency with which they come to signify in the consumer's mind a link between a particular trader and its particular goods or services prevents such names not only from meeting the requirement of distinctiveness but also the requirement of use in connection with goods or services.

In the specific context of the DNS it was asked early on whether the simple act of registering a domain name constitutes commercial use. When domain name disputes began to arise, it became clear to the trademark community that the emerging activity of 'cybersquatting', the act of registering a domain name comprised or constituted of a registered mark by someone other than the mark's owner,[28] had to be fit into the existing rubric of trademark infringement, which requires proof of use of the allegedly infringing mark as a trademark. This then necessitates proving commercial use. In many cases, domain names comprising registered trademarks were being registered without mark owners' authorization, but the websites operated under those domain names (if any website was operated at all) were not being used to engage in commercial activity. The names were not, in other words, being used on or in connection with goods or services.

What allowed courts to find trademark infringement was where the domain name registrant offered to sell the domain name, in most cases to the trademark owner. In one of the earliest 'cybersquatting' decisions in US courts, it was said of the defendant, Dennis Toeppen: 'At no time did Toeppen use intermatic.com in connection with the sale of any available goods or services. At no time has Toeppen advertised the intermatic.com domain name in association with any goods or services.'[29] It was nevertheless found that 'Toeppen's intention to arbitrage the "intermatic.com" domain name constitutes a commercial use.'[30] The same result could also be achieved by simply treating everything having to do with the internet as commercial in nature. This was suggested in a 1996 manual of trademark law and practice which was quoted by the court in its decision against Toeppen: 'Because Internet communications transmit instantaneously on a worldwide

28. In one of the early US court decisions on 'cybersquatting' facts, *Avery Dennison Corp. v. Sumpton*, 999 F. Supp. 1337, 1338 (C.D. Cal. 1998) the court described the practice in question as follows: 'Like all "cybersquatters," defendants merely "squat" on their registered domain names until someone else comes along who wishes to use them. Like all "cybersquatters," defendants usurp *all* of the accepted meanings of their domain names, so as to prevent others from using the same domain names in *any* of their accepted meanings. And like all "cybersquatters," defendants seek to make a financial return by exacting a price before consenting to allow others to use the domain names on which they have chosen to "squat."' *See* discussion in Heather A. Forrest, *Drawing a Line in the Constitutional Sand Between Congress and the Foreign Citizen 'Cybersquatter'*, 9(2) Wm. & Mary Bill Rts J. 461, 470–472 (2001).
29. *Intermatic Inc. v. Toeppen*, 947 F. Supp. 1227, 1233 (N.D. Ill. 1996).
30. *Intermatic Inc. v. Toeppen*, 947 F. Supp., at 1239.

basis there is little question that the "in commerce" requirement would be met in a typical Internet message, be it trademark infringement or false advertising.'[31]

In the years since, the US has devised specific legislative solutions such as the Anticybersquatting Consumer Protection Act to address the problem of cybersquatting and other activities characterized as DNS name-hijacking so that it is no longer necessary to fit such round peg problems into the square hole of trademark infringement. In that country and others, understanding of the internet has developed, as evidenced by the fact that not all registrations of trademarks as second-level domain names by someone other than the trademark owner are falling afoul of the UDRP, to which the majority of second-level domain registrants are bound.[32] It must be clarified, however, that commercial use is not a factor directly required under the UDRP as it is in trademark infringement. Offending domain name registrations under the UDRP are those that are, *inter alia*, used in bad faith pursuant to Clause 4(a)(iii). Three of the four non-exclusive examples of evidence of bad faith provided by Clause 4(b) are, however, based on commercial activity:

- (i) circumstances indicating that you have registered or you have acquired the domain name primarily for the purpose of selling, renting, or otherwise transferring the domain name registration to the complainant who is the owner of the trademark or service mark or to a competitor of that complainant, for valuable consideration in excess of your documented out-of-pocket costs directly related to the domain name; or
- (ii) you have registered the domain name in order to prevent the owner of the trademark or service mark from reflecting the mark in a corresponding domain name, provided that you have engaged in a pattern of such conduct; or
- (iii) you have registered the domain name primarily for the purpose of disrupting the business of a competitor; or
- (iv) by using the domain name, you have intentionally attempted to attract, for commercial gain, Internet users to your web site or other on-line location, by creating a likelihood of confusion with the complainant's mark as to the source, sponsorship, affiliation, or endorsement of your web site or location or of a product or service on your web site or location.

The notion that all internet activity and therefore all uses of domain names are inherently commercial seems to have predominated.[33] Instances in

31. *Ibid.*, quoting Jerome Gilson, *Trademark Protection and Practice* vol. 1, § 5.11[2], 5-234 (1996).
32. *See for example*, *St Moritz v. StMoritz.com,* WIPO Case No. D2000-0617; *New Zealand v. Virtual Countries,* WIPO Case No. D2002-0754.
33. Commonly adopted definitions of the term 'domain name' underscore this. *See for example*, Io Montes, Doctoral Dissertation in Law, Zürich, *Legal Framework for Domain*

which registration of domain names used on non-commercial, information-providing websites is deemed to constitute bad faith are not uncommon.[34] This is perhaps part of a broader trend in the field of intellectual property law attributable to the TRIPS Agreement and its origins in the WTO towards viewing all intellectual property subject matter as inherently commercial. In a seminal analysis of the TRIPS Agreement, only moral rights are offered as a clear example of 'the aspects of intellectual property that are not, in one form or another "trade-related"' and thus potentially not falling within the scope of the TRIPS Agreement.[35]

The international intellectual property treaty framework has historically drawn a line with respect to the recognition of rights in names between commercial and non-commercial use, those falling within the latter category being left available for public use and not subject to private property claims.[36] In taking the view that names in the DNS are inherently used commercially, the door is opened to proprietary claims even where names are not used on or in connection with goods or services, where they are used only in connection with the provision of information, commentary or opinion, as geographic names often are. Perhaps this is one reason to treat domain names as being a new type of property distinct from intellectual property, focusing only on the commercial interest of the subject matter in question.[37]

The far-reaching effects of the commercial characterization of otherwise non-commercial names are highlighted by the primarily commercial bases of rights relevant to geographic names. These are explored in particular in Chapter 8 below, but at this stage it suffices to highlight the fact that it is easier for otherwise non-commercial names such as geographic names to receive protection as trademarks where the context in which they are used is considered inherently commercial. On the other hand, if the use of geographic names is not considered inherently commercial, the protection available to them under existing intellectual property and related frameworks is automatically rendered quite limited.

5.3 COLLECTIVE AND CERTIFICATION MARKS

The traditional obstacles to registering geographic trademarks discussed above apply to what are termed 'standard' trademarks. The Paris Convention

Names 112 (2005) (defining the term 'domain name' as 'the virtual presence of a business in the on-line world that gives access to the cyber-market-place').

34. In the context of celebrity names, for example, *see* Chik, 46 (observing that '[e]ven when [use in commerce] was "weak", UDRP panels have largely been willing and able to find a protectable right').
35. Gervais, *The TRIPS Agreement,* 15.
36. This concept, called the 'public domain', is discussed in detail in Part III, Chapter 9, s. 9.2.5.2.2 below.
37. Chik, 44.

recognizes in Article 7*bis* another form of mark, called a 'collective mark'. The sole condition articulated in Article 7*bis* is that collective marks must belong to an association, but subparagraph (1) makes clear that associations need not 'possess an industrial or commercial establishment.' This has been interpreted to exclude States and other public bodies, whose marks are nevertheless likely to 'be protected by virtue of the rule of "national treatment" embodied in Article 2 of the Convention, and ... if these marks are at the same time official State signs or hallmarks indicating control and warranty – also by Article 6*ter*.'[38] Article 6*ter* is discussed in detail in the next chapter in the context of State sovereignty.

The criteria of collective marks' registrability are not harmonized by either the Paris Convention or the TRIPS Agreement to the same degree that standard trademark registration criteria are, but rather have been left to be determined by domestic legislation. Still, collective marks are a form of trademark, and as such they are required to be distinctive. This means that they must be capable of distinguishing goods or services – in this case, those of the members of an association from those of other associations. Conceptually similar to collective marks are certification marks, which connect a mark not with a particular association but with goods meeting particular, specified standards (which may, but need not, relate to geography).[39]

Registration of a collective or certification mark offers geographic names that communicate geographic characteristics (particularly geographic origin) distinct advantages.[40] Foremost, registration serves as proof of ownership just as it does for standard marks, despite the fact that ownership is an incongruous concept in this context: the association owns the mark and members of the association are authorized to use it. As such, some domestic laws prohibit or limit the transfer of collective marks.[41] It has also been suggested that registration may prevent a geographical indication from becoming generic.[42] Because they are forms of trademark, in the DNS context, collective or certification mark registration gives rise to standing to bring a claim under ICANN's Uniform Domain Name Dispute Resolution

38. Bodenhausen, 130 (internal citations omitted).
39. *See for example*, Lanham Act, 15 U.S.C. §1054 (US); Trade Marks Act 1995 (Austl.) s. 169; Trade Marks Act No. 194 of 1993 (S. Africa) s. 42. On the protection of geographical indications as certification marks under US law, *see* Lynne Beresford, *Geographical Indications: The Current Landscape*, 17 Fordham Intell. Prop. Media & Ent. L.J. 979, 983–984 (2006–2007).
40. Conrad, 21 (advocating the use of certification marks on an international level).
41. *See for example*, Trade Marks Act 1995 (Austl.) s. 166. On restrictions under US law, *see* David Snyder, *Enhanced Protections for Geographical Indications Under TRIPS: Potential Conflicts under the U.S. Constitutional and Statutory Regimes*, 18 Fordham Intell. Prop. Media & Ent. L.J. 1297, 1308 (2008).
42. O'Connor, *The Law of Geographical Indications*, 73 (citing by way of example the United States Lanham Act §1127, pursuant to which registered marks cannot be deemed generic provided the name remains geographically descriptive).

Policy ('UDRP') and the new Uniform Rapid Suspension ('URS') procedure, as well as standing to object under the *gTLD Applicant Guidebook* to a new gTLD application on the basis of existing legal rights. Registration as a collective or certification mark thus has the practical effect of transforming some geographic names from a situation of no recognition in the DNS to a situation of priority recognition.

5.4 GEOGRAPHIC TRADEMARKS: THE SWISS MODEL

The Swiss legislative project approved in late 2011[43] proposing amendments to the federal trademark law, RS 232.11 *Loi fédérale sur la protection des marques et des indications de provenance*, provides a model approach to protecting geographic names. In the new Chapter 2a, headed *Marque géographique*, nationally registered indications of source and geographical indications, protected cantonal wine designations and geographical indications regulated in a Federal Council ordinance are deemed registrable.[44] The geographic mark is intended to apply beyond the scope of food and beverages to include manufactured goods and services. Rather than confer exclusive rights, the mark would function similar to a collective mark.

It is likely significantly easier (although by no means a non-issue) to achieve the consensus needed to amend domestic law to expressly protect geographic names as trademarks than it is to amend international law. The domestic law solution removes the need for international consensus, but of course the rights created are limited to the territory in which they are recognized. This is nevertheless likely in the context of the DNS to be satisfactory as an immediate solution to the problem of unauthorized use of geographic names as domain names, since local concerns can be addressed in local law without loss of sovereignty.

This approach, if adopted by other Member States, will result in a less-harmonized global trademark law landscape (although potentially balanced by the emergence of a general principle of law). The TRIPS Agreement permits this given its nature as a minimum standards agreement that allows members to provide for higher levels of protection. The minimum standard of Article 15(1) requires that signs 'capable of distinguishing the goods or services of one undertaking from those of other undertakings, shall be capable of constituting a trademark.' Enabling other signs that may not be

43. L'Assemblée Fédérale, 'Loi sur la protection des marques et loi sur la protection des armoiries: Vers une réglementation différenciée', 11 Nov. 2011, http://www.parlament.ch/f/mm/2011/pages/mm-rk-n-2011-11-11.aspx.

44. RS 232.11 *Loi fédérale sur la protection des marques et des indications de provenance*, Art. 27a (nouveau), Feuille fédérale No 50, 15 Dec. 2009, at http://www.admin.ch/ch/f/ff/2009/index0_50.html.

able to meet this minimum standard to be capable of constituting a trademark provides a higher level of protection. Further, recognition in domestic law of a specific category of geographic trademark effectively enables the recognition of geographic names beyond a country's borders through ICANN contract-based policies such as the UDRP and URS. Both procedures are actionable only in respect of trademarks, and neither makes a distinction between types or forms of trademark.

5.5 CONCLUSIONS ON INTELLECTUAL PROPERTY RIGHTS IN GEOGRAPHIC NAMES

As the analysis of existing rights protection mechanisms undertaken in Chapter 3 reveals, there is a significant advantage to be gained in the online environment by having offline rights recognized, in particular as a trademark, given that existing rights protection mechanisms are almost exclusively based on trademark rights. Consistent with this, in ICANN's New gTLD Program, applicants of new gTLDs consisting of geographic names that are already protected in domestic trademark law are far better placed to have these rights transposed to the DNS and resist their use by others. Achieving such protection has, however, traditionally been a difficult exercise, but the fact that it is possible at least disproves the exclusivity of States' rights in geographic names. Further, it is unquestionably not the case that States inherently or automatically possess trademark rights in what they view as 'their' geographic names.

While it is conceptually not implausible to associate geographic names with intellectual property generally and trademarks specifically, it should nevertheless not be assumed that geographic names fall within either of these characterizations. Geographic names share many of the traditional characteristics of intellectual property subject matter, but they are not expressly mentioned within authoritative definitions of 'intellectual property' save for the special category of geographical indications. This does not stop States from protecting geographic names within domestic intellectual property law, as for example Switzerland has done through a specially targeted legislative initiative, but neither does it require States to do so.

Geographic names are also not expressly included within the scope of registrable trademarks as harmonized by the TRIPS Agreement. Standard trademark registration criteria, in particular the requirements of distinctiveness and use in connection with goods and services, clash with the primary function of geographic names as identifying a geographic location rather than a trader and its goods or services. Distinctiveness is less problematic in relation to collective and certification marks, which require instead a link in consumers' minds between a mark, particular goods and services, and a particular association or set of characteristics rather than a particular trader. In this way, rights can be recognized in geographic names, but only in the limited context of origin connotations, which may otherwise receive (as is discussed in Chapter 7) sui generis protection as geographical indications. Before narrowing the focus to examine the subset of geographic names that is geographical indications, the next chapter considers whether international law recognizes rights more broadly, in geographic names as such.

Chapter 6
Rights in Geographic Names as Such

This is my country
Land of my choice
This is my country
Hear my proud voice.
– 'This is My Country', American folksong, lyrics by Don Raye

6.1 THE CHANGING USE AND REGULATION OF GEOGRAPHIC NAMES

Regulation of the use of geographic names is difficult to characterize as a purely domestic matter in the face of increasing use of geographic names as internet domain names. Prior to the introduction of the DNS, outside of the diplomatic context geographic names had a relatively limited, territory-bound scope of use that could effectively be controlled through domestic law: they appeared principally in maps, road signs and official documents, in published works such as encyclopaedias, newspaper articles, scholarly works, academic texts, and less often in advertising, trademarks and trade names. When they began to be used online, geographic names came unmoored from the territory, and thus the legal jurisdiction, that they identify. Now they are potentially registrable as domain names by anyone, anywhere, for use in connection with any type of good or service. As active domain names they are potentially accessible by everyone, everywhere. Domestic legislation is ill-equipped to manage this situation.

International trademark law has also proven ill-equipped to regulate the use of geographic names, whether online or offline. As discussed in the previous chapter, geographic names have not traditionally been afforded trademark status due to their ordinarily non-commercial nature and, even where they are used in a commercial context, their lack of an inherent capability to link in consumers' minds the particular goods or services of one trader from those of another. It is further acknowledged by even the most ardent advocates of rights at the international level that domestic trademark legislation evidences anything but a consistent approach to recognizing trademark rights in geographic names. A 2011 survey shows a significant number of WIPO Member States have in place laws preventing the registration of country names as trademarks.[1] This speaks against the existence of a general principle of international law recognizing protection of geographic names as trademarks. Looking at these results another way, the fact that many States do allow registration of country name trademarks by private parties also weighs against the existence of a general principle of international law recognizing an exclusive right of government in geographic names.

If international law recognizes rights in geographic names as such, the findings of the previous chapter indicate that it must do so outside of trademark law. Nevertheless, most efforts to date regarding the recognition of rights, at least in respect of country names, have been directed at interpretations of or amendments to Article 6*ter* of the Paris Convention for the Protection of Industrial Property. That Article 'concerns *trademarks*, but its purpose is not to regulate their *protection as subjects of industrial property* but rather to *exclude them from becoming such subjects* in certain circumstances.'[2] From its proscription against 'use, without authorization by the competent authorities' is derived the position that their unavailability for registration by the public as trademarks equates to country names belonging exclusively to the State they identify. Yet WIPO has interpreted Article 6*ter*

1. WIPO Standing Committee on the Law of Trademarks, Industrial Designs and Geographical Indications (hereinafter 'WIPO SCT'), *Summary of the Replies to the Questionnaire Concerning the Protection of Names of States against Registration and Use as Trademarks*, WIPO Doc. SCT/24/6 (14 Feb. 2011) (available at http://www.wipo.int/edocs/mdocs/sct/en/sct_24/sct_24_6.pdf). For an example at the supranational level, *see* First Directive 89/104/EEC of the Council, of 21 Dec. 1988, to approximate the laws of the Member States relating to Trade Marks, OJ/L 40 of 11 Feb. 1989, p. 1, which provides at Art. 3(2)(b) and (c) for refusal on grounds of 'high symbolic value' or inclusion of 'badges, emblems and escutcheons other than those covered by Art. 6*ter* of the Paris Convention and which are of Public interest, unless the consent of the appropriate authorities to its registration has been given in conformity with the legislation of the Member State'. Another example is the Protocol on Harmonization of Norms on Intellectual Property in Mercosur in matters of Trademarks, Indications of Source and Appellations of Origin (5 Aug. 1995, entered into force 6 Aug. 2000), 2145 U.N.T.S. 40. Art. 9(2) of the Protocol requires that Member States prohibit the registration of signs that, *inter alia*, 'are formed with national symbols or symbols of any country; signs that are susceptible of falsely suggestion a relation with … national symbols of any country, or that offend their value or respectability.'
2. Bodenhausen, 95 (emphasis in original).

as not pertaining to country names, leading to the conclusion that their use (and the use of geographic names generally) in the DNS cannot be prevented under that Article.[3] Others have lent support to this conclusion,[4] but practice in notification of Article 6*ter* emblems in the time since the WIPO II Report warrants reconsideration of this issue. Because Article 6*ter* has featured so strongly in the discussion as the most likely source of rights in country names as such, it features first in this chapter.

Looking beyond international intellectual property treaties as a basis of rights in geographic names as such, this chapter also addresses the situation of States' claims to exclusionary rights in country names being articulated on the basis of sovereignty, as if possession of a State's name is linked to the status of statehood. Indeed, the rights conferred by Article 6*ter* of the Paris Convention are said to be directed at 'emblems constituting the symbol of the sovereignty of a State.'[5] Section 6.3 of this chapter considers the possible link between country names, sovereignty and statehood to determine whether claims to rights on this basis are supported by international law. Two separate questions are asked: first, whether having a name is a condition of statehood and second, whether having a name is a right of statehood. The limits of sovereignty are explored to delineate the authority of a State to select and use a name and interfere with others' selection and use of a name. Conclusions as to the existence under international law of rights in geographic names as such are summarized at the end of this chapter.

6.2 PARIS CONVENTION ARTICLE 6*TER* AND COUNTRY NAMES

6.2.1 ARTICLE 6*TER* (1)

6.2.1.1 Interpretation

The protection of country names under Article 6*ter* of the Paris Convention hinges upon the difference in wording between subsections (1)(a) and (1)(b)[6] of that Article. Article 6*ter* (1)(a) requires that Paris Union members prohibit registration as a trademark of emblems of national significance such as

3. WIPO, *WIPO II Report*, para. 284.
4. *See for example*, Froomkin, *When We Say US™, We Mean It!*; Mueller, *Governments and Country Names.*
5. WIPO, *General Information on Article 6ter*, http://www.wipo.int/article6ter/en/general_info.html.
6. **Paris Convention Art. 6*ter*:**

   (1) (a) The countries of the Union agree to refuse or to invalidate the registration, and to prohibit by appropriate measures the use, without authorization by the competent authorities, either as trademarks or as elements of trademarks, of armorial bearings, flags, and other state emblems, of the countries of the Union, official signs and hallmarks indicating control and warranty adopted by them, and any imitation from a heraldic point of view.

armorial bearings and national flags. Article 6*ter* (1)(b) contains a similar proscription in relation to IGOs except that it also expressly excludes the names of such organizations from trademark registration. This serves to highlight the absence of States' names in the wording of subsection (1)(a).[7] Relying on the principle of *expressio unius exclusio alterius*, WIPO has interpreted this subtle yet significant difference as not requiring that Member States exclude country names from registration as trademarks.[8] This interpretation is consistent with:

> the duty of a treaty interpreter to examine the words of the treaty to determine the intentions of the parties. This should be done in accordance with the principles of treaty interpretation set out in Article 31 of the Vienna Convention. But these principles of interpretation neither require nor condone the imputation into a treaty of words that are not there or the importation into a treaty of concepts that were not intended.[9]

Interpretations of the terms 'armorial bearings', 'other State emblems', 'official signs and hallmarks indicating control and warranty', and 'heraldic symbols' as including country names have been rejected. South Africa was an enthusiastic proponent of this interpretation within WIPO discussions, but the remark that this 'view has not been universally and definitely accepted'[10] suggests rather more support than may actually exist, and further conflicts with the acknowledgement made elsewhere that:

> other members of the Paris Union had made very laudable efforts at ensuring protection against the use of official State names as elements of trademarks, where such use constituted grounds for refusal of requests

---

> (b) The provisions of subparagraph (a), above, shall apply equally to armorial bearings, flags, other emblems, abbreviations, **and names**, of international intergovernmental organizations of which one or more countries of the Union are members, with the exception of armorial bearings, flags, other emblems, abbreviations, and names, that are already the subject of international agreements in force, intended to ensure their protection. (emphasis added)

7. WIPO, *WIPO II Report*, paras 278–285. Bodenhausen, 94–99.
8. WIPO, *WIPO II Report*, para. 281.
9. *India – Patent Protection for Pharmaceuticals and Agricultural Chemical Products*, WT/DS50/AB/R (W.T.O. App. Body Report 19 Dec. 1997). Susy Frankel, *WTO Application of 'the Customary Rules of Interpretation of Public International Law' to Intellectual Property*, 46 Va. J. Int'l L. 365, 388–389 (2005–2006). An alternative interpretation of Art. 6*ter* (1) is defended by Matthew Rimmer in *Virtual Countries: Internet Domain Names and Geographical Terms*, February 2003 Media Int'l Austl. Incorp. Culture & Pol'y 124, 132 (2003). Rimmer posits that an alternate interpretation of Art. 6*ter* 'is justified, on the one hand, in light of its spirit and underlying objectives, and, on the other hand, in view of recent technological evolutions, in particular the emergence of the Internet as a commercial medium and the importance of domain names as valuable signposts in this context.'
10. WIPO SCT, *The Protection of Country Names in the Domain Name System: Comments Submitted by the Government of the Republic of South Africa*, WIPO Doc. SCT/S2/6 (17 May 2002) (available at www.wipo.int/edocs/mdocs/sct/en/sct_s2/sct_s2_6.doc).

for trademark protection. However, the continued prevalence of such use in other countries provided clear evidence of the inconsistency of the efforts to provide protection to official State names.[11]

The 'prevalence of such use' offers support for WIPO's interpretation of Article 6*ter* (1)(a) in its WIPO II Report, as do attempts prior and subsequent to the WIPO II initiative to revise this Article to expressly include country names.

6.2.1.2 Proposed Revisions

A proposal[12] to revise Article 6*ter* (1)(a) to include country names as part of the 1980 Diplomatic Conference for the Review of the Paris Convention, though adopted,[13] did not ultimately result in amendments. This signifies an understanding amongst WIPO States that, at that time, country names were not included in the scope of Article 6*ter*. At the same time, this evidences a desire by some Member States at that time to achieve such an outcome by creating new law. The question thus arises as to the current legal significance of that previous state of affairs; despite the failure to achieve codification then, has new law since been created? Renewals of the effort to amend Article 6*ter* (1)(a) by the Jamaican delegation to WIPO's Standing Committee on the Law of Trademarks, Industrial Designs and Geographical Indications (the 'WIPO Standing Committee') offer insight. The Jamaican delegation's proposals notably go beyond the earlier attempt at revising Article 6*ter*, in that they have sought to impose a government consent requirement upon all applications for trademarks of official country names and homonymous representations of official names.[14]

It is clear from the Jamaican delegation's earliest proposal of 2009 that it believed as a starting point that new law is needed to protect country names.[15] This position is maintained in its revised proposal of 2014, in which it states:

11. WIPO SCT, *Report Adopted by the Standing Committee*, WIPO Doc. SCT/21/8, para. 309.
12. WIPO, *WIPO II Report*, paras 281–283 (discussing WIPO, *Basic Proposals (Supplement to Document PR/DC/3), Memorandum by the Director-General*). WIPO SCT, *Submission by the Russian Federation*, WIPO Doc. SCT/21/5 Annex 1, para. 1 (2 Mar. 2009) (available at http://www.wipo.int/edocs/mdocs/sct/en/sct_21/sct_21_5.pdf).
13. WIPO, *Diplomatic Conference on the Revision of the Paris Convention*, WIPO Doc. PR/SM/9, discussed in WIPO, *WIPO II Report*, para. 282.
14. WIPO SCT, *Proposal by Jamaica*, WIPO Doc. SCT/21/6 (30 Mar. 2009) (available at http://www.wipo.int/edocs/mdocs/sct/en/sct_21/sct_21_6.pdf).
15. WIPO SCT, *Report Adopted by the Standing Committee*, WIPO Doc. SCT/21/8, para. 309 (reporting the Jamaican delegation as speaking to 'the clear absence of provisions

> The SCT will recall that for over thirty years, concerns have been expressed by states internationally regarding the lack of international protection for country names and that proposals have been repeatedly made over the years for a review of the Paris Convention, in order to broaden the scope of Article 6ter to protect country names by including names of states within a special category of protected signs which currently includes armorial bearings, flags, other State emblems, official signs and hallmarks that are to be refused or invalidated as trademarks. This would have effectively led to the expansion of Article 6ter(1)(a) to include the protection of country names. Unfortunately, attempts to review Article 6ter of the Paris Convention have been so far unsuccessful.[16]

From this can be extrapolated the view that protection is not already extant. With the exceptions of the delegations of Brazil and Austria, which expressed the view that Article 6*ter* already offers sufficient protection to country names,[17] other members of the WIPO Standing Committee voiced no specific opposition to Jamaica's initial assessment. This can be interpreted as evidence of a general belief among members of the WIPO Standing Committee that international law on this issue does not yet exist, though it bears noting that not all members commented, nor was a vote on this specific point taken, nor was this issue debated in the General Assembly.

On the specifics of Jamaican delegation's 2009 proposed amendments to Article 6*ter*, members were more divided. The delegations of Iran (paragraph 312), Cuba (paragraph 314), Spain (paragraph 316), Greece (paragraph 325), Serbia (paragraph 328), Kenya (paragraph 329) and India (paragraph 332) expressed support.[18] The delegations of Colombia (paragraph 313), Australia (paragraph 315), South Africa (paragraph 317) and Germany (paragraph 318) expressed non-support.[19] In light of this it was

---

specifically prohibiting the use of official State names' and the proposed amendment to Art. 6*ter* being 'not only warranted, but timely'). A finding of *opinio juris* as to existing customary law cannot be based upon such forward-looking assertions: Michael Akehurst, *Custom as a Source of International Law*, 47 British Y.B. Int'l Law 1, 37 (1974–1975).

16. WIPO SCT, *Proposal by the Delegation of Jamaica*, WIPO Doc. SCT/31/4, Annex (21 Jan. 2014) (available at http://www.wipo.int/meetings/en/doc_details.jsp?doc_id=262359).
17. WIPO SCT, *Report Adopted by the Standing Committee*, WIPO Doc. SCT/21/8, para. 320 (comments of Brazil that it 'believed that the existing legal framework established under the Paris Convention and the TRIPS Agreement already provided enough grounds for the protection of State names') and para. 323 (comments of Austria that it saw 'no need to amend Article 6ter, the existing legal framework being sufficient to protect State names').
18. *Id.*, para. 309.
19. *Id.*, paras 308–343 (comments by Austria, Australia, Brazil, Colombia, Denmark, Germany, and the Republic of Korea).

decided[20] that the next step would be information-gathering through the drafting and circulation of a questionnaire[21] of members' domestic laws restricting the registration and use of country names (specified to include official State names, short-form names, common use names, translations, transliterations and adjectival use) as trademarks.

Responses to this questionnaire evidence a lack of consistency in the exclusion of country names from registration and use as a trademark, with a near 60/40 split.[22] That so many Member States responded in the negative to having in place limitations on country names – through trademark law, unfair competition law, general tort law or otherwise – supports the non-existence at this time of protection though Article 6*ter* (1)(a) for country names. This also weighs against the existence of a general principle of international law of exclusive State control or ownership of country names. The subsequently revised proposal submitted by Jamaica in consideration of the survey responses acknowledged this lack of consistency. Jamaica (joined by Barbados) proposed that 'there could be convergence among Members on an agreed approach to the protection of country names in the trademark/IP system having regard to differences that now exist in the protection afforded to country names across Member States.'[23] Potential such 'areas of convergence' identified by Jamaica are as follows:

- definition of 'country name' to encompass 'the official or formal name of the State, the name that is in common use, translation and transliteration of that name, the short name of the State, as well as use of the name in abbreviated form and as an adjective';
- refusal of applications on examination 'where the use of that name is descriptive of the place of origin of the goods or services';
- refusal of applications on examination 'where the use of that name renders the mark as a whole misleading, deceptive or false in relation to the origin of the goods or services'; and
- availability of mechanisms to prevent use that is likely to deceive the public'.[24]

---

20. *Id.*, para. 343.
21. WIPO SCT, *Draft Questionnaire Concerning the Protection of Names of States Against Registration and Use as Trademarks*, WIPO Doc. SCT/23/4 (15 Feb. 2010) (available at http://www.wipo.int/edocs/mdocs/stlt/en/sct_23/sct_23_4.pdf).
22. The results broadly found that 61% of survey respondents exclude country names from registration and 42% from use as trademarks for goods. In addition, 64% of survey respondents exclude country names from registration and 41% from use as trademarks for services.
23. WIPO SCT, *Proposal by the Delegations of Barbados and Jamaica*, WIPO Doc. SCT/27/6 para. 8 (18 Jun. 2012) (available at http://www.wipo.int/edocs/mdocs/sct/en/sct_27/sct_27_6.pdf).
24. WIPO SCT, *Protection of Country Names Against Registration and Use as Trademarks: Practices, Approaches and Possible Areas of Convergence*, WIPO Doc. SCT/35/4, 9 (25 Feb. 2016) (available at http://www.wipo.int/edocs/mdocs/sct/en/sct_35/sct_35_4.pdf).

As the Jamaican delegation has observed as to those States that have opted to exclude country names from trademark registration, this is not prohibited under the Paris Convention, but also not something they are obliged by that instrument or otherwise to do.[25] The case studies submitted to the Standing Committee by Jamaica, Lithuania, Mexico, Poland, Republic of Moldova, Turkey, Uganda and the US[26] evidence the varied ways in which countries which have opted to protect country names do so. Thus the Jamaican study 'confirm[s] ... that that the practice of States, as it relates to the protection of country names, is neither uniform nor comprehensive'.[27]

It is interesting to note the resemblance between Jamaica's proposals to restrict country names from registration as a trademark without government consent and the recommendation of the Governmental Advisory Committee to ICANN's Board of Directors to restrict creation of geographic new gTLDs without government consent. As to why the consent mechanism has come to be included in the *gTLD Applicant Guidebook* (and in less time) but not the Paris Convention, certain distinctions can be made. First, as new gTLD policy was being drafted and implemented, there was only one geographic gTLD already in existence: .asia. The *gTLD Applicant Guidebook*'s exclusion of country and territory name new gTLDs and imposition of a consent requirement on other geographic new gTLDs does not threaten the viability of vast numbers of existing registrations in the way that existing trademarks would be threatened by such a change.[28] It is worth noting, however, that had the *gTLD Applicant Guidebook* restrictions on geographic strings applied at the time that the .asia gTLD was created, the application would have been rejected as an application for the name of a macro-geographical (continental) region unless it secured authorization from all of the relevant governments throughout that region.[29]

---

25. WIPO SCT, *Proposal by the Delegation of Jamaica*, WIPO Doc. SCT/31/4, Annex ('The Paris Convention for the Protection of Industrial Property does not prescribe specific rules for the protection of country names, allowing Member States to adopt varied approaches to the matter.').
26. Case studies are accessible through the Standing Committee's electronic forum. WIPO, *Browse Comments: 2012 Country Names*, http://www.wipo.int/sct/en/comments/. WIPO Standing Committee on the Law of Trademarks, Industrial Designs and Geographical Indications, *Information on Cases and Case Studies Relevant to the Protection of Names of States and on Nation Branding Schemes*, WIPO Doc. SCT/27/5, (18 Jul. 2012) (available at http://www.wipo.int/edocs/mdocs/sct/en/sct_27/sct_27_5.pdf) (hereinafter '*Information on Cases and Case Studies*').
27. WIPO SCT, *Submission by the Delegation of Jamaica*, WIPO Doc. SCT/31/5, Annex at 1, (21 Jan. 2014) (available at http://www.wipo.int/edocs/mdocs/sct/en/sct_31/sct_31_5 .pdf).
28. Mueller, *Governments and Country Names*, 10 (positing that 'WIPO's caution was prodded in part by business trademark holders concerned about the potential confusion, and possible erosion of their rights, that might be caused by proliferating claims to names by governments, regions, and administrative entities').
29. ICANN, *gTLD Applicant Guidebook,* s. 2.2.4.1.2 (4) (referring to the UN's 'Composition of macro geographical (continental) regions, geographical sub-regions, and selected

Context is a second major difference: the GAC is an advisory body within ICANN, a private corporation. The WIPO Standing Committee, by contrast, is an advisory body within a UN specialist agency. There is the obvious difference (discussed in Chapter 4, above, in the context of non-State actors in the DNS norm-setting environment) in the law-making capacity of WIPO and ICANN; the potential for actions of the former to create binding legal obligations may serve as a disincentive to taking decisive action, while no such obligations are created by GAC advice. Different membership, voting procedures, expertise of participants, and the relative ability of what may be perceived as stronger or weaker members to influence or drive the recommendation-making process may also contribute to different outcomes.[30]

A further distinction can potentially be made as to the intended consequence of restrictions on geographic names from registration as trademarks or gTLDs. The Jamaican delegation has curiously stated that 'the intention of [its] proposal was not to create proprietary rights for States but rather to prevent unauthorized use of its name by individuals and companies.'[31] It is not clear how giving States the exclusive authority to prevent others' registration and use as a trademark of country names by means of a consent requirement underpinned by Article 6*ter* does not, by conventional understanding, equate to a property-type right in the name as such. WIPO's own articulation of the purpose of Article 6*ter* as being 'to protect'[32] emblems falling within its scope is indicative of a proprietary-type right in the name as such, rather than a non-proprietary limitation on the behaviour of others through, for example, consumer protection or unfair competition laws. Other provisions of the Paris Convention than 6*ter* are directed at behavioural limitations;[33] if the intention is to restrict use that is likely to confuse, amendment to Article 6*ter* is not necessary. Indeed, all of the above-mentioned 'areas of convergence' identified by Jamaica in its study are based on or derived not from exclusive ownership rights but avoidance of confusion. By contrast, no such denial has been expressed in the context

---

economic and other groupings' list, at http://unstats.un.org/unsd/methods/m49/m49regin.htm).

30. It has been suggested that both ICANN and WIPO suffer from sporadic attendance at meetings, particularly as regards developing country members, and this may have an impact on voting outcomes for both. On WIPO, *see* Coenraad Visser, *International intellectual property norm setting: Democratising the World Intellectual Property Organization?*, 32 S. Afr. Y.B. Int'l L. 222, 223–224 (2007). On the GAC, *see* Froomkin, *When We Say US™, We Mean It!*, 865–866.

31. WIPO SCT, *Report Adopted by the Standing Committee*, WIPO Doc. SCT/21/8, para. 311.

32. WIPO, *Article 6ter of the Paris Convention: Protection of State Emblems, and Names, Abbreviations and Emblems of International Intergovernmental Organizations*, http://www.wipo.int/article6ter/en/.

33. Unfair competition and related laws limiting commercial behaviour are the focus of Chapter 8.

of ICANN's consent or non-objection mechanism for geographic new gTLDs. One gets the sense from GAC members' comments that the consent or non-objection mechanism is driven by a desire to exert control of a proprietary nature over geographic names – at the very least in order to prevent the creation of property or other rights belonging to others.

In summary, the prevailing view is that Article 6*ter* does not require States to prevent the registration of country names as trademarks. Yet neither does that Article or other provisions of the Paris Convention prevent States from excluding country names from trademark registration on their own initiative. A survey of WIPO members' domestic law reveals a mixed practice in this regard, lending current support to WIPO's interpretation of Article 6*ter* (1)(a) as not encompassing a government right to protect country names. Further, the survey results lend support to the non-existence of a general principle of international law of excluding country names from trademark registration and, by corollary, to the non-existence of a general principle of international law of recognizing exclusivity of States' rights in country names.

6.2.2 Article 6*ter* (3): Interpretation

In order to facilitate the exclusion of national emblems from national trademark registers, Paris Convention Article 6*ter* (3) establishes a notice system whereby WIPO Member States communicate their national emblems to other members of the Union.[34] Communications pursuant to this provision are made by completing a 'Draft Request for Communication Under Article 6*ter* 3(a) of the Paris Convention for the Protection of Industrial Property by a State'.[35] Consistent with the prevailing interpretation of Article 6*ter* (1)(a) discussed in the preceding section, the request form does not invite notification of country names.[36] Notable, therefore, are the notifications made in 2008 by Iceland of its name in the English, Spanish/Castilian,

---

34. **Paris Convention Art. 6*ter*:**

> (3)(a) For the application of these provisions, the countries of the Union agree to communicate reciprocally, through the intermediary of the International Bureau, the list of State emblems, and official signs and hallmarks indicating control and warranty, which they desire, or may hereafter desire, to place wholly or within certain limits under the protection of this Article, and all subsequent modifications of such list. Each country of the Union shall in due course make available to the public the lists so communicated. Nevertheless such communication is not obligatory in respect of flags of States.

35. WIPO, *Article 6ter - Procedure for States*, http://www.wipo.int/article6ter/en/states.html.
36. The notification provides: 'On behalf of the Government of [official name of the country], I would like to request the communication, under Article 6ter(3)(a) of the Paris Convention for the Protection of Industrial Property (Paris Convention), to the States party to the Paris Convention and to the Members of the World Trade Organization (WTO) not party to the said Convention, of the [armorial bearings], [flag], [State emblem] and/or [official sign or hallmark indicating control and warranty] adopted by [official name of the country].'

French, Chinese, Arabic and Russian languages as State emblems.[37] The legal significance of Iceland's actions is ripe for consideration in light of the conclusions reached above as to the non-support of Article 6*ter* for encompassing country names.

Iceland's actions could only be supported by a restrictive interpretation of Article 6*ter* 3(a) (and thus Article 6*ter* (1)(a)) giving 'extreme deference to the sovereignty of states'.[38] The actual use of the restrictive approach by the PCIJ and its successor the ICJ is, however, limited, and on this and other bases its use has been cautioned against.[39] Furthermore, the US is recorded as having objected to Iceland's notifications;[40] since it is the only State to have done so, it could be questioned whether this signals tacit acceptance by other States. This is unlikely given that other States have not availed themselves of the notification process to notify State name-only emblems, although notifications have been made in which a country name is the prominent feature with the addition of a small emblem or sign.[41] These have essentially the same effect as name-only notifications because notified emblems 'are protected … against registration and use of trademarks which are identical to them *or incorporate them as elements thereof*'[42] (emphasis added). They function as stylized marks, however, and do not unambiguously evidence an intention to reserve a country name as the notification of an unstylized name only.

Looking beyond treaty obligations to the formation of custom, although practice by the entire international community of States is generally not seen as required, and although it may even in certain situations be considered sufficient that only a minority of States have acted in a particular way,[43] it is surely the case that the action of one State is insufficient evidence of a general or even specific custom of recognizing rights in country names through Article 6*ter* (3). Only if other States were doing so and these notifications consistently went unchallenged, and further if these actions were the product a sense of legal obligation and not simply diplomatic

---

37. Article 6*ter* Numbers IS8, IS9, IS10, IS11, IS12 and IS13, Notified as State Emblems in Circular Number 7596, 02 Apr. 2008, available at WIPO, *Article 6ter Structured Search*, http://www.wipo.int/ipdl/en/6ter/.
38. Richard K. Gardiner, *Treaty Interpretation* 53 (Oxford University Press 2008).
39. Hersch Lauterpacht, *Restrictive Interpretation and the Principle of Effectiveness in the Interpretation of Treaties*, XXVI British Y.B. Int'l L. 48, 62–67 (1949), discussed in Gardiner, *Treaty Interpretation*, 60–62.
40. Objections by the US are recorded as having been made on 30 Mar. 2009 for each of Art. 6*ter* notification Numbers IS8, IS9, IS10, IS11, IS12 and IS13. Available at WIPO, *Article 6ter Structured Search*, http://www.wipo.int.ipdl/en/6ter/ (input 'IS8', 'IS9', etc., into the 'Search' field or 'Iceland' in the 'State' search field).
41. An example is Canada's notification of State emblem CA16, available at WIPO, *Article 6ter Structured Search*, http://www.wipo.int/ipdl/en/6ter/.
42. Bodenhausen, 97.
43. Vladmir Duro Degan, *Sources of International Law* 182, Martinus Nijhoff 1997.

courtesy, could this be a basis for customary law recognizing States' rights in country names.

At this time, Iceland appears to be the only example of notification under Article 6*ter* (3) of a State emblem featuring only a country name. One reason for the isolation of this practice may be that States believe it too obvious to bother with an administrative process of notifying a desire to protect a name that they view as indisputably their own. Could it be that country names are so well-known that communication of an intention to assert exclusivity in them would be considered unnecessary because it is so obvious? Such a position is not so illogical when one considers that national flags have been exempt from the process of Article *6ter* notification since the 1958 Lisbon Conference of the Paris Convention for precisely this reason.[44] It would likewise not be unreasonable to suggest that in the modern world order, countries' names are just as, if not even more well-known than their flags. Perhaps the very obviousness of the ownership of both belies not merely a desire to preserve friendly relations but the observance of a legal obligation. Then again, the opposite may be true, where 'the absence of legal obligation *in such a context* is regarded as self-evident, just as, in municipal law, questions of good manners are treated as self-evidently not a matter for legal regulation.'[45]

Article 6*ter* (3)(a) of the Paris Convention expressly accommodates the fact that a flag so obviously belongs to the State that adopts it that the adopting State need not tell other States that it wishes to prevent its use or registration as a trademark.[46] This reasoning depends on an understanding that a flag, once adopted, is assumed to be easily and immediately identifiable as a particular State's own, not only by other heads of State and the diplomatic community but by people all over the world near or far from the State in question who would otherwise have contact with the flag if used as a trademark. Exclusion of flags from registration as a trademark is justified because their 'registration or use would violate the right of the State to control the use of symbols of its sovereignty'.[47] Yet are not country names

44. Daniel Gervais, *The TRIPS Agreement: Drafting History and Analysis* 662 n. 899 (4th ed., Sweet & Maxwell 2012), citing Bodenhausen, *Guide to the Application of the Paris Convention*, 100.
45. International Law Association, *Statement of Principles Applicable to the Formation of General Customary International Law: Final Report of the Committee on Formation of Customary (General) International Law*, s. 17(i) Commentary.
46. **Art. 6*ter*** (3)(a): For the application of these provisions, the countries of the Union agree to communicate reciprocally, through the intermediary of the International Bureau, the list of State emblems, and official signs and hallmarks indicating control and warranty, which they desire, or may hereafter desire, to place wholly or within certain limits under the protection of this Article, and all subsequent modifications of such list. Each country of the Union shall in due course make available to the public the lists so communicated. *Nevertheless such communication is not obligatory in respect of flags of States.* (emphasis added)
47. Bodenhausen, 96.

symbols of sovereignty just as much as, if not more so than, flags? If so, is there a custom or general principle of international law recognizing States' rights in country names, even if the Paris Convention does not explicitly require this? To answer this question, this study now turns to a fundamental principle of international law that is the cornerstone of the international legal order itself: sovereignty.

6.3 SOVEREIGNTY AND COUNTRY NAMES

Both the proposal made by the Jamaican delegation to the WIPO Standing Committee to expand the scope of Paris Convention Article 6*ter* (1) and the recommendation made by ICANN's GAC to restrict applications for new geographic gTLDs rely on sovereignty to justify preventing non-State use of country names.[48] Sovereignty has also been asserted as a basis for national control of country code TLDs.[49] Acknowledging the imprecision with which the term 'sovereignty' is used, as will be discussed further below, the impression one gets is that these are assertions of an inherent right of States to possess and control the use of their representative symbols, including their name. The seemingly inherent nature of the right suggests that it is derived from principles of natural law and the very conceptual and philosophical underpinnings of the international legal order. This is at least how the protection of State emblems by means of Article 6*ter* of the Paris Convention has been explained.[50]

Even if the protection of State emblems has as its origin the principle of sovereignty, one need look no further than the Paris Convention to identify international law expressly recognizing States' rights. It has been determined in the preceding section of this chapter that country names do not fall within this ambit; they are not specifically recognized in the Paris Convention or indeed any other international convention of universal scope as symbols of sovereignty meriting protection as such by means of an exclusion from trademark registration, or any other form of proprietary rights. States' names are nevertheless just as powerful and likely more universally recognizable identifiers than flags or other national symbols. The question therefore arises

48. *See* comments of the Delegation of Jamaica 'that its proposal was intended to protect the integrity and sovereignty of a State' in WIPO SCT, *Report Adopted by the Standing Committee*, WIPO Doc. SCT/21/8 (26 Nov. 2009) para. 311. The GAC's view is expressed in the context of Internationalized Domain Names that 'ICANN should consult with the Government or relevant public authority of the territory concerned to determine whether there may be any potential infringement of their sovereign rights regarding their country or territory name'. GAC, *GAC Communiqué: New Delhi*, 2, https://gacweb.icann.org/display/gacweb/GAC+31+Meeting+New+Delhi%2C+India+9-14+February+2008 (February 2008).
49. Von Arx & Hagen, 68.
50. Bodenhausen, 96.

as to whether possession and protection of States' rights in their names can alternatively be based on the status of statehood, either as a condition of statehood or a consequence of it.

Various sources identify a link between national flags as expressions or 'emblems' of sovereignty and national identity,[51] but less clearly articulated is a link between country names and sovereignty. If it were clear that sovereignty encompasses a right to possess and prevent others' use of a name, the issue of States' rights in country names and their use in the DNS would not be the open question that it is today. An answer can only be reached by piecing together historical and contemporary understandings of statehood in order to demarcate the legal connection, if any, between sovereignty, statehood and country name. This section of this chapter considers first whether having a name is a condition of statehood, and second, whether having a name is a right of statehood.

6.3.1 Name as a Condition of Statehood

6.3.1.1 Statehood and Possession of a Name

Foundational historical works on sovereignty and statehood offer little support for the position that statehood is conditioned on having a name. For example, Emerich de Vattel, whose seminal work *Le Droit des gens; ou, Principes de la loi naturelle appliqués à la conduit et aux affaires des nations et des souverains* is considered one of the foundations of modern nation-State theory, saw only self-government as necessary.[52] Yet where specific territories are identified as having achieved the status of sovereign statehood, they are commonly referred to by name. For example, Franciscus de Vittoria, another influential early contributor to international legal theory, described a 'perfect State' as 'one which is complete in itself, that is, which is not a part of another community, but has its own laws and its own council and its own

51. *See for example*, Am. Jur. 2d *Flag* §1 ('A national or state flag is an emblem of that nation or state's sovereignty and authority.'); Michael Billig, *Banal Nationalism* 40–41 (Sage Publications 1995) (discussing the powerful impact of even unwaved flags as symbols of nationality and nationhood); Arundhati Virmani, *National Symbols Under Colonial Domination: The Nationalization of the Indian Flag, March-August 1923*, 164 Past & Present 169 (1999); Yael Navaro-Yashin, *Confinement and the Imagination: Sovereignty and Subjectivity in a Quasi-State*, in *Sovereign bodies: Citizens, Migrants and States in the Postcolonial World* 103–104 (Thomas Blom Hansen & Finn Stepputat eds, Princeton University Press 2005) (discussing the importance of the flag of the Turkish Republic of Northern Cyprus to its sovereignty); *Sovereignty Flag Should Fly, says Maori Party*, nzherald.co.nz (31 Jan. 2007) (available at http://www.nzherald.co.nz/waitangi-day/news/article.cfm?c_id=1500878&objectid=10421769).

52. Emerich de Vattel, *Le Droit des Gens, ou Principes de la loi Naturelle, Appliqués à la conduite aux affaires des Nations et des Souverains*, vol. 1 Introduction, Bk I, ch I, §4 (1758).

magistrates, such as is the Kingdom of Castille and Aragon and the Republic of Venice and the like'.[53] Little can be drawn from this, however, because the examples to which Vittoria points are States in possession of a name rather than States lacking names. The latter situation is not contemplated.

Contemporary scholars have experienced difficulty in articulating a definition or identifying attributes of statehood. This is at least partly due to the traditionally complex question of the need for recognition; that issue[54] must be set aside as separate from a possible link between statehood and country name.[55] The definition of 'State' provided by Article 3 of the Montevideo Convention on Rights and Duties of States[56] (hereinafter the 'Montevideo Convention') is viewed as setting the standard despite that convention being a regional agreement only.[57] From it can be extrapolated four principal criteria: a permanent population; a defined territory; government; and capacity to enter into relations with other States.[58] Clearly, possession of a name is not one of these four criteria. Nor is it one of the other criteria that have been suggested over time, including permanence,

53. Franciscus de Vittoria, *De Indis et de Iure Belli Relectiones*, in *Relectiones Theologicae XII* (Ernest Nys ed.), reprinted in *The Classics of International Law* 169 para. 7 §§425-426 (James Brown ed., 1917).
54. On recognition, *see* James Crawford, *The Creation of States in International Law* 38, 89–95 (2d ed., Clarendon Press 2007).
55. Matthew C. R. Craven, *What's in a Name? The Former Yugoslav Republic of Macedonia and Issues of Statehood*, 16 Austl. Y.B. Int'l L. 199, 238 (1995) (arguing that a link between name choice and recognition 'offends the notion of sovereignty itself'). Louis Henkin et al., *International Law: Cases and Materials* 253 (3d ed., West 1993).
56. Convention on Rights and Duties of States adopted by the Seventh International Conference of American States (26 Dec. 1933, entered into force 26 Dec. 1934), 165 L.N.T.S. 19.
57. The definition of 'State' in the Restatement (Third) of Foreign Relations Law of the United States almost precisely mirrors that of the Montevideo Convention, and in comments to the Restatement it is said that this definition 'is well-established in international law'. *Restatement (Third) of the Foreign Relations Law of the United States* § 201 Comment a (1987). As to the effectiveness of the definition, *see* John Dugard, *Recognition and the United Nations* 123 (Cambridge University Press 1987). ('Although Rhodesia, Transkei, Boputhatswana, Venda, Ciskei and, possibly, the Turkish Republic of Northern Cyprus met or meet the traditional requirements of statehood expounded in the Montevideo Convention of 1933, it is absurd to contend that any of these entities […] acquired the status of "State".')
58. Even those who deem it inappropriate to view determinations of statehood as a checklist-based activity nevertheless tend to accept that certain fundamental characteristics 'constitute in legal terms the core of the concept of statehood'. Crawford, 42. Crawford qualifies this by arguing that the strictness of the elucidation of these characteristics in individual cases depends upon context and 'that the exclusive attributes of States do not prescribe specific rights, powers or capacities that all States must, to be States, possess: they are presumptions as to the existence of such rights, powers or capacities, rules that these exist unless otherwise stipulated. This must be so, since the actual powers, rights and obligations of particular States vary considerably. The legal consequences of statehood are thus seen to be – paradoxically – matters of evidence or rather of presumption.'

willingness and ability to observe international law, civilization, and legal order.[59] The requirements of membership in the UN are based first and foremost on having achieved statehood, but even these do not expressly require that aspiring members have a name.[60]

It is only plausible to take the position that possession of a name is a condition of statehood if it can be said that having a name, while not an express criterion of statehood, is a necessary or inherent aspect of a criterion of statehood. Considering in turn the four criteria identified by the Montevideo Convention as just noted, it could only be possible to interpret possession of a name as a necessary aspect of having the capacity to enter into relations with other States; the crux of this argument is that having a name is a necessary aspect of legal personality.[61] This will now be considered.

6.3.1.2 Name as a Necessary Aspect of Legal Personality

Having legal personality means being treated by the law as possessing the capacity to enter into formal relations with other legal persons and be held accountable for one's actions, as are natural, living persons.[62] States are 'the principal examples of international persons.'[63]

Without a name, it has been argued, it is not possible to be identified and therefore not possible to engage and transact with others:

> From the point of view of legal theory, the inherent right of a state to have a name can be derived from the necessity for a juridical personality to have a legal identity. In the absence of such an identity, the juridical person (such as a state) could – to a considerable degree (or even completely) – lose its capacity to conclude agreements and independently enter into and conduct its relations with other juridical persons. Therefore, the name of a state appears to be an essential element of its juridical personality and its statehood.[64] (emphasis in original)

This use of the term 'legal identity' helps to highlight that beyond their undeniably symbolic function, names primarily play a practical function in

59. *Id.*, 89–95.
60. Art. 4(1) of the Charter of the UN requires that applicants: (1) be a state; (2) be peace-loving; (3) accept the obligations of the UN Charter; (4) be able and willing to carry out these obligations.
61. Igor Janev, *Legal Aspects of the Use of a Provisional Name for Macedonia in the United Nations System*, 93 Am. J. Int'l L. 155, 160 (1999).
62. *Restatement (Third) of the Foreign Relations Law of the United States* § 206 comment c.
63. Henkin et al., 241. Vattel, 1 §2 ('[L'Etat] deviant une personne morale, qui a son etendement et sa volonté proper, et qui est capable d'obligations et de droits').
64. Janev, *Legal Aspects of the Use of a Provisional Name for Macedonia in the United Nations System*, 160; Igor Janev, *Some Remarks of the Legal Status of Macedonia in the United Nations Organization*, 53 Rev. Int'l Aff. 1108 (2002).

serving to identify things and distinguish them from others. Having some means by which to be identified and differentiated is certainly facilitative of engaging in relations with others, and contract law seeks as a general matter that parties be identifiable. A name is one means of distinguishing a party from another, but it is certainly not the only means; reference to geographical location, numbers and symbols could all be used, even if not as easily and memorably as names.[65] Each State could, for example, be assigned a number according to its order of accession to the UN, or it could be identified by its longitudinal and latitudinal coordinates or an image of its national flag. It could also be assigned a completely random and meaningless, yet unique, number. An analogy can be drawn with transactions between persons, in which context it is not strictly necessary that a party be referred to by name as opposed to another identifier, or that the identifiers used have semantic value or are unique as against all others. It is simply necessary to provide sufficient information to distinguish one from others.[66]

Nor is a name required of a legal person in order to express consent to be bound, bearing in mind that the voluntary expression of State consent is the cornerstone of positive international law. Just as illiterate persons can indicate their willingness to be bound to a legal instrument by stamping their fingerprint upon it or inscribing the letter 'X', so too could States communicate consent to be bound in a variety of visible ways. It is the expression of consent that is of consequence, not the form that expression takes or the possibility that others' expression of consent takes a similar form.

Another key aspect of relations between legal persons is participation in dispute resolution. In the international context one can look to the Statute as well as the Rules of the ICJ (hereinafter, the 'ICJ Rules)',[67] the latter of which specify the manner in which proceedings are to be initiated and conducted. Article 38(1) of the ICJ Rules requires in relevant part that an application to commence proceedings before the Court must 'indicate the party making it, the State against which the claim is brought, and the subject of the dispute'. Considering subject matter first, the *Island of Palmas Case (or Miangas)* [68] demonstrates that territorial disputes are resolvable even where the territory the subject of the dispute is referred to by multiple names.

---

65. Reference can be made here to domain names and the early decision to assign a name in addition to a number to identify hosts in the network. This is discussed in detail in Part I, Chapter 2, s. 2.1.3 above.
66. Janev, *Some Remarks on Legal Status*, 2 ('In the absence of such an identity, the juridical person, such as a state, could to a large extent (or even completely) loose [sic] its capacity to interact with other such juridical persons (e.g., conclude agreements, etc.) and independently enter into and conduct its external relations. The name of a state is, thus, an essential element of its juridical personality and, consequently, of its statehood.').
67. Rules of Court (14 Apr. 1978, entered into force 1 Jul. 1978, as amended 14 Apr. 2005), I.C.J. Acts & Docs 4.
68. *Island of Palmas Case (or Miangas)*, Hague Court Reports 2d. 83 (1932), (Perm. Ct. Arb. 1928), 2 U.N. Rep. Intl. Arb. Awards 829.

Turning to the naming of State parties, while Article 38(1) of the ICJ Rules does not expressly require that State parties have a name, names are typically used for this purpose. Article 38(1) does not preclude commencing proceedings before the Court against, for example, 'the State whose application for membership in the United Nations was made on [date]' or in a particular numbered document or 'the fiftieth State to join the United Nations', but these are not things that ordinarily occur in practice. One need look no further than the ICJ's docket for evidence of the practice and consistency of the use of States' names in proceedings.[69] It must be noted, however, that not all States have come before the ICJ and its predecessor, the PCIJ,[70] with a name of their own choosing. An example of this is the ongoing case brought in November 2008 by the 'former Yugoslav Republic of Macedonia' ('FYROM') against Greece,[71] a dispute which is comprehensively discussed in the next section of this chapter. The applicant's name in that case is a provisional one recommended by the UN Security Council, and not the name under which that country sought membership in the UN. The relevant question at this point in this enquiry is whether, without the provisional name, this country would have been prevented from raising its claim against Greece. In other words, was possession of a name (provisional or permanent) procedurally necessary to commencing the case?

Article 38(1) of the ICJ Rules requires identification of 'the party making' the application. It does not demand a particular format that identification must take. Identification of a party other than by its name would not run counter to ordinary meaning or defeat the object and purpose of the treaty as prescribed by Article 31(1) of the Vienna Convention, but the existence of a consistent subsequent practice 'in the application of'[72] Article 38(1) of the ICJ Rules supports an interpretation of this as calling for use of a State party's name.[73] Because all parties before the Court have had names, it is difficult to envisage what might otherwise occur. Presumably, names are used unless the party in question does not have a name, in which case some other identifier must – from a purely practical standpoint – be an acceptable substitute. Unless otherwise specified in the Rules, standing could not

---

69. On the significance of practice in treaty interpretation, *see* Vienna Convention on the Law of Treaties, Art. 31(3)(b). The ICJ docket is available at ICJ, *List of Cases referred to the Court since 1946 by date of introduction: List of contentious cases and advisory proceedings*, http://www.icj-cij.org/docket/index.php?p1=3&p2=2.
70. Publications of the Permanent Court of International Justice are available at ICJ, *Permanent Court of International Justice: Publications of the Permanent Court of International Justice (1922-1946)*, http://www.icj-cij.org/pcij/index.php?p1=9.
71. *Case Concerning the Application of Article 11, Paragraph 1, of the Interim Accord of 13 September 1995 (The Former Yugoslav Republic of Macedonia v. Greece)*, Memorial (I.C.J. 20 Jul. 2009) (available at http://www.icj-cij.org/docket/files/142/16354.pdf).
72. Vienna Convention on the Law of Treaties, Art. 31(3)(b).
73. Gardiner, 225–232.

logically be denied on the basis of non-possession of a name if possession of a name is not itself a condition of statehood.

This discussion reveals that a distinction must be made between practical necessity and legal necessity. It is undeniably the case that names facilitate the functions of the UN, and so much so that this could be characterized as necessary (as opposed to simply desirable) from a perspective of operational convenience. Yet from the ease of using names does not automatically follow a legal obligation. Neither can a general sense of legal obligation be easily inferred from existing evidence of practice in the functions of the UN. Rights in country names as such derived from States' possession of legal personality, or indeed derived from any other condition or right of statehood, cannot be based upon practicality or '(mere) comity (*courtoisie, comitas gentium*)'.[74]

Even if it is the case that State parties are required to be referred by name in ICJ proceedings, this does not equate to a strict prohibition against nameless parties' participation in proceedings, nor does it speak to exclusive rights of States in their names. There is no clear evidence of a felt sense of legal obligation to possess a name in order to participate as a UN member, and such a legal obligation is not expressly articulated in UN instruments. From these things and from the fungible nature of identifiers in legal transactions it can be concluded that possession of legal personality does not require possession of a name, and thus that States' claims to exclusive rights in country names should not be based upon their possession of legal personality.

6.3.2 Name as a Right of Statehood

6.3.2.1 A Right of States to Select a Name

Even if not required to achieve the status of statehood, possession of a name may alternatively be a right that accrues as a consequence of having achieved statehood. This reasoning makes a distinction between the capacities that must be possessed in order to achieve the status of statehood from capacities or rights that, once statehood is achieved, are imputed to the State. This bifurcated approach is reflected, for example, in the Restatement (Third) of the Foreign Relations Law of the United States[75] (the 'Restatement'), which

74. International Law Association, *Statement of Principles Applicable to the Formation of General Customary International Law: Final Report of the Committee on Formation of Customary (General) International Law*, Commentary to s. 2(vi).

75. The Restatements are treatises prepared and published by the American Law Institute on a variety of legal topics. They have the primary aim of providing guidance to judges and lawyers by clarifying and explaining fundamental legal subjects. The Third Restatement of the Foreign Relations Law of the US 'consists of international law as it applies to the

sets out the required elements of statehood in § 201 and then separately in § 206 the 'capacities, rights and duties of States' as:

(a) sovereignty over its territory and general authority over its nationals;
(b) status as a legal person, with capacity to own, acquire, and transfer property, to make contracts and enter into international agreements, to become a member of international organizations, and to pursue, and be subject to, legal remedies;
(c) capacity to join with other states to make international law, as customary law or by international agreement.

The wording of § 206 of the Restatement is illustrative of the general absence in international law and scholarship of an express attribution to States of a right to select or use a name. It is necessary, therefore, to consider whether such a right is implied because it is inherently an aspect of sovereignty, bearing in mind that sovereign rights derive from the 'simple fact' of the State's 'existence as a person under international law.'[76]

In determining whether possession and exclusive use of a name is a sovereign right of States, the advice offered by Justice Haynes of the High Court of Australia should be borne in mind: 'Sovereignty is a concept that legal scholars have spent much time examining. It is a word that is sometimes used to refer to very different legal concepts and for that reason alone, care must be taken to identify how it is being used.'[77] Similar concern is expressed, for example, in the comments to § 206 of the Restatement, which specify that its use in this context of States' rights 'implies a state's lawful control over its territory generally to the exclusion of other states, authority to govern in that territory, and authority to apply law there.'[78] The exercise of this control is a core right to inhere in all States.

United States, and domestic law that has substantial impact on the foreign relations of the United States or has other important international consequences.' ALI, *Restatement of the Law Third, Foreign Relations Law of the United States*, https://www.ali.org/publications/show/foreign-relations-law-united-states-rest/. The Restatement of the Foreign Relations Law of the United States of course offers the perspective of only the US as to international law, but the high regard in which its reporters are held mean that it has significance beyond that one country's borders: 'It should and will be consulted by lawyers in all parts of the world. For the lawyer in the United States, it may be a kind of authoritative codification. For lawyers in other countries, it is a valuable source of information about the foreign relations power in the United States and prevailing American views on international law.' Rudolf Bernhardt et al., *Book Review*, 86(3) Am. J. Int'l L. 608, 609 (1992) (reviewing *Restatement (Third) of the Foreign Relations Law of the United States*).

76. Convention on the Rights and Duties of States, Art. 4.
77. *Joosse v. Australian Securities and Investment Commission*, 159 A.L.R. 260, 263–264 (High Ct. Aust'l 1998).
78. *Restatement (Third) of the Foreign Relations Law of the United States* §206 comment (b).

As to whether there are more specifically articulated rights of States (which could include a right to a name), there are divergent views. Vattel's reliance in the eighteenth century on natural law to explain the origin of States' rights echoes in modern arguments supporting an inherent, 'inalienable right' of States to select and use a name.[79] These arguments can also be linked to a right to culture and heritage, similar to what was termed by an early twentieth century diplomat the right to 'national distinctiveness'.[80] Contrasting with these is the view that 'statehood does not involve any inherent substantive rights', but is 'rather a form of standing'.[81] The works of historical and contemporary scholars who support the notion of States' rights offer little support for a specific right of States to select and use a name. Nevertheless, it is difficult to oppose the idea that a State may choose and use a name by virtue of the exercise of sovereignty, and further that when it does so, it is free by virtue of that authority to place restrictions on others' use of its chosen name within its sovereign territory. The same can be said of national flags and domestic laws prohibiting their desecration.[82]

In other words, sovereignty does not require that a State select and use a name to identify itself, but rather bestows States with the inherent authority to do so if they so choose.[83] In practice, States do select a name. This is evidenced by the United Nations Terminology Bulletin Country Names (from which, not coincidentally, the names of ccTLDs are derived).[84] Although it is not expressly required under the UN Charter or the Rules of Procedure of the General Assembly, applications for UN membership refer to applicants by name:[85] indeed, compliance with Rule of

79. *See for example*, Janev, *Legal Aspects of the Use of a Provisional Name for Macedonia in the United Nations System*, 160.
80. F.A. Pezet, *The Future Relations of the United States with Latin America from the Latin American Viewpoint*, 7(2) Nat'l Conf. Foreign Rel. U.S. 287, 287 (1917).
81. Crawford, 44–45.
82. An interesting comparative analysis of flag desecration laws is provided by Ute Krüdewagen, *Political Symbols in Two Constitutional Orders: The Flag Desecration Decisions of the United States Supreme Court and the German Federal Constitutional Court*, 19(2) Ariz. J. Int'l & Comp. L. 679 (2002).
83. Janev, *Legal Aspects of the Use of a Provisional Name for Macedonia in the United Nations System*, 160 ('every state naturally has an inherent right to a name').
84. UN Terminology Bulletin No. 347/Rev. 1, *United Nations Terminology Bulletin Country Names* (available at http://unstats.un.org/unsd/methods/m49/m49alpha.htm). On the naming of ccTLDs, *see* Part I, Chapter 2, s. 2.4.2 above.
85. Recent examples include the Application of the Republic of Bosnia and Herzegovina at U.N. Doc. A/46/921 S23971 Annex (19 May 1992) ('On behalf of the Presidency of the Republic of Bosnia and Herzegovina and in conformity with the United Nations Charter, I am submitting the request of the Republic of Bosnia and Herzegovina to be admitted to the United Nations Organization as a full Member State.'); Application of the Democratic Republic of East Timor at U.N. Doc. A/56/953-S/2002/558 Annex (20 May 2002) ('In connection with the application by the Democratic Republic of East Timor for membership in the United Nations, we have the honour, on behalf of the Democratic Republic of East Timor and in our capacities as the President of the Republic and the

Procedure 134[86] would be difficult as a practical matter if this were not done. The applicant is then acknowledged by their designated name on acceptance.[87]

Sovereignty gives the State not only the authority to choose a name, but also to limit others' use of the selected name within its territory. There are, for example, reportedly 'thousands' of laws in Canada and 'probably millions' in the US, that 'bestow upon "public authorities" (which are often not elected bodies but government agencies, state-owned corporations, or non profit organizations) an absolute right to control particular signifiers.'[88] All States have the authority to select names and regulate their domestic use in this way, and have this authority equally, as articulated in the Montevideo Convention at Article 4: 'States are juridically equal, enjoy the same rights, and have equal capacity in their exercise.' Yet equality among States raises certain challenges in this context in that it does not prevent a State from selecting another State's name as its own; indeed, equality suggests that they are each equally entitled to make the same selection.

The question of States' rights in country names therefore does not end with name selection and use within the sovereign territory. It must further be considered whether States' authority to select a name is somehow limited by the rights of other States and relatedly, whether States have a right to be referred to by their chosen name.

6.3.2.2 A Right of States to Object to Another State's Name

It is entirely possible that one State might choose to be identified in the same or similar way as another. This duplication of identifiers could be said to have a direct impact on the States in question and those transacting with them.

Prime Minister, to declare that the Democratic Republic of East Timor accepts the obligations contained in the Charter of the United Nations and solemnly undertakes to fulfil them.'); Application of the Republic of Montenegro, U.N. Doc. A/60/890-S/2006/409 Annex (16 Jun. 2006) ('In line with the results of the referendum held in the Republic of Montenegro on 21 May 2006, organized in accordance with Article 60 of the Constitutional Charter of the State Union of Serbia and Montenegro, in my capacity as President of the Republic of Montenegro, I have the honour to request the admission of the Republic of Montenegro to membership in the United Nations.').

86. Rule 134 of the Rules of Procedure of the General Assembly of the UN provides: 'Any State which desires to become a Member of the United Nations shall submit an application to the Secretary-General. Such application shall contain a declaration, made in a formal instrument, that the State in question accepts the obligations contained in the Charter.'

87. Continuing with the above examples, *see* the Admission of the Republic of Bosnia and Herzegovina to membership in the United Nations, U.N. Doc. A/Res/46/237 (22 May 1992); Admission of the Democratic Republic of East Timor for admission to membership in the United Nations, U.N. Doc. A/Res/57/3 (2 Oct. 2002); Admission of the Republic of Montenegro for admission to membership in the United Nations, U.N. Doc. A/Res/60/264 (12 Jul. 2006).

88. Coombe, 135–136.

While on the one hand it might be said that the only limit to name choice is imagination, in practice, geographic name choices are drawn from a relatively limited field of reference that is, by its very nature, shared with neighbouring States: 'The names of the countries are usually associated with their geographical location and dimension. Geography, at any rate, political geography, as reflected in the boundary making and delimitation of frontiers, territorial, maritime and aerial or atmospheric, changes with time.'[89] As borders fluctuate and time passes, so too are history, culture, language and environmental conditions shared, and it is from this pool of shared experience that geographic names are often drawn. Thus the very same reasoning behind one State's choice of name could also underpin another (particularly neighbouring) State's choice of name.

It is clear why a State would prefer that other States not choose the same name, and this bears out in practice. The relative infrequency with which naming conflicts have arisen is nevertheless surprising when one considers the frequency with which new States have been created and old ones extinguished in modern times: it has been noted that more than 125 new States have been created or reconstituted since the coming into force of the UN Charter in 1945, not including name changes.[90] Even in this highly dynamic environment, the only major conflict is the ongoing dispute between Greece and the country provisionally referred to as the 'former Yugoslav Republic of Macedonia', or 'FYROM'. This dispute will next be critically analysed, but first, some comments must be made about its uniqueness. One conclusion to potentially be drawn from the scarcity of name choice disputes is that there is a customary rule of avoiding selecting a conflicting State name. The existence of such a rule is undermined, however, by the number of States with shared names[91] and the simple fact that in none of these cases has conflict arisen to the level of the Macedonia name dispute. What drives name choice (and, by corollary, avoidance of choosing what others have already chosen) may not be a sense of legal obligation but rather simply an overriding interest in avoiding confusion with other States – a practical preference to not be confused with others. Although (as concluded in the previous section of this chapter) possession of a name is not a necessary aspect of legal personality, it does make transacting with other legal persons

89. Sompong Sucharitkul, *The Inter-temporal Character of International and Comparative Law Regarding the Rights of the Indigenous Populations of the World*, 50 Am. J. Comp. L. 3, 10 (2002).
90. Crawford, 715 and Appendix 1. Note that the publication of this work in 2007 pre-dates the formation of South Sudan.
91. Examples of identical or materially similar country names include: (a) the Democratic Republic of the Congo and Republic of the Congo, (b) the Republic of Equatorial Guinea, the Republic of Guinea, the Republic of Guinea-Bissau, and the Independent State of Papua New Guinea, (c) the Democratic People's Republic of Korea and the Republic of Korea, and (d) Niger and Nigeria.

more convenient. Where similar names can be differentiated, these can be used without serious issue.

What then would lead a State to select a name insufficiently distinctive from or even objectionable to others? One possibility already alluded to in the previous paragraphs is that shared history and experiences could lead multiple States to select the same or similar representations and symbols of their sovereignty. Objection on this basis is defensible in principle only for neighbours or States otherwise currently or historically related. Exemplary of such a situation are neighbours Greece and the FYROM, one of the new nations borne out of dismembered Yugoslavia.

Responding to Greece's objection to Macedonia's application[92] for UN membership, the UN Security Council recommended that the country be 'provisionally referred to for all purposes within the United Nations as "the Former Yugoslav Republic of Macedonia" pending settlement of the difference that has arisen over the name of the State'.[93] The name is but one aspect of this long-running dispute; in earlier proceedings before the European Court of Justice (ECJ), Greece complained of large scale efforts to promote 'the idea of a unified Macedonia' through that country's chosen name (Republic of Macedonia), the wording of its constitution, and such activities as 'the circulation of maps, calendars and car stickers' and 'school history books' depicting the FYROM as encompassing Greek territory.[94] Also concerning to Greece was the FYROM's adoption of the 'Sun of Vergina' on its flag, this emblem having been discovered in excavations on Greek territory.[95] Greece demanded that the FYROM cease use of its chosen name and symbols and related activities, all of which it interpreted as territorial claims amounting to a threat of war.[96]

The ECJ's decision went not to resolving the name dispute, but rather to interim measures requested by the European Commission to suspend economic sanctions imposed by Greece against the FYROM, which request was ultimately rejected by the Court.[97] A subsequent Interim Accord between Greece and the FYROM required only undertakings to continue negotiation 'with a view to reaching agreement' on this matter.[98] In 2008, the

---

92. U.N. Doc. A/47/876-S/25147 (1992), discussed in detail in Michael C. Wood, *Participation of Former Yugoslav States in the United Nations and in Multilateral Treaties*, in *Max Planck Y.B. U.N. L.* 236–241 (Armin von Bogdandy ed., Martinus Nijhoff Publishers 1997).
93. S.C. Res. 817, 7 Apr. 1993, U.N. Doc. S/INF/49 (1993), at para. 2.
94. *Commission of the European Communities v. Hellenic Republic*, C-120/94 R I-03037 (E.C.J. 29 Jun. 1994), at para. 8.
95. *Id.*, para. 9.
96. *Id.*, para. 31.
97. *Id.*, para. 48.
98. Interim Accord (with related letters and translations of the Interim Accord in the Languages of the Contracting Parties), Greece-the former Yugoslav Republic of Macedonia, signed in New York 13 Sep. 1995, 1891 U.N.T.S. I-32193; 34 I.L.M. 1461 (13 Oct. 1995).

FYROM instituted proceedings before the ICJ asserting that the Interim Accord had been breached by Greece by its objection to the FYROM's application to join the North Atlantic Treaty Organization ('NATO').[99] In December 2011, the ECJ found[100] that Greece's objection violated the Interim Accord. The applicant's clear intentions to refer to itself by its constitutionally chosen name within NATO (which ultimately resolved to delay a decision on admission pending resolution of the name dispute) was considered not to render Greece's objection lawful. The Court seized the opportunity to highlight the fact that the dispute had been ongoing for sixteen years, and to remind the parties of their obligation under the Interim Accord to make good faith efforts towards its resolution.

This dispute is a unique constellation[101] and though it remains unresolved, an attempt can be made to draw conclusions on the legality of Greece's demand that its neighbour avoid adopting the name 'Macedonia' in order to broadly articulate limitations upon States' sovereign rights to select a name. Notably, leading scholars have avoided doing so.[102] One highly regarded text characterizes the matter as one of 'political guarantees ensuring that [the FYROM] had no territorial claims towards a neighbouring Community state'.[103] Another sees the dispute as illustrative of the potential problems inherent in States' sovereign authority, but makes no statement as to the legality of Greece's demands.[104] The problem, it has been said, is that this dispute:

> both clarifies and obscures the status of country names in international law. On the one hand, both the UN's and the EU's reactions suggest that Greece's claim that a country's choice of name could be a form of aggression was not, as an abstract matter, per se unreasonable. Thus, it appears that international law recognizes the theoretical possibility that a country's choice of name might amount to hostile propaganda against a neighbour, such as in 'the use of a denomination which implies

99. ICJ, Press Release, *The Former Yugoslav Republic of Macedonia Institutes Proceedings against Greece for a Violation of Article 11 of the Interim Accord of 13 September 1995*, No. 2008/40 (17 Nov. 2008) (available at http://www.icj-cij.org/docket/files/142/14881.pdf).
100. *Application of the Interim Accord of 13 September 1995 (the former Yugoslav Republic of Macedonia v. Greece)*, Judgment of 5 Dec. 2011.
101. Craven, *What's in a Name?*, 238 (characterizing this as 'the first occasion in which it has ever been suggested that a State, or for that matter a people, should not be the exclusive determinants of their own cultural and political symbols').
102. Demetrius Andreas Floudas, *Pardon? A Name for a Conflict? FYROM's Dispute with Greece Revisited*, in *The New Balkans: Disintegration and Reconstruction* (George A. Kourvetaris et al. eds, East European Monographs 2002).
103. Malcolm N. Shaw QC, *International Law* 452 (6th ed., Cambridge University Press 2008).
104. Colin Warbrick, *States and Recognition in International Law*, in *International Law* 241 (Malcom D. Evans ed., Oxford University Press 2006).

> territorial claims.' In so doing, it suggests that the presumed norm that countries control their names has been weakened; conversely, it suggests that the idea that one country has rights regarding another country's use of names might theoretically have more merit than many had previously suspected.[105]

These comments attribute to States a right to select a name, but posit that this right is not absolute. This is consistent with the principle of sovereignty, which gives the State supreme but not absolute authority within its territory. Interference in domestic matters is permitted by Article 2(7) of the UN Charter, as well as by customary international law. Further, the Friendly Relations Declaration requires that 'every State shall refrain from any action aimed at the partial or total disruption of the national unity or territorial integrity of any other State or country.'[106] If the right of a State to select and use a name is based on sovereignty, then this limitation must correspondingly apply, meaning that one State's name choice cannot constitute an unlawful interference with the sovereignty of another State. Such an interpretation is supported by the general principle of abuse of rights, which serves to limit a State's choice of name to the extent that the choice had the effect of 'inflict[ing] upon another State an injury which cannot be justified by a legitimate consideration of its own advantage.'[107] A link to the general principle of good faith is equally clear given that '[a] state that acts in good faith is unlikely to abuse its rights.'[108] A related principle of 'good neighbourliness' was raised by Judge ad hoc Roucounas and suggested in his dissenting opinion to have been breached by the FYROM.[109]

The determination as to whether one State's choice of name constitutes an unlawful interference with the sovereignty of another State or a breach of the principles of good faith, abuse of rights or good neighbourliness depends entirely on the facts in question.[110] As a result, it is impossible to develop universal rules around the selection of country names. In the Macedonia

---

105. Froomkin, *When We Say US™, We Mean It!*, 856, quoting the European Commission's 16 Dec. 1991 Guidelines on the Recognition of New States in Eastern Europe and in the Soviet Union, as reprinted in Danilo Türk, *Declaration on Yugoslavia*, 4(1) Eur. J. Int'l L. 73, 73 (1993).
106. *Declaration on Principles of International Law concerning Friendly Relations and Cooperation among States in accordance with the Charter of the United Nations*, GA/RES/2625(XXV), U.N. Doc. A/8082 (1970).
107. L. Oppenheim, *International Law: A Treatise* 345 (8th ed., H. Lauterpacht ed., Longmans, Green & Co. 1955).
108. Michael Byers, *Abuse of Rights: An Old Principle, a New Age*, 47 McGill L.J. 389, 406 (2002).
109. *Application of the Interim Accord of 13 September 1995 (the former Yugoslav Republic of Macedonia v. Greece)*, Judgment of 5 Dec. 2011 (Dissenting opinion of Judge ad hoc Roucounas).
110. Craven, *What's in a Name?*, 234, citing *Case Concerning Military and Paramilitary Activities in and Against Nicaragua (Nicaragua v. United States of America)*, I.C.J. Rep. 1986 (I.C.J. 27 Jun. 1986).

dispute, the European Commission Declaration on Yugoslavia required each former Yugoslav republic to declare that it had agreed, *inter alia*, 'to adopt constitutional and political guarantees "ensuring that it has no territorial claims" against a neighbouring E.C. country and that it would not use a name (e.g., Macedonia) that implied such claims and would conduct "no hostile propaganda activities" against a neighbouring E.C. country.'[111] This is likely as precise as rules could be articulated. This difficulty, along with the infrequency with which naming disputes have arisen,[112] may help to explain the non-existence of expressly acknowledged, detailed rules of international law on name selection.

There is no denying the potential for the choice of name by a State and even the purely internal, domestic use of the name to provoke (intentionally or unintentionally) changes in the world order. That part of the population in State A might be motivated by State B's choice of name to exercise a right of self-determination is a realistic possibility. Yet self-determination in its contemporary form is a right of peoples to be involved in a meaningful way in the constitution and maintenance of the systems that govern their lives.[113] The possibility that, as a right of peoples, self-determination encompasses a right to self- or group-identify using geographic names is explored in Chapter 9, below, along with other potential human rights bases of rights in geographic names.

6.3.2.3 A Right of States to Be Referred by Their Chosen Name

A separate but related question is whether States have a right to be referred to by their chosen name. As discussed above, there is a strong practical and diplomatic incentive for States to have a name, but this does not necessarily speak to the existence of a legal obligation to have a name either generally or for a particular purpose. It has been noted earlier in this chapter that there is a practice of using names in the functions of the UN, though there are no provisions in the UN Charter that require members to have a name. The use of names is directed in certain UN procedures, for example in General Assembly plenary voting.[114] Yet use of *a* name is one matter, while use of a State's *chosen name* is another; the issue here is specifically whether, to give

111. European Community, *Declaration on Yugoslavia and on the Guidelines on the Recognition of New States (Extraordinary European Political Cooperation Ministerial Meeting, Brussels, 16 Dec. 1991)*, 31 I.L.M. 1485 (1992).
112. There is another reported instance of a naming dispute in recent history, in which proposed changes to the name of the country of Uzbekistan were rejected on the basis of their being interpreted as territorial claims. Crawford, 68 n. 141, citing Karen Dawisha & Bruce Parrott, *Russia and the new states of Eurasia: the politics of upheaval* 85 (Cambridge University Press 1995).
113. Rupert Emerson, *Self-Determination*, 65 Am. J. Int'l L. 459, 465–466 (1971).
114. General Assembly of the United Nations, *Rules of Procedure and Comments*, Rule 87.

one specific example, the US is obliged to use the name 'Russian Federation' when referring to that country within or even beyond the UN context.

For the most part, the practice of using names in the UN is axiomatic. Names are ordinarily used – and without any special emphasis on their being used – in accordance with the wishes of the named UN member. One notable instance of special emphasis is the General Assembly's pronouncement 'that, in accordance with the desires of its people, South West Africa shall henceforth be known as "Namibia".'[115] Applications are ordinarily accepted using standardized language,[116] and the new member is then referred to by other members accordingly. The case of the FYROM is in this context again a unique constellation: the UN Security Council avoided making use of that country's chosen name when resolving on its membership application, instead recommending admission of the 'State whose application is contained in document S/25147', and then recommending the use of a provisional name.[117] The General Assembly then admitted the so-called former Yugoslav Republic of Macedonia using the standardized language just noted.

The Russian Federation provides an example of a different situation, that of an existing UN member changing its name. Leaving aside questions of continuation of membership[118] which lie outside the scope of this study, the Russian Federation's assumption of the Union of Soviet Socialist Republics' seat at the UN was characterized by then-President Yeltsin as a simple name change. He simply requested 'that the name "Russian Federation" should be used in the United Nations in place of the name "the Union of Soviet Socialist Republics".'[119] There is no record of objection to this request,[120] and the name 'Russian Federation' has accordingly since been used in the UN General Assembly and Security Council.[121]

Looking beyond these forums to the ICJ, it has been noted in the previous section of this chapter in the context of legal personality that there is uniform practice in referring to parties by name in ICJ disputes, and that

---

115. *Question of South West Africa*, G.A. Res. 2372(XXII), U.N. Doc. A/Res/2372(XXII) (12 Jun. 1968).
116. General Assembly resolutions on administration are worded as follows:

> The General Assembly,
> Having received the recommendation of the Security Council of [date] that [State name] should be admitted to membership in the United Nations,
> Having considered the application for membership of [State name],
> Decides to admit [State name] to membership in the United Nations.

See for example, Admission of the Republic of Montenegro to membership in the United Nations.
117. S.C. Res. 817, para. 2.
118. On continuation, *see* Yehuda Z. Blum, *Russia Takes Over the Soviet Union's Seat at the United Nations*, 3(2) Eur. J. Int'l L. 354 (1992).
119. U.N. Doc. 1991/RUSSIA, 1, excerpted in Blum, at 356.
120. Crawford, 677.
121. *See for example*, U.N.G.A. Res. A/RES/65/281 (17 Jun. 2011).

this practice is supported at least to some extent by the wording of Article 38(1) of the ICJ Rules. This Article does not expressly require that an official name be used, but presumably the name of a UN member as per its admission is the name that will be used. The 'Macedonia' case is illustrative: it was docketed as '*the former Yugoslav Republic of Macedonia v. Greece*'. That case nevertheless offers no particular support to the existence of a legal obligation to refer to parties by their chosen name except insofar as it evidences a sense of felt obligation on the FYROM's part to refer to itself by its provisional name as recommended by the UN Security Council. More assistance would have been offered were the roles of the parties in that case reversed (in other words, it would be interesting to see whether Greece would identify the respondent as something other than the 'former Yugoslav Republic of Macedonia'). Greece's counter-memorial and rejoinder did refer to the 'former Yugoslav Republic of Macedonia',[122] which is procedurally sensible, given that Greece was the respondent, but not expressly required by Article 49 of the ICJ Rules. It is also interesting to note that the respondent in the case against Greece before the ECJ was not identified as 'Greece' but rather as the 'Hellenic Republic' (the name under which it entered the Treaty Establishing the European Community).[123]

Of these instances just discussed, the language that most strongly supports a right of members to be referred to by their chosen name is that of the UN Security Council in directing other members to refer to the 'former Yugoslav Republic of Macedonia' and do so 'for all purposes within the United Nations'.[124] This, ironically, is not a case of a State being referred to by its chosen name, but rather a provisional name chosen by the UN to be used pending resolution of a naming dispute. Even if this or perhaps the Namibia case or standard practice offers a basis upon which a right of States to be referred to by their chosen name can be asserted, this is an extremely limited right which would prevent only the use of an alternative name within and for UN purposes. This would not prevent the use of alternative names (e.g., a reference to the United Kingdom of Great Britain and Northern Ireland by the slang name 'Old Blighty',[125] or even a reference to that country as 'Britain' or 'the UK') by a member of the GAC in ICANN discourse, a government official from commenting to the press, or even in

---

122. *Case Concerning the Application of Article 11, Paragraph 1, of the Interim Accord of 13 September 1995 (The Former Yugoslav Republic of Macedonia v. Greece)*, Counter-Memorial by Greece (I.C.J. 19 Jan. 2010) (available at http://www.icj-cij.org/docket/files/142/16356.pdf); *Case Concerning the Application of Article 11, Paragraph 1, of the Interim Accord of 13 September 1995 (The Former Yugoslav Republic of Macedonia v. Greece)*, Rejoinder of Greece (I.C.J. 27 Oct. 2010) (available at http://www.icj-cij.org/docket/files/142/16356.pdf).
123. Treaty Establishing the European Community (Consolidated Version) (25 Mar. 1957).
124. S.C. Res. 817, para. 2.
125. Michael Quinion, *World Wide Words: Blighty*, http://www.worldwidewords.org/qa/qa-bli1.htm.

international relations outside of the UN context, while acknowledging the potential detriment such actions might in some instances have in terms of good international relations. Much of State conduct around naming appears to have as its basis not clearly identifiable legal rules, but positive international relations with the aim of avoidance and resolution of disputes through good faith negotiations. The UN Security Council has encouraged this from Greece and the FYROM,[126] though as-yet those States have been unable to achieve resolution of their now two and a half decade running dispute.[127]

6.4 CONCLUSIONS ON RIGHTS IN GEOGRAPHIC NAMES AS SUCH

Two related bases have been explored in this chapter as potential sources of rights in geographic names under international law: Article 6*ter* of the Paris Convention for the Protection of Industrial Property and the principle of sovereignty. First, Article 6*ter* requires that States prohibit the registrability as trademarks of State flags and other emblems, as well as the emblems of IGOs. In this chapter, the interpretation of Article 6*ter* (1)(a) by WIPO has been confirmed with reference to recent survey evidence and as-yet unsuccessful attempts to amend that Article. The results of the questionnaire developed in 2011 by the WIPO Standing Committee indicate that many States are reserving country names from trademark registration even though they are not obliged under Article 6*ter* to do so. An isolated instance of the use of the notification procedure specified in Article 6*ter* (3) by Iceland has also been highlighted, but other actions and inactions in this space suggest that this is a unique interpretation of Article 6*ter* which does not constitute evidence of a custom of reserving rights in country names.

From discussions around proposed amendments to widen the scope of Article 6*ter* to include country names can be extrapolated the conclusion that there currently is no support in Article 6*ter* for recognizing rights in country names as such that could be called upon to justify their exclusive use by States and the prevention of their use by others – whether in the DNS context or elsewhere. The analysis documented in this chapter supports that conclusion. It is only logical to reach the same conclusion as respects subnational names. That said, Article 6*ter* does not prevent States from reserving rights in geographic names as such; it simply does not require that they do so. That a significant percentage of Paris Union Member States have opted not to recognize rights in country names in domestic law is indicative

126. S.C. Res. 817.

127. Lefteris Papadimas, *Macedonia Says 'Mountains to Climb' in Name Row with Greece*, Reuters, http://uk.reuters.com/article/uk-greece-macedonia-namedispute-idUKKBN0U01GJ20151217 (17 Dec. 2015).

of there not being a general principle of international law of recognizing States' rights in country names as such. The protection offered by ICANN through the *gTLD Applicant Guidebook* is therefore not strictly inconsistent with Article 6*ter*, as Article *6ter* does not require those protections, but they are nevertheless inconsistent with the intentions of Article *6ter* as evidenced by its precise wording. Furthermore, the reservation of country and territory names as gTLDs is neither supported nor justified by Article 6*ter*.

The second basis of rights evaluated in this chapter is the foundational international law principle of sovereignty. Governments have looked to the principle of sovereignty in order to justify what they view as an inherent right to prevent others' use of 'their' names. While there may be a growing body of examples of conflict over private parties' use of geographical names,[128] there are surprisingly few examples of name conflicts between States. As a result, there are very few constellations from which support of States' rights in country names can be drawn. In this chapter it has been considered that there are actually three rights potentially encompassed in a right of States to country names: a right to select a name, a right to object to another State's name, and a right to be referred to by a chosen name. In relation to none of these is there an express right contained in any international convention, though the ICJ Rules do refer to the identification of party names, while the UN General Assembly Rules refer to plenary voting according to name. At the same time, in relation to none of these is there an express denial of a corresponding right in any international convention.

From the as-yet unresolved dispute between Greece and the FYROM over the name 'Macedonia' can be extracted certain conclusions about States' rights to select and object to a name. This dispute is the manifestation of a rational tendency to select a name that happens to be based upon an identity or history that may be shared with neighbouring States. The escalation of this dispute into an international legal dispute is, however, unique. From it and other instances of name similarity can be deduced that there is no rule of international law preventing one State from selecting the same or similar name as another State's. This dispute suggests that a State's right to select a name is not absolute, but rather is limited by obligations not to encroach upon another State's sovereignty and to act in good faith. There are no clear rules to determine when this occurs, nor is it practicable to attempt to develop rules beyond the general proscription imposed upon the FYROM not to interfere with the territorial integrity of another State. Nor for the same reasons is it practicable to develop rules around objections to States' choice of name. These situations can only be resolved on a case-by-case basis, having due regard to the facts at issue.

As to the implications of these conclusions in the context of domain names, conflicting applications for new geographic gTLDs are inevitable:

128. For examples, *see* discussion of UDRP cases involving geographic names at Part II, Chapter 3, s. 3.3.1.2 above.

there are already in existence several constellations of similar country names which, although they have not previously been disputed in the offline context, could be the subject of a future challenge in the online context due to the technical requirement of absolute name uniqueness and the policy decision to prevent confusingly similar TLD strings. Although conflicting applications for a .macedonia new gTLD were not made in the 2012 applications period of the New gTLD Program, this is a real possibility in future expansion rounds if the prohibition on applications for country and territory names is lifted. It would be inappropriate to develop a single rule of priority on the basis of sovereignty, simply because sovereignty does not support such a rule. On this basis, as a matter of policy and to preserve the stability of the internet and its DNS, ICANN should consider refusing the creation of any geographic new gTLD for which competing applications have been submitted by rival States. This is supported and even required by the equality of States recognized by Article 4 of the Montevideo Convention.

Finally, to the extent that a right to be referred to by one's chosen name can be derived from practice within the UN and before the ICJ, that right is limited to those specific contexts and cannot be relied upon in other contexts such as the DNS. Further, the recognition of a right in that limited context is not alone determinative of the exclusivity of a State's rights in a particular name in that particular context, or certainly in any other context.

In short, the doctrine of sovereignty offers no support for a government's claim to exclusivity or priority over a geographic name and its use in the DNS, whether against another State or a private party. Further, the failure to include country names within the precise wording of Article 6*ter* of the Paris Convention opens the door to private parties possessing trademark rights in country names, as various countries have allowed through domestic law, and thus disproves government claims to exclusivity or priority.

Chapter 7
Rights in Geographical Indications

The protection of geographical indications is not only about the protection of names. It is about the protection of a certain quality and reputation that is attributable to a product that is made in a defined place. A mere name does not necessarily capture that concept of quality.[1]

7.1 GEOGRAPHICAL INDICATIONS AND WHY THEY PRESENT CHALLENGES

Geographic names that are used to denote the particular geographic origin of particular comestible products have since the early days of the Paris Convention for the Protection of Industrial Property held a special legal status separate from their potential registrability as trademarks. That status is, however, nowhere near as clearly defined or harmonized as it is for trademarks. When it comes to the recognition of rights under international law in geographical indications and related origin-connoting names, the question is therefore not whether rights are recognized, but whether the extent of their recognition is sufficient to have any impact upon their use in a particular context such as the DNS.

The TRIPS Agreement contains provisions respecting 'geographical indications', but since long before its coming into force there have been two separate international treaty frameworks directed at the recognition of rights

1. O'Connor, *The Law of Geographical Indications*, 18.

in origin-connoting geographic names. Entirely different agreements, one thing they have in common is a low number of signatories, as a result of which they could both reasonably be characterized as failures. Efforts through WIPO since the publication of the first edition of this book have been directly targeted at that problem, giving rise to the potential for (although not a guarantee of) a different landscape in the future. Until then, the regional level, where the EU in particular has constructed a robust protection framework out of Member States' traditions of recognizing rights,[2] remains the space in which protection of GIs is most robust and most harmonized. Past and present efforts on the issue of international recognition of geographical indications suggest that these are driven by Europe's (the so-called Old World) eagerness for other members of the international community to embrace its framework, or something closely resembling it.[3]

All members[4] of the WTO are required by the TRIPS Agreement to provide the means to protect geographical indications against use that would mislead the public or constitute unfair competition. It is up to members to determine how to meet this requirement. There is a vast range of approaches, including:

> unfair competition and consumer protection, passing off, sui generis protection of geographical indications via registration, passive protection where the concept of geographical indications is defined and protection available through courts but no registration system, trademarks with geographical references, collective, guarantee and certification trademarks, and administrative schemes of protection.[5]

What the TRIPS Agreement provides is not a right in geographical indications as such, but rather a limited right to prevent particular kinds of uses depending on the type of product to which the name relates. Importantly, as will be explored in detail throughout this chapter, a distinction is made between indications relating to wine and spirits and indications relating to other types of products.

This is as much as the WTO has – as-yet – managed to achieve in terms of reaching agreement among its members, and even getting to this point was difficult.[6] For those countries whose laws offer greater protection to geographical indications, including protection of indications as such, the TRIPS Agreement compromise offers little comfort because they see what is at stake

2. *Id.*, 123.
3. *See for example*, Cottier, *The Prospects for Intellectual Property in GATT*, 404.
4. WTO, *Understanding the WTO: The Organization, Members and Observers.*
5. O'Connor, *The Law of Geographical Indications*, 67.
6. Cottier, *The Prospects for Intellectual Property in GATT*, 404.

as being much more than mere names, but national identity.[7] On the other hand, for those countries in which geographical indications have not traditionally been protected, the TRIPS compromise represents the edge of a slippery slope; members' ability to offer greater protection than that required under the TRIPS Agreement (the so-called minimum standards framework) gives rise to 'a clear risk of excessive protection' and of needing to make fundamental changes to existing law.[8]

As with geographic names generally, recent discussions about an international standard of protection for geographical indications have been motivated by the use of these names in the online environment. The World Intellectual Property Organization's 'WIPO II' Report offered specific examples of unauthorized registrations of second-level domain names comprised of geographical indications, but as with geographic names generally, it was concluded that the TRIPS Agreement offered insufficient support for preventing this activity.[9] More than a decade later, the registration of second-level domain names comprised of geographical indications remains problematic, and potentially even exacerbated by ICANN's expansion of the top-level of the DNS. In early 2014, after new gTLD application evaluation results were released, a group of WIPO members notably proposed 'that the SCT [Standing Committee on the Law of Trademarks, Industrial Designs and Geographical Indications] start discussions in order to find a common solution to ensure the protection of geographical indications in the DNS, having regard in particular to the new gTLDs.'[10] As these new calls are made for recognition of geographical indications in future ICANN policy, it is imperative to examine the status of geographical indications under international law in order to anticipate, and in at least some instances preventatively address, specific issues.

This chapter begins with an introduction to the legal concept of a geographical indication and the international framework of protection that remains in development after more than 100 years. Mirroring the way in which geographical indications are separated in this framework, the analysis of legal rights that follows is divided into two parts, the first exploring rights in wine and spirit geographical indications, and the second exploring rights in geographical indications for other products.

---

7. Tomer Broude, *Taking 'Trade and Culture' Seriously: Geographical Indications and Cultural Protection in WTO Law*, 26 U. Pa. J. Int'l Econ. L. 623, 661–662 (2005).
8. Thomas Cottier, *The Agreement on Trade-Related Aspects of Intellectual Property Rights*, in *Trade and Intellectual Property Protection in WTO Law: Collected Essays* 145 (Cameron May 2005).
9. WIPO, *WIPO II Report*, paras 223–228 and 237–245.
10. WIPO Standing Committee on the Law of Trademarks, Industrial Designs and Geographical Indications, *Proposal by the Delegations of the Czech Republic, France, Germany, Hungary, Italy, Portugal, Republic of Moldova, Spain and Switzerland*, WIPO Doc. SCT/31/8 Rev.4 (23 Mar. 2015), Annex at 3 (available at http://www.wipo.int/edocs/mdocs/sct/en/sct_31/sct_31_8_rev_4.pdf).

7.1.1 Geographical Indications, Indications of Source and Appellations of Origin

The term 'geographical indication' is one of the three legal terms used to describe geographic names that identify a particular product as originating from a particular geographical location. 'Geographical indication' is the term used by the TRIPS Agreement, Article 22(1) of which states: 'Geographical indications are, for the purposes of this Agreement, indications which identify a good as originating in the territory of a Member, or a region or locality in that territory, where a given quality, reputation or other characteristic of the good is essentially attributable to its geographical origin.' Key to this definition are three points: first, its limitation to 'goods'; second, the required nexus of the good with a particular territory; and third, the demonstration of nexus through a 'quality, reputation or other characteristic' being 'essentially attributable' to geographical location. These three points differentiate geographical indications from 'indications of source' and 'appellations of origin', the two other legal terms used to describe geographic names that identify a particular product as originating from a particular geographical location.

The precise characteristics of each of these types of names are identified immediately below, but as an initial matter the existence of significant points of overlap between the three terms should be emphasized: all 'appellations of origin' are considered to fall within the definition of 'geographical indication' while at the same time are also 'considered to be a *species* of the *genus* "indications of source".'[11] It is nevertheless unwise to consider 'geographical indication' an 'umbrella term'; 'not all indications of source are covered by the definition of geographical indications since not all of them would necessarily have the "quality, reputation or other characteristic of the good which is essentially attributable to its geographical origin".'[12]

Of the three terms, 'indication of source' is the broadest and longest in use at the international level. What started as draft Article 6 at the 1880 Paris Conference would ultimately take shape in Article 10 of the Paris Convention for the Protection of Industrial Property as a prohibition on the use of false indications of the source of goods.[13] This prohibition was limited to the use of false indications only to the extent that they were used in conjunction with a false, fictitious, or deceptive trade name.[14] Such narrow drafting provoked a separate agreement in 1891, the Madrid Agreement for the Repression of False or Deceptive Indications of Source (the 'Madrid (Indications of Source) Agreement'), which made actionable any 'false or deceptive indication', whether direct or indirect, of the country or place of

11. Bodenhausen, 23 (internal citations omitted).
12. O'Connor, *The Law of Geographical Indications*, 24.
13. Conrad, 23.
14. *Ibid.*

origin.[15] Notably, no nexus to the territory in the form of characteristics or reputation specifically attributable to the geographical location was required under the Madrid (Indications of Source) Agreement. More than eighty years later, WIPO's Model Law for Developing Countries on Appellations of Origin and Geographical Indications maintained this position, defining 'indication of source' as 'any expression or sign used to indicate that a product or service originates in a country or region or a specific place'.[16]

Despite the liberalization of Article 10 achieved at the 1958 Paris Convention Revision Conference at Lisbon,[17] interest in yet stronger protection led to another, separate agreement, the Lisbon Agreement for the Protection of Appellations of Origin and their International Registration (the 'Lisbon Agreement').[18] Article 2(1) of the Lisbon Agreement defines the term 'appellation of origin' as 'the geographical name of a country, region, or locality, which serves to designate a product originating therein, the quality and characteristics of which are due exclusively or essentially to the geographic environment, including natural and human factors'. Unlike the Paris Convention and Madrid (Indications of Source) Agreement, the Lisbon Agreement applies only to geographic names and protects them as such; symbols and other signs are not protected. Thus it was that the Lisbon Agreement, until recently, could be said to offer stronger protection than the previous agreements but to a narrower set of indications. The 2015 Geneva Act of the Lisbon Agreement, which covers both appellations of origin and geographical indications,[19] is an attempt to resolve some of these differences in the hope of gaining more signatories.[20]

Although Articles 22, 23 and 24 of the TRIPS Agreement were based on the Lisbon Agreement, the TRIPS definition of 'geographical indication' marked a return to a broader scope of covered indications. The TRIPS Agreement does not require that an indication be a geographic name, but where an indication is geographic, it must relate to a single Member State only: country names qualify, but cross-border regional names like 'Caribbean' do not.[21] Notably, the 2015 Geneva Act of the Lisbon Agreement sidesteps use of the precise term 'geographical name', instead limiting its

15. Madrid Agreement for the Repression of False or Deceptive Indications of Source on Goods, Art. 1(1) (14 Apr. 1891), 828 U.N.T.S. 163.
16. WIPO, *Model Law for Developing Countries on Appellations of Origin*, PJ/91/2, No. 809(E)(1975).
17. Conrad, 23.
18. Lisbon Agreement for the Protection of Appellations of Origin and their International Registration (31 Oct. 1958, entered into force 25 Sep. 1966), 923 U.N.T.S. 205.
19. Geneva Act of the Lisbon Agreement on Appellations of Origin and Geographical Indications (20 May 2015, not yet in force), WIPO Doc. LI/DC/19 (hereinafter 'Geneva Act') Art. 2.
20. WIPO Special Union for the Protection of Appellations of Origin and their International Registration, *Assembly Report of the Twenty-third (6th Extraordinary) Session in Geneva, September 22 to 30, 2008*, LI/A/23/2.
21. O'Connor, *The law of geographical indications*, 52–53.

subject matter to 'any denomination protected in the Contracting Party of Origin *consisting of or containing the name of a geographical area, or another denomination known as referring to such area*'[22] and 'any indication protected in the Contracting Party of Origin *consisting of or containing the name of a geographical area, or another indication known as referring to such area*'.[23] (emphasis added)

The TRIPS Agreement requires that an indication 'identify' a 'good', as contrasted with the Lisbon Agreement's requirement that the geographical name 'designate' a 'product'. Although it has been concluded that this change in wording is of no legal effect,[24] this, too, is a gap filled by the Geneva Act.[25] Finally, the TRIPS Agreement allows for a good's non-physical reputation to be the basis of its nexus to the geographical location, while the Lisbon Agreement requires a physical tie in the form of quality and characteristics of a product as directly resulting from its geographical location. The Geneva Act of the Lisbon Agreement attempts to fill this gap by acknowledging that there are 'several different ways under national and regional laws' for recognizing rights in geographic origin-connoting names, and '[m]oreover, these laws do not all identify the subject-matter by the terms appellation of origin and geographical indication'.[26] Thus the Geneva Act incorporates all of these concepts within its stated subject matter.[27]

---

22. Geneva Act Art. 2(1)(i).
23. Geneva Act Art. 2(1)(ii).
24. Daniel Gervais, *The TRIPS Agreement: Drafting History and Analysis* 365 n. 438 (4th ed., Sweet & Maxwell 2012).
25. WIPO, *Diplomatic Conference for the Adoption of a New Act of the Lisbon Agreement for the Protection of Appellations of Origin and Their International Registration: Notes on the Basic Proposal for the New Act of the Lisbon Agreement on Appellations of Origin and Geographical Indications*, LI/DC/5 (22 Dec. 2014) para. 2.02 ('The term "good" has been used throughout the English version of the Draft Revised Lisbon Agreement, to align the terminology used with the one contained in the Agreement on Trade-Related Aspects of Intellectual Property Rights ("TRIPS Agreement").').
26. *Id.* para. 2.01.
27. Article 2 – Subject Matter:

> (1) [Appellations of Origin and Geographical Indications] This Act applies in respect of:
>
> (i) any denomination protected in the Contracting Party of Origin consisting of or containing the name of a geographical area, or another denomination known as referring to such area, which serves to designate a good as originating in that geographical area, where the quality or characteristics of the good are due exclusively or essentially to the geographical environment, including natural and human factors, and which has given the good its reputation; as well as
>
> (ii) any indication protected in the Contracting Party of Origin consisting of or containing the name of a geographical area, or another indication known as referring to such area, which identifies a good as originating in that geographical area, where a given quality, reputation or other characteristic of the good is essentially attributable to its geographical origin.
>
> (2) [Possible Geographical Areas of Origin] A geographical area of origin as described in paragraph (1) may consist of the entire territory of the Contracting Party of Origin or a region, locality or place in the Contracting Party of Origin. [This does not exclude the application of this Act in respect of a geographical area of origin, as described in paragraph (1), consisting of a trans-border geographical area, subject to Art. 5(4).]

Recent developments from Lisbon Agreement signatories notwithstanding, by reason of its inclusion in the TRIPS Agreement, to which all WTO members are bound, the term 'geographical indication' is the most authoritative of these three terms for origin-connoting names. Neither the Madrid (Indications of Source) Agreement nor the Lisbon Agreement has a critical mass of contracting parties, the former with thirty-six and the latter with twenty-eight.[28] The Geneva Act of the Lisbon Agreement, signed in 2015, will enter into force, per Article 29, 'three months after five eligible parties … have deposited their instruments of ratification or accession.' This was not yet completed as of late 2016.

In terms of an up-to-date exposition of rights, 'geographical indication' is the most appropriate term by reason of its use in the TRIPS Agreement and in the Doha trade round agenda.[29] This chapter thus primarily focuses on 'geographical indications' as these are defined in the TRIPS Agreement; where specific issues of overlap or conflict with the other two forms of rights ('appellations of origin' or 'indications of source') are present, these are identified. Likewise, where these overlaps or conflicts are touched upon by the Geneva Act of the Lisbon Agreement, this too is identified.

The goal of the first published edition of this work was to determine the status of geographical indications under international law at the point of launch of ICANN's New gTLD Program. In this second edition, this analysis is carried forward to late 2016, taking into account developments in the law, New gTLD Program application disputes, and new efforts in policy development for future expansion of the top-level of the DNS.

7.1.2 THREE CONVENTIONS, THREE GROUPS OF GOODS

The immediately preceding section of this chapter identifies three conventions that specifically address geographic names used to identify a particular product as originating from a particular geographical location: the Madrid (Indications of Source), Lisbon and TRIPS Agreements. These three conventions are distinguishable not only by the subject matter they protect ('indication of source', 'appellation of origin' and 'geographical indication', respectively) but also by the level of protection extended to their respective subject matters.

---

28. WIPO, *Lisbon Agreement (Total Contracting Parties: 28)*, http://www.wipo.int/treaties/en/ShowResults.jsp?lang=en&treaty_id=10; *WIPO, Madrid Agreement (Indications of Source) (Total Contracting Parties: 36)*, http://www.wipo.int/treaties/en/ShowResults.jsp?lang=en&treaty_id=3. Since the publication of the first edition of this work, Bosnia and Herzegovina notified its accession to both agreements in the first half of 2013, raising the total number of signatories from 27 to 28 in the case of the Lisbon Agreement and 35 to 36 in the case of the Madrid (Indications of Source) Agreement.
29. *Doha WTO Ministerial Declaration*, Art. 18, WTO Doc. WT/MIN(01)/DEC1 (20 Nov. 2001) (available at http://www.wto.org/english/thewto_e/minist_e/min01_e/mindecl_e.htm).

Of the three conventions, the (pre-Geneva Act) Lisbon Agreement offers the highest level of protection by recognizing rights in appellations of origin through a registration system comparable to the trademark system. Members are required by Article 1(2) to protect through domestic law all appellations of origin 'as such', meaning that only rights in the nature of exclusive property are recognized and recorded in the register. Mere limitations on the use of appellations through, for example, consumer protection, tort, unfair competition law or equitable principles are not sufficient. Specifically, domestic law must prohibit, pursuant to Article 3, all usurpation or imitation, including 'style' or 'type' indications. All appellations are treated equally, without regard to type of product, and appellations protected in the home country are immunized under Article 6 from 'genericization' in all signatory States. This means that protection can never be lost on the grounds that the public has come to equate the geographic name with a general type of product, unless this happens in the country of origin or for some other reason protected status is lost there.

This high level of protection, and in particular the protection against genericization, helps to explain the relatively low number of signatories[30] to this agreement. Some of these considerations are borne out in the Geneva Act of the Lisbon Agreement, with Article 10 leaving a signatory 'free to choose the type of legislation under which it establishes the protection stipulated in this Act, provided that such legislation meets the substantive requirements of this Act', while Article 13 safeguards other rights, including trademark rights. Provisions on genericization are, however, narrowly drafted.[31]

The Madrid (Indications of Source) Agreement, by contrast, covers a broader scope of indications but offers them a lower standard of protection,

---

30. Contracting parties comprise: Algeria, Boznia and Herzegovina, Bulgaria, Burkina Faso, Congo, Costa Rica, Cuba, Czech Republic, Democratic People's Republic of Korea, France, Gabon, Georgia, Greece (not in force), Haiti, Hungary, Iran (Islamic Republic of), Israel, Italy, Mexico, Montenegro, Morocco (not in force), Nicaragua, Peru, Portugal, Republic of Moldova, Romania (not in force), Serbia, Slovakia, Spain (not in force), the former Yugoslav Republic of Macedonia, Togo, Tunisia, Turkey (not in force). WIPO, *Lisbon Agreement (Total Contracting Parties: 28).*

31. 'On the other hand, statements made, upon adoption of the new Act, by a number of delegations of countries with trademark-based protection systems, made it very clear that the objective of an inclusive global system was not achieved and that there remain in the new Act a number of provisions that would make it very difficult, if not impossible, for countries relying on trademarks in order to protect geographical indications to join the Geneva Act. This is particularly the case with respect to (1) Art. 1 on the content of protection; and (2) Art. 12, which prevents a Contracting Party from considering a registered appellation of origin or geographical indication as having become generic as long as it is protected in the Contracting Party of Origin; or of the validity of the registered appellation of origin or geographical indication for an indefinite period of time without the need for renewal, or a requirement of use, or in spite of conduct leading to acquiescence.' INTA, *New Act of the Lisbon Agreement Encompasses All Geographical Indications, Allows Accession by Regional Organizations*, 70(11) INTA Bulletin (15 Jun. 2015), at http://www.inta.org/INTABulletin/Pages/LisbonAgreement_7011.aspx.

preventing only false and misleading use. The concept of use includes representations on a product as well as advertising and related communications – what the Agreement terms at Article 1(1) 'direct' and 'indirect'. Other than its broadening of protection to not merely false but misleading indications, there are few substantive differences between the Madrid (Indications of Source) Agreement and the protection offered under the Paris Convention.[32] On the issue of genericization, members are prevented by Article 4 from treating any indications for wine as generic terms. This protection is not extended to other products.

TRIPS Agreement members, by far the most numerous of these three conventions, are required to prevent the importation of goods that directly or indirectly use false indications under Article 10 of the Paris Convention, by virtue of that convention's inclusion by reference. This is despite the fact that Article 10 was not initially geared toward origin statements: Article 10(1) requires no nexus to a geographical location; false indication of the 'identity of the producer, manufacturer, or merchant' is actionable. Given the necessarily commercial nature of this right and its broader applicability to geographic names other than geographical indications, Article 10 is discussed in the next chapter, which focuses on unfair competition and related rights arising out of the commercial use of geographic names.

Articles 22 through 24 of the TRIPS Agreement are, on the other hand, specifically focused on geographical indications and are set out in that Agreement under a separate heading of that name. Nexus to territory is required, but 'any aspect or element of geographical origin, known or unknown, physical or human, may underpin a quality, reputation or other characteristic of a good identified as originating in a particular place.'[33] More clearly than the Madrid (Indications of Source) Agreement but unlike the Lisbon Agreement (or its Geneva Act), protected indications are divided into two groups by the type of product they identify: wines and spirits, and other products. The scope of protection afforded under the TRIPS Agreement to these two groups of products is explored next, and areas of conflict between this protection and the use of protected names in the DNS are identified.

7.2 RIGHTS IN GEOGRAPHICAL INDICATIONS UNDER THE TRIPS AGREEMENT

7.2.1 Scope of Protection for Wine and Spirit Geographical Indications

There has long been a practice in Europe of identifying wines by the name of the region from which they originate. Chianti has been identified as

32. O'Connor, *The Law of Geographical Indications*, 31.
33. *Id.*, 54.

possibly being the first legally defined geographical indication, its status having been declared by a Decree of Grand Duke Cosimo III dé Medici in 1716.[34] The name 'Champagne', the globally recognized icon for the many issues and questions surrounding the recognition of rights in geographical indications at an international level, is said to have been formally recognized in 1887 by the Angers Court for use only in connection with wines produced and grown in the Champagne region of France.[35] This was not the first recognition of a geographical indication in France, but rather the start of a period of momentum in which courts 'confirmed that the name of a locality belonged to all the inhabitants that had interest to exploit it to make the situation of their establishment known, and the place of origin or of manufacturing of their products.'[36]

The concern in early cases recognizing geographical indications seems not to have been the identification of particular characteristics of products as a nexus to the territory of origin; rather, the names served purely to link geographical location of fabrication with product.[37] Today, Article 22(1) of the TRIPS Agreement requires that there be a deeper nexus between territory and product: it is not sufficient that a good simply originate from a defined geographical location. For all products, not just wines and spirits, it must be shown that 'a given quality, reputation or other characteristic of the good is essentially attributable to its geographical origin.' In meeting this standard, 'any aspect or element of geographical origin, known or unknown, physical or human, may underpin a quality, reputation or other characteristic of a good identified as originating in a particular place.'[38]

A nod to their longstanding use in the 'Old World', Article 23 of the TRIPS Agreement accords a higher level of protection to wine and spirit geographical indications than it does to indications for other goods. Specifically, Article 23(1) sets a standard of absolute protection, meaning that it requires Member States to prevent all uses of a wine or spirit geographical indication on wines or spirits not originating in the identified geographical location, 'even where the true origin of the goods is indicated or the geographical indication is used in translation or accompanied by expressions such as "kind", "type", "style", "imitation" or the like.' Article 23(2) further prevents registration and requires invalidation of trademarks containing or consisting of a geographical name of a wine or spirit for wines or spirits.

To wines alone, the TRIPS Agreement directs further refinements in their current and future recognition. As to their current recognition, Article

34. Broude, 666.
35. Alessandro Stanziani, *Wine Reputation and Quality Controls: The Origin of the AOCs in 19th Century France*, 18 Eur. J. L. Econ. 149, 157–158 (2004).
36. *Id.*, 157 (internal citations omitted).
37. *Id.*, 157–158.
38. O'Connor, *The Law of Geographical Indications*, 54.

23(3) recognizes homonymous geographical indications, thus acknowledging the potential for a 'New World' wine region to have been named by its inhabitants after the 'Old World' wine region from which they emigrated. As to future recognition, Article 23(4) directs that negotiations be undertaken regarding the establishment of a 'multilateral system of notification and registration of geographical indications for wines eligible for protection' in their home country. This is the highest level of protection (and potential for future protection) offered to geographical indications under the TRIPS Agreement, and yet it still leaves many gaps into which unchallengeable uses may fall.

7.2.2 Issues for Wine and Spirit Geographical Indications as gTLD Strings

7.2.2.1 Top-Level Domains Offer a Service, Not Goods

The WIPO II Report highlighted 'two fundamental problems in endeavoring to apply the existing international legal framework to prevent the bad faith misuse of geographical indications in the DNS.'[39] The first of these is the limitation of protection to geographical indications used to identify goods. In respect of second-level domain names, it was concluded:

> The mere registration of a geographical indication as a domain name by someone with no connection whatsoever with the geographical locality in question, however cheap and tawdry a practice, does not appear to be, on its own, a violation of existing international legal rules with respect to false indications of source and geographical indications. Such a registration may violate existing standards if it is associated with conduct relating to goods. … one can imagine various hypothetical uses of domain name registrations with respect to goods which might be considered to constitute violations of the provisions on the protection of geographical indications in the TRIPS Agreement. However, there are many circumstances in which a domain name registration, even though constituting a false or unauthorized use of a geographical indication, may not constitute a violation of existing international rules because there is no relationship between the domain name and goods.[40]

An obvious corollary to the limitation to goods is the exclusion of services, which has been subjected to scrutiny. The term 'good' notably replaces 'product', the term used in the Lisbon and Madrid (Indications of Source) Agreements and the Paris Convention, and this has been interpreted as evidence of the drafters' intention to exclude services from Articles 22 and

39. WIPO, *WIPO II Report*, para. 239.
40. *Id.*, para. 240.

23: 'It seems that where negotiators wanted to indicate that a rule in respect of indications applied to services as well as goods, they said so.'[41] Others have also reached this conclusion.[42] Thus, for example, a registration of the domain name www.champagne.com must be prevented pursuant to Article 23(1) if the website operated under that name purported to sell or offer for sale sparkling wines not originating in Champagne, France or 'Champagne -type' sparkling wines. It could not be prevented if the website offered information about such products not in the context of advertising their sale, or if it offered other services (such as hospitality and tourism services offered by an hoteliers' association in the Champagne region). The existing international legal framework thus offers, in the words of the WIPO II Report, 'only a partial solution to the problem of' registration of geographical indications as second-level domain names.[43]

By contrast, the existing international legal framework offers no solution at all at the top-level of the DNS. The explanation for this lies in the fundamental differences between the top and lower levels of the DNS, which have been comprehensively discussed in Chapter 2. To summarize that discussion, second and lower level domain names have come to be used to identify the content of the websites to which they point. Use of a geographical indication in connection with goods is possible (though not inevitable) in that environment, where the domain name serves to identify goods offered for sale by means of an associated website. Use of a geographical indication in connection with goods is not possible, however, where the domain name serves to identify a communications portal for use by others for a variety of purposes (offering goods or services, expressing an opinion, reporting news, etc.) as top-level domains do. Top-level domains are themselves a service: the registry's primary function is to maintain an up-to-date listing of all of the second-level domain name registrations within that particular registry. This facilitates access to and between the registrants of those domain names, the registrants of domain names in other top-level domains, and internet users. In short, top-level domain registries have no inherent connection to goods. They provide an environment in which others can self-identify and make available information, which may or may not be connected to goods. A .football top-level domain, for example, would have only an indirect connection, if even any, to footballs. Rather, .football identifies itself as a space in which web users are able to communicate with

41. Gervais, *The TRIPS Agreement,* 368. As an example of an explicit application to services, Gervais points to Art. 24(6) of the TRIPS Agreement.
42. *See for example*, O'Connor, *The Law of Geographical Indications*, 53. It is also interesting to note the reference to Art. 22 in the Jamaican delegation's proposal regarding the scope of Art. 6*ter* of the Paris Convention, in which concern is expressed at that provision's failure to cover services. WIPO Standing Committee on the Law of Trademarks, Industrial Designs and Geographical Indications, *Report Adopted by the Standing Committee*, para. 311, SCT/21/8.
43. WIPO, *WIPO II Report*, para. 240.

others, most likely about things having to do with 'football', which term has multiple interpretations (an item of sports equipment as well as various forms worldwide of a sport called 'football'). The same can be said of a .champagne or a .chianti top-level domain.

The only relatable example provided by the 2012 New gTLD Program applications is that of .wine and .vin, both of which were introduced earlier in Part I, Chapter 1, section 1.3. Notably, 'wine' and 'vin' are generic terms, but their links to geographical indications in lower-level domain name registrations are obvious. Leaving that aside and focusing on the top-level, it bears noting that in applying for .wine, parent company Donuts envisioned a gTLD that 'is attractive and useful to end-users' precisely because of the improved, differentiated services, *not goods*, that it provides: 'search, self-expression, information sharing and the provision of legitimate goods and services. … this TLD will provide Internet users with opportunities for online identities and expression that do not currently exist.'[44]

This means that Article 23 of the TRIPS Agreement offers no protection against uses of geographical indications for wines and spirits at the top-level of the DNS. Even to the extent that the second 'fundamental problem' identified in the WIPO II Report – the lack of harmonization as to the recognition of geographical indications[45] – was somehow resolved, this would not change the outcome as regards geographical indications' use as a top-level domain. To impute a connection with goods to a top-level domain is to deny the very structure of the DNS. For this reason, expansion at the top-level cannot simply mirror the geographical indications community's attempts at managing growth at the second level; the issues are similar, but clearly not the same.

7.2.2.2 Homonymous Wine Geographical Indications Possible, TLDs Impossible

Another issue that can be managed at the second-level of the DNS but proves insurmountable at its top-level is that of homonyms. Article 23(3) of the TRIPS Agreement recognizes homonymous geographical indications for wines by requiring that they be protected and also that the States involved resolve conflicts by establishing means of differentiation. In so doing, States are to ensure not only that consumers are not misled, but also that the producers involved are treated equitably. This recognition is made 'subject to the provisions of paragraph 4 of Article 22', which prevent the use of geographical indications that are 'literally true as to the territory' but nevertheless 'falsely represent to the public that the goods originate in

44. ICANN, New gTLD Application Submitted to ICANN by: June Station, LLC, https://gtldresult.icann.org/application-result/applicationstatus/applicationdetails:downloadapplication/706?t:ac=706 (13 Jun. 2012).
45. WIPO, *WIPO II Report*, para. 241.

another territory'. Recognition of homonyms enables, for example, the coexistence of Rioja as a geographical indication identifying wines from the Rioja region of Spain as well as a geographical indication identifying wines from the Rioja region of Argentina.[46]

The sorts of 'creative solutions'[47] that might be employed to distinguish wines identified by homonymous names to achieve their coexistence as 'offline' geographical indications are of some assistance at the second level of the DNS, but of no effect at the system's top-level. Domain names require only absolute uniqueness, so variation at the second level, even minor, can serve to distinguish a www.riojaspain.com from a www.riojaargentina.com. Even easier, and indeed in direct acknowledgement of the territorial nexus of geographical indications, would be to distinguish homonym wines through the use of ccTLDs: www.rioja.es and www.rioja.ar. Yet this sort of identical-yet-different variation is not possible at the top-level of the DNS, where concerns about user confusion are captured in the *gTLD Applicant Guidebook* via rejection and objection on grounds of confusing similarity.[48] In other words, the bar is set higher than absolute uniqueness for top-level domain strings, and there is simply no way to accommodate homonyms for wines or indeed for any other products even if these were at some point to receive a consistent level of protection under international law. Put simply, there cannot be more than one .rioja internet top-level domain.

Even the availability of IDNs (domain names in non-Latin language scripts) is unlikely to offer a satisfactory answer to this problem given the likelihood that in addition to retaining the name of their 'Old World' region, emigrants also retained the language of their country of origin or at least a version of it insufficiently distinguishable from the original to survive objection on grounds of confusing similarity. Whether the States involved in a conflict over homonymous geographical indication new gTLDs could reach the sort of compromise called for by Article 23(3) is questionable. Also questionable is two States reaching agreement to share a gTLD, with the result that resolution of conflicting applications will be left to ICANN's

---

46. Based on the example offered by Daniel Gervais of Rioja regions and wines in both Argentina and Spain in *The TRIPS Agreement: Drafting History and Analysis*, 384 n. 479. This example is also used in Irene Calboli, *Expanding the Protection of Geographical Indications of Origin under TRIPS: 'Old' Debate or 'New' Opportunity?*, 10(2) Marq. Intell. Prop. L. Rev. 182, 192 (2006) (citing Felix Addor & Alexandra Grazioli, *Geographical Indications beyond Wines and Spirits: A Roadmap for a Better Protection for Geographical Indications in the WTO/TRIPS Agreement*, 5 J. World. Intell. Prop. 865, 879 (2002)). Iris V. Quadrio & Martin Chajchir, *Nineteenth Yearly Review of International Trademark Jurisprudence*, 102 Trademark Rep. 455, 468–469 at 'Argentina: II.C.3. Geographical Indications/Appellations of Origin' (2012).
47. Gervais, *The TRIPS Agreement,* 384.
48. ICANN, *gTLD Applicant Guidebook,* s. 3.2.2.1.

procedures for community priority evaluation and/or auction.[49] The result under either all-or-nothing approach is a losing party's exclusion from the top-level of the DNS. Even if a sufficiently different (and agreeable) alternative string exists, the gTLD applicant must wait until a subsequent application period to apply.

Member States likely to find themselves in this position should consider that 'if the solution adopted by a Member prejudiced the producers of another Member or could objectively mislead consumers, it could be argued that that Member had failed to comply with'[50] Article 23(3). Applying this logic to the New gTLD Program, a government's authorization of a geographical indication new gTLD application would violate Article 23(3) of the TRIPS Agreement if it 'prejudiced the producers' of products in another State identified by an identical geographical indication. It is not difficult to come to the conclusion that exclusion from the DNS root, if inclusion were indeed desired, could prejudice the holders of a competing geographical indication. Although likely to be few in number, conflict between homonymous geographical indications has the potential to be extremely problematic. It is imperative that the States likely to be embroiled in such conflicts (which should be easy to identify given that they would already presumably have taken action in the offline context pursuant to Article 23(3)) give consideration to this issue and develop strategies for addressing it.

Certain conceptual similarities can be drawn between these problems facing online recognition of homonyms and arguments against even their offline recognition, the practicality and fairness of which has been questioned. In the context of the negotiations that led to the Geneva Act of the Lisbon Agreement, the US delegation expressed the belief that the coexistence of homonymous geographical indications 'protected the late-comer', and therefore 'did not represent a particularly principled approach to the protection of private intellectual property rights', in that it 'undercut and undermined the original owner's right in a given territory.'[51] The first-in-time, first-in-right argument has a different dimension in the offline context, but at the core of both arguments lies the idea that conflicting indications will inevitably confuse, to the (offline) consumer and (online) user's detriment.

In conclusion, it appears impossible to extend the protection offered by Article 23 of the TRIPS Agreement to geographical indications for wines and spirits at the top-level of the DNS. Geographical indications for other products receive an even lower level of protection, and in the next section it

49. *Id.*, s. 4.1.
50. Gervais, *The TRIPS Agreement,* 385.
51. WIPO Special Union for the Protection of Appellations of Origin and their International Registration, *Assembly Report of the Twenty-third (6th Extraordinary) Session in Geneva, September 22 to 30, 2008*, LI/A/23/2, para. 13.

will be shown that these are also unable to be protected against unauthorized use as gTLDs.

7.2.3 Scope of Protection of Other Product Geographical Indications

While geographical indications for wine and spirits receive what is characterized as 'absolute' protection under the TRIPS Agreement, indications for all other products are said to receive only 'relative' protection.[52] Specifically, Article 22(2) requires that Members prevent any use of a geographical indication that is misleading as to the true geographic origin of the goods. It does so by requiring Member States to take steps to prevent any communication 'that indicates or suggests that the good in question originates in a geographical area other than the true place of origin'. Acts of competition or confusion with goods of a competitor are notably not limited, but this provision 'would seem to require at least trying to benefit from or denigrate the reputation of an industrial sector.'[53] Article 22 also brings geographical indications meeting the TRIPS definition of that term within the scope of Article 10*bis* of the Paris Convention, effectively expanding the scope of Article 10*bis* since it does not otherwise apply to origin statements.[54] The effect of this is explored in detail in Chapter 8.

As noted in the preceding section of this chapter, the TRIPS Agreement preserves the origin-connoting nature of geographical indications: specifically, Article 22 permits the nexus between good and territory to be not only particular physical characteristics but the intangible attribute of reputation. This is a significant point of departure from the (pre-Geneva Act) Lisbon Agreement, which limits protectable appellations of origin to those whose quality and characteristics are attributable to geographical location. The

52. Stephen A. Bowers, *Location, Location, Location: The Case against Extending Geographical Indication Protection under the TRIPS Agreement*, 31(2) A.I.P.L.A. Q. J. 129, 131 (2003); Thomas Cottier & Marion Panizzon, *Traditional Knowledge and Geographical Indications: Foundations, Interests and Negotiating Positions*, in *Trade and Intellectual Property Protection in WTO Law: Collected Essays* (Cameron May 2005); Lynne Beresford, *Geographical Indications: The Current Landscape. But* see Dwijen Rangnekar, *Demanding Stronger Protection for Geographical Indications: The Relationship between Local Knowledge, Information and Reputation*, #2004-11 United Nations University-INTECH Discussion Paper Series (2004) (arguing that it is inappropriate to consider Art. 23 as 'absolute' protection).

53. Gervais, *The TRIPS Agreement*, 371.

54. Conrad, 35–36 (further arguing at 36 that the TRIPS Agreement 'extends the purview of Article 10bis for the members of GATT/TRIPs without revealing that it is not simply the incorporation of a parallel treaty, but an extension of its scope' (internal citations omitted)).

TRIPS Agreement broadens the scope of protectable indications, but this does not impact upon the level of protection offered. Unlike the protection offered by Article 23 to geographical indications for wines and spirits, Article 22 does not require the prevention of 'kind', 'type', 'style', 'imitation' or similar uses of geographical indications for other products. This is subject only to the limitation in Article 22(4) prohibiting indications that are 'literally true as to the territory' but nevertheless 'falsely represent to the public that the goods originate in another territory'. It is worth noting for completeness that the 2015 Geneva Act of the Lisbon Agreement makes no distinction between wines and spirits and other types of products, thus achieving the extension of protection contemplated by, but not yet achieved through, the TRIPS Agreement.

Like unauthorized wine and spirit geographical indication TLD strings, unauthorized use of geographical indications for other products is not preventable. This is not simply because they receive a lower level of protection under the TRIPS Agreement relative to wine and spirit geographical indications, but because the protection they do receive is limited, as with wine and spirit geographical indications, to names identifying goods. As recognized in the WIPO II Report more than a decade ago, the use of geographical indications as second-level domain names to lure prospective consumers to a website offering products other than those true to geographical origin could fall within the scope of Article 22(2)(a).[55] Top-level domains' lack of connection to goods renders TLD strings comprised of non-wine or spirit geographical indications in all cases unpreventable.

This conclusion can be reached without consideration of another a key impediment to the recognition of rights at the international level in geographical indications, which is the lack of harmonization of protection at the international level. This was characterized as one of the 'fundamental problems' in the WIPO II Report.[56] In practical terms, the lack of harmonization means that a name protected in one jurisdiction may not be protected in others. This is the heart of the divide between countries that support recognition and those that do not, a division that has only become further entrenched in the negotiations called for by Article 23(4) of the TRIPS Agreement and the drafting of the Geneva Act of the Lisbon Agreement. In the remaining section of this chapter, those developments are explored as a foundation for considering the possible effect that the New gTLD Program will have on the future recognition of rights in geographical indications. Two other issues are additionally taken up given their relevance to new gTLD applications: the impact of an international register on the recognition of rights in the DNS and issues of priority between trademarks and geographical indications.

55. WIPO, *WIPO II Report*, para. 240.
56. *Id.*, para. 241.

7.3 OTHER ISSUES FACING GEOGRAPHICAL INDICATIONS IN THE DNS

7.3.1 International Notification and Registration System

A primary reason offered in the WIPO II Report for not including geographical indications within the scope of the Uniform Domain Name Dispute Resolution Policy ('UDRP') was the lack of harmonization at the international level on the recognition of rights and, therefore, the inability to point to one clear international owner of any given geographical indication.[57] In the TRIPS-plus environment, bilateral and multilateral trade agreements might, if sufficient in number of signatories and patched together, offer geographical indications the subject of those agreements a level of recognition that comes closer to being equivalent to a universal convention,[58] but this would require a significant amount of research to discern which indications these might be, if any. An international register would remove this problem, putting all on clear notice of the existence and owner of recognized geographical indications. This is the solution proposed by Article 23(4) of the TRIPS Agreement for geographical indications for wines.

The Lisbon Agreement's establishment of an international notification and registration system has far broader application in that it incorporates geographical indications for all products, not only wines. That agreement has already established an International Register which is maintained by WIPO on behalf of the twenty-eight signatories. Despite that relatively low number, the involvement of 'Old World' countries such as France, the Czech Republic, Italy and Portugal makes the total number of registrations significant; France alone has more than 500.[59] Appellations of origin registered under the Lisbon Agreement stand to benefit from their higher level of recognition in the New gTLD Program by reason of their being 'protected by a statute or treaty' and thus eligible for inclusion in the Trademark Clearinghouse,[60] the database of authenticated legal rights that underpins several rights protection mechanisms available in new gTLDs.

---

57. *Id.*, at Executive summary para. (iv) and paras 241–243.
58. Peter Drahos, *BITS and BIPS: Bilateralism in Intellectual Property*, 4 J. World Intell. Prop. 791, 802 (2001) ('The key point is that the MFN principle in TRIPS, when combined with bilateralism on intellectual property, will have the effect of spreading and setting new minimum standards of intellectual property faster than would have happened otherwise.'). Lucas S. Michels, *A Blueprint for International TRIPS-plus Geographical Indications Protections? An Analysis of Geographical Indication Protection Proposals in the European Union – India Bilateral Trade and Investment Agreement*, 15 Gonzaga J. Int'l L. 2 (2011–2012).
59. WIPO, *Appellations of Origin*, http://www.wipo.int/ipdl/en/lisbon/lisbon-map.jsp.
60. ICANN, *New gTLD Applicant Guidebook,* Trademark Clearinghouse, s. 3.2.5.

While the International Register is the Lisbon Agreement's most significant contribution to the cause of protecting geographical indicators at the international level, it is equally a deterrent for those who oppose recognition. This partly explains the absence of 'New World' wine producing countries such as the US, Australia, Chile and Argentina from the ranks of Lisbon Agreement signatories. This dichotomy continues to manifest itself in the negotiations called for by Article 23(4). Those negotiations, considered part of the TRIPS Agreement's 'built-in agenda',[61] commenced in 1998. The intervening years have seen little progress beyond a volley of proposals authored on the one side by the European Community[62] and on the other by Japan and the US, later joined by Canada and Chile.[63] Since the year 2000, these proposals have focused on two issues: first, the international notification system for wines and second, the extension of the additional degree of protection offered to wines and spirits to other products. For a time, the latter issue seemed to dominate discussions, with a surprising number of 'New World' countries joining in support[64] of extension amidst confusion as to whether the Doha Ministerial Declaration mandated this debate.[65] The Doha Ministerial Declaration set a deadline for decisions regarding the establishment of an international notification and registration system for the Fifth Session of the Ministerial Conference held in Cancun, in late 2003.[66] That deadline has come and gone, and although progress was reportedly made in early 2011 in drafting a 'composite text' that sets out all of the views thus far

61. WTO Council for Trade-Related Aspects of Intellectual Property Rights, *Report (1996) of the Council for TRIPS*, Part III, (1996) IP/C/8 96-4704.
62. WTO Council for Trade-Related Aspects of Intellectual Property Rights, *Implementation of Article 23.4 of the TRIPS Agreement Relating to the Establishment of a Multilateral System of Notification and Registration of Geographical Indications*, (2000) IP/C/W/107 Communication from the European Communities and their Member States, Rev. 1 00-2521.
63. WTO Council for Trade-Related Aspects of Intellectual Property Rights, *Proposal for a Multilateral System for Notification and Registration of Geographical Indications based on Article 23.4 of the TRIPS Agreement*, (1999) IP/C/W/133/Rev.1 Communication from Canada, Chile, Japan and the United States, Rev. 1 99-3125.
64. WTO Council for Trade-Related Aspects of Intellectual Property Rights, *Proposal from Bulgaria, Cuba, Czech Republic, Egypt, Iceland, India, Jamaica, Kenya, Liechtenstein, Mauritius, Nigeria, Pakistan, Slovenia, Sri Lanka, Switzerland, Turkey and Venezuela (Revision)*, (2001) IP/C/W/247/Rev.1 01-2491.
65. Gervais, *The TRIPS Agreement,* 50–51. To clarify, 'the Doha Declarations do not add to or diminish legal obligations. The question to be considered is whether there is flexibility within the WTO legal regime for binding legislative decisions that do not change obligations.' Steve Charnovitz, *The Legal Status of the Doha Declarations*, 5 J. Int'l Econ. L. 207, 210 (2002).
66. *Doha WTO Ministerial Declaration*, Art. 18, WT/MIN(01)/DEC1, 20 Nov. 2001 (available at http://www.wto.org/english/thewto_e/minist_e/min01_e/mindecl_e.htm).

expressed,[67] five years later no agreement has been reached.[68] Late in 2015, the Chairman of the Council for Trade-Related Aspects of Intellectual Property Rights Special Session recapped the progress of negotiations since 1997, noting from renewed discussions in 2014 and 2015 that it was clear that 'traditional differences on the substance and the scope of the negotiations persisted.'[69] Nor has agreement been reached on the issue of extension of protection, with no significant progress having been made since 2011.[70] Indeed, some argue that the failure of each initiative is inter-related, giving rise to doubts as to whether either can succeed.[71]

The 'Old World' and 'New World' divide likewise impacted upon the negotiation and adoption of the Geneva Act of the Lisbon Agreement. While the Working Group that developed the Act was motivated by reducing barriers to accession to the Lisbon Agreement,[72] only Lisbon signatories

67. WTO, *Multilateral System of Notification and Registration of Geographical Indications for Wines and Spirits: Report by the Chairman, Ambassador Darlington Mwape (Zambia) to the Trade Negotiations Committee*, TN/IP/21, (21 Apr. 2011) (available at http://www.wto.org/english/tratop_e/dda_e/chair_texts11_e/trips_e.doc).
68. Daniel Gervais, *Irreconcilable Differences? The Geneva Act of the Lisbon Agreement and the Common Law*, 53(2) Hous. L. Rev. 339, 343–344 (2015) ('No significant progress has been made on the TRIPS register since the entry into force of the TRIPS Agreement in 1995, despite a renewed appeal to WTO Members contained in the 2001 Doha Declaration.').
69. WTO Council for Trade-Related Aspects of Intellectual Property Rights Special Session, *Multilateral System of Notification and Registration of Geographical Indications for Wines and Spirits: Report by the Chairman, Ambassador Dacio Castillo (Honduras)*, TN/IP/23, (3 Dec. 2015) (available at https://www.wto.org/english/tratop_e/trips_e/gi1_docs_e.htm).
70. WTO, *Issues Related to the Extension of the Protection of Geographical Indications Provided for in Article 23 of the TRIPS Agreement to Products other than Wines and Spirits and those Related to the Relationship between the TRIPS Agreement and the Convention on Biological Diversity: Report by the Director-General*, WT/GC/W/633 and TN/C/W/61 (21 Apr. 2011) (available at https://www.wto.org/english/tratop_e/trips_e/giextension_cbd_dgreport_9jun08_e.doc).
71. Gervais, *Irreconcilable Differences?*, at 344 (attributing the lack of progress on developing an international register partly to the fact 'that WTO Members who are pushing for international protection of GIs disagree on the scope and purpose of their effort. Europe's focus has been on the establishment of the TRIPS Article 23.4 register. Other WTO Members, many of them developing countries, have insisted on an extension of the higher level of protection contained in Article 23.1 of TRIPS to products other than wines and spirits.').
72. WIPO Special Union for the Protection of Appellations of Origin and their International Registration, *Assembly Report of the Twenty-third (6th Extraordinary) Session in Geneva, September 22 to 30, 2008*, LI/A/23/2, (29 Sep. 2008) (available at http://www.wipo.int/edocs/mdocs/govbody/en/li_a_23/li_a_23_2.pdf) (*see for example* the record of comments of the Costa Rican delegation's belief 'that a significant opportunity was now being presented for the modernization of this international instrument and for allowing the Lisbon Agreement to attract more Member States' and the Mexican delegation's view of the 'need to enlarge the membership of the Lisbon Union'.).

were able to vote on the text,[73] preventing the very States the existing members of Lisbon hoped to attract from having a meaningful impact in the negotiations process. Furthermore, States opposing the Lisbon system were able to participate only as observers, [74] limiting their ability to protect their national systems' interests and approaches.

Were it not the case that geographical indications' connection to goods otherwise barred the applicability in the DNS of the protection afforded them under the TRIPS Agreement, an international notification and registration system would greatly facilitate the allocation of geographical indication new gTLDs. Such a system already exists to a certain extent at a domestic level even in countries that do not protect geographic indications as such.[75] This occurs through trademark law in cases where geographical indications are able, most commonly as a collective or certification mark, to satisfy registration criteria.[76] The availability of collective mark registration is but one of the many ways that TRIPS members have fulfilled their obligations to prevent misuse of geographical indications.[77]

One can envisage a notification system for rights in geographical indications functioning in a manner similar to the Trademark Claims service developed through ICANN's New gTLD Program. This service is intended to put would-be domain name applicants on notice of existing rights and offer them the choice of either terminating or continuing with a domain name application.[78] Owners of marks in the Trademark Clearinghouse are notified of completed registrations, thus putting them in a better position to challenge such registrations. The term 'owners' is not entirely appropriate in the context of geographical indications given their communal rather than individual nature,[79] but this fact does not impede the development of a register. The entrenched position of various non-Lisbon Union States against more specific international protection of geographical indications makes the

73. WIPO, *Diplomatic Conference for the Adoption of a New Act of the Lisbon Agreement for the Protection of Appellations of Origin and Their International Registration: Proposal by the Delegations of Argentina, Australia, Canada, Chile, Japan, New Zealand, Republic of Korea, Saudi Arabia, Singapore, United States of America and Uruguay*, LI/DC/9 (11 May 2015), http://www.wipo.int/edocs/mdocs/geoind/en/li_dc/li_dc_9.pdf, para. 3; WIPO Special Union for the Protection of Appellations of Origin and their International Registration, *Assembly Report of the Twenty-third (6th Extraordinary) Session in Geneva, September 22 to 30, 2008*, LI/A/23/2 (29 Sep. 2008) (available at http://www.wipo.int/edocs/mdocs/govbody/en/li_a_23/li_a_23_2.pdf), para. 35.
74. *Ibid.*
75. Justin Hughes, *Champagne, Feta, and Bourbon: The Spirited Debate about Geographical Indications*, 58 Hastings L.J. 299, 331 (2006) (discussing the level of regulatory intervention in France's protection of appellations and the US' use of trademark law).
76. Collective and certification marks are discussed in Part III, Chapter 5, s. 5.3 above.
77. *See* n. 5 above in this chapter. On the protection of geographical indications as collective marks under US law, *see* Beresford, 984.
78. The Trademark Clearinghouse is discussed in detail in Part II, Chapter 3, s. 3.2.2 above.
79. Conrad, 12; Calboli, 185.

establishment of such a system unlikely, however, without a broader consideration of where they (and indeed the Geneva Act of the Lisbon Agreement, if it achieves its goals of increasing the membership of the Lisbon Union) fit within the WTO Agreement framework and other issues arising under the Doha trade negotiations mandate.[80]

Understandably, it has been said that the overlap between WIPO-administered treaties and the TRIPS Agreement has complicated matters further. Commenting on the efforts of WIPO's Standing Committee on the Law of Trademarks, Industrial Designs and Geographical Indications, the US delegation posited that 'work of the SCT on geographical indications has been stymied for nearly a decade on the stated basis that no delegation wished to prejudice ongoing negotiations in other fora, such as, for example, the World Trade Organization (WTO).'[81] In essence, it may ultimately be accepted that the TRIPS Agreement is the high-water mark in terms of what the deeply divergent interests within the international community can agree on.

7.3.2 Conflict Between Trademarks and Geographical Indications

While it is certainly the case that registration as a standard, collective or certification mark has advantages for geographical indications, the availability of multiple forms of protection raises the potential for conflict between them. Despite having been considered conceptual 'equivalents' in the context of a comparison of EU and domestic legislation,[82] geographical indications and trademarks (all forms) are distinctly separate subject matter under international law, and the legal rights in them do not in all circumstances align. This equivalence is emphasized and complicated by a clear global divide between common law and civil law jurisdictions.[83]

The first problem lies in the issue of priority as between trademarks and geographical indications. In other words, where one rights holder claims rights in a trademark and another in the same name as a geographical indication, which one prevails? While the Paris Convention operates from a 'first-in-time, first-in-right' principle, it has been considered that this is

80. Cottier & Panizzon, *Traditional Knowledge and Geographical Indications*.

81. WIPO Standing Committee on the Law of Trademarks, Industrial Designs and Geographical Indications, *Proposal by the Delegation of the United States of America*, WIPO Doc. SCT/30/7 (31 Oct. 2013), Annex at 1 (available at http://www.wipo.int/edocs/mdocs/sct/en/sct_30/sct_30_7.pdf).

82. Lionel Bently & Brad Sherman, *The Impact of European Geographical Indications on National Rights in Member States*, 96 Trademark Rep. 850, 877–878 (2006). Bently and Sherman further note that the authors of *Kerly's Law of Trade Marks and Trade Names*, Britain's leading treatise on trademark law, support this view.

83. Gervais, *Irreconcilable Differences?*, at 346 (noting that '[n]o common law jurisdiction is party to the Lisbon Agreement.').

limited to trademarks as against other trademarks.[84] This does not resolve the conflict, but rather re-characterizes the issue to be resolved in terms of '"who has the better right to use a geographical name?", and not "who used a geographical name first?"'.[85]

The Lisbon Agreement, perhaps unsurprisingly given that it offers the highest level of protection of the existing international conventions, gives a measure of priority to protected appellations of origin. Article 5(3) of that agreement requires that States protect an internationally registered appellation unless it is declared within a year that the State is unable to ensure protection. Grounds for such a declaration are not specifically provided in the agreement, but it is presumed that an appellation's treatment as generic or the existence of prior rights would fall within this ambit.[86] Where a declaration is not made, conflicting prior rights must be phased out within two years pursuant to Article 5(6). The 2015 Geneva Act of the Lisbon Agreement continues this priority in Article 11(3), headed 'Use in a Trademark', by requiring signatories, '[w]ithout prejudice to Article 13(1)' … to '*ex officio* if its legislation so permits or at the request of an interested party, refuse or invalidate the registration of a later trademark if use of the trademark would result in' an offending use of the protected indication or appellation.

The presumed prevailing position on priority under the TRIPS Agreement is that Article 16 confers priority on a first registered trademark,[87] but this is not a universally held view.[88] Under the heading 'Rights Conferred', Article 16(1) gives trademark owners the exclusive right to prevent the use of 'identical or similar signs'. The loose definition of 'signs' in Article 15 (headed 'Protectable Subject Matter') suggests that this priority is conferred only as against other trademarks. Article 24(5), on the other hand, provides:

> Where a trademark has been applied for or registered in good faith, or where rights to a trademark have been acquired through use in good faith either:
>
> a. before the date of application of these provision in that Member as defined in Part VI; or
> b. before the geographical indication is protected in its country of origin;
>
> measures adopted to implement this Section shall not prejudice eligibility for or the validity of the registration of a trademark, or the

84. O'Connor, *The Law of Geographical Indications*, 115.
85. *Ibid.*
86. *Id.*, 115–116.
87. Burkhart Goebel, Presentation, *Geographical Indications and Trademarks: The Road from Doha* 8 (WIPO & USPTO Worldwide Symposium on Geographical Indications 9–11 Jul. 2003) WIPO/GEO/SFO/03/11.
88. *See for example*, O'Connor, *The Law of Geographical Indications*, 118 (concluding that trademarks and geographical indications receive equal protection under TRIPS).

right to use a trademark, on the basis that such a trademark is identical with, or similar to, a geographical indication.

On its face, Article 24(5) suggests a reprise of the first-in-time, first-in-right principle, whereby one party is able to use and the other not. Advocates of this interpretation call upon Article 16(1) for support, positing:

> [A] right to use must include the minimum rights in respect of trademarks under the Agreement. As such, this right to use would not simply mean a right to register and continue to use in spite of the presence of an identical or similar geographical indication, but in fact a right to exclude the geographical indication concerned.[89]

The important question is not only one of priority, but of whether the TRIPS Agreement permits coexistence between trademarks and geographical indications. It is very clearly the case that the TRIPS Agreement permits some coexistence of conflicting geographical indications due to its allowance for homonymous indications for wines in Article 23(3). The effect of Article 24(5) is greatly reduced if, read in conjunction with the reference to it in Article 24(1), it is interpreted as establishing a 'first-in-time, first-in-right' principle in respect of wine and spirit geographical indications only. The use in Article 24(5) of the term 'Section', however, suggests that it refers to the entire section 3 of the TRIPS Agreement, comprised of Articles 22, 23 and 24, 'and not to a "section" in the sense of an "article" as that term is used in the national laws of several countries.'[90] An alternate interpretation of Article 24(5) permits coexistence of conflicting geographical indications and trademarks as the natural consequence of Article 24(5) not obliging TRIPS members to:

> provide the protection of geographical indications if an identical or similar trademark has been registered in good faith. However, if this protection is provided (and there is clear possibility to provide this protection), it should not 'prejudice eligibility for or the validity of the registration of a trademark, or the right to use a trademark.' (emphasis in original)[91]

Neither interpretation can be supported by evidence of a relevant intention on the part of the TRIPS Agreement drafters, but both sides assert compatibility with the text of the Agreement itself.[92] While there are ways of avoiding or resolving conflict using the legal frameworks in place,[93] in the specific

89. Gervais, *The TRIPS Agreement,* 397.
90. *Id.*, 396.
91. O'Connor, *The Law of Geographical Indications*, 63.
92. *Ibid.* Gervais, *The TRIPS Agreement,* 396–398.
93. *European Communities – Protection of Trademarks and Geographical Indications for Agricultural Products and Foodstuffs – Complaint by Australia, Report of the Panel*, 150

context of the DNS it has been shown earlier in this chapter that coexistence at the top-level is likely impossible due to the technical requirement of absolute uniqueness braced by ICANN's disallowance of confusingly similar TLD strings. Conflicts can potentially be managed in second- and lower-level domain names through differentiation (unless a TLD registry operator implements policy to disallow confusingly similar domain name registrations by registrants, a policy that would be burdensome to police), but just as there cannot be two .rioja TLDs to represent both of the regions referred to by that name, there cannot be two .rioja TLDs to represent each of a geographical indication and a trademark.

The need to decide on priority as between applicants for new gTLDs will inevitably arise in top-level expansion: the ICANN community must not assume that because these conflicts did not arise in 2012, they will not arise in future application rounds. Where conflicts arise within a country, national laws can be relied upon. Where conflicts arise between applicants in different countries that treat geographical indications differently, some means of resolution is patently needed. Drawing from existing means of conflict resolution, the two clearest options that take into consideration the legal interest involved rather than simply resolving a dispute in favour of the party able to pay the most as in an auction are (i) to adopt a first-in-time, first-in-right rule; or (ii) to apply unfair competition principles. The latter are discussed in detail in the next chapter, though it can be said as an initial point that this is administratively the more complex approach. From the perspective of ease and efficiency of domain name registration, it is likely preferable to base priority on timing, although this creates inequities between countries with protection of geographical indications and countries without such protection.[94] ICANN's having undertaken to ensure that new gTLDs do not conflict with existing legal rights recognized under international law means that unfair competition issues must be considered. As this was not adequately done in drafting the *gTLD Applicant Guidebook*, forward-looking policy development efforts must address this failing.

7.3.3 Implications for Lisbon Agreement Signatories and Future Geneva Act Signatories

Prior to the Geneva Act, the protections offered by the Lisbon Agreement gave rise to a further issue with respect to new gTLDs by requiring members of the Lisbon Union to protect appellations of origin 'as such',[95] and to provide absolute protection 'against any usurpation or imitation, even if the

---

para. 7.686, WT/DS290/R 05-0936 (W.T.O. D.S.B. Panel 15 Mar. 2005) (finding that co-existence is a limited exception under TRIPS Art. 17); O'Connor, *The Law of Geographical Indications*, 119–121.

94. Conrad, 42–43. Rimmer, 12 (highlighting problems of free riding).

95. Lisbon Agreement Art. 1.

true origin of the product is indicated or if the appellation is used in translated form or accompanied by terms such as "kind," "type," "make," "imitation," or "the like".'[96] This level of protection contrasts sharply with that offered to geographical indications the TRIPS Agreement, which extends a higher level of protection only to geographical indications for wines and spirits and requires in relation to other indications that Member States prevent only uses in connection with goods and constituting an act of unfair competition pursuant to Article 10*bis* of the Paris Convention.

The protection against 'usurpation' offered by the Lisbon Agreement could operate to prevent the making of a new gTLD application for a string comprised of an appellation of origin notified under that agreement by an unauthorized party because the signatories are, as WIPO explains, 'under the obligation to provide a means of defence against any usurpation or imitation of an appellation of origin in their territory.'[97] The use of the term 'usurpation' is noted as being rather anomalous; '[t]he *travaux* define usurpation as the "illicit adoption" of an appellation (and provide "counter-feiting" as a possible synonym.'[98] Further, Article 3 makes no reference to 'goods', ensuring protection 'against *any* usurpation or imitation' (emphasis added). It is plausible that the registration of a new gTLD comprised of a notified appellation by a party not associated with the notification could be argued to constitute a 'usurpation'. If this argument were accepted, in order to comply with the Lisbon Agreement, signatories' domestic law would therefore need to prevent the registration of new gTLDs by those not otherwise entitled to do so.

If so, this creates an uneven playing field in ICANN's New gTLD Program. A new gTLD applicant in France would have to be prevented from applying for a .toscano new gTLD,[99] for example, but an applicant in China, not a signatory of the Lisbon Agreement, need not be so prevented. Similarly, a new gTLD applicant in Slovakia would need to be prevented from applying for a .pilsner[100] new gTLD, but an applicant in the US, a country with a

96. Lisbon Agreement Art. 3.

97. WIPO, *The Lisbon Agreement for the Protection of Appellations of Origin and their International Registration: Objective and Main Features, Protection to be Accorded*, http://www.wipo.int/lisbon/en/general/.

98. Gervais, *Irreconcilable Differences?*, at 348, citing Union Internationale pour la Protection de la Propriété Industrielle, Actes de la Conférence Réunie a Lisbonne du 6 au 31 Octobre 1958, at 814 (1863).

99. This is due to the existence of the registration Toscano: Notification No. 1001 by the I. Ministero delle Politiche Agricole Alimentari e Forestali Il. Consorzio per la tutela dell' Olio Extravergine di Oliva Toscano, accessible through WIPO Lisbon Express searchable database at http://www.wipo.int/ipdl/en/search/lisbon/search-struct.jsp.

100. This is due to the existence of the registration PLZEŇ/PILSEN PILS/PILSENER/PILSNER: Notification No. 1 by organizations in the Czech Republic, accessible through WIPO Lisbon Express searchable database at http://www.wipo.int/ipdl/en/search/lisbon/search-struct.jsp.

recognized beer industry but not a signatory of the Lisbon Agreement, need not be so prevented, and so on for all of the notified applications currently in the International Register of Appellations of Origin. ICANN's *gTLD Applicant Guidebook* does not itself give rise to a violation of the Lisbon Agreement, but Lisbon Union members must be aware of this possible interpretation of their obligations under that agreement in order to ensure that actions taken in the context of ICANN's New gTLD Program are not in breach.

As the ICANN community takes steps to plan a next round of new gTLD applications under the *gTLD Applicant Guidebook*, two specific points must be noted in this context. First, the absence of any applications in 2012 comprising a Lisbon-registered appellation of origin means that this problem is, as-yet, untested and unresolved. As with the issue of conflicting applications just noted in the previous section, this is something that forward-looking ICANN policy development must consider. Second, the Geneva Act of the Lisbon Agreement will, should it come into force and eventually become the dominant legal framework for protecting geographical indicators, simply continue the status quo as regards the use of such indicators in the DNS. While the 'as such' language of the Lisbon Agreement is replaced by language that leaves members 'free to choose the type of legislation under which it establishes the protection stipulated in this Act', Article 11(2) of the Geneva Act retains the sweeping Article 3 Lisbon Agreement protection of appellations of origin and indeed extends this to geographical indications for all products – not just wines and spirits. Further, the Geneva Act moves beyond 'usurpation and imitation' to a tripartite right that draws from TRIPS Articles 16(3) and 22(2), while also adding 'a form of dilution protection of well known marks'.[101] Each of the three prongs of Article 11 is explicitly targeted at preventing particular uses and practices in relation to goods. This focus on goods broadly removes top-level domains from the problem, but leaves the door open to case-by-case analysis of second- and lower-level domains.

7.4 CONCLUSIONS ON RIGHTS IN GEOGRAPHICAL INDICATIONS

All top-level domain strings constituted of geographical indications, regardless of the type of goods they identify, fall outside of the limited scope of protection offered to geographical indications under the TRIPS Agreement. This conclusion extends but is analogous to the one reached in the WIPO II Report, which found that the TRIPS Agreement was insufficient to prevent

101. Gervais, *Irreconcilable Differences?*, at 349.

registrations of second-level domain names lacking a connection to goods. Critically, top-level domains represent a service. They facilitate interaction with second-level domain name registrants and therefore do not have a direct connection to goods. While the establishment of an international register could facilitate the registration of domain names constituted of geographical indications, this would benefit only second- and lower-level domain names the use of which is directly connected to goods. The much-disputed international register, regardless of what form it could ultimately take, is of no consequence to geographical indications' use at the top-level of the DNS. This specific conclusion does not have any bearing on the presumed priority rights of governments to geographic names in ICANN's *gTLD Applicant Guidebook*, except to say that the potential for recognition of private parties' rights in geographical indications through a register inherently disproves the exclusivity of governments' rights in such names.

The holders of 'offline' legal rights in geographical indications are not, however, entirely foreclosed from exercising their rights in the New gTLD Program. Geographical indications 'protected by a statute or treaty'[102] are eligible for inclusion in the Trademark Clearinghouse, making them eligible to participate in sunrise processes and the Trademark Claims service in the launch of new gTLDs. Further, neither the *gTLD Applicant Guidebook* or the UDRP and Uniform Rapid Suspension ('URS') procedures differentiate standard trademarks from other forms of trademark. Registration of a geographical indication as a standard, collective or certification mark in countries in which registration criteria can be satisfied has the effect of elevating an indication to a higher level of recognition in DNS policy. Irrespective of whether they are recorded in an international register, that such rights are recognized (whether as a trademark or as an appellation of origin as such) again inherently disproves the exclusivity of governments' rights in such names.

Finally, special care may need to be taken by Lisbon Union members to take steps to prevent the 'usurpation or imitation' of notified indications through their use as a new gTLD by someone other than a notifying party. Future Geneva Act members may need to take similar care, depending on how their obligations are interpreted in terms of limitations to goods and consumers' use and interpretation of domain names. These are issues that must be taken into consideration in ICANN's Generic Names Supporting Organization policy development processes (including in particular the New gTLD Subsequent Procedures Policy Development Process which, as highlighted in Chapter 2 above,[103] notably includes within its scope the following: 'Review whether geographic names requirements are

102. ICANN, *New gTLD Applicant Guidebook,* Trademark Clearinghouse, s. 3.2.5.
103. *See* above Part I, Chapter 2, s. 2.5.

appropriate.'[104]) Input on these issues from the Governmental Advisory Committee will be critical to ensuring that the Policy Development Process achieves a result that is consistent not simply with government assumptions, but with international law as is then in force.

---

104. ICANN, *Working Group (WG) Charter: New gTLD Subsequent Procedures*, https://gnso.icann.org/en/issues/new-gtlds/subsequent-procedures-charter-21jan16-en.pdf (21 Jan. 2016), 4.f.

Chapter 8

Unfair Competition and Related Commercial Rights in Geographic Names

What is honest is not dishonest.[1]

8.1 UNFAIR COMPETITION LAW PRINCIPLES APPLIED TO GEOGRAPHIC NAMES

8.1.1 THE POTENTIAL OF UNFAIR COMPETITION LAW

Unfair competition law has high potential as a source of rights in geographic names given its traditional role as 'gap filler' where rights are not recognized in subject matter as such under intellectual property law or related sui generis regimes.[2] Even where IPRs are recognized, in many jurisdictions it is common practice to raise claims in the nature of unfair competition in addition to intellectual property infringement claims. That said, one must be careful to recognize the different natures of protection offered by these distinct sources of rights: in the specific context of the protection of names, trademark law protects the rights holder's private property interest in a name as such when used in connection with specified goods and/or services, while unfair competition law regulates commercial behaviour affecting competitors

1. *Angus v. Clifford*, 60 L.J. Rep. (N.S.) C.D. 456 (1891) (per Bowen, LJ).
2. On the traditional role of unfair competition law, *see* Gustavo Ghidini, *Intellectual Property and Competition Law: The Innovation Nexus* 112 (Edward Elgar 2006).

or consumers.[3] In other words, unfair competition law does not confer an exclusive proprietary right on an individual party, but rather aims to benefit the market as a whole. Whether this difference has any effect in actual practice is, however, questionable; it is said that 'there are overlaps for which a convincing theory has yet to be found.'[4]

Unfair competition law is based on a fundamentally simple understanding 'that dealings based on deceit are legally wrong.'[5] It is primarily addressed at the international level by the Paris Convention for the Protection of Industrial Property, Article 1(2) of which identifies 'the repression of unfair competition' as one of that convention's express objects.[6] Accordingly, Article 10*bis* (1) requires that members of the Paris Union provide 'effective protection against unfair competition', which Article 10*bis* (2) defines broadly as '[a]ny act of competition contrary to honest practices in industrial or commercial matters'. Relatedly, Article 10 requires members to prevent the 'direct or indirect use of a false indication of the source of the goods or the identity of the producer, manufacturer, or merchant.'

This definition of 'unfair competition' in the Paris Convention uses fairly broad, general terms, leaving Paris Union members to determine how best to meet their obligations in domestic law. The analysis undertaken in this chapter shows this nevertheless to be the most inclusive attempt to target unfair competition in an international convention to date. The TRIPS Agreement is notably silent on unfair competition save for limited references to Article 10*bis* of the Paris Convention found in Article 22(2)(b) in the context of prohibited uses of geographical indications and Article 39 in the context of protecting undisclosed confidential information. Article IX:6 of the GATT Agreement, which is discussed below in this chapter, merely requires members to 'co-operate' to prevent false representations of product origins.

Problematic from the perspective of protecting rights in geographic names is the fact that – as with the law of trademarks – the law of unfair competition has at its heart commercial activity. Indeed, it is said that 'the first prerequisite [of unfair competition] is that the conduct must not be private, social or political, but must be commercial.'[7] This and other core principles of unfair competition law place considerable strain on its ability to

3. WIPO, *Protection against Unfair Competition: Analysis of the Present World Situation*, WIPO Publication No. 725, 10 (1994).
4. Frauke Henning-Bodewig, *Unfair Competition law: European Union and Member States* 5 (Kluwer Law International 2006).
5. *Black's Law Dictionary* 1667 (Bryan A. Garner & Henry Campbell Black eds, West 2009) (definition of 'unfair competition').
6. Alternatively it has been posited that 'the aim of the PC was the international protection of industrial property rights and not the protection against unfair competition.' *Law against Unfair Competition: Towards a New Paradigm in Europe?* 54 (Reto M. Hilty & Frauke Henning-Bodewig eds, Springer 2007).
7. Henning-Bodewig, 1.

offer all geographic names (not simply subsets such as geographical indications or geographically named certification marks) blanket protection against unfair use. Gap filler it may be, but unfair competition law is not the solution to every problem. This is true even if the problem is a squarely commercial one (which for geographic names is frequently not the case) because '[n]ot everything that is regarded as "unfair" in the commercial sector falls under unfair competition law.'[8]

The aim of this chapter is to determine whether governments or others have rights under unfair competition law that justify or stand in the way of preventing the registration of geographic names as new gTLDs. It begins with an examination of the purposes and general principles of unfair competition law and their application to geographic names, then turns to an evaluation of four specific categories of commercial behaviour in order to identify situations in which registration of geographic new gTLDs could potentially be prevented. It is also pointedly considered whether the lodging of an application for a new gTLD without the authorization of an 'offline' rights holder constitutes an act of unfair competition such that limitations should be incorporated for geographical indications in ICANN's top-level domain policy implementation.

8.1.2 Purposes of Unfair Competition Law

Unfair competition law has long played a key role in the resolution of domain name disputes, albeit in a somewhat disguised form: the UDRP draws heavily from the unfair competition provisions of the Paris Convention.[9] The applicability of that policy to domain names constituted of trademarks (the only type of name actionable under the policy) should not, however, be automatically imputed to other subject matter, particularly when proposals to widen the scope of the UDRP have previously been rejected due to lack of support in international law.[10] Rather, it should be questioned as a starting point whether limiting the use of geographic names in the DNS on the basis of unfair competition – whether through the UDRP or otherwise – is consistent with the principles and purposes of unfair competition law.

There is no universally agreed singular purpose of unfair competition law, nor an all-inclusive enumeration of acts that constitute unfair competition.[11] Rather, this is an area of law that is 'deeply rooted' in domestic law and, as a result, has developed in different ways to prevent different forms of

8. *Id.*, 1.
9. WIPO, *WIPO I Report*, paras 172–174.
10. *See* above for discussion on the scope of the UDRP in Chapter 3, s. 3.3.1.2.
11. Henning-Bodewig, 19 (observing that 'relatively scant attention has been paid … to the international competition law anchored in Article 10bis and 10ter of the Paris Convention').

commercial behaviour in different jurisdictions.[12] The Paris Convention preserves these differences by leaving to its members the decision of how to identify and remedy unfair competition. In some countries, this means protecting competitors from each other's unscrupulous practices. Unfair competition law in the US and England, for example, has as its general focus the defendant who 'poaches upon the commercial magnetism of [a] symbol'.[13] Other countries, such as Spain and Germany, take a broader view of unfair competition law and use it to control not only acts that harm competitors but those that harm consumers.[14] This dual-headed protection is recognizable in Article 22 of the TRIPS Agreement, which sets out the protection available to geographical indications: while Article 22(2)(a) 'is aimed at representations misleading the public, i.e., consumers', Article 22(2)(b) 'protects the interests of producers and merchants' through the application of Article 10*bis* of the Paris Convention.[15]

An understanding of the types of behaviour captured by unfair competition law first requires an understanding of the purposes of unfair competition law. Identifying behaviour that is 'unfair' requires 'taking into account particularly the interests of those "concerned" by it, namely the parties involved in the operation of the marketplace.'[16] When one considers these interests, four central purposes of unfair competition law emerge. When geographic names are tested against these, there is reason to question the appropriateness of relying on unfair competition law to protect them.

8.1.2.1 Promote Honesty in Commercial Dealing

At the heart of unfair competition law is the notion of fairness and, by corollary, the prevention of unfairness, which Article 10*bis* (2) of the Paris Convention characterizes as acts 'contrary to honest trade practices'. Honesty in this context is less a moral concept than a normative concept derived from the marketplace in question. As such, it is measured according to 'what is actually usual in business life ("trade practices"),' and then 'corrected by the ethical aspect of "honest".'[17]

The focus on commercial dealings in unfair competition law is problematic for geographic names because many of their uses are non-commercial in nature (e.g., maps, signs, official documents and news reports). For these sorts of uses there is not a relevant trade or marketplace from which to draw the requisite standard of honesty in business. There can

12. *Introduction to Intellectual Property: Theory and Practice* 246–248 (WIPO ed., Kluwer Law International 1997).
13. *Mishawaka Rubber & Woolen Mfg. Co. v. S.S. Kresge Co.*, 316 U.S. 203, 205 (Sup. Ct. 1942).
14. Henning-Bodewig, 2–3. WIPO, *Protection against Unfair Competition*, 15–17.
15. Conrad, 36.
16. WIPO, *Protection against Unfair Competition*, 24–25.
17. Henning-Bodewig, 9.

be no commercial unfairness in the activity of providing information outside of trade in goods or services. This is not to suggest that honesty and fairness have no place in non-commercial contexts, but rather to highlight the fact that unfair competition laws cannot be relied upon to control that sort of behaviour.

Where unfair competition law has traditionally been applied in the context of geographic names is in the regulation of origin statements. Across trades and industries it has long been the expectation that where information is provided to convey the origin of a product, that information must be truthful. To behave otherwise cuts against the basic notion of honest trade practices; this is equally the case online as it is offline. Some statements are easily identifiable as connotative of origin, such as 'Made in the USA' and 'Swiss chocolate'. Geographic domain names at any level of the DNS are less easily discernible as per se connotative of origin, however. There are several reasons for this. The DNS is a global communications system the structure of which is not organized along territorial lines; for example, some ccTLDs are operated outside of the country represented by the country code and are targeted at domain name registrants with no connection to that country.[18] Further, there is no general rule in either generic TLDs or country code TLDs that applicants of geographic second-level domain names must be physically present in the geographic territory named. Whether geographic domain names constitute a dishonest statement of origin is therefore one of the core questions to be explored in detail in the next section of this chapter.

8.1.2.2 Promote and Protect Investment by Business

Consistent with justifications of intellectual property law on the basis of reward theory,[19] unfair competition laws are grounded in the belief that offering protection to intangible business assets such as goodwill and confidential information against unfair usurpation is a necessary incentive to ensure their creation.[20] Protection by means of unfair competition law is all the more important to businesses when their assets are not able to be

18. Tuvalu's .tv ccTLD is an example. Recognizing the unique online opportunities inherent in its ISO 3166-1 country code, the Tuvaluan government commenced a tender process for the marketing of.tv ccTLDs in the mid-1990s. Stephen Boland & Brian Dollery, *The Value and Viability of Sovereignty-Conferred Rights in MIRAB Economies: The Case of Tuvalu, University of New England Working Paper Series in Economics 2005-2009*, 17 (available at https://www.une.edu.au/__data/assets/pdf_file/0010/67969/econ-2005-9.pdf). Verisign has operated the .tv domain since its acquisition of The .tv Corporation at the end of 2001. *Verisign Acquires The .tv Corporation*, PR Newswire (7 Jan. 2002) (available at http://www.prnewswire.com/news-releases/verisign-acquires-the-tv-corporation-75291122.html). *See also* IANA, *Delegation Record for .TV*, http://www.iana.org/domains/root/db/tv.html.
19. *See for example*, Justin Hughes, *The Philosophy of Intellectual Property*, 77 Geo. L.J. 287, 305–310 (1988–1989).
20. *Restatement of the Law (Third): Unfair Competition* §1 Comment f (1995).

characterized (and therefore protected) as intellectual property. Justifying protection for geographic names on this basis is not, however, an easy fit.

Outside of their use as brands, it is difficult to conceptualize the creation of geographic names as occurring through some sort of planned, strategic, commercial process of asset generation. It is likewise difficult to characterize the creation of new geographic names as an activity that requires regulatory intervention to ensure its continuation. What immediately distinguishes the name 'France' from the name 'Polaroid' is that the latter has been created in a commercial environment for use in a commercial environment, and logically therefore derives its value from commercial attractiveness. The name 'Polaroid' must be distinctive – in other words, able to distinguish the goods or services on which it is used as originating from a particular trader – if it is to succeed in the marketplace. That distinctiveness can arise because the name is coined and has no other connotation or because it develops a reputation through use; either way, a certain degree of 'investment, labor, and strategic dissemination' is required in order to 'create[] a set of unique meanings in the minds of consumers'.[21] This is the primary function of a brand, the legal protection of which takes the form of a trademark.

Geographic names, by contrast, are not products of a commercially oriented development process and their primary function is not to create a link in consumers' minds between particular goods or services and a particular trader. Their primary function is to identify a particular geographic location. Even if no other connotation is generated in a person's mind by a geographic name, if the name serves to identify the correct place on the map to which it is attributed, it is a success. Achieving this sole purpose has not traditionally involved focus groups or market surveys; the choice of a geographic name is not tested for its ability to attract consumers. These observations are not made with the intention of suggesting that strategy has no role to play in the choice of geographic names; the dispute between Greece and the FYROM over the name 'Macedonia'[22] offers ample room for speculation about motives in countries' naming decisions. Rather, the intention here is to highlight the fact that businesses and countries take different things into consideration and do so for different reasons when making naming decisions. These differences call into question the appropriateness of justifying the protection of geographic names under unfair competition law on the basis of ensuring geographic names' continued use and creation.

Where investment in a corporate sense is being made in the context of geographic names is in goodwill. Countries are increasingly seen as brands,[23] with reputations that can be managed with a view to creating 'a desirable

21. Coombe, 61 (internal citations omitted).
22. The 'Macedonia' name dispute is discussed in detail in Part III, Chapter 6, s. 6.3.2 above.
23. FutureBrand, *Country Brand Index 2014-15*, http://www.futurebrand.com/uploads/CBI-14_15-LR.pdf. *See generally,* Forrest, *The New Frontier*, 133–134.

identity which consumers can relate to and want to build a repeat purchase relationship with'.[24] This is not a new phenomenon; governments and tourist bureaus have long been using reputation to entice the tourist consumer. What is new, however, is that more attention is being paid to geographic brands, whose effectiveness and value are now measured on an annual basis similar to the way in which the world's most valuable trademarks are ranked each year.[25]

In many countries, unfair competition law steps in to protect investment in goodwill, but protecting goodwill is not the same as protecting a name. This is because names and goodwill are two distinct (though related) concepts: goodwill is comprised, according to an oft-cited Australian judicial opinion, of 'elements',[26] of which the name is but one:

> As the differential profit advantage of a firm, goodwill may arise from superior efficiency, from convenience, from confidence, from nepotistic connections, from persuasive advertising, from successful infringement of a persuasive symbol, from threats of violence, and so on into a range of conduct entirely beyond the pale of the law.[27]

Correspondingly, the goodwill of a country or other geographic location (and thus its attractiveness to consumers) is likely to be influenced not only by its name but by its exports, the stability and form of its government, its culture and heritage, the friendliness of its people, its tourism, its topography, its propensity to experience natural disasters, etc.[28] The name is a powerful symbol which encapsulates these qualities and brings them to the public mind similar to the way in which the 'Polaroid' brand 'through much effort and the expenditure of large amounts of money had acquired a widespread reputation and much goodwill'.[29]

Geographic names are and have for ages been created and used despite a lack of explicit or implicit protection of them under international law. While there may be need of unfair competition law to protect governments' investments in goodwill in the tourism context, there is little need of unfair competition law to ensure the continued creation and use of geographic names. For this reason, protection of geographic names under unfair competition law can be more transparently characterized as fuelled by a

24. Allan Bonsall & John Harrison, *Brand Aid: The Secrets of Consumer Speak* 26 n. 21 (Estee Media 2006).
25. *See for example*, FutureBrand, Country Brand Index 2014-15; GFK, *Anholt-GFK Nation Brands Index*, http://nation-brands.gfk.com/.
26. *Commissioners of Inland Revenue v. Muller & Co's Margarine, Ltd*, A.C. 217, 223 (H.L. 1901).
27. Ralph S. Brown Jr., *Advertising and the Public Interest: Legal Protection of Trade Symbols*, 57 Yale L.J. 1165, 1199 (1948) (internal citations omitted).
28. GFK, *Anholt-GFK Nation Brands Index*.
29. *Polaroid Corp. v. Polaraid, Inc.*, 319 F.2d 830, 837 (7th Cir. 1963).

desire to preserve a monopoly in a name than a desire to encourage more names' creation and use.

8.1.2.3 Promote Competition and Efficiency in the Market

There is a great paradox inherent in unfair competition law, which is that the exercise of a right to demand that others not engage in anticompetitive conduct in the name of promoting competition has inherently and unavoidably anticompetitive consequences. Unfair competition law must strike a balance between 'protect[ing] the competitive position of the enterprise' and preventing 'business practices that hinder rather than promote the efficient operation of the market.'[30] It is not controversial to propose that a certain degree of competitive behaviour is needed to promote a healthy marketplace. It would not be appropriate, therefore, for unfair competition law to be overzealous in quashing acts aimed at gaining a competitive advantage. A seminal American text on unfair competition law succinctly explains the situation in this way:

> Every competitor seeks to win trade that would otherwise go to someone else. The ultimate end point of that process could conceivably be the complete elimination of one or more rivals as effective competitors. Yet there is no violation of the law so long as the rules of the 'game' are observed. Thus it is not the injury suffered by the complainant which makes competition unfair, it is the competitor's violation of a duty to keep his competition within certain bounds.[31]

The striking of those bounds is made all the more difficult when the behaviour at issue is potentially non-commercial in nature, as in the case of geographic names. Although they can be used commercially, geographic names' primary function as informational identifiers makes it difficult to distinguish competitive uses from anticompetitive uses. It is inappropriate to simply presume that all uses of geographic names are anticompetitive unless proven otherwise: such a drastic measure would have the benefit of preventing free riders, but could also seriously impinge upon the rights of the public to use geographic names in non-competitive, non-commercial ways.

The intention of unfair competition law is said first and foremost to be to protect the market as a whole, while 'the protection of monopolies in names is but a secondary and limiting policy.'[32] When potentially non-commercial subject matter such as a geographic name is involved, special consideration must be given to the balance between protecting whatever

---

30. *Restatement (Third) of the Foreign Relations Law of the United States* §1 Comment g.
31. Rudolf Callmann & Louis Altman, *Callmann on Unfair Competition, Trademarks and Monopolies* §1:9 (4th ed., Thomson-West 1997).
32. *Eastern Wine Corp. v. Winslow-Warren Ltd.*, 137 F.2d 955, 959 (C.C.A. 2d. 1943) (opinion of Frank, J).

interests a government may have in a name and protecting the public's right to use that name in a commercial or non-commercial context. If the use at issue is non-commercial, then unfair competition law is not the appropriate means of regulating that behaviour.

Commercial use is not in question for geographical indications due to their origin-connoting role and direct link to products, making unfair competition law particularly relevant to this specific type of geographic names. Accurate origin information can help consumers identify, distinguish and select goods and services, and it has been suggested that these things have a significant impact on the operation of a market.[33] Geographical indications are, however, a specifically defined subset of geographic name. By contrast, the assumption that all uses – commercial and non-commercial, online and offline, origin-connotative and otherwise – of any geographic name by someone other than a relevant government are unfair is overbroad, in that it places unjustified impediments on many uses of names not falling within the scope of unfair competition law.

If the balance in unfair competition law is tipped in entirely favour of government to the exclusion of others' use of the name, it is difficult to fulfil any of the other purposes of unfair competition law. At greatest risk are consumers, who suffer the effects of a legally supported monopoly.[34] The result of the great paradox of unfair competition law is that in the name of encouraging a competitive marketplace, consumers end up with fewer choices. That said, the law has long questioned consumers' ability to make choices, and in some countries, ensuring their protection is itself considered a purpose of unfair competition law.

8.1.2.4 Protect Consumers

Not all jurisdictions view unfair competition law as an appropriate means of protecting consumers from the unscrupulous behaviour of merchants. The aim of consumer protection law from an economic point of view is to reduce the knowledge and experience gap between buyer and seller.[35] This aim must be balanced with, *inter alia*, the right of freedom of expression, albeit with the recognition that commercial speech may be deemed to warrant less protection than non-commercial speech.[36] There is no universal standard as to what constitutes commercial speech, and the particular challenges of distinguishing commercial and non-commercial use in relation to domain

33. Bowers, 135. *Compare* Broude, 662–678.
34. Coombe, 65–66. Coombe highlights the anti-democratic effect of control over names in the context of trademarks, but her remarks could also logically apply to geographic names.
35. John Vickers, *Economics for Consumer Policy*, in P.J. Marshall (ed.), Proceedings of the British Academy Volume 125, 2003 Lectures (2005).
36. *See for example*, *Hertel v. Switzerland* (59/1997/843/1049) Eur. Ct. H.R. (1998).

names have been discussed in detail in Part III, Chapter 5, at section 5.2.2, above.

The long-held assumption that the consumer 'always aspires to follow the lead of the advertiser, and to have his hand guided in the supermarket'[37] has morphed almost seamlessly from the offline environment to the online environment. In fact, early cases of online confusion deemed it even more likely that consumers would suffer confusion on the internet than in the bricks-and-mortar environment because of the difficulties of determining the identity and legitimacy of a website's owner.[38] The comical aphorism, 'On the internet, nobody knows you're a dog',[39] precisely identifies this problem as well as the public's consciousness of it. It is this concern that motivated ICANN's Governmental Advisory Committee to limit registration of country names as second-level domain names in the newly delegated .info gTLD.[40] As to whether consumers actually require this sort of protection is, however, debatable.

Not all courts or scholars have assumed the gullibility of the (offline or online) consumer. In 1925 it was argued that there were many consumers for whom 'complete indifference reigns. The buyer cannot be deceptively confused if he does not care whether he gets Thinsies or Thins.'[41] Yet the way in which modern consumers use the internet to find information makes it unlikely that 'complete indifference reigns'. The average contemporary online shopper is likely more often savvy than ignorant; the vast numbers of results yielded by existing internet search methods and tools suggest that users may reasonably be presumed to have even lower expectations of immediately finding what they seek online than offline. In the California case of *The Network Network v. CBS, Inc.*[42] it was provocatively suggested more than a decade and a half ago:

> There is a difference between inadvertently landing on a website and being confused. Thousands of Internet users every day take a stab at what they think is the most likely domain name for a particular website.

---

37. Brown Jr, 1197 (internal citations omitted).
38. *See for example*, *Brookfield Communications, Inc. v. West Coast Entertainment Corp.*, 50 U.S.P.Q.2d (B.N.A.) 1545, 1559-1560 (9th Cir. 1999).
39. Peter Steiner, 69(20) New Yorker 61 (5 Jul. 1993).
40. The reservation of country names in the .info TLD is discussed in detail in Part II, Chapter 3, s. 3.2.1.1 above.
41. Brown Jr, 1197 (internal citations omitted).
42. The *Network Network v. CBS, Inc.*, 54 U.S.P.Q.2d (B.N.A.) 1150, 1155 (C.D. Cal. 2000). *Bruce Springsteen v. Jeff Burgar and Bruce Springsteen Club*, Case No. D2000-1532 (WIPO Arbitration and Mediation Center 25 Jan. 2001) (available at http://www.wipo.int/amc/en/domains/decisions/html/2000/d2000-1532.html) (remarking that 'it is relatively unlikely that any user would seek to go straight to the internet and open the site <brucespringsteen.com> in the optimistic hope of reaching the official Bruce Springsteen website. If anyone sufficiently sophisticated in the use of the internet were to do that, they would very soon realise that the site they reached was not the official site, and consequently would move on, probably to conduct a fuller search').

> Given the limited number of letters in the alphabet, and the tendency toward the use of abbreviations in commerce generally and in domain names in particular, it is inevitable that consumers will often guess wrong.

Similar views have been expressed outside of the US,[43] but they have not taken hold in domain name policy. That the WIPO II Report was aimed specifically at 'misleading'[44] uses of names in the DNS suggests that those who call for a measure of common sense and *caveat emptor* to be applied in the wilderness that is the internet are outnumbered by those who believe the average web user to be at a disadvantage. If such a disadvantage truly exists, then unfair competition law may indeed – in those countries that ascribe to unfair competition the purpose of protecting consumers – be a useful tool to address this problem. As the internet and our dependence upon it as an everyday means of communication grow, it is difficult to say whether users have become savvier and adjusted their expectations accordingly, or whether the potential for confusion has increased along with the volume of information available. The future applicability of unfair competition law to online commercial behaviour will depend heavily upon the way in which the DNS develops and is used after hundreds of new top-level domains are added to the root through ICANN's New gTLD Program.

In conclusion, it can be said that the protection of geographic names is not a natural fit within unfair competition law. It is difficult to draw analogies between governments and businesses, and geographic names' primary function as non-commercial identifiers means that to the extent that their protection under unfair competition law can be justified, that protection must necessarily be limited to preventing only those unfair uses that are distinctly commercial in nature and falling within the sorts of activities deemed 'unfair'. The simple act of adopting an existing geographic name as a brand and investing time, money and energy in developing its distinctiveness is not itself an unfair act; the vast numbers of geographic trademarks registered and used around the world is indisputable proof of this. Likewise, the simple act of registering a geographic domain name and investing time, money and energy into developing a distinctive web presence under it is not itself an unfair act; the elements of the UDRP see to this. Thus, unfair competition law has proven not to be needed to ensure the continued creation and use of geographic names, but it may have a role to play in protecting online consumers against being misled in countries that attribute to it that aim and where likelihood of being misled actually does exist.

Governments' interests in geographic names are not primarily commercial, though they may include certain commercial aspects as a result of the

43. *See for example*, Ueli Buri, Doctoral Dissertation in Law, Bern, *Die Verwechselbarkeit von Internet Domain Names nach schweizerischem Firmen-, Marken-, Namens- und Lauterkeitsrecht* (2000).
44. WIPO, *WIPO II Report*, v (Executive Summary).

increased attention to country branding. Ultimately, the multiple purposes of unfair competition law lend support for the view that the protection of governments' interests in geographic names should not automatically prevail over all other interests. Further, where government interests are protected through unfair competition law, this must be strictly limited to commercial uses of geographic names that fall within accepted understandings of what is 'unfair'.

8.1.3 ACTS OF UNFAIR COMPETITION

It is next relevant to consider whether the act of registering a geographic domain name falls within the definition of an 'act of unfair competition' provided by the Paris Convention. Article 10*bis* (2) sets up a two-part test to determine whether an act of unfair competition has occurred, seeking first to determine whether there is an 'act of competition' and then if so, whether that act is generally 'contrary to honest practices'.

8.1.3.1 Geographic TLDs: An 'Act of Competition'?

Unfair competition law seeks to control the unfair behaviour of commercial competitors for the benefit of the various parties identified in the preceding section of this chapter. As a starting point, there must be competition, because '[w]herever there is competition, there is unfair competition.'[45] The 'act of competition' sought to be prevented by Article 10*bis* (2) is conduct of a commercial nature which is likely to affect the players within a market. Most often such conduct is directed at a competitor, though it has been shown above that the harm occasioned by unfair conduct may have a wider impact. The question thus arises: are there competitors and competition of the sort envisioned by Article 10*bis* (2) in the use of names that is inherent in the DNS?

It is certainly the case that applicants for domain names at all levels of the system compete against other applicants for the ability to identify themselves by a particular name in the DNS. Since the system's earliest days, it has been possible at the second and lower levels for competing applications for a single name to be made. This led to the early adoption of a 'first come, first served' registration policy.[46] Competing applications at the top-level of the DNS have likewise been made, though the instances of such conflicts are far fewer than at lower levels of the system due to the controlled path of development at the top-level.[47] Continued open and uncapped top-level expansion is certain to generate an increase in the number of conflicting top-level domain applications. This is borne out by the applications received

45. Callmann & Altman, §1:1.
46. *See* Part II, Chapter 3, n. 111 above.
47. Top-level DNS development is discussed in Part I, Chapter 2, s. 2.4 above.

by ICANN in 2012: of the 1,930 new gTLD applications lodged, ICANN's analysis identified 751, nearly 40% of the total, in direct contention.[48]

Even so, competition in the context of gTLD applications is not quite competition for market share in the traditional sense. Domain name applicants are competitors in that they vie for control of a unique resource. Allocation of the unique resource has the effect of granting the right of entry into the market, similar to the effect of the granting of a business license or permit in a regulated market. To the extent that an applicant engages in unfair acts in the course of preparing or submitting its application for a new gTLD string, this could have the effect of harming other applicants, web users, and even the functionality and perceived legitimacy of the system as a whole.

It is less easy to characterize the situation as competitive once new gTLDs are created, however, because it is not quite clear that the registries of delegated new gTLD strings are actually in competition with other TLD registries. On the one hand, it could be said that the availability of far greater numbers of top-level domains in which to register domain names will increase competition among top-level domain registries. This was precisely the aim of the two 'proof of concept' top-level expansion efforts that preceded the launch of the New gTLD Program, but even now it has yet to fully bear out in practice.[49] On the other hand it must be questioned whether new gTLDs do in fact compete with each other, particularly in the case of 'sponsored' or 'community based' gTLDs that are targeted at or are even restricted to a defined segment of the internet community. Will the new .paris top-level domain compete, for example, with the new .eco top-level domain – or even any of the existing legacy top-level domains save the universal generic .com, .net and .org – for domain name registrants?

Article 10*bis* of Paris Convention notably requires action only when there are competitors, and it is not clear that competitors exist in this context. Member States have the freedom to 'grant protection against certain acts even if the parties involved are not competing against each other',[50] but this is not required under the Paris Convention or other international law.

8.1.3.2 Geographic Domain Names: 'Contrary to Honest Practices'?

The most fundamental question in the application of unfair competition law to geographic domain names is whether the simple act of registering a geographic domain name or applying for a TLD string is inherently 'contrary to honest practices' when that act is carried out by anyone other than the relevant government or public authority (in the case of a geographic name) or the geographical indication holder (in the case of a geographical

48. ICANN, *Program Statistics*, http://newgtlds.icann.org/en/program-status/statistics.
49. *See* above Part I, Chapter 2, n. 116.
50. WIPO, *Protection against unfair competition*, 18.

indication). Governments in particular have been quick to assume that the only legitimate interests in geographic domain names are their own. This point has been made not only in international law fora but in domestic courts and UDRP disputes. A group of such cases involve a US-based company called Virtual Countries, which registered during 1999 and 2000 various country names as second-level domain names and operated thirty-one websites under those names.[51] The complaint made by the government of New Zealand against Virtual Countries' registration of www.newzealand.com is illustrative of governments' general sentiment in this situation: 'Virtual Countries has no rights or legitimate interests in respect of the domain name [newzealand.com] because only the Complainant as Head of the Sovereign State of New Zealand, or its agencies, can have those rights or interests.'[52]

If the government is the only party with 'rights or legitimate interests' in geographic domain names, it must logically follow that the registration of geographic domain names without government authorization is inherently 'contrary to honest practices'. Yet as a universal rule this is problematic, because what are deemed honest practices in one country may not be so deemed in another. To the extent that 'honest practices' can be identified from international trade norms, then these should be considered,[53] but agreed standards of honesty in commercial behaviour have proven elusive even at a regional level.[54]

It is difficult to prove the existence of agreed standards of honesty at a global level given their wide use in a variety of contexts. The use of geographic names in non-commercial contexts in the offline environment is ordinarily not subject to a requirement of government approval. There are, of course, bound to be variations in domestic approaches, but teachers, schoolchildren, journalists, researchers and politicians in free speech-promoting societies usually need not seek government clearance before speaking or writing geographic names. Further, as the survey conducted in 2011 by the WIPO Special Committee on the Law of Trademarks, Industrial Designs and Geographical Indications evidences, many countries have taken steps to limit proprietary rights in geographic names as trademarks.[55] This has the practical effect of ensuring that geographic names remain accessible for public use.

---

51. *See for example*, *Virtual Countries, Inc. v. Republic of South Africa and South African Tourism Board*, No. 00 Civ. 84888 U.S. Dist. LEXIS (S.D.N.Y. 2001); *New Zealand v. Virtual Countries,* WIPO Case No. D2002-0754; *Puerto Rico Tourism Company v. Virtual Countries,* WIPO Case No. D2002-1129. *See also* discussion in Rimmer, *Virtual Countries*, 126.
52. *New Zealand v. Virtual Countries,* WIPO Case No. D2002-0754.
53. Bodenhausen, 144.
54. Henning-Bodewig, 20.
55. This survey is discussed in detail in Part III, Chapter 6, s. 6.2.1.2 above.

In the online environment, responses to third party use of geographic names are inconsistent. In some cases governments have been unable to convince UDRP panellists that unauthorized geographic domain name registrants have no legitimate interest in the names in question. The earlier-mentioned dispute between the government of New Zealand and Virtual Countries over the domain name www.newzealand.com is a notable example. The panel in that dispute considered it unnecessary to specifically address the question of Virtual Countries' legitimate interest in the domain name, but it was nevertheless pointed out that the use of the name on an operative, 'genuine' website 'although sketchy and badly in need of being updated' weighed in the registrant's favour.[56]

Further insight is provided by a subsequent dispute involving the domain name www.andalucia.com, in which the panel relied upon consensus views that had by that point emerged from UDRP decisions. In response to the question, 'Does a respondent automatically have a legitimate interest in a domain name comprised of a generic (dictionary) word(s)?'[57] the panel found:

> While the general rule is not necessarily, there is an exception, that is stated thusly: 'However: If a respondent is using a generic word to describe his product/business or to profit from the generic value of the word without intending to take advantage of complainant's rights in that word, then it has a legitimate interest.'
>
> ...
>
> The Panel finds that where, as here, a respondent is using a geographic indication to describe his product/business or to profit from the geographic sense of the word without intending to take advantage of complainant's rights in that word, then the respondent has a legitimate interest in respect of the domain name.[58]

56. *New Zealand v. Virtual Countries,* WIPO Case No. D2002-0754.
57. WIPO, *WIPO Overview of WIPO Panel Views on Selected UDRP Questions: 2.2 Does a Respondent Automatically Have a Legitimate Interest in a Domain Name Comprised of a Generic Word(s)?*, http://www.wipo.int/amc/en/domains/search/overview/index.html#15.
58. *Junta de Analucia Consejeria de Turismo, Comercio y Deporte, Turismo Andaluz, S.A. v. Andalucia.com Limited*, Case No. D2006-0749 (WIPO Arbitration and Mediation Center 13 Oct. 2006) (available at http://www.wipo.int/amc/en/domains/decisions/html/2006/d2006-0749.html). *See also Asphalt Research Technology, Inc. v. National Press & Publishing, Inc.*, Case No. D2000-1005 (WIPO Arbitration and Mediation Center 13 Nov. 2000) (available at http://www.wipo.int/amc/en/domains/decisions/html/2000/d2000-1005.html); *Porto Chico Stores, Inc. v. Otavio Zambon*, Case No. D2000-1270 (WIPO Arbitration and Mediation Center 15 Nov. 2000) (available at http://www.wipo.int/amc/en/domains/decisions/html/2000/d2000-1270.html); *Gorstew Limited v. Worldwidewebsales.com*, Case No. D2002-0744 (WIPO Arbitration and Mediation Center 23 Oct. 2002) (available at http://www.wipo.int/amc/en/domains/decisions/html/2002/d2002-0744.html).

Similar questions have arisen in respect of domain names comprised of geographical indications. The registrant of the domain name www.parmaham.com, for example, was not found to have a legitimate interest in the name 'parma ham',[59] but the result may have been different had the domain name at issue resolved to an active website. Taking a slightly different approach, the sole panellist in that dispute found that possession of the domain name by the respondent, who was not otherwise affiliated with the holder of the geographical indication, nevertheless did not constitute bad faith. It was noted that this finding would not necessarily preclude a finding of unfair competition under domestic law. An issue is potentially also raised in relation to Article 22 of the TRIPS Agreement, but only, as concluded in the previous chapter, if the website was related to goods (in the immediate example, Prosciutto di Parma).

As to whether the global online public perceives the registration of a geographic domain name by a registrant other than a relevant government as 'contrary to honest practices', this would be difficult to determine in a global marketplace. Despite concerns about globalization and a resultant homogenization of consumer tastes and preferences, there remain significant cultural and other differences that prevent the formulation of a single perception or interpretation of most names. It has already been argued in the previous chapter that this divergence of consumer interpretation remains one of the greatest challenges to recognizing rights in geographical indications at the international level. The same problem hinders their blanket protection under unfair competition law at the international level: terms which are in some countries protected as identifying a particular product originating from a particular geographical location are in other countries considered generic. As such, their use in the latter countries by someone other than producers of the product in the named location could not be considered dishonest.

Accordingly, if protection of geographic names is to be based on Article 10*bis* of the Paris Convention, this must result from a name-by-name, country-by-country determination of whether or not use of the name by a particular party without government authorization is 'honest practice'. This would be a resource-intensive undertaking, since not just the substance of the standard of honesty but even how it is determined that something is an 'honest practice' differs from country to country. Even *ex post* analysis of disputes involving similar names arising in multiple territories would present challenges, given the differing standards of 'unfairness' that may have been applied. Further, if it is the case that '[t]he most important factor for determining "unfairness" in the marketplace ... is derived from the *purpose* of unfair competition law',[60] there is little hope of arriving at any universal

59. *Consorzio del Proscuitto di Parma v. Domain Name Clearing Company, LLC*, Case No. D2000-0629 (WIPO Arbitration and Mediation Center 18 Sep. 2000) (available at http://www.wipo.int/amc/en/domains/decisions/html/2000/d2000-0629.html).

60. WIPO, *Protection against unfair competition*, 24-25.

standard, because the differing purposes of unfair competition law in various jurisdictions will lead to differing standards. In particular, what is considered fair in countries that carve consumer protection out from unfair competition law will differ from those countries that do not.[61]

It should thus not simply be assumed that the registration of a geographic domain name by a non-government registrant or the registration of a geographical indication domain name by a non-local producer falls squarely within the broadly worded definition of 'unfair competition' provided by Article 10*bis* (2) of the Paris Convention. Deeper consideration is needed to determine whether unauthorized registrations of geographic domain names fall within any of the specifically enumerated acts of unfair competition provided for under the Paris Convention. This will now be explored.

8.2 SPECIFIC ACTS OF UNFAIR COMMERCIAL BEHAVIOUR

Paragraph (1) of Article 10*bis* of the Paris Convention is of a general nature, not obliging States to create new law 'if their existing general legislation – for example, provisions of civil law directed against torts, or principles of common law – suffices to assure effective protection against unfair competition.'[62] Paragraphs (2) and (3) are less general in nature; while neither provides a comprehensive, authoritative list of impermissible acts of unfair competition, paragraph (2) offers the broad definition just discussed and paragraph (3) identifies three specific acts which, at a minimum, must be prohibited by members' domestic law. These acts seek to prevent unfair competition, on the one hand by stopping an enterprise from disparaging its competitors, and on the other hand by attempting to narrow the knowledge and experience gap between enterprise and consumer. Of these three acts that the convention specifically identifies as unfairly competitive, it is said that they share one aspect in particular:

> The common aspect of these most important, but by no means exhaustive, examples of unfair market behaviour is the attempt (by an entrepreneur) to succeed in competition without relying on his own achievements in terms of quality and price of his products and services, but rather by taking undue advantage of the work of another or by influencing consumer demand with false or misleading statements. Practices that involve such methods are therefore doubtful at the outset as to their fairness in competition.[63]

---

61. Henning-Bodewig, 21.
62. Bodenhausen, 143.
63. WIPO, *Protection against unfair competition*, 24.

It must be borne in mind that although Article 10*bis* (3) specifically identifies three behaviours as unfairly competitive, this list is not exhaustive; members are required to target all acts which would fall within the broad definition of unfair competition set out in Article 10*bis* (2), the relationship of which to geographic names generally and geographic domain names particularly has been discussed in the immediately preceding section of this chapter. Further, although geographic domain name registration is not expressly addressed by Article 10*bis* (3), and even to the extent that this provision is interpreted as not covering geographic domain name registration, there is nothing to prevent members from creating domestic law to that effect.

In addition to Article 10*bis*, which is specifically headed 'Unfair competition', Article 10 of the Paris Convention also addresses commercial behaviour that has the effect of harming competitors, consumers, or both. It makes actionable the use of false indications of source and thus is particularly relevant to the use of geographical indications. It is likewise applicable to other geographic names the use of which could be interpreted as connoting origin. The remainder of this chapter is devoted to an examination of these provisions in order to determine whether any of them offers grounds for restricting the registrability of geographic domain names, whether as new gTLD strings or at lower levels of the DNS.

8.2.1 False Indications of Source

The first attempt to control unfairly competitive acts at the international level took the form of preventions against false indications of source. At the 1880 conference that would result in the drafting of the Paris Convention, it was declared a priority that:

> Tout produit portant illicitement soit la marque d'un fabricant ou d'un commerçant établi dans l'un des pays de l'Union, soit une indication de provenance dudit pays, sera prohibé à l'entrée dans tous les autres États contractants, exclu du transit et de l'entrepôt, et pourra être l'objet d'une saisie suivie, s'il y a lieu, d'une action en justice.[64]

The prohibition against false indications of origin took shape as Article 10, in which indications were actionable only to the extent that they were used in conjunction with a false, fictitious, or deceptive trade name.[65] Since revision at the 1958 Lisbon Conference, Article 10 applies to all direct or indirect uses of a false indication of the source of goods. It is not expressly

64. Ministère des Affaires Étrangères de la France, *Conférence Internationale pour la Protection de la Propriété Industrielle,* 14.

65. Conrad, 23.

limited to geographical source, but that is identified as its most common application.[66]

Two things seriously hinder the applicability of Article 10 to geographic domain names. First, the indications of source covered by Article 10 are confined to those relating to goods, with the result that this provision is relevant only to second-level domain names corresponding to a website dealing in goods. Article 10 has no application to top-level domains because they bear no direct connection to goods. Rather, top-level domains represent the service of providing an online communications portal that others may, if they so choose, use to engage in commercial activity involving goods.

Second, even for those second-level domain names having a direct nexus to goods, or if a nexus between top-level domains and goods were thought to exist, Article 10 has no practical effect because the remedy for its breach is seizure of the falsely identified goods upon importation. This would have no effect on a domain name at any level of the DNS. Article 10 targets the cross-border movement of falsely identified goods; geographic domain names do not fall within this ambit.

Similar limitations arise in the application of Article IX:6 of the GATT Agreement, which deals with 'marks of origin'. It provides:

> The contracting parties shall co-operate with each other with a view to preventing the use of trade names in such a manner as to misrepresent the true origin of a product, to the detriment of such distinctive regional or geographical names of products of the territory of a contracting party as are protected by its legislation. Each contracting party shall accord full and sympathetic consideration to such requests or representations as may be made by any other contracting party regarding the application of the undertaking set forth in the preceding sentence to names of products which have been communicated to it by the other contracting party.

As an initial matter, the obligations imposed by this provision are significantly weaker than those imposed by Article 10 of the Paris Convention, requiring only 'co-operation with a view to' preventing false representations of origin. As with Article 10, the application of GATT Article IX:6 is not applicable to services. This likewise renders it only partially applicable to second-level domain names and entirely inapplicable to top-level domain strings. In addition, the capability of this provision to protect geographic names is hindered by its having been given a very narrow interpretation in the case of *Japan – Customs Duties, Taxes and Labelling Practices on Imported Wines and Alcoholic Beverages*.[67] The Panel in that case found that the use of terms such as 'Riesling' or 'chateau' by Japanese manufacturers

66. Bodenhausen, 139.

67. *Japan – Customs Duties, Taxes and Labelling Practices on Imported Wines and Alcoholic Beverages*, L6216 adopted 10 Nov. 1987, BISD 34S/83 (GATT Panel Report).

was not detrimental to the names of products produced by the European Communities.

Like the Paris Convention, the GATT Agreement does not expressly prevent members from offering greater protection to origin statements under domestic law than is required by their treaty obligations. On the contrary, GATT Article XX(d) allows contracting parties to adopt or enforce measures 'necessary to secure compliance with laws or regulations which are not inconsistent with the provisions of this Agreement, including those relating to [...] the protection of patents, trade marks, copyrights and the prevention of deceptive practices'. The term 'deceptive practices' has notably been interpreted to include 'false marking of geographical origin.'[68] There is, however, no scope for protection of non-commercial names under the GATT.

Neither Article 10 of the Paris Convention nor Article IX:6 of the GATT specifically offer rights that enable one party to prevent another's registration and use of a geographic top-level domain string. Some scope exists under these provisions for restricting registration of second and lower level domain names, but this is limited to the use of specifically origin-connoting geographic names used to identify websites offering goods. Member States are not prevented from enacting specific legislation preventing unauthorized registration of domain names as a false statement of origin, but any such rights would be enforceable only in the jurisdiction in which they are granted.

8.2.2 Acts Creating Confusion with a Competitor

Turning now to the first of the three acts that are specifically identified as unfairly competitive by the Paris Convention, Article 10*bis* (3)(i) prohibits 'all acts of such a nature as to create confusion by any means whatever with the establishment, the goods, or the industrial or commercial activities, of a competitor'. The term 'all acts' is sufficiently broad to be interpreted as including the registration and use of a name at any level of the DNS. The following two elements must additionally be satisfied for Article 10*bis* (3)(i) to justify a general rule of preventing their delegation to applicants without government authorization:

– The acts of applying for and operating a geographic gTLD, irrespective of the registrant's intent,[69] must be likely to create confusion with the government.

68. Daniel Gervais, *The TRIPS Agreement: Drafting History and Analysis* 8 (4th ed., Sweet & Maxwell 2012).

69. WIPO (ed.), *Introduction to Intellectual Property*, 254 (noting that while irrelevant to the determination of whether an act of unfair competition has taken place, intent may be deemed relevant to the determination of sanctions).

– Unauthorized geographic gTLD applicants and relevant governments must be competitors.

These steps are analysed in the subsections that follow.

8.2.2.1 Likelihood of Creating Confusion

It has been argued that society has become conditioned to 'assume that all the iconic indicia of consumer culture must be owned, and thus that *any* appearance of them must be approved by their official owners.'[70] If this is so, confusion is likely to result from the use of geographic names in the DNS, fuelled by the authoritative or official status of their presumptive owners. There are various means of determining confusion in domestic law, but most commonly it is established using a 'likelihood of confusion' test derived from trademark law.[71] This test has played a major role in trademark owners' efforts to extend their offline rights into the online environment. The standard applied is ordinarily that of 'an average (reasonable) consumer, having normal attentiveness with regard to the nature of the product or service or the place where it is offered'.[72] In the context of this study the following question arises: would the average, reasonable, normally attentive internet user be likely to be confused by geographic domain names registered by or delegated to parties other than governments? The following two fabricated examples are illustrative of this issue:

– When the average internet user in Country A sees the top-level domain .uruguay, do they understand it to be delegated to or affiliated with the country of Uruguay?
– When the average internet user in Country A sees the domain name 'mombasa.visit', do they understand this second-level domain in the .visit top-level domain to be registered by or affiliated with the city of Mombasa?

It is worth noting for completeness that these questions can of course be varied to take account of the many ways of representing names that have a geographic connotation, including long- and short-form names, colloquial names, abbreviations (including standardized codes) and others. The answers to these questions, whichever form of name they utilize, depend on a range of factors, of which several can be borrowed from trademark law:[73]

– The similarity between the geographic name and geographic domain name/string.

70. Coombe, 65 (internal citations omitted).
71. AIPPI, *Effective Protection against Unfair Competition under Article 10bis Paris Convention of 1883*, *AIPPI Y.B.* 1994/II, 398, 6.3. (1994).
72. *Id.*, 6.5.
73. WIPO (ed.), *Introduction to Intellectual Property*, 255.

- The reputation or degree of distinctiveness of the geographic name/ string and the location it names.
- The reputation of the government/s relevant to the name/string.
- Internet user sophistication regarding the DNS (e.g., some users will know that not all country code TLDs are operated by or formally affiliated with the government of the territory represented).[74]
- The relationship of the reasonable internet user to the name (local familiar names may be interpreted differently than non-local unfamiliar names).
- The existence of other, non-geographic meanings of the name (the names 'Turkey' and 'Orange', for example).
- The existence of multiple geographic locations having the same name (Melbourne, Australia and Melbourne, Florida, USA, for example).
- The relationship, if any, between a second-level domain name and the top-level domain in which it is registered (e.g., tokyo.japan could be assumed by the reasonable person to be associated with the government, while cooking.japan and japan.cooking could be understood differently).

Reliance upon the 'reasonable person' standard in the global context presents significant challenges because of the widely varied experience and knowledge of internet users across the globe. The reasonable internet user in one jurisdiction may be affected by the factors noted above in a different way than the reasonable internet user in another jurisdiction. Identifying a global standard would require capturing the many domestic standards and finding among them sufficient consistencies, to the extent that any exist. There is thus scant support for a general rule that any registration of a geographic domain name by a non-government registrant is likely to confuse.

There is greater scope for consistency in findings of likelihood of confusion when the domain name or string in question is a distinctive geographical indication.[75] The identification of a global 'reasonable person' standard is influenced by the fact that the ordinary use of a geographical identification is as an identifier of source. Consistent use of wine and spirit geographical indications resulting from the higher level of protection afforded them under Article 23 of the TRIPS Agreement increases the capacity for likelihood of confusion. The international register as proposed by Article 23[76] could, if it were to be established, have the effect of strengthening the public's awareness of the indications recorded by it.

74. Country code TLD administration is discussed at Part I, Chapter 2, s. 2.4.2 above. The example of Tuvalu's .tv ccTLD, which has no territorial restrictions and operates as if it were an open gTLD, is provided above in this chapter in n. 18.
75. WIPO (ed.), *Introduction to Intellectual Property*, 256–257.
76. The proposed international register is discussed in Part III, Chapter 7, s. 7.3.1 above.

Certain geographical indications may also benefit from widespread recognition through a patchwork of bi- and multilateral agreements between the origin country and trade partners. The EU in particular has made the recognition of geographical indications a key issue in agreements with its trade partners.[77]

In countries in which a geographical indication is interpreted as identifying a type of (rather than a particular) product, there is no connotation of origin and thus no likelihood of confusion. Courts tend to rely on the meaning of a term to the relevant public, as ascertained from such things as dictionary definitions, telephone directories, media sources and other publications, along with the use of the term made by the party claiming ownership, its competitors and others.[78] It would be interesting to consider whether the convention of using lower-case letters in domain names has any effect on public perception, given that geographical indications are often identified in written expression with capital letters following the convention of proper (i.e., non-generic) names.

These issues lead to the conclusion that name-by-name, jurisdiction-by-jurisdiction analysis is needed to determine whether registration as a domain name or delegation as a gTLD of geographical indications or other geographic names falls within the scope of Article 10*bis* (3)(i). It is overreaching for States to prevent registration of geographic domain names on the basis of the existence of a general rule among all Paris Union members that this activity is inherently likely to confuse.

8.2.2.2 Confusion with a Competitor

In cases in which likelihood of confusion is found, unauthorized registration/delegation of a geographic domain name will not fall within the scope of Article 10*bis* (3)(i) if the registrant/registry operator and government or geographical indication holder are not competitors. To clarify, the likelihood of confusion must exist between two parties in a market, with advantages

---

77. A summary of key EU bilateral agreements on geographical indications made in the ten years following the implementation of the TRIPS Agreement is provided in O'Connor and Company & Insight Consulting, *Geographical Indications and TRIPs: 10 Years Later … A Roadmap for EU GI Holders to Get Protection in other WTO Members*, http://trade.ec.europa.eu/doclib/docs/2007/june/tradoc_135088.pdf. Recently signed agreements addressing geographical indication protection include the Trade Agreement between the EU and Colombia and Peru (Annex XIII) and the EU-South Korea FTA (Chapter 10, sub-s. B). Trade Agreement between the European Union and its Member States, of the one part, and Colombia and Peru, of the other part, O.J. L 354, 21 Dec. 2012 (available at http://eur-lex.europa.eu/legal-content/EN/TXT/?qid=1479093383320&uri=CELEX:22012A1221(01); EU-South Korea Free Trade Agreement, O.J. L 127, 14 May 2011 (available at http://eur-lex.europa.eu/JOHtml.do?uri=OJ:L:2011:127:SOM:EN:HTML).
78. Xuan-Thao N. Nguyen, *Nationalizing Trademarks: A New International Trademark Jurisprudence?*, 39 Wake Forest L. Rev. 729, 744–745 (2004).

accruing to one competitor because consumers believe that competitor to be another competitor. General confusion about a market is not sufficient.

As noted earlier in this chapter, competition exists in the DNS but not in a clear, conventional sense. All new gTLD applicants compete against each other for monopoly control of a uniquely named domain. In the application process, a private geographic gTLD applicant may be in competition with a government applicant. Once the string is delegated to a successful applicant, the focus turns to operation of the TLD registry and the relevant question becomes whether the private geographic gTLD registry operator is in competition with the government of the named location. This depends upon the gTLD and its operator, in particular what the mission and purpose of the gTLD are and whether these are likely to cause confusion with the 'establishment, the goods, or the industrial or commercial activities' of the relevant government.

Automatic rejection of gTLD applications lacking government authorization is unsupportable under Article 10*bis* (3)(i) because this fails to take into account the mission and purpose of the proposed domain and whether these give rise to a competitive relationship. Further, it certainly cannot be assumed that all gTLD operators will be in competition with relevant governments. Domain names comprising a proprietary name and the derogatory word 'sucks' (so-called sucks sites) provide clear examples of potentially non-competing, non-commercial domains. This issue had not yet presented at the top-level of the DNS prior to the New gTLD Program, but three applications were made in the program for the top-level string '.sucks'.[79] One can point to registrations in the new gTLD resulting from the successful application lodged by Vox Populi Registry Inc. as examples of non-commercial speech that cannot be considered confusion with a competitor.[80]

The absence of a likelihood of confusion in all cases and the potential for confusion outside of a competitive relationship support a conclusion that Article 10*bis* (3)(i) does not oblige Paris Union Member States to prevent the unauthorized registration of geographical indications and other geographic names as domain names. Neither does Article 10*bis* (3)(i) prevent States from adopting and enforcing such a rule through domestic law.

79. ICANN, *Reveal Day 13 June 2012: New gTLD Applied-For Strings*, http://newgtlds.icann.org/en/program-status/application-results (13 Jun. 2012).

80. ICANN, *New Generic Top-Level Domains: Application Details (SUCKS)*, https://gtldresult.icann.org/application-result/applicationstatus/applicationdetails/54. Kevin Murphy, *Governments Probe Domain Land-Snatch: many.gTLDs.suck*, The Register (29 Jun. 2012) (available at http://www.theregister.co.uk/2012/06/29/domain_land_grab_under_the_microscope/). Murphy comments that the 'companies that have applied for .sucks … face an uphill battle selling their proposed benefits to the GAC and to ICANN's influential intellectual property lobby.'

8.2.3 False Allegations Discrediting a Competitor

As the second specifically identified act of prohibited unfair competition, Article 10*bis* (3)(ii) of the Paris Convention targets 'false allegations in the course of trade of such a nature as to discredit the establishment, the goods, or the industrial or commercial activities, of a competitor'. It is essentially a provision that protects a commercial enterprise from harm to its commercial reputation. With that in mind, it may be of even greater use to online businesses than offline businesses, because online reputation is potentially more difficult to build and therefore more valuable to the enterprise.[81] Yet while this may be the case for businesses and their brand-oriented domain names, it should not automatically be assumed to be so for those interested in geographic domain names.

It is helpful to begin by distinguishing Article 10*bis* (3)(i) from Article 10*bis* (3)(ii): misleading the public into confusion involves communicating something (usually positive) about one's own identity or products, while making a false allegation involves communicating something negative about another market player. In order for Article 10*bis* (3)(ii) to be called upon to prevent the unauthorized registration of geographic domain names or application for a gTLD comprising a geographic name, the act of registration/application must be interpreted as the making of a false allegation. Additionally, that false allegation must be of a discrediting nature. It is difficult to see how the simple act of registering a geographic domain or applying for a TLD string could satisfy either of these elements.

8.2.3.1 False Allegations

Making an application for a geographic gTLD such as .london or for a geographic second-level domain such as champagne.com cannot on its own be characterized as the making of a false allegation. That these actions should even be characterized as an 'allegation' is not at all obvious given the ordinary meaning of that term as 'a claim that someone has done something wrong, typically an unfounded one.'[82] There may be some scope for interpreting a geographic gTLD string as a claim the applicant makes about itself, but it is not logical to characterize a geographic gTLD as a claim about another party.

Even if domain names generally or geographic domain names specifically are understood in this manner, it is inappropriate to assume that the claim they make is false. Geographic names can be interpreted in a variety

81. Dan Jerker B. Svantesson, *The Right of Reputation in the Internet Era*, 23(3) Int'l Rev. L. Comp. & Tech. 169, 170 (2009) (positing that reputation has a much greater role to play online than off because 'online you simply do not have the same possibilities of building trust through means such as location, shop structure, etc.').

82. *The Concise Oxford English Dictionary* 34 (Catherine Soanes & Angus Stevenson eds, 11th ed. revised, Oxford University Press 2008).

of ways, including most obviously as the identifier of a particular geographic location. Only false allegations are expressly prohibited by this provision, and it is indubitably not the case that all of the possible interpretations of a geographic name are inherently false. The same can be said of domain names more generally. Here it helps to return to the discussion of what a domain name is, first and foremost the identifier of a particular location in the DNS. It is true that domain names have taken on initially unintended semantic significance, but to consider the act of applying for a top-level domain name the making of a false allegation is to push that significance to illogical limits. It should, however, be acknowledged that Paris Union members remain free to prohibit through domestic law true but nevertheless disparaging statements.[83]

8.2.3.2 Discrediting a Competitor

Even if it is found that a geographic domain name or string constitutes a false allegation, that allegation must be 'of such a nature as to discredit the establishment, the goods, or the industrial or commercial activities, of a competitor', what WIPO characterizes as an 'attack' on one's competitor.[84] The ordinary meaning of the verb form of the word 'discredit' as 'harm the good reputation of, cause (an idea or account) to seem false or unreliable'[85] serves to emphasize that the allegations at issue in Article 10*bis* (3)(ii), unlike the misleading activity targeted by Article 10*bis* (3)(i), are specifically directed at others in the market.

The act of lodging an application for a geographic domain name cannot, on its own, be said to constitute an attack on others. Such a finding could only be reached by considering the context in the geographic domain name is to be used, for example in conjunction with pejorative words. It could be said that a top-level domain such as .australiasucks or the domain name 'australia' registered in a new .sucks TLD ('australia.sucks') discredits everything about Australia, including its 'establishment', 'goods', and 'industrial or commercial activities'. Opinions are not actionable,[86] however, and it can be argued that registrants of such domain names are using the DNS to express an opinion rather than an objective fact.

Furthermore, discrediting though it may be, the use of a name in a 'sucks site' may be non-commercial in nature and made by a party not constituting a 'competitor'. Like Article 10*bis* (3)(i), Article 10*bis* (3)(ii) does not require that States prevent acts, however undesirable, against those who are not competitors. Accordingly, most countries limit disparagement to

83. AIPPI, 7.1.
84. WIPO (ed.), *Introduction to Intellectual Property,* 266.
85. Soanes & Stevenson (eds), *The Concise Oxford English Dictionary*, 409–410.
86. Lisa P. Ramsey, *Free Speech and International Obligations to Protect Trademarks*, 35 Yale J. Int'l L.J. 405, 421 (2010).

'cases where there is at least some sort of competitive relationship between the plaintiff and the defendant.'[87] Countries that do extend the scope of this provision are not required by Article 10*bis* (3)(ii) to do so, but neither are they prevented from doing so.

Restrictions on the registration of geographic domain names on the basis of their constituting a false allegation that discredits a competitor thus lack support from Article 10*bis* (3)(ii). Paris Union members are not obliged to prevent the registration of geographic names as domain names or strings, and it is difficult to see how Member States can rely on Article 10*bis* (3)(ii) as a basis for domestic law to that effect. A State's claim to rights on this basis appears less motivated by a desire to prevent unfair competition than a desire to foreclose all competition in order to prevent any slights against or encroachments upon the State's reputation. If that is the true intention, a more appropriate source of rights to consider is the trademark theory of dilution, the potential application of which to geographic names is discussed in the final section of this chapter.

8.2.4 Indications or Allegations Liable to Mislead the Public

Article 10*bis* (3)(iii) of the Paris Convention sets out the last of the three specifically prohibited acts of unfair competition, 'indications or allegations the use of which in the course of trade is liable to mislead the public as to the nature, the manufacturing process, the characteristics, the suitability for their purpose, or the quantity, of the goods.' The Austrian proposal from which this provision originated included the word 'origin', but its removal was motivated by objections raised by the US.[88] Origin statements or indications going to 'the *identity of the producer*, his *establishment* or his *industrial or commercial activities*' (emphasis in original) were thus beyond the reach of Article 10*bis*, and to the extent not covered by Article 10, relegated to domestic law.[89] The International Association for the Protection of Intellectual Property (AIPPI) has observed, however, that 'in general, all kinds of allegations, not restricted to those listed in Article 10*bis*, are covered by such protection, including allegations referring to the geographical origin of the products'.[90] Furthermore, despite the inapplicability on its face to geographical indications, this provision nevertheless 'became a launching point for'[91] the drafting of Articles 22, 23 and 24 of the TRIPS Agreement covering geographical indications. The end result is a curious one, in that Article 22(2)

87. WIPO (ed.), *Introduction to Intellectual Property*, 266.
88. J. Thomas McCarthy & Veronica Colby Devitt, *Protection of Geographical Denominations: Domestic and International*, 69 Trademark Rep. 199, 201–203 (1979).
89. Bodenhausen, 146 (internal citations omitted).
90. AIPPI, 8.1.
91. Hughes, *Spirited Debate*, 312.

of the TRIPS Agreement effectively extends the scope of protection under Article 10*bis* of the Paris Convention by bringing geographical indications, which are by definition origin statements, within its scope.[92]

8.2.4.1 Misleading

As with standards of truthfulness and fairness, the question of whether an indication or allegation is misleading inevitably varies from jurisdiction to jurisdiction.[93] Some countries tolerate exaggeration up to a point, but there is no universal agreement as to where that point lies.[94] This makes it difficult to enumerate specifically misleading acts at the international level. It is generally the case that in order to fall within the scope of Article 10*bis* (3)(iii), the indication or allegation in question need not be inherently false or actually result in a false impression in the consumer's mind. Rather, its misleading character is determined by the consumer's reaction, which 'may differ from country to country and may also depend on the kind of addressee (consumers or traders) and the type of goods or services. The Paris Convention leaves this question to member States'.[95]

The question in the context of geographic names' use in the DNS is whether their delegation to (top-level) or registration by (second- or lower-level) an applicant other than a government or geographical indication holder is inherently misleading to the average, reasonable internet user. As discussed in the context of the prohibition through Article 10*bis* (3)(i) of 'all acts of such a nature as to create confusion by any means whatever with the establishment, the goods, or the industrial or commercial activities, of a competitor', global reasonableness standards are difficult if not impossible to identify. It is extremely difficult to gauge public perception on a global scale, and attempts to do are very likely to reveal that the savvy and experience attributed to the average internet user differs from country to country and perhaps even within a country.

8.2.4.2 Limited to Goods

Even if geographic top-level domains are considered inherently misleading, there is an insurmountable obstacle to the application of Article 10*bis* (3)(iii), which is the limitation of that provision to 'indications or allegations' made about goods. As has been argued in the context of geographical indications in the previous chapter, unlike second-level domains (which may, although need not, have a direct connection to goods), top-level domains and their operators have no such connection. Rather, they provide a service by making

92. Conrad, 35–36.
93. AIPPI, 8.2.
94. WIPO (ed.), *Introduction to Intellectual Property*, 261–262 and 264.
95. *Id.*, 262.

available a communications portal. A .champagne gTLD, for example, could be a space in the DNS for domain name registrants to communicate commercial and non-commercial information about Champagne the region, Champagne the product originating from that region, or any number of other things.

While Article 10*bis* (3)(iii) may offer protection against the registration of geographic second-and lower level domain names to the extent that these are a) used in connection with goods and b) deemed misleading under domestic law as regards those goods, no such protection is afforded in the context of top-level domain strings. For the same reasons for which it was concluded in the previous chapter that there are no preventable uses of geographical indications at the top-level of the DNS, it can be concluded that Article 10*bis* (3)(iii) does not oblige Paris Union Member States to prevent geographic gTLD applications by non-State applicants. It is open to members to deem the registration of a geographic domain name at any level of the DNS by a party other than the relevant government or geographical indication holder inherently misleading, but this is not required by the Paris Convention. Nor is there any evident consistency amongst States adopting this broader approach.

8.3 PROTECTION OF REPUTATION

Although it seems logical to link a desire to prevent reputational harm with unfair commercial behaviour, the preceding analysis of Paris Convention Articles 10 and 10*bis* illustrates the very limited protection available to reputation through international unfair competition law. The concerns of governments and geographical indication holders about misappropriation of identity by others' use of geographic names are not limited to actions of competitors, nor does the term 'competitor' have much traction in this context. Even to the very limited extent that Articles 10 and 10*bis* protect these interests, they are clearly not sufficient bases for government claims to exclusive or priority rights in geographic names. Two further, related doctrines of rights protection will now be considered to determine their potential for filling the gaps left by unfair competition law: dilution and personality rights.

8.3.1 DILUTION

Dilution sits uneasily alongside unfair competition principles because its prevention of the use of a trademark in connection with even unrelated goods or services effectively makes competition in that sector impossible. Put simply: 'How could there be unfair competition when there was no competition?'[96] Dilution is therefore logically addressed in the Paris Convention not in Article 10*bis*, but rather separately in Article 6*bis*, which applies only to 'well-known' trademarks.

The function of the doctrine of dilution is to prevent the erosion by anyone – direct competitors or otherwise – of the reputation of famous trademarks.[97] The broader range of preventable acts fills in some of the gaps identified in the previous section of this chapter in terms of the applicability of unfair competition law to the use of geographic names in the DNS. It has already been suggested that dilution may be usefully applied at the second level of the DNS 'if a customer became confused about the owner of the domain name, purchased goods from a cybersquatter thinking they were made by the brand and lost confidence in the brand, thereby harming its reputation and value.'[98]

There is precedent for protecting geographic names under Article 6*bis* even where they are not registered as trademarks: Article 6*bis* has successfully been relied upon to support a claim to rights in the name of the government of the Spanish region of Catalunya, 'Generalitat de Catalunya'. In a UDRP dispute brought by the local government, the name in question was found to be protected on the basis of its well-known status and Spanish law's recognition of unregistered well-known marks.[99] The key in this and similar cases is domestic law's recognition of a geographic name as a trademark, which has the automatic effect of bringing the name within the scope of the UDRP. If domestic law does not consider the name a trademark, then the UDRP is inapplicable and the party asserting rights in the name can rely only on whatever other rights might be available under domestic law.

Setting aside the possibility of bringing a UDRP claim, the domestic applicability of dilution theory may extend beyond trademarks. This has significant potential for the protection of geographic names as a possible future development in international law. The protection of geographical indications in some European jurisdictions, for example, has been compared to the protection against dilution afforded to famous trademarks in the US,[100] which is where trademark dilution theory originated. Not coincidentally, then, have the European Commission's proposals for increased protection of geographical indications under the TRIPS Agreement been said to resemble a dilution or 'dilution plus' type of protection.[101]

96. Brown Jr, 1192.
97. Callmann & Altman, 22:15. On well-known marks and their potential reservation from domain name registrability, *see* Part II, Chapter 3, s. 3.2.1.3 above.
98. Elizabeth C. Woodard, *The UDRP, ADR, and Arbitration: Using Proven Solutions to Address Perceived Problems with the UDRP*, 19 Fordham Intell. Prop. Media & Ent. L. J. 1169, 1176 n. 31 (2009).
99. *Catalunya v. Wolf,* WIPO Case No. D2002-1124.
100. Hughes, Spirited Debate, 347–349.
101. *Id.*, 319.

In its 1996 Model Provisions on Protection against Unfair Competition, WIPO proposed amending Article 10*bis* (3) to include acts that damage goodwill or reputation.[102] Such an amendment would increase support for the protection of geographic names, in particular by eliminating the need for a competitive relationship between the parties, with the operative situation being 'any act or practice in the course of industrial or commercial activities'.[103] Interpreted broadly, as instructed by the accompanying Notes, this would include 'activities of professionals and non-profit making activities.'[104]

In summary, the proposed amendment to Article 10*bis* (3) has as-yet not been agreed upon and the 'model' provisions, which are directed at countries that are as an initial matter introducing unfair competition laws into national legislation in order to comply with their obligations under the TRIPS Agreement, are not binding. Nevertheless, these things are indicative of some desire at the international level to broaden the protection offered by dilution and to bring geographic names within the scope of unfair competition law.[105] Currently, the protection against dilution offered by Article 6*bis* of the Paris Convention is available only to geographic names recognized as well-known under domestic trademark law. Nor is Article 10*bis* (3), in its present wording, able to prevent damage to reputation except by competitors and in the very limited constellations identified in its subsections (i), (ii) and (iii).

8.3.2 Geographic Names and Personality Rights

There are strong conceptual links between unfair competition and the protection of personality or identity. Like individuals, governments are concerned about identity theft in the online environment. The recognition of personality rights in geographic names could address States' concerns by preventing unauthorized parties from holding themselves out as the government or its authorized representative on the internet. This sort of protection ordinarily has as its focus the reputation of persons; it must therefore be questioned whether international law recognizes personality rights of States such that these rights might be called upon by governments to prevent unauthorized applications for geographic gTLDs.

WIPO has considered this question in the context of protecting personal names from unauthorized registration as second-level domain names, and concluded that the domestic nature of personality protection and the diversity of domestic approaches are obstacles to the existence of an international

---

102. WIPO, *Model Provisions on Protection Against Unfair Competition*, WIPO Pub. No. 832 (1996).
103. *Id.*, 62 Art. 1(1).
104. Henning-Bodewig, 24.
105. Gervais, *The TRIPS Agreement,* 369.

norm of protection of personal names.[106] In jurisdictions where protection exists for personal names, this generally takes the form of personality law, which derives from individuality and personhood.[107] Such a theory could recognize that a State's identification with a symbolic name gives rise to a 'personality stake'[108] in that name; the use of that name by another could plausibly be interpreted as analogous to appropriation of an individual's interest in his or her personality.[109] Yet the characteristics of individuality and personhood underpinning protection are unique to human beings and lacking in other forms of legal person. On this basis, personality theory has been deemed to be of limited application to protecting corporations' trademarks.[110] The same logic refutes governments' claims to geographic names on the basis of personality.

Even where human personality rights are recognized in domestic law,[111] they cannot be characterized as rights in a name as such.[112] First, they are limited to protecting commercial value in a name,[113] and ordinarily this stands to benefit only famous persons. Even then, not all uses of the famous person's name can be prevented; in particular, non-commercial, informational uses are not preventable where the right to free speech is protected.[114] In the context of domain names, it is certainly not the case that any person can object to a registration of his or her name as a domain name on the basis of personality theory, and in any event the multiplicity of names will make it virtually impossible for every person with a common name to have his or her own domain name.

If a personality theory of statehood exists, to the extent that it is based upon existing personality doctrines respecting persons, the protection it offers is likewise limited. Though their relatively low numbers and global notoriety create commercial value in States' names, the benefit to States of a personality theory would be limited to preventing commercial uses of a country name. Most subnational geographic names will have more difficulty in demonstrating requisite fame than country names. Non-commercial use of geographic names in diplomatic, official, descriptive or informative contexts – realistically a large proportion of the possible uses of geographic names – cannot be prevented. A complete prohibition on the unauthorized registration

106. WIPO, *WIPO II Report*, para. 178.
107. Melville B. Nimmer, *The Right of Publicity*, 19 Law & Contemp. Probs. 203 (1954).
108. Hughes, *The Philosophy of Intellectual Property*, 340–341.
109. Leon Green, *The Right to Privacy*, 27 Ill. L. Rev. 237 (1932).
110. Anupam Chander, *The New, New Property*, 81 Texas L. Rev. 715, 748 (2003), citing Margaret Jane Radin, *Reinterpreting Property* 12–13 and 112 (University of Chicago Press 1993).
111. Madow, 132 n. 23 and n. 24.
112. WIPO, *WIPO II Report*, para. 172.
113. Madow, 130.
114. WIPO, *WIPO II Report*, para. 196 (contemplating the 'chilling effect on free speech' if personal names were to be protected under the UDRP).

of geographic domain names on this basis would require as a conceptual first step deeming the act of registration, irrespective of the nature of the proposed use of the domain, an inherently commercial activity.[115]

The internet has undeniably given rise to concerns about misappropriated identity and corresponding harm to reputation. There is nevertheless no international legal framework currently in place to prevent the harm that could potentially result from the registration of a geographic domain name by a party not authorized by a relevant government to do so. There are conceptual obstacles to applying human personality rights to non-human interests, and even if this were not the case, human personality rights are not recognized as an international norm. A theory of State personality is not yet extant, and its future development would likely require significant departure from existing notions underpinning personality protection available to persons.

8.4 CONCLUSIONS ON COMMERCIAL RIGHTS IN GEOGRAPHIC NAMES

This chapter has challenged justifications of restrictions on geographic names in the DNS on the basis of international unfair competition law. Governments' claims to rights in geographic names on this basis appear to be grounded more in a desire to exercise control than to promote honesty in commercial dealing, promote and protect commercial investment, promote competition or protect consumers. One is ultimately inclined to agree with the comments made in a 1945 decision of the US Second Circuit Court of Appeals that 'the doctrine of so-called "unfair competition" is really a doctrine of "unfair intrusion on a monopoly".'[116]

As a starting point, the notion of 'competitors' in the context of the top-level of the DNS is strained. It is prudent to question whether an applicant for a new geographic gTLD is a competitor, in the ordinary sense of that term, with existing TLD registries, other applicants for new gTLDs, or governments relevant to a geographic name. If not, unfair competition law as provided for in Article 10*bis* of the Paris Convention is inapplicable to geographic gTLDs. Yet even if this conceptual challenge is overcome, there remain other considerable obstacles to applying international unfair competition law at the top-level of the DNS.

Preventing the registration of geographic gTLDs cannot be justified on the basis of all registrations being a false indication of the source of goods or an indication or allegation liable to mislead the public about goods,

---

115. On the inherently commercial nature of internet transactions and the effect that such a determination would have on DNS law and policy, *see* Part III, Chapter 5, s. 5.2.2 above.
116. *Standard Brands v. Smidler*, 151 F.2d 34, 40 (C.C.A. 2d 1945) (concurring opinion of Frank, J.).

because top-level domains and the registries that operate them lack the requisite connection to goods. The then-Director General of WIPO pursued the inclusion of services in Article 10*bis* (3) in 1977,[117] but the attempt was unsuccessful. This provision remains applicable only to goods and therefore cannot be applied to the top-level of the DNS.

Whether a TLD string can on its own constitute an allegation discrediting a competitor is doubtful. Dilution theory, which is conceptually at odds with unfair competition law but relatedly targets commercial behaviour that causes harm, is recognized in international law, but at this stage applies only to well-known trademarks. It remains to be seen whether this form of protection will ultimately be universally adopted through the Geneva Act of the Lisbon Agreement[118] or otherwise extended to geographical indications through the TRIPS Agreement or some other instrument. Nor is there a norm in international law recognizing personality rights in respect of States.

There is scope for protecting the rights of geographical indication holders (which, unlike government interests, do have a clearly and directly commercial application) by preventing their registration as top-level domain strings, but this protection depends in large part on the distinctiveness of the indication. Until awareness is achieved more broadly, whether through an international register or otherwise, few names will benefit from this protection. Like geographic names generally, geographical indications are subject to a name-by-name, jurisdiction-by-jurisdiction analysis as to their distinctiveness and likelihood of creating confusion.

These considerations lead to the conclusion that neither Article 10 nor Article 10*bis* of the Paris Convention obliges Paris Union members to prohibit as acts of unfair competition the unauthorized registration of geographic names or geographical indications as top-level domain strings. The same conclusion is reached with respect to Article 6*bis* of the Paris Convention and GATT Article IX:6. It is important to emphasize, however, that Article 10*bis* (3) is not exhaustive; the broader definition of 'unfair competition' provided in Article 10*bis* (2) makes this clear. While the three specifically enumerated acts of unfair competition 'are important examples of unfair competition and may even cover the majority of acts committed in practice … there exist manifold other ways and means to commit unfair competition which do not fall into any of these three categories.'[119] WIPO's Model Laws are evidence of a view that the unfair competition provisions of the Paris Convention require clarification and strengthening.

117. McCarthy & Devitt, 204. Services were included in the first TRIPS negotiation draft, but later removed. Conrad, 34 n. 101.

118. Geneva Act of the Lisbon Agreement on Appellations of Origin and Geographical Indications (20 May 2015, not yet in force), WIPO Doc. LI/DC/19 (discussed in detail below in Part III, Chapter 7).

119. AIPPI, para. 1.

It is also important to emphasize that although the Paris Convention does not specifically oblige States to prevent the registration of geographic domain names as false indications of origin or as acts of unfair competition, it does not prevent members from enacting domestic law to that effect. Unfair competition law remains a domestic source of rights with the subject matter protected as well as the means of protection left open for States to decide. Greater protection for geographic names generally and geographical indications specifically, through unfair competition or anti-dilution law, may motivate the marketplace to provide better, more accurate information or perhaps even better quality products. In the context of the DNS, this may upset the delicate balance between laws protecting commercial signs, competition law and free speech. Although there was found in 1925 'no substantial precedent to indicate the degree of control of an industry through trade symbols which would be held a restraint of trade or an attempt to monopolize any part of trade or commerce', the process of evaluating new gTLD applications and delegating new gTLDs could just bring about the sort of 'scheme of industrial dominion'[120] that was then speculated of.

120. Brown Jr, 1202.

Chapter 9
Human Rights in Geographic Names

What are we? A nation? A region? In the Internet we are a community of interest.[1]

9.1 LINKING GEOGRAPHIC DOMAIN NAMES WITH HUMAN RIGHTS

9.1.1 Human Rights, Internet Access, and Identity

In the relatively short time since its being made accessible to the public, the internet has come to play an integral role in peoples' daily lives. This is so much the case that it can now be plausibly argued that obstacles impeding a person's ability to access and use the internet have the effect of impinging upon that person's ability to survive and thrive in the modern world. Much has been written about the potential benefits of technology to humankind and the continuation and development of cultures, languages and communities;[2] indeed, this has been a prime reason for expanding the top-level of the DNS since the privatization of the internet with the formation of ICANN, a non-profit corporate body specifically charged with 'reflecting' in its

1. Gerrand, *Cultural Diversity in Cyberspace*, quoting Amadeu Abril i Abril.
2. *See for example*, Celia Lury, *Cultural Rights: Technology, Legality, and Personality* (Routledge 1993); Kyra Landzelius ed., *Native on the Net* (Routledge 2006); *Intellectual Property and Traditional Cultural Expressions in a Digital Environment* (Christoph Beat Graber & Mira Burri-Nenova eds, Edward Elgar 2008).

decision-making processes 'the functional, geographic and cultural diversity of the Internet'.[3] As ICANN continues to expand the top-level of the DNS, an argument can be made that blocking or rejecting an application for a new gTLD can have the practical effect of denying the applicant (and, to the extent that the application is made on behalf of a community, that community) the capability of expressing itself online and having an online identity. Given the fundamental nature of the internet to contemporary humanity, it is therefore imperative that any restrictions placed by ICANN on the creation of new generic top-level domains are closely examined with the rights of the persons and communities affected by them in mind.

The implications of the technology underpinning the DNS, in particular the requirement of absolute name uniqueness, have been discussed in earlier chapters of this book in the context of internet governance issues, but there are also major societal implications embedded in the decision-making processes that result in a greater number of gTLDs. Conceptual links can be drawn between the societal implications of these decisions and the fundamental attributes of humanity that are acknowledged and protected through human rights law. The aim of this final chapter is to explore those implications and the potential of human rights as a basis for challenging States' assumptions of exclusive rights in geographic names and control over their use in the DNS.

The relevance of human rights to new gTLD policy were recognized by ICANN's Generic Names Supporting Organization ('GNSO') in its policy development process that ultimately recommended expansion: in its 2007 recommendations to the Board of Directors, the GNSO expressly identified the Universal Declaration of Human Rights ('UDHR') and the International Covenant on Civil and Political Rights ('ICCPR') as potential sources of existing legal rights, conflict with which it advised avoiding.[4] These instruments and others are considered in this chapter as possible sources of human rights in geographic names which may conflict with a policy that gives States exclusive or priority control over their use in the DNS.

Some human rights lack a precise definition, making it difficult to determine whether particular actions fall within their scope. This can be seen as an advantage or a disadvantage to those who seek to challenge States' rights in geographic names. It is on the one hand an advantage that human rights treaties and customs are in a state of development; if a claim can plausibly be based on any of the universal aspects of humanity protected by human rights law, it may be more favourably received than a claim to rights

3. ICANN, *Bylaws (As amended 1 October 2016)*, Art. 1 s. 1.2(b)(ii).
4. GNSO, *Final Report on the Introduction of New Generic Top-Level Domains*, Recommendation 3.

based on capitalistic attitudes to property ownership.[5] It is nonetheless a disadvantage that no specific human right to possess, control or use a geographic name has been codified or crystallized in international law. Standing in the way of such a precisely articulated right coming into existence is a reluctance to interpret the term 'human rights' too liberally for fear of diluting the effectiveness of human rights law in redressing major wrongs.[6] Yet even without such specificity, certain internationally recognized human rights of a broader nature, such as the rights to national identity, self-determination, freedom of expression, culture, language and property, as well as the doctrine of common heritage of mankind, may potentially be called upon in support of a right of persons or peoples to use geographic names.

Precisely because of the lack of specificity in articulating the bounds of human rights, the intention here is not to catalogue all of the rights that could potentially be interpreted as encompassing a right to use geographic names in the DNS. Rather, the intention is to focus on key rights for which there is a compelling connection to geographic names and explore the strengths and weaknesses of those connections. Before commencing this analysis, it is important first to identify the core concepts of the international human rights law framework into which this discussion fits. This chapter thus begins with a discussion of the subjects and sources international human rights law, explaining their particular relevance to geographic names and their use in the DNS. This foundation is then built upon by examining five specific human rights: the right to self-determination, the right to national identity, the right to freedom of expression, the right to culture and the right to language. The substance of each of these rights is discussed in order to evaluate their potential for encompassing a right of persons or peoples make use of a geographic name in the DNS.

Recalling earlier chapters' consideration of the links between geographic names and property rights, the third section of this chapter explores the potential for geographic names' recognition as the property or, conversely, non-property of mankind. It begins with a discussion of the recognition in international law of a right to property, then progresses to consideration of the intellectual property-based concept of the public domain. This chapter ends by turning to natural resources law to consider the applicability the concept of the common heritage of mankind. Conclusions on human rights relating to geographic names are then summarized.

---

5. Michael F. Brown, *Who Owns Native Culture?* 40 (Harvard University Press 2003).
6. Richard B. Bilder, *An Overview of International Human Rights Law*, in *Guide to International Human Rights Practice* 15 (Hurst Hannum ed., Transnational Publishers 2004).

9.1.2 Distinguishing Human Rights and Intellectual Property Rights

There 'is little doubt' as to the intention of human rights law as 'endow[ing] individuals directly with basic rights'[7] under international law. These rights 'apply always and everywhere',[8] but an individual's being acknowledged as having the capacity to possess rights 'does not necessarily imply the capacity to exercise those rights oneself'.[9] Rather, human rights law imposes obligations on (in some cases, all) States to respect and promote human rights on the individual's behalf. In addition to the obligation upon them not to infringe human rights, States are obliged to protect these rights against interference by private parties.[10] Increasingly, international law recognizes not just individual but collective or community rights, as it comes to be acknowledged that modern State theory and the fundamental precepts of international law derived from it inadequately capture 'the multiple, overlapping spheres of community, authority, and interdependency that actually exist in the human experience.'[11] Identity (whether online or offline) is not purely individualistic: rights affecting identity must take into account individual and collective interests, and these must be balanced not just between individuals as against other individuals and communities, but between the individual and his or her own community.[12]

This tension is also inherent in intellectual property law, with its traditional aim of protecting the creative efforts and outputs of identifiable individual creators. The almost-complete ignorance in the TRIPS Agreement of community-generated creative works has provoked debate about the need

7. Rene Provost, *International Human Rights and Humanitarian Law* 18 (Cambridge University Press 2002).
8. *Id.*, 19, quoting Report on Human Rights in Armed Conflict, U.N. Doc. A/8052 (1970) 13, para. 25.
9. *Peter Pázmány University v. Czechoslovakia*, P.C.I.J. Reports Ser. A/B No. 61, 231 (P.C.I.J. 1933).
10. If ICANN's New gTLD Program policy of recognizing exclusive rights of States to geographic names is deemed inconsistent with international law under any of the bases explored in this study, this gives rise to an interesting possibility that the US has an obligation under human rights law to compel ICANN, an American corporation, to revise its policy of requiring government consent or non-objection to applications for geographic new gTLDs. This issue lies beyond the scope of this study but is identified here for later consideration. On the obligation to protect, *see generally*, Manfred Nowak, *U.N. Covenant on Civil and Political Rights: CCPR Commentary* 448 (2d ed. revised, N.P. Engel 2005).
11. S. James Anaya, *Indigenous Peoples in International Law* 101 (2d ed., Oxford University Press 2004).
12. As an example of a situation requiring balancing of the rights of individuals vis-à-vis their community, Anaya points (at 136) to the Human Rights Committee's decision in the case of *Kitok v. Sweden*, Communication No. 197/1985, *Report of the Human Rights Committee*, U.N. GOAR, 43rd Sess., Supp. No. 40, at 207, U.N. Doc. A/43/40, Annex 7(G) (1988) (views adopted 27 Jul. 1988).

for sui generis protection regimes based on or beyond the existing intellectual property law framework.[13] In the meanwhile, human rights law offers an alternative means of protecting and preserving communities' culture, language and ways of life.[14]

Despite this apparent overlap, it must be borne in mind that the aims of intellectual property law and the rights it protects are not equivalent to the aims and protections afforded by human rights law. The UN's Committee on Economic, Social and Cultural Rights makes this clear in its General Comment No. 17,[15] which explains the rationale of Article 15(1)(c) of the International Covenant on Economic, Social and Cultural Rights ('ICESCR'). That provision sets out the 'right of everyone to benefit from the protection of the moral and material interests resulting from any scientific, literary or artistic production of which he or she is the author'. In distinguishing this right from the rights that accrue to authors and inventors under intellectual property laws, the Committee explained:[16]

> The right of everyone to benefit from the protection of the moral and material interests resulting from any scientific, literary or artistic production of which he or she is the author is a human right, which derives from the inherent dignity and worth of all persons. This fact distinguishes Article 15, paragraph 1 (c), and other human rights from most legal entitlements recognized in intellectual property systems. Human rights are fundamental, inalienable and universal entitlements belonging to individuals and, under certain circumstances, groups of individuals and communities. Human rights are fundamental as they are inherent to the human person as such, whereas intellectual property rights are first and foremost means by which States seek to provide incentives for inventiveness and creativity, encourage the dissemination of creative and innovative productions, as well as the development of cultural identities, and preserve the integrity of scientific, literary and artistic productions for the benefit of society as a whole.

---

13. *See for example*, Thomas Cottier & Marion Panizzon, *Legal Perspectives on Traditional Knowledge: The Case for Intellectual Property Protection*, 7 J. Int'l Econ. L. 371 (2004); Jeannette Mwangi, *TRIPS and Agricultural Biotechnology: Implications for the Right to Food in Africa*, in *Human Rights and Intellectual Property Rights: Tensions and Convergences* 241–288 (Mpazi Sinjela ed., Martinus Nijhoff 2007).
14. Dominic McGoldrick, *Culture, Cultures, and Cultural Rights*, in *Economic, Social and Cultural Rights in Action* 454 (Mashood A. Baderin & Robert McCorquodale eds, Oxford University Press 2007).
15. *The right of everyone to benefit from the protection of the moral and material interests resulting from any scientific, literary or artistic production of which he or she is the author (Article 15, paragraph 1(c), of the Covenant)* U.N. Doc. E/C.12/GC/17 (available at http://www.un.org/en/ga/search/view_doc.asp?symbol=E/C.12/GC/17).
16. *Id.*, para. 1.

Human rights are further distinguished from IPRs by their indefinite duration and the essentially personal, rather than financial, interests they protect.

These fundamental differences offer unique perspectives when human rights are considered in the interpretation of laws recognizing IPRs. These differences also give rise to a clear potential for conflict in the exercise of human rights with the exercise of IPRs; protection afforded to one party in respect of a particular aspect of culture or identity or product of intellectual effort (a geographic name, for example) under one system could be afforded to a different party under the other, or a right recognized under one may not be recognized at all under the other. Prominent scholars have found evidence of this in case law, yet this issue is not effectively addressed by either the TRIPS Agreement or human rights instruments.[17]

9.1.3 Sources of Human Rights Law

The sources of international human rights law are the same as those relied upon in other areas of international law, and are identified in Article 38(1) of the Statute of the ICJ. Of the three principal sources set out in Article 38(1) it bears noting that treaties possess a special relevance in the human rights context; there are now a significant number of treaties in force between States regarding matters of human rights, and leading scholars characterize treaties as being of 'paramount importance'[18] to international human rights law. Particularly significant among these is the UN Charter, to which nearly all States throughout the world are bound and by which they are united to the common general purpose of 'promoting and encouraging respect for human rights and for fundamental freedoms for all without distinction as to race, sex, language, or religion'.[19] In addition to this broadly worded obligation there are a number of 'core'[20] treaties of global effect that deal with specific aspects of human rights.[21] Beyond these, numerous bi- and multilateral

17. On the lack of a general cultural exception in WTO agreements, *see* Mary E. Footer & Christoph Beat Graber, *Trade Liberalization and Cultural Policy*, 3(1) J. Int'l Econ. L. 115 (2000); Deborah Z. Cass, *The Constitutionalization of the World Trade Organization: Legitimacy, Democracy, and Community in the International Trading System* (Oxford University Press 2005). On the balance between free speech and free trade, *see* *Human Rights and International Trade* (Thomas Cottier, Joost Pauwelyn & Elisabeth Bürgi Bonanomi eds, Oxford University Press 2006).
18. Bruno Simma & Philip Alston, *The Sources of Human Rights Law: Custom, Jus Cogens, and General Principles*, Aust'l Y.B. Int'l L. 82, 85 (1988-1989).
19. Charter of the UN, Art. 1(3) (26 Jun. 1945, entered into force 24 Oct. 1945) 59 Stat. 1031; TS 993; 3 Bevans 1153.
20. United Nations, *The Core International Human Rights Instruments and their monitoring bodies*, http://www.ohchr.org/EN/ProfessionalInterest/Pages/CoreInstruments.aspx.
21. These include the ICCPR (16 Dec. 1966, entered into force 23 Mar. 1976) 999 U.N.T.S. 171; ICESCR (16 Dec. 1966, entered into force 3 Jan. 1976) 993 U.N.T.S. 3; International Convention on the Elimination of All Forms of Racial Discrimination, (21 Dec. 1965, entered into force 4 Jan. 1969) 660 U.N.T.S. 195; Convention on the

treaties contribute to the significant and growing framework of international human rights conventions.

Given the fundamental nature of human rights to all mankind, customary human rights law is also important in that its universal applicability allows for the exercise of rights even in the absence of a State's membership in treaties recognizing human rights.[22] That said, proving the existence of a customary rule is not without difficulty, as has already been shown in previous chapters of this book in the contexts of other bases of rights, because it requires broad empirical analysis of State practice and *opinio juris*. In the human rights context, the imprecision of the definition and scope of particular rights creates additional challenges in proving the existence of customary rules. In spite of this, there is broad agreement that certain basic human rights have assumed the status of customary international law,[23] though exactly which rights have done so is debated. Commonly on such a list are freedoms from genocide, slavery, torture and racial discrimination.[24] There is also support for recognizing certain rights of indigenous peoples as having crystallized into customary norms.[25]

Exposition of customary human rights law is further complicated by a degree of overlap between custom and general principles of international law. This is exemplified by the treatment of the right of self-determination, which is relevant to the use of geographic names by peoples in their full and free participation in representative government. The right of self-determination, which is discussed in detail in the next section of this chapter, has been characterized as having its origins in general principle,[26] in

---

Elimination of All Forms of Discrimination against Women (18 Dec. 1979, entered into force 3 Sep. 1981) U.N. GAOR Supp. (No. 46) at 193, U.N. Doc. A/34/46; Convention against Torture and Other Cruel, Inhuman or Degrading Treatment or Punishment, (10 Dec. 1984, entered into force 26 Jun. 1987) 39 U.N. GAOR Supp. (No. 51) at 197, U.N. Doc. A/39/51 (1984); Convention on the Rights of the Child (20 Nov. 1989, entered into force 2 Sep.1990) 44 U.N. GAOR Supp. (No. 49) at 167, U.N. Doc. A/44/49 (1989); International Convention on the Protection of the Rights of All Migrant Workers and Members of their Families (18 Dec. 1990, entered into force 1 Jul. 2003) 47 U.N. GAOR Supp. (No. 49A) at 262, U.N. Doc. A/47/49 (1990); Convention on the Rights of Persons with Disabilities (13 Dec. 2006, entered into force 3 May 2008) U.N. Doc. A/61/611; International Convention for the Protection of All Persons from Enforced Disappearance (20 Dec. 2006, entered into force 23 Dec. 2010) U.N. Doc. A/61/488.

22. Provost, 55.
23. Bilder, 10, citing Hurst Hannum, *The Status of the Universal Declaration of Human Rights in National and International Law*, 25 Ga. J. Int'l & Comp. L. 287 (1995-1996).
24. *See for example*, Gillian D. Triggs, *International Law: Contemporary Principles and Practices* 951–952 (2d ed., LexisNexis Butterworths 2011); *Restatement (Third) of the Foreign Relations Law of the United States* §702.
25. Anaya, *Indigenous Peoples in International Law*, 64.
26. *See for example*, Hurst Hannum, *The Right of Self-Determination in the Twenty-First Century*, 55 Wash. & Lee L. Rev. 773, 775 (1998).

custom,[27] and arguably either principle or custom.[28] If a general practice becomes established State practice, the question becomes the origin of the norm. It is not necessary for the purposes of this study, however, to pinpoint the origin of a particular norm; the critical concern here is whether a norm exists, not how it originated.

Finally, in identifying the sources of international human rights law, mention must be made of the significance of so-called soft law because, as with the development of norms respecting the internet, much of the dialogue respecting human rights occurs outside the formal rubric of Article 38(1) of the Statute of the ICJ.[29] UN General Assembly resolutions, for example, are recommendations only and not legally binding on members. They are nevertheless of high significance because of their capacity to influence State practice. Likewise, the Universal Declaration of Human Rights is not a legally binding instrument; as stated in its Preamble, it is 'a common standard of achievement for all peoples and all nations.'[30] It too 'has force as a morally, though not legally, binding document, as a yardstick by which to measure the development of the rule of law, and its authority is enhanced by the universality of its acceptance by Members of the United Nations.'[31] These and other non-binding instruments establish standards that can result in changes to State behaviour and ultimately lead to the formal, voluntary, observable assertions of consensus by States needed to generate a rule of customary international law.[32] With this in mind, such standards are considered in this chapter as a fundamental aspect of the potential future recognition of (if not a formal source of existing) rights in geographic names under international human rights law.

9.2 PARTICULAR HUMAN RIGHTS RELEVANT TO GEOGRAPHIC NAMES

National identity, expression, culture and language are all interconnected, symbiotic elements of human existence: nations and national identity are frequently formed out of linguistic communities, and culture is the product of the ways in which and languages with which humans express themselves.

27. *See for example*, Triggs, 952.
28. *See for example*, Theodor Meron, *Human Rights and Humanitarian Norms as Customary Law* 97 (Clarendon Press 1989).
29. So-called soft law and its broader relevance to this study is discussed in Part II, Chapter 4, s. 4.2.3 above.
30. An alternative view is asserted in M.G. Kaladharan Nayar, *Human Rights: The United Nations and United States Foreign Policy*, 19(3) Harv. Int'l L.J. 813, 816-817 (1978) (arguing that the Universal Declaration in its entirety is customary international law).
31. Ruth Donner, *The Regulation of Nationality in International Law* 191 (2d ed., Transnational Publishers 1994).
32. Simma & Alston, 90.

It is difficult, therefore, to partition these rights into discrete analytical sections and evaluate their relevance to geographic names without a certain degree of overlap. Further, the precise parameters of the rights to national identity and self-determination, expression, culture and language are not settled. Notwithstanding these challenges, compelling arguments can be made linking geographic names with each.

The analysis in this chapter is structured to first identify the theoretical connections between a particular human right and geographic names. Where appropriate because of a deviation with an ordinary understanding of rights holders under international law, beneficiaries of the right in question are identified. The legal basis, substance and limitations of each right are then discussed in order to evaluate potential conflicts with the *gTLD Applicant Guidebook* requirement of government consent or non-objection to applications for geographic new gTLDs. Conclusions are made at the end of the analysis of each right, and then summarized together at the end of the chapter.

9.2.1 Right to National Identity and Right of Self-determination

9.2.1.1 Connections Between National Identity and Geographic Names

Human beings have long identified themselves by reference to nationality. It has been said that this is 'not inevitable … [but] is extremely important for how people define themselves.'[33] In the day-to-day human experience, national identity is not only a complex legal concept deriving from State sovereignty, but also a social concept deriving from the innate human processes of self- and group-identification. The oft-quoted English philosopher John Stuart Mill aptly described this social aspect, what he termed the 'feeling of nationality', as potentially 'generated by various causes':

> Sometimes it is the effect of identity of race and descent. Community of language, community of religion, greatly contribute to it. Geographical limits are one of its causes. But the strongest of all is identity of political precedents; the possession of national history and consequent community of recollections; collective pride and humiliation, pleasure and regret, connected with the same incidents in the past. None of these

33. James Summers, *Peoples and International Law: How Nationalism and Self-Determination Shape a Contemporary Law of Nations* 20 (Martinus Nijhoff 2007) (internal citations omitted).

> circumstances however are either indispensable, or necessarily sufficient by themselves.[34]

The tendency to relate as individuals and groups with nations (though acknowledging the difficulty inherent in defining the term 'nation'[35]) is, in this view, a fundamental aspect of the human experience. This helps to explain the multipurpose role of geographic names in human lives and specifically why a geographic name such as 'France' can serve not only the practical function of identifying a particular geographic location on a map but also the symbolic function of, to use Mill's term, the 'feeling of nationality' that is shared by the people of that location.

Effective articulation of one's 'feeling of nationality' is dependent upon having the freedom to make use of names and symbols representative of nationality. By corollary, governments' exertions of exclusive control over the use of national names and symbols impede the dynamic and ongoing processes of individual and group self-identification, ultimately impinging upon democratic freedom.[36] These tensions have crept into the online world, where they are likely amplified by three additional factors: the global reach of the internet as a communications medium, governments' limited ability to exert control due to their narrow role in internet governance, and the 'tremendous potential [of the internet] as a staging ground for identity-claims'.[37] The integral role that domain names play in online identification is unmistakably clear and has been so since the commercial launch of the DNS. Indeed, the primary reason for increasing the number of available gTLDs has been said to be to offer greater opportunity for under-represented communities to stake such identity-claims in the internet.[38]

Even a cursory review of ICANN's efforts at DNS policy-making reveals that most have had as their aim relieving what was identified early on as the 'considerable amount of tension [that] has unwittingly been created between, on the one hand, addresses on the Internet in a human-friendly form which carry the power of connotation and identification and, on the other hand, the recognized rights of identification in the real world ... .'[39] Particular attention has been paid to trademark rights; the efforts of that community to transpose its legal rights in the so-called real (in other words, 'offline') world to the policy norms of the 'online' world have been explored in detail in Chapter 3.

---

34. John Stuart Mill, *Considerations on Representative Government* 294 (Parker, Son & Bourn 1861).
35. James Mayall, *Nationalism and International Society* 2 (Cambridge University Press 1990).
36. Coombe, 143.
37. Kyra Landzelius, *Introduction: Native on the Net*, in *Native on the Net* 14 (Kyra Landzelius ed., Routledge 2006).
38. ICANN, *gTLD Applicant Guidebook,* Preamble.
39. WIPO, *WIPO I Report*, para. 22.

The trademark community's experience is illustrative of the trend of relying on offline identity to justify claims to online identity, but the ubiquity of the internet in contemporary human experience could just as easily give rise to the inverse situation, where online identity is used to justify claims to offline identity. Illustrative of this situation is the Occupied Territory of Palestine's experience in seeking the creation of its own ccTLD. Creation of a .ps domain was initially refused because of the absence of the two-letter country code 'PS' from the International Standardization Organization's ISO 3166-1 list, inclusion in which requires UN recognition.[40] Interim measures involving the creation of a Palestinian second-level domain within the .int gTLD, which would have resulted in domain names taking the form www.examplename.palestine.int, were justified on the basis of Palestine's status as a Permanent Observer to the UN.[41] Palestinians were otherwise forced to choose between global gTLDs like .com and Israel's .is ccTLD.[42]

This example shows that in the modern world, offline and online identity are inextricably intertwined, and that achieving recognition of identity in the online world may for some be a milestone in an ongoing struggle for recognition of identity in the offline world.[43] It further shows that despite the trend of globalization, the world order is still heavily reliant upon States and State theory for legitimization. Palestine's status remains an issue of debate, but as a first step a .ps ccTLD required, and as a second step became part of, Palestine's claims to sovereignty. This helps to explain the significance attributed to .ps in its Domain Registration Policy, which states: 'Domain names under the .ps domain and the contents they point to, are considered virtual extensions of the Palestinian sovereignty with applicability of Palestinian law to the said extensions'.[44] The significance of the .ps domain has not been lost on the Palestinian internet community. In an early 2001 article, Ghassan Qadah, then-administrator of .ps and senior technology advisor to the Palestinian National Authority, characterized the ccTLD as an 'important symbol for the Palestinian state,'[45] the creation of which

40. The process of ccTLD creation and delegation is discussed in Part I, Chapter 2, s. 2.4.2 above.
41. IANA, *Report on Request for Delegation of the.ps Top-Level Domain*, http://www.iana.org/reports/ps-report-22mar00.htm (22 Mar. 2000).
42. Oscar S. Cisneros, *Dot-PS: Domain Without a Country*, Wired.com (12 Jan. 2001) (available at http://archive.wired.com/politics/law/news/2001/01/41135?currentPage=all).
43. 'The Palestinians' main objective was to achieve recognition for themselves not merely as refugees deserving of help on humanitarian grounds, but as a people with political aspirations.' David Hirst, *The Gun and the Olive Branch: The Roots of Violence in the Middle East* 461–462 (Thunder's Mouth Press/Nation Books 2003).
44. Palestinian National Internet Naming Authority, *PNINA Registration Policies and Procedures for Registering Domains under the .ps ccTLD*, s. 2.2, http://www.pnina.ps/domains/registration-policy/.
45. Cisneros.

represented a breakthrough in legitimacy in the eyes of the global community.

The process of creating and delegating ccTLDs remains tied to the ISO-3166-1 standard, and those seeking their creation today will face the same challenges faced by the proponents of the .ps ccTLD more than a decade and a half ago. Prior to the launch of the New gTLD Program, comparable difficulties were faced by applicants for new gTLDs, whose chance of success was severely hampered by ICANN's discretion and the tight quantitative limits placed on the two 'proof of concept' gTLD expansion rounds. The New gTLD Program is so significant because it is without quantitative limits: any application for a new gTLD meeting the criteria set out in the *gTLD Applicant Guidebook* should result in the creation of the applied-for string. It is, at last, a real opportunity for previously unsuccessful as well as first-time applicants to stake identity claims in the DNS.

Geographic new gTLDs may be desired by those who identify in the offline world with existing, recognized nations or territories and wish to transpose their offline identity into the online environment, just as trademark owners have done with their offline trademark rights. The human rights to expression, culture and language which are discussed in the subsequent sections of this chapter are most relevant to that situation. Others, like the proponents of the .ps ccTLD, may hope to facilitate the realization of their offline political aims through recognition of their online identity in the form of a top-level domain. For those applicants, ICANN's New gTLD Program represented (and future expansion efforts represent) an opportunity to establish an online national (or regional, local, etc.) identity as a platform to acquiring offline national identity. The right of self-determination, also inherently linked to identity,[46] is likewise potentially relevant in that context. Before delving into the substance, scope and limitations of the rights of national identity and self-determination, however, a distinction should be made between their respective beneficiaries.

9.2.1.2 Beneficiaries of the Right to National Identity and Right of Self-Determination

An initial distinction can be made between the right to national identity and the right of self-determination: in the case of the former, international law recognizes the rights of individuals, while in the latter, international law recognizes the rights of peoples.[47] In other words, while the right to national

46. Karen Knop, *Interpretation and Identity*, in *Diversity and Self-Determination in International Law* (Cambridge University Press 2002).
47. Common Art. 1(1) of the ICCPR and the ICESCR provide: 'All peoples have the right of self-determination.' Further, the United Nations Charter provides in Art. 1(2) that one of the purposes of the United Nations is to '[t]o develop friendly relations among nations

identity follows the pattern of individual human rights, self-determination is collective in nature. This is not to suggest that individual rights may not also have the effect of protecting collective interests, but rather to emphasize that international law singles out certain groups for additional protection through the right of self-determination.[48]

The term 'peoples' is not clearly defined in the international conventions in which it is used, nor has a generally accepted definition emerged from the interpretation of those conventions.[49] This raises particular challenges, although it has been suggested that the very fact of its being undefined is what makes the term 'peoples' so significant: 'If it is claimed that a group is a people there is no agreed standard against which that claim can be measured. It is purely a matter of perception. ... [This] may be a problem for lawyers, but it lubricates the politics of nationalism.'[50] Distinctions have been made between the terms 'peoples' and 'populations', with the former being 'generally regarded as implying a greater and more positive recognition of group identity and corresponding attributes of community.'[51] For reasons that are discussed in detail in the next section of this chapter, having the status of a 'people' has been equated with claims to independent statehood. The term 'populations', on the other hand, has traditionally been used to signify a lower level of recognition in international law, and it is this term that States prefer when a claim to rights is seen as a threat to sovereignty. This is a distinction that relies on a narrow positivist view,[52] and it has proven to be an obstacle to communities that do not fit within, and in some cases do not even aspire to fit within, the State-centric model.

A clear illustration of this problem is found in the efforts of indigenous peoples to achieve recognition under international law. It is in this context that much of the discussion of the beneficiaries of human rights takes place. The world's population has been said to include roughly 300 million indigenous people,[53] yet despite their numbers and the fact that they inhabit almost every part of the world, it is difficult to assess with precision their status under international law because of this problem of terminology. Some States are reluctant to use the phrase 'indigenous peoples' in the international

---

based on respect for the principle of equal rights and self-determination of *peoples*, and to take other appropriate measures to strengthen universal peace' (emphasis added). By contrast, Art. 15(1) of the Universal Declaration of Human Rights recognizes the right of 'everyone ... to a nationality'.

48. Brownlie, 579–580.
49. Martti Koskenniemi, *National Self-Determination Today: Problems of Legal Theory and Practice*, 43(2) Int'l & Comp. L.Q. 241 (1994).
50. Summers, xlii (internal citations omitted).
51. Anaya, *Indigenous Peoples in International Law*, 60.
52. *Id.*, 101. *See also* Knop, 53–54.
53. Alessandro Fodella, *International Law and the Diversity of Indigenous Peoples*, 30 Vt. L. Rev. 565, 566 (2006).

law context because 'it is too close to the concept of "people"'[54] and thus the right of self-determination. In spite of this it has been argued that it is 'in any case proper to conclude that, as a matter of already existing international law, the principle or right of self-determination applies in one way or another to indigenous peoples.'[55] Why some States might continue to find this problematic turns on certain outdated conceptions of the substance of the contemporary right of self-determination.

9.2.1.3 Legal Basis, Status, and Substance of the Right of Self-Determination

The right of self-determination is expressed in the UN Charter, which provides in Article 1(2) that one of the purposes of the UN is to 'develop friendly relations among nations based on respect for the principle of equal rights and self-determination of peoples, and to take other appropriate measures to strengthen universal peace'. This is supported by obligations under Article 55 to promote economic and social cooperation. The right of self-determination is codified as common Article 1(1) in the International Covenant on Civil and Political Rights ('ICCPR') and the International Covenant on Economic, Social and Cultural Rights ('ICESCR'), by virtue of which peoples 'freely determine their political status and freely pursue their economic, social and cultural development.'

Because of its acknowledged[56] *jus cogens* [57] status, the right of self-determination 'informs and complements other general principles of international law, viz., of State sovereignty, the equality of states, and the equality of peoples within a State.'[58] Historically, the substance of the right of self-determination has been conjoined with its remedial aspects, the 'most controversial'[59] and prominent of which is secession. With the demise of

54. Summers, xliii. Anaya, *Indigenous Peoples in International Law*, 61–72.
55. Anaya, *Indigenous Peoples in International Law*, 112. *See also* Glenn T. Morris, *In Support of the Right of Self-Determination for Indigenous Peoples under International Law*, 29 German Y.B. Int'l L. 277 (1986).
56. Crawford, 101; Brownlie, 580-581; Triggs, 995.
57. Art. 53 of the Vienna Convention on the Law of Treaties identifies *jus cogens* as 'a norm accepted and recognized by the international community of States as a whole as a norm from which no derogation is permitted and which can be modified only by a subsequent norm of general international law having the same character.'
58. Brownlie, 582. Francisco Forrest Martin, *Delineating a Hierarchical Outline of International Law Sources and Norms*, 65(2) Saskatchewan L. Rev. 341, 343 (2002).
59. Sarah Joseph et al., *The International Covenant on Civil and Political Rights: Cases, Materials, and Commentary* 101 (Oxford University Press 2000). *See also* Anaya, *Indigenous Peoples in International Law*, 99 ('In its most prominent modern manifestation within the international system, self-determination has promoted the demise of colonial institutions of government and the emergence of a new political order for subject peoples.'). On the historical connection between self-determination and colonialization with specific examples, *see* Nathaniel Berman, *Sovereignty in Abeyance: Self-Determination and International Law*, 7 Wis. Int'l L.J. 51, 84–103 (1988).

colonialism and the inclusion of the right of self-determination in the ICCPR, however, it has been observed that a shift occurred from an externally focused right to an internally focused[60] right which:

> ceased to be a rule applicable only to specific territories (at first, the defeated European powers; later, the overseas trust territories and colonies) and became a right of everyone. It also, at least for now, stopped being a principle of exclusion (secession) and also became one of inclusion: the right to participate. The right now entitles peoples in all states to free, fair and open participation in the democratic process of governance freely chosen by each state.[61]

Accordingly, contemporary articulations of the right of self-determination recognize the right of peoples 'to be full and equal participants in the creation of the institutions of government under which they live and, further, to live within a governing institutional order in which they are perpetually in control of their own destinies.'[62] The right is thus called upon to help peoples 'assert their identities, to preserve their languages, cultures, and traditions and to achieve greater self-management and autonomy, free from undue interference from central governments.'[63] This broad understanding of self-determination acknowledges the human need to associate in and self-identify as members of groups,[64] and not be unduly restricted in doing so. The right to self-determination so understood can be seen to prevent States from exercising control over identity symbols (such as geographic names) without the input of the peoples who identify with those symbols.

The right of self-determination does not, however, shed light on the existence of an exclusive right of States in geographic names. Rather, what the right of self-determination does is prevent States from taking unilateral, unconsulted decisions respecting the name by which a 'people' identifies. Unilateral, unconsulted decisions regarding the control of geographic names in the DNS could in this way be deemed analogous to State practices in the offline world that have the effect of forcibly incorporating indigenous peoples into a majority society to the detriment of their group identity, which in turn affects their ability to exercise their economic, social and cultural rights.[65] Arguably, a decision by a central government to deny a 'people' the

60. Rupert Emerson, *Self-Determination*, 465–466; Joseph et al., 101–104; Triggs, 996.
61. Thomas M. Franck, *The Emerging Right to Democratic Governance*, 86 Am. J. Int'l L. 46, 58–59 (1992).
62. Anaya, *Indigenous Peoples in International Law*, 113 (internal citations omitted).
63. Australian Government Delegation, Speaking Notes on Self-Determination, 2 (24 Jul. 1991), quoted in Anaya, *Indigenous Peoples in International Law*, 111.
64. Thomas M. Franck, *Clan and Superclan: Loyalty, Identity and Community in Law and Practice*, 90 Am. J. Int'l L. 359, 376–382 (1996) (discussing 'identity as a personal act of self-determination').
65. As an example of such a case, *see* Inter-American Commission on Human Rights, *Report on the Situation of Human Rights of a Segment of the Nicaraguan Population of Miskito*

ability to identify online by a particular name could prevent the group's preservation and expression of its identity, which could logically be seen to impinge upon the group's ability to exercise its economic, social and cultural rights. A government's compelling a 'people' to self-identify under a particular online identity without consultation or consent is equally problematic. The will of the people and their own understanding of identity must lead.

Finally but importantly, the right of self-determination prevents particular actions taken by States. It does not prevent actions by non-State actors, amongst which notable in the context of this study is ICANN. A challenge could not be raised by a 'people' against ICANN asserting that its policies regarding geographic new gTLDs violate their right to self-determination. Similarly, such a group could not rely upon the right of self-determination to challenge a private actor (i.e., a corporation) applicant for a domain name. It would need to be considered whether such a challenge could be raised against the US in order to compel ICANN, a corporation registered in that jurisdiction, to change its policy.[66]

9.2.1.4 Legal Basis, Substance, and Limitations of the Right to National Identity

There is 'a growing consciousness [of the existence of a] personal right to compose one's identity',[67] and much has been written about national identity in particular national contexts.[68] International law recognizes a right to national identity,[69] but that right is of only limited application to geographic names.

Origin and Resolution on the Friendly Settlement Procedure Regarding the Human Rights Situation of a Segment of the Nicaraguan Population of Miskito Origin, O.A.S. Doc. OEA/Ser.L/V/II.62, doc. 10, rev. 3 (1983) OEA/Ser/L/V/II.62, doc. 26 (1984) (*Case No. 7964 (Nicaragua)*). On the links between participation and economic, social and cultural rights, *see* Richard Burchill, *Democracy and the Promotion and Protection of Socio-Economic Rights*, in *Economic, Social and Cultural Rights in Action* 375–379 (Mashood A. Baderin & Robert McCorquodale eds, Oxford University Press 2007).

66. *See* n. 10 above in this chapter.
67. Franck, *Clan and Superclan*, 359.
68. *See for example*, Ahmet Içduygu & Özlem Kaygusuz, *The Politics of Citizenship by Drawing Borders: Foreign Policy and the Construction of National Citizenship Identity in Turkey*, 40(6) Middle Eastern Studies 26 (2004); Aneta Mihaylova, *National versus Regional Identity: The 'Other' Romanians in Greater Romania*, 1(2006) Balkan Studies 9 (2006); Nan Seuffert, *Jurisprudence of National Identity: Kaliedoscopes of Imperialism and Globalisation from Aotearoa New Zealand* (Ashgate 2006); Lauren Gilbert, *National Identity and Immigration Policy in the U.S. and the European Union*, 14(1) Colum. J. Eur. L. 99 (2007-2008); Jo Eric Khushal Murkens, *'We Want our Identity Back': The Revival of National Sovereignty in the German Federal Constitutional Court's Decision on the Lisbon Treaty*, 2 Bundesverfassungsgericht 530 (2010).
69. *See generally*, Donner.

The most direct articulation of a right to national identity can be found in Article 8 of the Convention on the Rights of the Child, which requires that 'States Parties undertake to respect the right of the child to preserve his or her identity, including nationality, name and family relations as recognized by law without unlawful interference.' Commentary indicates that 'the purpose of this provision is to prevent a child from being afforded less protection by the society and the State because he is stateless', not to 'make it an obligation for States to give their nationality to every child born in their territory.'[70] In other words, the concern is that children have some nationality rather than that they have a particular nationality.

Article 24(3) of the ICCPR recognizes the 'special'[71] right of all children to 'acquire a nationality'. Article 15(1) of the Universal Declaration of Human Rights, by contrast, recognizes the right of 'everyone … to a nationality', while Articles 6 and 33 of the Declaration on the Rights of Indigenous Peoples similarly do so in respect of indigenous persons. These provisions support the conclusion that a person's possession of some national identity is protected, but this has no bearing on a person's right to possess a particular nationality.

The latter issue is one left to domestic law, as provided for in the 1930 Convention on Certain Questions in Relation to the Conflict of Nationality Laws[72] and confirmed in the seminal *Nottebohm* case, in which it was said that it 'is for every sovereign State … to settle by its own legislation the rules relating to the acquisition of its nationality, and to confer that nationality by naturalization granted by its own organs in accordance with that legislation.'[73] International law thus only imposes upon States an obligation to ensure that each person has an identity.

It is difficult to see how this right could be infringed by a policy of exclusive state control of geographic names, unless a decision to deny a person the right to identify him/herself online using a particular name puts that person's possession of having *any* nationality at all at risk. At the same time, neither does the right to national identity offer specific support to States' claims of exclusivity in geographic names. A person's right to use a particular name in order to identify him or herself is more logically characterized in terms of a right of self-expression, so it is to this particular human right that focus now turns.

---

70. UN Office of the UN High Commissioner for Human Rights, *International Human Rights Instruments,* UN Doc. HRI/GEN/1/Rev.9 (Vol. I), CCPR General Comment No. 17: Art. 24 (Rights of the child), para. 8 (27 May 2008) (available at http://www.ohchr.org/Documents/HRBodies/TB/HRI-GEN-1-REV-9-VOL-I_en.doc).
71. Nowak, 560.
72. Convention on Certain Questions in Relation to the Conflict of Nationality Laws, Art. 1. (12 Apr. 1930, entered into force 1 Jul. 1937) 179 L.N.T.S. 89.
73. *Nottebohm Case (second phase), Judgment of April 6th,* 19 jj, I.C.J. Reports 1955, pp. 4, 20–21. For an identification of rules commonly adopted by States to determine nationality, *see* Brownlie, 388–394.

9.2.2 Right to Freedom of Expression

9.2.2.1 Connections Between Free Expression and Geographic Names

The tendency with which human beings identify themselves according to their nationality has been highlighted in the previous section of this chapter in order to draw a connection between geographic names and the human rights of national identity and self-determination. The same tendency can be relied upon in connecting geographic names and the human right to freedom of expression. Geographic names are integral to human vocabulary. Beyond their obvious roles as identifiers of a particular geographical location and their necessity in articulations of national identity, geographic names also help individuals to describe and articulate opinions and ideas about the world, its people, politics, culture, environment and products. Their broad range of uses, non-commercial and commercial, is evidenced by the multiplicity of potential sources of rights in them as identified and discussed in this and earlier chapters.

While being mindful of the sorts of restrictions against false or misleading use that have been examined in the previous chapter, it is difficult to discuss the world without being able to use the names that identify the subject of discussion. It has been remarked that '[a] news reporter cannot very well be expected to refer to "the football club based in Manchester, England" every time he or she wishes to report on the exploits of Manchester United.'[74] Taking this example one step further and focusing on geographic names rather than on trademarks, neither can a reporter (or indeed a school pupil, a journalist, a researcher or a person at the dinner table) be rationally expected to refer to 'the football club based in the second most populous urban district in the country that occupies two-thirds of the island nation located between roughly 54.5 and 52.2 degrees latitude and through which the prime meridian runs'.

Requiring that we communicate in this way when referring to geographic names would almost surely chill communication, and this is not an end to which a society that favours intellectual and social development aspires.[75] This helps to explain why the right to free expression is considered one of the most fundamental of all human rights, and it opens the door to a correlative human right to express one's self using geographic names. Placing the articulation of geographic names in the DNS exclusively in the control of States arguably impinges upon this right, bearing in mind the

74. Frederick M. Abbott et al., *International Intellectual Property in an Integrated World Economy* 271 (Aspen 2007).

75. Joseph et al., 386.

potentially commercial as well as non-commercial nature of expression involving geographic names.[76]

9.2.2.2 Legal Basis, Substance, and Limitations of the Right to Freedom of Expression

The right to free expression is 'not infrequently termed the core of the [International] Covenant [on Civil and Political Rights] and the touchstone for all other rights guaranteed therein.'[77] Article 19 of the ICCPR sets out the scope of the right as well as its limitations:

> 1. Everyone shall have the right to hold opinions without interference.
> 2. Everyone shall have the right to freedom of expression; this right shall include freedom to seek, receive and impart information and ideas of all kinds, regardless of frontiers, either orally, in writing or in print, in the form of art, or through any other media of his choice.
> 3. The exercise of the rights provided for in paragraph 2 of this article carries with it special duties and responsibilities. It may therefore be subject to certain restrictions, but these shall only be such as are provided by law and are necessary:
>   (a) For respect of the rights or reputations of others;
>   (b) For the protection of national security or of public order (ordre public), or of public health or morals.

Paragraph 1 acknowledges the 'right to hold opinions'. This right is interpreted as absolute in its passive form (possession), but pursuant to paragraphs 2 and 3, not absolute in its active form (expression).[78] This means that a person may hold whatever opinions he/she wishes in his/her mind, but the communication of those opinions to others may be restricted in certain situations.[79] The use of the term 'opinions' here is perhaps misleadingly limiting; it has been noted that the use of the phrase 'information and ideas of all kinds' in paragraph 2 was intended to signal that 'every communicable type of subjective idea and opinion, of value-neutral news and information, of commercial advertising, art works, political commentary regardless of how critical, pornography, etc., is protected',[80] including information and ideas expressed in commercial contexts or of a commercial nature.[81]

---

76. *See* above at Part III, Chapter 8, n. 35 and accompanying discussion on the need to balance consumer protection with freedom of expression.
77. Nowak, 438 (internal citations omitted).
78. Joseph et al., 387.
79. *See for example*, *Faurisson v. France*, 4 I.H.R.R. 444 (Hum. Rts. Comm. 1996).
80. Nowak, 444.
81. *See for example*, *Ballantyne, Davidson, McIntyre v. Canada*, U.N. Doc. CCPR/C/47/D/359/1989 and 385/1989/Rev.1 (1993).

The broadly worded range of protected types and means of expression make it clear that the right to free expression applies to all types of expression, including expression made on the internet and irrespective of whether online activity is considered inherently commercial. This is a particularly significant point to the question of whether international law recognizes rights in geographic names, because many of the other bases of rights explored in the previous chapters of this book (trademarks, geographical indications, prevention of unfair competition, dilution, personality rights) rely on commercial activity. The right to free expression notably also applies irrespective of whether the act in question is considered political – even politically critical – expression.[82] It could thus potentially be called upon to defend the registration of a geographic domain name with a connotation that is considered undesirable by a relevant government.[83]

The right to freedom of expression may only be restricted in furtherance of the aims specified in ICCPR Article 19(3), about which it is recorded that 'more than 30 concrete proposals for restrictions'[84] were made in the drafting process. Of these, 'most related to expression that instigates or incites to criminal actions or violent overthrow of the government, reveals State or trade secrets, undermines friendly relations with other States, impairs the independence of the judiciary, infringes rights of personality (honour, good reputation) or is pornographic or blasphemous.'[85] The final text takes a different approach, identifying not specific instances in which expression can be restricted, but rather permissible purposes justifying restriction. Of these, the purposes of protecting national security and public order ('ordre public') and ensuring respect for the rights of others have greater relevance to geographic names than the purposes of protecting public health or morals.

Protection of national security focuses on activities that pose 'serious cases of political or military threat to the entire nation'.[86] Commonly falling within this ambit are disclosures of State secrets.[87] This is clearly not relevant to the use of geographic names, save in the rare constellation in which revelation of a particular name in State secrets has the effect of identifying the State in question. The primary issue in such a case is, in any event, the revelation of the secret rather than the use of the State's name. Such a

82. The individual's right to engage in politically critical expression has been deemed paramount even where States have based this on national security and public order. *See for example*, *Mukong v. Cameroon*, 2 I.H.R.R. 131 (Hum. Rts. Comm. 1995).
83. An example is the www.tamilnet.com website, discussed in Mark Whitaker, *Internet Counter Counter-Insurgency: TamilNet.com and Ethnic Conflict in Sri Lanka*, in *Native on the Net* 255–271 (Kyra Landzelius ed., Routledge 2006).
84. Nowak, *U.N. Covenant on Civil and Political Rights: CCPR Commentary*, 457.
85. *Ibid.*
86. *Id.*, 463–464.
87. Joseph et al., 400.

constellation would also implicate the right to freedom of information recognized in Article 2(1) of the UNESCO Convention on the Protection and Promotion of the Diversity of Cultural Expressions, which is qualified by Article 19(3) allowing for restrictions on the basis of '[r]espect of the rights or reputations of others' and 'protection of national security or of public order (ordre public), or of public health or morals'. Yet in practice, national security has been treated more broadly, merging with 'public order', which is directed at activities that affect the 'peaceful and effective functioning of society'.[88] Accordingly, restrictions are commonly aimed at the sorts of expressions 'which may incite crime, violence or mass panic',[89] but would also apply to expressions advocating the overthrow or de-stabilization of a government.

While geographic names could be (and indeed have been, as the Catalonian linguistic community's experience with the .cat gTLD application demonstrates[90]) interpreted as an expression of destabilizing sentiments, this is countered by the fact that geographic names are not inherently politically threatening. They are not inherently fighting words, nor are they inherently directed at inciting the sorts of grave situations to which national security and public order are directed. They could plausibly be seen to indirectly play a role in inciting 'crime, violence, or mass panic', but such a determination is entirely dependent on the context in which they are used, bearing in mind the need to 'specify the precise nature of the threat allegedly posed by the author's exercise of freedom of expression.'[91]

A stronger case can be made that a second- or lower level domain name has the potential to incite 'crime, violence or mass panic' than a gTLD string because of the connection between lower level domain names and content. The function of a top-level domain, by contrast, is not to identify content but to provide a service, a channel of communication. An indirect link to content could be made by targeting a top-level domain at particular domain name registrants (e.g., a policy of restricting domain name registration to members of an anti-government group), but this is clearly an exception and not the rule. Restricting all uses of geographic names on this basis would surely prove excessive and unnecessary. Rather, the determination that a name disrupts national security or public order can be made on a case-by-case basis only.

This conclusion has special significance to applications for new gTLDs because of the provision within the *gTLD Applicant Guidebook* of a 'limited public interest objection' (what in earlier drafts was termed the 'morality and

88. *Id.*, 396.
89. *Id.*, 396 and 401, citing *Kim v. Republic of Korea* (574/94) and *Park v. Republic of Korea* (628/95).
90. The .cat gTLD application is discussed in Part I, Chapter 1, s. 1.2.2.4 above.
91. *Keun-Tae Kim v. Republic of Korea*, para. 12.5, U.N. Doc. CCPR/C/64/D/574/1994 (U.N. Hum. Rts. Comm. 1999).

public order exception').[92] Each objection made on this ground must likewise be considered on a case-by-case basis. In relying on this objection, governments must take care to specify the precise nature of the threat to national security or public order. A statement of discomfort with an applied-for name, as is made possible by the *gTLD Applicant Guidebook* in its provision for 'early warning' by the Governmental Advisory Committee,[93] will not suffice to satisfy States' obligations under Article 19(3)(b) of the ICCPR.

Lastly, restrictions on expression are permitted for the purpose of ensuring 'respect of the rights or reputations of others'. This study could hopefully be of use in this regard. The existence of multiple sources of potentially conflicting or overlapping rights in geographic names revealed in this study requires that States consider and prioritize in the application of Article 19(3)(a) of the ICCPR these multiple interests proportionately in domestic law. It is not at all clear how this can be achieved in the context of the DNS, however, given that the delegation of a new gTLD to one applicant has the practical effect of denying all others across the globe the use of that name as a top-level domain string. This problem is exacerbated by a policy of rejecting strings on the basis of confusing similarity.[94]

Recent experience suggests that the winner in a contest between self-expression rights and property rights is increasingly likely to be a property rights holder.[95] This raises interesting implications that go beyond mere domain name disputes into the realm of freedom and liberty, and the formation of DNS policy offers an opportunity to explore these. The challenge that arises not only in the exercise of the right to freedom of expression but all of the human rights considered in this chapter is that to the extent that persons or 'peoples' have a right to use a geographic name, and to the extent that they wish to exercise that right in the DNS (a point which is not axiomatic, as the examples of applications from 2012 provided in Chapter 1 section 1.3 aptly demonstrate), that right can only practically be exercised in the context of top-level domains by one registry operator (or, in respect of a community based application, by one operator on behalf of a community). These issues lie beyond the scope of this study, but are raised here for future discussion, and perhaps more usefully, private negotiations between competing applicants.

---

92. ICANN, *gTLD Applicant Guidebook,* s. 3.2.1. On the potential applicability of the so-called limited public interest objection to geographic new gTLD applications, *see* Part I, Chapter 1, s. 1.2.2.4 above.

93. ICANN, *gTLD Applicant Guidebook,* s. 1.1.2.4. ICANN, *New gTLD Program Explanatory Memorandum: Early Warning.*

94. ICANN, *gTLD Applicant Guidebook,* s. 2.2.1.1.2.

95. Wendy Gordon, *A Property Right in Self-Expression: Equality and Individualism in the Natural Law of Intellectual Property*, 102 Yale L.J. 1533, 1537 (1993) (positing that '[t]he incantation "property" seems sufficient to render free speech issues invisible').

A more general question is whether the right to freedom of expression encompasses a right to express oneself using a geographic name. This is a right the exercise of which depends entirely on context. It would be difficult to specify beyond the general limitations articulated in Article 19(3) of the ICCPR situations in which a person's expression of a geographic name must categorically be prohibited. ICANN should for that reason avoid imposing such a blanket prohibition in new gTLD policy. It is further the case that Article 19 of the ICCPR does not require the prohibition of expression in any form or for any purpose; rather, it gives States the possibility of imposing restrictions where these can be duly justified. This neither specifically proves nor denies the existence of an exclusive right of States to geographic names, though it does at least suggest that multiple interests may exist in names, which in turn suggests non-exclusivity. It also indicates that where restrictions imposed by States have the effect of impinging upon free expression, those restrictions must be for one of the purposes identified in Articles 19(3)(a) or (b). The likelihood of those circumstances being present in the context of an application to ICANN for a new gTLD is remote. In summary, arguments justifying restrictions on geographic gTLDs for the purposes of national security or public order must be individually scrutinized rather than assumed, and one-size-fits-all policy giving governments exclusive rights is not justified.

9.2.3 Right to Culture

9.2.3.1 Connections Between Culture and Geographic Names

Although certainly not confined by geographical boundaries, culture is inherently linked to geography. Many aspects of culture are drawn from the land, with climate, topography, presence of natural resources, proximity to neighbours and sea access, among other things, having an impact on how people interpret their surroundings.[96] These interpretations and the ways in which people express them through such things as music, arts, literature, lifestyle, religious beliefs and traditions meld together to form culture, which the United Nations Educational, Scientific and Cultural Organization ('UNESCO') defines as the 'set of distinctive spiritual, material, intellectual, and emotional features of a society or a social group'.[97] The people that share these features often, though not always, also share geographical location. Sometimes the link between geography and culture is not recent, relying

96. Johanna Gibson, *The Lay of the Land: the Geography of Traditional Cultural Expression*, in *Intellectual Property and Traditional Cultural Expressions in a Digital Environment* 182–204 (Christoph Beat Graber & Mira Burri-Nenova eds, Edward Elgar 2008); Triggs, 319–323.

97. Universal Declaration on Cultural Diversity, Preamble, adopted by the UNESCO General Conference on 2 Nov. 2001, 31C/Resolution 25.

instead on historic places. An example of this is Indonesia's attempt to develop a national culture following independence through initiatives that included the creation of a new national motto expressed in an ancient language no longer in use but 'connected to the past of ancient feudal kingdoms on Java and Bali, with few remaining links to the rest of Indonesia'.[98] One can also point to geographic name changes motivated by decolonization and inspired by names of places of historical significance, including Bombay/Mumbai[99] and Burma/Myanmar.[100]

Geographic names can be considered representative or symbolic of a nation and its culture, though the appropriateness of the term 'national culture' is debatable. Few, if any, modern States are mono-cultural.[101] To the extent that there is a recognized 'national culture', this is likely to be the culture of a dominant majority, the promotion of which at one extreme risks eliminating minority cultures. At the other extreme lies the appropriation of minorities' cultural symbols into national culture without the support or permission of the affected minorities.[102] The focus in discussions of protecting and promoting cultural rights is therefore less on nations and more on minority and particularly indigenous groups within nations, based on the assumption 'that majorities can take care of, and protect, their own dominant culture.'[103]

Indigenous peoples' culture is particularly linked to geography because the characterization of a people as 'indigenous' generally points to the inhabitation of a particular geographic territory.[104] Western thinking on indigenousness tends to go one step further by identifying the group as the first inhabitants of a territory, meaning that they lived in the geographic location prior to the arrival of colonizing outsiders.[105] The cultural rights of indigenous peoples so-defined are therefore called upon to 'preserve, develop and transmit to future generations their ancestral territories, and their ethnic

98. Christoph Antons, *Traditional Cultural Expressions and Their Significance for Development in a Digital Environment: Examples from Australia and Southeast Asia*, in *Intellectual Property and Traditional Cultural Expressions in a Digital Environment* 289 (Christoph Beat Graber & Mira Burri-Nenova eds, Edward Elgar 2008).
99. *See generally,* Thomas Blom Hansen, *Wages of Violence: Naming and Identity in Postcolonial Bombay* (Princeton University Press 2001).
100. *See generally*, Gustaaf Houtman, *Mental Culture in Burmese Crisis Politics: Aung San Suu Kyi and the National League for Democracy* 43–47 (Institute for the Study of Languages & Cultures of Asia & Africa 1999).
101. McGoldrick, 450.
102. *See for example*, *Harold Joseph Thomas v. David George Brown & James Morrison Vallely Tennant*, 215 F.C.A. (Fed. Ct. Aust'l 1997).
103. McGoldrick, 452.
104. Anaya, *Indigenous Peoples in International Law*, 3; Landzelius, *Introduction: Native on the Net*, 34 n. 5 (offering the following definition of 'indigenous' as 'conventional': 'disadvantaged descendants of those peoples that inhabited a territory prior to formation of a state').
105. Jeremy Waldron, *Indigeneity? First Peoples and Last Occupancy*, 1 N.Z. J. Pub. & Int'l L. 55 (2002).

identity, as the basis of their continued existence as peoples, in accordance with their own cultural patterns, social institutions and legal systems'.[106] In other parts of the world, indigenousness is not seen as dependent on colonization or minority status; in some countries 'the majority or even the whole population'[107] is characterized as indigenous. In practice, the lack of an agreed definition of 'indigenous people' makes it difficult to apply these understandings to real-life disputes. Further, as recognized at the beginning of this chapter, some States are reluctant to formally recognize the link between 'indigenous peoples' and territory out of concerns that this could lead to claims of independent statehood.[108]

Even without an agreed legal definition of 'indigenous peoples', it is clear that indigenousness involves a connection to geographic territory. For many indigenous groups, the relationship with land and their environment has great significance to their culture.[109] For these groups in particular, the names used to identify the land may have a cultural meaning beyond mere identification; members may wish to call upon the human right to culture to protect this from misuse or misappropriation by others who do not comprehend its significance.[110] Further, to deprive such a group of the free use of its name may impinge upon its ability to interact materially and intellectually, to preserve and create its culture.

9.2.3.2 Legal Basis and Substance of the Right to Culture

The human right to culture is widely recognized in human rights law instruments, both binding and non-binding: it is provided for in varying terms in the Universal Declaration of Human Rights (Articles 22 and 27), the ICESCR (Article 15(1)(a)), the ICCPR (Article 27), the Convention on the Rights of the Child (Article 30) and the Declaration on the Rights of Indigenous Peoples (Articles 8, 11 and 31), and it is the focus of UNESCO's Convention on the Protection and Promotion of Cultural Diversity of Cultural Expressions[111] and the Convention for the Safeguarding of Intangible Cultural Heritage.[112] Each of these instruments refers in some way to a right to participate in or practice a culture, but none expressly acknowledges a right to possess a culture. Article 15(1)(a) of the ICESCR is

---

106. Landzelius, *Introduction: Native on the Net*, 34 n. 5, quoting International Work Group for Indigenous Affairs (www.iwgia.org).
107. Antons, 291.
108. Anaya, *Indigenous Peoples in International Law*, 65. *See also* discussion earlier in this chapter, at Part III, Chapter 9, s. 9.2.1.3, on the right of self-determination.
109. Fodella, 565–566.
110. Antons, 296.
111. Convention on the Protection and Promotion of the Diversity of Cultural Expressions (18 Dec. 1990, entered into force 18 Mar. 2007) 33C/Res. 42.
112. Convention for the Safeguarding of the Intangible Cultural Heritage (17 Oct. 2003, entered into force 20 Apr. 2006) 32C/Res. 32.

illustrative of this point: it specifically recognizes 'the right of everyone (a) To take part in cultural life', and 'the participatory element has been interpreted as including a right to express one's own cultural life.'[113] Yet it must logically be said that a 'right to participate in a culture can only exist if there is a culture'.[114] This argument is supported by the specific obligation imposed upon States by Article 15(2) to 'conserve, develop and diffuse culture.'

Beyond this right of all persons to 'take part' in culture, members of minorities are specifically afforded rights to 'enjoy' their cultures. Article 27 of the ICCPR relevantly provides:

> In those States in which ethnic, religious or linguistic minorities exist, persons belonging to such minorities shall not be denied the right, in community with the other members of their group, to enjoy their own culture, to profess and practice their religion, or to use their own language.

The cultural rights of children of minority groups are recognized in similar terms in Article 30 of the Convention on the Rights of the Child.[115] Articles 8, 11 and 31 of the Declaration on the Rights of Indigenous Peoples[116] relatedly call for the recognition of cultural rights of indigenous peoples.

Certain difficulties arise in the application of cultural rights to support States' claims of exclusive rights in geographic names and their use in the

113. McGoldrick, 453.
114. *Id.*, 454.
115. Convention on the Rights of the Child, Art. 30 (20 Nov. 1989, entered into force 2 Sep. 1990), 44 U.N. GAOR Supp. (No. 49) at 167, U.N. Doc. A/44/49 (1989): 'In those States in which ethnic, religious or linguistic minorities or persons of indigenous origin exist, a child belonging to such a minority or who is indigenous shall not be denied the right, in community with other members of his or her group, to enjoy his or her own culture, to profess and practise his or her own religion, or to use his or her own language.'
116. UN Declaration on the Rights of Indigenous Peoples, adopted by the General Assembly 2 Oct. 2007, G.A. Res. A/RES/61/295:
    - Art. 8(1): Indigenous peoples and individuals have the right not to be subjected to forced assimilation or destruction of their culture.
    - Art. 11(1): Indigenous peoples have the right to practise and revitalize their cultural traditions and customs. This includes the right to maintain, protect and develop the past, present and future manifestations of their cultures, such as archaeological and historical sites, artefacts, designs, ceremonies, technologies and visual and performing arts and literature.
    - Art. 31(1): Indigenous peoples have the right to maintain, control, protect and develop their cultural heritage, traditional knowledge and traditional cultural expressions, as well as the manifestations of their sciences, technologies and cultures, including human and genetic resources, seeds, medicines, knowledge of the properties of fauna and flora, oral traditions, literatures, designs, sports and traditional games and visual and performing arts. They also have the right to maintain, control, protect and develop their intellectual property over such cultural heritage, traditional knowledge, and traditional cultural expressions.

DNS. First, the substance of the right to culture is very much in debate because of the fact that culture 'is not a static concept: cultures change all the time'.[117] Nor is culture a universal concept such that it could be definitively said that a right to control or use geographic names is an essential aspect of all cultures. Jurisprudence in this area reveals that a determination that the right to culture encompasses a right to control or use a geographic name depends upon the importance of the name in question to the existence of the particular culture in question.

A further issue arises in that even if it is determined that the use of a geographic name is integral to a particular culture, it is not axiomatic that a policy of exclusive State control over geographic names either supports or impinges upon the right of persons, children or minorities to take part in or enjoy their culture. That Article 15 of the ICESCR specifically provides for the 'right *freely* to participate' (emphasis added) is significant, however, in that restrictions on the right to use a geographic name are patently inhibitive of *free* participation. In the context of the DNS and given the integral role played by the internet in creating, preserving and communicating culture,[118] a policy of requiring government authorization of applications for geographic new gTLDs would arguably require involvement of the State to a degree that impinges upon *free* participation in online cultural life. While there are no cases on these specific facts, an analogy can be drawn from other 'offline' constellations. In the case of *Ominayak v. Canada*,[119] for example, it was argued that the survival of the Lubicon Lake Band people depended upon their connection to the land, which was integrally connected to their culture. Because of this integral connection between land and culture, Article 27 of the ICCPR was deemed infringed by the Canadian government having allowed the provincial government of Alberta to grant leases for oil and gas exploration on lands belonging to the Lubicon Lake Band. A similar argument could be made in a situation where a State denies members of a cultural group the ability to identify themselves in the online environment using a geographic domain name or string.

In summary, there is no general right to culture that universally and in all cases supports a corresponding right of members of cultural groups to control or make use of a geographic name. Such a right does exist, but is limited to members of a cultural group in which the particular geographic

---

117. Lyndel V. Prott, *Cultural Rights as Peoples' Rights in International Law*, in *The Rights of Peoples* 95 (James Crawford ed., Oxford University Press 1992).
118. Kathryn Bowrey, *Law & Internet Cultures* (Cambridge University Press 2005); Mira Burri-Nenova, *The Long Tail of the Rainbow Serpent: New Technologies and the Protection and Promotion of Traditional Cultural Expressions*, in *Intellectual Property and Traditional Cultural Expressions in a Digital Environment* 205–236 (Christoph Beat Graber & Mira Burri-Nenova eds, Edward Elgar 2008).
119. *Ominayak, Chief of the Lubicon Lake Band v. Canada*, Communication No. 267/1984, Report of the Human Rights Committee U.N. GOAR, 45th Sess., Supp. No. 40, Vol. 2, at 1, U.N. Doc. A/45/40, Annex 9(A) (1990).

name is integral. Nevertheless, the existence of this right serves to refute the exclusivity of rights claimed by States in geographic names. It also places restrictions on State decision-making respecting the use of geographic names by non-State others.

9.2.3.3 Promoting Cultural Diversity

Beyond the individual's right to participate in culture, there is also increasing emphasis in international legal discourse on humanity's interest in cultural diversity.[120] These interests have not yet developed into norms that recognize rights to culture, however. UNESCO's Convention on the Protection and Promotion of Cultural Diversity of Cultural Expressions (the 'UNESCO Convention') is the most prominent example: it does not create rights respecting culture or cultural diversity. The obligations set out in that convention are not absolute, being articulated in the following terms: in Article 6, 'each Party *may* adopt measures aimed at protecting and promoting the diversity of cultural expressions within its territory' (emphasis added) and in Article 7, '*shall endeavour to* create in their territory an environment which encourages individuals and social groups' (emphasis added). This has no bearing on the existence or exclusivity of State rights in geographic names, but the UNESCO Convention is nevertheless indirectly relevant to DNS policy on geographic names.

Geographic names per se are not inherently an element of cultural diversity,[121] but their use in the context of the DNS has tremendous potential in terms of facilitating cultural diversity by providing a channel for the creation and dissemination of cultural expression. States party to the UNESCO Convention are not specifically obliged to enact measures respecting domain names in order to promote or preserve cultural diversity. The UNESCO Convention does recognize that in making decisions to promote or protect cultural diversity, States may have to prioritize conflicting interests. This is critical in the context of competing claims arising from the exercise of cultural rights, the possibility of which is not sufficiently acknowledged or addressed by other multilateral treaties respecting the right to culture, including the ICCPR and the ICESCR.

---

120. *See for example*, Cottier, *The Agreement on Trade-Related Aspects of Intellectual Property Rights*, 170; Fodella, *International Law and the Diversity of Indigenous Peoples*; *Accommodating Cultural Diversity* (Stephen Tierney ed., Ashgate 2007); *Cultural Diversity, Heritage and Human Rights: Intersections in Theory and Practice* (Michele Langfield et al. eds, Routledge 2010).

121. The term 'cultural diversity' is defined in Art. 4(1) of the UNESCO Convention as 'the manifold ways in which the cultures of groups and societies find expression. These expressions are passed on within and among groups and societies. … [It] is made manifest not only through the varied ways in which the cultural heritage of humanity is expressed, augmented and transmitted through the variety of cultural expressions, but also through diverse modes of artistic creation, production, dissemination, distribution and enjoyment, whatever the means and technologies used'.

Prioritization of competing cultural interests is, understandably, entirely avoided by ICANN in the *gTLD Applicant Guidebook*. The rough guidance offered by the UNESCO Convention as to how such competing claims might be addressed could nevertheless be useful to identifying the considerations that should be borne in mind in the resolution of disputes involving culturally significant gTLD strings.

9.2.3.4 Cultural Property

Another growing area of discourse in the area of cultural rights relates to cultural property.[122] The notion of culture as property is largely based upon Western intellectual property doctrines, but at the same time also awkwardly depends on the application of those doctrines to 'cross-cultural claims that cannot be addressed solely by reference to values that have traditionally been embedded within the legal commentaries on property.'[123] While the use of the term 'property' in this discourse unmistakably 'implies control in the form of an ability to alienate, exploit and exclude others'[124] as possessed by a single individual, the added cultural element implies a different rationale for this protection than pure commercial interest. Thus cultural property differs from other forms of property in significant ways:

> first, that it is 'owned' in common or, at least, publicly; secondly, that the ownership rights focus on preservation, access and the sharing of benefits associated with it; and thirdly, that the role of cultural property rights is to prevent or limit the privatization of cultural property.[125]

Discussion of legal protection for cultural property diverges into two broad themes: protection of 'cultural expressions' and protection of 'traditional knowledge'. For neither of these terms is there an agreed definition and likewise for neither is there yet an agreed legal protection framework. These

---

122. *See generally,* John Henry Merryman, *Two Ways of Thinking About Cultural Property*, 80(4) Am. J. Int'l L. 831 (1986); Lyndel V. Prott, *Problems of Private International Law for the Protection of the Cultural Heritage*, 217 Recueil des Cours de l'Academie de la Haye 301 (1989); Fiona Macmillan, *Human Rights, Cultural Property and Intellectual Property: Three Concepts in Search of a Relationship*, in *Intellectual Property and Traditional Cultural Expressions in a Digital Environment* (Christoph Beat Graber & Mira Burri-Nenova eds, Edward Elgar 2008); Jürgen Bröhmer & Jennifer Greaney, *Der Schutz der Kulturgüter der australischen Ureinwohner*, in *Verfassung – Völkerrecht – Kulturgüterschutz* (Michaela Wittinger, Rudolf Wendt & Georg Ress eds, Duncker & Humblot 2011).
123. Tatiana Flessas, *Cultural Property Defined, and Redefined as Nietzschean Aphorism*, 24 Cardozo L. Rev. 1067, 1068 n. 3 (2003), quoted in *The Resolution of Cultural Property Disputes: Some Issues of Definition* 55 (Kathryn Last ed., Kluwer Law International 2004).
124. *The Resolution of Cultural Property Disputes* 55 (Kathryn Last ed.).
125. Macmillan, *Human Rights, Cultural Property and Intellectual Property*, 91.

concepts are nevertheless arguably the principal focus of today's international intellectual property law development efforts. The volume of scholarship on cultural expressions and traditional knowledge means that an examination of whether either of these encompasses a particular subject matter such as geographic names constitutes a study unto itself. Such a detailed enquiry lies outside of the scope of this work, but the considerable recent effort expended at the international level in the contexts of human rights, international trade law[126] and intellectual property law[127] demands that the potential of cultural expressions and traditional knowledge as existing or future sources of rights in geographic names be raised here for later, thorough consideration.

9.2.3.4.1 Geographic Names as Cultural Expressions

The term 'cultural expression' has been encountered in earlier sections of this chapter in the context of the human right to culture and the promotion of cultural diversity. There it was noted that the UNESCO Convention creates no binding obligations on State parties with respect to cultural expressions, which are defined in Article 4(3) as 'those expressions that result from the creativity of individuals, groups and societies, and that have cultural content.' What the UNESCO Convention does is acknowledge the role that cultural expressions play in society and, controversially, the 'complementarity of economic and cultural aspects of development'.[128] With these things in mind, the UNESCO Convention offers States guidance on the implementation of measures aimed at promoting and protecting the diversity of cultural expressions.

---

126. The scope for protecting cultural property in international trade law beyond the narrow issue of geographical indications (which is discussed later in this chapter in the context of traditional knowledge) is being considered, but as the UN Sub-Commission for the Protection and Promotion of Human Rights resolution on 'Intellectual Property and Human Rights' warns, it is necessary to be aware of 'actual or potential conflicts that exist between the implementation of TRIPS and the realization of economic, social and cultural rights.' UN Sub-Commission on Human Rights, *Resolution 2000/7: Intellectual Property Rights and Human Rights*, U.N. Doc. E/CN.4/SUB.2/RES/2000/7 (2000). For detailed discussion on this issue, *see for example*, Pamela Samuelson, *Implications of the Agreement on Trade Related Aspects of Intellectual Property Rights for Cultural Dimensions of National Copyright Laws*, 23(1–2) J. Cult. Econ. 95 (1999); John Henry Merryman, *Cultural Property, International Trade and Human Rights*, 19 Cardozo Arts & Ent. L.J. 51 (2001); Cottier, *The Agreement on Trade-Related Aspects of Intellectual Property Rights*; Fiona Macmillan, *Copyright, the World Trade Organization and Cultural Self Determination*, in *New Directions in Copyright Law* (Fiona Macmillan ed., Edward Elgar 2007).
127. *See for example*, Cottier & Panizzon, *Legal Perspectives on Traditional Knowledge*; Peter K. Yu, *Intellectual Property and Human Rights in the Nonmultilateral Era*, 64 Fla. L. Rev. 1045, 1072 (2012).
128. Convention on the Protection and Promotion of the Diversity of Cultural Expressions, Art. 2(5).

WIPO takes a different approach, focusing instead on intellectual property law frameworks. In 2011, its Intergovernmental Committee on Intellectual Property and Genetic Resources, Traditional Knowledge and Folklore (the 'Intergovernmental Committee') released draft articles on the protection of 'traditional cultural expressions' (or 'TCEs', as they are also known).[129] In draft alternative forms,[130] the articles propose to define the subject matter of protection using key intellectual property (of which in particular copyright) terminology.

The protection envisaged by draft Article 3 is, in both proposed options, likewise broadly reliant upon intellectual property terminology. The text remains under discussion, with the most recent version published in June 2014.[131] On the other hand, the 'Glossary of Key Terms Related to Intellectual Property and Genetic Resources, Traditional Knowledge and Traditional Cultural Expressions' published as part of the Intergovernmental Committee's twentieth session in 2012[132] evidences the need to extend beyond intellectual property in understanding these culture-based concepts. A more significant difference between the UNESCO Convention and the WIPO Draft Articles than terminology is the fact that the latter creates rights and clear obligations respecting cultural expressions, whilst the former does not.

---

129. WIPO Intergovernmental Committee on Intellectual Property and Genetic Resources, Traditional Knowledge and Folklore (hereinafter 'WIPO IGC'), *The Protection of Traditional Cultural Expressions: Draft Articles*, WIPO Doc. WIPO/GRTKF/IC/18/4 Rev. (14 Apr. 2011) (available at http://www.wipo.int/edocs/mdocs/tk/en/wipo_grtkf_ic_18/wipo_grtkf_ic_18_4_rev.pdf).

130. WIPO IGC, *The Protection of Traditional Cultural Expressions: Draft Articles Rev. 2 (September 23, 2016)*, WIPO Doc. WIPO/GRTKF/IC/31/FACILITATORS TEXT REV. 2 (30 Sep. 2016), (available athttp://www.wipo.int/edocs/mdocs/tk/en/wipo_grtkf_ic_31/wipo_grtkf_ic_31_facilitators_text_rev_2.pdf). WIPO IGC, *Like-Minded Countries Contribution to the Draft Articles on the Protection of Traditional Cultural Expressions*, WIPO Doc. WIPO/GRTKF/IC/22/5 (27 Apr. 2012) (available at http://www.wipo.int/edocs/mdocs/tk/en/wipo_grtkf_ic_22/wipo_grtkf_ic_22_5.pdf).

131. WIPO IGC, *The Protection of Traditional Cultural Expressions: Draft Articles*, WIPO Doc. WIPO/GRTKF/IC/28/6 (2 Jun. 2014) (available at http://www.wipo.int/edocs/mdocs/tk/en/wipo_grtkf_ic_28/wipo_grtkf_ic_28_6.pdf).

132. WIPO IGC, *Glossary of Key Terms Related to Intellectual Property and Genetic Resources, Traditional Knowledge and Traditional Cultural Expressions*, WIPO Doc. WIPO/GRTKF/IC/20/INF/13 (7 Dec. 2012) (available at http://www.wipo.int/edocs/mdocs/tk/en/wipo_grtkf_ic_20/wipo_grtkf_ic_20_inf_13.pdf) (introduced as follows: The present document draws, as far as possible, from previous glossaries of the IGC and from existing United Nations and other international instruments. The document also takes into account definitions and glossaries which can be found in national and regional laws and draft laws, multilateral instruments, other organizations and processes and in dictionaries. Further, definitions are based on working documents of the IGC, other WIPO documents and documents of other work programs of WIPO. That said, the proposed definitions are not exhaustive. Other terms may also be relevant to intellectual property and genetic resources, traditional knowledge, and traditional cultural expressions and the terms selected may also be defined in other ways.').

Both instruments attribute a relatively wide scope of subject matter as falling within 'cultural expressions', but they do so using different approaches, with UNESCO focusing on cultural content and WIPO focusing on the form of expression. This is a direct result of the differing motivations of human rights law and intellectual property law. Despite these differences, an argument can be made that geographic names fall within the scope of the protected subject matters of both of these instruments. WIPO's Draft Articles are the most clearly applicable given their express inclusion in subparagraph (a) of 'names' as covered subject matter. Falling within the UNESCO Convention's definition of 'cultural expression', on the other hand, depends on a name's having such a strong link to a culture that it can be considered 'cultural content'. The requirement that protected subject matter 'result from the creativity of individuals, groups and societies' may prove an obstacle to geographic names' protection given that they are often inspired by historic, geographic or other features rather than the product of human creativity. In this geographic names differ from things that would typically be characterized as creative cultural expressions, such as music, dance, stories and artworks.

Even if geographic names fall within either of these definitions of cultural expressions, no binding obligations have as-yet been created for their protection. Surveys conducted as part of WIPO's Cultural Heritage Project[133] evidence the fact that protection of TCEs is at this stage still a work in progress even at the domestic level. Work within WIPO's Intergovernmental Committee to finalize the Draft Articles is ongoing and appears to be making progress. This is an area of high potential for the recognition of rights in geographic names in the (perhaps even near) future, but not currently a source of legal rights in geographic names under international law.

9.2.3.4.2 Geographic Names as Traditional Knowledge

While the term 'cultural expression' tends to focus upon the results of creativity (the *what* of culture), the term 'traditional knowledge' tends to focus upon creative energies themselves (the *how* of culture). Though it too lacks an agreed definition, 'traditional knowledge' is broadly understood as something of value to a community because of its production and use by that community often (though not necessarily) over a lengthy period of time.[134] It is also frequently associated with the relationship between people and the environment in which they live. Accordingly, traditional knowledge may include knowledge of 'plants and animals and their properties; minerals and

133. WIPO, *Creative Heritage Project: Surveys of Existing Practices, Protocols and Policies*, http://www.wipo.int/tk/en/resources/surveys.html.

134. Antony Taubman & Matthias Leistner, *Analysis of Different Areas of Indigenous Resources: Traditional Knowledge*, in *Indigenous Heritage and Intellectual Property, Genetic Resources, Traditional Knowledge and Folklore* 59–60 (Silke von Lewinski ed., Kluwer Law International 2008).

soils and their properties; combinations of organic and inorganic matters; processes and technologies; means of enhancing individual health and welfare; means of enhancing collective health and welfare; [and] artistic expressions.'[135] The medicines, healing practices, religious ceremonies, handicrafts and other ways of life that are derived from this knowledge are valuable to the communities that develop and use them in terms of the community's continued ability to survive and thrive, but they may also have commercial value to outsiders. The incidence of outsiders appropriating and using traditional knowledge, particularly when this occurs without compensation, has given rise to interest in its protection.

The potential subject matter of traditional knowledge covers a broad range of activities. This is reflected in the variety of participants involved in efforts to protect it at the international level, including WIPO, the WTO, the UN's Food and Agriculture Organization, the UN Conference on Trade and Development, UNESCO, and the World Health Organization.[136] There are not yet any multilateral conventions of global force that specifically protect 'traditional knowledge' as a discrete subject matter, though the Convention on Biological Diversity[137] represents a significant step forward for the protection of the biological resources upon which many forms of traditional knowledge are based.

In conjunction with its work on protecting traditional cultural expressions, WIPO's Intergovernmental Committee is also engaged in efforts to protect traditional knowledge, though it has been said that international protection of TCEs is more 'mature';[138] this appears so, with the most recently published draft articles released in September 2016. [139] These draft articles on the protection of traditional knowledge remain under development, and similar to the draft articles on traditional cultural expressions, the

135. Bernard O'Connor, *Protecting Traditional Knowledge. An Overview of a Developing Area of Intellectual Property Law*, 6(5) J. World Intell. Prop. 677, 677-678 (2005). Thomas Cottier, *The Protection of Genetic Resources and Traditional Knowledge: Toward More Specific Rights and Obligations in World Trade Law*, 1 J. Int'l Econ. L. 555 (1998).
136. Cottier & Panizzon, *Legal Perspectives on Traditional Knowledge*.
137. Convention on Biological Diversity (5 Jun. 1992, entered into force 29 Dec. 1993) 1760 U.N.T.S. 79; 31 I.L.M. 818.
138. WIPO, *A New Dawn for Custodians of TK in Africa*, WIPO Magazine (December 2010) (available at http://www.wipo.int/wipo_magazine/en/2010/06/article_0008.html).
139. WIPO IGC, *The Protection of Traditional Knowledge: Draft Articles Rev. 2 (September 23, 2016)*, WIPO Doc. WIPO/GRTKF/IC/31/FACILITATORS TEXT REV. 2 (30 Sep. 2016) (available at http://www.wipo.int/edocs/mdocs/tk/en/wipo_grtkf_ic_31/wipo_grtkf_ic_31_facilitators_text_rev_2.pdf). WIPO IGC, *Like-Minded Countries Contribution to the Draft Articles on the Protection of Traditional Knowledge*, WIPO Doc. WIPO/GRTKF/IC/21/5 (2012) (available at http://www.wipo.int/edocs/mdocs/tk/en/wipo_grtkf_ic_21/wipo_grtkf_ic_21_5.pdf).

definition of 'traditional knowledge',[140] eligibility criteria (draft Article 1) and the scope of protection (draft Article 3) are at this stage drafted in optional forms.

Meanwhile, regional frameworks for the protection of traditional knowledge are also gaining ground, the most notable of which being the African Regional Intellectual Property Organization ('ARIPO') Swakopmund Protocol on the Protection of Traditional Knowledge and Expressions of Folklore (the 'Swakopmund Protocol'),[141] which entered into force on 11 May 2015.[142] It is instructive in terms of its broad but relatively concise definition of 'traditional knowledge'[143] and detailed criteria[144] of protectability which directly link knowledge to a particular community and its cultural identity.

Names are notably not expressly included in the definition of 'traditional knowledge' in the Swakopmund Protocol or in either of the definitional

140. Alt 1: Traditional knowledge, for the purposes of this instrument, is knowledge that is created, maintained, and developed by indigenous [peoples], local communities, [and nations/states], and that is linked with, or is an integral part of, the national or social identity and/or cultural heritage of indigenous [peoples], local communities, [and nations/states]; that is transmitted between or from generation to generation, whether consecutively or not; which subsists in codified, oral, or other forms; and which may be dynamic and evolving, and may take the form of know-how, skills, innovations, practices, teachings or learnings.].
Alt 2: Traditional knowledge, for the purposes of this instrument, is knowledge that is created, maintained, controlled, protected and developed by indigenous [peoples], local communities, [and nations] and that is directly linked with the social identity and/or cultural heritage of indigenous [peoples] and local communities; that is transmitted from generation to generation, whether consecutively or not; which subsists in codified, oral, or other forms; and which may be dynamic and evolving, and may take the form of know-how, skills, innovations, practices, teachings or learnings.].
WIPO IGC, *The Protection of Traditional Knowledge: Draft Articles*, Use of Terms ('Traditional knowledge').

141. Swakopmund Protocol on the Protection of Traditional Knowledge and Expressions of Folklore, WIPO Lex No. TRT/AP010/001 (9 Aug. 2010, entered into force 11 May 2015).

142. African Regional Intellectual Property Organization, *Entry into force of the ARIPO Swakopmund Protocol on the Protection of Traditional Knowledge and Expressions of Folklore*, http://www.aripo.org/news-events-publications/news/item/54-entry-into-force-of-the-aripo-swakopmund-protocol-on-the-protection-of-traditional-knowledge-and-expressions-of-folklore.

143. Swakopmund Protocol, Art. 2.1: '"traditional knowledge" shall refer to any knowledge originating from a local or traditional community that is the result of intellectual activity and insight in a traditional context, including know-how, skills, innovations, practices and learning, where the knowledge is embodied in the traditional lifestyle of a community, or contained in the codified knowledge systems passed on from one generation to another. The term shall not be limited to a specific technical field, and may include agricultural, environmental or medical knowledge, and knowledge associated with genetic resources.'

144. Swakopmund Protocol, Art. 4.

options in WIPO's Draft Articles on the Protection of Traditional Knowledge. It is questionable whether a geographic name could be interpreted to implicitly fall within the sorts of knowledge protected under either, given that they focus on how knowledge is generated rather than the form of its expression.

Even if a connection cannot be drawn between traditional knowledge and geographic names as a general matter, such a connection can potentially be drawn between traditional knowledge and goods identified by geographical indications.[145] This is because geographical indications implicitly represent the *how* element that geographic names as a general matter do not. Those who support the recognition and protection of geographical indications recognize that the aim of their protection goes beyond the mere name to 'protection of a certain quality and reputation that is attributable to a product that is made in a defined place.'[146] This quality and reputation is frequently derived not only from particular characteristics of the geographical territory from which a product originates, but from the human interaction with that territory and the knowledge employed to transform elements in their natural state into distinctive products.[147]

It has been shown in Chapter 7 that the international intellectual property law framework offers only limited protection to geographical indications against unauthorized use. Geographical indications as presently recognized thus have little capacity to protect the cultural aspects that inhere in them. Specifically, geographical indications are considered not to possess:

> the independent capacity to protect local cultures of production, consumption or identity, or to prevent the erosion of cultural diversity. Market forces inevitably induce changes in local production methods and consumption preferences, in spite of the GIs that should, in theory, play a role in preserving them, and the proliferation of GIs has itself diluted the claims of special reputation, typicity, and cultural identity of GI-endowed locales.[148]

Traditional knowledge protection has been proposed as a means of addressing these inadequacies and facilitating the protection of both a geographical

145. Cottier & Panizzon, *Legal Perspectives on Traditional Knowledge*.
146. O'Connor, *The Law of Geographical Indications*, 18. Conrad, 13.
147. Dev Gangjee, *Melton Mowbray and the GI Pie in the Sky: Exploring Cartographies of Protection*, 2006(3) Intell. Prop. Q. 291, 300-308 (2006) (discussing 'the link between product and place'). Stephen R. Munzer & Phyllis Chen Simon, *Territory, Plants, and Land-Use Rights among the San of Southern Africa: A Case Study in Regional Biodiversity, Traditional Knowledge, and Intellectual Property*, 17 Wm. & Mary Bill Rts J. 831 (2009).
148. Broude, 678. Rhonda Chesmond, *Protection or Privatisation of Culture? The Cultural Dimension of the International Intellectual Property Debate on Geographical Indications of Origin*, 29(9) Eur. Intell. Prop. Rev. 379 (2007).

indication as such and the cultural knowledge it represents.[149] This is an interesting future possibility, but the scope that traditional knowledge protection currently offers for recognizing rights in geographic names (of which geographical indications in particular) is only speculative. Taking guidance from the Swakopmund Protocol, geographic names are not expressly provided for, and a plain reading of the definition and eligibility criteria of 'traditional knowledge' renders it unlikely that these will be interpreted to implicitly include geographic names.

9.2.4 RIGHT TO LANGUAGE

Closely linked to the right to culture is the right to language. Culture and language are symbiotic aspects of life; many forms of cultural expression use language, and the words that comprise languages are constantly evolving and being drawn from speakers' cultural interactions and experiences. This is not unique to modern civilization; the German writer Johann Wolfang von Goethe observed the following of late eighteenth century life: 'So unübersetzlich sind die Eigenheiten jeder Sprache; denn vom höchsten bis zum tiefsten Wort bezieht sich alles auf Eigentümlichkeiten der Nation, es sei nun in Charakter, Gesinnungen oder Zuständen.' ['It is impossible to translate the idiosyncrasies of each language; every word, from the most arcane down to the simplest, is permeated by the particular nature of the nation, be it in character, outlook or circumstances.'][150]

Modern technologies seem to be moving human societies away from such culturally and nationally distinct languages, however. The ease and affordability of global cultural dissemination via the internet contributes to the growing trend of linguistic homogenization, and it has been estimated that as much as '95 per cent of the languages today will have no long-term prospects of survival'.[151] The death of languages is linked to the death of cultures, and this is generally viewed as undesirable.[152] Paradoxically, the internet may have just as much of a role to play in reversing this trend as it has had in its creation by helping waning linguistic communities to overcome challenges to communication such as geographical isolation, unsupportive

149. Cottier & Panizzon, *Traditional Knowledge and Geographical Indications*; Olufunmilayo B. Arewa, *TRIPS and Traditional Knowledge: Local Communities, Local Knowledge, and Global Intellectual Property Frameworks*, 10 Marquette Intell. Prop. L. Rev. 155 (2006).

150. Johann Wolfgang von Goethe, *Italienische Reise 1786-1788* Teil 1 (Den 5. Oktober, nachts), 80 (Hirmer Verlag 1961) (trans. Dinah Cannell in Konrad Schröder, *Languages*, in *What is Europe? Aspects of European Cultural Diversity* 13 (Monica Shelley & Margaret Winck eds, Routledge 1995).

151. Schröder, *Languages*, 14.

152. *See for example*, Gerrand, *Cultural Diversity in Cyberspace*.

government language policies and political conflict. One step in this direction is ICANN's introduction in 2010 of Internationalized Domain Names ('IDNs'), enabling domain names to be represented in non-Latin scripts.[153] The introduction of IDN new gTLDs promises even greater possibilities for linguistic communities to promote, preserve and develop their language in the online world, although the low percentage of applications they comprised in 2012[154] may mean that bigger impacts will be delayed until subsequent calls for new gTLD applications, or perhaps never realized.

It is not surprising that much of the discussion surrounding human rights and language takes place within the context of minority rights. As is the case with cultural rights, it can be argued that the majority is sufficiently well equipped to protect its linguistic interests, but that its doing so puts the continued existence of minority languages at risk. Article 27 of the ICCPR is clearly relevant given its recognition of the right of persons of 'ethnic, religious or linguistic' minority groups to, *inter alia*, 'use their own language'. Article 30 of the International Convention on the Rights of the Child additionally recognizes the right of a child belonging to a minority or indigenous group to 'use his or her own language'. These are, however, the only instruments of global effect to specifically recognize a right to language.

To clarify, the Charter of the UN recognizes at Article 1(3) a right of non-discrimination on the basis of language, as do Articles 2(1) of the ICCPR and 2(2) of the ICESCR, but this is not axiomatically subject to interpretation as a right *to* language. The Committee on the Elimination of Discrimination has recommended that States' obligations to prevent discrimination be interpreted as ensuring 'that indigenous communities can exercise their rights to practise and revitalize their cultural traditions and customs and to preserve and to practise their languages',[155] but even this is not expressly a right to language. Nor does the additional protection offered to indigenous people and minorities by Articles 27 and 30 of the ICCPR and International Convention on the Rights of the Child, respectively, expressly recognize a right to language. Rather, protection in both of these instruments is articulated in terms of a right to *use* or *practice* a language, similar to the way in which the right *to participate in* culture is recognized in the ICESCR, rather than a right *to* culture. The analysis of the right under Article 15 of the

153. On IDNs, *see* Part I, Chapter 1, s. 1.2.2.3 above.

154. IDN strings comprised 6%, or 116 of 1,930, of applied-for strings in the first round of the New gTLD Program. ICANN, *New Generic Top-Level Domains: Quick Facts about Applied-for New gTLD Strings*, http://newgtlds.icann.org/en/program-status/statistics/applications-quick-facts-13jun12-en.pdf (13 Jun. 2012).

155. UN Office of the UN High Commissioner for Human Rights, International Human Rights Instruments, UN Doc. HRI/GEN/1/Rev.9 (Vol. II), *General Recommendation XXIII on the rights of indigenous peoples* 285 (27 May 2008) (available at http://www.ohchr.org/Documents/HRBodies/TB/HRI-GEN-1-REV-9-VOL-II_en.doc).

ICESCR 'to take part in the cultural life of the community' cited earlier in this chapter is aptly recalled here; borrowing those words, the right to use a language logically 'can only exist if there is a'[156] language. This statement seems sensible in the context of the right to language, but nevertheless lacks support in international law in the way that the right to culture is supported through Article 15(2) of the ICESCR, which requires States to take steps necessary for culture's conservation and development. In spite of this, it is posited that:

> normative expectations converge at least to the extent that states feel an obligation to provide some affirmative support for the use of indigenous languages and to ensure that indigenous people do not suffer discrimination for failure to speak the dominant language of the state in which they live.[157]

The scope for a broader right of indigenous peoples to language is supported by the Declaration on the Rights of Indigenous Peoples, Article 13(1) of which is of particular relevance here. It provides: 'Indigenous peoples have the right to revitalize, use, develop and transmit to future generations their histories, languages, oral traditions, philosophies, writing systems and literatures, **and to designate and retain their own names for communities, places** and persons' (emphasis added). The Declaration on the Rights of Indigenous Peoples is not binding and thus not a formal source of rights in geographic names, but the language just emphasized suggests at a minimum that there is some recognition at the international level of the importance of geographic names to indigenous peoples. Otherwise, nothing in the ongoing discourse on legal rights in geographic names suggests that there is currently a custom or general principle of recognizing this right of indigenous peoples to 'retain their own names for communities [and] places'.

Recognition of the human right to language in international law thus appears to be limited to particular segments of the human population and the particular context of preventing discrimination. While there are regional agreements that provide for rights respecting language,[158] these are also limited to the non-discrimination context and do not create specific rights to language that might support a correlative right to use or control a geographic name. Nor has support for a right to language been found outside of human rights law in the area of international trade law.[159]

156. McGoldrick, 454. *See* discussion above in this chapter at s. 9.2.3.2.

157. Anaya, *Indigenous Peoples in International Law*, 139 (internal citations omitted).

158. For example, the European Convention on Human Rights recognizes at Art. 14 a right to non-discrimination on the basis of language. Convention for the Protection of Human Rights and Fundamental Freedoms (4 Nov. 1950, entered into force 3 Sep. 1953) E.T.S. 5; 213 U.N.T.S. 221.

159. Broude, 682 (concluding that the potential for using trade-restrictive measures to preserve language, 'a national treasure of sorts', under GATT Art. XX(f) is very low).

Against this backdrop it must be considered whether actions of the State that have the effect of preventing a particular linguistic community from having an online identity in the form of a geographic internet top-level domain could be interpreted as discrimination on the basis of language. In cases in which language and geographic territory share a name, a restriction by government on the linguistic community's application for that domain name or string could plausibly constitute discrimination by preventing that community from expressing itself on the internet. On the other hand, a policy of State control of geographic names would not be discriminatory if, for example, domain name registration within gTLDs were open to members of the linguistic community. Further, the policy underpinning the operation of the domain and use of domain names registered within it could not discriminate against in-language content and users. A hypothetical example would be a decision by the government of the UK to apply for a .cymru gTLD in which domain name registrants are prohibited from registering Welsh-language names or displaying Welsh-language content.[160]

The human right to language thus appears at present to offer scant support for a right of any party to make use of or exercise control over geographic names. Application of the right to language is limited to preventing State actions that discriminate on the basis of language; a government taking steps to prevent a linguistic community's access to the internet could, in certain circumstances, constitute a breach of this right. It does not automatically follow, however, that the recognition of exclusive State rights in a geographic domain name is discriminatory. That said, neither does the human right to language prove the existence of an exclusive right of States to geographic names; what it does is obligate States using geographic names not to do so in ways that discriminate against linguistic communities. Fundamentally, the right inheres in individuals; this directly contradicts States' claims that geographic names 'belong to' the State and does not support States' exclusive control of geographic names. That being the case, it is not for the State to decide whether individuals wish to exercise this right, whether by applying for a new gTLD or otherwise.

9.2.5 Right to Property

Several forms of property have been explored in this and earlier chapters as potential bases of rights under international law in geographic names: in the context of human rights, cultural property (including cultural expressions and

160. This example did not eventuate in the actual application process; the .cymru application made by Nominet UK, the registry operator of the UK's .uk ccTLD, specifically supports 'the registration of internationalized domain names (IDNs) to support the Welsh language'. ICANN, *Application Details, String: CYMRU*, Question 23, http://gtldresult.icann.org/application-result/applicationstatus/applicationdetails/1420.

traditional knowledge), and in the context of intellectual property, trademarks and geographical indications. These regimes protect exclusive individual – and to a lesser extent collective – rights to property in a particular form or satisfying particular criteria. What remains as a final area of enquiry is to consider whether geographic names can be considered as either the property of individuals or, alternatively, belonging to all humankind. The starting point in answering these questions is the recognition in international law of an individual's right to property and its potential applicability to geographic names. This then leads to a discussion of the notion of public property, what was termed '*res publicae*' in Roman law. Lastly, it is shown that these historic notions of property remain a feature of contemporary legal frameworks, appearing in the intellectual property context in the concept of the public domain.

9.2.5.1 The Human Right to Property and Individuals' Rights in Geographic Names

A human right to property remains elusive and indefinite in international law. It is recognized most clearly in the non-binding UN Declaration on Human Rights, Article 17 of which provides:

> (1) Everyone has the right to own property alone as well as in association with others.
> (2) No one shall be arbitrarily deprived of his property.

A right to property is not provided for in either the ICCPR or the ICESCR, though both address property in the context of non-discrimination.[161] 'There is reason to believe, however, that it was the precise formulation of the contours of the right to property, rather than disagreement over its existence in some form, that proved the stumbling block (and even then, only narrowly so).'[162] This is supported by the express recognition of a right to property in regional agreements, amongst which the European Convention on Human Rights,[163] the African Charter on Human and Peoples

161. ICCPR, Arts 2(1), 24(1) and 26(1); ICESCR, Art. 2(2).
162. Francisco Forrest Martin et al., *International Human Rights Law and Practice: Cases, Treaties and Materials* 868–869 (Kluwer Law International 1997) citing William A. Schabas, *The Omission of the Right to Property in the International Covenants*, 4 Hague Y.B. Int'l L. 135 (1991).
163. Art. 1 of the Optional Protocol to the Convention provides:

> Every natural or legal person is entitled to the peaceful enjoyment of his possessions. No one shall be deprived of his possessions except in the public interest and subject to the conditions provided for by law and by the general principles of international law.
>
> The preceding provisions shall not, however, in any way impair the right of a State to enforce such laws as it deems necessary to control the use of property in accordance with the general interest or to secure the payment of taxes or other contributions or penalties.

Rights[164] and the American Convention on Human Rights.[165] Further support for the existence of a right to property can be derived from the non-binding UN General Assembly Resolution on Respect for the Right of Everyone to Own Property Alone as Well as in Association with Others and Its Contribution to the Economic and Social Development of Member States.[166]

Although it may broadly (even if not universally) be agreed that a human right to property exists in some form in international law, there is disagreement as to the precise substance of the right and limitations to it.[167] This is less problematic in the regional instruments just noted. Article 17(2) of the European Charter on the Fundamental Rights of the European Union,[168] for example, specifically states: 'Intellectual property shall be protected.' The European Convention on Human Rights is another example; although a right to property is not expressly provided for, analysis shows that protection of intellectual property, including trademarks, bears out in cases.[169]

The most common and general aspect of the right to property at the international level is its protection of individuals 'against wrongful state action'.[170] Whether protection against arbitrary and uncompensated taking of property is the only protection offered by an international law-based right to property is unclear but possible. Related arguments may be made to the effect that a taking constitutes a violation of the TRIPS Agreement's guarantees of protection to trademarks and geographical indications.[171] Another broader possibility that is philosophically supported by the belief that property rights are directly linked to economic prosperity[172] is its encompassing a positive right to acquire and possess at least *some* property. Even this broader view

---

164. African Charter on Human and Peoples' Rights, Art. 14 (27 Jun. 1981, entered into force 21 Oct. 1986) O.A.U. Doc. CAB/LEG/67/3 Rev 5, discussed in Mashood A. Baderin, *The African Commission on Human and Peoples' Rights and the Implementation of Economic, Social and Cultural Rights in Africa*, in *Economic, Social and Cultural Rights in Action* 151–153 (Mashood A. Baderin & Robert McCorquodale eds, Oxford University Press 2007).
165. American Convention on Human Rights, Art. 21 (22 Nov. 1969, entered into force 17 Jul. 1978) 1144 U.N.T.S. 123.
166. *Respect for the right of everyone to own property alone as well as in association with others and its contribution to the economic and social development of Member States*, 14 Dec. 1990, UN General Assembly Doc. A/RES/45/98.
167. *Restatement (Third) of the Foreign Relations Law of the United States* §711 comment d.
168. Charter of Fundamental Rights of the European Union, OJ 2000/C 364/01.
169. Goebel, 7.
170. Forrest Martin et al., *International Human Rights Law and Practice*, 866.
171. *See for example, Australia – Certain Measures Concerning Trademarks and Other Plain Packaging Requirements Applicable to Tobacco Products and Packaging*, WT/DS434/1; *Australia – Certain Measures Concerning Trademarks, Geographical Indications and Other Plain Packaging Requirements Applicable to Tobacco Products and Packaging*, WT/DS435/1; *Australia – Certain Measures Concerning Trademarks and Other Plain Packaging Requirements Applicable to Tobacco Products and Packaging*, WT/DS441/1.
172. *Ibid.*

does not extend so far as to justifying claims to acquire or own *particular* property, however. Nor have claims based solely on a right to property been accepted in international courts.[173]

While there are regional laws that support a right to property as protecting particular property,[174] international law does not go so far. International law does, however, offer support for the claim that a property right recognized in a geographic name (e.g., as a trademark, geographical indication or as cultural property) cannot arbitrarily be taken away. In the specific context of the New gTLD Program, this should motivate governments (including in the exercise of the GAC Early Warning procedure) to articulate clear reasons for denying support of a geographic new gTLD application made by an applicant possessing property rights such as a geographic trademark or geographical indication.

9.2.5.2 Collective Property Rights in Geographic Names

9.2.5.2.1 Geographic Names as Public Property: 'Res Publicae'

Various societies and political ideologies have held to varying degrees the belief that some things in life are the property of the public at large. In law, this has roots in the Roman concept of '*res publicae*', in which public access was ensured by operation of law.[175] Classic examples of *res publicae* include highways, railways, harbours, ports and bridges. These things 'are overwhelmingly the physical spaces required for mobility—lanes for travel, transportation, navigation, and communication among distant locations.'[176] Their desirability to the public and use by all, in addition to their susceptibility to a certain degree of control to ensure their orderly use,[177] justifies ownership by all.

Taking the view that geographic names are public property starts with a determination that they are property, something that the law has been notably reticent to do at least in the context of their registrability as trademarks.[178] Article 6*ter* of the Paris Convention is argued to have been

---

173. *See for example*, *L.E.S.K. v. the Netherlands*, U.N. Human Rights Committee, Communication No. 381/1989 U.N. Doc. CCPR/C/45/D381/1989 (1992); *K.J.L. v. Finland*, U.N. Human Rights Committee, Communication No. 544/193 U.N. Doc. CCPR/C/49/D/544/1993 (views adopted by the Human Rights Committee 3 Nov. 1993); *Koné v. Senegal*, U.N. Human Rights Committee, Communication No. 386/1989 U.N. Doc. CCPR/C/52/D/386/1989 (views adopted by the Human Rights Committee 21 Oct. 1994), as cited in Forrest Martin et al., *International Human Rights Law and Practice*, 875.
174. Goebel, 7.
175. Carol M. Rose, *Romans, Roads, and Romantic Creators: Traditions of public property in the information age*, 66 L. & Contemp. Probs. 89 (2003).
176. *Id.*, 97.
177. *Id.*, 99.
178. *See* discussion of geographical names' protectability as a trademark in Part III, Chapter 5, s. 5.2 above.

motivated by national emblems' incapability of propertization.[179] Debates surrounding the protection of cultural expressions, traditional knowledge and biological resources centre on the appropriateness of propertization.[180] It is also said that '[f]rom an indigenous perspective, a song or story is not a commodity or a form of property but "one of the manifestations of an ancient and continuing relationship between people and their territory".'[181] Nor are plants and animals, healing methods, or ways of life easily characterized as property.

Characterizations of the internet and its DNS as *res publicae* [182] should be scrutinized. It would be difficult if not impossible to maintain a *res publicae* space in the current environment of natural monopoly that results from the technical rule of absolute name uniqueness. The proviso that the public must be willing to 'behave in an orderly fashion'[183] in a *res publicae* space requires an absolute willingness on the part of unsuccessful gTLD applicants to relinquish aspirations of extending offline rights into the online environment.

Even if the communications network underpinning the internet is deemed public property, this does not mean that all of the traffic and content upon it is also public property. Reference can be made back to physical *res publicae* spaces: the use of a public highway or port by privately owned vehicles and ships does not transform those vehicles and ships into public property. Likewise, if the internet is considered public property, its use to communicate information does not transform that information into public property. The information may be public property, but if so, this is irrespective of its transmission via the internet. That said, the line between 'lanes and means of communication … [and] the content of communication'[184] is difficult to draw. This is certainly an issue for domain names because they have a tendency to connote content while also identifying the source of information and its location in the internet.

---

179. Antony Taubman, *The Public Domain and International Intellectual Property Law Treaties*, in *Intellectual Property: The Many Faces of the Public Domain* 82 (Hector Macqueen & Charlotte Waelde eds, Edward Elgar 2007).
180. Anupam Chander & Madhavi Sunder, *The Romance of the Public Domain*, 92 Cal. L. Rev. 1331, 1368 (2004).
181. Wend B. Wendland, *'It's a Small World (After All)': Some Reflections on Intellectual Property and Traditional Cultural Expressions*, in *Intellectual Property and Traditional Cultural Expressions in a Digital Environment* 150 (Christoph Beat Graber & Mira Burri-Nenova eds, Edward Elgar 2008), quoting Erica-Irene Daes, Special Rapporteur of the (then) Sub-Commission on Prevention of Discrimination and Protection of Minorities and Chair of the Working Group on Indigenous Populations, *Study on the Protection of the Cultural and Intellectual Property of Indigenous Peoples*, E/CN.4/Sub.2/1993/28, 28 Jul. 1993, para. 22.
182. Rose, 100 (identifying the internet as 'the most obvious example of res publicae in Intellectual Space').
183. *Id.*, 99.
184. *Id.*, 104.

Just as *'[p]ublic* roads and open systems of transportation make *private* property more valuable'[185] (emphasis in original), the internet and other modern communications mediums make privately owned names and symbols more valuable, encouraging their commoditization despite the incongruity in some cases of that approach with the beliefs of their creators. As has been shown in earlier sections of this chapter, recent trends in the propertization of cultural expressions and traditional knowledge tend to follow existing property regimes. In the DNS context, this is consistent with the broad understanding of domain names as property or something conceptually comparable. The existence of these other potential sources of legal rights in geographic names renders it even more remote that they might be considered generally, or in the specific context of the DNS, public property.

9.2.5.2.2 Geographic Names as Part of the Public Domain

It is a widely accepted premise of intellectual property law that new creation depends upon the existence of a stock of ideas and expressions that is open and available to all; in some legal systems, this philosophy justifies the very existence of intellectual property laws as temporary means of private propertization.[186] The things falling outside of private property rights, whether at the expiry of protection or not protectable in the first place, are considered to be in the 'public domain'. There are three ways of characterizing the public domain: as property belonging to all – the notion of public property just discussed,[187] as 'res nullius' – the 'property of no one',[188] or as the 'opposite of property' – something not falling within the characterization of property.[189]

There is no agreed definition of 'public domain', but there is consistency in terms of its focus on access rather than ownership, as this definition illustrates: 'Resources for which legal rights to access and use for free (or for nominal sums) are held broadly.'[190] Articulated in this way in terms of access and use, the notion of the public domain is inconsistent with property rights, which confer 'control in the form of an ability to alienate, exploit and exclude others'.[191] Nevertheless, even access and use can give rise to

185. Chander & Sunder, 1345.
186. Hughes, *The Philosophy of Intellectual Property*, 323–325.
187. *See for example*, Rose, 100.
188. *See for example*, Indigenous World Association and Indigenous Media Network, *Review of Developments Pertaining to the Promotion and Protection of the Rights of Indigenous Peoples, Including their Human Rights and Fundamental Freedoms: Joint Statement from the Indigenous World Association and Indigenous Media Network. UN High Commission on Human Rights*, E/CN.4/Sub.2/AC.4/2005/CRP.3, http://www.ohchr.org/Documents/Issues/IPeoples/WG/E-CN4-Sub2-AC4-2005-CRP3.doc (13 Jul. 2005).
189. *See for example*, James Boyle, *Foreword: The Opposite of Property?*, 66 L. & Contemp. Probs. 1 (2003).
190. Chander & Sunder, 1338.
191. Last (ed.), *The Resolution of Cultural Property Disputes*, 55.

feelings that might be mistaken for property, particularly property owned by the State as:

> a form of domain defined not merely by the absence of exclusive private rights but by a positive sense of public ownership or collective sovereignty. This is domain as dominion: the sense of 'domain' recalled in the concept of 'eminent domain', the sovereign's residual entitlement to assume use of private property for public use, based on a superior form of sovereign dominion over property.[192]

Intellectual property laws traditionally make a distinction between property and the public domain, subject matter falling into the former category being protected and subject matter falling into the latter category not protected.[193] This is helpful to achieving a foundational understanding of what the public domain comprises, but it has been argued that it is not appropriate to conclude from this simplified explanation that intellectual property and the public domain are somehow opposed, as if 'the public domain is a bulwark against propertization and an alternative to intellectual property.'[194] Rather, there is a cyclic symbiosis between property rights and the public domain, an idea which has as its roots in Lockean 'labour theory': energies are exerted upon ideas and information in the public domain and thus take on the status of private property, which status they relinquish when the term of protection ends.[195] Falling into the public domain, they become available to others for use in creating new intellectual property. In this way, the public domain is a driver of propertization 'because it offers a sphere of free works upon which capitalists can draw without either seeking consent or drawing liability.'[196]

The subject matter in the public domain is not itself appropriable, but can be used to create appropriable subject matter that ultimately joins the stock of non-appropriable subject matter. This is precisely what concerns indigenous communities if cultural heritage is to be considered public domain:

> Placing our knowledge into the public domain turns it into a freely available resource for commercial utilization. Thus, it also creates the pre-condition for using non-indigenous Intellectual Property Rights (IPR) regimes to patent 'inventions' based upon our knowledge. … We therefore strongly reject the application of the public domain concept to

192. Taubman, *The Public Domain and International Intellectual Property Law Treaties*, 60–61, citing Grotius, *In Hugonis Grotii Jus Belli Et Pacis Commentatio.* De Jure Belli, Book I, iii. §6.
193. *See generally*, Jessica Litman, *The Public Domain*, 39 Emory L.J. 965 (1990).
194. Chander & Sunder, 1343.
195. On Locke's labour theory and its application in justifying IPRs, Hughes, *The Philosophy of Intellectual Property*, 296–329.
196. Chander & Sunder, 1343.

> any aspect that relates to our cultures and identities, including human and other genetic information originating from our lands and waters.[197]

On the other hand, the non-appropriable nature of the public domain aligns it with the Roman law concept of *res communes*, which 'encapsulates what might be called the Impossibility Argument against private property: The character of some resources makes them incapable of "capture" or any other act of exclusive appropriation.'[198] Classic examples of *res communes* are oceans and water; they are needed and used by all, but it is physically impossible to exert exclusive control over them.[199]

In the non-physical world, languages, alphabets, facts and laws of nature all fit the description of being needed by all and incapable of possession or propertization by individuals.[200] The symbols protected by Article 6*ter* have also been considered to fit this description.[201] These examples highlight the distinction made in Roman law between *res publicae* and *res communes*: *res publicae* are contained spaces over which some degree of control is possible. This distinction has since blurred, and intellectual property law appears to have played a role in that process.[202]

A characterization of geographic names as falling in the public domain[203] does not necessarily equate to a 'right' of the public to them, however. On the contrary, claims to rights in the public domain lack support because of the very notion of the commons as a non-proprietary environment:

> Rather, we all have the privilege or liberty to do what we like with these works (for example, stage a Shakespeare play); the only corollary is that other persons have no right to prevent us from so doing (for example, the direct descendant of William Shakespeare has no right to prevent me staging Macbeth).[204]

Applying this thinking to geographic names, the public may not so much have a right to use a geographic name (suggesting a corresponding duty on the part of others, including the State, not to interfere in that interest) but rather a 'privilege or liberty' to use them – as domain names or otherwise –

197. Indigenous World Association and Indigenous Media Network, *Joint Statement*.
198. Rose, 93.
199. *Ibid.*, citing William A. Hunter, *Introduction to Roman Law* 59–60 (9th ed. revised, Oxford University Press 1934).
200. On traditional knowledge and the public domain, Cottier & Panizzon, *Legal Perspectives on Traditional Knowledge*, 374–376.
201. Taubman, *The public domain and international intellectual property law treaties*, 82.
202. Rose, 94–95.
203. Rimmer, 131.
204. Cahir, 39–40.

within the bounds of other norms surrounding their use such as those established by unfair competition law.[205]

If they do form part of the public domain, geographic names should be made available for domain name registration by any member of the public. This is not because each member of the public has a legal right to have such a space delegated to their control by ICANN: no one member of the public has a greater claim than another. The 'first come, first served' approach to domain name registration reflects this view perfectly, but the perfect application of the public domain to the DNS ends there. In the offline world, things in the public domain are available to all, and their transformative use by one does not prevent transformative use by another. In the online world, multiple simultaneous users of a domain name cannot exist: the technical requirement of absolute name uniqueness means that domain names start out as available to all, but they lose that status once they are delegated (top-level) or registered (second and lower levels). The plot (e.g., boy meets girl, they fall in love, their love is forbidden by family relations) remains in the public domain for others to use even after *Romeo and Juliet* is written, but a geographic name is effectively removed from the pool of available names when it is delegated to a registry operator or registered by a domain name registrant. There can only be one .africa, one .switzerland, one .paris, and only one kenya.africa, restaurant.geneva and one champagne.wine.

In conclusion, although the law does not recognize a right of the public to subject matter in the public domain, when the use at issue takes the form of a domain name, the practical outcome is difficult to distinguish from a legal right. While there is no right to prevent another person from making an application for a geographic gTLD string or registering a domain name comprised of a term falling within the public domain, there is a technological impediment to doing so that gives rise to an exclusive, property-type right once the name has been expressed in that way.

9.3 GEOGRAPHIC NAMES AS THE COMMON HERITAGE OF MANKIND

The final basis of rights considered in this study is a concept that has its roots in natural resources law, but also has clear links to cultural rights.[206] It is

205. Taubman, *The Public Domain and International Intellectual Property Law Treaties*, 58–59.

206. *See for example*, Liu Lina, *Ownership of Underwater Cultural Heritage in the Area*, 1 Creighton Int'l & Comp. L.J. 60 (2011); Derek Fincham, *The Distinctiveness of Property and Heritage*, 115 Penn St. L. Rev. 641 (2011); Joseph P. Fishman, *Locating the International Interest in Intranational Cultural Property Disputes*, 35 Yale J. Int'l L. 3347 (2010); Siegfried Wiessner, *Re-enchanting the World: Indigenous Peoples' Rights as Essential Parts of a Holistic Human Rights Regime*, 15 UCLA J. Int'l L. & Foreign Aff. 239 (2010).

acknowledged from the outset that this discussion could sit apart from human rights in this book, but it has been purposefully placed here in order to highlight the conceptual connections between cultural rights, the public domain and common heritage. This is broadly consistent with the doctrine of common heritage of mankind coming to be embraced within human rights law, for example, as a tenet recognized in the preamble of the UN Declaration on the Rights of Indigenous Peoples.[207]

The principle of common heritage of mankind has as its starting point a concept similar to that of the public domain, but to this is added a social responsibility framework. Common heritage of mankind proposes that 'all people would be expected to share in the management of a common space area' and economic benefits from the exploitation of that space 'would be shared internationally.'[208] Its traditional application in the context of natural resources also gives rise to two further aspects, namely that the use of the area 'must be limited exclusively to peaceful purposes' and that scientific research conducted therein 'would be freely and openly permissible, so long as the environment of the common space area was in no way physically threatened or ecologically impaired.'[209] The deep sea bed is the most commonly identified common heritage of mankind space.[210]

There are not obvious reasons for treating geographic names, like the deep sea bed, as a common resource managed and accessible by all, with the profits of any economic exploitation to be divided globally and equally. On the contrary, several compelling bases of private legal rights in geographic names have been identified in this study, and the existence of these rights weighs against treating geographic names as a communal resource. Private rights also underpin domain names, the fundamental building blocks of the DNS. Some argue that this is not the most appropriate model, that the internet should 'be exploited for the benefit of the people of the world',[211] and that its governance by a corporation is inappropriate to achieve that aim.

For the internet to be managed as a common resource, its fundamental components must all be shared internationally and decisions respecting its development must be geared to achieving total equality of access. These notions are not prima facie inconsistent with the object of ICANN, the California non-profit public benefit corporation established to oversee

207. UN Declaration on the Rights of Indigenous Peoples (2 Oct. 2007) G.A. Res. A/RES/61/295.

208. Christopher C. Joyner, *Legal Implications of the Concept of the Common Heritage of Mankind*, 35(1) Int'l & Comp. L. Q. 190, 191–192 (1986) (internal citations omitted).

209. *Id.*, 192.

210. Dolliver M. Nelson, *Reflections on the 1982 Convention on the Law of the Sea*, in *The Law of the Sea: Progress and Prospects* 33–34 (Richard Barnes & David Ong eds, Oxford University Press 2006). Antarctica is also put forward as a potential common heritage space. J.M. Spectar, *Saving the Ice Princess: NGOs, Antarctica & International Law in the New Millenium*, 23 Suffolk Transnational L. Rev. 57 (1999).

211. Chander, *The New, New Property*, 750.

domain name system policy, as articulated in the 'Core Values' in section 1.2 of its 1 October 2016 Bylaws. The transition of ICANN in 2016 from US government contractor to independent entity confirms ICANN's legitimacy in the eyes of the global internet community and the failure (at least for now) of apparent attempts to shift operational and policy control over the DNS to an international intergovernmental organization. To be precise, the transition to an independent ICANN was expressly conditioned upon avoidance of that outcome, with the US Department of Commerce stating that 'it would not accept a plan that replaced NTIA's [the National Telecommunications and Information Administration] role with a government-led or intergovernmental organization solution.'[212]

Shifting the internet and its DNS out of the private sector-led 'multi-stakeholder'[213] model championed by ICANN and into shared global management (e.g., to the International Telecommunications Union ('ITU')) no longer seems necessary given that ICANN's independence has the equivalent effect of quashing claims to 'ownership' by any sovereign, or even by all mankind. This conceptually should turn the focus unambiguously towards universal access and the motivation in policy decision-making conclusively towards the long-term greater good.[214] Yet while such radical thinking is in many ways a desirable path for the internet to take, it would unquestionably be fraught with practical and legal difficulties too numerous to list here. These difficulties do not make treating the internet as the common heritage of mankind impossible, but this is not an outcome to be taken lightly or assumed to be inevitable, even from ICANN's ambitious transition to independence.

Additionally, while it is conceptually not difficult to apply such thinking to the governance model, the same is not true for the domain names that are the primary components of the system under governance. These have (if unintentionally) come to be viewed if not as property, then something analogous – a sort of 'third generation' or 'virtual property'.[215] If treating the internet as we treat the deep sea bed requires treating domain names as belonging to all mankind, any property or related proprietary rights in domain names, the most fundamental components of the DNS, should arguably be extinguished. Such an outcome is entirely antithetical to the way

212. 'The NTIA's legacy role has long been a source of irritation to foreign governments and prompted calls by some governments to push for the UN, International Telecommunications Union, or another intergovernmental organisation to take over stewardship of the DNS.' National Telecommunications and Information Administration – US Department of Commerce, *Q and A on IANA Stewardship Transition*, https://www.ntia.doc.gov/other-publication/2016/q-and-iana-stewardship-transition-0 (16 Aug. 2016).

213. *Ibid.*

214. Joyner, 194.

215. David Nelmark, *Virtual Property: The Challenges of Regulating Intangible, Exclusionary Property Interests Such as Domain Names*, 3(1) Northwestern J. Tech. & Intell. Prop. 1 (2004). Chik, *Lord of Your Domain, But Master of None*.

the DNS currently operates, and also raises issues of takings of property as discussed earlier in this chapter in the context of the human right to property. At this point in time it is difficult to imagine the occurrence of such a massive shift in thinking.

Sharing the proceeds of exploiting common heritage resources internationally – this is, after all, the social conscience component upon which the principle of common heritage of mankind is based – is also antithetical to the way we presently view and use the privatized internet. In the face of ICANN's non-profit status, questions have notably been raised about its use of the 'approximately USD 350 million'[216] generated by new gTLD applications.[217] ICANN's response, that 'the community will be consulted as to how that excess should be used',[218] while supportive of the multi-stakeholder governance model, does not equate to sharing the proceeds of exploiting common heritage resources internationally.

In summary, the current model of internet governance leverages the spirit of the doctrine of the common heritage of mankind without embracing it fully. To do so would require fundamental changes, not just to the governance model itself, but to the now firmly established and jealously defended private rights in the domain names so fundamental to the Domain Name System. Treating the internet, the DNS, and names used in that context as the common heritage of mankind thus reveals itself to be an interesting theory, but one that is implausible in practice at this point in time.

9.4 CONCLUSIONS ON HUMAN RIGHTS ENCOMPASSING RIGHTS TO GEOGRAPHIC NAMES

It is human nature to identify with the communities in which one lives. Modern multi-layered societies give rise to the likelihood that each person makes multiple associations, linking him or herself to a family, a local community, a professional community, a linguistic community, a subnational region, a nation, a supranational region. One association is no less important than the other in generating a complete picture of who a person is as a human being and how the person perceives his or her place in this world and wishes

216. ICANN, *TAS Interruption: Update (21 May 2012)*, http://newgtlds.icann.org/en/announcements-and-media/latest.

217. *See for example* R. Shawn Gunnarson, *Modest Proposals for gTLD Profits*, CircleID (27 Oct. 2011) (available at http://www.circleid.com/posts/modest_proposals_for_gtld_profits); Michael Berkens, *Beckstrom: 'I Took ICANN From $57 Million Under Management To $444 Million'*, The Domains (25 Jun. 2012) (available at http://www.thedomains.com/2012/06/25/beckstrom-i-took-icann-from-57-million-under-management-to-444-million/).

218. ICANN, *Frequently Asked Questions: 1.7 Is ICANN Initiating the New gTLD Program to Make Money?*, http://newgtlds.icann.org/en/applicants/customer-service/faqs/faqs-en.

others to perceive him or her. To limit a person's ability to articulate this sense of belonging is arguably to limit his or her freedom, and therefore violate the most fundamental aspects of his or her humanity. There are thus clear links between human rights and human beings' innate habit of self-identification.

This chapter has considered the most prominent links between human rights and geographic self-identification by analysing the rights to national identity and self-determination, freedom of expression, culture, language and property, as well as the doctrines of the public domain, public property, and common heritage of mankind. Of these, the right to freedom of expression and cultural rights have in particular been shown to offer clear bases for a person's right to use a geographic name. These rights are not absolute, but they do require consideration by States in making, reacting and responding to applications for geographic new gTLDs. New gTLD registries should also consider the issues noted in this chapter when developing supplemental policies that restrict the registration of geographic names as domain names in their newly created gTLDs.

The human right to freedom of expression as protected under international law recognizes a person's right not to have access to a geographic name prevented unless this poses a rationally articulated threat to national security or public order. Geographic names are not inherently threatening to national security or public order. Although the contexts in which they are used could give rise to such an interpretation, the existence of threats can only be determined on a case-by-case basis, so a universal rule restricting control of geographic names on this basis is inappropriate. States' objections to geographic domain names or strings should be scrutinized to ensure that they 'specify the precise nature of the threat allegedly posed by'[219] the applicant's registration of that name in the DNS.

The human right to culture has also been shown to recognize a person's right to use a geographic name; this right is limited in terms of who may claim it (members of an identifiable cultural group) and when it may be claimed (where the name is integral and there is a risk of direct harm to the culture as a result of the State's action). Analogous arguments have been successfully made linking non-interference with land to the existence, practice and preservation of culture. In the context of the DNS and given the integral role played by the internet in creating, preserving and communicating culture, government actions preventing a cultural group from possessing an online identity and a space in which to freely express and practice its culture could be seen to impinge upon free participation in online cultural life, if the community desires to engage online. Importantly, just as it should not be assumed that governments have superior rights in geographic names, it should not be assumed that the citizenry they govern wish for them to exercise any such rights on their behalf.

219. *Keun-Tae Kim v. Republic of Korea*, para. 12.5.

It is therefore a principal conclusion of this study that the individual's human right to freedom of expression and the individual's human right to culture stand in the way of a policy of recognizing exclusive rights of States in geographic names' use in the DNS. It is inappropriate to assume that only States have rights in geographic names, or that States' actions inherently further the rights of affected individuals, or that these rights necessarily always trump the rights of other parties. Going forward, changes to ICANN's *gTLD Applicant Guidebook* respecting geographic names are warranted to acknowledge the existence of the rights of non-State others in geographic names. In the interim, States should consider the impact of these rights upon their decision-making in relation to new gTLDs and reflect this consideration in their input through GAC representatives into ICANN's policy development processes.

Although the other rights examined in this chapter offer only scant support for the existence of rights in geographic names, some nevertheless serve to limit State action and should therefore also be borne in mind going forward in DNS policy-making. The human right of self-determination gives to 'peoples' a right to be involved in decision-making respecting geographic names and their use in the DNS. The human right of nationality ensures that State decisions regarding geographic names do not put a person's possession of a (though not a *specific*) nationality at risk. The human right to language prevents State actions respecting geographic names and their use in the DNS that discriminate on the basis of language.

This is the current and most visible protection available under international human rights law to geographic names, bearing in mind that this area is involved in an ongoing state of development and additional rights may be recognized even in the not-too-distant future. An agreement on the protection of cultural expressions remains a work in progress, as does an agreement on the protection of traditional knowledge. Custom may also develop out of the provision in the Declaration of the Rights of Indigenous Peoples for indigenous peoples to 'retain their own names for communities, [and] places'.

Notwithstanding the existence of human rights encompassing a right to geographic names, there remains the practical problem in the context of the DNS of exclusivity; even if persons or peoples have these rights, it is practically impossible for more than one claimant or group of claimants to exercise them by registering them as domain names, given the technological requirement of absolute name uniqueness. Neither the law nor ICANN have provided an adequate means of prioritizing or accommodating these interests; ICANN's approach in new gTLD allocation is to resolve otherwise unresolvable conflicts by auction.[220] While this avoids ICANN having to make overt value judgments on specific gTLD applications, it embeds in the

220. ICANN, *gTLD Applicant Guidebook*, s. 4.2.2.

New gTLD Program as a whole a value judgment of prioritizing exceptionally funded applicants. On the other side of the coin, affected interested communities must engage proactively and constructively with the DNS expansion process; States' international obligations to their citizens are not satisfied by GAC representatives raising non-specific complaints expressing merely general notions of discomfort with a new gTLD application with no reference to relevant provisions of law.

ICANN, too, bears responsibility in this regard: as gTLD policy matures, and having affirmatively proved the existence of some rights and disproved others, due consideration to these rights and their role in cultural diversity may require the ICANN Board to make decisions. Having taken on the responsibility of ensuring that new gTLD policy is consistent with rights recognized in international law, ICANN has as its disposal legal counsel and the full complement of laws and soft law instruments to assist it in this process. Decisions (or the avoidance of taking decisions) cannot any longer be justified on the basis of uncertainty as to whether legal rights are recognized, or on the basis of fear of a particular government's response to their acknowledgement; justifications must be transparent, precisely articulated, substantive, and not inconsistent with recognized and applicable law. Of particular potential value in the context of human rights is the guidance offered by the UNESCO Convention on the Protection and Promotion of the Diversity of Cultural Expressions.

Summary of Conclusions

The internet makes information easily, cheaply and instantaneously accessible without regard to borders, language or cultural differences. As a result, there is wider use and a correspondingly higher likelihood that others will have exposure to uses of geographic names. This is precisely the situation that ICANN attempts to manage in the internet Domain Name System ('DNS') through policy on geographic names implemented as the *gTLD Applicant Guidebook*. The approach taken is twofold: first, to bar applications constituted of country and territory names, and second, to require government authorization for applications constituted of other types of geographic names. This approach is based on untested assumptions about the existence and exclusivity or priority status of governments' rights in geographic names.

This study has been undertaken to remove the need for policy-making on the basis of assumptions about States' rights in geographic names. The legal bases of rights examined in this study fall into two broad, overlapping categories: bases that recognize the potential for States' rights in geographic names, and bases that recognize the potential for non-State others' rights in geographic names. Importantly, none of the bases within either category proves the exclusivity or priority of States' rights. Within both categories, certain bases disprove the exclusivity of States' rights, while others neither prove nor disprove exclusivity. As to each, the following findings have been made and conclusions reached:

(1) Within the first category of legal bases recognizing rights of States in geographic names fall the principle of sovereignty, trademarks, geographical indications, the right to prevent unfair competition and the protection against dilution afforded well-known trademarks. While rights are potentially available to States under each of these bases, none is absolute. The principle of sovereignty must logically

incorporate an ability of States to control geographic names within State borders, but attempts to exercise control outside of borders risks impingement on other States' sovereignty. The principle of sovereignty and its related doctrines thus disprove exclusivity as between States, while offering scant guidance as to how disputes between States can be resolved. Further, the principle of sovereignty does not conclusively create or incorporate substantive, proprietary legal rights in geographic names. The other bases of law falling within this category that do create substantive, proprietary rights are not exclusively available to States and do not prioritize the recognition of States' rights over those of non-State others.

(2) Within the second category of legal bases recognizing the rights of non-State others in geographic names (and therefore disproving the exclusivity of States' rights) fall trademarks, geographical indications, and human rights to expression and culture. The human rights to expression and culture are expressly unavailable to States, with the result that any rights States do have in geographic names cannot as a blanket proposition be considered exclusive. The fact that many countries do not prohibit the use or registration of geographic terms as a trademark and the recognition (albeit limited) afforded geographical indications under international law further support a finding that States' rights in geographic names are not exclusive. With the exception of geographical indications, none of these bases of rights expressly cover geographic names, but all offer the potential for recognition provided that certain criteria are met or factual circumstances are established.

(3) Also falling within the second category of legal bases recognizing rights of non-State others in geographic names are bases that neither specifically prove nor disprove exclusivity of States' rights, because they do not recognize proprietary rights in geographic names as such and instead place behavioural limitations upon their use. Into this grouping fall the right to prevent confusion with a competitor and the protection against dilution afforded well-known marks, as well as the human rights to nationality, self-determination, language and property. Restrictions on geographic names and their use in the DNS on these bases must be individually, contextually scrutinized. A blanket policy of restriction based on exclusive proprietary-style government rights is therefore not supported by these bases of international law.

(4) Not falling within either of these two broad categories because of their current lack of recognition at the international level are State personality rights and cultural property rights.

(5) As new gTLD policy development recommences and enters a new phase, it is critical to make absolutely explicit the following point, which was implicit in the first edition of this work: the application

of the above findings leads to the conclusion that the assumption of exclusivity of States' rights in geographic names is incorrect, as this fails to acknowledge the recognition under international law of non-State others' rights in geographic names. Such an acknowledgement is called for by the adoption by ICANN's Board of Directors of the recommendation of the Generic Names Supporting Organization, empowered under ICANN's Bylaws to develop policy for gTLDs,[1] to ensure that new gTLDs do not 'infringe the existing legal rights of others that are recognized or enforceable under generally accepted and internationally recognized principles of law'.[2] If the rationale for the reservation of country and territory names, the imposition of an authorization requirement on other geographic names, and/or the issuance of a Governmental Advisory Committee Early Warning notice or advice is based upon exclusive government rights in geographic names, this cannot stand, and the *gTLD Applicant Guidebook* must be amended. If a rationale for restrictions imposed on geographic gTLDs by the *gTLD Applicant Guidebook* has not been articulated or is not required to be articulated, this too must be corrected in future versions and their applications.

(6) The application of these findings additionally leads to the conclusion that although rights of non-State others in geographic names are recognized under international law, in particular through the human rights of expression and culture, those bases do not require recognition in DNS policy as private property rights in geographic names as such. This being the case, it is appropriate that geographic names as such are not per se mandatorily actionable on these bases under new gTLD rights protection measures (the Legal Rights Objection, the Trademark Claims service and the Uniform Rapid Suspension procedure). Where proprietary legal rights are recognized for a given name, however, these should be capable of reflection in the New gTLD Program rights protection mechanisms.

(7) It has also been shown that geographic names receive the greatest protection under international law and in DNS policy when they satisfy the criteria for registration as trademarks. The conclusions reached in this study lead to a prediction that the New gTLD Program will be the catalyst for significant changes in domestic trademark laws, with Switzerland as a model. These changes will have the effect of bringing geographic names within the scope of

1. ICANN, *Bylaws*, Art. 11, s. 11.1, https://www.icann.org/resources/pages/governance/bylaws-en (as amended 1 Oct. 2016).
2. GNSO, *Final Report on the Introduction of New Generic Top-Level Domains*, Recommendation 3, http://gnso.icann.org/issues/new-gtlds/pdp-dec05-fr-parta-08aug07.htm (8 Aug. 2007).

domestic trademark subject matter, which will have the concomitant effect of bringing geographic names within the scope of legal rights recognized and protected in DNS policy.

The focus in this study on legal rights reflects the fact that governments' assertions of control over geographic names have to date been articulated (explicitly or implicitly) in proprietary legal rights terms. Having disproven in this study a basis in international law for exclusive proprietary-style government rights in geographic names and precisely identified the limited bases upon which (and conditions in which) governments' rights can be recognized (albeit not exclusively), the discourse could most helpfully shift away from the language of exclusive proprietary rights to the concern for preventing any likely harm to internet users and consumers. This must be given due consideration in current and future new gTLD policy development, while bearing in mind that the simple act of registering a geographic domain name is not inherently or automatically an unfair commercial practice (indeed there are numerous UDRP decisions to support this conclusion), that international unfair competition norms require the identification of market competitors, and that generalized confusion is not sufficient to enliven those norms. Further, it must be noted that, to date, no data has been presented to support an overarching conclusion that private use of a geographically relevant name in the DNS is inherently likely to confuse or harm internet users. Given differing global markets, users and standards of commercial 'unfairness' and general behaviour, future policy would be most effective if it ensured that concerns are addressed through domestic norms rather than an awkwardly compromised global norm.

This book began by quoting the words of Timothy Denton, a lawyer and consultant specializing in internet domain name policy. His words appear at the start of this work as a prompt not to simply accept assumptions about legal rights in geographic names, but they could just as logically be placed here as an overarching summary of the delicate interplay between legal rights and internet DNS policy at this critical, dynamic period in the system's development. Lawyers and technologists may debate the theoretical need to do something about the inconsistencies identified in this book between geographic names' treatment in the *gTLD Applicant Guidebook* and international law, but in practice it is impossible to divorce the DNS from the 'real'[3] (or 'offline') world in which it operates. Contemporary society may be in a transition period between the supremacy of law and the supremacy of technology, but for now the two are inextricably intertwined and interdependent. Questions about technology cannot be answered without an understanding of the impact of law, and vice versa. States' reactions to proposed new

3. WIPO, *Final Report of the WIPO Internet Domain Name Process: The Management of Internet Names and Addresses: Intellectual Property Issues*, para. 22, http://www.wipo.int/amc/en/processes/process1/report/index.html (30 Apr. 1999).

internet top-level domains may in the future result in changes to the recognition of rights under international law in geographic names through treaty, custom or general principles of international law. ICANN's *gTLD Applicant Guidebook* may at some point in the future be considered evidence of the crystallization of recognition in international law of rights in geographic names. The two processes – development of domain name policy and development of international law – are interrelated, and are likely to remain so for the foreseeable future.

From Denton's words can be distilled a need for dialogue within the ICANN community to ensure that the conflicts that arise along the path of DNS development do not result in its stagnation. In a similar vein it was once remarked in the ISOC: 'If the Internet stumbles, it will not be because we lack for technology, vision, or motivation. It will be because we cannot set a direction and march collectively into the future.'[4] This study, and its continuation in this second edition, has been undertaken with the intention of contributing to the setting of direction in current and future policy development on geographic names and their treatment in DNS, with the hope that the conclusions reached will facilitate, rather than impede, our collective march into the future.

4. Barry M. Leiner et al., *A Brief History of the Internet*, Internet Society, http://www.internetsociety.org/internet/what-internet/history-internet/brief-history-internet.

Bibliography

Abbott, Frederick M.; Cottier, Thomas; and Gurry, Francis. *International Intellectual Property in an Integrated World Economy*. Aspen Publishers, 2007.

African Regional Intellectual Property Organization, *Entry into force of the ARIPO Swakopmund Protocol on the Protection of Traditional Knowledge and Expressions of Folklore*. Available at http://www.aripo.org/news-events-publications/news/item/54-entry-into-force-of-the-aripo-swakopmund-protocol-on-the-protection-of-traditional-knowledge-and-expressions-of-folklore.

AIPPI. *Effective protection against unfair competition under Article 10bis Paris Convention of 1883*. AIPPI Y.B. 1994/II, 398 (1994).

Akehurst, Michael. *Custom as a Source of International Law.* 47 British Y.B. Int'l Law 1 (1974–1975).

Alexander, Fiona M. Letter to Rod Beckstrom, President and CEO, ICANN (2 Dec. 2000). Available at http://forum.icann.org/lists/5gtld-guide/msg00013.html.

ALI, *Publications Catalog: Restatements of the Law – Foreign Relations Law of the United States*. Available at https://www.ali.org/publications/#publication-type-restatements (*Restatement (Third) of the Foreign Relations Law of the United States* § 201 Comment a (1987)).

Alvarez, José E. *Positivism Regained, Nihilism Postponed*. 15 Michigan J. Int'l L. 747 (1994).

Alvarez, José E. *International Organizations as Law-makers*. Oxford University Press, 2005.

Amazon EU S.à.r.l. v. ICANN (.AMAZON), International Centre for Dispute Resolution, Expert Report of Professor Heather Ann Forrest, Dr.(iur.), LL.M., J.D., B.A., 23, 26 Feb. 2016. Available at https://www.icann.org/en/system/files/files/irp-amazon-export-report-forrest-02mar16-en.pdf.

Amazon EU S.à.r.l. v. ICANN (.AMAZON), International Centre for Dispute Resolution, Request by Amazon EU S.à.r.l. for Independent Review,

19–20, 1 Mar. 2016. Available at https://www.icann.org/en/system/files/files/irp-amazon-request-redacted-02mar16-en.pdf.

American Jurisprudence 2d. *Flag*.

Anaya, S. James. *Customary International Law*, 92 Am. Soc. Int'l L. Proc. 41 (1998).

Anaya, S. James. *Indigenous Peoples in International Law*. 2d ed. Oxford University Press, 2004.

Anticybersquatting Consumer Protection Act, 15 U.S.C. § 1125(d)(1)(b)(i)(I).

Antons, Christoph. *Traditional Cultural Expressions and Their Significance for Development in a Digital Environment: Examples from Australia and Southeast Asia*. In *Intellectual Property and Traditional Cultural Expressions in a Digital Environment*. Christoph Beat Graber & Mira Burri-Nenova eds Edward Elgar, 2008.

Arewa, Olufunmilayo B. *TRIPS and Traditional Knowledge: Local Communities, Local Knowledge, and Global Intellectual Property Frameworks*. 10 Marquette Intell. Prop. L. Rev. 155 (2006).

Asociación PuntoGal. *Official web[site] of Asociación PuntoGal*. http://www.puntogal.org.

Baderin, Mashood A. *The African Commission on Human and Peoples' Rights and the Implementation of Economic, Social and Cultural Rights in Africa*. In *Economic, Social and Cultural Rights in Action*. Mashood A. Baderin and Robert McCorquodale eds Oxford University Press, 2007.

Beat Graber, Christoph and Burri-Nenova, Mira eds *Intellectual Property and Traditional Cultural Expressions in a Digital Environment*. Edward Elgar, 2008.

Beckham, Brian. *WIPO Arbitration and Mediation Center Observations on ICANN's Proposed Measures for Letter/Letter Two-Character ASCII Labels to Avoid Confusion with Corresponding Country Codes*. (4 Aug. 2016). Available at https://forum.icann.org/lists/comments-proposed-measures-two-char-08jul16/msg00006.html.

Bella, Timothy. *The '7 Dirty Words' Turn 40, but They're Still Dirty. The Atlantic* (24 May 2012). Available at http://www.theatlantic.com/entertainment/archive/2012/05/the-7-dirty-words-turn-40-but-theyre-still-dirty/257374/.

Bently, Lionel and Sherman, Brad. *The Impact of European Geographical Indications on National Rights in Member States*. 96 Trademark Rep. 850 (2006).

Beresford, Lynne. *Geographical Indications: The Current Landscape*. 17 Fordham Intell. Prop. Media & Ent. L.J. 979 (2006–2007).

Berkens, Michael. *Beckstrom: 'I Took ICANN From $57 Million Under Management To $444 Million', The Domains* (25 Jun. 2012). Available at http://www.thedomains.com/2012/06/25/beckstrom-i-took-icann-from-57-million-under-management-to-444-million/.

Berman, Nathaniel. *Sovereignty in Abeyance: Self-Determination and International Law*. 7 Wis. Int'l L.J. 51 (1988).

Bernhardt, Roger; Beyerlin, Ulrich; Doehring, Karl; and Frowein, Jochen Abr. *Book Review*. 86(3) Am. J. Int'l L. 608 (1992).

Berniker, Mark. *NeuLevel Settles Internet Domain Class-Action Suit*. InternetNews.com (2 Jan. 2003). Available at http://www.internetnews.com/xSP/article.php/1563201/NeuLevel+Settles+Internet+Domain+ClassAction+Suit.htm.

Bettinger, Torsten ed. *Domain Name Law and Practice: An International Handbook*. Oxford University Press, 2005.

Bilder, Richard B. *An Overview of International Human Rights Law*. In *Guide to International Human Rights Practice*. Hurst Hannum ed. Transnational Publishers, 2004.

Billig, Michael. *Banal Nationalism*. Sage Publications, 1995.

Biofuels Journal. *New dotCoop Internet Domain Offers Trademark/Brand Protection for Companies Who Can't Get.coop Sites*. (15 May 2002). Available at http://www.biofuelsjournal.com/articles/new_dotcoop_internet_domain_offers_trademark_brand_protection_for_companies_who_can_t_get__coop_sites-15011.html.

Blum, Yehuda Z. *Russia Takes Over the Soviet Union's Seat at the United Nations*. 3(2) Eur. J. Int'l L. 354 (1992).

Bodenhausen, Georg Hendrik Christiaan. *Guide to the Application of the Paris Convention for the Protection of Industrial Property as revised at Stockholm in 1967*. United Bureaux for the Protection of Intellectual Property, 1968.

Boland, Stephen and Dollery, Brian. *The Value and Viability of Sovereignty-Conferred Rights in MIRAB Economies: The Case of Tuvalu*. University of New England Working Paper Series in Economics 2005-9, 17. Available at https://www.une.edu.au/__data/assets/pdf_file/0010/67969/econ-2005-9.pdf.

Bonsall, Allan and Harrison, John. *Brand Aid: The Secrets of Consumer Speak*. Estee Media, 2006.

Bowers, Stephen A. *Location, Location, Location: The Case Against Extending Geographical Indication Protection under the TRIPS Agreement*. 31(2) A.I.P.L.A. Q. J. 129 (2003).

Bowrey, Kathryn. *Law & Internet Cultures*. Cambridge University Press, 2005.

Boyle, Alan and Chinkin, Christine. *The Making of International Law*. Oxford University Press, 2007.

Boyle, James. *Foreword: The Opposite of Property?* 66 L. & Contemp. Probs. 1 (2003).

Brierly, James Leslie. *The Law of Nations: An Introduction to the International Law of Peace*. 6th ed. revised. Oxford University Press, 1963.

Bröhmer, Jürgen and Greaney, Jennifer. *Der Schutz der Kulturgüter der australischen Ureinwohner*, in *Verfassung – Völkerrecht – Kulturgüterschutz*. Michaela Wittinger, Rudolf Wendt and Georg Ress eds Duncker & Humblot, 2011.

Broude, Tomer. *Taking 'Trade and Culture' Seriously: Geographical Indications and Cultural Protection in WTO Law*. 26 U. Pa. J. Int'l Econ. L. 623 (2005).

Brown Jr, Ralph S. *Advertising and the Public Interest: Legal Protection of Trade Symbols*. 57 Yale L.J. 1165 (1948).

Brown, Michael F. *Who Owns Native Culture?* Harvard University Press, 2003.

Brownlie, Ian. *Principles of Public International Law*. 7th ed. Oxford University Press, 2008.

Burchill, Richard. *Democracy and the Promotion and Protection of Socio-Economic Rights*. In *Economic, Social and Cultural Rights in Action*. Mashood A. Baderin and Robert McCorquodale eds Oxford University Press, 2007.

Buri, Ueli. *Die Verwechselbarkeit von Internet Domain Names nach schweizerischem Firmen-, Marken-, Namens- und Lauterkeitsrecht*. Doctoral Dissertation in Law, Bern. 2000.

Burri-Nenova, Mira. *The Long Tail of the Rainbow Serpent: New Technologies and the Protection and Promotion of Traditional Cultural Expressions*. In *Intellectual Property and Traditional Cultural Expressions in a Digital Environment*. Christoph Beat Graber and Mira Burri-Nenova eds Edward Elgar, 2008.

Byers, Michael. *Abuse of Rights: An Old Principle, a New Age*. 47 McGill L.J. 389 (2002).

Cahir, John. *The Public Domain: Right or Liberty?* In *Intellectual Property: The Many Faces of the Public Domain*. Hector Macqueen and Charlotte Waelde eds Edward Elgar, 2007.

Calboli, Irene. *Expanding the Protection of Geographical Indications of Origin under TRIPS: 'Old' Debate or 'New' Opportunity?* 10(2) Marq. Intell. Prop. L. Rev. 182 (2006).

Callmann, Rudolf & Louis Altman. *Callmann on Unfair Competition, Trademarks and Monopolies*. 4th ed. Thomson-West, 1997.

Cass, Deborah Z. *The Constitutionalization of the World Trade Organization: Legitimacy, Democracy, and Community in the International Trading System*. Oxford University Press, 2005.

ccNSO. *Cross-Community Working Group on Use of Country/Territory Names as TLDs*. Available at http://ccnso.icann.org/workinggroups/ccwg-unct.htm.

ccNSO. *Non-PDP Study Group on Use of Names for Countries and Territories*. Available at http://ccnso.icann.org/workinggroups/unct wg.htm.

CCWG Accountability. *Supplemental Final Proposal on Work Stream 1 Recommendations* (23 Feb. 2016). Available at https://www.icann.org/en/system/files/files/ccwg-accountability-supp-proposal-work-stream-1-recs-23feb16-en.pdf.

CENTR. *CENTR Best Practice Guidelines for ccTLD Managers: Version 2 Adopted 10 May 2001*. Available at http://www.icann.org/en/cctlds/centr-2nd-best-practices-20may01.htm.

Cerf, Vint. *RFC 2468: I Remember IANA*. *RFC Editor* (17 Oct. 1998). Available at http://www.rfc-editor.org/rfc/rfc2468.txt.

Chander, Anupam. *The New, New Property*. 81 Texas L. Rev. 715 (2003).

Chander, Anupam and Sunder, Madhavi. *The Romance of the Public Domain*. 92 Cal. L. Rev. 1331 (2004).

Charnovitz, Steve. *The Legal Status of the Doha Declarations*. 5 J. Int'l Econ. L. 207 (2002).

Cheng, Bin. *United Nations Resolutions on Outer Space: 'Instant' International Customary Law?* 5 Indian J. Int'l L. 23 (1965).

Chesmond, Rhonda. *Protection or Privatisation of Culture? The Cultural Dimension of the International Intellectual Property Debate on Geographical Indications of Origin*. 29(9) Eur. Intell. Prop. Rev. 379 (2007).

Chik, Warren B. *Lord of Your Domain, But Master of None: The Need to Harmonize and Recalibrate the Domain Name Regime of Ownership and Control*. 16 Int'l J. L. Info. Tech. 8 (2008).

Chodosh, Hiram E. *Neither Treaty nor Custom: The Emergence of Declarative International Law*. 26 Texas Int'l L.J. 87 (1991).

CircleID. *Key Members of Congress Call for Permanent ICANN-US Tie, CircleID Internet Infrastructure*. (5 Aug. 2009). Available at http://www.circleid.com/posts/key_members_of_congress_call_for_permanent_icann_us_tie/.

Cisneros, Oscar S. *Dot-PS: Domain Without a Country*. Wired.com. (12 Jan. 2001). Available at http://archive.wired.com/politics/law/news/2001/01/41135?currentPage=all.

Clapham, Andrew. *Human Rights Obligations of Non-State Actors*. Oxford University Press, 2006.

Clark, David D. *RFC 814: Name, Addresses, Ports and Routes*. *RFC Editor* (Jul. 1982). http://www.rfc-editor.org/rfc/rfc814.txt.

Clinton, William J. and Gore Jr., Albert. *A Framework For Global Electronic Commerce*. Office of the Executive. Available at http://clinton4.nara.gov/WH/New/Commerce/.

Coerper, M.G. *The Protection of Geographical Indications in the United States of America, with Particular Reference to Certification Marks*. 29(7/8) Industrial Property 232 (1990).

Conrad, Albrecht. *The Protection of Geographical Indications in the TRIPS Agreement*. 86 Trademark Rep. 11 (1996).

Coombe, Rosemary J. *The Cultural Life of Intellectual Properties: Authorship, Appropriation, and the Law*. Duke University Press, 1998.

Cottier, Thomas; Pauwelyn, Joost and Bürgi Bonanomi, Elisabeth eds. *Human Rights and International Trade*. Oxford University Press, 2006.

Cottier, Thomas. *The Prospects for Intellectual Property in GATT*. 28 Common Mkt. L. Rev. 383 (1991).

Cottier, Thomas. *The Impact of New Technologies on Multilateral Trade Regulation and Governance*. 72 Chicago-Kent L. Rev. 415 (1996).

Cottier, Thomas. *The Protection of Genetic Resources and Traditional Knowledge: Toward More Specific Rights and Obligations in World Trade Law*. 1 J. Int'l Econ. L. 555 (1998).

Cottier, Thomas. *The Agreement on Trade-Related Aspects of Intellectual Property Rights*. In *Trade and Intellectual Property Protection in WTO Law: Collected Essays*. Cameron May, 2005.

Cottier, Thomas and Panizzon, Marion. *Legal Perspectives on Traditional Knowledge: The Case for Intellectual Property Protection*. 7 J. Int'l Econ. L. 371 (2004).

Cottier, Thomas and Panizzon, Marion. *Traditional Knowledge and Geographical Indications: Foundations, Interests and Negotiating Positions*. In *Trade and Intellectual Property Protection in WTO Law: Collected Essays*. Cameron May, 2005.

Craven, Matthew C. R. *What's in a Name? The Former Yugoslav Republic of Macedonia and Issues of Statehood*. 16 Austl. Y.B. Int'l L. 199 (1995).

Crawford, James. *The Creation of States in International Law*. 2d ed. Clarendon Press, 2007.

Cringely, Robert X. *Nerds 2.0.1 (film)*. Available at http://www.sci.sdsu.edu/~stewart/cs440/nerds_2_0_1.html.

CSTB. *Signposts in Cyberspace: The Domain Name System and Internet Navigation*. National Academies Press, 2005.

Danilenko, Gennadiĭ Mikhaĭlovich. *Law-Making in the International Community*. Martinus Nijhoff, 1993.

Dawisha, Karen and Parrott, Bruce. *Russia and the New States of Eurasia: The Politics of Upheaval*. Cambridge University Press, 1995.

de Vittoria, Franciscus. *De Indis et de Iure Belli Relectiones*. In *Relectiones Theologicae XII*. Ernest Nys ed. Reprinted in *The Classics of International Law*. James Brown ed. 1917.

Degan, Vladmir Duro. *Sources of International Law*. Martinus Nijhoff, 1997.

Dengate-Thrush, Peter. Letter to Janis Karklins, Chairman of the Governmental Advisory Committee and Ambassador of Latvia to France. (22 Dec. 2009). Available at https://www.icann.org/en/system/files/files/dengate-thrush-to-karklins-22sep09-en.pdf.

Dengate-Thrush, Peter and Beckstrom, Rod. Letter to GNSO Council Members. (12 Oct. 2009). Available at http://gnso.icann.org/correspondence/beckstrom-to-gnso-council-12oct09-en.pdf.

Denton, Timothy. *RE: [gnso-rn-wg] Comments on ICANN/IANA Reserved Names Reports, 28 Feb. 2007*. Available at http://forum.icann.org/lists/gnso-rn-wg/msg00169.html.

Diamond, S.A. *The Historical Development of Trademarks*. 73 Trademark Rep. 22 (1983).

Dinwoodie, Graeme B. *The International Intellectual Property Law System: New Actors, New Institutions, New Sources*. 98 Am. Soc. Int'l L. Proc. 213 (2004).

DNSO Working Group-A, *DNSO WG-A Final Report to the Names Council.* 29 Jul. 1999. Available at http://www.dnso.org/dnso/notes/19990729.WGA-report.html.

DNSO Working Group B. *Working Group B (WG-B) Report*. Presented to DNSO Names Council on 15 May 2000. Available at http://www.dnso.org/wgroups/wg-b/Arc00/msg00963.html.

Domein Registreren, *.tel Sunrise Terms & Conditions*. (Jun. 2008). Archived at https://www.domein-registreren.nl/tel-voorwaarden_533.html.

Donner, Ruth. *The Regulation of Nationality in International Law*. 2d ed. Transnational Publishers, 1994.

Donuts. *Domains Protected Marks List Overview*. Available at http://www.donuts.domains/services/dpml/dpml-overview.

Donuts. *Comment on Proposed Measures for Letter/Letter Two-Character ASCII Codes. ICANN* (17 Aug. 2016). Available at https://forum.icann.org/lists/comments-proposed-measures-two-char-08jul16/pdfNH7eezpMIp.pdf.

dotBERLIN GmbH & Co. KG. *.berlin: Die Top-Level-Domain Für Berliner*. Available at http://dotberlin.de.

dotCYM. *April 2007 Newsletter*. Available at http://www.dotcym.org/home/?p=56.

Drahos, Peter. *BITS and BIPS: Bilateralism in Intellectual Property*. 4 J. World Intell. Prop. 791 (2001).

Dugard, John. *Recognition and the United Nations*. Cambridge University Press, 1987.

Emerson, Rupert. *Self-Determination*. 65 Am. J. Int'l L. 459 (1971).

Emerson, Chad D. *Wasting Time in Cyberspace: The UDRP's Inefficient Approach Toward Arbitrating Internet Domain Name Disputes*. 34 U. Baltimore L. Rev. 161 (2004).

Employ Media. *Trade Name Period version 1.0*. Formerly at http://www.employmedia.com/tradenameperiod.html (2005), archived at http://www.archive.org/web/web.php.

European Community. *Declaration on Yugoslavia and on the Guidelines on the Recognition of New States (Extraordinary European Political Cooperation Ministerial Meeting, Brussels, 16 Dec. 1991)*. 31 I.L.M. 1485 (1992).

EU-South Korea Free Trade Agreement, O.J. L 127, 14 May 2011. Available at http://eur-lex.europa.eu/JOHtml.do?uri=OJ:L:2011:127:SOM:EN:HTML.

Festa, Paul. *Controversial Domains Go to Civil Rights Groups. CNET News* (1 May 1998). Available at https://www.cnet.com/news/controversial-domains-go-to-civil-rights-groups/.

Fincham, Derek. *The Distinctiveness of Property and Heritage*. 115 Penn St. L. Rev. 641 (2011).

Fishman, Joseph P. *Locating the International Interest in Intranational Cultural Property Disputes*. 35 Yale J. Int'l L. 3347 (2010).

Fitzmaurice, Malgosia. *Actors and Factors in the Evolution of Treaty Norms (An Empirical Study)*. 4 Austrian Rev. Int'l & Eur. L. 1 (1999).

Flessas, Tatiana. *Cultural Property Defined, and Redefined as Nietzschean Aphorism*. 24 Cardozo L. Rev. 1067 (2003).

Floudas, Demetrius Andreas. *Pardon? A Name for a Conflict? FYROM's Dispute with Greece Revisited*, in *The New Balkans: Disintegration and Reconstruction*. George A. Kourvetaris et al. eds East European Monographs, 2002.

Fodella, Alessandro. *International Law and the Diversity of Indigenous Peoples*, 30 Vt. L. Rev. 565 (2006).

Footer, Mary E. and Beat Graber, Christoph, *Trade Liberalization and Cultural Policy*. 3(1) J. Int'l Econ. L. 115 (2000).

Forrest, Heather A. *Comments on the Scope of the Legal Rights Objection [3gtld-dispute] Chronological Index*. (23 Nov. 2009). Available at http://forum.icann.org/lists/3gtld-dispute/.

Forrest, Heather A. *Domain Name Allocation and Government Super-Prioritization: Lessons Learned from the UDRP Keep ICANN Out of the Business of Deciding What Is or is Not a Country*. 18(1) Vanderbilt J. Ent. & Tech. L. 1 (2015).

Forrest, Heather A. *Drawing a Line in the Constitutional Sand Between Congress and the Foreign Citizen 'Cybersquatter'*. 9(2) Wm. & Mary Bill Rts J. 461 (2001).

Forrest, Heather A. *The New Frontier: Country Brands and Their Legal Status under Australian Trade Mark Llaw*. 20(3) Austl. Intell. Prop. J. 127 (2009).

Forrest Martin, Francisco. *Delineating a Hierarchical Outline of International Law Sources and Norms*. 65(2) Saskatchewan L. Rev. 341 (2002).

Forrest Martin, Francisco; Schnably, Stephen J.; Slye, Ronald C.; Wilson, Richard; Falk, Richard; Simon, Jonathan S. and Koren, Edward. *International Human Rights Law and Practice: Cases, Treaties and Materials*. Kluwer Law International, 1997.

Franck, Thomas M. *The Emerging Right to Democratic Governance*. 86 Am. J. Int'l L. 46 (1992).

Franck, Thomas M. *Clan and Superclan: Loyalty, Identity and Community in Law and Practice*. 90 Am. J. Int'l L. 359 (1996).

Frankel, Susy. *WTO Application of 'the Customary Rules of Interpretation of Public International Law' to Intellectual Property*. 46 Va. J. Int'l L. 365 (2005–2006).

Frischmann, Brett and Weber Waller, Spencer. *Revitalizing Essential Facilities*. 75 Antitrust L.J. 1 (2008).

Froomkin, A. Michael. *Wrong Turn in Cyberspace: Using ICANN to Route Around the APA and the Constitution.* 50 Duke L.J. 17 (2000).

Froomkin, A. Michael. *ICANN's Uniform Dispute Resolution Policy: Causes and (Partial) Cures*. 67 Brooklyn L. Rev. 605 (2002).

Froomkin, A. Michael. *When We Say USTM, We Mean It!* 41 Houston L. Rev. 839 (2004–2005).

Fundació.cat. *Normativa del domini.cat*. Available at http://fundacio.cat/ca/domini/sobre-el-cat/normativa.

Fundació.cat. *.CAT Domain Name Registration Agreement (English version)*. Available at http://fundacio.cat/sites/default/files/cat-registrationagrmt.pdf.

Fung, Brian. *Amazon Wants to Control '.amazon.' But so Does Half of South America. The Washington Post* (23 Jun. 2015). Available at https://www.washingtonpost.com/news/the-switch/wp/2015/06/23/amazon-wants-to-control-amazon-but-so-does-practically-half-of-south-america/.

FutureBrand, *Country Brand Index 2014-15*. Available at http://www.futurebrand.com/uploads/CBI-14_15-LR.pdf.

GAC. *GAC Early Warning – Submittal --- (Early Warnings received from GAC Member(s) after the EW Deadline: Application 1-868-66341 (WINE))*. Available at https://gacweb.icann.org/display/gacweb/Early+Warnings+received+from+GAC+Member%28s%29+after+the+EW+Deadline?preview=/27132095/27197596/GAC%20EW%20Submission-Iran-1-1223-37711%20(WINE).docx.

GAC. *Two-Letter Second-Level Domains*. Available at https://gacweb.icann.org/display/gacweb/Two-Letter+Second-Level+Domains.

GAC. *Meeting 10 Communiqué: Montevideo 7-8 September 2001. ICANN*. Available at https://gacweb.icann.org/display/gacweb/GAC+10+Meeting+Montevideo%2C+Uruguay+-+7-8+September+2001.

GAC. *Principles Regarding New gTLDs. ICANN* (28 Mar. 2007). Available at https://archive.icann.org/en/topics/new-gtlds/gac-principles-regarding-new-gtlds-28mar07-en.pdf.

GAC. *GAC Communiqué: New Delhi. ICANN* (Feb. 2008). Available at https://gacweb.icann.org/display/gacweb/GAC+31+Meeting+New+Delhi%2C+India+9-14+February+2008.

GAC. *About the GAC. ICANN* (2011). Available at https://gacweb.icann.org/display/gacweb/About+the+GAC.

GAC. *GAC indicative scorecard on new gTLD outstanding issues listed in the GAC Cartagena Communiqué*. (23 Feb. 2011). Available at http://www.icann.org/en/topics/new-gtlds/gac-scorecard-23feb11-en.pdf.

GAC. *GAC Early Warning – Submittal Amazon-BR-PE-58086. ICANN* (20 Nov. 2012). Available at https://gacweb.icann.org/download/attachments/27131927/Amazon-BR-PE-58086.pdf?version=1&modificationDate=1353452622000&api=v2.

GAC. *GAC Early Warning – Submittal Patagonia-AFR-78254*. (20 Nov. 2012). Available at https://gacweb.icann.org/display/gacweb/GAC+Early+Warnings?preview=/27131927/27197990/Patagonia-AR-78254.pdf.

GAC. *GAC Early Warning – Submittal Vin-FR-23177*. (20 Nov. 2012). Available at https://gacweb.icann.org/display/gacweb/GAC+Early+Warnings?preview=/27131927/27197919/Vin-FR-23177.pdf.

GAC. *GAC Communiqué – Buenos Aires, Argentina. ICANN* (20 Nov. 2013). Available at https://gacweb.icann.org/download/attachments/28278854/FINAL_Buenos_Aires_GAC_Communique_20131120.pdf?version=1&modificationDate=1390424520000&api=v2.

GAC. *GAC Communiqué – Singapore. ICANN* (27 Mar. 2014). Available at https://gacweb.icann.org/display/GACADV/2014-03-27-spa.

GAC. *The Protection of Geographic Names in the New gTLDs [sic] Process: V3 – August 29 2014. ICANN*. Available at https://gacweb.icann.org/display/gacweb/Community+Input+-+The+protection+of+Geographic+Names+in+the+New+gTLDs+process?preview=/35455403/35622234/Geo%20names%20in%20new%20gTLDs%20Updated%20%20V3%20%2029%20august%202014%5B4%5D.pdf.

GAC. *GAC Working Group to Examine the Protection of Geographic Names in Any Future Expansion of gTLDs: Working Papers. ICANN* (27 Jun. 2016). Available at https://gacweb.icann.org/display/gacweb/GAC+Working+Group+to+Examine+the+Protection+of+Geographic+Names+in+any+Future+Expansion+of+gTLDs?preview=/39944662/41944013/GAC%20Geo-names%20WG%20-%20Working%20Papers%20.pdf.

Gangjee, Dev. *Melton Mowbray and the GI Pie in the Sky: Exploring Cartographies of Protection*. 2006(3) Intell. Prop. Q. 291 (2006).

Gardiner, Richard K. *Treaty Interpretation*. Oxford University Press, 2008.

Garner, Bryan A. and Campbell Black, Henry eds *Black's Law Dictionary*. West, 2009.

Garnham, Nicholas. *Constraints on Multimedia Convergence*. In *Information and Communication Technologies: Visions and Realities*. William H. Dutton ed. Oxford University Press, 2001.

Geist, Michael. *Fair.com? An Examination of the Allegations of Systemic Unfairness in the ICANN UDRP*. Available at http://aix1.uottawa.ca/~geist/geistudrp.pdf.

Gerien, Scott and Passarelli, Christopher. *Challenges for Geographical Indications (GIs) in the Context of the ICANN New Generic Top-Level Domains (gTLDs): A Manual for GIs Groups to Navigate the New Environment. oriGIn* (2016). Available at http://www.origin-gi.com/images/stories/PDFs/English/oriGIn_Publications_2010/GI_gTLDs_JAN2016_WEB_VERSION.pdf.

Gerrand, Peter. *Cultural Diversity in Cyberspace: The Catalan Campaign to Win the New .cat Top Level Domain*. 11(1–2) First Monday (2006).

Gervais, Daniel. *The TRIPS Agreement: Drafting History and Analysis*. 4th ed. Sweet & Maxwell, 2012.

Gervais, Daniel. *Irreconcilable Differences? The Geneva Act of the Lisbon Agreement and the Common Law*. 53(2) Hous. L. Rev. 339 (2015).

GFK, *Anholt-GFK Nation Brands Index*. Available at http://www.gfkamerica.com/practice_areas/roper_pam/nbi_index/index.en.html.

Ghidini, Gustavo. *Intellectual Property and Competition Law: The Innovation Nexus*. Edward Elgar, 2006.

Gibson, Johanna. *The Lay of the Land: The Geography of Traditional Cultural Expression*. In *Intellectual Property and Traditional Cultural Expressions in a Digital Environment*. Christoph Beat Graber and Mira Burri-Nenova eds Edward Elgar, 2008.

Gilbert, Lauren. *National Identity and Immigration Policy in the U.S. and the European Union*. 14(1) Colum. J. Eur. L. 99 (2007–2008).

Global Name Registry. *What is .name: Defensive Registrations*. (2001). Formerly at http://www.gnr.com/whatis.htm, archived at http://www.archive.org/web/web.php.

GNSO. *GNSO Issues Report: Introduction of New Top-Level Domains Draft version 1.3. ICANN*. (5 Dec. 2005). Available at http://gnso.icann.org/issues/new-gtlds/gnso-issues-rpt-gtlds-05dec05.pdf.

GNSO. *Reserved Name Working Group Report: Working Document 16 Mar. 2007. ICANN*. Available at http://gnso.icann.org/drafts/rn-wg-fr19mar07.pdf.

GNSO. *Reserved Names Working Group Final Report. ICANN* (23 May 2007). Available at http://gnso.icann.org/issues/new-gtlds/final-report-rn-wg-23may07.htm.

GNSO. *Final Report on the Introduction of New Generic Top-Level Domains. ICANN* (8 Aug. 2007). Available at http://gnso.icann.org/issues/new-gtlds/pdp-dec05-fr-parta-08aug07.htm.

GNSO. *Motion on Selected Trademark Issues from the ICANN Board of Directors: GNSO Council Resolution 20091028-3. ICANN* (28 Oct. 2009). Available at http://gnso.icann.org/resolutions/#200910.

GNSO. *Council Resolution 20151217: Initiation of a Policy Development Process (PDP) on New gTLD Subsequent Procedures. ICANN* (17 Dec. 2015). Available at https://gnso.icann.org/en/council/resolutions#201512.

GNSO. *Council Resolution 20160218-3: Initiation of a Policy Development Process (PDP) on a Review of All Rights Protection Mechanisms in All Generic Top-Level Domains (gTLDs). ICANN* (18 Feb. 2016). Available at http://gnso.icann.org/en/council/resolutions#20160218-3.

GNSO. *PDP Review of All Rights Protection Mechanisms in All gTLDs*. ICANN (Last updated 15 Mar. 2016). Available at https://gnso.icann.org/en/group-activities/active/rpm.

Goebel, Burkhart. *Geographical Indications and Trademarks: The Road from Doha*. Presentation, WIPO & USPTO Worldwide Symposium on Geographical Indications 9–11 Jul. 2003. WIPO/GEO/SFO/03/11. Available at http://www.wipo.int/meetings/en/doc_details.jsp?doc_id=78713.

Gordon, Wendy. *A Property Right in Self-Expression: Equality and Individualism in the Natural Law of Intellectual Property*. 102 Yale L.J. 1533 (1993).

Green, Leon. *The Right to Privacy*. 27 Ill. L. Rev. 237 (1932).

Greenhalgh, Christine and Dixon, Padraig. *The Economics of Intellectual Property: A Review to Identify Themes for Future Research*. University of Oxford Department of Economics Discussion Paper Series No. 135, Dec. 2002. Available at http://www.economics.ox.ac.uk/Research/wp/pdf/paper135.pdf.

Guillon, Jean. *.WINE New gTLD is Here, Thanks to Politicians*. *CircleID* (5 Oct. 2015). Available at http://www.circleid.com/posts/201451005_wine_new_gtld_is_here_thanks_to_politicians/.

Gunnarson, R. Shawn. *Modest Proposals for gTLD Profits*. *CircleID* (27 Oct. 2011). Available at http://www.circleid.com/posts/modest_proposals_for_gtld_profits).

Haas, Marie-Emmanuelle. *The Origin of the UDRP: NSI's 1995 domain name dispute policy*. *DomainesInfo* (23 Jul. 2009). Available at http://www.domainesinfo.fr/english/302/the-origin-of-the-udrp-nsi-s-1995-domain-name-dispute-policy.php.

Hannum, Hurst. *The Right of Self-Determination in the Twenty-First Century*. 55 Wash. & Lee L. Rev. 773 (1998).

Hansen, Thomas Blom. *Wages of Violence: Naming and Identity in Postcolonial Bombay*. Princeton University Press, 2001.

Helfer, Lawrence R. *Regime Shifting: The TRIPS Agreement and New Dynamics of International Intellectual Property Lawmaking*. 29 Yale J. Int'l L. 1 (2004).

Henkin, Louis; Crawford Pugh, Richard; Schachter, Oscar and Smit, Hans. *International Law: Cases and Materials*. 3d ed. West, 1993.

Henning-Bodewig, Frauke. *Unfair Competition Law: European Union and Member States*. Kluwer Law International, 2006.

Hilty, Reto M. and Henning-Bodewig, Frauke eds. *Law Against Unfair Competition: Towards a New Paradigm in Europe?* Springer, 2007.

Hirst, David. *The Gun and the Olive Branch: The Roots of Violence in the Middle East*. Thunder's Mouth Press/Nation Books, 2003.

Holstein-Childress, Victoria. *Lex Cyberus: The UDRP as a Gatekeeper to Judicial Resolution of Competing Rights to Domain Names*. 109 Penn St. L. Rev. 565 (2004).

Houtman, Gustaaf. *Mental Culture in Burmese Crisis Politics: Aung San Suu Kyi and the National League for Democracy*. Institute for the Study of Languages & Cultures of Asia & Africa, 1999.

Howse, Robert. *The Canadian Generic Medicines Panel: A Dangerous Precedent in Dangerous Times*. 3 J. World Int. Prop. 493 (2000).

Hughes, Justin. *The Philosophy of Intellectual Property*. 77 Geo. L.J. 287 (1988–1989).

Hughes, Justin. *Champagne, Feta, and Bourbon: The Spirited Debate about Geographical Indications*. 58 Hastings L.J. 331 (2006).

IAB. *A Brief History of the Internet Advisory/Activities/Architecture Board*. Available at http://www.iab.org/about/history.html.

IAHC. *Final Report of the International Ad Hoc Committee: Recommendations for Administration and Management of gTLDs*. (4 Feb. 1997). Formerly at http://www.iahc.org/draft-iahc-recommend-00.html, archived at http://www.archive.org/web/web.php.

IAHC. *Memorandum of Understanding on the Generic Top-Level Domain Space of the Internet Domain Name System (gTLD-MoU)*. 28 Feb 1997. Archived at http://www.archive.org/web/web.php.

IANA. *Root Zone Database: List of TLDs and Administrators*. Available at http://www.iana.org/domains/root/db#.

IANA. *Delegation Record for.TV*. Available at http://www.iana.org/domains/root/db/tv.html.

IANA. *Report on Request for Delegation of the .ps Top-Level Domain*. Available at http://www.iana.org/reports/ps-report-22mar00.htm.

IANA. *Qualifying Top-Level Domain Strings: Eligible Countries for Country-Code TLDs*. Available at http://www.iana.org/help/eligible-tlds.

ICANN. *ccTLD Agreements*. Available at http://www.icann.org/en/cctlds/agreements.html.

ICANN. *Charter Eligibility Dispute Resolution Policy*. Available at https://www.icann.org/resources/pages/cedrp-2012-02-25-en.

ICANN. *Charter Eligibility Dispute Resolution Policy Rules*. Available at https://www.icann.org/resources/pages/rules-fd-2012-02-25-en.

ICANN. *Eligibility Requirements Dispute Resolution Policy*. Available at http://www.icann.org/en/udrp/erdrp-policy.html.

ICANN. *Frequently Asked Questions: 1.7 Is ICANN initiating the New gTLD Program to Make Money?*. Available at http://newgtlds.icann.org/en/applicants/customer-service/faqs/faqs-en.

ICANN. *Information Page for Sponsored Top-Level Domains: A Summary of Documents and Reports Associated with the Second 'Proof of Concept' Top-Level Domain Expansion Round*. Available at http://www.icann.org/en/tlds/stld-apps-19mar04/.

ICANN. *Intellectual Property Defensive Registration Challenge Policy*. Available at https://www.icann.org/resources/pages/ipdrcp-2012-02-25-en.

ICANN. *ICP-1: Internet Domain Name System Structure and Delegation (ccTLD Administration and Delegation)*. Available at http://www.icann.org/en/icp/icp-1.htm.

ICANN. *Monthly Registry Reports*. Available at https://www.icann.org/resources/pages/registry-reports.

ICANN. *New Generic Top-Level Domains – Applicant Guidebook*. Available at https://newgtlds.icann.org/en/applicants/agb.

ICANN. *New Generic Top-Level Domains: Community Priority Evaluation*. Available at https://newgtlds.icann.org/en/applicants/cpe.

ICANN, *New Generic Top Level Domains: Competition, Consumer Trust and Consumer Choice Review*. Available at https://newgtlds.icann.org/en/reviews/cct.

ICANN. *New gTLD Program Application Process Archive*. Available at http://archive.icann.org/en/tlds/app-index.htm.

ICANN. *New gTLD Agreement Specifications AIRFORCE: Specification 11 Public Interest Commitments*. Available at https://gtldresult.icann.org/application-result/applicationstatus/applicationdetails:downloadpicposting/1109?t:ac=1109.

ICANN. *Qualification Challenge Policy*. Available at https://www.icann.org/resources/pages/proqcp-2012-02-25-en.

ICANN. *Restrictions Dispute Resolution Policy*. Available at https://www.icann.org/resources/pages/rdrp-2012-02-25-en.

ICANN. *Specification 11: Public Interest Commitments (Donuts)*. Available at https://gtldresult.icann.org/application-result/applicationstatus/applicationdetails:downloadpicposting/706?t:ac=706.

ICANN. *Statement of Registrar Accreditation Policy*. Available at http://www.icann.org/en/registrars/policy_statement.html#lllj.

ICANN. *Two-Character Letter/Letter Label Comments and Mitigation Measures*. Available at https://www.icann.org/resources/two-character-comments.

ICANN. *Preliminary Report: ICANN Meeting in Berlin 27-29 May 1999*. Available at http://archive.icann.org/en/meetings/berlin/berlin-resolutions.html#1.

ICANN. *Minutes of the Meeting of the Initial Board.* (26 Aug. 1999). Available at https://www.icann.org/resources/board-material/minutes-1999-08-26-en.

ICANN. *Uniform Domain Name Dispute Resolution Policy (adopted 26 Aug. 1999)*. Available at http://www.icann.org/en/udrp/udrp-policy-24oct99.htm.

ICANN. *Second Staff Report on Implementation Documents for the Uniform Dispute Resolution Policy*. (24 Oct. 1999). Available at http://archive.icann.org/en/udrp/udrp-second-staff-report-24oct99.htm.

ICANN. *Amendment 1 to ICANN/DOC Memorandum of Understanding*. (4 Nov. 1999). Available at https://archive.icann.org/en/nsi/amend1-jpamou-04nov99.htm.

ICANN. *Report (Part One) of Working Group C (New TLDs) Presented to Names Council. ICANN* (21 Mar. 2000). Available at https://archive.icann.org/en/dnso/wgc-report-21mar00.htm.

ICANN. *New TLD Application Process Overview*. (3 Aug. 2000). Available at http://www.icann.org/en/tlds/application-process-03aug00.htm.

ICANN. *Criteria for Evaluating New TLD Proposals*. (15 Aug. 2000). Available at http://www.icann.org/en/tlds/tld-criteria-15aug00.htm.

ICANN. *TLD Application Review Update*. (13 Oct. 2000). Available at http://www.icann.org/en/tlds/tld-review-update-13oct00.htm.

ICANN. *TLD Applications Lodged: 2 Oct. 2000*. (Corrected to 10 Oct. 2000). Available at http://www.icann.org/en/tlds/tld-applications-lodged-02oct00.htm.

ICANN. *.info Registry Agreement*. (signed 11 May 2001). Available at https://www.icann.org/resources/unthemed-pages/index-d0-2001-05-11-en.

ICANN. *Registrar Accreditation Agreement*. (17 May 2001). Available at https://www.icann.org/resources/unthemed-pages/raa-2001-05-17-en.

ICANN. *Amendment 3 to ICANN/DOC Memorandum of Understanding*. (25 May 2001). Available at https://www.icann.org/resources/unthemed-pages/amend3-jpamou-2001-05-25-en.

ICANN. *Regular Meeting of the Board Minutes*. (10 Sep. 2001). Available at https://www.icann.org/resources/board-material/minutes-2001-09-10-en.

ICANN. *Board of Directors Resolution 02.43: Geographic and Geopolitical Names in .info*. (14 Mar. 2002). Available at https://www.icann.org/resources/board-material/minutes-2002-03-14-en.

ICANN. *Board of Directors Resolution 02.44*. (14 Mar. 2002). Available at https://www.icann.org/resources/board-material/minutes-2002-03-14-en.

ICANN. *New TLD Evaluation Process Planning Task Force Final Report*. (31 Jul. 2002). Available at https://archive.icann.org/en/committees/ntepptf/final-report-31jul02.htm.

ICANN. *Minutes of Special Meeting of the Board of Directors: Resolution 02.97A*. (23 Aug. 2002). Available at https://www.icann.org/resources/board-material/minutes-2002-08-23-en.

ICANN. *ICANN Resolutions: 2003-10-31 - Adoption of GNSO Council Domain Deletion Policy Recommendations*. (31 Oct. 2003). Available at https://features.icann.org/2003-10-31-adoption-gnso-council-domain-deletion-policy-recommendations.

ICANN. *New sTLD Application*. (15 Dec. 2003). Available at http://www.icann.org/en/tlds/new-stld-rfp/new-stld-application-parta-15dec03.htm.

ICANN. *New sTLD RFP Application: .asia Part B Application Form*. (19 Mar. 2004). Available at http://archive.icann.org/en/tlds/stld-apps-19mar04/asia.htm.

ICANN. *New sTLD RFP Application: .cat Part B Application Form*. (19 Mar. 2004). Available at http://archive.icann.org/en/tlds/stld-apps-19mar04/cat.htm.

ICANN. *Status Report on the sTLD Evaluation Process*. (19 Mar. 2004). Available at https://archive.icann.org/en/tlds/stld-apps-19mar04/stld-status-report.pdf.

ICANN. *sTLD Application Process Appendix A: sTLD Selection Criteria*. (19 Mar. 2004). Available at http://www.icann.org/en/tlds/stld-apps-19mar04/PostAppA.pdf.

ICANN. *.jobs Registry Agreement*. (5 May 2005). Available at https://www.icann.org/resources/unthemed-pages/jobs-agreement-2012-02-25-en.

ICANN. *.travel Sponsored TLD Registry Agreement*. (signed 5 May 2005). Available at https://www.icann.org/resources/unthemed-pages/travel-agreement-2006-04-12-en.

ICANN. *.mobi TLD Sponsorship Agreement*. (signed 10 Jul. 2005). Available at https://www.icann.org/resources/unthemed-pages/mobi-2012-02-25-en.

ICANN. *.cat TLD Sponsorship Agreement*. (signed 23 Sep. 2005). Available at https://www.icann.org/resources/unthemed-pages/cat-agreement-2005-09-23-en.

ICANN. *.tel Registry Agreement*. (30 May 2006). Available at https://www.icann.org/resources/unthemed-pages/tel-2012-02-25-en.

ICANN. *New Agreement Means Greater Independence in Managing the Internet's System of Unique Identifiers*. (29 Sep. 2006). Available at https://www.icann.org/news/announcement-2006-09-29-en.

ICANN. *.asia Registry Agreement*. (6 Dec. 2006). Available at https://www.icann.org/resources/unthemed-pages/asia-2012-02-25-en.

ICANN. *.INFO Agreement Appendix 6: List of Reserved TLD Strings*. (8 Dec. 2006). Available at https://www.icann.org/en/system/files/files/info-appx-06-pdf-22aug13-en.pdf.

ICANN. *Board of Directors Resolution 2008.06.26.02, Adopted Board Resolutions, Paris*. (26 Jun. 2008). Available at https://www.icann.org/resources/board-material/resolutions-2008-06-26-en.

ICANN. *DNS Stability: The Effect of New Generic Top Level Domains on the Internet Domain Name System*. (6 Feb. 2008). Available at http://archive.icann.org/en/topics/dns-stability-draft-paper-06feb08.pdf.

ICANN. *Draft New gTLD Agreement Specification 5: Schedule of Reserved Names at the Second Level in gTLD Registries*. (24 Oct. 2008). Available at https://archive.icann.org/en/topics/new-gtlds/reserved-names-24oct08-en.pdf.

ICANN, *New gTLD Program: New gTLD Program in Brief*. (2009). Available at https://archive.icann.org/en/topics/new-gtlds/factsheet-new-gtld-program-oct09-en.pdf.

ICANN. *Welcome to the New gTLD Applicant Guidebook Version 2 (V2) Public Comment Forum*. (2009). Available at http://archive.icann.org/en/topics/new-gtlds/comments-2-en.htm.

ICANN. *Draft Applicant Guidebook, version 2*. (18 Feb. 2009). Available at https://archive.icann.org/en/topics/new-gtlds/draft-rfp-clean-18feb09-en.pdf.

ICANN. *Board of Directors Resolution 2009.03.06.06*. (6 Mar. 2009). Available at http://www.icann.org/en/minutes/resolutions-06mar09.htm#07.

ICANN. *Registrar Accreditation Agreement*. (21 May 2009). Available at https://www.icann.org/resources/pages/ra-agreement-2009-05-21-en.

ICANN. *Affirmation of Commitments by the United States Department of Commerce and the Internet Corporation for Assigned Names and Numbers*. (30 Sep. 2009). Available at https://www.icann.org/resources/pages/affirmation-of-commitments-2009-09-30-en.

ICANN. *For GNSO Consideration: Trademark Clearinghouse*. (Oct. 2009). Available at http://www.icann.org/en/topics/new-gtlds/draft-proposed-procedure-tm-clearinghouse-04oct09-en.pdf.

ICANN. *Draft Applicant Guidebook, Version 3*. (2 Oct. 2009). Available at https://archive.icann.org/en/topics/new-gtlds/draft-rfp-clean-04oct09-en.pdf.

ICANN. *New gTLD Program: Uniform Rapid Suspension (URS) Summary and Analysis of Public Comments*. (4 Oct. 2009). Available at http://www.icann.org/en/topics/new-gtlds/summary-analysis-urs-comments-04oct09-en.pdf.

ICANN. *Transcript: Affirmation of Commitments Consultation*. (27 Oct. 2009). Available at http://sel.icann.org/node/7481.

ICANN. *ICANN Bringing the Languages of the World to the Global Internet*. (30 Oct. 2009). Available at http://www.icann.org/en/announcements/announcement-30oct09-en.htm.

ICANN. *.post Sponsored TLD Agreement* (11 Dec. 2009). Available at https://www.icann.org/resources/unthemed-pages/post-2015-10-30-en.

ICANN. *Registration Abuse Policies Working Group Initial Report*. (12 Feb. 2010). Available at http://gnso.icann.org/issues/rap-wg-initial-report-12feb10-en.pdf.

ICANN. *Board of Directors Resolution 2010.11.05.02: New gTLDs Cross-Ownership Issues for Registries and Registrars*. (5 Nov. 2010). Available at http://www.icann.org/en/minutes/resolutions-05nov10-en.htm.

ICANN. *New gTLDs Proposed Final Applicant Guidebook Public Comment Summary*. (21 Feb. 2011). Available at http://www.icann.org/en/topics/new-gtlds/summary-analysis-proposed-final-guidebook-21feb11-en.pdf.

ICANN, *Updated: New gTLDs: Briefing Papers for ICANN Board-GAC Consultations*. (21 Feb. 2011, updated 23 Feb. 2011). Available at https://www.icann.org/news/announcement-6-2011-02-21-en.

ICANN. *ICANN Board Notes on the GAC New gTLD Scorecard*. (4 Mar. 2011). Available at http://www.icann.org/en/topics/new-gtlds/board-notes-gac-scorecard-04mar11-en.pdf.

ICANN. *New gTOLD [sic] Session: ICANN 40. ICANN* (13 Mar. 2011). Available at http://archive.icann.org/en/meetings/siliconvalley2011/bitcache/Transcript_%20New%20gTLD%20Session-vid=23275&disposition=attachment&op=download.pdf.

ICANN. *Board of Directors Resolutions 2011.03.18.23-2011.03.18.25 Approval of ICM Registry Application for.XXX: Adopted Board Resolutions, Silicon Valley/San Francisco*. (18 Mar. 2011). Available at https://www.icann.org/resources/board-material/resolutions-2011-03-18-en#5.

ICANN. *.xxx Registry Agreement (31 Mar. 2011)*. Available at https://www.icann.org/resources/agreement/xxx-2011-03-31-en.

ICANN. *New gTLD Program Explanatory Memorandum: GAC and Government Objections; Handling of Sensitive Strings; Early Warning*. (15 Apr. 2011). Available at https://archive.icann.org/en/topics/new-gtlds/gac-objections-sensitive-strings-15apr11-en.pdf.

ICANN. *Approval of the New gTLD Program: Resolution 2011.06.20.01*. (20 Jun. 2011). Available at https://www.icann.org/resources/board-material/resolutions-2011-06-20-en.

ICANN. *Current State of the UDRP: ICANN – Singapore Transcript*. (22 Jun. 2011). Available at http://archive.icann.org/en/meetings/singapore2011/bitcache/The%20Current%20State%20of%20the%20UDRP-vid=26007&disposition=attachment&op=download.txt.

ICANN. *Workshop on the Current State of the UDRP: Overview & Analysis of the Preliminary Issue Report*. (22 Jun. 2011). Available at http://archive.icann.org/en/meetings/singapore2011/bitcache/Workshop%20on%20the%20Current%20State%20of%20the%20UDRP_%20Overview%20&%20Analysis%20of%20the%20Preliminary%20Issue%20Report-vid=25871&disposition=attachment&op=download.pdf.

ICANN. *Program Statistics*. (2012). Available at http://newgtlds.icann.org/en/program-status/statistics.

ICANN. *gTLD Applicant Guidebook: Version 2012-01-11*. (11 Jan. 2012). Available at http://newgtlds.icann.org/en/applicants/agb/guidebook-full-11jan12-en.pdf.

ICANN. *Statement on TLD Application System*. (12 Apr. 2012). Available at http://newgtlds.icann.org/en/announcements-and-media/latest.

ICANN. *TAS Interruption: Update*. (21 May 2012). Available at http://newgtlds.icann.org/en/announcements-and-media/latest.

ICANN. *Applicant Guidebook: New gTLD Applicant Guidebook 4 June 2012*. Available at https://newgtlds.icann.org/en/applicants/agb.

ICANN. *New Generic Top-Level Domains: Quick Facts about Applied-for New gTLD Strings*. (13 Jun. 2012). Available at http://newgtlds.icann.org/en/program-status/statistics/applications-quick-facts-13jun12-en.pdf.

ICANN. *Reveal Day 13 June 2012: New gTLD Applied-For Strings*. (13 Jun. 2012). Available at https://www.icann.org/news/announcement-2012-06-13-en.

ICANN. *Memorandum on the Trademark Clearinghouse 'Strawman Solution'*. (20 Mar. 2013). Available at https://newgtlds.icann.org/en/about/trademark-clearinghouse/strawman-solution-memo-20mar13-en.pdf.

ICANN. *New gTLD Program – Initial Evaluation Report (AMAZON)*. (12 Jul. 2013). Available at http://newgtlds.icann.org/en/program-status/application-results/ie-1-1315-58086-en.pdf.

ICANN. *Transcription ICANN Toronto Meeting: Commercial Stakeholder Group (CSG) Meeting Tuesday 16 October 2012 at 9:45 local time.* Available at http://archive.icann.org/en/meetings/toronto2012/bitcache/Transcript_%20Commercial%20Stakeholder%20Group%20(CSG)-vid=42195&disposition=attachment&op=download.pdf.

ICANN. *New gTLD Program – Initial Evaluation Report (SPA)*. (7 Jun. 2013). Available at https://newgtlds.icann.org/sites/default/files/ier/0riusp5e5hoes40ji6vlayi6/ie-1-1309-81322-en.pdf.

ICANN. *New gTLD Program – Initial Evaluation Report (广州 – Guangzhou)*. (6 Sep. 2013). Available at https://newgtlds.icann.org/sites/default/files/ier/driuswlu8rlevoagl5ml1si9/ie-1-1121-22691-en.pdf.

ICANN. *2013 Registrar Accreditation Agreement*. (17 Sep. 2013). Available at https://www.icann.org/resources/pages/approved-with-specs-2013-09-17-en.

ICANN. *New gTLD Program – Initial Evaluation Report (BAR)*. (4 Oct. 2013). Available at https://newgtlds.icann.org/sites/default/files/ier/9812hf75ri5droaslu2iacie/ie-1-1870-98363-en.pdf.

ICANN, *Final Report on the Protection of IGO and INGO Identifiers in All gTLDs*. (10 Nov. 2013). Available at http://gnso.icann.org/en/issues/igo-ingo-final-10nov13-en.pdf.

ICANN. *Public Interest Commitment Dispute Resolution Procedure*. (19 Dec. 2013). Available at https://newgtlds.icann.org/en/applicants/agb/picdrp-19dec13-en.pdf.

ICANN. *Registry Agreement*. (9 Jan. 2014). Available at https://newgtlds.icann.org/sites/default/files/agreements/agreement-approved-09jan14-en.htm.

ICANN. Letter from Stephen D. Crocker, Chair, ICANN Board of Directors, to Heather Dryden, Chair, Governmental Advisory Committee, 31 Mar. 2014. Available at https://www.icann.org/en/system/files/correspondence/crocker-to-dryden-07apr14-en.pdf.

ICANN. *Resolutions – Applications for .vin and .wine/GAC Communiqué-Singapore*. (4 Apr. 2014) Available at https://features.icann.org/applications-vin-and-wine-gac-communiqu%C3%A9-%E2%80%93-singapore.

ICANN. *.WINE and .VIN: Where Does ICANN Stand?* (14 May 2014). Available at https://www.icann.org/news/blog/wine-and-vin-where-does-icann-stand.

ICANN. *New gTLD Program – Community Priority Evaluation Report (.OSAKA)*. (29 Jun. 2014). Available at https://www.icann.org/sites/default/files/tlds/osaka/osaka-cpe-1-901-9391-en.pdf.

ICANN. *ICANN Finalizes Process for Requests for Release of Two-Character ASCII Labels*. (1 Dec. 2014). Available at https://www.icann.org/news/announcement-2014-12-01-en.

ICANN. *.aarp Registry Agreement: Specification 13 .BRAND TLD Provisions*. (21 May 2015). Available at https://www.icann.org/sites/default/files/tlds/aarp/aarp-spec13-21may15-en.pdf.

ICANN. *Rights Protection Mechanisms Review: Revised Report*. (11 Sep. 2015). Available at https://newgtlds.icann.org/en/reviews/rpm/rpm-review-11sep15-en.pdf.

ICANN. *Cross-Community Working Group – Framework for Use of Country and Territory Names as TLDs (CWG-UCTN) {Strawman} Options Paper*. (21 Sep. 2015). Available at https://community.icann.org/display/CWGOUCNT/Output+and+Draft+Documents?preview=/49354211/56143211/Options%20Paper%2015%20October%202015%20.doc.

ICANN. *New gTLD Program Community Priority Evaluation Report (.GAY)*. (8 Oct. 2015). Available at https://www.icann.org/sites/default/files/tlds/gay/gay-cpe-rr-1-1713-23699-en.pdf.

ICANN. *Case Study: .BAR*. (11 Nov. 2015). Available at https://newgtlds.icann.org/en/announcements-and-media/case-studies/bar-us-letter-11nov15-en.pdf.

ICANN. *Working Group (WG) Charter: New gTLD Subsequent Procedures*. (21 Jan. 2016). Available at https://gnso.icann.org/en/issues/new-gtlds/subsequent-procedures-charter-21jan16-en.pdf.

ICANN. *Transcript GNSO Council Public Meeting Marrakech – 9 March 2016 at 13:30 UTC*. Available at https://webcache.googleusercontent.com/search?q=cache:fKxMYHvf-60J:https://meetings.icann.org/en/marrakech55/schedule/wed-gnso-council/transcript-gnso-council-09mar16-en.pdf+&cd=1&hl=en&ct=clnk&gl=au.

ICANN. *ICANN Board Transmits IANA Stewardship Transition Proposal and Enhancing ICANN Accountability Recommendations to NTIA*. (10 Mar. 2016). Available at https://www.icann.org/resources/pages/board-ntia-transmissions-2016-06-13-en.

ICANN. *Public Meetings: GNSO New gTLD Subsequent Procedures PDP WG –Transcript [EN]*. (10. Mar. 2016). Available at https://meetings.icann.org/en/marrakech55/schedule/thu-new-gtld-subsequent-procedures/transcript-new-gtld-subsequent-procedures-10mar16-en.pdf.

ICANN. *Charter for Proposed PDP to Review all Rights Protection Mechanisms in All gTLDs*. (15 Mar. 2016). Available at http://gnso.icann.org/en/drafts/rpm-charter-15mar16-en.pdf.

ICANN. *Review of all Rights Protection Mechanisms (RPMs) in All gTLDs PDP Working Group – Questions Raised in the Charter*. (15 Mar. 2016).

Available at https://community.icann.org/display/RARPMRIAGPWG/Questions+raised+in+the+Charter.

ICANN. *A 'Grand' Milestone: New gTLD Program Reaches 1,000th Delegation*. (25 May 2016). Available at https://www.icann.org/news/blog/a-grand-milestone-new-gtld-program-reaches-1-000th-delegation.

ICANN. *Proposed Measures for Letter/Letter Two-Character ASCII Labels to Avoid Confusion with Corresponding Country Codes*. (8 Jul. 2016). Available at https://www.icann.org/en/system/files/files/proposed-measures-two-char-08jul16-en.pdf.

ICANN. *Draft Work Plan for Phase One of the PDP on Review of all RPMs in all gTLDs – 12 July 2016*. Available at https://community.icann.org/display/RARPMRIAGPWG/Work+Plan?preview=/59643840/60491167/Work%20Plan%20-%2012%20July.pdf.

ICANN. *Registry Stakeholder Group Statement on Proposed Measures for Letter/Letter Two-Character ASCII Codes*. (16 Aug. 2016). Available at https://forum.icann.org/lists/comments-proposed-measures-two-char-08jul16/msg00014.html.

ICANN. *Bylaws*. (As amended, 1 Oct. 2016). Available at https://www.icann.org/resources/pages/governance/bylaws-en.

ICANN. *Adopted Board Resolutions: Regular Meeting of the ICANN Board 8 November 2016 - Resolution 2016.11.08.15*. Available at https://www.icann.org/resources/board-material/resolutions-2016-11-08-en#2.a.rationale.

Içduygu, Ahmet and Kaygusuz, Özlem. *The Politics of Citizenship by Drawing Borders: Foreign Policy and the Construction of National Citizenship Identity in Turkey*. 40(6) Middle Eastern Studies 26 (2004).

ICJ. *List of Cases Referred to the Court since 1946 by Date of Introduction: List of Contentious Cases and Advisory Proceedings*. Available at http://www.icj-cij.org/docket/index.php?p1=3&p2=2.

ICJ. *Permanent Court of International Justice: Publications of the Permanent Court of International Justice (1922-1946)*. Available at http://www.icj-cij.org/pcij/index.php?p1=9.

ICJ. Press Release. *The former Yugoslav Republic of Macedonia institutes proceedings against Greece for a violation of Article 11 of the Interim Accord of 13 September 1995*. No. 2008/40, 17 Nov. 2008. Available at http://www.icj-cij.org/docket/files/142/14881.pdf.

ICM Registry. *Launch Plan and Related Policies*. (2012). Available at https://www.icmregistry.com/about/policies/launch/Launch-Plan-and-Related-Policies.pdf.

Indigenous World Association and Indigenous Media Network. *Review of Developments Pertaining to the Promotion and Protection of the Rights of Indigenous Peoples, Including their Human Rights and Fundamental Freedoms: Joint Statement from the Indigenous World Association and Indigenous Media Network. UN High Commission on Human Rights*. E/CN.4/Sub.2/AC.4/2005/CRP.3 (13 Jul. 2005). Available at http://

www.ohchr.org/Documents/Issues/IPeoples/WG/E-CN4-Sub2-AC4-2005-CRP3.doc.

.INFO. *History of .INFO*. Available at http://info.info/why-info/history-info.

Information Sciences Institute USC Viterbi School of Engineering. *About Jon Postel*. (16 Sep. 2008). Available at http://www.postel.org/postel.html.

INTA. *New Act of the Lisbon Agreement Encompasses All Geographical Indications, Allows Accession by Regional Organizations*. 70(11) INTA Bulletin (15 Jun. 2015). Available at http://www.inta.org/INTABulletin/Pages/LisbonAgreement_7011.aspx.

Intellectual Property Constituency. *The Intellectual Property Constituency Impact Statement Regarding the Introduction of New gTLDs*. Available at http://www.ipconstituency.org/assets/ipc-position-papers/2007/IPC%20Impact%20Statement%20re%20new%20gTLDs.pdf.

Intellectual Property Interests Constituency. *Comments of Intellectual Property Interests Constituency Re: 'Draft Applicant Guidebook' for New gTLDs*. (15 Dec. 2008). Available at http://ipconstituency.org/PDFs/IPC%20comments%20re%20new%20TLD%20DAG%20submitted%20121508%20%282060018%29.pdf.

Intellectual Property Constituency. *IPC Comments on Proposed Measures for Letter/Letter Two-Character ASCII Codes*. (17 Aug. 2016). Available at https://ipc.memberclicks.net/assets/ipc-position-papers/2016/2016_08august_17%20ipc%20comments%20on%20letter%20letter%20ascii%20codes.pdf.

International Law Association Committee on Formation of Customary (General) International Law. *Statement of Principles Applicable to the Formation of General Customary International Law: Final Report of the Committee on Formation of Customary (General) International Law*. 2000.

InternetNews.com. *NSI Faces Seven Filthy Words Suits*. (3 May 1999). Available at http://www.internetnews.com/bus-news/article.php/109461/NSI+Faces+Seven+Filthy+Words+Suits.htm.

IPC and Marques. *The Perfect Sunrise? How Pre-launch Rights Protection Mechanisms and Successful Registry Operations Go Hand in Hand. ICANN* (Jun. 2008). Available at https://archive.icann.org/en/topics/new-gtlds/perfect-sunrise-jun08-en.pdf.

IPRota. *Taking Control: Safeguarding Brand Owners' Rights in .XXX*. (May 2011). Available at http://eo2.commpartners.com/users/inta/downloads/110803_XXX-Whitepaper.pdf.

IRT. *Final Report on Trademark Protection in New gTLDs*. ICANN (29 May 2009). Available at http://www.icann.org/en/topics/new-gtlds/irt-final-report-trademark-protection-29may09-en.pdf.

Isenberg, Doug. *WIPO Domain Name Dispute Filings Rise 4.5% in 2015*. (13 Jan. 2016). Available at http://www.gigalaw.com/2016/01/13/wipo-udrp-2015/.

ISO. *Country Codes: ISO 3166*. Available at http://www.iso.org/iso/home/standards/country_codes.htm#2012_iso3166_MA.

ISO. *Online Browsing Platform (OBP)*. Available at https://www.iso.org/obp/ui/#search.

Janev, Igor. *Legal Aspects of the Use of a Provisional Name for Macedonia in the United Nations System*. 93 Am. J. Int'l L. 160 (1999).

Janev, Igor. *Some Remarks of the Legal Status of Macedonia in the United Nations Organization*. 53 Rev. Int'l Aff. 1108 (2002).

Joseph, Sarah; Schultz, Jenny and Castan, Melissa. *The International Covenant on Civil and Political Rights: Cases, Materials, and Commentary*. Oxford University Press, 2000.

Joyner, Christopher C. *Legal Implications of the Concept of the Common Heritage of Mankind*. 35(1) Int'l & Comp. L. Q. 190 (1986).

Karklins, Janis. Letter to Paul Twomey, ICANN CEO and President. (26 May 2009). Available at http://www.icann.org/en/correspondence/karklins-to-twomey-26may09-en.pdf.

Kiss, Alexandre. *Abuse of Rights*. In *Encyclopedia of Public International Law*. Vol. 1. R. Bernhardt ed. North-Holland, 1992.

Kleinrock, Leonard. *Information Flow in Large Communication Nets. RLE Quarterly Progress Report*. (Jul. 1961). Available at http://www.lk.cs.ucla.edu/data/files/Kleinrock/Information%20Flow%20in%20Large%20Communication%20Nets0.pdf.

Klensin, John C. *Reflections on the DNS, RFC 1591, and Categories of Domains*. *RFC Editor* (29 Jan. 2011). Available at http://tools.ietf.org/html/draft-klensin-1591-reflections-03.

Knop, Karen. *Interpretation and Identity*. In *Diversity and Self-Determination in International Law*. Cambridge University Press, 2002.

Kokott, Juliane. *Soft Law Standards under Public International Law*. In *International Standards and the Law*. Peter Nobel ed. Staempfli, 2005.

Koskenniemi, Martti. *National Self-Determination Today: Problems of Legal Theory and Practice*. 43(2) Int'l & Comp. L.Q. 241 (1994).

Koskenniemi, Martti. *From Apology to Utopia: The Structure of International Legal Argument*. Cambridge University Press, 2005.

Krüdewagen, Ute. *Political Symbols in Two Constitutional Orders: The Flag Desecration Decisions of the United States Supreme Court and the German Federal Constitutional Court*. 19(2) Ariz. J. Int'l & Comp. L. 679 (2002).

Landzelius, Kyra. *Introduction: Native on the Net*. In *Native on the Net*. Kyra Landzelius ed. Routledge, 2006.

Langfield, Michele et. al., eds. *Cultural Diversity, Heritage and Human Rights: Intersections in Theory and Practice*. Routledge, 2010.

Lanham Act, 15 U.S.C. § 1054 (US).

L'Assemblée Fédérale. *Loi sur la protection des marques et loi sur la protection des armoiries: Vers une réglementation différenciée*. (11 Nov.

2011). Available at http://www.parlament.ch/f/mm/2011/pages/mm-rk-n-2011-11-11.aspx.

Last, Kathryn. ed. *The Resolution of Cultural Property Disputes: Some Issues of Definition*. Kluwer Law International, 2004.

Lauterpacht, Hersch. *Restrictive Interpretation and the Principle of Effectiveness in the Interpretation of Treaties*. XXVI British Y.B. Int'l L. 48 (1949).

Lawrence, David M. *Private Exercise of Governmental Power*. 61 Indiana L.J. 647 (1985–1986).

'Lectric Law Library. *NSI Domain Dispute Resolution Policy*. Available at http://www.lectlaw.com/files/inp08.htm.

'Lectric Law Library. NSI Domain Dispute Policy, Rev. 01. Effective 23 Nov. 1995. Available at http://www.lectlaw.com/files/inp13.htm.

Leiner, Barry M.; Cerf, Vinton G.; Clark, David D.; Kahn, Robert E.; Kleinrock, Leonard; Lynch, Daniel C.; Postel, Jon; Roberts, Larry G. and Wolff, Stephen. *A Brief History of the Internet*. Available at http://www.internetsociety.org/internet/what-internet/history-internet/brief-history-internet.

Lenard, Thomas M. and White, Lawrence J. *Improving ICANN's Governance and Accountability: A Policy Proposal*. 23(2) Info. Econ. & Pol'y 189 (2011).

Lessig, Lawrence. *The Future of Ideas: The Fate of the Commons in a Connected World*. Random House, 2001.

Lina, Liu. *Ownership of Underwater Cultural Heritage in the Area*. 1 Creighton Int'l & Comp. L.J. 60 (2011).

Lindsay, David. *International Domain Name Law: ICANN and the UDRP*. Hart Publishing, 2007.

Lipton, Jacqueline D. *Bad Faith in Cyberspace: Grounding Domain Name Theory in Trademark, Property, and Restitution*. 23(2) Harvard J.L. & Tech. 447 (2010).

Litman, Jessica. *The Public Domain*. 39 Emory L.J. 965 (1990).

Litman, Jessica. *Essay: The DNS Wars: Trademarks and the Internet Domain Name System*. 4 J. Small & Emerging Bus. L. 149 (2000).

Little, Trevor. *Think Geographic Name Protection in New gTLDs Won't Impact Your Brand? Think again, World Trademark Law Review* (16 Oct. 2014). Available at http://www.worldtrademarkreview.com/Blog/detail.aspx?g=63cc4191-082f-431e-87bb-980bbf02b7b6.

Loi fédérale sur la protection des marques et des indications de provenance. Art. 27a (nouveau), RS 232.11, Feuille fédérale No 50, 15 Dec. 2009.

Lury, Celia. *Cultural Rights: Technology, Legality, and Personality*. Routledge, 1993.

Lynn, Stuart. *A Plan for Action Regarding New gTLDs. ICANN* (18 Oct. 2002). Available at http://www.icann.org/en/committees/ntepptf/new-gtld-action-plan-18oct02.htm.

MacLean, Don. Speech. *Herding Schrödinger's Cats: Some Conceptual Tools for Thinking about Internet Governance*. ITU Workshop on Internet Governance, 26–27 Feb. 2004. Available at www.itu.int/osg/spu/forum/intgov04/contributions/itu-workshop-feb-04-internet-governance-background.pdf.

Macmillan, Fiona. *Copyright, the World Trade Organization and Cultural Self Determination*. In *New Directions in Copyright Law*. Fiona Macmillan ed. Edward Elgar, 2007.

Macmillan, Fiona. *Human Rights, Cultural Property and Intellectual Property: Three Concepts in Search of a Relationship*. In *Intellectual Property and Traditional Cultural Expressions in a Digital Environment*. Christoph Beat Graber and Mira Burri-Nenova eds Edward Elgar, 2008.

Madow, Michael. *Private Ownership of Public Image: Popular Culture and Publicity Rights*. 81 Cal. L. Rev. 127 (1993).

Mann, F. A. *Reflections on a Commercial Law of Nations*. 33 British Y.B. Int'l L. 20 (1957).

Marikar, Sheila. *Do Carlin's 'Seven Dirty Words' Still Shock? Comedians Argue for More Curses on TV, Critics Say It Won't Happen Soon*. *ABC News*. (24 Jun. 2008). Available at http://abcnews.go.com/Entertainment/story?id=5229910&page=1.

Martin, Charles. *The Meaning of Distinctiveness in Trade-mark Law*. 45(5) Ill. L. Rev. 535 (1950–1951).

Mayall, James. *Nationalism and International Society*. Cambridge University Press, 1990.

McCarthy, J. Thomas and Colby Devitt, Veronica. *Protection of Geographical Denominations: Domestic and International*. 69 Trademark Rep. 199 (1979).

McCullagh, Declan. *The Domain Name List is Dwindling*. *Wired.com*. (14 Apr. 1999). Available at http://archive.wired.com/science/discoveries/news/1999/04/19117.

McDonough, Molly. *Tightening Domain Reins: California Court Puts a Damper on '.biz' Addition, Calls Application Process a Lottery*. ABA Journal 23 (Dec. 2001).

McGoldrick, Dominic. *Culture, Cultures, and Cultural Rights*. In *Economic, Social and Cultural Rights in Action*. Mashood A. Baderin and Robert McCorquodale eds Oxford University Press, 2007.

Meron, Theodor. *Human Rights and Humanitarian Norms as Customary Law*. Clarendon Press, 1989.

Merryman, John Henry. *Two Ways of Thinking About Cultural Property*. 80(4) Am. J. Int'l L. 831 (1986).

Merryman, John Henry. *Cultural Property, International Trade and Human Rights*. 19 Cardozo Arts & Ent. L.J. 51 (2001).

Michels, Lucas S. *A Blueprint for International TRIPS-plus Geographical Indications Protections? An Analysis of Geographical Indication Protection Proposals in the European Union – India Bilateral Trade and Investment Agreement*. 15 Gonzaga J. Int'l L. 2 (2011–2012).

Mihaylova, Aneta. *National versus Regional Identity: the 'Other' Romanians in Greater Romania*. 1 (2006) Balkan Studies 9 (2006).

Mill, John Stuart. *Considerations on Representative Government*. Parker, Son & Bourn, 1861.

Mills, David L. *RFC 799: Internet Domain Names*. *RFC Editor* (Sep. 1981). Available at http://www.rfc-editor.org/rfc/rfc799.txt.

Ministère des Affaires Étrangères de la France. *Conférence Internationale pour la Protection de la Propriété Industrielle*. Imprimerie Nationale, 1880.

Mitchell, Andrew D. *Legal Principles in WTO Disputes*. Cambridge University Press, 2008.

Mockapetris, Paul. *RFC 882: Domain Names Concepts and Facilities*. *RFC Editor* (Nov. 1983). Available at http://www.rfc-editor.org/rfc/rfc882.txt.

Montes, Io. Doctoral Dissertation in Law, Zürich. *Legal Framework for Domain Names* (2005).

Morando, James W. and Nadan, Christian H. *Can Trademark Law Regulate the Race to Claim Internet Domain Names*. 13 Computer Lawyer 10 (1996).

Morris, Glenn T. *In Support of the Right of Self-Determination for Indigenous Peoples under International Law*. 29 German Y.B. Int'l L. 277 (1986).

Mueller, Milton L. *Rough Justice: A Statistical Assessment of ICANN's Uniform Dispute Resolution Policy*. 17(3) Information Society (2001).

Mueller, Milton L. Speech. *Governments and Country Names: ICANN's Transformation into an Intergovernmental Regime*. Pacific Telecommunication Council, Jan. 2002.

Mueller, Milton L. *Ruling the Root: Internet Governance and the Taming of Cyberspace*. MIT Press, 2002.

Mueller, Milton L. *NTIA Plays Chicken with the IANA Contract*. (10 Mar. 2012). Available at http://www.internetgovernance.org/2012/03/10/ntia-plays-chicken-with-the-iana-contract/.

Munzer, Stephen R. and Simon, Phyllis Chen. *Territory, Plants, and Land-Use Rights among the San of Southern Africa: A Case Study in Regional Biodiversity, Traditional Knowledge, and Intellectual Property*. 17 Wm. & Mary Bill Rts J. 831 (2009).

Murkens, Jo Eric Khushal. *'We Want Our Identity Back': The Revival of National Sovereignty in the German Federal Constitutional Court's Decision on the Lisbon Treaty*. 2 Bundesverfassungsgericht 530 (2010).

Murphy, Kevin. *Governments Probe Domain Land-Snatch: many. gTLDs.suck. The Register* (29 Jun. 2012). Available at http://www.theregister.co.uk/2012/06/29/domain_land_grab_under_the_microscope/.

Murphy, Kevin. *Told You So? Four New gTLDs Given Geographic Surprise, Others Given a Pass. Domain Incite.* (7 Mar. 2013). Available at http://domainincite.com/12166-told-you-so-four-new-gtlds-given-geographic-surprise-others-given-a-pass.

Murphy, Kevin. *Ten More New gTLDs Get ICANN Contracts. Domain Incite* (13 Dec. 2013). Available at http://domainincite.com/15299-ten-more-new-gtlds-get-icann-contracts.

Murphy, Kevin. *The Price of.bar Was $100,000 to a School. Domain Incite* (30 Jun. 2014). Available at http://domainincite.com/17002-the-price-of-bar-was-100000-to-a-school.

Murphy, Kevin. *Donuts Makes Private Deal with Wine-Makers. Domain Incite* (21 Jun. 2015). Available at http://domainincite.com/18739-donuts-makes-private-deal-with-wine-makers.

Murray, Andrew D. *The Regulation of Cyberspace: Control in the Online Environment.* Routledge-Cavendish, 2007.

Mwangi, Jeannette. *TRIPS and Agricultural Biotechnology: Implications for the Right to Food in Africa.* In *Human Rights and Intellectual Property Rights: Tensions and Convergences.* Mpazi Sinjela ed. Martinus Nijhoff, 2007.

National Telecommunications and Information Administration. *Improvement of Technical Management of Internet Names and Addresses.* 63 Fed. Reg. 8826–8833 (20 Feb. 1998).

National Telecommunications and Information Administration. *Management of Internet Names and Addresses.* 63 Fed. Reg. 31,741, 31,745 (10 Jun. 1998).

National Telecommunications and Information Administration. *NTIA Announces Intent to Transition Key Internet Domain Name Functions.* (14 Mar. 2014). Available at https://www.ntia.doc.gov/press-release/2014/ntia-announces-intent-transition-key-internet-domain-name-functions.

National Telecommunications and Information Administration – US Department of Commerce. *Q and A on IANA Stewardship Transition.* (16 Aug. 2016). Available at https://www.ntia.doc.gov/other-publication/2016/q-and-iana-stewardship-transition-0.

NSF Network Technical Advisory Group. *RFC 985: Requirements for Internet Gateways [Draft]. RFC Editor* (May 1986). Available at http://www.rfc-editor.org/rfc/rfc985.txt.

Navaro-Yashin, Yael. *Confinement and the Imagination: Sovereignty and Subjectivity in a Quasi-State*, in *Sovereign Bodies: Citizens, Migrants and States in the Postcolonial World.* Thomas Blom Hansen & Finn Stepputat eds Princeton University Press, 2005.

Nayar, M. G. Kaladharan. *Human Rights: The United Nations and United States Foreign Policy.* 19(3) Harv. Int'l L.J. 813 (1978).

Nelmark, David. *Virtual Property: The Challenges of Regulating Intangible, Exclusionary Property Interests Such as Domain Names.* 3(1) Northwestern J. Tech. & Intell. Prop. 1 (2004).

Nelson, Dolliver M. *Reflections on the 1982 Convention on the Law of the Sea.* In *The Law of the Sea: Progress and Prospects.* Richard Barnes & David Ong eds Oxford University Press, 2006.

Network Solutions Inc. *NSI Domain Name Dispute Policy Revision 02.* (Effective 9 Sep. 1996). Reproduced in Michael Tanner, *Trademarks, Internet Domain Names, and the NSI: How Do We Fix a System that Is Already Broken?* 3(2) J. Tech. L.& Pol'y, Appendix.

Network Working Group. *RFC 3172: Management Guidelines & Operational Requirements for the Address and Routing Parameter Area Domain ('arpa'). RFC Editor* (Sep. 2001). Available at http://www.rfc-editor.org/rfc/rfc3172.txt.

NeuLevel Inc. *IP Claims Service: Terms of Use.* Available at http://www.webfusion.co.uk/terms-and-conditions/biz-terms/.

NeuLevel Inc. *Start-up Trademark Opposition Policy and Rules for .biz.* (Adopted 11 May 2001). Available at http://www.wipo.int/amc/en/docs/stoprules.pdf.

NeuStar Inc. *.US Domain Name Registration Terms and Conditions Version 2.1.* Available at http://web.neustar.biz/policies/docs/neustar_registrar_terms.pdf.

Nguyen, Xuan-Thao N. *Nationalizing Trademarks: A New International Trademark jurisprudence?* 39 Wake Forest L. Rev. 729 (2004).

Nimmer, Melville B. *The Right of Publicity.* 19 Law & Contemp. Probs. 203 (1954).

Nominet. *Second Level Registration in .uk: Nominet Consultation Document.* (1 Jul. 2013). Available at https://ico.org.uk/media/about-the-ico/consultation-responses/2013/2135/consultation-second-level-domain-registration-in-uk-july-2013.pdf.

Nowak, Manfred. *U.N. Covenant on Civil and Political Rights: CCPR Commentary.* 2d ed. revised. N.P. Engel, 2005.

Nurton, James. *Sunrise Meets Sunset for .info.* (Sep. 2001). Managing Intellectual Property.

Nurton, James. *Top Level Domains: Mapping a TLD strategy.* (Jul./Aug. 2001). Managing Intellectual Property.

nzherald.co.nz. *Sovereignty Flag Should Fly, Says Maori Party.* (31 Jan. 2007). Available at http://www.nzherald.co.nz/waitangi-day/news/article.cfm?c_id=1500878&objectid=10421769.

O'Connor, Bernard. *The Law of Geographical Indications.* Cameron May, 2004.

O'Connor, Bernard. *Protecting Traditional Knowledge. An Overview of a Developing Area of Intellectual Property Law.* 6(5) J. World Intell. Prop. 677 (2005).

O'Connor and Company & Insight Consulting. *Geographical Indications and TRIPs: 10 Years Later ... A Roadmap for EU GI Holders to Get Protection in Other WTO Members*. Available at http://trade.ec.europa.eu/doclib/docs/2007/june/tradoc_135088.pdf.

OECD Working Party on Telecommunication and Information Services Policies. *Generic Top Level Domain Names: Market Development and Allocation Issues*. DSTI/ICCP/TISP(2004)2/FINAL. (13 Jul. 2004). Available at http://www.oecd.org/dataoecd/56/34/32996948.pdf.

Olsen, John R.; Maniatis, Spyros M.; Wood, Nick and Zografos, Daphne. *Domain Names: Global Practice and Procedure*. Sweet & Maxwell, 2007.

Olson, Mancur. *The Logic of Collective Action: Public Goods and the Theory of Groups*. Harvard University Press, 1971.

Oppenheim, Lassa. *Science of International Law: Its Tasks and Method*. 2(2) Am. J. Int'l L. 313 (1908).

Oppenheim, Lassa. *International Law: A Treatise*. 8th ed. H. Lauterpacht ed. Longmans, Green & Co., 1955.

Palestinian National Internet Naming Authority. *PNINA Registration Policies and Procedures for Registering Domains under the .ps ccTLD*. Available at http://www.pnina.ps/domains/registration-policy/.

Papadimas, Lefteris. *Macedonia Says 'Mountains to Climb' in Name row with Greece. Reuters*. (17 Dec. 2015). Available at http://uk.reuters.com/article/uk-greece-macedonia-namedispute-idUKKBN0U01GJ20151217.

Passa, Jérôme. *Opinion Report. ICANN* (22 Mar. 2014). Available at https://www.icann.org/en/system/files/files/analysis-wine-vin-22mar14-en.pdf.

Petroski, Karen. *Special Issue: The Many Fates of Legal Positivism – Is Post-Positivism Possible?* 12 German L.Rev. 663 (2011).

Pezet, F. A. *The Future Relations of the United States with Latin America from the Latin American Viewpoint*. 7(2) Nat'l Conf. Foreign Rel. U.S. 287 (1917).

Pitofsky, Robert; Patterson, Donna and Hooks, Jonathan. *The Essential Facilities Doctrine Under U.S. Antitrust Law*, 70 Antitrust L.J. 443 (2002).

PLZEŇ/PILSEN PILS/PILSENER/PILSNER: Notification No. 1 by organizations in the Czech Republic. Available at http://www.wipo.int/ipdl/en/search/lisbon/search-struct.jsp.

Postel, Jon. *RFC 1083: IAB Official Protocol Standards. RFC Editor* (Dec. 1988). Available at http://www.rfc-editor.org/rfc/rfc1083.txt.

Postel, Jon. *Domain Name System Structure and Delegation: RFC 1591. RFC Editor* (Mar. 1994). Available at http://www.rfc-editor.org/rfc/rfc1591.txt.

Postel, Jon and J. Reynolds. *Domain Requirements: RFC 920. RFC Editor* (Oct. 1984). Available at http://www.rfc-editor.org/rfc/rfc920.txt.

Pritz, Kurt. Letter to The Honorable Robert Goodlatte, US House of Representatives. *Response to Questions*. (7 Jun. 2011). Available at http://www.icann.org/en/correspondence/pritz-to-goodlatte-07jun11-en.pdf.

Pritz, Kurt. Testimony before the US House Committee on the Judiciary, Subcommittee on Intellectual Property, Competition and the Internet, Hearing on New Generic Top-Level Domains (gTLD). (4 May 2011). Available at https://www.gpo.gov/fdsys/pkg/CHRG-112shrg74251/html/CHRG-112shrg74251.htm.

PR Newswire. *Verisign Acquires The .tv Corporation*. (7 Jan. 2002). Available at http://www.prnewswire.com/news-releases/verisign-acquires-the-tv-corporation-75291122.html.

PRNewswire. *New .Pro Internet Registry Now Accepting Defensive Registrations for Trademarks and Brand Names: 'Sunrise' Period Allows Major Brands, Others to Protect Names*. (5 Apr. 2004). Available at http://www.prnewswire.com/news-releases/new-pro-internet-registry-now-accepting-defensive-registrations-for-trademarks-and-brand-names-72334052.html.

Prott, Lyndel V. *Problems of Private International Law for the Protection of the Cultural Heritage*. 217 Recueil des Cours de l'Academie de la Haye 301 (1989).

Prott, Lyndel V. *Cultural Rights as Peoples' Rights in International Law*. In *The Rights of Peoples*. James Crawford ed. Oxford University Press, 1992.

Provost, Rene. *International Human Rights and Humanitarian Law*. Cambridge University Press, 2002.

PROWG, *Protecting the Rights of Others Working Group (PROWG) Final Report: Annex One Registry Summaries. ICANN* (1 Jun. 2007). Available at http://gnso.icann.org/files/gnso/drafts/GNSO-PRO-WG-final-01Jun07.pdf.

Public Domain Registry. *Dotmobi: When Can I Start Registering?* Available at http://www.publicdomainregistry.com/dotmobi/.

Quadrio, Iris V. and Chajchir, Martin. *Nineteenth Yearly Review of International Trademark Jurisprudence*. 102 Trademark Rep. 455 (2012).

Quinion, Michael. *World Wide Words: Blighty*. Available at http://www.worldwidewords.org/qa/qa-bli1.htm.

Quittner, Joshua. *Billions Registered: Right Now, There Are No Rules to Keep You from Owning a Bitchin' Corporate Name as Your Own Internet Address*. 2.10 Wired.com (Oct. 1994). Available at https://www.wired.com/1994/10/mcdonalds/.

Radin, Margaret Jane. *Reinterpreting Property*. University of Chicago Press, 1993.

Rains, Christopher P. *A Domain By Any Other Name: Forging International Solutions for the Governance of Internet Domain Names*. 13 Emory Int'l L.Rev. 355 (2000).

Ramsey, Lisa P. *Free Speech and International Obligations to Protect Trademarks*. 35 Yale J. Int'l L. 405 (2010).

Rangnekar, Dwijen. *Demanding Stronger Protection for Geographical Indications: The Relationship between Local Knowledge, Information and Reputation*. #2004-11 United Nations University-INTECH Discussion Paper Series (2004).

Restatement of the Law (Third): Unfair Competition (1995).

Ribeiro, John. *US Lawmakers Back Amazon.com's Bid for .amazon Domain. PCWorld.* (24 Jun. 2015). Available at http://www.pcworld.com/article/2940032/us-lawmakers-back-amazoncoms-bid-for-amazon-gtld.html.

Rimmer, Matthew. *Virtual Countries: Internet Domain Names and Geographical Terms*. Feb. 2003 Media Int'l Austl. Incorp. Culture & Pol'y 124 (2003).

Rose, Carol M. *Romans, Roads, and Romantic Creators: Traditions of Public Property in the Information Age*. 66 L. & Contemp. Probs. 89 (2003).

Samuels, Jeffrey M. and Samuels, Linda B. *Internet Domain Names: The Uniform Dispute Resolution Policy*. 40 Am. Bus. L. J. 885 (2003).

Samuelson, Pamela. *Implications of the Agreement on Trade Related Aspects of Intellectual Property Rights for Cultural Dimensions of National Copyright Laws*. 23(1–2) J. Cult. Econ. 95 (1999).

Schröder, Konrad. *Languages*. In *What is Europe? Aspects of European Cultural Diversity*. Monica Shelley and Margaret Winck eds Routledge, 1995.

Seuffert, Nan. *Jurisprudence of National Identity: Kaliedoscopes of Imperialism and Globalisation from Aotearoa New Zealand*. Ashgate, 2006.

Sevcik, Peter and Wetzel, Rebecca. *Stop Comparing the Internet to the Highway System. NetworkWorld* (6 Aug. 2008). Available at http://www.networkworld.com/article/2345535/data-center/stop-comparing-the-internet-to-the-highway-system.html.

Shaw QC, Malcolm N. *International Law*. 6th ed. Cambridge University Press, 2008.

Shewchuk, Ryan. *The UDRP and the ACPA: What Are They, and Which Should Be Used?* 2 Asper Rev. Int'l Bus. & Trade L. 85 (2002).

Simma, Bruno and Alston, Philip. *The Sources of Human Rights Law: Custom, Jus Cogens, and General Principles*. Aust'l Y.B. Int'l L. 82 (1988–1989).

Simma, Bruno and Paulus, Andreas L. *Symposium on Method in International Law, The Responsibility of Individuals for Human Rights Abuses in Internal Conflicts: A Positivist View*. 93(2) Am. J. Int'l L. 302 (1999).

Smith, Graham J. H. *Internet Law and Regulation*. 3d ed. Sweet & Maxwell, 2002.

Smith, J. Theodore. Student Author. *'1-800-RIPOFFS.COM': Internet Domain Names are the Telephone Numbers of Cyberspace*. 1997 U. Ill. L. Rev. 1169 (1997).

Smith, Nicholas and Wilbers, Erik. *The UDRP: Design Elements of an Effective ADR Mechanism.* 15(2) Am. Rev. Int'l Arb. 215 (2004).

Snyder, David. *Enhanced Protections for Geographical Indications Under TRIPS: Potential Conflicts under the U.S. Constitutional and Statutory Regimes.* 18 Fordham Intell. Prop. Media & Ent. L.J. 1297 (2008).

Soanes, Catherine and Stevenson, Angus eds *The Concise Oxford English Dictionary.* 11th ed. revised. Oxford University Press, 2008.

Spectar, J.M. *Saving the Ice Princess: NGOs, Antarctica & International Law in the New Millenium.* 23 Suffolk Transnational L. Rev. 57 (1999).

Stanziani, Alessandro. *Wine Reputation and Quality Controls: The Origin of the AOCs in 19th Century France.* 18 Eur. J. L. Econ. 149 (2004).

Statistical Office of Montenegro. *Statistical Yearbook 2015: Review by Municipalities.* Chapter 28.4 (Review by Municipalities, Population and Households by Municipalities. Available at http://www.monstat.org/eng/publikacije_page.php?id=1312.

Steiner, Peter. *Illustration.* 69(20) New Yorker 61 (5 Jul. 1993).

STI. *Recommendations.* ICANN. Available at https://gnso.icann.org/en/issues/sti/sti-wt-recommendations-11dec09-en.pdf.

Su, Zaw-Sing and Postel, Jon. *RFC 819: The Domain Naming Convention for Internet User Applications. RFC Editor* (1 Aug. 1982). Available at http://www.rfc-editor.org/rfc/rfc819.txt.

Sucharitkul, Sompong. *The Inter-temporal Character of International and Comparative Law Regarding the Rights of the Indigenous Populations of the World.* 50 Am. J. Comp. L. 3 (2002).

Summers, James. *Peoples and International Law: How Nationalism and Self-Determination Shape a Contemporary Law of Nations.* Martinus Nijhoff, 2007.

Summit Strategies International. *Evaluation of New gTLDs: Policy and Legal Issues.* (10 July 2004). Available at http://archive.icann.org/en/tlds/new-gtld-eval-31aug04.pdf .

Svantesson, Dan Jerker B. *The Right of Reputation in the Internet Era.* 23(3) Int'l Rev. L. Comp. & Tech. 169 (2009).

SWITCH. *Legal Information: Legal Basis and Dispute Resolution Service for .ch domain names.* Available at https://www.nic.ch/terms/.

Symbolics.com. *About Symbolics.* Available at http://symbolics.com/about-symbolics/.

Michael Tanner, *Trademarks, Internet Domain Names, and the NSI: How Do We Fix a System that Is Already Broken?* 3(2) J. Tech. L.& Pol'y, Appendix.

Tarmizi, Mohamed Sharil. *Reservation of Country Names in Dot Info: ICANN Board Resolutions of 10 September 2001 and 14 March 2002.* (9 Sep. 2003). Hard copy on file with author.

Tatham, David. *Well Known Trade Marks: A CLIP Seminar Report.* Intellectual Property Institute, 1997.

Taubman, Antony. *The Public Domain and International Intellectual Property Law Treaties*. In *Intellectual Property: The Many Faces of the Public Domain*. Hector Macqueen and Charlotte Waelde eds Edward Elgar, 2007.

Taubman, Antony and Leistner, Matthias. *Analysis of Different Areas of Indigenous Resources: Traditional Knowledge*. In *Indigenous Heritage and Intellectual Property, Genetic Resources, Traditional Knowledge and Folklore*. Silke von Lewinski ed. Kluwer Law International, 2008.

The Dot Asia Organisation. *.ASIA General Registry Policies Final Draft*. (2007). Available at http://www.dot.asia/draft/DotAsia-General-Policies--FINALDRAFT-v-1-0.pdf.

The Dot Asia Organisation. *.ASIA Pioneer Domains Program Policies version 2.0*. (2007). Archived at http://pioneer.domains.asia/ascii/policies/DotAsia-PDP-Policies--2007-07-11.pdf.

The Dot Asia Organisation. *.ASIA Sunrise Policies*. (10 Aug. 2007). Available at http://www.dot.asia/policies/DotAsia-Sunrise-Policies--COMPLETE-2007-08-10.pdf.

The Dot Asia Organisation. *.ASIA Charter Eligibility Requirement Policies*. (15 Aug. 2007). Available at http://www.dot.asia/policies/DotAsia-Charter-Eligibility--COMPLETE-2007-08-15.pdf.

The Dot Asia Organisation. *DotAsia Sunrise Challenge Policy*. (Effective 31 Oct. 2007). Available at http://www.dot.asia/draft/DotAsia-Sunrise-Challenge--DRAFT.pdf.

The Economist. *New Internet Addresses: .patience*. (25 Jul. 2013). Available at http://www.economist.com/blogs/schumpeter/2013/07/new-internet-addresses-0.

Thirlway, Hugh. *The Sources of International Law*. In *International Law*. Malcom D. Evans ed. Oxford University Press, 2010.

Thürer, Daniel. *Soft Law*. In *Max Planck Encyclopedia of Public International Law*. Rüdiger Wolfrum ed. Oxford University Press, 2010.

Tierney, Stephen ed. *Accommodating Cultural Diversity*. Ashgate, 2007.

Tralliance. *.travel Registry Policies*. Available at http://www.travel.travel/wp-content/uploads/2008/12/122008trmcpoliciesfinal.pdf.

Trade Agreement between the European Union and its Member States, of the one part, and Colombia and Peru, of the other part, O.J. L 354, 21 Dec. 2012.

Trade Marks Act 1995 (Austl.).

Trade Marks Act No. 194 of 1993 (S. Africa).

Triggs, Gillian D. *International Law: Contemporary Principles and Practices*. 2d ed. LexisNexis Butterworths, 2011.

United Nations. *The Right of Everyone to Benefit from the Protection of the Moral and Material Interests Resulting from Any Scientific, Literary or Artistic Production of which He or She is the Author (Article 15, paragraph 1(c), of the Covenant)*. U.N. Doc. E/C.12/GC/17. Available at http://www.un.org/en/ga/search/view_doc.asp?symbol=E/C.12/GC/17.

United Nations, *The Core International Human Rights Instruments and Their Monitoring Bodies*. Available at http://www.ohchr.org/EN/ProfessionalInterest/Pages/CoreInstruments.aspx.

United Nations. *United Nations Terminology Bulletin Country Names*. UN Terminology Bulletin No. 347/Rev. 1. Available at http://unstats.un.org/unsd/methods/m49/m49alpha.htm.

United Nations. *Question of South West Africa*, G.A. Res. 2372(XXII), U.N. Doc. A/Res/2372(XXII) (12 Jun. 1968).

United Nations. *Declaration on Principles of International Law concerning Friendly Relations and Cooperation among States in accordance with the Charter of the United Nations*. GA/RES/2625(XXV), U.N. Doc. A/8082 (1970).

United Nations. *Application of the Republic of Bosnia and Herzegovina*. U.N. Doc. A/46/921 S23971 Annex (19 May 1992).

United Nations. *Admission of the Republic of Bosnia and Herzegovina to membership in the United Nations*. U.N. Doc. A/Res/46/237 (22 May 1992).

United Nations. S.C. Res. 817, 7 Apr. 1993, U.N. Doc. S/INF/49 (1993).

United Nations. Sub-Commission on Human Rights. *Resolution 2000/7: Intellectual Property Rights and Human Rights*. U.N. Doc. E/CN.4/SUB.2/RES/2000/7 (2000).

United Nations. *Application of the Democratic Republic of East Timor*. U.N. Doc. A/56/953-S/2002/558 Annex (20 May 2002).

United Nations. *Admission of the Democratic Republic of East Timor for admission to membership in the United Nations*. U.N. Doc. A/Res/57/3 (2 Oct. 2002).

United Nations. *Application of the Republic of Montenegro*. U.N. Doc. A/60/890-S/2006/409 Annex (16 Jun. 2006).

United Nations. *Admission of the Republic of Montenegro for admission to membership in the United Nations*. U.N. Doc. A/Res/60/264 (12 Jul. 2006).

United Nations Declaration on the Rights of Indigenous Peoples, adopted by the General Assembly. 2 Oct. 2007, G.A. Res. A/RES/61/295.

United Nations. General Assembly Res. A/RES/65/281 (17 Jun. 2011).

United Nations Office of the United Nations High Commissioner for Human Rights. *International Human Rights Instruments,* UN Doc. HRI/GEN/1/Rev.9 (Vol. I), CCPR General Comment No. 17: Article 24 (Rights of the child) (27 May 2008). Available at http://www.ohchr.org/Documents/HRBodies/TB/HRI-GEN-1-REV-9-VOL-I_en.doc).

United Nations Office of the United Nations High Commissioner for Human Rights. *International Human Rights Instruments*. UN Doc. HRI/GEN/1/Rev.9 (Vol. II), *General Recommendation XXIII on the Rights of Indigenous Peoples*, 27 May 2008. Available at http://www.ohchr.org/Documents/HRBodies/TB/HRI-GEN-1-REV-9-VOL-II_en.doc.

United Nations Economic Commission for Europe. UN/LOCODE Country Subdivisions ISO 3166-2 – Montenegro. Available at http://www.unece.org/fileadmin/DAM/cefact/locode/Subdivision/meSub.htm.

Universal Declaration on Cultural Diversity, adopted by the UNESCO General Conference on 2 Nov. 2001, 31C/Resolution 25.

US Department of Commerce. *.edu Cooperative Agreement and Subsequent Amendments*. (Last amended 16 Oct. 2007). Available at http://www.ntia.doc.gov/ntiahome/domainname/educa (no longer accessible but archived at http://www.archive.org/web/web.php).

US Department of Commerce and ICANN. *Memorandum of Understanding Between the US Department of Commerce and Internet Corporation for Assigned Names and Numbers*. (Last updated 31 Dec. 1999). Available at https://www.ntia.doc.gov/page/1998/memorandum-understanding-between-us-department-commerce-and-internet-corporation-assigned-.

Vattel, Emerich de. *Le Droit des Gens, ou Principes de la loi Naturelle, Appliqués à la conduite aux affaires des Nations et des Souverains*. vol. 1. 1758.

Vaughan, Owen. *RFC 2240: A Legal Basis for Domain Name Allocation. RFC Editor* (Nov. 1997). Available at http://www.rfc-editor.org/rfc/rfc2240.txt.

Verisign. *The Domain Name Industry Brief 9(1)*. (Mar. 2012). Available at https://www.verisign.com/assets/domain-name-brief-march2012.pdf.

Verisign. *The Domain Name Industry Brief 9(2)*. (Jul. 2012). Available at http://www.verisigninc.com/assets/domain-name-brief-july2012.pdf.

Verisign. *The Domain Name Industry Brief 13(2)*. (Jul. 2016). Available at https://www.verisign.com/assets/domain-name-report-july2016.pdf.

Vickers, John. 'Economics for Consumer Policy', in *Proceedings of the British Academy*. P.J. Marshall (ed.) Volume 125, 2003 Lectures (2005).

Virally, Michel. *The Sources of International Law*, in *Manual of Public International Law*. Max Sorensen ed. Macmillan, 1968.

Virmani, Arundhati. *National Symbols Under Colonial Domination: The Nationalization of the Indian Flag, March-August 1923*. 164 Past & Present 169 (1999).

Visser, Coenraad. *International Intellectual Property Norm Setting: Democratising the World Intellectual Property Organization?* 32 S. Afr. Y.B. Int'l L. 222 (2007).

Von Arx, Kim G. and Hagen, Gregory R. *Sovereign Domains: A Declaration of Independence of ccTLDs from Foreign Control*. 9 Richmond J L & Tech 4 (2002).

von Goethe, Johann Wolfgang. *Italienische Reise 1786-1788*. Hirmer Verlag, 1961.

Waldron, Jeremy. *Indigeneity? First Peoples and Last Occupancy*. 1 N.Z. J. Pub. & Int'l L. 55 (2002).

Wang, Minqin. *Regulating the Domain Name System: Is the '.BIZ' Domain Name Distribution Scheme an Illegal Lottery?* U. Ill. L.Rev. 245 (2003).

Warbrick, Colin. *States and Recognition in International Law*. In *International Law*. Malcom D. Evans ed. Oxford University Press, 2006.

Wass, Erica Schlesinger. *Introduction: Lots of Dots*. In *Addressing the World: National Identity and Internet Country Code Domains*. Erica Schlesinger Wass ed. Rowman & Littlefield, 2003.

Wass, Erica Schlesinger. *The United States' .US: Striving for the American Dream*. In *Addressing the World: National Identity and Internet Country Code Domains*. Erica Schlesinger Wass ed. Rowman & Littlefield, 2003.

Watson, Richard W. *RFC 273: More on Standard Host Names*. *RFC Editor* (18 Oct. 1971). Available at http://www.rfc-editor.org/rfc/rfc273.txt.

Watts, Jonathan. *Amazon v the Amazon: Internet Retailer in Domain Name Battle*. *The Guardian*. (25 Apr. 2013). Available at http://www.theguardian.com/environment/2013/apr/25/amazon-domain-name-batt le-brazil.

Weber, Rolf H. *Shaping Internet Governance: Regulatory Challenges*. Schulthess Juristische Medien, 2009.

Weise, Elizabeth. *Judge Denies Block on Internet Address Transfer*. USA Today. (1 Oct. 2016). Available at http://www.usatoday.com/story/tech/news/2016/09/30/judge-denies-block-internet-address-transfer-icann-ia na-ip-address-texas/91349184/.

Wendland, Wend B. *'It's a Small World (After All)': Some Reflections on Intellectual Property and Traditional Cultural Expressions*. In *Intellectual Property and Traditional Cultural Expressions in a Digital Environment*. Christoph Beat Graber and Mira Burri-Nenova eds Edward Elgar, 2008.

Whitaker, Mark. *Internet Counter Counter-Insurgency: TamilNet.com and Ethnic Conflict in Sri Lanka*. In *Native on the Net*. Kyra Landzelius ed. Routledge, 2006.

Wiessner, Siegfried. *Re-enchanting the World: Indigenous Peoples' Rights as Essential Parts of a Holistic Human Rights Regime*. 15 UCLA J. Int'l L. & Foreign Aff. 239 (2010).

Wiessner, Siegfried and Willard, Andrew R. *Symposium on Method in International Law, Policy-Oriented Jurisprudence and Human Rights Abuses in Internal Conflict: Toward a World Public Order of Human Dignity*. 93 Am. J. Int'l L. 316 (1999).

WIPO. *Appellations of Origin*. http://www.wipo.int/ipdl/en/lisbon/lisbon-map.jsp.

WIPO. *Article 6ter of the Paris Convention: Protection of State Emblems, and Names, Abbreviations and Emblems of International Intergovernmental Organizations*. Available at http://www.wipo.int/article6ter/en/.

WIPO, *Article 6ter - Procedure for States*. Available at http://www.wipo.int/article6ter/en/states.html.

WIPO. *Article 6ter Structured Search*. Available at http://www.wipo.int/ipdl/en/6ter/.

WIPO. *Creative Heritage Project: Surveys of Existing Practices, Protocols and Policies*. Available at http://www.wipo.int/tk/en/resources/surveys.html.

WIPO. *General Information on Article 6ter*. Available at http://www.wipo.int/article6ter/en/general_info.html.

WIPO. *General Information on STOP*. Available at http://www.wipo.int/amc/en/domains/gtld/biz/stop/index.html.

WIPO. *Joint Recommendation Concerning Provisions on the Protection of Well-Known Marks*. WIPO Doc. A/34/13. Available at http://www.wipo.int/edocs/pubdocs/en/marks/833/pub833.pdf.

WIPO. *Lisbon Agreement (Total Contracting Parties: 28)*. Available at http://www.wipo.int/treaties/en/ShowResults.jsp?lang=en&treaty_id=10.

WIPO. *The Lisbon Agreement for the Protection of Appellations of Origin and their International Registration: Objective and Main Features, Protection to be Accorded*. Available at http://www.wipo.int/lisbon/en/general/.

WIPO. *Madrid Agreement (Indications of Source) (Total Contracting Parties: 36)*. Available at http://www.wipo.int/treaties/en/ShowResults.jsp?lang=en&treaty_id=3.

WIPO. *Search Appellations of Origin (Lisbon Express)*. Available at http://www.wipo.int/ipdl/en/search/lisbon/search-struct.jsp.

WIPO. *WIPO: Member States*. Available at http://www.wipo.int/members/en/.

WIPO. *WIPO Arbitration and Mediation Center - Domain Name Disputes (New gTLDs: WIPO Guide to the Afilias Sunrise Registration Challenge Policy for .info*. Available at http://www.wipo.int/amc/en/domains/gtld/info/sunrise/guide.html.

WIPO. *WIPO End Report on Case Administration under the Sunrise Challenge Policy for.mobi and the Premium Name Trademark Application Rules for .mobi*. Available at http://www.wipo.int/amc/en/domains/reports/mobi/report/index.html.

WIPO. *WIPO Overview of WIPO Panel Views on Selected UDRP Questions*. Available at http://www.wipo.int/amc/en/domains/search/overview/index.html#15.

WIPO. *Model Law for Developing Countries on Appellations of Origin*. PJ/91/2, No. 809(E)(1975).

WIPO. *WIPO Diplomatic Conference on the Revision of the Paris Convention*. Doc PR/DC/4, 30 Aug. 1979. Available at http://www.wipo.int/mdocsarchives/PR_DC_1%20to%2020_1980/PR_DC_4_E.pdf.

WIPO. *Protection Against Unfair Competition: Analysis of the Present World Situation*. WIPO Publication No. 725 (1994).

WIPO. *Model Provisions on Protection Against Unfair Competition*. WIPO Pub. No. 832 (1996).

WIPO ed. *Introduction to Intellectual Property: Theory and Practice*. Kluwer Law International, 1997.

WIPO. *Interim Report of the WIPO Internet Domain Name Process, The Management of Internet Names and Addresses: Intellectual Property Issues*. (23 Dec. 1998). Available at http://www.wipo.int/amc/en/processes/process1/rfc/3/index.html.

WIPO. *Final Report of the WIPO Internet Domain Name Process: The Management of Internet Names and Addresses: Intellectual Property Issues*. (30 Apr. 1999). Available at http://www.wipo.int/amc/en/processes/process1/report/index.html.

WIPO. *The Recognition of Rights and the Use of Names in the Internet Domain Name System: Report of the Second WIPO Internet Domain Name Process*. (3 Sep. 2001). Available at http://www.wipo.int/amc/en/processes/process2/report/html/report.html.

WIPO. *ccTLD Best Practices for the Prevention and Resolution of Intellectual Property Disputes: version 1*. (20 Jun. 2001). Available at http://www.wipo.int/export/sites/www/amc/en/docs/bestpractices.pdf.

WIPO. *General Assembly Twenty-Eighth (13th Extraordinary) Session, Geneva, 23 Sept. – 1 Oct*. WIPO Doc. WO/GA/28/3, 24 Jun. 2002. Available at http://www.wipo.int/meetings/en/details.jsp?meeting_id=4650.

WIPO. *Letter to ICANN regarding Proposed New gTLDs Procedure*. 13 Mar. 2009. Available at http://www.wipo.int/export/sites/www/amc/en/docs/icann130309.pdf.

WIPO. *A New Dawn for Custodians of TK in Africa*. WIPO Magazine (Dec. 2010). Available at http://www.wipo.int/wipo_magazine/en/2010/06/article_0008.html.

WIPO. *Browse Comments: 2012 Country Names*. Available at http://www.wipo.int/sct/en/comments/.

WIPO. *Diplomatic Conference for the Adoption of a New Act of the Lisbon Agreement for the Protection of Appellations of Origin and Their International Registration: Notes on the Basic Proposal for the New Act of the Lisbon Agreement on Appellations of Origin and Geographical Indications*. WIPO Doc. LI/DC/5 (22 Dec. 2014). Available at http://www.wipo.int/meetings/en/details.jsp?meeting_id=35202.

WIPO, *Diplomatic Conference for the Adoption of a New Act of the Lisbon Agreement for the Protection of Appellations of Origin and Their International Registration: Proposal by the Delegations of Argentina, Australia, Canada, Chile, Japan, New Zealand, Republic of Korea, Saudi Arabia, Singapore, United States of America and Uruguay*, LI/DC/9 (11 May 2015). Available at http://www.wipo.int/edocs/mdocs/geoind/en/li_dc/li_dc_9.pdf.

WIPO General Assembly. *Report of the Twenty-Eighth (13th Extraordinary) Session*. WIPO Doc. WO/GA/28/7 CORR, 1 Oct. 2002. Available at http://www.wipo.int/edocs/mdocs/govbody/en/wo_ga_28/wo_ga_28_7.pdf.

WIPO Intergovernmental Committee on Intellectual Property and Genetic Resources, Traditional Knowledge and Folklore. *The Protection of Traditional Cultural Expressions: Draft Articles*. WIPO Doc. WIPO/GRTKF/IC/18/4 Rev. 14 Apr. 2011. Available at http://www.wipo.int/edocs/mdocs/tk/en/wipo_grtkf_ic_18/wipo_grtkf_ic_18_4_rev.pdf.

WIPO Intergovernmental Committee on Intellectual Property and Genetic Resources, Traditional Knowledge and Folklore. *The Protection of Traditional Cultural Expressions: Draft Articles*. WIPO Doc. WIPO/GRTKF/IC/28/6 (2 Jun. 2014) (available at http://www.wipo.int/edocs/mdocs/tk/en/wipo_grtkf_ic_28/wipo_grtkf_ic_28_6.pdf).

WIPO Intergovernmental Committee on Intellectual Property and Genetic Resources, Traditional Knowledge and Folklore. *Like-Minded Countries Contribution to the Draft Articles on the Protection of Traditional Cultural Expressions*. WIPO Doc. WIPO/GRTKF/IC/22/5 (2012). Available at http://www.wipo.int/edocs/mdocs/tk/en/wipo_grtkf_ic_22/wipo_grtkf_ic_22_5.pdf.

WIPO Intergovernmental Committee on Intellectual Property and Genetic Resources, Traditional Knowledge and Folklore. *Like-Minded Countries Contribution to the Draft Articles on the Protection of Traditional Knowledge*. WIPO Doc. WIPO/GRTKF/IC/21/5 (2012) Available at http://www.wipo.int/edocs/mdocs/tk/en/wipo_grtkf_ic_21/wipo_grtkf_ic_21_5.pdf.

WIPO Intergovernmental Committee on Intellectual Property and Genetic Resources, Traditional Knowledge and Folklore. *Glossary of Key Terms Related to Intellectual Property and Genetic Resources, Traditional Knowledge and Traditional Cultural Expressions*. WIPO Doc. WIPO/GRTKF/IC/20/INF/13 (2012). Available at http://www.wipo.int/edocs/mdocs/tk/en/wipo_grtkf_ic_20/wipo_grtkf_ic_20_inf_13.pdf.

WIPO Intergovernmental Committee on Intellectual Property and Genetic Resources, Traditional Knowledge and Folklore. *The Protection of Traditional Cultural Expressions: Draft Articles*. WIPO Doc. WIPO/GRTKF/IC/28/6 (2 Jun. 2014) Available at http://www.wipo.int/edocs/mdocs/tk/en/wipo_grtkf_ic_28/wipo_grtkf_ic_28_6.pdf.

WIPO Intergovernmental Committee on Intellectual Property and Genetic Resources, Traditional Knowledge and Folklore. *The Protection of Traditional Cultural Expressions: Draft Articles Rev. 2 (September 23, 2016)*. WIPO Doc. WIPO/GRTKF/IC/31/FACILITATORS TEXT REV. 2 (30 Sep. 2016). Available at http://www.wipo.int/edocs/mdocs/tk/en/wipo_grtkf_ic_31/wipo_grtkf_ic_31_facilitators_text_rev_2.pdf.

WIPO Special Union for the Protection of Appellations of Origin and their International Registration. *Assembly Report of the Twenty-third (6th Extraordinary) Session in Geneva, September 22 to 30, 2008*, LI/A/23/2.

WIPO Standing Committee on the Law of Trademarks, Industrial Designs and Geographical Indications. *First Special Session on the Report of the Second WIPO Internet Domain Name Process, Geneva, November 29 to*

December 4, 2001. SCT/S1/6 (7 Dec. 2001). Available at http://www.wipo.int/amc/en/processes/sct/documents/index.html.

WIPO Standing Committee on the Law of Trademarks, Industrial Designs and Geographical Indications. *The Protection of Country Names in the Domain Name System: Comments Submitted by the Government of the Republic of South Africa*. WIPO Doc. SCT/S2/6 (17 May 2002). Available at www.wipo.int/edocs/mdocs/sct/en/sct_s2/sct_s2_6.doc.

WIPO Standing Committee on the Law of Trademarks, Industrial Designs and Geographical Indications. *Second Special Session on the Report of the Second WIPO Internet Domain Name Process, Geneva, May 21-24, 2002*. SCT/S2/8 (24 May 2002). Available at http://www.wipo.int/amc/en/processes/sct/documents/index.html.

WIPO Standing Committee on the Law of Trademarks, Industrial Designs and Geographical Indications. *Report of the Ninth Session, Geneva, November 11 to 15, 2002*.SCT/9/9 (2 May 2003). Available at http://www.wipo.int/edocs/mdocs/sct/en/sct_9/sct_9_9.pdf.

WIPO Standing Committee on the Law of Trademarks, Industrial Designs and Geographical Indications. *Proposal by Jamaica*. WIPO Doc. SCT/21/6 (30 Mar. 2009). Available at http://www.wipo.int/edocs/mdocs/sct/en/sct_21/sct_21_6.pdf.

WIPO Standing Committee on the Law of Trademarks, Industrial Designs and Geographical Indications. *Report Adopted by the Standing Committee*. WIPO Doc. SCT/21/8 (26 Nov. 2009). Available at http://www.wipo.int/edocs/mdocs/sct/en/sct_21/sct_21_8.pdf.

WIPO Standing Committee on the Law of Trademarks, Industrial Designs and Geographical Indications. *Submission by the Russian Federation*. WIPO Doc. SCT/21/5 (2 Mar. 2009). Available at http://www.wipo.int/edocs/mdocs/sct/en/sct_21/sct_21_5.pdf.

WIPO Standing Committee on the Law of Trademarks, Industrial Designs and Geographical Indications. *Draft Questionnaire Concerning the Protection of Names of States Against Registration and Use as Trademarks*. WIPO Doc. SCT/23/4 (15 Feb. 2010). Available at http://www.wipo.int/edocs/mdocs/stlt/en/sct_23/sct_23_4.pdf.

WIPO Standing Committee on the Law of Trademarks, Industrial Designs and Geographical Indications. *Summary of the Replies to the Questionnaire Concerning the Protection of Names of States against Registration and Use as Trademarks*. WIPO Doc. SCT/24/6 (14 Feb. 2011). Available at http://www.wipo.int/edocs/mdocs/sct/en/sct_24/sct_24_6.pdf.

WIPO Standing Committee on the Law of Trademarks, Industrial Designs and Geographical Indications. *Proposal by the Delegations of Barbados and Jamaica*. WIPO Doc. SCT/27/6 (18 Jun. 2012). Available at http://www.wipo.int/edocs/mdocs/sct/en/sct_27/sct_27_6.pdf.

WIPO Standing Committee on the Law of Trademarks, Industrial Designs and Geographical Indications. *Information on Cases and Case Studies Relevant to the Protection of Names of States and on Nation Branding*

Schemes. WIPO Doc. SCT/27/5 (18 Jul. 2012). Available at http://www.wipo.int/edocs/mdocs/sct/en/sct_27/sct_27_5.pdf.

WIPO Standing Committee on the Law of Trademarks, Industrial Designs and Geographical Indications. *Proposal by the Delegation of the United States of America*, WIPO Doc. SCT/30/7 (31 Oct. 2013). Available at http://www.wipo.int/edocs/mdocs/sct/en/sct_30/sct_30_7.pdf.

WIPO Standing Committee on the Law of Trademarks, Industrial Designs and Geographical Indications. *Proposal by the Delegation of Jamaica*, WIPO Doc. SCT/31/4 (21 Jan. 2014). Available at http://www.wipo.int/meetings/en/doc_details.jsp?doc_id=262359.

WIPO Standing Committee on the Law of Trademarks, Industrial Designs and Geographical Indications. *Proposal by the Delegations of the Czech Republic, France, Germany, Hungary, Italy, Portugal, Republic of Moldova, Spain and Switzerland*, WIPO Doc. SCT/31/8 Rev. 4 (23 Mar. 2015). Available at http://www.wipo.int/edocs/mdocs/sct/en/sct_31/sct_31_8_rev_4.pdf.

WIPO Standing Committee on the Law of Trademarks, Industrial Designs and Geographical Indications. *Protection of Country Names Against Registration and Use as Trademarks: Practices, Approaches and Possible Areas of Convergence*, WIPO Doc. SCT/35/4 (25 Feb. 2016). Available at http://www.wipo.int/edocs/mdocs/sct/en/sct_35/sct_35_4.pdf).

Wood, Michael C. *Participation of Former Yugoslav States in the United Nations and in Multilateral Treaties*. In *Max Planck Y.B.U.N. L.* 236–241. Armin von Bogdandy ed. Martinus Nijhoff Publishers, 1997.

Woodard, Elizabeth C. *The UDRP, ADR, and Arbitration: Using Proven Solutions to Address Perceived Problems with the UDRP*. 19 Fordham Intell. Prop. Media & Ent. L. J. 1169 (2009).

WTO. *Doha WTO Ministerial Declaration*. WTO Doc. WT/MIN(01)/DEC1 (20 Nov. 2001). Available at http://www.wto.org/english/thewto_e/minist_e/min01_e/mindecl_e.htm.

WTO. *Issues Related to the Extension of the Protection of Geographical Indications Provided for in Article 23 of the TRIPS Agreement to Products Other Than Wines and Spirits and Those Related to the Relationship between the TRIPS Agreement and the Convention on Biological Diversity: Report by the Director-General*. WT/GC/W/633 and TN/C/W/61 (21 Apr. 2011). Available at https://www.wto.org/english/tratop_e/trips_e/giextension_cbd_dgreport_9jun08_e.doc.

WTO. *Multilateral System of Notification and Registration of Geographical Indications for wines and Spirits: Report by the Chairman, Ambassador Darlington Mwape (Zambia) to the Trade Negotiations Committee*. TN/IP/21 (21 Apr. 2011). Available at http://www.wto.org/english/tratop_e/dda_e/chair_texts11_e/trips_e.doc.

WTO. *Understanding the WTO: The Organization, Members and Observers, 164 members since 29 July 2016 (with dates of membership)*. Available at https://www.wto.org/english/thewto_e/whatis_e/tif_e/org6_e.htm.

WTO Council for Trade-Related Aspects of Intellectual Property Rights. *Report (1996) of the Council for TRIPS*. IP/C/8 96-4704. 1996.

WTO Council for Trade-Related Aspects of Intellectual Property Rights. *Implementation of Article 23.4 of the TRIPS Agreement Relating to the Establishment of a Multilateral System of Notification and Registration of Geographical Indications*. IP/C/W/107. Communication from the European Communities and their Member States. Rev. 1 00-2521. (2000).

WTO Council for Trade-Related Aspects of Intellectual Property Rights. *Proposal for a Multilateral System for Notification and Registration of Geographical Indications based on Article 23.4 of the TRIPS Agreement*. IP/C/W/133/Rev.1. Communication from Canada, Chile, Japan and the United States, Rev. 1 99-3125. (1999).

WTO Council for Trade-Related Aspects of Intellectual Property Rights. *Proposal from Bulgaria, Cuba, Czech Republic, Egypt, Iceland, India, Jamaica, Kenya, Liechtenstein, Mauritius, Nigeria, Pakistan, Slovenia, Sri Lanka, Switzerland, Turkey and Venezuela (Revision)*. IP/C/W/247/Rev.1 01-2491. 2001.

WTO Council for Trade-Related Aspects of Intellectual Property Rights Special Session. *Multilateral System of Notification and Registration of Geographical Indications for Wines and Spirits: Report by the Chairman, Ambassador Dacio Castillo (Honduras)*. TN/IP/23, 3 Dec. 2015.

Yu, Peter K. *The Origins of ccTLD Policymaking*. 12 Cardozo J. Intl & Compar. L. 387 (2004).

Yu, Peter K. *Intellectual Property and Human Rights in the Nonmultilateral Era*. 64 Fla. L. Rev. 1045 (2012).

.zadna. *Second Level Domain General Policy – 1 April 2015*. Available at http://www.zadna.org.za/uploads/files/ZA_SLD_General_Policy_final_1_April_2015.pdf.

Zakon, Robert Hobbes. *Hobbes' Internet Timeline Version 10.1*. (Last updated 15 Dec. 2010). Available at http://zakon.org/robert/internet/timeline/#Growth.

Zook, Matthew. Email to Heather Forrest: *Domain Counts* (15 Sep. 2012) (on file with author).

ZookNIC Internet Intelligence. *History of gTLD Domain Name Growth*. Available at http://www.zooknic.com/Domains/counts.html.

International Treaties and Agreements

Agreement on Trade-Related Aspects of Intellectual Property Rights, Marrakesh Agreement Establishing the World Trade Organization, Annex 1C (15 Apr. 1994) 1869 U.N.T.S. 299, 33 I.L.M. 1197.

African Charter on Human and Peoples' Rights (27 Jun. 1981, entered into force 21 Oct. 1986) O.A.U. Doc. CAB/LEG/67/3 Rev 5.

American Convention on Human Rights (22 Nov. 1969, entered into force 17 Jul. 1978) 1144 U.N.T.S. 123.

Berne Convention for the Protection of Literary and Artistic Works (9 Sep. 1886) 828 U.N.T.S. 221.

Charter of Fundamental Rights of the European Union, OJ 2000/C 364/01.

Charter of the United Nations (26 Jun. 1945, entered into force 24 Oct. 1945) 59 Stat. 1031.

Convention against Torture and Other Cruel, Inhuman or Degrading Treatment or Punishment (10 Dec. 1984, entered into force 26 Jun. 1987) 39 U.N. GAOR Supp. (No. 51) at 197, U.N. Doc. A/39/51 (1984).

Convention Establishing the World Intellectual Property Organization (14 Jul. 1967, entered into force 26 Apr. 1970) 828 U.N.T.S. 3.

Convention for the Protection of Human Rights and Fundamental Freedoms (4 Nov. 1950, entered into force 3 Sep. 1953) E.T.S. 5, 213 U.N.T.S. 221.

Convention for the Safeguarding of the Intangible Cultural Heritage (17 Oct. 2003, entered into force 20 Apr. 2006) 32C/Res. 32.

Convention on Biological Diversity (5 Jun. 1992, entered into force 29 Dec. 1993) 1760 U.N.T.S. 79; 31 I.L.M. 818.

Convention on Certain Questions in Relation to the Conflict of Nationality Laws (12 Apr. 1930, entered into force 1 Jul. 1937) 179 L.N.T.S. 89.

Convention on Rights and Duties of States adopted by the Seventh International Conference of American States (26 Dec. 1933, entered into force 26 Dec. 1934) 165 L.N.T.S. 19.

Convention on the Elimination of All Forms of Discrimination against Women (18 Dec. 1979, entered into force 3 Sep. 1981) U.N. GAOR Supp. (No. 46) at 193, U.N. Doc. A/34/46.

Convention on the Protection and Promotion of the Diversity of Cultural Expressions (18 Dec. 1990, entered into force 18 Mar. 2007) 33C/Res. 42.

Convention on the Rights of Persons with Disabilities (13 Dec. 2006, entered into force 3 May 2008) U.N. Doc. A/61/611.

Convention on the Rights of the Child (20 Nov. 1989, entered into force 2 Sep. 1990) 44 U.N. GAOR Supp. (No. 49) at 167, U.N. Doc. A/44/49 (1989).

General Agreement on Tariffs and Trade 1994 (15 Apr. 1994, entered into force 1 Jan. 1995) 1867 U.N.T.S. 187, 33 I.L.M. 1153.

Geneva Act of the Lisbon Agreement on Appellations of Origin and Geographical Indications (20 May 2015, not yet in force) WIPO Doc. LI/DC/19.

Interim Accord (with related letters and translations of the Interim Accord in the Languages of the Contracting Parties), Greece-the former Yugoslav Republic of Macedonia, signed in New York 13 Sep. 1995, 1891 U.N.T.S. I-32193, 34 I.L.M. 1461 (13 Oct. 1995).

International Convention on the Elimination of All Forms of Racial Discrimination, (21 Dec. 1965, entered into force 4 Jan. 1969) 660 U.N.T.S. 195.

International Convention for the Protection of All Persons from Enforced Disappearance (20 Dec. 2006, entered into force 23 Dec. 2010) U.N. Doc. A/61/488.

International Convention for the Protection of Performers, Producers of Phonograms and Broadcasting Organisations (26 Oct. 1961, entered into force 18 May 1964) 496 U.N.T.S. 43.

International Convention on the Protection of the Rights of All Migrant Workers and Members of their Families (18 Dec. 1990, entered into force 1 Jul. 2003) 47 U.N. GAOR Supp. (No. 49A), U.N. Doc. A/47/49 (1990).

International Covenant on Civil and Political Rights (16 Dec. 1966, entered into force 23 Mar. 1976) 999 U.N.T.S. 171.

International Covenant on Economic, Social and Cultural Rights (16 Dec. 1966, entered into force 3 Jan. 1976) 993 U.N.T.S. 3.

Lisbon Agreement for the Protection of Appellations of Origin and their International Registration (31 Oct. 1958, entered into force 25 Sep. 1966) 923 U.N.T.S. 205.

Madrid Agreement for the Repression of False or Deceptive Indications of Source on Goods (14 Apr. 1891) 828 U.N.T.S. 163.

Nice Agreement Concerning the International Classification of Goods and Services for the Purposes of the Registration of Marks of 15 Jun. 1957, as revised at Stockholm on 14 Jul. 1967 (entered into force 12 Nov. 1969) 828 U.N.T.S. 191.

Paris Convention for the Protection of Industrial Property (20 Mar. 1883, last revised 14 Jul. 1967 and as amended 28 Sep. 1979) 828 U.N.T.S. 305.

Protocol on Harmonization of Norms on Intellectual Property in Mercosur in matters of Trademarks, Indications of Source and Appellations of Origin (5 Aug. 1995, entered into force 6 Aug. 2000) 2145 U.N.T.S. 40.

Protocol Relating to the Madrid Agreement Concerning the International Registration of Marks (28 Jun. 1989, entered into force 1 Dec. 1995) 82 Trademark Rep. 58.

Rules of Court (14 Apr. 1978, entered into force 1 Jul. 1978, as amended 14 Apr. 2005) I.C.J. Acts & Docs 4.

Statute of the International Court of Justice (26 Jun. 1945, entered into force 24 Oct. 1945) 3 Bevans 1179; 59 Stat. 1031; T.S. No. 993; 39 A.J.I.L. Supp. 215.

Swakopmund Protocol on the Protection of Traditional Knowledge and Expressions of Folklore, WIPO Lex No. TRT/AP010/001 (9 Aug. 2010, entered into force 11 May 2015).

Trademark Law Treaty (27 Oct. 1994, entered into force 1 Aug. 1996) 2037 U.N.T.S. 35.

Treaty Establishing the European Community (25 Mar. 1957).

Treaty on Intellectual Property in Respect of Integrated Circuits (26 May 1989) 28 I.L.M. 1477.

Vienna Convention on the Law of Treaties (23 May 1969, entered into force 27 Jan. 1980) 1155 U.N.T.S. 331.

Cases and Dispute Resolution Decisions

Angus v. Clifford, 60 L.J. Rep. (N.S.) C.D. 456 (1891).

Application of the Interim Accord of 13 September 1995 (the former Yugoslav Republic of Macedonia v. Greece), Judgment of 5 Dec. 2011.

Asphalt Research Technology, Inc. v. National Press & Publishing, Inc., Case No. D2000-1005 (WIPO Arbitration and Mediation Center 13 Nov. 2000) (available at http://www.wipo.int/amc/en/domains/decisions/html/2000/d2000-1005.html).

Australia – Certain Measures Concerning Trademarks and Other Plain Packaging Requirements Applicable to Tobacco Products and Packaging, WT/DS434/1.

Australia – Certain Measures Concerning Trademarks, Geographical Indications and Other Plain Packaging Requirements Applicable to Tobacco Products and Packaging, WT/DS435/1.

Australia – Certain Measures Concerning Trademarks and Other Plain Packaging Requirements Applicable to Tobacco Products and Packaging, WT/DS441/1.

Avery Dennison Corp. v. Sumpton, 999 F. Supp. 1337, 1338 (C.D. Cal. 1998).

BAA plc, Aberdeen Airport Limited v. Mr H Hashimi, Case No. D2004-0717 (WIPO Arbitration and Mediation Center 21 Oct. 2004) (available at http://www.wipo.int/amc/en/domains/decisions/html/2004/d2004-0717.html).

Ballantyne, Davidson, McIntyre v. Canada, U.N. Doc. CCPR/C/47/D/359/1989 and 385/1989/Rev.1 (1993).

Brisbane City Council v. Warren Bolton Consulting Pty Ltd, Case No. D2001-0047 (WIPO Arbitration and Mediation Center 7 May 2001) (available at http://www.wipo.int/amc/en/domains/decisions/html/2001/d2001-0047.html).

Brisbane City Council v. Joyce Russ Advertising Pty Ltd, Case No. D2001-0069 (WIPO Arbitration and Mediation Center 14 May 2001) (available at http://www.wipo.int/amc/en/domains/decisions/html/2001/d2001-0069.html).

Brookfield Communications, Inc. v. West Coast Entertainment Corp., 50 U.S.P.Q.2d (B.N.A.) 1545, 1559-1560 (9th Cir. 1999).

Bruce Springsteen v. Jeff Burgar and Bruce Springsteen Club, Case No. D2000-1532 (WIPO Arbitration and Mediation Center 25 Jan. 2001) (available at http://www.wipo.int/amc/en/domains/decisions/html/2000/d2000-1532.html).

Canada – Patent Protection of Pharmaceutical Products (Generic Medicines), WT/DS114/R (W.T.O. D.S.B. Panel 17 Mar. 2000) (available at http://www.wto.org/english/tratop_e/dispu_e/cases_e/ds114_e.htm).

Case Concerning the Application of Article 11, Paragraph 1, of the Interim Accord of 13 September 1995 (The Former Yugoslav Republic of Macedonia v. Greece), Memorial (I.C.J. 20 Jul. 2009) (available at http://www.icj-cij.org/docket/files/142/16354.pdf).

Case Concerning the Application of Article 11, Paragraph 1, of the Interim Accord of 13 September 1995 (The Former Yugoslav Republic of Macedonia v. Greece), Counter-Memorial by Greece (I.C.J. 19 Jan. 2010) (available at http://www.icj-cij.org/docket/files/142/16356.pdf).

Case Concerning the Application of Article 11, Paragraph 1, of the Interim Accord of 13 September 1995 (The Former Yugoslav Republic of Macedonia v. Greece), Rejoinder of Greece (I.C.J. 27 Oct. 2010) (available at http://www.icj-cij.org/docket/files/142/16356.pdf).

City of Hamina v. Paragon International Projects Ltd, Case No. D2001-0001 (WIPO Arbitration and Mediation Center 12 Mar. 2001) (available at http://www.wipo.int/amc/en/domains/decisions/html/2001/d2001-0001.html).

Commission of the European Communities v. Hellenic Republic, C-120/94 R I-03037 (E.C.J. 29 Jun. 1994).

Commissioners of Inland Revenue v. Muller & Co's Margarine, Ltd, A.C. 217, 223 (Aust'l H.L. 1901).

Consorzio del Proscuitto di Parma v. Domain Name Clearing Company, LLC, Case No. D2000-0629 (WIPO Arbitration and Mediation Center 18 Sep. 2000) (available at http://www.wipo.int/amc/en/domains/decisions/html/2000/d2000-0629.html).

Deer Valley Resort Company v. Intermountain Lodging and Registration Center, Case No. FA474344 (National Arbitration Forum 27 Jun. 2005) (available at http://www.adrforum.com/domaindecisions/474344.htm).

Eastern Wine Corp. v. Winslow-Warren Ltd., 137 F.2d 955, 959 (C.C.A. 2d. 1943).

ePrize v. NeuLevel, No. BC257632 (Cal. Super. Ct., filed 10 Sep. 2001).

European Communities – Protection of Trademarks and Geographical Indications for Agricultural Products and Foodstuffs – Complaint by

Australia, Report of the Panel. WT/DS290/R 05-0936 (W.T.O. D.S.B. Panel 15 Mar. 2005).

Excelentisimo Ayuntamiento de Barcelona v. Barcelona.com Inc., Case No. D2000-0505 (WIPO Arbitration and Mediation Center 4 Aug. 2000) (available at http://www.wipo.int/amc/en/domains/decisions/html/2000/d2000-0505.html).

Faurisson v. France, 4 I.H.R.R. 444 (Hum. Rts. Comm. 1996).

FC Bayern München AG v. Peoples Net Services Ltd, Case No. D2003-0464 (WIPO Arbitration and Mediation Center 15 Jul. 2003) (available at http://www.wipo.int/amc/en/domains/decisions/html/2003/d2003-0464.html).

Federal Communications Commission v. Fox Television Stations, Inc., 132 S. Ct. 2037 (U.S. Sup. Ct. 2012).

Federal Communications Commission v. Pacifica Foundation, 434 U.S. 1008 (U.S. Sup. Ct. 1978).

Federal Communications Commission v. Pacifica Foundation, 438 U.S. 726 (U.S. Sup. Ct. 1978).

Generalitat de Catalunya v. Thomas Wolf, Wolf Domains, WIPO Case No. D2002-1124. (WIPO Arbitration and Mediation Center 14 Apr. 2003) (available at http://www.wipo.int/amc/en/domains/decisions/html/2002/d2002-1124.html).

Gorstew Limited v. Worldwidewebsales.com, Case No. D2002-0744 (WIPO Arbitration and Mediation Center 23 Oct. 2002) (available at http://www.wipo.int/amc/en/domains/decisions/html/2002/d2002-0744.html).

Harold Joseph Thomas v. David George Brown & James Morrison Vallely Tennant, 215 F.C.A. (Fed. Ct. Aust'l 1997).

Her Majesty the Queen, in right of her Government in New Zealand v. Virtual Countries, WIPO Case No. D2002-0754 (WIPO Arbitration and Mediation Center 27 Nov. 2002) (available at http://www.wipo.int/amc/en/domains/decisions/html/2002/d2002-0754.html).

Hertel v. Switzerland (59/1997/843/1049) Eur. Ct. H.R. (1998).

India – Patent Protection for Pharmaceuticals and Agricultural Chemical Products, WT/DS50/AB/R (W.T.O. App. Body Report 19 Dec. 1997).

Inter-American Commission on Human Rights. Report on the Situation of Human Rights of a Segment of the Nicaraguan Population of Miskito Origin and Resolution on the Friendly Settlement Procedure Regarding the Human Rights Situation of a Segment of the Nicaraguan Population of Miskito Origin. O.A.S. Doc. OEA/Ser.L/V/II.62, Doc. 10, Rev. 3 (1983); OEA/Ser/L/V/II.62, doc. 26 (1984) (Case No. 7964 (Nicaragua)).

Intermatic Inc. v. Toeppen, 947 F. Supp. 1227, 1233 (N.D. Ill. 1996).

Island of Palmas Case (or Miangas), Hague Court Reports 2d. 83 (1932), (Perm. Ct. Arb. 1928), 2 U.N. Rep. Intl. Arb. Awards 829.

Japan – Customs Duties, Taxes and Labelling Practices on Imported Wines and Alcoholic Beverages, L6216 adopted 10 Nov. 1987, BISD 34S/83 (GATT Panel Report).

Joosse v. Australian Securities and Investment Commission, 159 A.L.R. 260, 263-264 (High Ct. Aust'l 1998).

Junta de Analucia Consejeria de Turismo, Comercio y Deporte, Turismo Andaluz, S.A. v. Andalucia.com Limited, Case No. D2006-0749 (WIPO Arbitration and Mediation Center 13 Oct. 2006) (available at http://www.wipo.int/amc/en/domains/decisions/html/2006/d2006-0749.html).

Keun-Tae Kim v. Republic of Korea, U.N. Doc. CCPR/C/64/D/574/1994 (U.N. Hum. Rts. Comm. 1999).

K.J.L. v. Finland, U.N. Human Rights Committee, Communication No. 544/193 U.N. Doc. CCPR/C/49/D/544/1993.

Koné v. Senegal, U.N. Human Rights Committee, Communication No. 386/1989 U.N. Doc. CCPR/C/52/D/386/1989.

Kur-und Verkehrsverein St Moritz v. StMoritz.com, Case No. D2000-0617 (WIPO Arbitration and Mediation Center 17 Aug. 2000) (available at http://www.wipo.int/amc/en/domains/decisions/html/2000/d2000-0617.html).

L.E.S.K. v. the Netherlands, U.N. Human Rights Committee, Communication No. 381/1989 U.N. Doc. CCPR/C/45/D381/1989 (1992).

Mishawaka Rubber & Woolen Mfg. Co. v. S.S. Kresge Co., 316 U.S. 203, 205 (Sup. Ct. 1942).

Morris Communications Corp. v. PGA Tour, Inc., 364 F.3d 1288 (11th Cir. 2004), *cert. denied.*

Morris Communications Corp. v. PGA Tour, Inc., 543 U.S. 919, 125 S.Ct. 87, 160 L.Ed.2d 203 (US Sup. Ct. 2004).

Mukong v. Cameroon, 2 I.H.R.R. 131 (Hum. Rts. Comm. 1995).

National A-1 Advertising, Inc. v. Network Solutions, Inc., 121 F.Supp. 2d 156 (Dist. Ct. N.H. 2000).

Network Network v. CBS, Inc., 54 U.S.P.Q.2d (B.N.A.) 1150, 1155 (C.D. Cal. 2000).

North Sea Continental Shelf Cases (Federal Republic of Germany/Denmark; Federal Republic of Germany/Netherlands), I.C.J. 43 (I.C.J. 1969).

Nottebohm Case (second phase), Judgment of April 6th, 19 jj, I.C.J. Reports 1955.

Ominayak, Chief of the Lubicon Lake Band v. Canada, Communication No. 267/1984, Report of the Human Rights Committee U.N. GOAR, 45th Sess., Supp. No. 40, Vol. 2, at 1, U.N. Doc. A/45/40, Annex 9(A) (1990).

Panavision Int'l v. Toeppen, 141 F.3d 1316 (9th Cir. 1998).

Peter Pázmány University v. Czechoslovakia, P.C.I.J. Reports Ser. A/B No. 61, 231 (P.C.I.J. 1933).

Polaroid Corp. v. Polaraid, Inc., 319 F.2d 830 (7th Cir. 1963).

Porto Chico Stores, Inc. v. Otavio Zambon, Case No. D2000-1270 (WIPO Arbitration and Mediation Center 15 Nov. 2000) (available at http://www.wipo.int/amc/en/domains/decisions/html/2000/d2000-1270.html).

Puerto Rico Tourism Company v. Virtual Countries, Inc., Case No. D2002-1129 (WIPO Arbitration and Mediation Center 14 Apr. 2003) (available at http://www.wipo.int/amc/en/domains/decisions/html/2002/d2002-1129.html).

Right of Passage over Indian Territory (Portugal v. India), Merits Judgment I.C.J. Reports (I.C.J. 1960).

Seven Words LLC v. Network Solutions, 260 F.3d 1089 (9th Cir. Ct. App. 2001).

Seven Words LLC v. Network Solutions, Inc., (Seven Words I), D.C. No. CV-99-02816-SVW (C.D. Cal. 1999).

Seven Words LLC v. Network Solutions, Inc., (Seven Words II), D.C. No. CV-99-06722-SVW (C.D. Cal. 1999).

Skipton Building Society v. Peter Colman, Case No. D2000-1217 (WIPO Arbitration and Mediation Center 1 Dec. 2000) (available at http://www.wipo.int/amc/en/domains/decisions/html/2000/d2000-1217.html).

Smiley v. ICANN, No. BC254659 (Cal. Super. Ct. filed 23 Jul. 2001).

South West Africa Cases (Ethiopia v. South Africa; Liberia v. South Africa) (Second Phase), 4 I.C.J. 48, (I.C.J. 1966).

Standard Brands v. Smidler, 151 F.2d 34, 40 (C.C.A. 2d 1945).

State of Arizona; State of Texas; State of Oklahoma; State of Nevada v. National Telecommunications and Information Administration (NTIA); United States of America; United States Department of Commerce; Penny Pritzker, in her Official Capacity as Secretary of Commerce; Lawrence E. Strickling in his Official Capacity as Assistant Secretary for Communications and Information and Administrator of NTIA, Case 3:16-cv-00274 (28 Sep. 2016).

Sydney Airport v. Crilly, WIPO Case No. D2005-0989.

Sydney Markets Limited v. Nick Rakis, Case No. D2001-0932 (WIPO Arbitration and Mediation Center, 8 Oct. 2001) (available at http://www.wipo.int/amc/en/domains/decisions/html/2001/d2001-0932.html).

The Case of the S.S. 'Lotus', Ser. A., no. 10, p. 18 P.C.I.J. 18 (P.C.I.J. 1927).

The Paris Pages v. Woohoo T&C Ltd, Case No. FA110763 (National Arbitration Forum, 10 Jul. 2002) (available at http://www.adrforum.com/domaindecisions/110763.htm).

United States – Import Prohibition of Certain Shrimp and Shrimp Products, WT/DS58/AB/R, AB-1998-4 (W.T.O. D.S.B. App. Body 12 Oct. 1998).

United States – Section 211 Omnibus Appropriations Act of 1998, 41 I.L.M. 654 (W.T.O. D.S.B. App. Body 2 Jan. 2002).

Verizon Communications Inc. v. Law Offices of Curtis v. Trinko, LLP, 540 U.S. 398 (2004).

Veuve Clicquot Ponsardin v. Net-Promotion, Inc., Case No. D2000-0347 (WIPO Arbitration and Mediation Center 14 Jun. 2000) (available at http://www.wipo.int/amc/en/domains/decisions/html/2000/d2000-0347.html).

Virtual Countries, Inc. v. Republic of South Africa and South African Tourism Board, No. 00 Civ. 84888 U.S. Dist. LEXIS (S.D.N.Y. 2001).

Weber-Stephen Products Co. v. Armitage Hardware & Building Supply, Inc., No. 00 C 1738, 2000 U.S. Dist. LEXIS 6335 (N.D. Ill. 2000).

Wembley National Stadium Limited v. Bob Thomson, Case No. D2000-1233 (WIPO Arbitration and Mediation Center, 16 Nov. 2000) (available at http://www.wipo.int/amc/en/domains/decisions/html/2000/d2000-1233.html).

Referenced New gTLD Applications (2012)

. 广东 (Guangdong)	Xinhua News Agency Guangdong Branch 新华通讯社广东分社	https://gtldresult.icann.org/application-result/applicationstatus/applicationdetails/140
广州 (.guangzhou)	Guangzhou YU Wei Information Technology Co., Ltd.	https://gtldresult.icann.org/application-result/applicationstatus/applicationdetails/1379
.airforce	United TLD Holdco Ltd.	https://gtldresult.icann.org/application-result/applicationstatus/applicationdetails/1109
.amazon	Amazon EU S.à.r.l.	https://gtldresult.icann.org/application-result/applicationstatus/applicationdetails/984
.bar	United TLD Holdco Ltd.	https://gtldresult.icann.org/application-result/applicationstatus/applicationdetails/1121
.bar	Punto 2012 Sociedad Anonima Promotora de Inversion de Capital Variable	https://gtldresult.icann.org/application-result/applicationstatus/applicationdetails/246

.barcelona	Municipi de Barcelona	https://gtldresult.icann.org/application-result/applicationstatus/applicationdetails/320
.berlin	dotBERLIN GmbH & Co. KG	https://gtldresult.icann.org/application-result/applicationstatus/applicationdetails/1777
.cartier	Richemont DNS Inc.	https://gtldresult.icann.org/application-result/applicationstatus/applicationdetails/1152
.catalonia	Generalitat de Catalunya	https://gtldresult.icann.org/application-result/applicationstatus/applicationdetails/318
.corsica	Collectivité Territoriale de Corse	https://gtldresult.icann.org/application-result/applicationstatus/applicationdetails/1697
.cymru	Nominet UK	https://gtldresult.icann.org/application-result/applicationstatus/applicationdetails/1420
.hamburg	Hamburg Top-Level Domain GmbH	https://gtldresult.icann.org/application-result/applicationstatus/applicationdetails/1351
.indians	Reliance Industries Limited	https://gtldresult.icann.org/application-result/applicationstatus/applicationdetails/1005
.ipiranga	Ipiranga Produtos de Petroleo S.A.	https://gtldresult.icann.org/application-result/applicationstatus/applicationdetails/1509

.lasalle	Jones Lang LaSalle Incorporated	https://gtldresult.icann.org/application-result/applicationstatus/applicationdetails/1160
.madrid	Communidad de Madrid	https://gtldresult.icann.org/application-result/applicationstatus/applicationdetails/416
.osaka	Interlink Co., Ltd.	https://gtldresult.icann.org/application-result/applicationstatus/applicationdetails/1781
.paris	City of Paris	https://gtldresult.icann.org/application-result/applicationstatus/applicationdetails/1450
.patagonia	Patagonia, Inc.	https://gtldresult.icann.org/application-result/applicationstatus/applicationdetails/1466
.quebec	PointQuébec Inc	https://gtldresult.icann.org/application-result/applicationstatus/applicationdetails/556
.rocher	Ferrero Trading Lux S.A.	https://gtldresult.icann.org/application-result/applicationstatus/applicationdetails/1371
.scot	Dot Scot Registry Limited	https://gtldresult.icann.org/application-result/applicationstatus/applicationdetails/417
.spa	Asian Spa and Wellness Promotion Council Limited	https://gtldresult.icann.org/application-result/applicationstatus/applicationdetails/123

.sucks	Vox Populi Registry Inc.	https://gtldresult.icann.org/ application-result/ applicationstatus/ applicationdetails/54
.swiss	Swiss Confederation	https://gtldresult.icann.org/ application-result/ applicationstatus/ applicationdetails/906
.sydney	State of New South Wales, Department of Premier and Cabinet	https://gtldresult.icann.org/ application-result/ applicationstatus/ applicationdetails/200
.thai	Better Living Management Company	https://gtldresult.icann.org/ application-result/ applicationstatus/ applicationdetails/27
.tirol	punkt Tirol GmbH	https://gtldresult.icann.org/ application-result/ applicationstatus/ applicationdetails/461
.tokyo	GMO Registry Inc.	https://gtldresult.icann.org/ application-result/ applicationstatus/ applicationdetails/1790
.virgin	Virgin Enterprises Limited	https://gtldresult.icann.org/ application-result/ applicationstatus/ applicationdetails/378
.vin	Holly Shadow, LLC	https://gtldresult.icann.org/ application-result/ applicationstatus/ applicationdetails/679
.wien	punkt.wien GmbH	https://gtldresult.icann.org/ application-result/ applicationstatus/ applicationdetails/1564

.wine	June Station, LLC	https://gtldresult.icann.org/application-result/applicationstatus/applicationdetails/706
.wine	Afilias Limited	https://gtldresult.icann.org/application-result/applicationstatus/applicationdetails/1831
.wine	dot Wine Limited	https://gtldresult.icann.org/application-result/applicationstatus/applicationdetails/1204

Index

M

N

P

R

INFORMATION LAW SERIES

1. Egbert J. Dommering & P. Bernt Hugenholtz, *Protecting Works of Fact: Copyright, Freedom of Expression and Information Law,* 1991 (ISBN 90-654-4567-6).
2. Willem F. Korthals Altes, Egbert J. Dommering, P. Bernt Hugenholtz & Jan J.C. Kabel, *Information Law Towards the 21st Century,* 1992 (ISBN 90-654-4627-3).
3. Jacqueline M.B. Seignette, *Challenges to the Creator Doctrine: Authorship, Copyright Ownership and the Exploitation of Creative Works in the Netherlands, Germany and The United States,* 1994 (ISBN 90-654-4876-4).
4. P. Bernt Hugenholtz, *The Future of Copyright in a Digital Environment, Proceedings of the Royal Academy Colloquium,* 1996 (ISBN 90-411-0267-1).
5. Julius C.S. Pinckaers, *From Privacy Toward a New Intellectual Property Right in Persona,* 1996 (ISBN 90-411-0355-4).
6. Jan J.C. Kabel & Gerard J.H.M. Mom, *Intellectual Property and Information Law: Essays in Honour of Herman Cohen Jehoram,* 1998 (ISBN 90-411-9702-8).
7. Ysolde Gendreau, Axel Nordemann & Rainer Oesch, *Copyright and Photographs: An International Survey,* 1999 (ISBN 90-411-9722-2).
8. P. Bernt Hugenholtz, *Copyright and Electronic Commerce: Legal Aspects of Electronic Copyright Management,* 2000 (ISBN 90-411-9785-0).
9. Lucie M.C.R. Guibault, *Copyright Limitations and Contracts: An Analysis of the Contractual Overridability of Limitations on Copyright,* 2002 (ISBN 90-411-9867-9).
10. Lee A. Bygrave, *Data Protection Law: Approaching its Rationale, Logic and Limits,* 2002 (ISBN 90-411-9870-9).
11. Niva Elkin-Koren & Neil Weinstock Netanel, *The Commodification of Information,* 2002 (ISBN 90-411-9876-8).
12. Mireille M.M. van Eechoud, *Choice of Law in Copyright and Related Rights: Alternatives to the Lex Protectionis,* 2003 (ISBN 90-411-2071-8).
13. Martin Senftleben, *Copyright, Limitations and the Three-Step Test: An Analysis of the Three-Step Test in International and EC Copyright Law,* 2004 (ISBN 90-411-2267-2).
14. Paul L.C. Torremans, *Copyright and Human Rights: Freedom of Expression – Intellectual Property – Privacy,* 2004 (ISBN 90-411-2278-8).
15. Natali Helberger, *Controlling Access to Content: Regulating Conditional Access in Digital Broadcasting,* 2005 (ISBN 90-411-2345-8).
16. Lucie M.C.R. Guibault & P. Bernt Hugenholtz, *The Future of the Public Domain: Identifying the Commons in Information Law,* 2006 (ISBN 978-90-411-2435-7).

17. Irini Katsirea, *Public Broadcasting and European Law: A Comparative Examination of Public Service Obligations in Six Member States*, 2008 (ISBN 978-90-411-2500-2).
18. Paul L.C. Torremans, *Intellectual Property and Human Rights: Enhanced Edition of Copyright and Human Rights*, 2008 (ISBN 978-90-411-2653-5).
19. Mireille van Eechoud, P. Bernt Hugenholtz, Stef van Gompel, Lucie Guibault & Natali Helberger, *Harmonizing European Copyright Law: The Challenges of Better Lawmaking*, 2009 (ISBN 978-90-411-3130-0).
20. Ashwin van Rooijen, *The Software Interface between Copyright and Competition Law: A Legal Analysis of Interoperability in Computer Programs*, 2010 (ISBN 978-90-411-3193-5).
21. Irini A. Stamatoudi, *Copyright Enforcement and the Internet*, 2010 (ISBN 978-90-411-3346-5).
22. Wolfgang Sakulin, *Trademark Protection and Freedom of Expression: An Inquiry into the Conflict between Trademark Rights and Freedom of Expression under European Law*, 2011 (ISBN 978-90-411-3415-8).
23. Stef van Gompel, *Formalities in Copyright Law: An Analysis of their History, Rationales and Possible Future*, 2011 (ISBN 978-90-411-3418-9).
24. Nadezhda Purtova, *Property Rights in Personal Data: A European Perspective*, 2012 (ISBN 978-90-411-3802-6).
25. Brad Sherman & Leanne Wiseman, *Copyright and the Challenge of the New*, 2012 (ISBN 978-90-411-3669-5).
26. Ewa Komorek, *Media Pluralism and European Law*, 2012 (ISBN 978-90-411-3894-1).
27. Joris van Hoboken, *Search Engine Freedom: On the Implications of the Right to Freedom of Expression for the Legal Governance of Web Search Engines*, 2012 (ISBN 978-90-411-4128-6).
28. Natali Helberger, Lucie Guibault, Marco Loos, Chantal Mak, Lodewijk Pessers & Bart van der Sloot, *Digital Consumers and the Law: Towards a Cohesive European Framework*, 2012 (ISBN 978-90-411-4049-4).
29. Tatiana-Eleni Synodinou, *Codification of European Copyright Law: Challenges and Perspectives*, 2012 (ISBN 978-90-411-4145-3).
30. Heather Ann Forrest, *Protection of Geographic Names in International Law and Domain Name System Policy*, Second Edition, 2017 (ISBN 978-90-411-8839-7).
31. Sari Depreeuw, *The Variable Scope of the Exclusive Economic Rights in Copyright*, 2014 (ISBN 978-90-411-4915-2).
32. Vikrant Narayan Vasudeva, *Open Source Software and Intellectual Property Rights*, 2014 (ISBN 978-90-411-5228-2).
33. Frederik J. Zuiderveen Borgesius, *Improving Privacy Protection in the Area of Behavioural Targeting*, 2015 (ISBN 978-90-411-5990-8).

34. Paul L.C. Torremans, *Intellectual Property Law and Human Rights*, Third Edition, 2015 (ISBN 978-90-411-5836-9).
35. Irini A. Stamatoudi, *New Developments in EU and International Copyright Law*, 2016 (ISBN 978-90-411-5991-5).
36. Lodewijk W.P. Pessers, *The Inventiveness Requirement in Patent Law: An Exploration of Its Foundations and Functioning*, 2016 (ISBN 978-90-411-6731-6).
37. Susy Frankel & Daniel Gervais, *The Internet and the Emerging Importance of New Forms of Intellectual Property*, 2016 (ISBN 978-90-411-6789-7).
38. Axel M. Arnbak, *Securing Private Communications: Protecting Private Communications Security in EU Law – Fundamental Rights, Functional Value Chains, and Market Incentives*, 2016 (ISBN 978-90-411-6737-8).
39. Christina Angelopoulos, *European Intermediary Liability in Copyright: A Tort-Based Analysis*, 2017 (ISBN 978-90-411-6835-1).

www.ingramcontent.com/pod-product-compliance
Lightning Source LLC
LaVergne TN
LVHW020002031026
849161LV00023B/831
* 9 7 8 9 0 4 1 1 8 8 3 9 7 *